THE BLACKWELL COMPANION TO MEDICAL SOCIOLOGY

BLACKWELL COMPANIONS TO SOCIOLOGY

The *Blackwell Companions to Sociology* provide introductions to emerging topics and theoretical orientations in sociology as well as presenting the scope and quality of the discipline as it is currently configured. Essays in the Companions tackle broad themes or central puzzles within the field and are authored by key scholars who have spent considerable time in research and reflection on the questions and controversies that have activated interest in their area. This authoritative series will interest those studying sociology at advanced undergraduate or graduate level as well as scholars in the social sciences and informed readers in applied disciplines.

The Blackwell Companion to Medical Sociology

Edited by

William C. Cockerham

Blackwell
Publishing

© 2001, 2005 by Blackwell Publishing Ltd

BLACKWELL PUBLISHING
350 Main Street, Malden, MA 02148-5020, USA
108 Cowley Road, Oxford OX4 1JF, UK
550 Swanston Street, Carlton, Victoria 3053, Australia

First published 2001
First published in paperback 2005 by Blackwell Publishing Ltd

Library of Congress Cataloging-in-Publication Data

The Blackwell companion to medical sociology / edited by William C. Cockerham.
    p. cm. — (Blackwell companions to sociology)
    Includes bibliographical references and index.
    ISBN 0-631-21703-7 (alk. paper) — ISBN 1-4051-2266-8 (pbk.: alk. paper)
    1. Medical sociology—Miscellanea. 2. Social medicini—Miscellanea. I. Cockerham,
William C. II Series.

RA418.B5736   2001
306.4′61—dc21

00—0033714

A catalogue record for this title is available from the British Library.

Set in 10.5/12.5pt Sabon
by Kolam Information Services Pvt. Ltd, Pondicherry, India
Printed and bound in the United Kingdom
by TJ International, Padstow, Cornwall

The publisher's policy is to use permanent paper from mills that operate a sustainable forestry
policy, and which has been manufactured from pulp processed using acid-free and elementary
chlorine-free practices. Furthermore, the publisher ensures that the text paper and cover board
used have met acceptable environmental accreditation standards.

For further information on
Blackwell Publishing, visit our website:
www.blackwellpublishing.com

Contents

Africa

The Middle East

Asia and the Pacific Region

Contributors

Masahira Anesaki, Ph.D., Professor of Sociology, Nihon University School of Medicine, Tokyo, Japan.

Ellen Annandale, Ph.D., Senior Lecturer in Sociology, Leicester University, Leicester, England.

Ofra Anson, Ph.D., Senior Lecturer, Faculty of Health Sciences, Ben-Gurion University of the Negev, Beer-Sheva, Israel.

Sara Arber, Ph.D., Professor and Head, Department of Sociology, University of Surrey, Guildford, England.

B. Singh Bolaria, Ph.D., Professor of Sociology, University of Saskatchewan Saskatoon, Saskatchewan, Canada.

Carol A. Boyer, Ph.D., Assistant Professor and Associate Director, Institute for Health, Health Care Policy, and Aging Research, Rutgers University, New Brunswick, New Jersey, USA.

Roberto Castro, Ph.D., Coordinator of the Research Program on Health, Violence, and Society, Regional Center for Multidisciplinary Research, National Autonomous University of Mexico, Cuernavaca, Mexico.

Meei-shia Chen, Ph.D., Professor and Director, Department of Public Health, College of Medicine, National Cheng Kung University, Tainan, Taiwan.

William C. Cockerham, Ph.D., Professor of Sociology, Medicine, and Public Health and Chair, Department of Sociology, University of Alabama at Birmingham, Birmingham, Alabama, USA.

Harley D. Dickinson, Ph.D., Professor of Sociology and Director of the Social Research Unit, University of Saskatchewan Saskatoon, Saskatchewan, Canada.

Elena Dmitrieva, Ph.D., Assistant Professor of Sociology and Politics and Chair of Communicative Technologies, Nevsky Institute of Language and Culture, St. Petersburg, Russia.

David Field, Ph.D., Professor, Center for Palliative Care Studies, Institute of Cancer Research, London, England.

Eugene Gallagher, Ph.D., Professor of Behavioral Sciences, College of Medicine, University of Kentucky, Lexington, Kentucky, USA.

Örjan Hemström, Ph.D., Research Associate in the Department of Sociology, Stockholm University, and at the National Institute for Working Life, Stockholm, Sweden.

Professor Hana Janečková, Ph.D., Assistant Professor, School of Public Health, Postgraduate Medical School, Prague, Czech Republic.

Olaf von dem Knesebeck, Ph.D., Assistant Professor, Department of Medical Sociology, Düsseldorf University, Düsseldorf, Germany.

Eero Lahelma, Ph.D., Professor of Medical Sociology, Department of Public Health, University of Helsinki, Finland.

Deborah Lupton, Ph.D., Associate Professor in Cultural Studies and Cultural Policy and Director, Centre for Cultural Risk Research, Charles Sturt University, Bathurst, Australia.

Professor Tsunetsugu Munakata, Dr. H.Sc., Professor of Health Behavioral Science, Institute of Health and Sports Sciences, University of Tsukuba, Tsukuba, Japan.

Sarah Nettleton, Ph.D., Senior Lecturer in Social Policy and Social Work, University of York, Heslington, York, England.

Charles Ngwena, LL.B., L.L.M., Associate Professor, Faculty of Law, Department of Procedural Law, Vista University, Bloemfontein, South Africa.

Everardo Duarte Nuñes, Sc.D., Professor of Social Sciences, College of Medical Sciences, Campinas State University, São Paulo, Brazil.

Kristina Orfali, Ph.D., Assistant Director, MacLean Center for Clinical Medical Ethics, University of Chicago, Chicago, Illinois, USA.

Nina Ostrowska, Ph.D., Deputy Director, Institute of Philosophy and Sociology Polish Academy of Sciences, Warsaw, Poland.

Bernice A. Pescosolido, Ph.D., Professor of Sociology, Indiana University, Bloomington, Indiana, USA.

Stella Quah, Ph.D., Associate Professor of Sociology, National University of Singapore.

H. C. J. van Rensburg, Ph.D., Professor and Director, Centre for Health Systems Research and Development, University of the Free State, Bloemfontein, South Africa.

Elianne Riska, Ph.D., Academy Professor of Sociology, Åbo Akademi University, Åbo, Finland.

Judith T. Shuval, Ph.D., Louis and Pearl Rose Professor of Medical Sociology and Director, Programme in the Sociology of Health, School of Public Health, Hebrew University of Jerusalem, Jerusalem, Israel.

Professor Johannes Siegrist, Ph.D., Professor and Director, Department of Medical Sociology, Düsseldorf University, Düsseldorf, Germany.

Fred Stevens, Ph.D., Professor of Medical Sociology, University of Maastricht, Maastricht, The Netherlands.

Hilary Thomas, Ph.D., Senior Lecturer in Sociology, University of Surrey, Guildford, England, and President of the European Society for Health and Medical Sociology.

Preface

The Blackwell Companion to Medical Sociology is the first, truly global book reflecting the range of work taking place in medical sociology. Medical sociology, also referred to as health sociology or the sociology of health and illness, is a subdiscipline of sociology that has experienced tremendous growth worldwide. This growth began in the late 1940s when medical sociology first appeared on a systematic basis in the United States and then spread to other countries. Medical sociology has become one of the largest and most popular areas of sociology, but it also has multidisciplinary roots in medicine which have been important in its development. The growth of the field is seen in the numerous books, journals and journal articles, professional associations, and conferences devoted to the topic around the world. Consequently, it is time for a globally-oriented book to be published that expresses the work of the subdiscipline.

The term "medical sociology" is used in the title of this book because it is the traditional name of the field even though its work extends beyond medical practice to the entire social spectrum related to health and illness. The book itself consists of two parts – Substantive Topics and Regional Perspectives. The 26 chapters have been written by subject matter experts and residents of the particular countries and regions of the world being described. An exception is the chapter on the Arab world, written by Eugene Gallagher of the University of Kentucky, who is the foremost authority in the world on medical sociology in the Arab countries. Part I is concerned with substantive topics in medical sociology, generally like theory, culture, gender, and social stratification, while Part II deals with regional perspectives from the Americas, Western Europe, Russia and Eastern Europe, Africa, the Middle East, and Asia and the Pacific Region.

Part I has nine chapters, which begins with my discussion of medical sociology and sociological theory. The evolution of theoretical thought in the field from

Talcott Parsons in the 1950s to the twenty-first century is reviewed and it is concluded that medical sociology is not atheoretical; on the contrary, it has a rich and diverse theoretical foundation. Chapter 2, by Stella Quah of the National University of Singapore, discusses the relevance of culture for health and reviews the research on this topic. Chapter 3, by Sarah Nettleton of the University of York in Great Britain, deals with an increasingly popular and promising new topic in medical sociology with a highly active theoretical discourse: the sociology of the body.

Next come chapters on health and social stratification, a basic subject, by Eero Lahelma of the University of Helsinki in Finland; women's health and gender, another central topic, by Sara Arber and Hilary Thomas of the University of Surrey in Great Britain; and two chapters on stress – one on the workplace by Johannes Siegrist of the University of Düsseldorf in Germany and the other on migration by Judith Shuval of the Hebrew University of Jerusalem in Israel. Part I concludes with chapters on health professions and occupations by Elianne Riska of Åbo Akademi University in Finland, and modern health systems by Fred Stevens of the University of Maastricht in The Netherlands. All of the contributors in Part I are medical sociologists and are on the faculties of their various universities.

Part II, on regional perspectives, begins with the section on the Americas, leading with a chapter on health care delivery in the United States by Bernice Pescosolido of Indiana University and Carol Boyer of Rutgers University. Next are chapters on the evolution of health care in Canada by B. Singh Bolaria and Harley D. Dickinson of the University of Saskatchewan, medical sociology in Mexico by Roberto Castro of the National Autonomous University of Mexico, and social science and health in Brazil by Everardo Duarte Nuñes of Campinas State University in São Paulo.

The section on western Europe follows and includes chapters on medical sociology in Great Britain by Ellen Annandale of the University of Leicester and David Field of the Institute of Cancer Research in London; the French "paradox" concerning a rich diet and high life expectancy, along with a discussion of French health generally, health care, and health policy by Kristina Orfali of the University of Chicago; medical sociology in Germany by Olaf von dem Knesebeck and Johannes Siegrist of the University of Düsseldorf; and health and society in Sweden by Örjan Hemström of the University of Stockholm. These contributors are medical sociologists and most are university professors. Exceptions are David Field, who is a researcher at the Institute of Cancer Research in London and Kristina Orfali, a native of France, who currently serves as the Assistant Director of the MacLean Center for Clinical Medical Ethics at the University of Chicago.

Regional perspectives continue with a section on the health problems of Russia and eastern Europe, with a chapter on the health transition and medical sociology in Russia by Elena Dmitrieva of the Russian Naval Academy in St. Petersburg; the macrosocial context of health in Poland by Nina Ostrowska of the Institute of Philosophy and Sociology of the Polish Academy of Sciences in Warsaw; and the transformation of the health system in the Czech Republic by Hana Janečková of the Postgraduate Medical School in Prague. Dmitrieva is on the faculty at the Nevsky Institute of Language and Culture in St. Petersburg, Russia, and is one of the country's new generation of medical sociologists, Ostrowska is the Deputy Director of the Institute of Philosophy and Sociology in Warsaw, and Janečková is on the faculty at the School of Public Health in Prague's Postgraduate Medical School.

The section on Africa consists of a chapter by H. C. J. van Rensburg of the University of the Free State and Charles Ngwena of Vista University in South Africa. Van Rensburg is Director of the Centre for Health Systems Research and Development at the University of the Free State and Ngwena is on the law faculty at Vista University. Both schools are in Bloemfontein, South Africa.

The Middle East chapters on the Arab world are by Eugene Gallagher of the University of Kentucky and on health and health care in Israel by Ofra Anson of Ben-Gurion University of the Negev.

The book concludes with the section on Asia and the Pacific Region with chapters on medicine and health care in Australia by Deborah Lupton of Charles Sturt University in Bathurst; sociobehavioral factors in health and illness in Japan by Masahira Anesaki of the Nihon University School of Medicine in Tokyo and Tsunetsugu Munakata of the University of Tsukuba in Tsukuba, Japan; and the transformation of health care in the People's Republic of China by Meei-shia Chen of the National Cheng Kung University in Taiwan. All of these contributors are medical sociologists on the faculties of their respective institutions.

Finally, I would like to acknowledge the hard work and able assistance of Chris Snead, Sara Daum and Emily Norman, doctoral students in medical sociology at the University of Alabama at Birmingham. Their efforts were extremely important in keeping this global project organized and on schedule; they also made valuable contributions in editing, as did Anthony Grahame of Brighton, England, on behalf of Blackwell Publishers. Additional thanks go to Acquisitions Editor Susan Rabinowitz and Assistant Editor Ken Provencher at the Blackwell office in Malden, Massachusetts for their ideas and support in the conceptualization and completion of this project. I also thank my wife, Cynthia, for suggesting the cover for this volume and my children – Laura, Geoffrey, Sean, and Scott–for their lifelong social support. This book is dedicated to the memory of my father, Carl Reese Cockerham.

William C. Cockerham
Birmingham, Alabama

Part I
Substantive Topics

1

Medical Sociology and Sociological Theory

William C. Cockerham

The link between medical sociology and sociological theory is crucial to the subdiscipline. Theory binds medical sociology to the larger discipline of sociology more extensively than any other aspect of the sociological enterprise. Theory is also what usually distinguishes research in medical sociology from socially-oriented studies in allied fields, like public health and health services research. Whereas seminal sociological contributions in quantitative and qualitative data collection and analysis, along with many fundamental concepts on social behavior, have been subsumed by multidisciplinary approaches in several fields, sociological theory allows medical sociology to remain unique among the health-related social and behavioral sciences.

This could be considered as a somewhat surprising statement because medical sociology has often been described in the past as atheoretical. It is true that much of the work in the field historically has been applied, intended to help solve a clinical problem or policy issue, rather than develop theory or utilize it as a tool to further understanding. Medical sociology was not established until after World War II when the American government provided extensive funding through the National Institutes of Health for joint sociological and medical research projects. The same situation prevailed in western Europe, where, unlike in the United States, few medical sociologists were affiliated with university sociology faculties and connections to the general discipline of sociology were especially weak (Claus 1982; Cockerham 1983). It was primarily through the stimulus of the availability of government funding that sociologists and health professionals embraced medical sociology as a new subdiscipline. Funding agencies were not interested in theoretical work, but sponsored research that had some practical utility in postwar society as western governments had come to realize that social factors were important for health.

By the end of the twentieth century, however, this situation had changed significantly. Most research in medical sociology remains oriented toward practical problem solving, but the use of sociological theory in this endeavor is now widespread. There has been a general evolution of work in medical sociology that combines both applied and theoretical perspectives, with the utilization of theory becoming increasingly common as a framework for explaining or predicting health-related social behavior. At the same time, medical sociology moved away from a state of dependence upon medicine for defining and guiding research agendas to a position of relative independence. Although the relationship between medical sociology and medicine has been important, it has not always been harmonious (Gerhardt 1989). Medical sociology tended to side with patients and call attention to instances of poor treatment, while some physicians have been contemptuous of medical sociologists in clinical settings. Yet medicine nurtured, funded, and sponsored medical sociology early in its development and continues to do so today. In fact, one could arguably state that medicine has supported medical sociology with funding and job positions to a much greater extent than sociology. It can also be claimed that the increased use of theory in medical sociology represents more of an effort on the part of medical sociologists to establish and reinforce links to the parent discipline, than vice versa. In many ways, medicine has been a better ally of medical sociology than sociology.

While medical sociology is moving closer to sociology, it has generally removed itself from a subordinate position to medicine. There are four reasons for this development. First, the shift from acute to chronic diseases as the primary causes of death in contemporary societies has made medical sociology increasingly important to medicine. This is because of the key roles of social behavior and living conditions in the prevention, onset, and course of chronic disorders. Medical sociologists bring more expertise to the analysis of health-related social conditions than physicians who typically receive little or no training in this area. Second, medical sociology has moved into a greater partnership with medicine as it has matured and fostered a significant body of research literature, much of it relevant to clinical medicine and health policy. Third, success in research has promoted the professional status of medical sociologists, both in relation to medicine and sociology. And fourth, medical sociology has generally set its own research agenda, which includes medical practice and policy as an *object* of study. In the case of malpractice, failure to police incompetent practitioners, limited access to quality care for the poor, and placing professional interest ahead of the public's interest, medical sociologists have been significant critics of medicine. In doing so, they have established themselves as objective professionals.

The movement of medical sociology toward greater connections with general sociology reflects the desire of a mature subdiscipline to expand its analytic capabilities and reinforce its potential. Changing social conditions associated with the transition in society from the postindustrial to the current late modern or postmodern period requires all of sociology to account for altered circumstances and formulate new concepts. This situation suggests that not only is medical sociology connecting with general sociology, but that sociology is moving toward a closer affiliation with it – given the considerations of health increasingly evident in the everyday social lives of people and medical sociology's capacity for explaining it. Under the current conditions of social change, medical sociologists are making greater use of sociological theory because theory promotes the explanatory power of their empirical findings. This development has led some to suggest that medical sociology may indeed prove to be the "leading edge" in some areas of the development of contemporary theory (Turner 1992). Whether or not this assertion will be fully realized is not yet certain, but it is clear that medical sociology has a strong theoretical orientation that is continuing to evolve. The remainder of this chapter will therefore provide a general review of the theoretical work in medical sociology that has taken place to date.

PARSONS, DURKHEIM, AND STRUCTURAL-FUNCTIONALISM

From 1946 to 1951, the new field of medical sociology was almost completely an applied area of research. Medical sociologists worked with psychiatrists and other physicians on government-funded projects to largely address medical problems; few were employed in university departments of sociology in the United States and they were generally absent from sociology faculties in Europe and Asia. However, a pivotal event occurred in 1951 that oriented medical sociology toward theoretical concerns and initiated the establishment of its academic credentials. This was the publication of Talcott Parsons' long anticipated book, *The Social System*, which established the author at the time as the dominant figure in American sociology (Ritzer 2000). Anything Parsons published attracted great attention because he was thought to be charting a course for all of sociology. This book, providing a structural-functionalist model of society, contained Parsons' concept of the sick role and was the first time a major sociological theorist included an analysis of the function of medicine in his view of society. Parsons (1951: 428–9) was interested in the differing roles of professionals in capitalistic and socialist societies and decided to include physicians and their relationship to their clients in his analysis because this topic was an area of long-standing interest and one in which he felt he had familiarity. Parsons himself had undergone training in psychoanalysis in the 1950s at the Boston Psychoanalytic Institute when he was on the faculty at Harvard University (Smelser 1998).

This experience had grounded him in the theories of Sigmund Freud which became an important influence on his own work, along with the ideas of the classic sociological theorists Emile Durkheim and Max Weber. Parsons had completed his doctoral studies at Heidelberg University in Germany in the mid-1920s where he participated in the "Weber Circle" that continued to meet regularly to discuss sociology after Weber's death at the home of his widow, Marianne Weber. Parsons subsequently translated Weber's book on the *Protestant Ethic and the Spirit of Capitalism* (1958) into English, and reintroduced the work of both Weber and Durkheim to European sociologists after the disruption of their work during World War II. Freud's concepts of transference and counter-transference helped Parsons draw analogies between the roles of parent–child and physician–patient important in his notion of the sick role. Freud's structure of the personality and theory of the unconscious also assisted Parsons in developing his ideas on the motivation of sick persons to either recover or desire the "secondary gain" of privileges and exemption from normal social roles that accompany sick-role legitimation (Gerhardt 1989). Parsons also incorporates Durkheim's ideas on moral authority and Weber's analysis of religion into his discussion of the normative requirement to visit physicians when sick and the dominant position of the physician in the doctor–patient role relationship.

Parsons' concept of the sick role is a clear and straightforward statement of four basic propositions outlining the normative pattern of physician utilization by the sick and their respective social roles. Parsons not only constructed the first theoretical concept directly applicable to medical sociology, but by utilizing the work of Durkheim and Weber, he did so within the parameters of classical sociological theory. His formulation was recognized as "a penetrating and apt analysis of sickness from a distinctly sociological point of view" (Freidson 1970a: 228), which indeed it was. Parsons also influenced the study of professions by using the medical profession as the model for professions based on expertise and a service orientation. Although extensive criticism was to subsequently lessen the acceptance of the Parsonian approach to theory, this outcome does not negate the significant influence Parsons initially had on promoting debate and research in medical sociology. Parsons, more so than any other sociologist of his time, made medical sociology academically respectable by providing it with its inaugural theoretical orientation (Cockerham and Ritchey 1997).

However, structural-functionalism, with its emphasis on value consensus, social order, stability, and functional processes at the macro-level of society, had a short-lived period as the leading theoretical paradigm in medical sociology. Robert Merton and his colleagues extended the structural-functionalist mode of analysis to the socialization of medical students in their book, *The Student Physician* (1957), but other major works in medical sociology were not forthcoming. Structural-functionalism itself was under assault by critics in the 1960s and early 1970s and lost considerable influence.

Durkheim (1950), who was generally responsible for the theory in sociology, emphasized the importance of macro-level social processes, structures, norms, and values external to individuals that integrated them into the larger society and shaped their behavior. People were depicted as constrained in exercising free will by the social order. Durkheim's (1951) only work that had a direct application to medical sociology was his theory of suicide in which the act of taking one's life was determined by the individual's ties to his or her community or society. This is seen in his typology of three major types of suicide: (1) egoistic (social detachment), (2) anomic (state of normlessness), and (3) altruistic (a normative demand for suicide). The merit of his concept is that it shows the capability of the larger society to create stressful situations where people are forced to respond to conditions not of their own choosing. Thus, Durkheim helps us to not only understand the social facets of suicide, but to recognize that macro-level social events (like economic recessions) can affect health in a variety of ways through stress and that the effects of stress can be mitigated through social support (Thoits 1995; Cockerham 1998). Indirectly, Durkheim (1964) also influenced the study of health professions in noting the transition from mechanical to organic social solidarity, with its emphasis upon specialization, in the modern division of labor.

However, symbolic interactionists objected to the relegation of individuals to relatively passive roles in large social systems, while conflict theorists found structural-functionalism inadequate in explaining the process of social change and the social functions of conflict. The theory's emphasis on equilibrium and consensus also seemed to favor maintenance of the status quo and support for dominant elites (Ritzer 2000), at a time (the 1960s) of widespread social protest against authority in the West. Structural-functionalism in general and Parsons in particular suffered a serious fall in popularity, although Parsons' work enjoyed a mild resurgence in the 1990s (Robertson and Turner 1991; Callinicos 1999). Parsons' concept of the sick role, however, has remained a central theoretical proposition in medical sociology, despite challenges. It is still utilized as a basic ("ideal-type") explanation for physician–patient encounters in which the model of interaction is primarily that of guidance on the part of the physician and cooperation by the patient in clinics or patient care office settings.

SYMBOLIC INTERACTION

The first major theoretical perspective to challenge Parsons and structural-functionalist theory in medical sociology was symbolic interaction, based largely on the work of George Herbert Mead (1934) and Herbert Blumer (1969). Symbolic interaction maintained that social reality is constructed on a micro-level by individuals interacting with one another on the basis of shared symbolic meanings. Human beings were seen to possess the capacity to think, define situations, and construct their behavior on the basis of their definitions and interpretations. "It is the position of symbolic interaction," states Blumer (1969: 55), "that the social action of the actor is *constructed* by him [or her]; it is not a mere release of activity brought about by the play of initiating factors on his [or her] organization." Social life was therefore produced by interacting agents choosing their own behavior and acting accordingly, not by large-scale social processes and structures channeling behavior down option-less pathways. Symbolic interaction not only had its particular (micro-level) orientation toward theory construction, but also its own qualitative research methodologies of participant observation that focused on small group interaction and natural social settings. A related approach was ethnomethodology which featured description of taken-for-granted meanings in natural settings, rather than analysis.

The major figures in early medical sociology working in the symbolic interactionist tradition were Anselm Strauss and Erving Goffman. Strauss joined with Howard Becker and others in their now classic study of medical school socialization, *Boys in White* (Becker et al. 1961). Strauss made his own contributions to theory and methods in a number of areas, including seminal work on the social process of death and dying (Glaser and Strauss 1965, 1968); observation of the "negotiated order" of hospital routine featuring a minimum of "hard and fast" regulations and a maximum of "innovation and improvisation" in patient care, especially in emergency treatment (Strauss et al. 1963); and formulation of grounded theory methodology featuring the development of hypotheses from data *after* its collection, rather than before (Glaser and Strauss 1967).

Goffman, who became a major theorist in sociology generally, began his research career in medical sociology by using participant observation to study the life of mental hospital patients. His classic work in this area, *Asylums* (1961), presented the concept of "total institutions" that emerged as an important socio-logical statement on the social situation of people confined by institutions. His observations also led to the development of his notions of impression manage-ment and the dramaturgical perspective in sociology that views "life as a theatre" and "people as actors on a stage," as well as his concept of stigma (Goffman 1959, 1967).

With the introduction of symbolic interactionist research into an area pre-viously dominated by structural-functionalism, medical sociology became an arena of debate between two of sociology's major theoretical schools. By the mid-1960s, symbolic interaction came to dominate a significant portion of the literature in the field. One feature of this domination was the numerous studies conducted in reference to labeling theory, a variant of symbolic interaction, and the controversy it provoked. Labeling theory held that deviant behavior is not a quality of the act a person commits but rather is a consequence of the definition applied to that act by others (Becker 1973). That is, whether or not an act is considered deviant depends upon how other people react to it. Although labeling theory pertained to deviance generally, the primary center of argument was focused on the mental patient experience, with Thomas Scheff (1999) the prin-cipal proponent of the labeling approach. Labeling theory was also employed in studies of the medical profession as seen in Eliot Freidson's (1970b) alternative concept of the sick role.

By the 1980s, however, symbolic interaction entered a period of decline in medical sociology. Many of its adherents had been "rebels" intentionally sub-verting the dominant paradigm of structural-functionalism and giving voices to women and marginal social groups like mental patients, the physically-handicapped, and the aged and their caretakers by entering their social world and observing it. Yet, as Norman Denzin (1991) points out, between 1981 and 1990, the canonical texts in the field had shifted from Mead to Blumer and Blumer himself was under attack on several methodological and substantive issues – but most importantly for not advancing the field to meet his own early criticisms; moreover, practitioners of the perspective were getting older ("the graying of interactionism"), the number of students espousing interactionism was decreasing, and the old enemy (structural-functionalism) had been largely vanquished. Unfortunately, symbolic interaction had taken on the image of a "fixed doctrine" and, except for Mead's (1934) concept of the "generalized other," was unable to satisfactorily link small group processes with social phe-nomena reflecting the behavioral influences of the larger society. It was particu-larly unable to account for interaction between institutions or societal-level processes that affect each other, not just individuals. In addition, labeling theory, despite its merits in accounting for the powerful behavioral effects of "labels" placed on people, had not been able to explain the causes of deviance (other than the reaction of the social audience), nor whether deviants themselves share common characteristics like poverty, stress, or family background.

But it would be a mistake to relegate symbolic interaction to history, as participant observation remains the primary form of qualitative research in medical sociology. Participant observation and ethnomethodology are still the best methods for recording social behavior from the personal standpoint of those being studied and the settings within which they lead their usual lives. Annandale (1998) reports that interactionism has been the dominant theoretical perspective in medical sociology in Great Britain as seen in the majority of published studies. The observed patterns of behavior and first-person accounts of social situations bring a sense of "real life" to studies that quantitative research is unable to capture. While symbolic-interaction theory has not moved far beyond the original concepts of Mead and Blumer, it persists as an important theoretical approach to the study and explanation of social behavior among small groups of people interacting in ways that are relevant for health.

A relatively new area of research in medical sociology helping to revive symbolic interaction is the sociology of emotions, a topic that had been neglected in the past. Research in this field seeks to understand the link between social factors and emotions, since emotions are expressed either in response to social relationships or situations or both. Symbolic interactionism fills in the analytic gap between organic or biological approaches to the study of emotions and approaches like social constructionism that ignores biological processes and focuses more or less exclusively on the social and cultural components of emotions (Williams and Bendelow 1996). Interaction between people plays perhaps the major role in the activation and expression of emotions (Freund 1990). Thus, emotions are biological responses to social situations and the interaction between people involved in those situations. According to Simon Williams (1998), emotions, as existentially embodied states, also connect "personal troubles" to social structure in ways that affect health and shape patterns of disease. Williams finds, for example, that feelings of stress, helplessness, depression, sense of coherence, insecurity, and lack of control have been shown to be associated with increased levels of mortality and morbidity.

CONFLICT THEORY

Conflict theory, with its roots in the work of Karl Marx and Max Weber, joined symbolic interaction in significantly reducing the influence of structural-functionalism, but has failed to date to establish a major foothold in medical sociology. Conflict theory is based on the assumption that society is composed of various groups struggling for advantage, that inequality is a basic feature of social life, and conflict is the major cause of social change. Marx's perspective in conflict theory is seen in the rejection of the view expressed by structural-functionalism that society is held together by shared norms and values. Conflict theory claims that true consensus does not exist; rather, society's norms and values are those of the dominant ⟨...⟩ ⟨...⟩sed by them on the less privileged to maintain their advantaged po⟨...⟩ ⟨...⟩ adds, however, that social inequality is not based on just money ⟨...⟩y, and relationships to the means of production, but also on status ⟨...⟩tical influence. Since all social systems contain such inequality, conflict ⟨...⟩tably results and conflict, in turn, is responsible for social change.

Whereas the Marxian-oriented features of conflict theory have emphasized class struggle, other theorists have moved toward emphasizing conflicts that occur between interest groups and the unequal distribution of political power (Dahrendorf 1959). According to Bryan Turner (1988), modern societies are best understood as having a conflict between the principles of democratic politics (emphasizing equality and universal rights) and the organization of their economic systems (involving the production, exchange, and consumption of goods and services, about which there is considerable inequality). Therefore, while people have political equality, they lack social equality. This unresolved contradiction is relatively permanent and a major source of conflict. Ideologies of fairness are constantly challenged by the realities of inequalities, and they influence governments to try to resolve the situation through politics and welfare benefits.

This situation represents one of conflict theory's most important assets for medical sociology; namely, the capacity to explain the politics associated with health reform. Conflict theory allows us to chart the maneuvers of various entities, like the medical profession, insurance companies, drug companies, the business community, and the public, as they struggle to acquire, protect, or expand their interests against existing government regulations and programs and those under consideration. Other conflict approaches are connected more directly to classical Marxism by relying on class struggle to explain health policy outcomes (Navarro 1994) and the disadvantages of the lower and working classes in capitalist medical systems where the emphasis is on profit (McKinley 1984; Waitzkin 1983). While a major focus of conflict theory in medical sociology is on the role of competing interests in health care delivery and policy, other interests concern the sources of illness and disability in work environments, working-class health, differences in health lifestyles, and capitalist ideologies supportive of physician–patient interaction (Waitzkin 1983, 1989, 1991; McKinlay 1984; Navarro 1986; Blane 1987).

However, there are inherent limitations in the use of conflict theory in medical sociology. While some health situations are affected by conflict-related conditions, others are not. People may maintain their health or become sick and these outcomes can have little or nothing to do with conflict, politics, interest-group competition, class struggles, and the like. Moreover, Marxism began losing influence from the late 1970s onward. As Alex Callinicos (1999) points out, political events sank Marxist theory in the universities. First, French scholars turned their back on Marxism as a "theory of domination" in response to Soviet labor camps, the cold war, and the crackdown on Solidarity in Poland in 1981, followed by similar reactions elsewhere in Europe and Latin America. "The process of retreat was slower in the English-speaking world," states Callinicos (1999: 261), "but by the beginning of the 1990s, under the impact of postmodernism and the collapse of 'existing socialism' in Eastern Europe and the Soviet Union, Marx was a dead dog for most intellectuals there as well."

As a political doctrine. Marxist–Leninism also failed to construct healthy social conditions and an adequate health care delivery system in the former Soviet Union and eastern Europe. This region experienced a 30-year rise (1965–95) in adult male mortality, which is unprecedented for a group of industrialized societies under stable administrations in peacetime (Field 1995; Cockerham 1997, 1999). The epicenter of the downturn in life expectancy was in Russia where male longevity fell nearly six years during this period. The greatest potential of conflict theory for medical sociology thus lies in its non-Marxist aspects, as interest-group competition in welfare states proves more relevant for health concerns than class struggle.

MAX WEBER

None of the classical theorists – Comte, Spencer, Simmel, Marx, Durkheim, and Weber – concerned themselves with medical sociology. Weber, however, has had the greatest direct influence on the field. His most important contributions are associated with his concepts of formal rationality and lifestyles. Weber (1978) distinguished between two major types of rationality: formal and substantive. Formal rationality is the purposeful calculation of the most efficient means and procedures to realize goals, while substantive rationality is the realization of values and ideals based on tradition, custom, piety, or personal devotion. Weber described how, in western society, formal rationality became dominant over its substantive counterpart as people sought to achieve specific ends by employing the most efficient means and, in the process, tended to disregard substantive rationality because it was often cumbersome, time-consuming, inefficient, and stifled progress. This form of rationality led to the rise of the West and the spread of capitalism. It is also linked to the development of scientific medicine and modern social structure through bureaucratic forms of authority and social organization that includes hospitals (Hillier 1987). The rational goal-oriented action that takes place in hospitals tends to be a flexible form of social order based on the requirements of patient care, rather than the rigid organization portrayed in Weber's concept of bureaucracy (Strauss et al. 1963). But his perspective on bureaucracy nevertheless captures the manner in which authority and control are exercised hierarchically and the importance of organizational goals in hospital work (Hillier 1987).

Weber's notion of formal rationality has likewise been applied to the "depro-fessionalization" of physicians. Deprofessionalization means a decline in power resulting in a decline in the degree which a profession maintains its professional characteristics. Eliot Freidson's (1970a, 1970b) seminal work on the medical profession in the 1970s had captured American medicine's professional domin-ance in its relations with patients and external organizations. Medicine was *the* model of professionalism, with physicians having absolute authority over their work and ranked at or near the top of society in status. However, George Ritzer and David Walczak (1988) noted the loss of absolute authority by physicians as their treatment decisions came under increasing scrutiny in the late twentieth century by patients, health care organizations, insurance companies, and government agencies.

Ritzer and Walczak found that government policies emphasizing greater control over health care costs and the rise of the profit motive in medicine identified a trend in medical practice away from substantive rationality (stressing ideals like serving the patient) to formal rationality (stressing rules, regulations, and efficiency). Government and insurance company oversight in reviewing and approving patient care decisions, and the rise of private health care business corporations, decreased the autonomy of medical doctors by hiring them as employees and controlling their work – joined with greater consumerism on the part of patients – to significantly reduce the professional power and status of physicians. Thus, the "golden age" of medical power and prestige ended, as medicine's efforts to avoid regulation left open an unregulated medical market that invited corporate control and public demands for government control to contain costs. Frederic Hafferty and Donald Light (1995: 138) predict that "the basic overall thrust of professionalism is toward a loss and not a continuation or strengthening of medicine's control over its work."

Weber's work also provides the theoretical background for the study of health lifestyles. Weber (1978) identified life conduct (*Lebensführung*) and life chances (*Lebenschancen*) as the two central components of lifestyles (*Lebensstil*). Life conduct refers to choice or self-direction in behavior. Weber was ambiguous about what he meant by life chances, but Ralf Dahrendorf (1979:73) analyzed Weber's writings and found that the most comprehensive concept of life chances in his terminology is that of "class position" and that he associated the term with a person's probability of finding satisfaction for interests, wants, and needs. He did not consider life chances to be a matter of pure chance; rather, they are the chances that people have in life because of their social situation.

Weber's most important contribution to conceptualizing lifestyles is to identify the dialectical interplay between choices and chances as each works off the other to shape lifestyle outcomes (Abel and Cockerham 1993; Cockerham, Abel, and Lüschen 1993). That is, people choose their lifestyle and the activities that characterize it, but their choices are constrained by their social situation. Through his concept of *Verstehen* or interpretive understanding, Weber seems to favor the role of choice as a proxy for agency over chance as representative of structure in lifestyle selection, although both are important. Weber also made the observation that lifestyles are based not so much on what people produce, but what they consume. By connecting lifestyles to status, Weber suggests that the means of consumption not only *expresses* differences in social and cultural practices between groups, but *establishes* them as social boundaries (Bourdieu 1984).

Health lifestyles are collective patterns of health-related behavior based on choices from options available to people according to their life chances (Cockerham and Ritchey 1997; Cockerham, Rütten, and Abel 1997). These life chances include class, age, gender, ethnicity, and other relevant structural variables that shape lifestyle choices. The choices typically involve decisions about smoking, alcohol use, diet, exercise, and the like. The behaviors resulting from the interplay of choices and chances can have either positive or negative consequences for health, but nevertheless form a pattern of health practices that constitute a lifestyle. Although positive health lifestyles are intended to produce good health, the ultimate aim of such lifestyles is to be healthy in order to use (consume) it for something, such as the capability to work, feel and look good, participate in sports and leisure activities, and enjoy life (d'Houtaud and Field 1984). Health lifestyles originated in the upper middle-class, yet have the potential to spread across class boundaries in varying degrees of quality (Cockerham et al. 1988). While Weber did not consider the health aspects of lifestyles, his concepts allow us to view them as (1) associated with status groups and principally a collective, rather than individual, phenomenon; (2) patterns of consumption, not production; and (3) formed by the dialectical interplay between choices and chances.

THEORY IN THE TWENTY-FIRST CENTURY

The twentieth century ended with massive social changes causing both sociology and medical sociology to adjust to new realities and forge new theoretical orientations, as well as adapt older ones to account for the changes. As Bernice Pescosolido and Jennie Kronenfeld (1995: 9) explain:

> We stand at a transition between social forms. The society that created the opportunity for the rise of a dominant profession of medicine, for a new discipline of sociology, and for a spinoff of the subfield of medical sociology, is undergoing major change. As the larger social system unravels in the face of rapid social change, established problems, solutions, and understandings are challenged because they do not as successfully confront current realities.

It is clear that the breakup of the industrial age is occurring and, as Ulrich Beck (1992) explains, a "new modernity" is emerging. "Just as modernization dissolved the structure of feudal society in the nineteenth century and produced the industrial society," states Beck (1992: 10), "modernization today is dissolving industrial society and another modernity is coming into being." With the twenty-first century at hand, we have already witnessed the collapse of communism in the former Soviet Union and eastern Europe, the multiculturalization of Europe and North America, the rise of cultural and sexual politics, changing patterns of social stratification, the increasing importance of information as an economic commodity, and the dominance of the service sector in the global economy. Changing social circumstances have resulted in new theoretical approaches in medical sociology which will be reviewed in this section: poststructuralism, postmodernism, the work of Pierre Bourdieu, and critical realism.

POSTSTRUCTURALISM: FOUCAULT, THE SOCIOLOGY OF THE BODY, AND FEMINIST THEORY

Poststructualism emerged out of a short-lived structuralist perspective that was popular in France in the 1960s. Structuralism has its roots in linguistics, most notably the semiotic (sign systems) theory of Ferdinand de Saussure, and is largely based on the work of the anthropologist Claude Lévi-Strauss. Both structuralism and poststructuralism developed theories which analyzed culture in terms of signs, symbolic codes, and language, and took the position that the individual was not autonomous but constrained in social action by discourse (Best and Kellner 1991). Structuralism, however, depicted social meaning as a product of signification, a process maintained by traditional and universal structures forming a stable and self-contained system. Poststructuralists rejected the notion that there were universal rules organizing social phenomena into compact systems, as well as structuralism's failure to account for the motivations of users of language and its ahistorical approach to analysis. One approach to poststructuralism is the work of Jacques Derrida that helped lay a foundation for the emergence of postmodern theory. Derrida's (1978) analysis (deconstruction) of texts suggested that written language was not socially constraining, nor were its meanings stable and orderly. Depending upon the context in which they were used, meanings could be unstable and disorderly.

The leading representative of poststructuralism is Michel Foucault who focused on the relationship between knowledge and power. Foucault provided social histories of the manner in which knowledge produced expertise that was used by professions and institutions, including medicine, to shape social behavior. Knowledge and power were depicted as being so closely connected that an extension of one meant a simultaneous expansion of the other. In fact, Foucault often used the term "knowledge/power" to express this unity (Turner 1995). The knowledge/power link is not only repressive, but also productive and enabling, as it is a decisive basis upon which people are allocated to positions in society. A major contribution of Foucault to medical sociology is his analysis of the social functions of the medical profession, including the use of medical knowledge as a means of social control and regulation, as he studied madness, clinics, and sexuality. Foucault (1973) found two distinct trends emerging in the history of medical practice; "medicine of the species" (the classification, diagnosis, and treatment of disease) and "medicine of social spaces" (the prevention of disease). The former defined the human body as an object of study subject to medical intervention and control, while the latter made the public's health subject to medical and civil regulation. The surveillance of human sexuality by the state, church, and medicine subjected the most intimate bodily activities to institutional discourse and monitoring. Thus, bodies themselves came under the jurisdiction of experts on behalf of society (Armstrong 1987; Turner 1992; Peterson and Bunton 1997).

Foucault's analysis of the body also led to the development of a new specialty, the sociology of the body, with Turner's book *The Body and Society* (1996, originally published in 1984), the seminal work in this area. Theoretical developments concerning the sociological understanding of the control, use, and the phenomenological experience of the body, including emotions, have been most pronounced in Great Britain where this subject has become a major topic in medical sociology. One area of inquiry is the dialectical relationship between the physical body and human subjectivity or the "lived" or phenomenological experience of having and being in a body. As Deborah Lupton (1998: 85) explains: "The body-image shapes the ways in which individuals understand and experience physical sensations and locate themselves in social space, how they conceptualize themselves as separated from other physical phenomena, how they carry themselves, how they distinguish outside from inside and invest themselves as subject or object."

Another area of investigation is the social construction of bodies, illness, and emotions. In medical sociology, the social constructionist approach is closely tied to Foucault and analyzes the body as a product of power and knowledge (Bury 1986; Nettleton 1995; Annandale 1998). It focuses on examining the manner in which people shape, decorate, present, manage, and socially evaluate the body. Chris Shilling (1993), for example, points out that social class has a profound influence on how people develop their bodies and apply symbolic values to particular body forms. Schilling (1993: 140) finds that bodies are forms of physical capital with their value determined by "the ability of dominant groups to define their bodies and lifestyles as superior, worthy of reward, and as, metaphorically and literally, the embodiment of class."

Judith Lorber (1997) and others (Radley 1993) argue that illness is also socially constructed in that the expression of symptoms is shaped by cultural and moral values, experienced through interaction with other people, and influenced by particular beliefs about health and illness. The result, claims Lorber, is a transformation of physiological symptoms into a diagnosis, socially appropriate illness behavior, and a modified status. When it comes to emotions, social constructionism emphasizes the social, rather than biological nature of emotional states (James and Gabe 1996). It takes the position that emotions vary cross-culturally and socially in their meaning and expression; consequently, they are first and foremost social and cultural constructions (Williams and Bendelow 1996).

Feminist theory in medical sociology also has poststructural roots, especially in regard to social constructionist accounts of the female body and its regulation by a male-dominated society. Social and cultural assumptions are held to influence our perceptions of the body, including the use of the male body as the standard for medical training, the assignment of less socially desirable physical and emotional traits to women, and the ways in which women's illnesses are socially constructed (Martin 1987; Lupton 1994; Annandale and Clark 1996; Lorber 1997; Clarke and Olesen 1999). Other feminist theory is grounded in conflict theory or symbolic interaction, and deals with the sexist treatment of women patients by male doctors and the less than equal status of female physicians in professional settings and hierarchies (Fisher 1984; West 1984; Riska and Wegar 1993). There is, however, no unified perspective among feminist theorists other than a "woman-centered" perspective that examines the various facets of women's health and seeks an end to sexist orientations in health and illness and society at large (Nettleton 1995; Annandale and Clark 1996; Annandale 1998; Clarke and Olesen 1999; Lengermann and Niebrugge-Brantley 2000).

Regardless of its widespread influence on many facets of contemporary theory in medical sociology, poststructuralism has its critics. Some argue that poststructuralism has been overtaken and surpassed by postmodern theory or, at best, cannot be easily distinguished from postmodernism (Ritzer 2000). Others suggest that the perspective does not take limits on power into account, nor explain relations between macro-level power structures other than dwell on their mechanisms for reproduction; moreover, there is a disregard of agency in post-structural concepts, especially those of Foucault (Giddens 1987; Münch 1993). Anthony Giddens, for example, notes Foucault's history tends to have no active subjects at all and concludes: "It is history with the agency removed." Yet Foucault's knowledge/power equation, applied to social behavior and poststructuralism in general, is important for a number of topics in medical sociology (Petersen and Bunton 1997).

POSTMODERNISM

There is considerable disagreement about the nature and definition of post-modernity, but a common theme is the breakup of modernity and its postindustrial social system that is bringing new social conditions. Postmodernism was generally ignored by sociologists until the mid-1980s when primarily British social scientists decided it was worthy of serious attention (Bertens 1995). Postmodernism emerged out of poststructuralism as a more inclusive critique of modern sociological theory and grand narratives; it rejected notions of continuity and order and called for new concepts explaining the disruptions of late modern social change (Best and Kellner 1991). Rather, it argued that there was no single coherent rationality and the framework for social life had become fragmented, diversified, and decentralized (Turner 1990). Its sociological relevance rested in its depiction of the destabilization of society and the requirement to adjust theory to new social realities. However, there have been few works to date in medical sociology explicitly adopting postmodern themes. Exceptions include highly abstract and poststructuralist-oriented discourses on health and the definition of the body (Fox 1993), along with works concerning the fragmentation of modern society and medical authority leaving individuals with greater self-control over their bodies (Glassner 1989) and increased personal responsibility for their health (Cockerham et al. 1997).

Postmodern theory has been criticized for a number of reasons, including its failure to explain social conditions after the rupture with modernity is complete, lacking an adequate theory of agency, being too abstract, not providing clear conceptualizations, and not having empirical confirmation (Best and Kellner 1991; Ritzer 2000). While its demise has been announced in Britain (Williams 1999), it is still popular in France and has gained adherents in the United States (Ritzer 2000). The advantage of postmodern theory is that modern society is indeed shifting into a new form with social conditions different from the recent past (the 1960s and 1970s) and the perspective provides a theoretical framework, despite its diffuse literature, for explaining many of the changes. Its ultimate fate is therefore unknown.

PIERRE BOURDIEU

Identified as the leading intellectual in contemporary France, Bourdieu's work focuses on how the routine practices of individuals are influenced by the external structure of their social world and how these practices, in turn, reproduce that structure (Jenkins 1992). Through his key concept of habitus, Bourdieu connects social practices to culture, structure, and power (Swartz 1997). Bourdieu (1990) describes the habitus as a mental scheme or organized framework of perceptions (a structured structure operating as a structuring structure) that predisposes the individual to follow a particular line of behavior as opposed to others that might be chosen. These perceptions are developed, shaped, and maintained in memory and the habitus through socialization, experience, and the reality of class circumstances. While the behavior selected may be contrary to normative expectations and usual ways of acting, behavioral choices are typically compatible with the dispositions and norms of a particular group, class, or the larger society; therefore, people tend to act in predictable and habitual ways even though they have the capability to choose differently. Through selective perception, the habitus adjusts aspirations and expectations to "categories of the probable" that impose boundaries on the potential for action and its likely form.

Of all Bourdieu's works, the one most relevant for medical sociologists remains his book *Distinction* (1984) in which he systematically accounts for the patterns of cultural consumption and competition over definitions of taste of the French social classes. It includes an analysis of food habits and sports that describes how a class-oriented habitus shaped these particular aspects of health lifestyles. Cockerham (1997, 1999) follows Bourdieu's theoretical framework in identifying negative health lifestyles as the primary social determinant of the late twentieth-century downturn in life expectancy in Russia and eastern Europe. The group most responsible for reduced longevity were middle-age, working-class males. The living conditions of these men and their relatively low and powerless position in the social structure produced a habitus fostering unhealthy practices (heavy drinking and smoking, disregard for diet, and rejection of exercise) that resulted in a lifestyle promoting heart disease, accidents, and other health problems leading to a shortened life span. These behaviors were norms established through group interaction, shaped by the opportunities available to them, and internalized by the habitus. The structure of everyday life both limited and molded health-related choices to the extent that lifestyles led to premature deaths.

According to Williams (1995), the merit of Bourdieu's analysis for understanding the relationship between class and health lifestyles lies in his depiction of the relative durability of various forms of health-related behavior within particular social classes and the relatively seamless fashion in which he links agency and structure. "In particular," states Williams (1995: 601), "the manner in which his arguments are wedded to an analysis of the inter-relationship between class, capital, taste, and the body in the construction of lifestyles...is both compelling and convincing." Although Bourdieu has been criticized for overemphasizing structure at the expense of agency and presenting an overly deterministic model of human behavior (Münch 1993), he nevertheless provides a framework for medical sociologists to conceptualize health lifestyles and for sociologists generally to address the agency-structure interface.

CRITICAL REALISM

Critical realism is a new theoretical perspective that has recently emerged in Great Britain and is based on the work of philosopher Roy Bhaskar (1994, 1998) and sociologist Margaret Archer (1995; Archer et al. 1998). Critical realist theory argues that social constructionism does not account for agency and provides an "oversocialized" view of individuals overemphasizing the effects of structure, while other theorists, like Bourdieu and Giddens, opt for a "seamless" approach to agency and structure, but the operations of the two in reality are not synchronized. Consequently, critical realism, in opposition to poststructuralism, treats agency and structure as fundamentally distinct but interdependent dimensions that need to be studied separately in order to understand their respective contributions to social practice. The "analytical decoupling of structure and agency" is necessary, states Williams (1999: 809), "not in order to abandon their articulation, but, on the contrary, so as to examine their *mutual interplay across time*; something which can result both in *stable reproduction* or *change* through the *emergence* of new properties and powers."

Critical realism takes the position that social systems are open to process and change and that people as agents and actors have the critical capacity, reflexivity, and creativity to shape structure, yet, in turn, are shaped by structure. But the key factor for the critical realist is the capacity of the individual to transform structure and produce variable outcomes (Archer 1995). Structure, for its part, is relatively enduring, although it can be modified, and deep structures have generative mechanisms going beyond the observable that influence behavior. A goal of critical realism is to connect agency and structure in a way that the distinctive properties of both can be realistically accounted for without being reduced to a single entity. Space limitations preclude a more extensive discussion of critical realism and its recent emergence has not yet evoked major criticisms, nor has the perspective achieved widespread prominence to date. Among the few studies in medical sociology employing critical realism is an examination of the body from the standpoint of chronic illness and disability, which focuses on the interrelationship of biological and social factors in shaping outcomes (Williams 1999).

CONCLUSION

The notion that medical sociology is atheoretical is wrong, although there have been past problems in this regard. This chapter has provided a brief account of the history and variety of viewpoints in sociological theory that have been utilized within the field and provided influential statements on the relationship between society and health. Beginning with Parsons and structural-functionalism, medical sociology in reality has a rich theoretical tradition spanning more than 50 years and incorporating the work of both classical and contemporary theorists. Debates in general sociology, such as those involving the opposition of symbolic interactionists and conflict theorists to structural-functionalism and the current agency versus structure issue, became points of theoretical contention in medical sociology as well. The trend in twenty-first century sociological theory that seems to be aligning more with structural concerns, as seen in poststructuralism, is reflected in medical sociology, along with the counter perspective of critical realism. Although the ultimate direction of theory in medical sociology this century is uncertain, the theoretical basis for work in the field is extensive and its potential explanatory power is exciting. Medical sociology has become a theoretical subdiscipline.

References

Abel, Thomas and William C. Cockerham. 1993. "Lifestyle or Lebensführung? Critical Remarks on the Mistranslation of Weber's 'Class, Status, Party'." *Sociological Quarterly* 34: 551–6.

Annandale, Ellen. 1998. *The Sociology of Health and Medicine: A Critical Introduction.* Cambridge: Polity Press.

Annandale, Ellen and Judith Clark. 1996. "What is Gender? Feminist Theory and the Sociology of Human Reproduction." *Sociology of Health and Illness* 18: 17–44.

Archer, Margaret S. 1995. *Realist Social Theory: The Morphogenetic Approach.* Cambridge: Cambridge University Press.

Archer, Margaret, Roy Bhasker, Andrew Collier, Tony Lawson, and Alan Norrie. 1998. *Critical Realism: Essential Readings.* London: Routledge.

Armstrong, David. 1987. "Bodies of Knowledge: Foucault and the Problem of Human Anatomy." pp. 59–76 in G. Scambler (ed.), *Sociological Theory and Medical Sociology.* London: Tavistock.

Beck, Ulrich. 1992. *Risk Society: Towards a New Modernity.* London: Sage.

Becker, Howard S. 1973. *Outsiders: Studies in the Sociology of Deviance*, 2nd edition. New York: Free Press.

Becker, Howard S., Blanche Greer, Everett Hughes, and Anselm Strauss. 1961. *Boys in White: Student Culture in Medical School.* Chicago: University of Chicago Press.

Bertens, Hans. 1995. *The Idea of the Postmodern.* London: Routledge.

Best, Steven and Douglas Kellner. 1991. *Postmodern Theory: Critical Interrogations.* New York: Guilford.

Bhaskar, Roy. 1994. *Plato Etc.: The Problems of Philosophy and Their Resolution.* London: Verso.

——. 1998. *The Possibility of Naturalism: A Philosophical Critique of the Contemporary Human Sciences.* London: Routledge.

Blane, David. 1987. "The Value of Labour-Power and Health." Pp. 8–36 in G. Scambler (ed.), *Sociological Theory and Medical Sociology.* London: Tavistock.

Blumer, Herbert. 1969. *Symbolic Interactionism.* Englewood Cliffs, NJ: Prentice-Hall.

Bourdieu, Pierre. 1984. *Distinction: A Social Critique of the Judgement of Taste.* London: Routledge.

——. 1990. *The Logic of Practice.* Cambridge: Polity Press.

Bury, Michael. 1986. "Social Constructionism and the Development of Medical Sociology." *Sociology of Health and Illness* 8: 137–69.

Callinicos, Alex. 1999. *Social Theory: A Historical Introduction.* Cambridge: Polity Press.

Clarke, Adele E. and Virginia L. Olesen (eds.). 1999. *Revisioning Women, Health, and Healing.* London: Routledge.

Claus, Elizabeth. 1982. *The Growth of a Sociological Discipline: On the Development of Medical Sociology in Europe*, vol. I. Leuven, Belgium: Sociological Research Institute, Katholieke Universiteit Leuven.

Cockerham, William C. 1983. "The State of Medical Sociology in the United States, Great Britain, West Germany, and Austria." *Social Science and Medicine* 17: 1513–27.

——. 1997. "The Social Determinants of the Decline of Life Expectancy in Russia and Eastern Europe." *Journal of Health and Social Behavior* 38: 117–30.

——. 1998. *Medical Sociology*, 7th edition. Upper Saddle River, NJ: Prentice-Hall.

——. 1999. *Health and Social Change in Russia and Eastern Europe.* London: Routledge.

Cockerham, William C., Thomas Abel, and Guenther Lueschen. 1993. "Max Weber, Formal Rationality, and Health Lifestyles." *Sociological Quarterly* 34: 413–25.

Cockerham, William C., Gerhard Kunz, and Guenther Lueschen. 1988. "Social Stratification and Health Lifestyles in Two Systems of Health Care Delivery: A Comparison of the United States and West Germany." *Journal of Health and Social Behavior* 29: 113–26.

Cockerham, William C. and Ferris J. Ritchey. 1997. *Dictionary of Medical Sociology.* Westport, CT: Greenwood Press.

Cockerham, William C., Alfred Rütten, and Thomas Abel. 1997. "Conceptualizing Contemporary Health Lifestyles: Moving Beyond Weber." *Sociological Quarterly* 38: 321–42.

Dahrendorf, Ralf. 1959. *Class and Conflict in Industrial Society.* Stanford, CA: Stanford University Press.

——. 1979. *Life Chances.* Chicago: University of Chicago Press.

Denzin, Norman K. 1991. *Symbolic Interactionism and Cultural Studies.* Oxford: Blackwell.

Derrida, Jacques. 1978. *Writing and Difference.* Chicago: University of Chicago Press.

d'Houtaud, A. and Mark G. Field. 1984. "The Image of Health: Variations in Perception by Social Class." *Sociology of Health and Illness* 6: 30–59.

Durkheim, Emile. 1950 [1895]. *The Rules of Sociological Method.* New York: Free Press.

——. 1951 [1897]. *Suicide: A Study in Sociology.* Glencoe, IL: Free Press.

——. 1964 [1893]. *The Division of Labor in Society.* New York: Free Press.

Field, Mark. 1995. "The Health Crisis in the Former Soviet Union: A Report from the 'Post-War' Zone." *Social Science and Medicine* 41: 1469–78.

Fisher, Sue. 1984. "Doctor–Patient Communication: A Social and Micro-Political Performance." *Sociology of Health and Illness* 6: 1–27.

Foucault, Michel. 1973. *The Birth of the Clinic.* London: Tavistock.

Fox, Nicholas J. 1993. *Postmodernism, Sociology and Health.* Buckingham: Open University Press.

Freidson, Eliot. 1970a. *Profession of Medicine.* New York: Dodd & Mead.

——. 1970b. *Professional Dominance.* Chicago: Aldine.

Freund, Peter. 1990. "The Expressive Body: A Common Ground for the Sociology of Emotions and Health and Illness." *Sociology of Health and Illness* 12: 452–77.

Gerhardt, Uta. 1989. *Ideas about Illness: An Intellectual and Political History of Medical Sociology.* London: Macmillan.

Giddens, Anthony. 1987. *Social Theory and Modern Sociology*. Stanford, CA: Stanford University Press.

Glaser, Barney G. and Anselm M. Strauss. 1965. *Awareness of Dying*. Chicago: Aldine.

——. 1967. *The Discovery of Grounded Theory*. Chicago: Aldine.

——. 1968. *Time for Dying*. Chicago: Aldine.

Glassner, Barry. 1989. "Fitness and the Postmodern Self." *Journal of Health and Social Behavior* 30: 180–91.

Goffman, Erving. 1959. *The Presentation of Self in Everyday Life*. New York: Anchor.

——. 1961. *Asylums*. Anchor.

——. 1967. *Stigma: Notes on the Management of Spoiled Identity*. Engelwood Cliffs, NJ: Prentice-Hall.

Hafferty, Frederic W. and Donald W. Light. 1995. "Professional Dynamics and the Changing Nature of Medical Work." *Journal of Health and Social Behavior*, Extra Issue: 132–53.

Hillier, Sheila. 1987. "Rationalism, Bureaucracy, and the Organization of Health Services: Max Weber's Contribution to Understanding Modern Health Care Systems." Pp. 194–220 in G. Scambler (ed.), *Sociological Theory and Medical Sociology*. London: Tavistock.

James, Veronica and Jonathan Gabe (eds.). 1996. *Health and the Sociology of Emotions*. Oxford: Blackwell.

Jenkins, Richard. 1992. *Pierre Bourdieu*. London: Routledge.

Lengermann, Patricia Madoo and Jil Niebrugge-Brantley. 2000. "Contemporary Feminist Theory." pp. 307–55 in G. Ritzer, *Modern Sociological Theory*. New York: McGraw-Hill.

Lorber, Judith. 1997. *Gender and the Social Construction of Illness*. London: Sage.

Lupton, Deborah. 1994. *Medicine as Culture: Illness, Disease, and the Body in Western Culture*. London: Sage.

——. 1998. "Going with the Flow: Some Central Discourses in Conceptualizing and Articulating the Embodiment of Emotional States." Pp. 82–99 in S. Nettleton and J. Watson (eds.), *The Body in Everyday Life*. London: Routledge.

McKinlay, John (ed.). 1984. *Issues in the Political Economy of Health Care*. London: Tavistock.

Martin, Emily. 1987. *The Woman in the Body*. Milton Keynes: Open University Press.

Mead, George H. 1934. *Mind, Self, and Society*. Chicago: University of Chicago Press.

Merton, Robert K., George G. Reader, and Patricia Kendall. 1957. *The Student Physician*. Cambridge, MA: Harvard University Press.

Münch, Richard. 1993. *Sociological Theory*. Chicago: Nelson-Hall.

Navarro, Vicente. 1986. *Crisis, Health, and Medicine: A Social Critique*. London: Tavistock.

——. 1994. *The Politics of Health Policy*. Oxford: Blackwell.

Nettleton, Sarah. 1995. *The Sociology of Health and Illness*. Cambridge: Polity Press.

Parsons, Talcott. 1951. *The Social System*. New York: Free Press.

Pescosolido, Bernice and Jennie J. Kronenfeld. 1995. "Health, Illness, and Healing in an Uncertain Era: Challenges from and for Medical Sociology." *Journal of Health and Social Behavior*, Extra Issue: 5–33.

Petersen, Alan and Robin Bunton (eds.). 1997. *Foucault, Health, and Medicine*. London: Routledge.

Radley, Alan (ed.). 1993. *Worlds of Illness: Biographical and Cultural Perspectives On Health and Disease*. London: Routledge.

Riska, Elianne and Katarina Wegar (eds.). 1993. *Gender, Work, and Medicine*. London: Sage.

Ritzer, George. 2000. *Modern Sociological Theory*, 5th edition. New York: McGraw-Hill.

Ritzer, George and David Walczak. 1988. "Rationalization and the Deprofessionalization of Physicians." *Social Forces* 67: 1–22.

Robertson, Roland and Bryan S. Turner (eds.). 1991. *Talcott Parsons: Theorist of Modernity*. London: Sage.

Scheff, Thomas J. 1999. *Being Mentally Ill*, 3rd edition. Hawthrone, NY: Aldine de Gruyter.

Shilling, Chris. 1993. *The Body and Social Theory*. London: Sage.

Smelser, Neil J. 1998. *The Social Edges of Psychoanalysis*. Berkeley: University of California Press.

Strauss, Anselm, Leonard Schatzman, Danuta Ehrlich, Rue Bucher, and Melvin Sabshin. 1963. "The Hospital and its Negotiated Order." Pp. 147–69 in E. Freidson (ed.), *The Hospital in Modern Society*. New York: Free Press.

Swartz, David. 1997. *Culture and Power: The Sociology of Pierre Bourdieu*. Chicago: University of Chicago Press.

Thoits, Peggy A. 1995. "Stress, Coping, and Social Support Processes: Where Are We? What Next?" *Journal of Health and Social Behavior*, Extra Issue: 53–79.

Turner, Bryan S. 1988. *Status*. Milton Keynes: Open University Press.

——. 1990. "The Interdisciplinary Curriculum: From Social Medicine to Postmodernism." *Sociology of Health and Illness* 12: 1–23.

——. 1992. *Regulating Bodies*. London: Routledge.

——. 1995. *Medical Power and Social Knowledge*, 2nd edition. London: Sage.

——. 1996. *The Body and Society*, 2nd edition. London: Sage.

Waitzkin, Howard. 1983. *The Second Sickness: Contradictions of Capitalist Health Care*. New York: Free Press.

——. 1989. "A Critical Theory of Medical Discourse: Ideology, Social Control, and the Processing of Social Context in Medical Encounters." *Journal of Health and Social Behavior* 30: 220–39.

——. 1991. *The Politics of Medical Encounters*. New Haven, CT: Yale University Press.

Weber, Max. 1958 [1904–5]. *The Protestant Ethic and the Spirit of Capitalism*, translated by T. Parsons. New York: Scribner's.

——. 1978 [1922]. *Economy and Society*, 2 vols., edited and translated by G. Roth and C. Wittich. Berkeley: University of California Press.

West, Candace. 1984. "When the Doctor is a 'Lady': Power, Status, and Gender in Physician–Patient Encounters." *Symbolic Interaction* 7: 87–106.

Williams, Simon J. 1995. "Theorising Class, Health and Lifestyles: Can Bourdieu Help Us?" *Sociology of Health and Illness* 17: 577–604.

——. 1998. "'Capitalising' on Emotions? Rethinking the Inequalities in Health Debate." *Sociology* 32: 121–39.

——. 1999. "Is Anybody There? Critical Realism, Chronic Illness and the Disability Debate." *Sociology of Health and Illness* 21: 797–819.

Williams, Simon J. and Gillian Bendelow. 1996. "Emotions, Health and Illness: The 'Missing Link' in Medical Sociology." Pp. 25–53 in V. James and J. Gabe (eds.), *Health and the Sociology of Emotions*. Oxford: Blackwell.

2

Health and Culture

STELLA QUAH

Is culture relevant to the study of health and illness? Almost with one voice, sociologists and anthropologists affirm it is. Such a consensus is exceptional in these disciplines which have produced the bulk of systematic research on health-related behavior by applying a wide variety of approaches and conceptual perspectives. Today we know that culture is not just one of many factors associated with health but is the context within which health-related behavior unfolds. This chapter explains why culture is significant in health-related behavior. The discussion unfolds in three steps. We shall first deal with the definition of culture. Then we will consider the link between culture and health behavior. Finally, we will focus on the link between culture and healing systems.

DEFINING CULTURE

The meaning of the term "culture" varies widely across disciplines and conceptual perspectives. To keep within the scope of this volume, the focus is on the contributions of sociology and anthropology. We begin with an historical glance at the efforts made to define and understand "culture."

The Classics

One enduring contribution is that of Emile Durkheim, a pioneer of the discipline of sociology. In his *Rules of Sociological Method*, first published in 1895, Durkheim proposed guidelines for the study of social phenomena as *social facts*. He argued that social facts are "representations" of society in the mind of the individual. They are ways of thinking, feeling, and acting external to the person. Such "facts" include myths, popular legends, religious conceptions, moral beliefs, and social beliefs and practices in general. By treating social values, beliefs, and customs as social facts, Durkheim promoted the systematic study of culture. Durkheim's concepts of a collective social consciousness and social solidarity also encompass culture. He saw social solidarity and, particularly, collective consciousness as reflective of culture and concurrently present within and external to the individual. Taylor and Ashworth (1987: 43) propose that these ideas are applicable to the study of medical sociology phenomena, such as attitudes toward death and the link between "changing forms of social solidarity and changing perceptions of health, disease, and medicine."

One of Durkheim's contemporaries was Max Weber. Weber's work during the first two decades of the twentieth century brilliantly marked the initiation of the sociological analysis of culture. Among his voluminous published work, two studies are particularly relevant: *The Protestant Ethic and the Spirit of Capitalism* (1905) and *Economy and Society* (published in English in 1968). Weber highlighted the importance of culture as values and beliefs coexisting and shaping social action within the micro-cosmos of the individual actor as well as at the level of collectivities, institutions, and the larger society. In particular, Weber's conceptualization of *ethnic group* and *traditional action* offers the most relevant insights to the study of culture.

Weber defined *ethnic* groups as "human groups" characterized by a "subjective belief in their common descent" given their real or perceived similarities in one or more characteristics: physical types or race, customs, language, religion, and in "perceptible differences in the conduct of everyday life" (Weber 1978: 389–90). The impact of these subjectively perceived similarities on social action is heightened by yet another crucial feature of ethnicity: "the belief in a specific *honor* of their members, not shared by outsiders, that is, the sense of *ethnic honor.*" Weber (1978: 391) explained:

> palpable differences in dialect and differences of religion in themselves do not exclude sentiments of common ethnicity...The conviction of the excellence of one's own customs and the inferiority of alien ones, a conviction which sustains the sense of ethnic honor, is actually quite analogous to the sense of honor of distinctive status groups.

Weber's concept of *traditional action* (one of four in his typology of social action) is similarly relevant to the link between culture and health. Weber defines *traditional* action as social action "determined by ingrained habituation." *Traditional* action, he wrote, "is very often a matter of almost automatic reaction to habitual stimuli that guide behavior in a course which has been repeatedly followed. The great bulk of all everyday action to which people have become habitually accustomed approaches this type" (Weber 1978: 4). As will be discussed, these insights into the substance of ethnicity and traditional action elucidate the pervasiveness of customs, beliefs, and practices of different ethnic or cultural communities upon their health-related behavior. Weber's analyses have inspired subsequent research and contributed to the understanding of the pervasiveness of culturally inspired and culturally sustained health practices. Probably because of the profound influence and widespread incorporation of his conceptual insights into the body of general knowledge of sociology, these

Weberian contributions are seldom cited directly in current medical sociology research. A notable exception is the analysis of Weber's legacy in medical sociology by Uta Gerhardt (1989) and his concept of lifestyles (Cockerham 1998).

The interest in culture was passed along to subsequent generations of social scientists. By 1951, Clyde Kluckhohn reported many different definitions of culture (1951) and many more have appeared since. Yet, in spite of the plurality of definitions, some common strands are found in the cumulative work of anthropologists and sociologists that make up the fundamental fabric of this important concept. Kluckhohn (1951: 86) defined "culture" in the widest sense, as a community's "design for living." He pointed out that despite the wide variety of definitions, he and A. L. Kroeber (1952) found, in their critical review of definitions, an "approximate consensus" that he (Kluckhohn 1951: 86) summarized as follows:

> Culture consists in patterned ways of thinking, feeling, and reacting, acquired and transmitted mainly by symbols, constituting the distinctive achievements of human groups, including their embodiments in artifacts;... traditional (i.e. historically derived and selected) ideas and especially their attached values.

Kluckhohn proposed that the concept of culture be used as "a map" or "abstract representation" of the distinctive features of a community's way of life. This method is akin to the *ideal type*, the analytical tool introduced by Weber ([1925] 1946) to identify general characteristics, patterns, and regularities in social behavior.

A direct connection between culture and health was articulated by Bronislaw Malinowski (1944: 37) who considered culture as a functional response to satisfy "the organic and basic needs of man and of the race." He (Malinowski 1944: 36) defined culture as "the integral whole" encompassing "human ideas and crafts, beliefs and customs...A vast apparatus, partly material, partly human and partly spiritual, by which man is able to cope with the concrete, specific problems that face him." Malinowski saw those problems as human "needs" that prompted "cultural responses." These needs were metabolism, reproduction, bodily comforts, safety, movement, growth, and health. However, in his (Malinowski 1944: 93) view, health is implied in all the other six human basic needs, in addition to the need for "relief or removal of sickness or of pathological conditions." Malinowski (1944: 91) proposed "hygiene" as the "cultural response" to *health*. Hygiene involves all "sanitary arrangements" in a community, "native beliefs as to health and magical dangers," "rules about exposure, extreme fatigue, the avoidance of dangers or accidents," and the "never absent range of household remedies" (Malinowski 1944: 108).

Another valuable contribution to the understanding of culture was provided by sociologist Talcott Parsons. Parsons was greatly influenced as a student by Durkheim and Weber. Among his colleagues, he acknowledged the influence of Kluckhohn concerning "the problems of culture and its relation to society" (1951: xi). Parsons conceptualized social action as taking place within a three-dimensional context comprising personality, culture, and the social system

(1951: 17). He (Parsons 1951: 327) defined culture as "ordered systems of symbols" that guide social action and are "internalized components of the personalities of individual actors and institutionalized patterns of social systems." For Parsons (1951: 11), the shared symbolic systems are fundamental for the functioning of the social system and they represent "a *cultural tradition*." Parsons argued that a cultural tradition has three principal components or systems: value-orientations, beliefs, and expressive symbols (1951: 326–7).

Parson's preoccupation with a balanced analysis of values and motives that would prevent us from falling into the extremes of "psychological" or "cultural" determinism, led him to invest considerable effort into the discussion of culture. Parsons (1951: 15) identified three main features:

> First, that culture is *transmitted*, it constitutes a heritage or a social tradition; secondly, that it is *learned*, it is not a manifestation, in particular content, of man's genetic constitution; and third, that it is *shared*. Culture, that is, is on the one hand the product of, on the other hand a determinant of, systems of human interaction.

Parsons' concepts of culture and cultural traditions and his identification of culture as transmitted, learned, and shared, together with the contributions from Durkheim, Weber, Kluckhohn, and Malinowski form the significant inheritance from the social science pioneers on the study of culture. An additional heritage of the study of culture is the cross-fertilization of insights and research from sociology and anthropology. Most current studies on culture and on the link between culture and health have built on this rich patrimony.

By identifying the fundamental components of culture, the collective wisdom inherited from the classics permit us to consider culture and ethnicity as the same phenomenon. Although Margaret Mead (1956) and Benjamin Paul (1963) proposed that cultural differences cut across racial and religious lines, these two factors are very much part of the cultural landscape within which individuals and groups operate. This idea is captured well by Stanley King (1962) who proposed that what constitutes an ethnic group is the combination of "common backgrounds in language, customs, beliefs, habits and traditions, frequently in racial stock or country of origin" and, more importantly, "a consciousness of kind" (1962: 79). It is important to keep in mind that, from the perspective of individuals and collectivities, these ethnic similarities may be factual or perceived and may include a formal religion. The sharing of the same geographical settlement is not as important as it was once thought, mainly because large migrations (voluntary or not) of people from different ethnic groups have resulted in the formation of diaspora beyond their ancestral lands and the subsequent increase of multiethnic settlements. The process of assimilation (becoming a member of the host culture) is commonly observed when individuals settle in a new country. Living in close proximity to each other leads individuals from different ethnic groups into another process, *pragmatic acculturation*; that is, the process of culture borrowing motivated by the desire to satisfy specific needs (Quah 1989: 181). Inspiration from the classics has guided the identification of these processes. Assimilation and *pragmatic acculturation* have been found to influence health behavior significantly. These processes will be discussed in more detail later. But first, let us review some of the contemporary leading ideas on culture and health.

Main Contemporary Research Trends

The contributions of the classics are the foundation of our understanding of culture and of its impact on behavior. As we shall see, the research conducted over the past five decades have supported their interpretation of culture. The corpus of contemporary sociological and anthropological research on culture is expanding rapidly and in different directions. Some "neoclassical approaches" have sprang out of the work of Weber, Durkheim, and Marx but have taken a life of their own as, for example, interpretations of religion, studies of social control, and feminist perspectives of the body and gender (Alexander 1990).

Attention to the body as an important subject of social analysis was brought up by Michael Foucault's work on *The Order of Things* (1970), *The Birth of the Clinic* (1973), and *Discipline and Punish* (1977). He eschewed research in favor of formulating assumptions, but his effort at awakening alertness to the symbolic and perceived meaning of the body is, to me, his vital contribution. Research findings over the past decade show that the symbolic meaning of the body in relation to health and illness, manipulation, completeness and mutilation, varies substantially across cultures. One of the most recent and dramatic illustrations of this finding is the cultural interpretation of female genital cutting (FGC) by western groups advocating the eradication of FGC as opposed to the symbolic meaning of FGC held by some African communities that are struggling to preserve it (Greer 1999).

On the effort to elucidate how culture affects the individual's behavior, the work of Erving Goffman (1968a, 1968b) using the symbolic-interactionist perspective is important. Goffman focuses on the person's subjective definition of the situation and the concept of stigma. He proposes a three-stage stigmatization process (1968b): the person's initial or "primary" deviation from a normative framework; the negative societal reaction; and the person's "secondary" reaction or response to the negative reaction that becomes the person's "master-status." It is clear that Goffman's "normative framework" is socially constructed based on the community's predominant culture. Disability and disease, particularly mental illness (1968a), are typically perceived as stigma and trigger the stigmatization process. Unfortunately, Goffman and many of his followers have neglected to apply his conceptual approach fully to their own studies: they overlook cross-cultural comparisons (see for example Strauss 1975; Locker 1983; Scambler 1984).

The preceding discussion might lead some readers to believe that there is consensus on what is culture and how to study it. Drawing a sketch of the current situation in cultural studies, Jeffrey Alexander (1990) indicates that one point of agreement is "their emphasis on the autonomy of culture from social structure." On the other hand, he finds in the contemporary literature on culture "extraordinary disagreement over what is actually inside the cultural system itself." Is it symbols, or values, or feelings, or metaphysical ideas? He proposes that culture might embrace all these because culture cannot be understood "without reference to subjective meaning" and "without reference to social structural constraints." For the same reason he favors a multidisciplinary approach to the study of culture (1990: 25–6).

The multidisciplinary approach is indeed one of two main trends in contemporary research on the link between culture and health. Focusing on the understanding of culture and health behavior, the disciplines of sociology and anthropology have produced research findings confirming that culture or ethnicity influence health behavior and attitudes significantly. The research work advanced over the second half of the twentieth century is characterized by a second main trend: although several conceptual perspectives on the influence of culture are discussed and explored, no dominant theory has yet emerged to explain that influence systematically.

Rene Fox (Parsons and Fox 1952a, 1952b; Fox 1976, 1989), has contributed to the advance in the search for evidence on the impact of values and beliefs on health behavior at the micro-level through her analysis of individuals and at the macro-level by focusing on institutional aspects of medical care such as the medical school and the hospital. She demonstrated the advantages of close collaboration between sociology and anthropology in the study of health-related behavior, particularly on the aspect of culture. Some of her contributions will be discussed in the subsequent sections.

A final note before moving on to culture and health: The inclusion of ethnicity has become fashionable in medical research in the past two decades but it appears that little is learned from social science research. Reviewing the uses of the ethnicity concept in articles published in the *American Journal of Public Health* from 1980 to 1989, Ahdieh and Hahn (1996) found that "there was little consensus in the scientific [medical] community regarding the meaning or use of terms such as race, ethnicity or national origin" (1996: 97–8). Efforts have been made to assist health care practitioners to appreciate the complexity of culture (LaVeist 1994; Williams 1994). The social sciences and, in particular sociology and anthropology, remain the disciplines most dedicated to the study of culture or ethnicity *per se* and of its association with health and illness phenomena.

CULTURE AND HEALTH BEHAVIOR

The conceptual insights of the classic and contemporary sociologists and anthropologists on the significance of culture are confirmed by research on health behavior over the past four decades. A complete review of the vast body of sociological and anthropological literature dealing with the influence of culture upon the individual's health behavior is a formidable task beyond the scope of this chapter. Instead, I will highlight the nuances and significance of cultural variations in health behavior by discussing relevant findings within the framework of three types of health-related behavior: namely, *preventive health behavior, illness behavior,* and *sick-role behavior.* The two former concepts were proposed by Kasl and Cobb (1966). The concept of *sick-role* behavior was formulated by Talcott Parsons (1951: 436–8).

Preventive health behavior refers to the activity of a person who believes he or she is healthy for the purpose of preventing illness (Kasl and Cobb 1966: 246). Kasl and Cobb labeled this "health behavior" but the term *preventive* differentiates it clearly from the other two types of health-related behavior. Kasl and Cobb (1966: 246) defined *illness behavior* as the activity undertaken by a person who feels ill for the purpose of defining the illness and seeking a solution. In the sense intended for this discussion, *illness behavior* encompasses the time span between a person's first awareness of symptoms and his or her decision to seek expert assistance or "technically competent" help (to borrow Parsons' [1951: 437] term). *Illness behavior* thus defined includes activities such as initial self-medication or self-treatment, and discussion of the problem with non-expert family members and others within one's primary or informal social network. *Sick-role behavior* is the activity undertaken by a person who considers himself or herself ill for the purpose of getting well (based on Parsons 1951: 436–8). *Sick-role behavior* is typically preceded by *illness behavior* and encompasses the sick person's formal response to symptoms, that is, the seeking of what he or she perceives as "technically competent" help. The sick person may seek technically competent or expert advice from whoever he or she perceives as or believes to be an expert including traditional healers, modern medical healing practitioners, or a combination of these. *Sick-role behavior* also includes the relations between patient and healer, and the subsequent activity of the person as a patient.

Culture and Preventive Health Behavior

Preventive health behavior refers to the activity of a person who believes he or she is healthy for the purpose of preventing illness (Kasl and Cobb 1966: 246). In addition to the study of healthy individuals, relevant research on preventive health behavior also covers studies on substance addiction or abuse (drugs, alcohol, cigarettes) that seek to understand the path toward addiction and to identify the factors involved. The subjective evaluation of one's own health status may propel or retard preventive action against disease. Many studies on preventive health behavior report data on self-health evaluation but it is not common to report variations in the cultural meaning attached to health status. As health status is in many respects a value, cultural variations are commonly found in people's evaluation of their own health status and the way in which they evaluate it.

The study by Lew-Ting, Hurwicz, and Berkanovic (1998) illustrates this phenomenon in the case of the Chinese. The Chinese use the traditional idea of "ti-zhi" or "constitution" to denote "a long-term, pervasive characteristic that is central to their sense of self" and clearly different from the western concept of health status. The latter is "a more temporal, fluctuating state" that varies with "the experience of illness" (1998: 829). This is an illustration of the cultural similarity in the definition of constitution among people of the same ethnic group (Chinese elderly) living in two different parts of the world. In contrast, residing in the same geographical location does not secure a common meaning of health status. For example, significant cultural differences in self-evaluated health status were observed among three cultural groups living in close proximity of each other in south-central Florida (Albrecht, Clarke, and Miller 1998).

Among the latest studies relevant to the prevention of substance abuse, in this case of alcohol, is the work of Gureje, Mavreas, Vazquez-Baquero, and Janca (1997). People in nine cities were interviewed by Gureje and his colleagues on their values and perceptions concerning the meaning of drinking alcohol. The nine cities were Ankara (Turkey), Athens (Greece), Bangalore (India), Flagstaff (Arizona), Ibadan (Nigeria), Jebal (Romania), Mexico City, Santander (Spain), and Seoul (South Korea). These authors reported a "remarkable congruence" in the practitioners' criteria to diagnose alcoholism. But they found significant variations among people across the nine cities concerning "drinking norms, especially with regard to *wet* and *dry* cultures" (1997: 209). A *wet* culture, they stated, is that where alcohol drinking is permitted or encouraged by the social significance attached to the act of drinking and to the social context within which drinking takes place. In a *dry* culture alcohol drinking is discouraged or prohibited altogether. They cited two of the earliest alcohol studies by Bunzel (1940) and Horton (1943) which suggested the strong influence of culture on alcohol drinking. Their own study adds to the increasing body of research findings showing that the difficulties encountered in the prevention of alcoholism are greater in some cultures than in others.

The investigation into the relative influence of culture upon alcohol abuse was found by Guttman (1999) to be equivocal in situations where acculturation takes place. Guttman refers to the common definition of acculturation that is, "the process whereby one culture group adopts the beliefs and practices of another culture group over time" (1999: 175). His study of alcohol drinking among Mexican immigrants in the United States highlighted several problems. He found it difficult to identify clearly the boundaries between cultures sharing the same geographical area. This problem has been overcome in some studies by following the symbolic-interactionist postulate of the importance of subjective definition of self and of the situation and correspondingly accepting the subjects' self-identification as members of a given culture (see Quah 1993). Some researchers assume that the length of time spent in the host country leads to acculturation and thus use other indicators, such as the proportion of the immigrant's life spent in the host country (cf. Mandelblatt et al. 1999).

A second and more critical difficulty in the study of preventive and other types of health behavior involving alcoholism and other health disorders among immigrants is their concurrent exposure to multiple cultural influences. In this regard, Guttman's finding in the United States is similar to findings from immigrant studies in other countries. He observed that immigrants "are participants not only in the dissolution of older cultural practices and beliefs but are also constantly engaged in the creation, elaboration, and even intensification of new cultural identities" (Guttman 1999: 175). However, the presence of multiple cultural influences does not necessarily lead to the creation of new identities. Other outcomes are possible. A significant outcome is what I label *pragmatic acculturation*: the borrowing of cultural elements (concepts, ways of doing things, ways of organizing and planning) and adapting them to meet practical needs. Pragmatic acculturation is practiced in the search for ways to prevent illness, or trying different remedies to deal with symptoms (illness behavior), or seeking expert help from healers from other cultures (Quah 1985, 1989, 1993). Individuals "borrow" healing options from cultures other than their own, but they may or may not incorporate those options or more aspects of the other cultures into their lives permanently. The borrowing and adapting is part of the ongoing process of dealing with health and illness. Solutions from other cultures tend to be adopted, or adapted to one's own culture, if and for as long as they "work" to the satisfaction of the user.

Yet another angle of analysis in the study of culture and health is the identification of cultural differences in health behavior among subgroups of a community or country assumed to be culturally homogeneous. Such is the case of differences commonly found between "rural" and "urban" ways of life and ways of thinking in the same country. One of the numerous illustrations of this phenomenon is the study on preventive health education on AIDS in Thailand by Lyttleton (1993) that documented the urban–rural divide. The message of public preventive information campaigns designed in urban centers was not received as intended in rural villages. The concept of promiscuity that was at the center of the Thai AIDS prevention campaigns was associated by the villagers with the visiting of "commercial sex workers" only and not with the practice of "sleeping with several different village women" (1993: 143). The misperceptions of preventive public health campaigns occur between the rural, less educated, and dialect-speaking groups on the one hand, and the urban, educated civil servants and health professionals who design the campaigns, on the other hand. The misperception of the campaign message is not the only problem. An additional serious obstacle to reach the target rural population is the medium used to disseminate preventive health information. The Thai villagers perceived new technology including television broadcasts from Bangkok as "belonging to a different world – both physically and socioculturally" and, consequently, "increased exposure to these messages simply reinforces the [villagers'] perception that they are not locally pertinent" (Lyttleton 1993: 144).

Culture and Illness Behavior

As mentioned earlier, illness behavior refers to the activity undertaken by a person who feels ill for the purpose of defining the illness and seeking a solution (Kasl and Cobb 1966). What people do when they begin to feel unwell, the manner in which people react to symptoms, and the meaning they attach to symptoms have been found to vary across cultures.

Reviewing the work of Edward Suchman (1964, 1965) on illness behavior and ethnicity, Geertsen and his colleagues (1975) concluded that there was indeed an association between the two phenomena. They found that "Group closeness and exclusivity increases the likelihood" of a person responding to a health problem "in a way that is consistent with his subcultural background" (1975: 232). Further detailed data on the correlation between ethnicity and illness behavior was reported by, among others, Robertson and Heagarty (1975); Kosa and Zola (1975); and by Sanborn and Katz (1977) who found significant cultural variations in the perception of symptoms. In fact, the relative saturation of the literature regarding the ethnicity-illness behavior link was already manifested in Mechanic's observation in the late 1970s: "Cultures are so recognizably different that variations in illness behavior in different societies hardly need demonstration" (1978: 261).

Nevertheless, the number of studies documenting the association between culture and illness behavior has increased continuously. One of the most common research themes is mental illness, given that mental illness symptoms are primarily manifested through alterations in what is culturally defined as "normal" or "acceptable" social interaction. A prominent contributor to the study of culture and mental illness is Horacio Fabrega (1991, 1993, 1995). Summarizing the crux of current research in sociology and anthropology, Fabrega states that "empirical studies integral to and grounded in sound clinical and epidemiological research methods...have succeeded in making clear how cultural conventions affect manifestations of disorders, aspects of diagnosis, and responses to treatment" (1995: 380).

The reaction of others, particularly the family and people emotionally close to the symptomatic person, plays an important part in determining how the affected person reacts, that is, how he or she defines and handles symptoms. Such reaction varies across cultures. McKelvy, Sang, and Hoang (1997) found that, in contrast to Americans, "the Vietnamese traditional culture has a much more narrower definition of mental illness." They are more tolerant of behavioral disturbance triggered by distress. The Vietnamese define someone as mentally ill only if the person is "so disruptive" that he or she "threatens the social order or the safety of others"; even then, the family is the first source of care that may include "physical restraint." The person is taken to the hospital if the family is unable to control him or her (1997: 117).

Research conducted from the perspective of psychiatry tends to put a stronger emphasis on the importance of culture: the cultural definition of symptoms is seen as determining the disease outcome. Hahn and Kleinman (1983) proposed that beliefs in the etiology and prognosis of disease are as important to disease causation as microorganisms or chemical substances. Adler (1994) found this premise evident in the case of the sudden nocturnal death syndrome or SUNDS among the Hmong refugees in the United States. Adler explains "in the traditional Hmong worldview the functions of the mind and the body are not dichotomized and polarized" (1994: 26). Consequently, Adler identified a series of pathological circumstances leading to SUNDS. As refugees, the Hmong lost their traditional social support and were pressed to adapt to a different culture. The "severe and ongoing stress related to cultural disruption and national resettlement" as well as "the intense feelings of powerlessness regarding existence in the US," and their "belief system in which evil spirits have the power to kill men who do not fulfill their religious obligations" together led "the solitary Hmong male" to die of SUNDS (1994: 52).

Illness behavior typically involves a "wait-and-see" attitude as the first reaction to symptoms, followed by self-medication; if the problem is judged to have worsened, then the person might be prepared to seek expert advice. In this process, cultural patterns of behavior may be superseded by formal education.

In a comparative analysis of Chinese, Malays, and Indians, I found that education explains the practice of self-medication with modern over-the-counter medications better than culture. There was a significant difference among the three groups in the keeping of non-prescription and traditional medications at home. Yet, education served as an "equalizer" for self-medication with modern (i.e. western) medicines. The more educated a person is the more inclined he or she would be to practice self-medication with "modern" over-the-counter medicines before (or instead of) seeking expert advice, irrespective of his or her ethnic group (Quah 1985). A similar finding is reported by Miguel, Tallo, Manderson, and Lansong (1999) in the treatment of malaria in the Philippines.

Culture and Sick-Role Behavior

To recapitulate what was discussed in the first section, *sick-role behavior* is the activity undertaken by a person who considers himself or herself ill for the purpose of getting well (based on Parsons 1951: 436–8). Sick-role behavior encompasses the sick person's response to symptoms, in particular, the seeking of what he or she perceives as "technically competent" help (to borrow Parsons' term), as well as doctor–patient or healer–patient interaction. Lyle Saunders (1954) was among the first sociologists to observe that cultural differences in medical care manifested in the problems encountered when the physician and the patient were from different ethnic groups.

One of the earliest and most significant investigations on the actual influence of culture on sick-role behavior was Mark Zborowski's (1952, 1969) analysis of cultural differences in responses to pain. Investigating differences among war veterans warded in an American hospital, he observed that the Italian-American and Jewish-American patients differed significantly from the "old American" and Irish-American patients in their expression of pain and description of their symptoms. Zborowski proposed that cultural differences such as socialization, time-orientation, and the array of values outlining what is appropriate behavior in cultural communities explained the differences he observed among the four groups of patients. Along the same line of investigation, Irving Zola (1966) pursued the analysis of how culture shapes the subjective perception of symptoms. His research confirmed the findings reported by Zborowski on the presence of cultural differences in perception of, and reaction to, symptoms and pain. Zola continued his probe into the impact of cultural differences on the doctor–patient relationship, the perception of illness and the importance given to health matters in different cultural communities (1973, 1983). Andrew Twaddle (1978) conducted an exploratory replication of Zborowski's study, comparing 26 American married males who classified themselves as "Italian Catholics," "Protestants," and "Jewish." Twaddle found that Parsons' configuration of "sick role" varied among these groups.

Recent studies continue to confirm the impact of culture on the doctor–patient relation and, correspondingly, on patient outcomes. Nitcher (1994) observed the use of the traditional term "mahina ang baga" (weak lungs) by doctors and lay persons in the Philippines. Nitcher found that doctors use the term when diagnosing tuberculosis in an effort to spare the patient the social stigma of the disease. However, "weak lungs" is a very ambiguous term in everyday discourse, thus, the unintended consequence is a negative patient outcome. Nitcher states "the sensitivity of clinicians to [the] social stigma [of tuberculosis] is laudatory." But he correctly points out that "the use of the term *weak lungs* has [serious] consequences" for public health because the diagnosis "*weak lungs* is not deemed as serious as TB" and thus people, especially the poor, do not comply with the prescribed treatment which is a "six-month course of medication" (Nitcher 1994: 659).

A major direct implication of the concept of role is the symbolic, perceived or actual presence of others. Sick-role behavior implies the presence of the healing expert (irrespective of what healing system is at work). A large body of research into the doctor–patient relationship has produced interesting information confirming the relevance of culture. An expected finding is that cultural similarities, such as physical appearance and language, among other characteristics, between doctor (or healer) and patient facilitate the relationship and increase the possibility of positive patient outcomes (Kleinman 1980: 203–58; Cockerham 1998: 168–81). A note of caution: similarities in culture do not secure success in the doctor–patient relationship. Many other aspects come into play, from ecological factors (Catalano 1989) to the differential understanding of metaphors (Glennon 1999). The structural features of the healer–patient relationship, such as how is the interaction conducted and who is involved, also vary across cultures. Haug and her colleagues (1995) found interesting differences in the manner in which the doctor–patient interaction develops in Japan and the United States. Kleinman (1980: 250–310) shows that the relationship is not always a dyad as in some communities the patient's family is often directly involved. In some communities the quality of the interpersonal relationship built between patient and healer is paramount and may become as significant to the patient as "the technical quality" of the medical care received (Haddad, Fournier, Machouf, and Yatara 1998).

Recent publications have addressed the need of physicians and other health care personnel to be informed on the importance of cultural differences that may affect the doctor–patient interaction. Three of the latest works will suffice as illustrations. *The Cultural Context of Health, Illness and Medicine* by Martha O. Loustaunau and Elisa J. Sobo (1997) introduces the role of culture in an easy style devoid of conceptual arguments and thus suitable for health care practitioners who simply wish to improve their interaction with patients. Using a similar approach, the *Handbook of Diversity Issues in Health Psychology* edited by Pamela M. Kato and Traci Mann (1996) offers basic information for practitioners on the impact of ethnicity on health. The third example is Malcolm MacLachlan's (1997) book on *Culture and Health* that covers the analysis of culture in more detail and introduces some conceptual discussion. His book is also addressed to the medical profession but, compared to the other two, MacLachlan's is more suitable for health care practitioners interested in a social science analysis of culture and health. It is relevant to note that MacLachlan is a clinical psychologist but follows (albeit without citations) the sociological and anthropological conceptualization of ethnicity discussed earlier in this chapter:

that ethnicity encompasses a way of life and common origin as well as a consciousness of kind (1997: 3).

Following the same premise on the significance of the presence of others, another important aspect of sick-role behavior is the availability of an informal, social support network for the sick individual. The emotional, social, and instrumental support received from one's informal network of family and friends tend to guide the attitudes and actions of the ill person before, during, and after consulting experts. Just as cultural variations are observed among sick people searching for help from healing experts (whether traditional or modern), the seeking of emotional and social support and the presence and quality of informal social support from family and friends also vary across cultures. A recent example of studies supporting these assumptions is the study conducted by Kagawa-Singer, Wellisch, and Durvasula (1997). They compared Asian-American and Anglo-American women's situations after breast cancer diagnosis and found that the subjective meaning of the disease and the presence and use of family as the first source of social support varied between the two groups of patients.

CULTURE AND HEALING SYSTEMS

The options available to people seeking health care vary greatly across countries and cultures. As Cockerham explains (1998: 128), even in a modern, developed country like the United States, people may not look at modern medicine as the only or right option. In the discussion of culture and health, reference must be made to the wide range of healing options found in most societies today. For the sake of clarity and expediency, it is useful to consider all healing options as falling into three general categories: the modern or *western biomedicine* system; *traditional* medicine systems; and *popular* medicine. A medical system is understood as "a patterned, interrelated body of values and deliberate practices governed by a single paradigm of the meaning, identification, prevention and treatment of...illness and/or disease" (Press 1980: 47). Traditional medical systems flourished well before western biomedicine and their history goes back more than one millennium. Three ancient healing traditions are considered to be the most important: the Arabic, Hindu, and Chinese healing traditions (Leslie 1976: 15–17). However, there is a revival of interest in cultural traditions today around the two best-known traditional medicine systems: traditional Chinese medicine (Unschuld 1985) and Hindu or Ayurvedic medicine (Basham 1976). Popular medicine refers to "those beliefs and practices which, though compatible with the underlying paradigm of a medical system, are materially or behaviorally divergent from official medical practice" (Press 1980: 48). Popular medicine is also labeled "alternative" medicine or therapies (Sharma 1990).

In contrast to the modest attention given by researchers to power and dominance in the traditional healing system, the intense concern with the preponderance and power of western biomedicine is evident in the work of Foucault (1973) and Goffman (1968a, 1968b), and has been documented and analyzed in detail by Freidson (1970), Starr (1982), and Conrad and Schneider (1992) among others. These authors have referred to western biomedicine as practiced in western industrialized countries mainly in North America and western Europe. Interestingly, however, by the end of the twentieth century the predominance of western biomedicine is apparent in other countries as well (Quah 1995).

Healing systems are constantly evolving and two features of their internal dynamics are relevant here: divergence and pragmatic acculturation. Divergence in a healing system is the emergence of subgroups within the system supporting different interpretations of the system's core values. The comparative study of medical schools by Renée Fox (1976) serves as a good illustration of cultural divergence. She investigated the assumed resilience of six value-orientations (in Parsons' sense) at the core of western biomedicine: rationality, instrumental activism, universalism, individualism, and collectivism, all of which comprise the ethos of science and detached concern, a value she assigned specifically to western biomedicine practitioners. Fox observed that these values of biomedicine are subject to reinterpretations across cultures. She found "considerable variability in the form and in the degree to which they [the six value-orientations] are institutionalized" (Fox 1976: 104–6) even within the same country as illustrated by the situation in four major medical schools in Belgium in the 1960s representing basic cultural rifts: "Flemish" versus "French," and "Catholic" versus "Free Thought" perspectives.

A manifestation of pragmatic acculturation in a healing system is the inclination of its practitioners to borrow ideas or procedures from other systems to solve specific problems without necessarily accepting the core values or premises of the system or systems from which they do the borrowing. To illustrate: some traditional Chinese physicians use the stethoscope to listen to the patient's breathing, or the sphygmomanometer to measure blood pressure, or the autoclave to sterilize acupuncture needles, or a laser instrument instead of needles in acupuncture (see Quah and Li 1989; Quah 1989: 122–59). The study by Norheim and Fonnebo (1998) illustrates the practice of pragmatic acculturation among young western biomedicine practitioners in Norway who learned and practiced acupuncture. Norheim and Fonnebo reported that general practitioners were more inclined than specialists to use acupuncture with their patients, and that the majority of all 1,466 practitioners interviewed had "already undergone acupuncture or indicated that they would consider doing so" (1998: 522). Pragmatic acculturation has also facilitated the provision of western biomedical services to peoples from other cultures. Ledesma (1997) and Selzler (1996) studied the health values, health beliefs, and the health needs of Native Americans. These researchers stressed the importance of taking the cultures of Native Americans into consideration for the provision of relevant western biomedical services to their communities. Adapting the type and mode of delivery of modern health care services to serve the needs of traditional peoples is not a new preoccupation but it is now receiving more serious attention from health care providers. In today's parlance the process is called making the medical services more "user-friendly." Although pragmatic acculturation requires the western biomedicine practitioners to change or adapt their usual practices and assumptions, it is deemed worthwhile if it attains the objective of delivering health care to communities in need.

The presence and relative success of groups and institutions (for example, the medical profession, hospitals, and other health care organizations) involved in the provision of health care unfold in the context of culture. Arthur Kleinman (1980) highlights the relevance of the "social space" occupied by health systems. He identified significant differences among ethnic communities and the subsequent impact of cultural perceptions of mental illness upon the structure of mental health services. The influence of culture on the provision of mental health services has been studied widely. In the recent investigation on mental health in Vietnam by McKelvy, Sang, and Hoang (1997), cited earlier, they found that "There is no profession specifically dedicated to hearing the woes of others. Talk therapy is quite alien to the Vietnamese" (1997: 117). The Vietnamese's traditional perception of child behavior and their "narrow" definition of mental illness help to explain their skepticism on the need for child psychiatric clinics.

THE PERVASIVENESS OF CULTURE

The conclusion of this chapter is that culture has, does, and will continue to influence health-related behavior. There is a wealth of social science and, in particular, medical sociology research demonstrating the pervasiveness of cultural values and norms upon preventive health behavior, illness behavior, and sick-role behavior among individuals and groups as well as at the macro-level of healing systems.

The preceding discussion has highlighted three additional features of the study of culture in health and illness. The first of these features is the remarkable confluence of different and even opposite schools of thought in sociology concerning the need to analyze culture as an independent phenomenon, and the influence of culture upon agency and structure. The affective nature and subjectivity of one's perceived identity as member of an ethnic group and the permeability of cultural boundaries, are ideas found implicitly or explicitly in Durkheim, Weber, Parsons, as well as Goffman, Foucault, and Habermas, among others. The second feature is the divergence of healing systems. Healing systems are not always internally consistent; different interpretations of the core values or principles of the system may be held by subgroups within the system. The third feature is pragmatic acculturation, that is, the borrowing from other cultures of elements, ways of thinking and ways of doing things, with the objective of solving specific or practical problems. This borrowing is very prevalent and is found in all types of health-related behavior.

Finally, a comprehensive review of the relevant literature is not possible in this chapter given the enormous body of medical sociology research on health and culture. Instead, illustrations and the list of references are offered for each main argument in this discussion in the hope that the reader be enticed to pursue his or her own journey into this engaging research topic.

References

Adler, Shelley R. 1994. "Ethnomedical Pathogenesis and Hmong Immigrants' Sudden Nocturnal Deaths." *Culture, Medicine and Psychiatry* 18: 23–59.

Ahdieh, L. and R. A. Hahn. 1996. "Use of Terms 'Race', 'Ethnicity', and 'National Origin': A Review of Articles in the American Journal of Public Health, 1980–1989." *Ethnicity and Health* 1: 95–8.

Albrecht, Stan L., L. L. Clarke, and M. K. Miller. 1998. "Community, Family, and the Race/Ethnicity Differences in Health Status in Rural Areas." *Rural Sociology* 63: 235–52.

Alexander, Jeffrey C. 1990. "Analytic Debates: Understanding the Relative Autonomy of Culture." Pp. 1–27 in J. C. Alexander and Steven Seidman (eds.), *Culture and Society. Contemporary Debates*. Cambridge: Cambridge University Press.

Basham, A. L. 1976. "The Practice of Medicine in Ancient and Medieval India." Pp. 18–43 in Charles Leslie (ed.), *Asian Medical Systems: A Comparative Study*. Berkeley: University of California Press.

Bunzel, R. 1940. "The Role of Alcoholism in Two Central American Cultures." *Psychiatry* 3: 361–87.

Catalano, Ralph. 1989. "Ecological Factors in Illness and Disease." Pp. 87–101 in Howard E. Freeman and Sol Levine (eds.), *Handbook of Medical Sociology*, 4th edition. Englewood Cliffs, NJ: Prentice-Hall.

Cockerham, William C. 1998. *Medical Sociology*, 7th edition. Englewoods Cliffs: Prentice-Hall.

Conrad, Peter and Joseph W. Schneider. 1992. *Deviance and Medicalization. From Badness to Sickness*, Expanded edition. Philadelphia: Temple University Press.

Durkheim, Emile. 1938. *The Rules of Sociological Method*, 8th Edition. New York: The Free Press.

Fabrega, Horacio. 1991. "Psychiatric Stigma in Non-Western Societies." *Contemporary Psychiatry* 326: 534–51.

——. 1993. "A Cultural Analysis of Human Behavioral Breakdowns: An Approach to the Ontology and Epistemology of Psychiatric Phenomena." *Culture, Medicine and Psychiatry* 17: 99–132.

——. 1995. "Cultural Challenges to the Psychiatric Enterprise." *Comprehensive Psychiatry* 36: 377–83.

Freidson, Eliot. 1970. *Profession of Medicine: A Study of the Sociology of Applied Knowledge*. New York: Dodd Mead.

Foucault, Michael. 1970. *The Order of Things: An Archaeology of the Human Sciences*. London: Tavistock.

——. 1973. *The Birth of the Clinic: An Archeology of Medical Perception*. London: Tavistock.

——. 1977. *Discipline and Punish: The Birth of the Prison*. London: Allen Lane.

Fox, Renée C. 1976. "The Sociology of Modern Medical Research." Pp. 102–14 in Charles Leslie (ed.), *Asian Medical Systems: A Comparative Study*. Berkeley: University of California Press.

——. 1989. *Medical Sociology. A Participant Observer's View*. New York: Prentice-Hall.

Geertsen, R., M. R. Klauber, M. Rindflesh, R. L. Kane, and R. Gray. 1975. "A Re-Examination of Suchman's Views on Social Factors in Health Care Utilization." *Journal of Health and Social Behavior* 16: 226–37.

Gerhardt, Uta. 1989. *Ideas about Illness: An Intellectual and Political History of Medical Sociology*. New York: New York University Press.

Glennon, Cheryl D. 1999. "Conceptual Metaphor in the Health Care Culture (Health Communicators)." Unpublished Ph.D. Dissertation. San Diego: University of San Diego.

Goffman, Erving. 1968a. *Asylums: Essays on the Social Situation of Mental Patients and other Inmates*. Harmondsworth: Penguin.

——. 1968b. *Stigma. Notes on the Management of Spoilt Identity*. Harmondsworth: Penguin.

Greer, Germaine. 1999. *The Whole Woman*. New York: Knopf.

Gureje, O., V. Mavreas, J. L.Vazquez-Baquero, and A. Janca. 1997. "Problems Related to Alcohol Use: A Cross-Cultural Perspective." *Culture, Medicine and Psychiatry* 21: 199–211.

Guttman, M. C. 1999. "Ethnicity, Alcohol, and Assimilation." *Social Science and Medicine* 48: 173–84.

Habermas, J. 1981. *Theory of Communicative Action, Vol. 1. Reason and the Rationalization of Society*. Cambridge: Polity Press.

Haddad, Slim, Pierre Fournier, Nima Machouf, and Fissinet Yatara. 1998. "What Does Quality Mean to Lay People? Community Perceptions of Primary Health Care Services in Guinea." *Social Science and Medicine* 47: 381–94.

Hahn, Robert A. and Arthur Kleinman. 1983. "Belief as Pathogen, Belief as Medicine: 'Voodoo Death' and the 'Placebo Phenomenon' in Anthropological Perspective." *Medical Anthropology Quarterly* 14: 6–19.

Haug, Marie, H. Akiyama, G. Tryban, K. Sonoda, and M. Wykle. 1995. "Self-Care: Japan and the U.S. Compared." Pp. 313–24 in William C. Cockerham (ed.), *The Sociology of Medicine. International Library of Critical Writings in Sociology*. Aldershot: Elgar. Reprinted from *Social Science and Medicine* 1991, 33: 1011–22.

Horton, D. J. 1943. "The Functions of Alcohol in Primitive Societies: A Cross-Cultural Study." *Quarterly Studies of Alcohol* 4: 195–320.

Kagawa-Singer, Marjorie, David K. Wellisch, and Ramani Durvasula. 1997. "Impact of Breast Cancer on Asian American and Anglo American Women." *Culture, Medicine and Psychiatry* 21: 449–80.

Kasl, S. V. and S. Cobb. 1966. "Health Behavior, Illness Behavior, and Sick Role Behavior." *Archives of Environmental Health* 12: 246–55.

Kato, Pamela M. and Traci Mann (eds.). 1996. *Handbook of Diversity Issues in Health Psychology*. New York: Plenum Press.

King, Stanley H. 1962. *Perceptions of Illness and Medical Practice*. New York: Russell Sage Foundation.

Kleinman, Arthur. 1980. *Patients and Healers in the Context of Culture*. Berkeley: University of California Press.

Kluckhohn, Clyde. 1951. "The Study of Culture." Pp. 86–101 in Daniel Lerner and Harold D. Lasswell (eds.), *The Policy Sciences. Recent Developments in Scope and Method*. Stanford, CA: Stanford University Press.

Kosa, J. and I. K. Zola. 1975. *Poverty and Health. A Sociological Analysis*, revised edition. Cambridge, MA: Harvard University Press.

Kroeber, A. L. and C. Kluckhohn. 1952. "Culture: A Critical Review of Concepts and Definitions." *Papers of the Peabody Museum*, vol. 47. Cambridge, MA: Harvard University.

LaVeist, T. 1994. "Beyond Dummy Variable and Sample Selection: What Health Services Researchers Ought to Know about Race as a Variable." *Health Services Research* 29: 1–16.

Ledesma, Rita V. 1997. "Cultural Influences upon Definitions of Health and Health Sustaining Practices for American Indian Children." Unpublished Ph.D. Dissertation. Los Angeles: University of California.

Leslie, Charles (ed.). 1976. *Asian Medical Systems. A Comparative Study.* Berkeley: University of California Press.

Lew-Ting, Chih-Yin, M. L. Hurwicz, and E. Berkanovic. 1998. "Personal Constitution and Health Status among Chinese Elderly in Taipei and Los Angeles." *Social Science and Medicine* 47: 821–30.

Locker, D. 1983. *Disability and Disadvantage: The Consequences of Chronic Illness.* London: Tavistock.

Loustaunau, Marth O. and Elisa J. Sobo. 1997. *The Cultural Context of Health, Illness and Medicine.* Westport, CT: Bergin & Garvey.

Lyttleton, Chris. 1993. "Knowledge and Meaning: The AIDS Education Campaign in Rural Northeast Thailand." *Social Science and Medicine* 38: 135–46.

MacLachlan, Malcolm. 1997. *Culture and Health.* Sussex: Wiley.

Malinowski, Bronislaw. 1944. *A Scientific Theory of Culture and Other Essays.* Chapel Hill: University of North Carolina.

Mandelblatt, Jeanne S., K. Gold, A. S. O'Malley, K. Taylor, K. Cagney, J. S. Hopkins, and J. Kerner. 1999. "Breast and Cervix Cancer Screening Among Multiethnic Women: Role of Age, Health and Source of Care." *Preventive Medicine* 28: 418–25.

McKelvy, Robert S., David L. Sang, and Cam Tu Hoang. 1997. "Is There a Role for Child Psychiatry in Vietnam?" *Australian and New Zealand Journal of Psychiatry* 31: 114–19.

Mead, Margaret. 1956. "Understanding Cultural Patterns." *Nursing Outlook* 4: 260–2.

Mechanic, David. 1978. *Medical Sociology*, 2nd edition. New York: The Free Press.

Miguel, Cynthia A., V. L. Tallo, L. Manderson, and M. A. Lansong. 1999. "Local Knowledge and Treatment of Malaria in Agusan del Sur, The Philippines." *Social Science and Medicine* 48: 607–18.

Nitcher, Mark. 1994. "Illness Semantics and International Health: The Weak Lung/TB Complex in the Philippines." *Social Science and Medicine* 38: 649–63.

Norheim, Arne Johan, and Vinjar Fonnebo. 1998. "Doctors' Attitudes to Accupuncture – A Norwegian Study." *Social Science and Medicine* 47: 519–23.

Parsons, Talcott. 1951. *The Social System.* London: Routledge & Kegan Paul Ltd.

Parsons, Talcott and Renée Fox. 1952a. "Introduction." *Journal of Social Issues* 8: 2–3.

——. 1952b. "Illness, Therapy, and the Modern Urban Family." *Journal of Social Issues* 8: 31–44.

Paul, Benjamin. 1963. "Anthropological Perspectives on Medicine and Public Health." *Annals of the American Academy of Political and Social Science* 346: 34–43.

Press, I. 1980. "Problems of Definition and Classification of Medical Systems." *Social Science and Medicine* 14B: 45–57.

Quah, Stella R. 1985. "Self-Medication in Singapore." *Singapore Medical Journal* 26: 123–9.

——. 1989. *The Triumph of Practicality. Tradition and Modernity in Health Care Utilization in Selected Asian Countries.* Singapore: Institute of Southeast Asian Studies.

——. 1993. "Ethnicity, Health Behavior, and Modernization: The Case of Singapore." Pp. 78–107 in Peter Conrad and Eugene B. Gallagher (eds.), *Health and Health Care in Developing Countries: Sociological Perspectives.* Philadelphia: Temple University Press.

——. 1995. "The Social Position and Internal Organization of the Medical Profession in the Third World: The Case of Singapore." Pp. 485–501 in William C. Cockerham (ed.), *The Sociology of Medicine. International Library of Critical Writings in Sociology*. Aldershot: Elgar. Reprinted from *Journal of Health and Social Behavior* 1989, 30: 450–66.

Quah, Stella R. and Jing-Wei Li. 1989. "Marriage of Convenience: Traditional and Modern Medicine in the People's Republic of China." Pp. 19–42 in Stella R. Quah (ed.), *The Triumph of Practicality. Tradition and Modernity in Health Care Utilization in Selected Asian Countries*. Singapore: Institute of Southeast Asian Studies.

Robertson, Leon and M. Heagarty. 1975. *Medical Sociology: A General Systems Approach*. New York: Nelson Hall.

Sanborn, K. O. and M. M. Katz. 1977. "Perception of Symptoms Behavior Across Ethnic Groups." Pp. 236–40 in Y. H. Poortinga (ed.), *Basic Problems in Cross-Cultural Psychology*. Amsterdam: International Association for Cross-Cultural Psychology.

Saunders, Lyle. 1954. *Cultural Differences and Medical Care*. New York: Russell Sage Foundation.

Scambler, G. 1984. "Perceiving and Coping with Stigmatizing Illness." Pp. 35–43 in *The Experience of Illness*, edited by Ray Fitzpatrick et al. London: Tavistock.

Selzler, Bonnie Kay. 1996. "The Health Experiences of Dakota Sioux and Their Perceptions of Culturally Congruent Nursing Care." Unpublished Ph.D. Dissertation. Denver: University of Colorado Health Sciences Center.

Sharma, Ursula M. 1990. "Using Alternative Therapies: Marginal Medicine and Central Concerns." Pp. 127–39 in Pamela Abbot and Geoff Payne (eds.), *New Directions in the Sociology of Health*. London: Falmer Press.

Starr, Paul. 1982. *The Social Transformation of American Medicine*. New York: Basic Books.

Strauss, A. L. 1975. *Chronic Illness and the Quality of Life*. St Louis: Mosby.

Suchman, Edward. 1964. "Socio-Medical Variations Among Ethnic Groups." *American Journal of Sociology* 70: 319–31.

——. 1965. "Social Patterns of Illness and Medical Care." *Journal of Health and Human Behavior* 6: 2–16.

Taylor, Steve and Clive Ashworth. 1987. "Durkheim and Social Realism: An Approach to Health and Illness." Pp. 37–58 in Graham Scambler (ed.), *Sociological Theory & Medical Sociology*. London: Tavistock Publications.

Twaddle, Andrew C. 1978. "Health Decisions and Sick Role Variations: An Exploration." Pp. 5–15 in Howard D. Schwartz and Cary S. Kart (eds.), *Dominant Issues in Medical Sociology*. Reading, MA: Addison-Wesley. [First published in *Journal of Health and Social Behavior*, 10 (June, 1969), 105–15].

Unschuld, Paul U. 1985. *Medicine in China. A History of Ideas*. Berkeley: University of California Press.

Weber, Max. 1905. *The Protestant Ethic and the Spirit of Capitalism*. Translated by Talcott Parsons. New York: Scribner.

——. 1946 [1925]. *From Max Weber: Essays in Sociology*. Edited and translated by Hans H. Gerth and C. Wright Mills. New York: Oxford University Press.

——. 1978 [1968]. *Economy and Society*. Berkeley: University of California Press.

Williams, D. 1994. "The Concept of Race in Health Services Research, 1966–1990." *Health Services Research* 29: 261–74.

Zborowski, Mark. 1952. "Cultural Components in Response to Pain." *Journal of Social Issues* 8: 16–30.

——. 1969. *People in Pain*. San Francisco: Jossey-Bass.

Zola, Irving K. 1966. "Culture and Symptoms – An Analysis of Patients' Presentation of Complaints." *American Sociological Review* 31: 615–30.

——. 1973. "Pathways to the Doctor – From Person to Patient." *Social Science and Medicine* 7: 677–87.

——. 1983. *Socio-Medical Inquiries: Recollections, Reflections, and Reconsiderations*. Philadelphia: Temple University Press.

3

The Sociology of the Body

SARAH NETTLETON

In Tom Stoppard's (1967) play *Rosencrantz and Guildenstern are Dead* the two central characters lament the precariousness of their lives. Rosencrantz seeks solace in life's only certainty when he comments that "the only beginning is birth and the only end is death – if we can't count on that what can we count on." To this he might have added that he could reliably count on the fact that he had a body. The "fact" that we are born, have a body, and then die is of course something that does *seem* to be beyond question. It is something that we can hold on to, as we live in a world that appears to be ever more uncertain and risky (Giddens 1991; Beck 1992). But is this fact so obvious? Ironically, the more sophisticated our medical, technological, and scientific knowledge of bodies becomes the more uncertain we are as to what the body actually is. For example, technological developments have meant that boundaries between the physical (or natural) and social body have become less clear. With the development of assisted conception, when does birth begin? With the development of life extending technologies, when does the life of a physical body end? With the development of prosthetic technologies, what constitutes a "pure" human? It seems the old certainties around birth, life, bodies, and death are becoming increasingly complex. It is perhaps not surprising, therefore, that attempts to understand the social and ethical significance of the body have become central to recent sociological debates. Attempts to develop a sociological appreciation of the body have been especially important in the subdiscipline of the sociology of health and illness. The aim of this chapter is to delineate some of the key developments in the sociological theorizing of the body and to assess their significance for a number of substantive issues in medical sociology.

To meet this aim the chapter will first, review the main "perspectives" on the *sociology of the body* and the key social theorists who have informed each of these approaches. Second, the chapter will outline the parameters of the *sociology of embodiment.* Two key concepts which have emerged from these sociologies of the body and embodiment – *body projects* and the *lived body* – will also be discussed. Finally, a number of substantive issues which are central to medical sociology will be discussed with a view to highlighting the value of incorporating the body into the analysis of issues associated with health and illness. These issues are: illness and injury; health care work; medical technology; and health inequalities.

SOCIOLOGICAL PERSPECTIVES ON THE SOCIOLOGY OF THE BODY

There is now a copious literature on the sociology of the body which spans a range of perspectives. There are, however, alternative ways in which the body is understood and analyzed, with the most obvious approaches being rooted within the physical sciences, and classified as being part of a naturalistic perspective (Shilling 1993; Nettleton 1995). In this chapter, however, we will focus on three main *sociological* approaches. First, those which draw attention to the *social regulation* of the body, especially the way in which social institutions regulate, control, monitor, and use bodies. Our bodies are, of course, highly politicized; whilst we might like to think that we own and have control of our own bodies and what we do with them – we do not. This fact has perhaps become most strikingly evident as a result of feminist analyses of the ways in which medicine has controlled the bodies of women (Martin 1989; Oakley 1993). It is also evident in contemporary debates on topics such as euthanasia, organ transplantation, and abortion.

A second perspective within the sociology of the body literature is that which focuses on the ontology of the body. A number of theorists have asked the question – what exactly *is* the body? Their answer is that in late modern societies we seem to have become increasingly *uncertain* as to what the body actually is. For most sociologists the body is to a greater or lesser extent socially constructed. However, there are a number of variants of this view with some arguing that the body is simply a fabrication – an effect of its discursive context, and others maintaining that bodies display certain characteristics (e.g. mannerisms, gait, shape) which are influenced by social and cultural factors.

The third approach pays more attention to the way the body is experienced or *lived*. Whilst this *phenomenological* approach accepts that the body is to some extent socially fashioned it argues that an adequate sociology must take account of what the body, or rather embodied actor, actually does. In this sense it is perhaps more accurately described as a *sociology of embodiment* rather than a sociology of the body. This approach to the study of the body has gained much currency in recent years. It has to some extent emerged as a result of critical and creative debates within this field of study which have attempted to counter the dominant structuralist approach that concentrates on the social regulation of bodies. Some authors have become aware that this was a missing dimension of their earlier work. For example, in the Introduction to the second edition of his influential book *The Body and Society,* Turner (1996: 33) wrote that his earlier work will "now be corrected by a greater focus on the phenomenology of experience." This said, research which has outlined the ways in which bodies are socially regulated and socially constructed remains central to our understanding of the body in society.

Social Regulation of Bodies

In his book, *Regulating Bodies*, Turner (1992) suggests that late modern societies are moving toward, what he refers to as a "somatic society"; that is, a social system in which the body constitutes the central field of political and cultural activity. The major concerns of society are becoming less to do with increasing production, as was the case in industrial capitalism, and more to do with the regulation of bodies. Turner (1992: 12–13) writes:

> our major political preoccupations are how to regulate the spaces between bodies, to monitor the interfaces between bodies, societies and cultures...We want to close up bodies by promoting safe sex, sex education, free condoms and clean needles. We are concerned about whether the human population of the world can survive global pollution. The somatic society is thus crucially, perhaps critically structured around regulating bodies.

The concerns of the somatic society are also evidenced by the concerns of contemporary political movements such as feminist groupings, pro-and anti-abortion campaigns, debates about fertility and infertility, disability, and the Green movement.

This idea emerges from Turner's earlier work (1984) which examined the ways in which bodies are controlled within society and finds that it is the institutions of law, religion, and medicine that are most preoccupied with such regulation. The role of religion, law, and medicine are especially evident at the birth and death of bodies. Whilst the control of bodies by the church has gone into decline, the control of bodies by the medical profession is in the ascendancy. He argues, echoing the earlier writings of Zola (1972) and Conrad and Schneider (1980), that as society has become more secularized it has also become more medicalized with medicine now serving a moral as well as a clinical function:

> Medical practice in our time clearly does have a moral function, especially in response to AIDS and IVF programmes for unmarried, single women, but these moral functions are typically disguised and they are ultimately legitimized by an appeal to scientific rather than religious authority...medicine occupies the space left by the erosion of religion. (Turner 1992: 23)

Developing an analytical framework which works at two levels – the bodies of individuals and the bodies of populations – Turner identifies four basic, social tasks which are central to social order. We might refer to these as the four 'r's. First, *reproduction*, which refers to the creation of institutions which govern populations over time to ensure the satisfaction of physical needs, for example the control of sexuality. Second, the need for the *regulation* of bodies, particularly medical surveillance and the control of crime. Third, *restraint*, which refers to the inner self and inducements to control desire and passion in the interests of social organization. Fourth, the *representation* of the body, which refers to its physical presentation on the world's stage.

Turner's conceptualization of these four 'r's owes a great deal to the ideas of Foucault, especially his writings on normalization and surveillance. These draw attention to the ways in which bodies are monitored, assessed, and corrected within modern institutions. A central theme which runs through Foucault's (1976, 1979) work is that the shift from pre-modern to modern forms of society involved the displacement of what he terms *sovereign power*, wherein power resided in the body of the monarch, by *disciplinary power*, wherein power is invested in the bodies of the wider population. Disciplinary power refers to the way in which bodies are regulated, trained, maintained, and understood and is most evident in social institutions such as schools, prisons, and hospitals. Disciplinary power works at two levels. First, individual bodies are trained and observed. Foucault refers to this as the anatomo-politics of the human body. Second, and concurrently, populations are monitored. He refers to this process as "regulatory controls: a bio-politics of the population" (Foucault 1981: 139). It is these two levels – the individual and the population – which form the basis of Turner's arguments about regulating bodies which we have discussed above. Foucault argues that it is within such institutions that knowledge of bodies is produced. For example, the observation of bodies in prisons yielded a body of knowledge we now know as criminology and the observation of bodies in hospitals contributed to medical science. In fact it was the discourse of pathological medicine in the eighteenth century which formed the basis of the bodies in western society that we have come to be familiar with today. The body, Foucault argued, is a fabrication which is contingent upon its discursive context (see Armstrong 1983).

Through these discussions we can see that the regulation of bodies is crucial to the maintenance of social order. This observation forms the basis of Mary Douglas's (1966, 1970) work on the representation of the symbolic body. The ideas of Mary Douglas – an anthropologist – have been drawn upon extensively by medical sociologists. She argues that the perception of the physical body is mediated by the social body. The body provides a basis for classification, and in turn the organization of the social system reflects how the body is perceived.

> The social body constrains the way the physical body is perceived. The physical experience of the body, always modified by the social categories through which it is known, sustains a particular view of society. There is a continual exchange of meanings between the two kinds of bodily experience so that each reinforces the categories of the other. As a result of this interaction the body itself is a highly restricted medium of expression. (Douglas 1970: xiii)

Thus, according to Douglas, the body forms a central component of any classificatory system. Working within a Durkheimian tradition she maintains that all societies have elements of both the sacred and the profane, and that demarcation between the two is fundamental to the functioning of social systems. Thus societies respond to disorder by developing classificatory systems which can designate certain phenomena as "matter out of place." "Where there is dirt there is system... This idea of dirt takes us straight into the field of symbolism and promises a link-up with more obviously symbolic systems of purity" (Douglas 1966: 35). Anything which transcends social, or bodily, boundaries will be regarded as pollution. Ideas, therefore, about bodily hygiene tell us as much about our cultural assumptions as they do about the "real" body and our medical knowledge of it. Furthermore any boundaries that are perceived to be vulnerable or permeable will need to be carefully regulated or monitored to prevent transgressions (Nettleton 1988).

Social changes have bodily correlates in that what bodies are permitted to do, and how people use their bodies, is contingent upon social context. The work of Elias (1978, 1982) demonstrates this on a very grand scale. Elias is concerned with the link between the state and state formations and the behaviours and manners of the individual. He offers a *figurational sociology*; this means that he works at the level of social configurations, rather than societies. In fact, for Elias, societies are the outcome of the interactions of individuals. In his studies of *The Civilizing Process* (first published in 1939 in German) Elias (1978) examines in detail changes in manners, etiquette, codes of conduct, ways of dressing, ways of sleeping, ways of eating, and changing ideas about shame and decency associated with bodies.

According to Elias, the civilizing process began in the middle ages within court societies where social mobility became more fluid and peoples' futures could be determined not only by their birthrights, as had been the case under the feudal system, but also by the extent to which they were in favour with the sovereign or his/her advisers. In short, people were more inclined to be on their "best behaviour." Medieval personalities were characteristically unpredictable and emotional, they were inclined to be indulgent, and there were virtually no codes surrounding bodily functions. However, within court, societies codes of body management were developed and copious manuals were written on how to and where to sleep and with whom, how to behave at meals, appropriate locations for defecation, and so on. Changes in behavior impacted on social relations and, as social relations transformed, so the compulsions exerted over others became internalized. This process, according to Elias, was accelerated in the sixteenth century. People came to have greater self-control over behaviors associated with the body and a heightened sense of shame and delicacy:

> The individual is compelled to regulate his [sic] conduct in an increasingly differentiated, more even and more stable manner... The more complex and stable control of conduct is increasingly instilled in the individual from his earliest years as an automatism, a self compulsion that he cannot resist. (Elias 1982: 232–3)

This civilizing process involves three key progressive processes (Shilling 1993: 164–7): *socialization*; *rationalization*; and *individualization*. *Socialization* refers to the way in which people are encouraged to hide away their natural functions.

Thus the body comes to be regarded more in social rather than natural terms. In fact we find many natural functions offensive or distasteful; for example, if someone sitting next to us on a bus vomits over our clothes or if someone willingly urinates in an "inappropriate" part of our house. *Rationalization* implies that we have become more rational as opposed to emotional and are able to control our feelings. Finally, *individualization* highlights the extent to which we have come to see our bodies as encasing ourselves as separate from others. It is important therefore that we maintain a socially acceptable distance between ourselves and others. Furthermore how we "manage" and "present" our bodies (cf. Goffman 1959) has become especially salient in a late modern context. Some argue that this is because the body has become a prime site for the formation and maintenance of the modern self and identity.

Uncertain Bodies in Late Modern Societies

Giddens (1991) and a number of other commentators such as Beck (1992) and Douglas (1986) have argued that a key feature of such contemporary societies is *risk*. Doubt, Giddens argues, is a pervasive feature which permeates into every-day life "and forms a general existential dimension of the contemporary social world." Within our posttraditional societies, our identities and our sense of self are not givens. We can no longer hang on to our "traditional place" in society with respect to our social class, family, gender, locality, and so on. Rather, our self and identity becomes a "reflexively organised endeavour." Less and less can we rely on continuous biographical narratives but these tend to be flexible and continually revised (see also Featherstone and Hepworth 1991). The reflexive self is one which relies on a vast array of advice and information provided by a myriad of sources.

What has all this got to do with the body? Well a number of theorists have suggested that the body has come to form one of the main sites through which people develop their social identities. Whilst the environment and the social world seem to be "out of control," the body becomes something of an anchor. Giddens points out that the self is embodied and so the regularized control of the body is a fundamental means whereby a biography of self-identity is maintained. Giddens (1991:218) states:

> The body used to be one aspect of nature, governed in a fundamental way by processes only marginally subject to human intervention. The body was a "given," the often inconvenient and inadequate seat of the self. With the increasing invasion of the body by abstract systems all this becomes altered. The body, like the self, becomes a site of interaction, appropriation and re-appropriation, linking reflexively organised processes and systematically ordered expert knowledge. [...]. Once thought to be the locus of the soul...the body has become fully available to be "worked upon by the influences of high modernity" [...] In the conceptual space between these, we find more and more guidebooks and practical manuals to do with health, diet, appearance, exercise, lovemaking and many other things.

According to this thesis, therefore, we are more uncertain about our bodies, we perceive them to be more pliable and are actively seeking to alter, improve, and refine them.

The idea that contemporary societies are characterized by change and adaptability has also been articulated by Emily Martin (1994) in her empirical study of contemporary ideas about immunity in North America. By way of data collected via interviews, analyses of documents, participant observation, and informal exchanges, she (Martin 1994: xvii) found that "flexibility is an object of desire for nearly everyone's personality, body and organisation." Flexibility is associated with the notion of the immune system which now underpins our thinking about the body, organizations, machines, politics, and so on. In her interviews with ordinary men and women the idea of developing a strong immune system appeared to be in common currency. To be effective, that is to protect the body against the threats of disease and illness, the immune system must be able to change and constantly adapt. Martin's study not only provides a valuable analysis of late modernity but also reveals how our accounts and interpretations of our bodies are historically and socially contingent, and that they are not "immune" from broader social transformations (see also the discussion about the work of Elias above). How we experience our bodies is invariably social, and one of the central thrusts of modern times is that we feel compelled to work at creating a *flexible* and therefore adaptable and socially acceptable body.

Shilling (1993) also argues that the body might best be conceptualized as an *unfinished* biological and social phenomenon, which is transformed, within limits, as a result of its participation in society. The body is therefore in a continual state of "unfinishedness"; the body is "seen as an entity which is in the process of becoming; *a project* which should be worked at and accomplished as part of an individual's self-identity" (Shilling 1993: 5 – my emphasis). *Body projects* become more sophisticated and more complex in a context where there is both the knowledge and technology to transform them in ways that would have been regarded as the province of fiction. There is now a vast array of medical technologies and procedures to choose from if we want to shape, alter, and recreate our bodies – from various forms of assisted conception, to gene therapy, to forms of cosmetic surgery and so on. Shilling points out that there is of course an irony here. As we expand our "knowledge" and "expertise" the more uncertain we become as to what the body actually is and what its boundaries are. Reviewing the impact of medical technologies and the body, Williams (1997: 1047) suggests: "From plastic surgery to virtual medicine, our previously held and cherished beliefs about the body and the 'limits' of corporeality are being 'placed in brackets' and the body has thus become 'ever more elusive and problematic'."

Whilst the above discussion has highlighted the body as an unfinished and malleable entity which has become central to the formation of the late modern *reflexive* self, other more postmodern analyses have suggested that the body is not so much *uncertain* as *un/hyperreal*. In other words the body has disappeared – there is no distinction between bodies and the images of bodies. Drawing of the work of Baudrillard, Frank (1992) challenges the conventional idea that the body of the patient forms the basis of medical practice. It is the *image* of the body which now forms the basis of medical care.

> Real diagnostic work takes place away from the patient; bedside is secondary to screen side. For diagnostic and even treatment purposes, the image on the screen becomes the "true" patient, of which the bedridden body is an imperfect replicant, less worthy of attention. In the screens' simulations our initial certainty of the real (the body) becomes lost in hyperreal images that are better than the real body. (Frank 1992: 83)

There is a myriad of such images in the medical centre – CAT scan images, x-rays, angiograms, magnetic resonance imaging (MRI) videotapes, and so on. Although seeking to root ideas in empirical evidence is sometimes regarded as antithetical to postmodern ideas, a study of the use of these types of diagnostic tests for people with chronic back pain did seem to support the fact that medical practitioners rely on test results rather than the patients accounts of their pain. The image of the body is more legitimate than the body itself. For example, one participant in their study who experienced chronic back pain said that the doctors –

> are not listening to what you say... [they] try to tell you backaches are psychosomatic and your back couldn't be hurting, [that] there's nothing, no reason for it to hurt. X-rays don't show anything and you don't really have a backache. Oh yes I do, yes I do... but backaches are hard to see. Unless there's something that's a visible thing, it's kind of your word against who's looking. (Cited in Rhodes et al. 1999: 1191)

Perhaps more profound impact of the production of images is in relation to pregnancy. Writing in German from a historical perspective, Barbare Duden (1993) argues that the use of technologies which enable the fetus to be visually represented has contributed to the transformation of an unborn fetus into *a life*. The imagining of the unborn has meant that the fetus has become an emblem, a "billboard image," which has come into the limelight. Her (Duden 1993: 7) study addresses the following puzzle:

> How did the female peritoneum acquire transparency? What set of circumstances made the skinning of women acceptable and inspired public concern for what happens in her innards? And finally, the embarrassing question: how was it possible to mobilize so many women as uncomplaining agents of this skinning and as willing?

The images which are produced by a scanning ultramicroscope produce images which those who are trained appropriately can "read." However, this is something that has to be learned. Duden (1993: 29) describes the experience of a Puerto Rican woman, new to New York, who is asked to look at such images when she visits the antenatal clinic:

The graph that she is asked to look at during her visit to the clinic only serves to mystify her experience. In ways that she cannot fathom, expert professionals claim to know something about her future child, much more, in fact, than she could ever find out by herself.

In an amazingly short space of the time "the scan" has become a routine and ubiquitous experience for most pregnant women in many western societies. In popular discourse, women – and especially men – can be heard to say that "it was only then," when they saw the image of the fetus, did they feel that it was "real."

There is a tension here then, between the way the body is experienced or *lived* and the way the body is observed and described by "medical experts." In those circumstances where the voice of the body is silenced the person is likely to become alienated from those who aim to "practice" upon his or her body. In some respects this tension captures the difference between a sociology of the body and a sociology of embodiment. This difference is described neatly by Bendelow and Williams (1998: 123) who write:

> Whilst the former translates, in corporeal terms, into a treatment of the body as simply one amongst many topics which sociologists can study from "outside"...the latter, in contrast, refuses to slip into this deceptive Cartesian view of the world – one which treats mind and body as distinctly separate entities – taking the embodiment of its practitioners as well as its subjects seriously through a commitment to a lived body and its being in the world.

Sociology of Embodiment

A sociology of embodiment has developed out of a critique of the literature on the body which has failed to incorporate the voices of bodies as they are experienced or lived (Nettleton and Watson 1998). Drawing on phenomenological analyses this approach has argued that much of the existing literature has failed to challenge a whole series of dualisms such as: the split between mind and body; culture and nature; and reason and emotion. Such socially created dualisms are pernicious, it is argued, not only because they are false, but also because they serve to reinforce ideologies and social hierarchies. "These dualisms," Bendelow and Williams (1998: 1) argue, "have been mapped onto the gendered division of labour in which men, historically, have been allied with the mind, culture and the public realm of production, whilst women have been tied to their bodies, nature, and the private sphere of domestic reproduction." But most important, from a sociological point of view they hinder any effective theorizing which must assume the inextricable interaction and oneness of mind and body. Studies of pain and emotion have, perhaps more than any other, revealed that the body and the mind are not separate entities (Morris 1991; Burkitt 1997; Bendelow and Williams 1998).

Phenomenology: the "lived body"

The phenomenological perspective focuses on the "lived body"; the idea that consciousness is invariably embedded within the body. The human being is an embodied social agent. The work of Merleau-Ponty, in particular his text *The Phenomenology of Perception*, has been revisited, and it is regarded by many as critical to our appreciation of embodiment (see for example, Csordas 1994; Crossley 1995). Essentially he argued that all human perception is embodied, we cannot perceive anything and our senses cannot function independently of our bodies. This does not imply that they are somehow "glued" together, as the Cartesian notion of the body might suggest, but rather there is something of an oscillation between the two. This idea forms the basis of the notion of "embodiment." As Merleau-Ponty (1962) writes:

> Men [sic] taken as a concrete being is not a psyche joined to an organism, but movement to and fro of existence which at one time allows itself to take corporeal form and at others moves toward personal acts....It is never a question of the incomprehensive meeting of two casualties, nor of a collision between the order of causes and that of ends. But by an imperceptible twist an organic process issues into human behaviour, an instinctive act changes direction and becomes a sentiment, or conversely a human act becomes torpid and is continued absent-mindedly in the form of a reflex. (Merleau-Ponty 1962: 88, cited by Turner 1992: 56)

Thus while the notion that embodied consciousness is central here, it is also highlighted that we are not always conscious or aware of our bodily actions, we do not routinely tell our body to put one leg in front of the other if we want to walk, or to breath in through our nose if we want to smell a rose. The body in this sense is "taken for granted," or as Leder puts it, the body is "absent."

> Whilst in one sense the body is the most abiding and inescapable presence in our lives, it is also characterised by its absence. That is, one's own body is rarely the thematic object of experience...the body, as a ground of experience...tends to recede from direct experience. (Leder 1990: 1)

Within this perspective, the lived body is presumed to both construct and be constructed by, and within, the lifeworld. The lived body is an intentional entity which gives rise to this world. As Leder (1992: 25) writes elsewhere:

> in a significant sense, the lived body helps to constitute this world as experienced. We cannot understand the meaning and form of objects without reference to bodily powers through which we engage them – our senses, motility, language, desires. The lived body is not just one thing *in* the world but a way in which the world comes to be.

We can see therefore that it is analytically possible to make a distinction between *having* a body, *doing* a body, and *being* a body. Turner (1992) and others have found the German distinction between *Leib* and *Korper* to be instructive here. The former refers to the experiential, animated, or living body (the body-for-itself), the latter refers to the objective, instrumental, exterior body (the body-in-itself).

This approach highlights that the concepts of the "lived body" and the notion of "embodiment" reminds us that the self and the body are not separate and that experience is invariably, whether consciously or not, embodied. As Csordas (1994: 10) has argued, the body is the "existential ground of culture and self," and therefore he prefers the notion of "embodiment" to "the body," as the former implies something more than a material entity. It is rather a "methodological field defined by perceptual experience and mode of presence and engagement in the world." This idea that the self is embodied is also taken up by Giddens (1991: 56–7), who also emphasizes the notion of day-to-day *praxis*. The body is not an external entity but is experienced in practical ways when coping with external events and situations. How we handle our bodies in social situations is of course crucial to our self and identity and has been empirically and extensively explored by Goffman and other symbolic interactionists, as well as Garfinkel (Heritage 1984) and other ethnomethodologists. Indeed, the study of the management of bodies in everyday life and how this serves to structure the self and social relations has a long and important history within sociology. It highlights the preciousness of the body as well as the remarkable ability of humans to sustain bodily control through day to day situations. Many of these themes have been explored by sociologists who have studied how people *experience* illness.

THE SOCIOLOGY OF THE BODY: SOME ILLUSTRATIVE ISSUES

Illness and Injury and Lived Bodies

The literature on the experience of chronic illness and disability had drawn attention to many of the themes discussed above prior to the more recent emergence of the body and embodiment literature; most particularly the fundamental link between the *self* and the body. A number of researchers (e.g. Charmaz 1987) have documented how this occurs in the case of chronic illness. Here the relationship between the body and self is seriously disrupted. As we have just seen Leder, in his book *The Absent Body*, has argued how ordinarily we do not consistently reflect on our bodies; we take for granted the fact that they can function as we require them to. However, for the sick person the body, as Toombs (1992) suggests, undergoes a metamorphosis and becomes a "diseased body," which is separated and alienated from the self. Toombs, when describing her own experience of multiple sclerosis, reveals how, when living with a chronic illness, "one feels inescapably embodied" (Toombs 1992: 134). What is more, she (Toombs 1992: 127) says that "the breakdown in body is experienced as a fundamental transformation in one's whole way of being," thus, there is "an alteration of one's sense of self."

A number of writers have emphasized that in our day-to-day lives our bodies are "absent" (Leder 1990) or are taken for granted. We only become aware of them when they are in pain or suffer from disease or illness – when they are (*dys*)functional. Simon Williams (1996) has illustrated this well by drawing on the findings or research into chronic illness. He demonstrates how the experience of chronic illness involves a move from an "initial" state of embodiment (a state in which the body is taken for granted in the course of everyday life) to an oscillation between states of (*dys*)embodiment (embodiment in a dysfunctional state) and "re-embodiment." Attempts to move from a dys-embodied state to a re-embodied state require a considerable amount of "biographical work," or what Gareth Williams (1984) terms "narrative reconstruction." This theme is also demonstrated by Seymour (1998) in her empirical study of 24 men and women who experienced profound and permanent body paralysis as a result of spinal injuries. As the title of her book, *Remaking the Body*, suggests, as men and women go about remaking their bodies they "remake their worlds." Through listening to the accounts of these men and women she argues that she was able to appreciate the crucial role of embodiment in the reconstitution of the self. Whilst the participants she spoke to have had to endure profound bodily changes and difficulties, she maintains that they have retained their "selves." Seymour (1998: 178) states:

> this damage [the spinal injury] has disturbed, but not destroyed, their embodied selves. These people still inhabit and possess their bodies; their bodies are still resources with which they may explore new possibilities and opportunities for re-embodiment.

The problem with the literature on the lived body (from within the sociology of embodiment), and the notion of body projects and the reflexive self (from within the sociology of the body), is that they both assume a competent mind. In a moving paper by David Webb, he describes the impact on individuals and their families of traumatic brain injury (TBI) which he describes as a silent epidemic of our modern times. In Britain, 15 people are taken to the hospital every hour with a head injury. Most are the result of traffic accidents, and young men are the most common victims. This modern epidemic ironically means that the victims are unable to participate in one of the key aspects of late modernity. As Webb (1998: 545–9) explains:

> Indeed the case here is that with a physiologically damaged brain comes the likelihood of a fractured mind, and that consequently this will have a bearing on the person's capacity to existentially "live their body" – to reflexively experience it [. . .] [H]igh modernity revolves around a mentalist discourse in which greater importance is given to the mind than the sociological talk of "body matters" suggests.

Many assumptions are made, therefore, that when we reflect upon the following – how we feel about ourselves; how we view our past; how we assess and plan our futures – we have a socially acceptable – competent – mental capacity to do so. Our mental capacity depends upon our "normal" functioning of the brain, which in turn may also be contingent upon the "acceptable" functioning of the rest of our bodies. This issue is explored in the context of hospice care and is discussed in the next section of this chapter.

HEALTH CARE WORK

How can these theorizations on the body and embodiment help us to make sense of health care in practice? The most obvious and extensively researched areas concern the ways in which bodies have become regulated, controlled, and medicalized in areas of pregnancy and childbirth (Oakley 1993) and death and dying (Seale 1998). But more recently, qualitative studies of health caring work within formal settings have revealed the analytic value of the conceptual developments outlined above. For example, Julia Lawton's (1998) study of care within a hospice attempts to understand why it is that some patients remain within the hospice to die whilst others are more likely to be discharged and sent home to die. To address this health policy puzzle, Lawton argues that we need to focus on the *body* of the dying person. She found that those patients cared for within the hospice were those whose bodies became "*unbounded.*" By this she means that the diseases they were suffering from involved a particular type of bodily deterioration and disintegration which required very specific forms of symptom control. The most common examples being:

> incontinence of urine and faeces, uncontrolled vomiting (including faecal vomit), fungating tumours (the rotting away of a tumour site on the surface of the skin) and weeping limbs which resulted from the development of gross oedema in the patient's legs or arms. (Lawton 1998: 128)

It is these forms of bodily (dys)functions that people living in western society cannot tolerate rather than the process of dying itself. Indeed in those cases where the boundedness of their bodies could be reinstated, patients would be discharged. To address the question, Why are unbounded bodies unacceptable in western societies?, Lawton draws upon much of the sociological theorizing outlined above – especially the work of Douglas and Elias. The unbounded body is perceived symbolically, according to Douglas, as a source of dirt – it is "matter out of place." The increasingly "civilized" body, according to Elias, has become "individualised" and private, and the "natural" functions of the body are removed from public view.

The fact that natural or intimate bodily functions are problematic for health care practitioners has also been explored by Lawler (1991), who again draws upon the ideas developed by Elias and Douglas in her study of nursing care in an Australian hospital. Quintessentially, the work of nurses is about caring for bodies. This becomes a problem when nurses have to attend to those bodily functions (defecating, grooming, etc.) which in a "civilized" society have become taboo. Consequently, nurses have to learn how to negotiate social boundaries and create new contexts so that both the patient and the nurse can avoid feelings of shame and embarrassment.

There is a further fascinating finding highlighted in Lawton's study, and this relates to the link that we have discussed above between the notion of self and physical body. The two are meshed together. We saw in our discussion of Webb's (1998) paper that the functioning reflexive self relied on the competent mind. Lawton's work demonstrates that even where there is a "competent" mind, the lack of bodily controls (see also Featherstone and Hepworth 1991 and Nettleton and Watson 1998: 14–17) affects a person's capacity to continue with their life projects or their reflexive self. In fact, patients who had the least control over their bodily functions exhibited behavior which suggested a total loss of self and social identity, once their bodies became severely and irreversibly unbounded. Take Lawton's account of Deborah for example:

> When Deborah's bodily deterioration escalated, I observed that she had suddenly become a lot more withdrawn. After she had been on the ward for a couple of days she started asking for the curtains to be drawn around her bed to give her more privacy. A day or so later she stopped talking altogether, unless it was really necessary (to ask for a commode, for example), even when her family and other visitors were present. Deborah spent the remaining ten days of her life either sleeping or staring blankly into space. She refused all food and drink.... One of the hospice doctors concluded that "for all intents and purposes she [had] shut herself off in a frustrated and irreversible silence." (Lawton 1998: 129)

Both Webb and Lawton's papers are pertinent to late modern societies, in that the salience of the loss of self is linked to features of contemporary societies. The emphasis was on bodily controls and the boundedness of the body in Lawton's study. In Webb's analysis, by contrast, TBI would clearly alter who a person "is" and their capacity to "act" in any context. But its prevalence is related to modern ways of living (fast cars). Webb (1998: 548–50) comments:

> In high modernity the body has a diminishing *productive* significance, and it becomes increasingly a site more of recreational indulgence than labour power as such. In this context, it is catastrophic to be denied the opportunity to participate in the identity constituting reflexivity of late modernity (Giddens 1991). [...] There is, in short, no clarity about the categorisation of those who are head injured. The person becomes "someone else," an everyday recognition that it is the mind (more than the body) which signifies what it is to be a person. If the mind itself is seriously impaired then it is no longer able to mobilise the body to create the *physical capital* which might compensate for the run on *mental capital* occasioned through head injury.

The experience of TBI also brings into sharp relief another feature of late modernity and that is the fact that (medical) technologies have their limits. As Webb points out, in cases of physical impairment very often technology can offer something – some means by which motor coordination or whatever can be facilitated. This is not so when physical injury impairs the mind; here, technological resolutions to disability are almost invariably impossible (Webb 1998: 547).

TECHNOLOGY AND THE BODY

Whilst technological "advances" do have their limits, there is no do doubt that they have served to contribute to our reconceptualization of what constitutes the "body." The boundaries between the physical and the social body become increasingly fuzzy, and, as we have suggested above, we are less certain as to what the body actually is, or has the potential to do. During the last few decades developments in a number of areas of medical and related technologies have contributed these uncertainties. For example, bodies have bits added to them to enable them to function more effectively. Prosthetics – the use of artificial body parts, such as limbs – of course has a long history. But the list of body parts has grown in recent decades to include cardiac pacemakers, valves, ear implants, and even polyurethane hearts (Synnott 1993). Such developments have become increasingly sophisticated as they have developed in concert with advances in molecular biology. This has led some authors to talk about the emergence of *cyborgs* – the marriage between a human organism and machines (Featherstone and Hepworth 1991) which has been defined thus:

> Cyborgs are hybrid entities that are neither wholly technological nor completely organic, which means that the cyber has the potential to disrupt persistent dualisms that set the natural body in opposition to the technologically recrafted body, but also to refashion our thinking about the theoretical construction of the body as both a material entity and a discursive process. These bodies are multiple consti-tuted parts of cybernetic systems – what we now recognise as social and inform-ational networks. (Balsamo 1996: 11)

Thus the cyborg is neither a "natural body" nor simply a machine.

New reproductive technologies (NRTs) comprise a range of methods to assist conception which have been around for some decades. However, more recent technological developments, in conjunction with the more extended use of technologies such as GIFT, hormonal treatments, and so on, have altered the boundaries of what was or was not physically possible for a growing number of women (Edwards et al. 1999). People are presented with more choices than ever before, people are presented with a wider array of possibilities, and people are also having to learn how to negotiate and deal with new identities. For example, as Edwards et al. (1999: 1) point out:

> To a greater or lesser extent, part of everyone's identity as a person is derived from knowledge about their birth and about how they were brought up [...] The late twentieth-century development of the means to alter what many would have said were immutable processes of birth has created a new and complex vehicle for conceptualising connections.

The certainties of "birth" as an immutable process are therefore altered. This can make the negotiation of a reflexive identity very complex indeed.

A further "technological" development, that impacts upon our notions of who and what we are, is in relation to the, so called, *New Genetics*. The Human Genome Project is an international initiative that identifies particular genes which are associated with diseases and, more controversially, behaviors (Conrad and Gabe 1999). This project, completed in 2000, gives rise to a new discourse within which we can come to talk about our selves. It comprises a new twist to the notion that our "biology is our destiny." The prospect is that medical science will be able to predict with a significant degree of precision our *pre-disposition* to a wide range of diseases such as cancers, heart disease, diabetes, and so on.

More knowledge, more information, and yet ever more uncertainty. Although the degree of accuracy, or rather certainty, associated with molecular genetic predictive testing is greater than that of traditional probablistic clinical genetics, many uncertainties still remain and, in large measure, predictive tests can rarely ever be completely certain. They also raise a host of social and ethical considerations (see Davison et al. 1994 for a thorough exploration of these issues for social researchers). In relation to our discussion here, the main point is that the language of the new genetics has implications for how we think about, talk about, and experience our bodies. When we reflect upon our selves and our identities, we increasingly do so with recourse to our genes. As Spallone (1998) has pointed out, the word "gene" has replaced the looser notions of "the biological" and "hereditary." So rather than say, as we might have done 15 years ago, "it runs in the family," or "it's inherited," we hear ourselves saying, "it must be in their/my genes" (Spallone 1998: 50). Spallone also cites James Watson, the first director of the US Human Genome Initiative, who said: "We used to think our fate was in the stars. Now we know, in large measure, our fate is in our genes."

We noted above how "bits" are added to bodies, but another salient issue is the fact that body organs can be transplanted from one body to another due to advances in *organ donation and transplantation* surgery. In the summer of 1999 in England, a 15-year-old girl who refused consent to a heart transplant had her case overruled by the high court. She was reported to have said: "Death is final – I know I can't change my mind. I do not want to die, but I would rather die than have the transplant and have someone else's heart." Again, as with medical practices associated with the new genetics, this issue raises ethical issues. Who should make decisions about people's bodies – should it be lawyers, medical practitioners, relatives, or the "owner" of the body itself? But this issue also highlights the malleability of bodies in the modern age. Is it my body if parts of it belonged to someone else? A study of patients who had undergone organ transplant surgery found that patients felt that they needed to work at "restructuring their sense of self" (Sharp 1995). The author reports that there was a tension between the need to both personalize and the need to objectify bodies and organs. Thus, as Williams (1997) has pointed out, organ transplantation poses many questions about self-identity:

> Medical personnel put great stress on objectification; the heart, for example, is "only a pump." Yet recipients experience conflict between this mechanistic/reductionist view of the body and their wider cultural beliefs about the embodied nature of self identity and the "sacred" nature of the heart as the very core of the person. (Williams 1997: 1044)

This albeit brief and partial discussion of medical technological developments and the body serves to highlight a key theme running throughout this chapter. That is the idea that in late modern contexts there is a growing array of uncertainties associated with the body. The emergence of sophisticated medical knowledges and practices in fields associated with reproduction, genetics, and immunology have increased the complexities and choices which people face when reflecting upon their bodies and their *embodied* identities. Thus it is perhaps not surprising that sociologists have become increasingly preoccupied with the embodied basis of social action.

There is a further twist to the emerging debates within the sociology of the body and embodied sociology, and this relates to an area of medical sociology which has a much longer history – the study of health inequalities. A vein of research and debate is emerging within this area of study which draws upon: the lived body; the physiological basis of the body; and social structure.

SOCIAL INEQUALITIES AND THE SOCIOLOGY OF EMBODIMENT

A basic tenet of medical sociology is that social circumstances – in particular material and social deprivation – become inscribed upon people's bodies. In other words, it is argued that health status is socially determined. The reasons why social circumstances, and more especially social inequalities, impact upon health status has been researched and debated for over a century. Surprisingly, perhaps, the literatures on the sociology of the body and the sociology of embodiment are providing some important clues as to why health is socially patterned in this way. It seems then that "unhealthy societies" (Wilkinson 1996), or rather unequal societies, are associated with unhealthy bodies. This is not just a result of *material* deprivation and poverty – the harmful effects of poor housing, poor food, and living conditions *per se* – though these are undoubtedly important. But what is also important is one's class position. Essentially those people who are lower down the social hierarchy, and have the least control over their circumstances, are more likely to be ill. The reason for this is that they are more likely to experience prolonged stress and negative emotions, which in turn have physiological consequences. This psychosocial perspective on health inequalities has been summarized by Elstad (1998) who points to a growing body of research which demonstrates how certain aspects of social life such as: a sense of control; perceived social status; strength of affiliations; self esteem; feelings of ontological insecurity, and so on, lead to variations in health outcomes. This has been most fully explored in relation to male paid employment but also in relation to the housing circumstances of men and women (Nettleton and Burrows 2000).

It seems that how people reflect upon, feel about, and internalize their social position or their social circumstances is critical. Drawing from work in physiological anthropology, in particular studies of non-human primates, researchers have found that primates who were lower down the social hierarchy, and most importantly had least control and power, exhibited more detrimental physiological changes in times of stress. Authors have argued that this may help to explain the fact that numerous studies have consistently found that people in social environments who have limited autonomy and control over their circumstances suffer proportionately poor health. The key issue here is the degree of social cohesion. Greater social cohesion means that people are more likely to feel secure and "supported" and are less likely to respond negatively when they have to face difficulties or uncertainties. In turn, it is social inequality that serves to undermine social cohesion and the quality of social fabric. Freund (1990) has argued that people express "somatically" the conditions of their existence. What he calls "emotional modes of being" are very likely to be linked to ones structural position. He (Freund 1990: 461) writes:

> Subjectivity, social activity and the social structural contexts interpenetrate. It is this relationship that comes to be physically embodied in many ways. Irregularity of breathing may accompany muscular tension and experiences of ontological insecurity and the anger or fear that is part of this insecurity.

Thus, for example, if we are in a social environment which is threatening we may be "scared stiff." Freund (1990: 471) is able to postulate this theory because he believes that:

> Emotions and the feeling they express are embodied in neurohormonal and other aspects of bodyliness. They form communicative "fields" between the body and between body–mind and social existence.[1]

This link becomes evident when we mesh together the "lived body" and the structural perspectives on the body. How people experience their structural context, the meanings and interpretations they ascribe to it, in turn impacts upon their physical bodies. This is the new development here. Hitherto, the literature on health inequalities has tended to be limited to the physical body and so works within a Cartesian model which brackets off the mind. Experience and meanings were only elicited to try and understand why people might engage in "unhealthy" activities such as smoking (e.g. Graham 1987). The lived body approach which collapses these dualisms therefore provides us with fresh insights into one of the main concerns for sociologists of health and illness. This said, hitherto the empirical studies have been restricted to class and socioeconomic inequalities rather than others associated with gender and race – where issues of social control and ascribed social status are particularly salient.

CONCLUSION

This chapter has reviewed some of the key theoretical perspectives within the literature on the sociology of the body and the sociology of embodiment. Drawing on these approaches it has discussed a number of substantive issues which are of interest to those working within medical sociology. Thus it has attempted to show that a "sociology of the body" has added a new dimension to matters which have traditionally been of interest to this field of study. A key theme running throughout this chapter is that the more knowledge and information we have about bodies, the more uncertain we become as to what bodies actually are. Certainties about seemingly immutable processes associated with birth and death, for example, become questioned. Furthermore, how we experience and live our bodies has also become central to how we think about our *selves*. Thus any comprehensive analysis of the experience health, illness, or health care should take cognisance of the body (what ever that is!) itself.

Note

1   Of course, for sociologists working within a social constructionist perspective, the interest here might be more to do with the current rise and salience of these psycho–physiological discourses within medical sociology.

References

Armstrong, D. 1983. *Political Anatomy of the Body: Medical Knowledge in Britain in the Twentieth Century*. Cambridge: Cambridge University Press.

Balsamo, A. 1996. *Technologies of the Gendered Bodies: Reading Cyborg Women*. London: Duke University Press.

Beck, U. 1992. *Risk Society: Towards a New Modernity*. London: Sage.

Bendelow, G. and S. Williams (eds). 1998. *Emotions in Social Life: Critical Themes and Contemporary Issues*. London: Routledge.

Burkitt, D. 1997. "Social Relationships and Emotions." *Sociology* 31: 37–55.

Charmaz, K. 1987. "Struggling for a Self: Identity Levels of the Chronically Ill." In J. A. Roth and P. Conrad (eds.), *Research in the Sociology of Health Care, volume 6, The Experience and Management of Chronic Illness*. Greenwich, CT: JAI Press.

Conrad, P. and J. Gabe. 1999. "Introduction: Sociological Perspectives on the New Genetics: An Overview." *Sociology of Health and Illness* 21: 505–16.

Conrad, P. and J. W. Schneider. 1980. *Deviance and Medicalization: From Badness to Sickness*. St Louis: Mosby.

Crossley, N. 1995. "Merleau-Ponty, the Elusive Body and Carnal Sociology." *Body and Society* 1: 43–64.

Csordas, T. J. 1994. *Embodiment and Experience: The Existential Ground of Culture and Self*. Cambridge: Cambridge University Press.

Davison, C., S. Macintyre, and G. Davey Smith. 1994. "The Potential Impact of Predictive Genetic Testing for Susceptibility to Common Chronic Diseases: A Review and a Proposed Research Agenda." *Sociology of Health and Illness* 16: 340–71.

Douglas, M. 1966. *Purity and Danger: An Analysis of the Concepts of Pollution and Taboo*. London: Routledge and Kegan Paul.

——. 1970 *Natural Symbols: Explorations in Cosmology*. London: Cresset Press.

——. 1986. *Risk Acceptability According to the Social Sciences*. London: Routledge and Kegan Paul.

Duden, B. 1993. *Disembodying Women: Perspectives on Pregnancy and the Unborn*. London: Harvard University Press.

Edwards, J., S. Franklin, E. Hirsch, F. Price, and M. Strathern. 1999. *Technologies of Procreation: Kinship in the Age of Assisted Conception*, 2nd edition. London: Routledge.

Elias, N. 1978. *The Civilising Process, Volume 1, The History of Manners*. Oxford: Blackwell.

——. 1982. *The Civilising Process, Volume 2, State Formation and Civilisation*. Oxford: Blackwell.

Elstad, J. I. 1998. "The Psycho-social Perspective on Social Inequalities in Health." *Sociology of Health and Illness* 20: 598–618.

Featherstone, M. and M. Hepworth. 1991. "The Mask of Aging and the Postmodern Lifecourse." In M. Featherstone, M. Hepworth, and B. Turner (eds.), *The Body: Social Processes and Cultural Theory*. London: Sage.

Foucault, M. 1976. *The Birth of the Clinic: An Archaeology of Medical Perception*. London: Tavistock.

——. 1979. *Discipline and Punish, the Birth of the Prison*. Harmondsworth: Penguin.

——. 1981. *The History of Sexuality: An Introduction*. Harmondsworth: Penguin.

Frank, A. 1992. "Twin Nightmares of the Medical Simulacrum: Jean Baudrillard and David Cronenberg." In W. Stearns and W. Chaloupka (eds.), *Jean Baudrillard: The Disappearance of Art and Politics*. London: Macmillan.

Freund, P. E. S. 1990. "The Expressive Body: A Common Ground for the Sociology of Emotions and Health and Illness." *Sociology of Health and Illness* 12: 452–77.

Giddens, A. 1991. *Modernity and Self-Identity: Self and Society in the Late Modern Age*. Cambridge: Polity Press.

Goffman, E. 1959. *The Presentation of Self in Everyday Life*. Harmondsworth: Penguin.

Graham, H. 1987. "Women's Smoking and Family Health." *Social Science and Medicine* 32: 507–15.

Heritage, J. 1984. *Garfinkel and Ethnomethodology*. Cambridge: Polity Press.

Lawler, J. 1991. *Behind the Screens: Nursing Somology and the Problem of the Body*. London: Churchill Livingstone.

Lawton, J. 1998. "Contemporary Hospice Care: The Sequestration of the Unbounded Body and 'Dirty Dying'." *Sociology of Health and Illness* 20: 121–43.

Leder, D. 1990. *The Absent Body*. Chicago: Chicago University Press.

——. 1992. "Introduction." In D. Leder (ed.), *The Body in Medical Thought and Practice*. London: Kluwer Academic.

Martin, E. 1989. *The Woman in the Body: A Cultural Analysis of Reproduction*. Milton Keynes: Open University Press.

——. 1994. *Flexible Bodies: The Role of Immunity in American Culture from the Days of Polio to the Age of AIDS*. Boston, MA: Beacon Press.

Morris, D. 1991. *The Culture of Pain*. Berkeley, CA: University of California Press.

Nettleton, S. 1988. "Protecting a Vulnerable Margin: Towards an Analysis of How the Mouth Came to be Separated from the Body." *Sociology of Health and Illness* 10: 156–69.

——. 1995. *The Sociology of Health and Illness*. Cambridge: Polity Press.

Nettleton, S. and J. Watson (eds.). 1998. *The Body in Everyday Life*. London: Routledge.

Nettleton, S. and R. Burrows. 2000. "When a Capital Investment Becomes an Emotional

Loss: The Health Consequences of the Experience of Mortgage Repossession in England." *Housing Studies* (Forthcoming).

Oakley, A. 1993. *Essays on Women, Medicine and Health*. Edinburgh: Edinburgh University Press.

Rhodes, L. A., C. A. McPhillips-Tangum, C. Markham, and R. Klenk. 1999. "The Power of the Visible: The Meaning of Diagnostic Tests in Chronic Back Pain." *Social Science and Medicine* 48: 1189–203.

Seale, C. 1998. *Constructing Death: The Sociology of Dying and Bereavement*. Cambridge: Cambridge University Press.

Seymour, W. 1998. *Remaking the Body*. London: Routledge.

Sharp, L. A. 1995. "Organ Transplantation as a Transformative Experience: Anthropological Insights into the Restructuring of the Self." *Medical Anthroplogy Quarterly* 93: 357–89.

Shilling, C. 1993. *The Body and Social Theory*. London: Sage.

Spallone, P. 1998. "The New Biology of Violence: New Geneticisms for Old?" *Body and Society* 4: 47–66.

Stoppard, T. 1967. *Rosencrantz and Guildenstern are Dead*. London: Faber and Faber.

Synnott, A. 1993. *The Body Social: Symbolism, Self and Society*. London: Routledge.

Toombs, S. K. 1992. "The Body in Multiple Sclerosis: A Patient's Perspective." In D. Leder (ed.) *The Body in Medical Thought and Practice*. London: Kluwer Academic Publishers.

Turner, B. S. 1984. *The Body and Society*, 1st edition. Oxford: Blackwell.

——. 1992. *Regulating Bodies: Essays in Medical Sociology*. London: Routledge.

——. 1996. *The Body and Society*, 2nd edition. Oxford: Blackwell.

Webb, D. 1998. "A 'Revenge' on Modern Times: Notes on Traumatic Brain Injury." *Sociology* 32: 541–56.

Wilkinson, R. 1996. *Unhealthy Societies: The Afflictions of Inequality*. London: Routledge.

Williams, G. 1984. "The Genesis of Chronic Illness: Narrative Reconstruction." *Sociology of Health and Illness* 6: 175–200.

Williams, S. 1996. "The Vicissitudes of Embodiment across the Chronic Illness Trajectory." *Body and Society* 2: 23–47.

Williams, S. 1997. "Modern Medicine and the 'Uncertain Body': From Corporeality to Hyperreality?" *Social Science and Medicine* 45: 1041–9.

Williams, S. and G. Bendelow. 1998. *The Lived Body: Sociological Themes, Embodied Issues*. London: Routledge.

Zola, I. K. 1972. "Medicine as an Institution of Social Control." *Sociological Review* 20: 487–504.

4

Health and Social Stratification

Eero Lahelma

It is a basic assumption in medical sociology that social divisions shape people's health and illness. That poor health emerges from poor living conditions has been known for a long time. However, such views are not necessarily shared by lay people. There is, in fact, a paradox between the lay and expert conceptions of the reasons for poor health. While lay people may not recognize the bearing of adverse conditions for poor health, it is clear to medical sociologists and epidemiologists that health, illness, and death are profoundly determined by the social conditions in which people live (Blaxter 1997).

This chapter will draw on medical sociological research on the social patterning of health, illness, and death. The particular focus is on the associations between social stratification and health. It has become habitual to speak about *health inequalities* when examining morbidity and mortality differentials across various dimensions of social stratification, such as social class, education, or income (Townsend and Davidson 1982).

A broad, comparative perspective is used and evidence is drawn from different countries and, where possible, from international comparisons. For lack of comparable data, the scope is restricted to the (post-)industrialized or western countries. However, it should be borne in mind that the broadest health divide is found between the developed and the developing world. This has been emphasized, for example, in the *Health for All by the Year 2000* strategy by the WHO (1985) and is apparent from other contributions to this book as well. Being restricted western countries one should also remember the dramatic decline in the health situation of the postsocialist countries, particularly Russia, due to the turbulent sociopolitical development (Cockerham 1997; Bobak et al. 1998; Palosuo 1998).

THE CHALLENGE

If health is divided very unequally between the rich and the poor countries one can ask what kind of health divisions can be found within and between the developed countries. Although social inequalities in health in the western countries are widely recognized they have also been challenged. In the 1960s it was predicted by an American scholar Charles Kadushin (1964) that health inequalities would be disappearing. According to his conclusion "in modern western countries the relationship between social class and the prevalence of illness is certainly decreasing and most probably no longer exists." Kadushin's view was a limited one since he contended that the reasons for equality in health were primarily related to lack of absolute subsistence problems and physical want in the western countries. Although he presented evidence to support the conclusions, other scholars did not share his views and subsequent research has not been able to confirm a predicted egalitarian health development.

Again in the 1990s, sociological debate on the late or postmodern changes has emerged on the "death of class." This would imply that class inequalities give way to new divisions in society (Lee and Turner 1996; Scambler and Higgs 1999). The dominant view is that hierarchical socioeconomic divisions in general are losing their significance for a deconstructed social structure, whereas a weaker position suggests that new social divisions, such as those related to employment status, consumption patterns, and identity, have emerged which are more salient than social class for understanding social inequalities including health.

It is a reasonable argument that social structures are changing and this will affect the social patterning of the determinants of health as well. As a result, theories, concepts, and empirical approaches to health inequalities are in constant need to be rethought (Scambler and Higgs 1999). However, it would be a very profound transformation of the western societies if universal social hierarchies had become non-existent, and consequently health inequalities had disappeared as we turn to the third Millennium. In fact, health provides an interesting case study for an examination of the challenge of whether and what kind of universal social structural inequalities continue to exist in the contemporary western societies.

THE TRADITION

Examining health inequalities has a long history which has particularly deep roots in Britain. This tradition has examined a variety of social conditions producing ill health and premature death. Analyses have included – in addition to the overall level of health – health among the worst off and the distribution of health across social classes and other social divisions.

The documenting and monitoring of social divisions in the population's health can be traced back to such scholars as John Graunt and William Petty in the mid-seventeenth century. In one of the first studies on health inequalities from 1662, based on London Bills of Mortality, Graunt reported that those living in London had a shorter life than those living in the countryside, due to poor living conditions such as pollution in the city (see Whitehead 1997).

In the 1830s there was a breakthrough in British public health policies and documenting health divisions in the population. The New Poor Law Act of 1834 and Public Health Act of 1848 aimed to tackle the serious health problems related to industrial poverty. The authorities had as their task to monitor the health situation and the *General Report on the Sanitary Conditions of the Labouring Population of Great Britain* was published by Edwin Chadwick in 1842. This report showed that in Liverpool the average age at death was 35 years for the gentry and professionals, whereas it was 22 years for tradesmen and their families and 15 years for laborers, mechanics, and servants. Chadwick's report was a seminal work for the subsequent examination of health inequalities (see Macintyre 1997).

In addition to Chadwick, William Farr from the British Registrar General's office strongly influenced the monitoring of health inequalities by providing further documents, such as the *Decennial Supplement*, reporting on the associations of the social position with health and mortality. A debate between Chadwick and Farr illuminates different emphasizes in the early health inequalities scholarship (Hamlin 1995). While Chadwick's view was a more medical one emphasizing the prevention of infectious diseases by hygienic measures, Farr's view was a broader one including also social and economic determinants of health. This debate bears significance to a subsequent division of approaches. Medical sociology and social epidemiology usually examine a variety of social determinants shaping health, illness, and death in the population at large, whereas the medical model examines specific programs directed toward the treatment of those already affected by diseases. This division is related to the "prevention paradox," which implies that a large population has to be approached in order to prevent a small number of people from falling ill (Rose 1992).

Significant public health developments and documentation can be found in many other western countries as well. In the Nordic countries a special feature was early development of population statistics. In the Swedish empire the world's oldest population statistics were established in 1748. These nationwide statistics were immediately utilized in research (Lahelma et al. 1996). For example, Abraham Bäck, a chief medical officer, reported in 1765 that "Many types of pestilence rage deeply among the lower classes, whereas only few among the richer people fall ill . . . As I search for the reasons for illnesses and unfair mortality among the peasantry and lower classes in towns, in the first place come poverty, squalor, lack of subsistence, anxiety and distress" (see Lundberg 1998). Thus health inequalities were identified early as an issue for the Swedish public health policy.

In Germany the founder of modern cellular pathology, Rudolf Virchow, writing in the revolutionary months of 1848, drew a connection between a typhoid epidemic and living conditions among the mining population in Upper Silesia. This signified a new relationship between medicine and sociology which

Virchow himself encapsulated by stating that "Medicine is social science and politics nothing but medicine on a grand scale." In other words, medicine was also social science and its task was to contribute to the health and well-being of the population at large, not only those already hit by diseases. According to Virchow health must be a democratic right of each citizen rather than a privilege of the well-positioned few. This has had far-reaching consequences for modern medical sociology examining health inequalities within broad populations (Gerhardt 1989: 271–2).

The new socio-medical ideas spread all over Europe and northern America in the nineteenth century. For example, in Finland, a small country in the northern European periphery, a wave of socio-medical research burst out in the 1840s. A strong emphasis was put on the social disadvantages contributing to serious public health problems among the worst off and leading to sharp inequalities in health and death. Carl Qvist, a medical doctor, examined in the 1870s social class inequalities in mortality caused by a cholera epidemic and drew a methodological conclusion: "The division of the population into classes according to either estate and living conditions or occupations and work is one of the most difficult tasks of population statistics." This conclusion, still valid today, provided a challenge for further research until World War I. In 1916 the chief medical officer of Finland, Akseli Koskimies, crystallized the research program for health inequalities stating that the task of such research "was to examine a person as member of a particular class, economic group; as such a person is susceptible to the health hazards common and characteristic to one's own class" (see Lahelma et al. 1996).

However, the wave of health inequalities research in the nineteenth century in many European countries and the USA showed a relative decline in the early twentieth century as medicine adopted a new biomedical paradigm and differentiated into subspecialties (Claus 1983; Rosen 1993; Krieger and Fee 1996). Gradually, modern social sciences emerged and research on health inequalities adopted new approaches.

The British Registrar General, T. H. C. Stevenson, developed an occupational class scheme in the early twentieth century. This was first used in a study which showed a clear social class gradient in infant mortality. What was debated, however, was what were the reasons for such inequalities. First of all, the hereditarians and eugenists applied Darwin's ideas of natural selection to social inequalities in health. They claimed that social class expressed genetic endowment. This was seen in the poorer health among the lower classes which contained high proportions of men and women from "tainted stock." Secondly, in contrast, Stevenson and other environmentalists suggested the importance of poor living conditions as reasons for poor health and premature death. Thirdly, it was also emphasized that unhealthy or feckless behaviours contribute to the observed health inequalities. These three explanations – hereditarian, environmental, and behavioural – prefigured the types of explanation to be further discussed much later in the twentieth century (Macintyre 1997).

One of Stevenson's successors was Richard Titmuss. His studies on trends in infant mortality using census data added significantly to previous work as evidence was obtained on changes over time (Titmuss 1943). Although infant mortality had declined over the early twentieth century in all classes measured by the father's occupation, the decline was slowest in the lowest class. As a result, inequalities in infant mortality had not decreased, but widened.

The emergence of the welfare state in Britain and in Scandinavia was based on broad social policies to combat the "Five giants of Want, Disease, Ignorance, Squalor, and Idleness" as put by William Beveridge (1942). In Scandinavian research on the welfare state, an emphasis has been on citizens' possibilities to lead a good life. Living conditions are studied looking at avoidable inequalities among population subgroups, such as social classes (Erikson and Uusitalo 1987). To be in good health and to be able to perform one's daily activities is a basic prerequisite for leading a good life. Therefore, social inequalities in morbidity and mortality provide essential information on people's living conditions. All the more so as health has a high priority among the subareas of welfare. This high priority is linked to the fact that good health is needed within most subareas of life, such as employment or housework (Allardt 1975; Johansson 1979).

More recent documentations of health inequalities include the *Black Report on Health Inequalities* (Townsend and Davidson 1982), which again found social inequalities in health and death. This report gave a strong incentive for health inequalities research all over the developed world (see also Davey Smith et al. 1990; Macintyre 1997). The Black Report also influenced the European strategy for *Health for All by the Year 2000* by the WHO, with equity in health as a primary target (WHO 1985). In 1997 the British Labor government commissioned a new *Independent Inquiry into Inequalities in Health* (1998). This inquiry reviewed the British evidence since the Black Report, but also put forward a detailed program "to improve health of the worst off and to narrow the health gap."

Since the Black Report research, inquiries, and programs on health inequalities have spread all over the western world. The main message from these can be encapsulated in the invariance: *The poorer the social position, the poorer the health*. Subsequent research has elaborated the nature of the association and suggested reasons for health inequalities in different countries.

THE DETERMINANTS OF HEALTH

Taken as a whole, the variety of social factors determining the patterning of the population's health is broad and complex. Based on evidence from the medical sociological and epidemiological research tradition, such factors have been summarized by Göran Dahlgren and Margaret Whitehead (1991) in figure 4.1.

Individuals are found in the center. First of all, they bear constitutional factors contributing to their health. Age and sex/gender are biologically as well as socially determined, since our social roles and positions are strongly affected by the phase of life course and gender. Secondly, individual lifestyles and

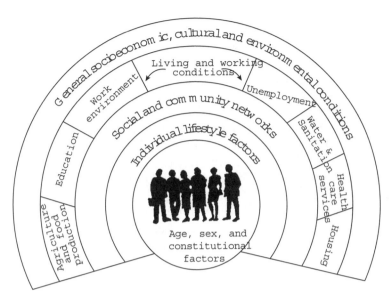

Figure 4.1 Main determinants of health
Source: Dahlgren and Whitehead 1991.

behaviors, such as smoking, drinking, eating and exercising, are likely to be health-damaging or health-promoting. Thirdly, individuals do interact with each other in communities and the mutual support provided helps sustain the health of its members. Fourthly, people's material living and working conditions influence their ability to maintain good health. These conditions vary a lot between individuals, groups, and whole societies. Fifthly, social, structural, cultural, and other environmental factors characterizing communities and whole societies contribute to people's health and its social patterning.

An examination of health inequalities will concentrate on the social structural influences included in the outermost layer of Dahlgren and Whitehead's model. However, in accordance with the research tradition, the model emphasizes interrelationships between the determinants effective at different levels. Therefore, an examination of social inequalities in health needs to make frequent reference to other layers of the social determinants as well. Particularly, attention should be paid to how gender and life course shape the social patterning of health.

THE DIMENSIONS OF HEALTH

The Black Report (Townsend and Davidson 1982) and studies earlier on in the health inequalities research tradition have relied mostly on mortality and main causes of death. Very often only men have been included. The main reason for these limitations is availability of data. Additionally, mortality data has advantages in being reliable and valid in most countries, and allowing comparisons between countries. Therefore, mortality continues to be a major indicator in the examination of health inequalities.

However, mortality data do have drawbacks. A methodological problem is that combining death records with population censuses may produce mismatches in the data, called the numerator-denominator bias. Such problems do not exist where universal person numbers are available and permit linking different data sources at the individual level. During the last few decades this possibility has been open mostly in the Nordic countries (e.g. Valkonen and Martelin 1999). The main drawback with mortality data in the examination of the population's health is that it does not adequately reflect the burden of ill health among living people. There are health problems which cause a lot of pain and suffering as well as costs for sick leave, treatment, and care, but which are not fatal. These include, for example, musculoskeletal problems and most problems of mental health; both are prevalent in the adult population. From a welfare perspective, besides mortality data, we need data on the manifold dimensions of health and illness, including their social consequences.

Data on inequalities in ill health often derive from population surveys using interviews or mail questionnaires. Information on ill health and the social status is obtained from the same individuals responding to the survey. Health measures are by their very nature self-reported, instead of being medically confirmed diagnoses or other kind of data. Rather than being a limitation, working directly with people's own reports is an inherent characteristic of many medical sociological studies: the aim is not medical treatment, but an examination of people's well-being and ability to perform their everyday activities.

Often-used health measures include such generic indicators as perceived or self-assessed general health and (limiting) long-standing illness. These have been recommended as suitable for comparative research by a WHO report (de Bruin et al. 1996). Additionally, functional capacities, disabilities, symptoms, pain, and various summary indices of health can be used in studies (see e.g. Bowling 1991, 1995). Also statistics, records from health services, and qualitative self-reports provide data for medical sociological studies. Most measures reflect *illnesses* indicating health problems as experienced by people, or *sicknesses* indicating social consequences of health problems, but less often *diseases* indicating medical conditions (Blaxter 1989).

All self-reported indicators share the characteristics of being bound to people's own perceptions and the surrounding cultures. Therefore, the disposition to report ill health may vary between individuals and groups, such as social classes, as well as whole countries. For example, it has been suggested that at similar true limiting long-standing illness levels manual and non-manual workers may report different levels of limitation because of the differential nature of their work (Blane et al. 1993). Subsequent research suggests that the limiting long-standing illness measure rather underestimates than overestimates socioeconomic inequalities in health (Elstad 1996; Macintyre et al. 1999).

THE DIMENSIONS OF SOCIAL STRATIFICATION

Social stratification is a comprehensive concept encompassing the positioning of people in the social structure by their social status (Liberatos et al. 1988; Krieger et al. 1997). A person's social status is related to various assets which are distributed unequally in society, such as power, prestige, material and non-material resources. Classifications of social stratification do contain qualitative elements, such as the difference between farmers and workers, as well as hierarchical elements, such as the difference between upper and lower professionals or white-collar employees as well as manual and non-manual workers. Some stratification schemes are fully hierarchical and form ordinal scales, such as those based on the amount of prestige, income, or education. Some others contain partial hierarchies, which are typical to employment status and occupational social class. Whatever the classification used, hierarchies and social divisions which are in principle avoidable, are taken as foci in the examination of health inequalities.

A stratification approach views social statuses across the whole social structure emphasizing hierarchical positions. Within such a perspective systematic inequalities are expected between all hierarchical strata under scrutiny, with those at the bottom of the ladder having poorer health than those in the middle and at the top. An alternative perspective suggests that only the worst off differ from all other groups. Such a marginal perspective would predict that the disadvantaged groups, such as poor or excluded people, have poorer health than other groups, but the moderately wealthy do not necessarily differ from the rich (Najman 1993).

A perspective closely related to the marginal one predicts that a threshold can be found below which health is poorer than in the higher strata. Such a threshold might be found for income or for education since it has been suggested, for example, that the amount of money available up to a certain level contributes to people's well-being, but an additional increase of money after that has no impact whatsoever (Warr 1987).

Whether a structural, marginal, or threshold perspective is valid for an examination of health inequalities cannot be resolved a priori. Also time periods and countries are likely to differ from each other. Furthermore, different stratification schemes and criteria can be used. As social structures change and new social divisions emerge, it is important to use multidimensional measurements and be open to new types of health inequalities. This will also help respond to the challenges suggested by late modernist social theorizing (see Scambler and Higgs 1999).

There are a number of options to measure social stratification in empirical studies on health inequalities. The following concentrates on structural measures classifying people across the whole social ladder. The main classification schemes include: first, occupational divisions, such as employment status and occupational social class; secondly, educational attainment; and thirdly, income.

Occupational Classifications

Employment status divides people into classes according to their main activity, i.e. whether they are gainfully employed or non-employed. First, employment status distinguishes between those who are engaged in paid employment, be they employees or self-employed. Secondly, the main groups of the non-employed include unemployed, those doing housework ("housewives"), disabled or retired, and full-time students. Being non-employed may increase the risk of poor health, but employment status is subject to reverse causality as well. Those with poor health may drift out of the labour market into non-employed positions (Arber 1997).

Occupational social class divisions relate people by their current occupation to the social structure. The individual approach uses a person's own occupation (Arber 1997). When currently non-employed, the last occupation can be used. However, some people have never been employed and have no past occupation. In many countries a substantial proportion of women remain outside paid employment all their life. In such cases the conventional approach can be used and a person's missing occupational status can be substituted by his/her partner's occupation.

The benefits of the occupational classification schemes include links to traditional macro-sociological class divisions as presented by classical sociologists. These traditional divisions attach people to social structures based on their relationship to production (Marx) or their status and power related to different occupations (Weber). The main drawback with occupational classifications is that they are suitable for those who have an occupation, but less so for those who are outside employment. A gender bias is likely depending on the proportion of women who are non-employed. Also many classifications are more detailed for male-dominated than female-dominated jobs. Another difficulty in using occupational divisions relates to changes of occupational structures over time as well as variations between countries. Some occupations decline while new ones emerge. For example, farmers in most developed countries form a small group only, whereas some decades ago they may have still been a substantial group. Similar variations in the occupational structure between countries can be found.

Occupational social class groupings typically distinguish between (1) non-manual employees, such as upper and lower professional or white-collar employees; (2) skilled and unskilled manual workers; (3) self-employed and entrepreneurs; and (4) farmers. An example is the aforementioned British Registrar General's occupational social class scheme (table 4.1).

The special feature of the Registrar General's scheme is that the classification is understood as a fully ordinal scale. This classification has been very much used in British documentations and research on health inequalities. As this is an old measure it is particularly susceptible to the criticism emphasizing changes in occupational structures as well as disregarding female employment. New social class classifications have been developed (see Rose and O'Reilly 1997), but the

Table 4.1 British Registrar General's occupational social class scheme

	Social class	Examples of occupations
I	Professional, higher administrative	Lawyer, doctor
II	Managerial and technical/intermediate	Manager, teacher, nurse
IIIN	Skilled non-manual	Clerk, police, secretary
IIIM	Skilled manual	Cook, bus driver, carpenter
IV	Partly skilled	Post worker, farm worker, security guard
V	Unskilled	Cleaner, car park attendant, building laborer

Registrar General's scheme continues to have discriminatory power in studies on health inequalities (e.g. Drever and Whitehead 1997).

As occupational social class is closely related to available material resources and living conditions, including working environment, it is reasonable to assume that class will shape people's health.

Education

Education as a measure of social stratification reflects people's social status in a broad manner and is related not only to their material but also non-material resources. The significance of educational attainment may even increase in competitive societies which need a better labor force. Education can be measured using highest passed examinations or years of completed education. Educational classifications have some advantages as compared to occupational ones. First, each individual can be allocated to educational groupings irrespective of his/her employment status. Secondly, education remains broadly stable across the life-course. Thirdly, education is equally suitable for men and women. Fourthly, the amount of completed education forms an ordinal scale. Fifthly, education is better comparable across countries than occupation (Valkonen 1989). The draw-backs of this measure include that educational structures change over time. A major difficulty with education is its skewness which varies across cohorts. The distribution of education is particularly skewed for older people of whom a great majority has completed basic education only.

Education by its very nature gives people knowledge and qualifications. Therefore, education shapes people's health consciousness and health behaviors, and through these affects their health and illness.

Income

Income is the third main measure of social stratification. It most clearly indicates material resources, the availability of money. Gross and net income can be measured. Gross income can be taken as an indicator of the social status, whereas net income reflects closely the available resources. As many people live in families, household income is a more accurate measure of their available resources than individual income. Household income measures need to be "equivalized," taking into account the size of the household. This yields a measure of net household disposable income, often used in studies on health inequalities (Cavelaars et al. 1998a). Usually, income is used to allocate people across the whole social ladder, but also marginal approaches can be used to distinguish poor people. Classifications use absolute sums of income as well as relative income groups, for example quintiles of equal size.

The main advantage of income measures is that they, in principle, allow accurate measurement and ordinal scales. The main drawback is that causal relationships are difficult to establish. A person's income may contaminate with his/her own health since, on the one hand, poor income is likely to contribute to poor health; but on the other hand, poor health is equally likely to contribute to a lowered income. The latter takes place as people with health problems drift to less well-paid jobs and outside the labor market. In cross-sectional studies the direction of causation is difficult to determine. A second problem with income is its close relationship with employment status. Usually those without employment also have a low income. For example, women doing housework lack individual income. To cope with this problem, household income is needed. A third drawback is that the measurement of income is often problematic since self-reports of income are inaccurate and biased. Additionally, many people refuse to report on their incomes.

In addition to individual or household income, the association between the income distribution and health at the aggregate level has been examined (Kaplan et al. 1996; Kennedy et al. 1998). It is argued that the relative position, not the absolute amount of money available, in the income distribution contributes to poor health and mortality through lack of cohesion and stress (Wilkinson 1996).

Interrelationships

Above, special features of each of the main dimensions of social status have been emphasized. Finally, it should be noted that these dimensions, as well as further measures of social stratification, such as housing tenure, car ownership or consumption, are interrelated and together give a comprehensive view of people's multiple social positioning. A schematic presentation is given in figure 4.2.

First of all, the social class of origin of a person, i.e. his/her parents' social status, influences the social status of destination, i.e. his/her own achieved status. Secondly, people's own education gives them basic resources and qualifications usually in youth. Education is causally prior to employment status and occupational class. Educational qualifications are important at the labor market and lead people to various occupational classes. Being without or with poor educational qualifications a person runs the risk of low status jobs, unemployment, and other forms of non-employment. Occupation class and employment status, together with education, contribute to a person's income level.

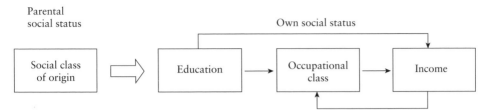

Figure 4.2 Associations between main dimensions of social status

Education is a very basic measure of social stratification and is a marker of other measures as well. So is occupation since in western societies many material and other resources are strongly dependent on the individual's labor market position (Arber 1997). In addition to using separately the measures of social status, summary indices combining several dimensions of the social stratification are sometimes used. However, their usefulness is limited to the extent that the measures are closely correlated and the direction of causation is similar. Finally, many other characteristics, such as gender and life course, modify the stratification pattern and should be taken into account in the examination of health inequalities. For example, assessing young people's social position is a complicated task; their own status is not yet crystallized, since their education may still continue, but they are non-employed and therefore have low incomes.

TYPES OF EXPLANATION AND CAUSALITY

Social inequalities in health are often described using the above measures of health and social status. However, the ultimate aim of research is a deeper understanding and explanation of health inequalities. Rather than being only descriptive, studies need to illuminate questions, such as "What is the causal direction of the associations found between health status and social status?" and "What are the reasons for the found associations?" Reference has already been made to the causal direction of the association between health and the social status. On the one hand, a person's social status is likely to affect his/her health, on the other hand, poor health may affect the social status through low income and lead sometimes to a non-employed social position.

Explanations

Various types of explanation have been advanced to explain the observed social inequalities in health. A major effort to approach the potential explanations was included in the Black Report (Townsend and Davidson 1982). The report presented a typology which included four types of explanation: (1) artefact, (2) natural or social selection, (3) materialist or structuralist, and (4) cultural or behavioral explanations. These types have been much discussed and a further

Table 4.2 "Hard" and "soft" explanations for health inequalities

	"Hard" version	*"Soft" version*
Artefact	No relation between class and mortality; purely an artefact of measurement	Magnitude of observed class gradients will depend on the measurement of both class and health
Natural/social selection	Health determines class position, therefore class gradients are morally neutral and "explained away"	Health can contribute to achieved class position and help to explain observed gradients
Materialist/structural	Material, physical, conditions of life associated with the class structure are the complete explanation for class gradients in health	Physical and psycho-social features associated with the class structure influence health and contribute to observed gradients
Cultural/behavioral	Health-damaging behaviors freely chosen by individuals in different social classes explain away social class gradients	Health-damaging behaviors are differentially distributed across social classes and contribute to observed gradients

Source: Macintyre 1997.

development was presented by Sally Macintyre (1997), who emphasized the explanations *not* being mutually exclusive. She distinguished between "hard" and "soft" versions of the four types of explanation (table 4.2).

1   *The artefact explanation* in its hard version suggests that the observed association between social status and health is spurious and non-existent due to measurement error of the studied variables. A soft version recognizes that the measurement of social status and health does not fully produce the observed association, but nevertheless may contribute to its magnitude. An example thereof is the numerator/denominator problem in Britain, since census data and death certificates are not linked at the individual level, and the social position given in the death certificates may differ from those given in the census.

2   *Natural or social selection explanation* is related to the direction of causality. The hard version of this selectionist explanation implies that the association between the social status and health is a real one, but that health determines social status rather than the other way round. People are recruited to social classes by their health and therefore poor people are in low social status groups. Avoidable inequalities in health are explained away and are outside any sociological or political concern. According to the soft version, recruitment to employment or education is not fully determined by health-related selection, but nevertheless selective entry to social status groups can contribute to the production of health inequalities to a greater or lesser extent. For example, illness in childhood may affect school performance and through this contribute to adult social status, or those with illness in adulthood may be excluded from

the labor market. Thus, the soft versions of the selection explanation are closely related to discrimination of people at important arenas of life.

3 *Materialist or structuralist explanations* are those most often searched for in research. Many scholars think that these are important explanations, and some scholars think that these are the only important explanations for social inequalities in health. According to the hard version, occupational social class, together with income and wealth, determines people's physical and material living conditions, such as working conditions and housing, and these produce an unequal distribution of health in the population. According to the soft version, living conditions determined by occupational class include additionally psychosocial factors. In this way the soft version takes into account social and cultural capital available to people, to which also education contributes.

4 *Cultural/behavioral explanations* in the hard version imply that the observed health inequalities can be explained away by health damaging behaviors, such as smoking, drinking, or poor diet. The soft version suggests that health-damaging behaviors may be unequally distributed across social status groups and to a greater or lesser extent contribute to health inequalities. For example smoking, which is more prevalent among low status people, contributes to a number of health problems. Thus health inequalities are not explained away, but the final explanation is pushed back and one can ask what are the reasons for the unequal distributions of health behaviors.

The hard versions of the above explanations for health inequalities are too fundamentalist to direct research and sticking to these may only obscure the richness of empirical associations between health and social status. The typology of the four main explanations in itself distinguishes important areas where explanations need to be searched for. The soft versions, contrary to the hard ones, allow alternative hypotheses to be formulated. Hypotheses may suggest a particular explanation or their combination depending on the aim of research, and predict the relative strength of the various explanations.

Causes

The causation from social status to ill health or death is a very complex process. An example thereof is a model from the British Whitehall Study (Marmot et al. 1991). As presented in figure 4.3, the model summarizes a number of causal factors included in the materialist as well as behavioral explanation. To cover also the possibility of the selection explanation reverse associations could be added to the figure, for example from health outcomes to work and social structure. Reverse causation is direct when poor health contributes to poor social status, and indirect when parents' social status contributes both to a person's own social status and his/her health (West 1991).

The model also includes early life, which is a biologically and psychosocially important phase of life with regard to adult social status as well as health. Health, together with social and economic living conditions in childhood, contribute to adult health and health inequalities. The social status of origin acquired in childhood correlates with the class of destination achieved in adulthood, and these both are associated with inequalities in adult health.

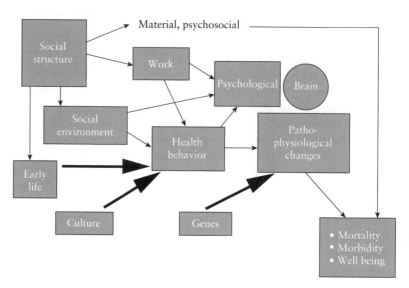

Figure 4.3 Summary of main causal associations between the social environment and health

Source: Independent Inquiry into Inequalities in Health 1998.

Genetic and pathophysiological influences are included in the model. So far very little is known about the mutual relationships between the biological, psychological, and social processes producing poor health. General susceptibility to ill health as well as specific etiological processes leading to diseases can be distinguished (Marmot et al. 1984). A disadvantaged position is likely to contribute to poor health in general and to a large number of diseases. Additionally, specific etiological factors related to particular social and occupational positions contribute to particular diseases, such as smoking or asbestos to lung cancer.

An exclusively "hard" emphasis on a particular type of explanation is likely to lead to unfruitful controversies. For example, one can ask whether health inequalities are caused by material living conditions *or* by health-damaging behaviors? An exclusive individualist interpretation of the influence of health behaviors leads easily to blaming the victim him/herself for the health-damaging behaviors, instead of trying to understand the social processes leading to such behaviors. On the other hand, sticking exclusively to material living conditions omits other potentially important simultaneous influences, such as those related to health behaviors. Another controversy concerns the bi-directional causality between social status and health. Looking at one direction only overlooks either the contribution of poor conditions to health, or social exclusion and discrimination based on poor health. A third example of a controversy is that between living conditions *per se* and the relative social position as determinants of health inequalities. An exclusive emphasis on absolute living conditions, such as poverty, overlooks the potential significance of relative deprivation, whereas an exclusive relative emphasis overlooks the contribution of absolute scarcity of resources to health inequalities.

The alternative explanations should be taken as hypotheses allowing further analysis instead of being established positions. Unwarranted controversies between the different explanations lead to a one-sided and distorted scientific picture of the production of health inequalities. Additionally they obscure policy options, which have potential beneficial and egalitarian consequences.

The Patterning of Health by Social Status

There is now ample evidence showing that health inequalities by social status exists all over the developed world. A summary up to the 1970s was provided by the Black Report (Townsend and Davidson 1982). This was substantially completed by Margaret Whitehead in the *Health Divide* report (Townsend et al. 1990). There are further reviews adding to the evidence, for example by Davey Smith et al. (1990) and Macintyre (1997), and further British documentations, including the latest *Decennial Supplement* (Drever and Whitehead 1997) and the *Independent Inquiry into Inequalities in Health* (1998). A number of state of the art collections on health inequalities have been produced (e.g. Fox 1989; Illsley and Svensson 1990; Vågerö and Illsley 1992; Lahelma and Rahkonen 1997; Bartley et al. 1998; Marmot and Wilkinson 1999).

Studies have examined health inequalities by the different dimensions of social status, analyzing various health outcomes. To illuminate the nature of the invariance on health inequalities the patterning of health by social status is examined among Finnish adult men and women in the mid-1990s (Lahelma et al. 1997; Rahkonen et al. 2000). An examination of perceived health by main measures of own social status, that is employment status, occupational social class (current or last occupation), education (highest examination passed), and income (net household income per consumption unit classified into quintiles), shows very clear results for men and women (table 4.3). Among the employment status groups the employed have the best health, whereas the unemployed and housewives, and retired people, most of whom are on work disability pension, have clearly poorer health. Occupational social class shows the best health is among the white-collar classes, particularly the upper white collar, whereas the poorest health is found among workers and farmers. Education and income, both ordinal measures, give a very clear gradient: the lower the education or income, the poorer the health.

Perceived health shows a very clear gradient across the various dimensions of social status, for men as well as women. Not only do the worst off show poor health, but an unequal distribution of health across the whole social ladder is evident. Often the highest social status groups are in a particularly advantaged position in terms of their health. Looking at other health indicators, such as limiting long-standing illness, we would find a very similar patterning of health inequalities.

Further evidence based on mortality among Finnish men and women confirms the above patterning of inequalities found for dimensions of ill health (Valkonen and Martelin 1999). Life expectancy at age 35 for men and women is distributed very unequally by social class: the upper white-collar class, particularly for men,

Table 4.3 Age-adjusted prevalence of perceived health as below good (in percentages) by main measures of social status among Finnish men and women in 1994

	Men	Women
Employment status		
Employed	28	25
Unemployed	37	33
Housewives	–	31
Retired/disabled	79	75
Social class		
Upper white-collar	21	20
Lower white-collar	30	26
Manual workers	36	36
Entrepreneurs/self-employed	33	27
Farmers	35	40
Education		
Higher	21	17
Secondary	32	27
Lower	37	35
Net household income		
Highest quintile	23	19
Fourth	30	28
Third	33	31
Second	34	33
Lowest quintile	37	32
N	3220	3087

Source: Rahkonen et al. 2000.

shows much longer life expectancy than any other social class (figure 4.4). Manual men and women have the shortest life expectancy, and other classes fall in-between. The gap in life expectancy between the upper white collar and manual class is six years for men and three years for women in Finland. The patterning of mortality by education is very similar to that by social class (Martikainen and Valkonen 1995).

The above examples use data from one country only. Inequalities in ill health and mortality by various dimensions of the social status are persistent even in an advanced welfare state such as Finland. Examples could have been taken from other western countries and the general picture would be very similar. However, there are also differences between countries. These are shown by available comparative research on health inequalities.

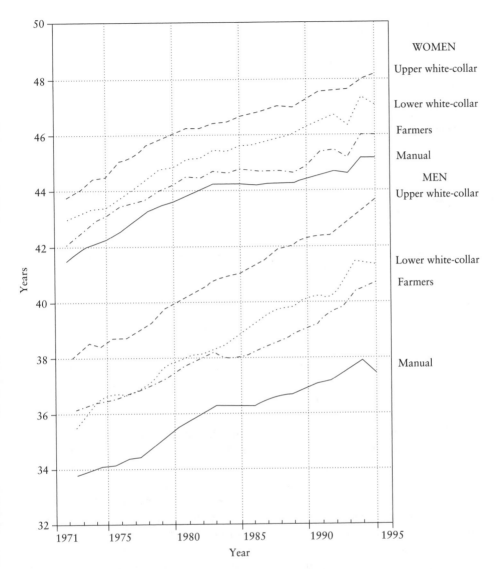

Figure 4.4 Life expectancy at age 35 by social class among Finnish men and women during the period 1971–95

Source: Valkonen and Martelin 1999.

Table 4.4   Mortality for manual vs. non-manual men aged
45–56 in nine European countries

	Mortality ratio: manual vs. non-manual
France	1.71
Finland	1.53
England/Wales	1.44
Sweden	1.41
Spain	1.37
Italy	1.35
Norway	1.34
Switzerland	1.34
Denmark	1.33

Source: Mackenbach et al. 1997.

THE INTERNATIONAL EVIDENCE

Comparative studies allow for testing whether similar social inequalities in ill
health and death can be found in different countries, what are the differences in
the social patterning of health, and how does the size of health inequalities vary
between countries? Most comparative studies on health inequalities have
included a limited number of countries only. One of the first comparative studies
examined inequalities in limiting long-standing illness by social class and education in Denmark, Finland, Norway, and Sweden in the early 1970s (Karisto et al.
1978). A clear gradient following the health inequalities invariance was found
for each country. These Nordic results were further confirmed for the 1980s
(Rahkonen et al. 1994). Another study compared educational inequalities in
mortality in the 1970s in seven European countries and found again a clear
gradient (Valkonen 1989). The gradient was steeper for men than for women.
Largest inequalities in mortality were found for France, whereas inequalities
were smallest in the Scandinavian countries. However, differences between
countries were not very large. By cause of death inequalities were smallest for
cancer, average for cardiovascular causes, and largest for accidents and external
causes.

The broadest international comparison of health inequalities so far was made
by the EU Working Group on Socioeconomic Inequalities in Health (Mackenbach et al. 1997). The study aimed to examine health inequalities in as many
European countries as possible, for mortality as well as morbidity, with special
reference to the size of relative inequalities between countries. Existing data
sources from various countries were used and harmonized to be as comparable
as possible. Educational inequalities for perceived health as below good could
be studied in 11 countries (Mackenbach et al. 1997; Cavelaars et al. 1998b).

According to Relative Index of Inequality – a regression based measure (Mackenbach and Kunst 1997) – the size of inequalities in perceived health varied between countries for men as well as women (figure 4.5). Gender differences in inequalities in each country were not very large. For both men and

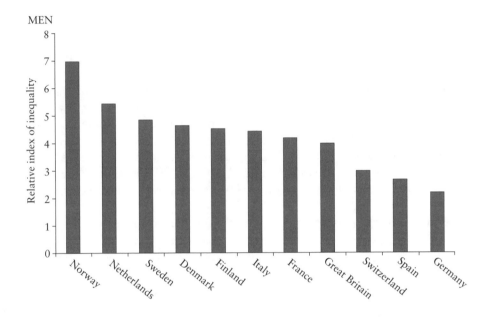

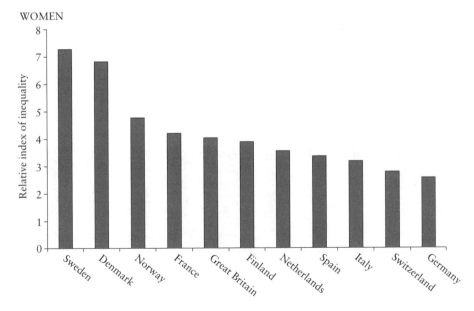

Figure 4.5 Perceived health by education in 11 European countries. Relative Index of Inequality

Source: Cavelaars et al. 1998b.

women there was a tendency for the Nordic countries to show larger than average health inequalities, whereas Germany and Switzerland showed small inequalities.

Occupational social class and income inequalities in perceived health could be found as well. The international pattern for social class was broadly in accordance with that for education (Caverlaars et al. 1998c). However, for income, the pattern was different since the Nordic countries did not stand out as having large inequalities as for education. On the contrary, inequalities in perceived health by income in these countries were now smaller than average (Cavelaars et al. 1998a).

Inequalities in mortality by occupational social class could be studied for men only (Mackenbach et al. 1997). This was done by comparing mortality in two broad occupational groups, manual vs non-manual, in nine European countries in the 1980s (table 4.4 and figure 4.6). Although a rough measure, the two broad classes are likely to be very similar in different countries. France shows largest inequalities, as was found also for the 1970s. Out of the Nordic countries Finland has large inequalities, but other Nordic countries average or small inequalities.

The international patterning, particularly for perceived health inequalities, is unexpected, given that the Nordic countries are highly developed welfare states emphasizing egalitarian policies. However, inequalities in ill health could be found for other measures of ill health as well, although the international pattern was not fully similar with that found for perceived health.

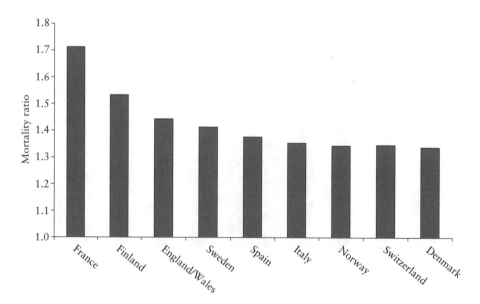

Figure 4.6 Mortality for manual vs. non-manual men aged 45–56 in 9 European countries

Source: Mackenbach et al. 1997.

The patterning of health inequalities is under further debate, and the reasons for the found inequalities and the variation of their size by country are not yet well understood. However, the differential international patterning of inequalities in morbidity and mortality suggests that the reasons are not necessarily identical. The European comparative study looked only at relative inequalities. Looking at absolute inequalities in morbidity and mortality by various measures of the social status might add to the picture. Furthermore, the significance of methodological issues, particularly for morbidity, needs further elaboration.

A major effort to find out potential determinants of health inequalities in the European comparative study concerned smoking. The results give an example which may help explain the production of health inequalities (Cavelaars et al. 1998d). Educational inequalities in smoking are particularly large in the Nordic countries whereas the southern European countries show negligible or even reverse inequalities in smoking; in other words, people with higher education are more often smokers. This suggests that the southern countries are still in an earlier phase of the "smoking epidemic." Lacking the unequal social patterning of smoking might then contribute to health inequalities. Looking at causes of death can be taken as supporting this line of reasoning, since overall inequalities in mortality in the Nordic countries were largely determined by unequal cardio-vascular mortality, whereas a similar gradient is virtually non-existent in the southern European countries.

CHANGES OVER TIME

There has been considerable debate concerning the trend in health inequalities: whether they are widening, narrowing, or remaining stable over time (Marmot and Dowall 1986; Whitehead and Diderichsen 1997; Lahelma et al. 2000). Analyzing time trends in health is a challenging task and part of the debate is related to methodological difficulties. How to study changes? Should one measure absolute or relative differentials? How to take into account changes in the size of social status groups over time? Relatively little is known about time trends in health inequalities, and particularly little is known about the international variation of time trends in health inequalities.

Trends in mortality inequalities in the 1970s in seven European countries showed that in France and England, where inequalities already were relatively large, further widening occurred, whereas in the Nordic counties inequalities in mortality remained broadly stable (Valkonen 1989). In no single country did inequalities show a narrowing trend.

More recent international evidence on the trends of mortality inequalities is so far very limited. For Finnish men as well as women widening mortality inequalities and an overall decline in mortality can be seen since the early 1970s (see figure 4.4). For British men and women a similar widening trend in mortality by social class can be found (Harding et al. 1997). In Finland the decline in mortality from cardiovascular diseases, particularly among men, has been much faster in the higher social status groups than in the lower ones, and this largely accounts for the widening trend of mortality inequalities (Martikainen and Valkonen 1995).

Changes in morbidity differentials will not necessarily follow a similar pattern as those found for mortality. Studies from Finland and Sweden suggest that from the 1980s to 1990s health inequalities have remained broadly stable among men and women (Fritzell and Lundberg 1994; Lahelma et al. 1997; Fritzell 1999; Lundberg et al. 1999). A comparison of health inequalities in Britain and Finland from the 1980s to 1990s showed a contrasting trend in these two countries (Lahelma et al. 2000). In Britain perceived health and limiting long-standing illness inequalities widened or remained stable, whereas in Finland they declined or remained stable.

Finally, reference is made to Norwegian evidence on time trends in health inequalities which deviates from other countries, but has potential future significance for the other affluent countries as well. According to a recent study (Dahl and Birkelund 1999) health inequalities among the Norwegian employed labor force have narrowed by the mid-1990s and become virtually invisible. However, simultaneously ill health among non-employed men and women has become more prevalent resulting into a widening gap between the non-employed and the employed. This trend is likely to be due to health-related selection out of the employed labor force: the Norwegian labor market has become more selective and reluctant to accept less competitive employees who are discriminated against and even excluded from paid jobs. Once non-employed, people with health problems have poor chances of re-employment. As a result, health inequalities tend to be polarized between the employed and non-employed, but may not be found within employed people only.

The significance of the Norwegian development will become evident as research on the trends of health inequalities from other countries accumulates. However, available evidence on the main trends of health inequalities over the last few decades has suggested rather a stable or widening development. It is possible that different countries show contrasting trends in health inequalities as the evidence from Britain and Finland suggests (Lahelma et al. 2000). It is also worth noticing that in the western countries the response to major social transformations in terms of health inequalities is not a straightforward, but a complex one. An example thereof is Finland where unemployment skyrocketed in the early 1990s from 2–3 percent to 18 percent, but so far health inequalities have remained stable or even narrowed (Lahelma et al. 1997).

POLICY AND FUTURE PERSPECTIVES

Evidence from international comparisons as well as a large number of national studies confirms the universal social patterning of ill health and mortality in the developed world. The health inequalities invariance – *the poorer the social position, the poorer the health* – holds true even in the most advanced countries. Thus the evidence contrasts hypotheses suggesting universal hierarchical social structures giving way to new divisions, such as age, identity, or other. Health has provided a case which shows persistent continuities in class and other inequalities by social status. A death of class development cannot be found, at least so far, for morbidity and mortality in advanced societies. Regarding the persistence of health inequalities they are likely to continue in the foreseeable future. Therefore, health inequalities need to be given a high priority in the future medical sociological and epidemiological research as well as political agenda.

Having emphasized the universal patterning of health inequalities it is equally important to recognize that there are variations between countries and over time. Additionally, for example, gender and life course modify health inequalities. Whether occupational social class differences in health will be transformed outside the labor market in the future and whether a stricter polarization of health status will develop between the employed and non-employed as the Norwegian evidence suggested, remains a hypothesis to be tested in other countries as well. The universal patterning of health inequalities may have partly common reasons in hierarchically organized societies. However, to understand the variation between countries, concrete analyses and country-specific explanatory factors are needed.

Explanations for health inequalities have included a variety of factors which should not be taken in an exclusive way, as suggested by Macintyre (1997) in her distinction between the "hard" and "soft" versions of explanations. Four particularly important areas of factors, which all provide partial explanations for health inequalities and their size, can be identified on the basis of current evidence. First, living conditions at work (Lundberg 1991) and at home (Bartley et al. 1992; Arber and Lahelma 1993; Hunt and Annandale 1993) contribute to health inequalities and their size. Secondly, health behaviors, such as smoking (Cavelaars et al. 2000), drinking (Mäkelä et al. 1997), and diet (Pekkanen et al. 1995; Roos et al. 1998) are all factors which contribute to health inequalities. A third area includes early influences on health: economic and social conditions in childhood have a bearing on adult health inequalities (Lundberg 1993; Rahkonen et al. 1997a). Fourthly, selective social mobility (Lundberg 1993; Rahkonen et al. 1997b) and discrimination, for example, at the labor market (Bartley and Owen 1996; Dahl and Birkelund 1999) also play a role in the production of health inequalities. In other words, health, directly or indirectly, can influence people's placing into different social positions which then contributes to health inequalities between social status groups.

The patterning of observed health inequalities is usually very clear and the size of absolute health inequalities often large. For example, life expectancy at age 35 among Finnish men with higher education is close to six years longer than that for men with basic education only (Martikainen and Valkonen 1995). A large part of this gap is in principle avoidable. In other words, narrowing the health gap between social status groups provides a large potential not only for improving equality in health, but also producing a substantial improvement in the overall public health. If health among the worst off groups could be improved closer to the best off groups, this would bring about advantages to the population's health so large that it is difficult to imagine other equally effective policy options. At the international level the size of health inequalities shows substantial variation. This, in turn, suggests that countries with particularly large health inequalities show a particularly large potential for narrowing the health gap between social status groups.

The significance of health inequalities has been recognized at the international level as well as in many countries. The *Health for All by the Year 2000* strategy of the WHO emphasizes the need to reduce health inequalities (WHO 1985). Two recent British reports reviewed the international evidence on policy options to reduce social inequalities in health referring to individual, community, macro-economic, and cultural factors as well as to the role of health services (Benzeval et al. 1995; Independent Inquiry into Inequalities in Health 1998). Particularly the *Independent Inquiry into Inequalities in Health* suggests concrete measures to improve the living conditions and health among disadvantaged groups. Emphasis is laid on social and health services which are often overlooked as reasons for health inequalities. Although little is known about the significance of health services, available evidence suggests that health services may contribute to health inequalities (Keskimäki 1997).

Research on health inequalities has often examined relative health inequalities only, for example whether and to what extent health is poorer among the manual relative to the non-manual classes. The relative strategy indicates the existence of health inequalities and allows hypotheses to be forwarded and explanations to be searched for. However, this is likely to be an inadequate strategy for egalitarian health policies, since for policy purposes measures which bring about maximal public health benefits are needed. It is then import-ant to know how large health improvements can be achieved and how many people can be covered by using a particular measure. For example, two years more of life expectancy among upper white-collar women brings about moder-ate relative benefits for a class which already has a longer life than other classes. This class is also relatively small and therefore the impact to women's overall life expectancy also remains moderate. In contrast, two years more of life expec-tancy for manual women would bring about a much larger relative benefit, since life expectancy is much shorter in this class. Also, as the manual class is larger than the upper white-collar class, two years longer life among manual women brings about a substantial extension to women's overall life expectancy.

Absolute measures, for example how many deaths or diseases could be pre-vented or how many years longer life expectancy can be achieved by a measure, are indispensable for the evaluation of the efficiency of health and welfare policies in the population and in each social status group (Independent Inquiry into Inequalities in Health 1998).

In conclusion, egalitarian policies need a multiple strategy aiming simulta-neously at improving the health of the worst off groups, reducing the gap between all other social status groups, and improving the overall level of health in the whole target population. To be able to successfully implement policies the evidence from research should be better communicated to lay people as well. This would help people articulate their needs, suggest initiatives, and participate in egalitarian policies to reduce health inequalities.

References

Allardt, Erik. 1975. *Att ha, att älska, att vara. Om välfärden i Norden* [Having, loving and being. Welfare in the Nordic countries]. Lund: Argos.

Arber, Sara. 1997. "Insights about the Non-Employed, Class and Health: Evidence from the General Household Survey." In D. Rose and K. O'Reilly (eds.). *Constructing Classes: Towards a New Social Classification for the UK*. Swindon: Office for National Statistics: 78–92.

Arber, Sara, and Eero Lahelma. 1993. "Inequalities in Women's and Men's Ill Health: Britain and Finland Compared." *Social Science & Medicine* 37: 1055–68.

Bartley, Mel, Jennie Popay, and Ian Plewis. 1992. "Domestic Conditions, Paid Employment and Women's Experience of Ill Health." *Sociology of Health and Illness* 14: 313–43.

Bartley, Mel, and Clive Owen. 1996. "Relation between Socioeconomic Status, Employment and Health during Economic Change, 1973–93." *British Medical Journal* 313: 445–9.

Bartley, Mel, David Blane, and George Davey Smith (eds.). 1998. *Sociology of Health Inequalities*. Oxford: Blackwell.

Benzeval, Michaela, Ken Judge, and Margaret Whitehead (eds.). 1995. *Tackling Inequalities In Health*. London: King's Fund.

Beveridge, William. 1942. *Social Insurance and Allied Services*. London: HMSO.

Blane, David, Chris Power, and Mel Bartley. 1993. "The Measurement of Morbidity in Relation to Social Class." In T. Abel, S. Geyer, U. Gerhardt, J. Siegrist, and W. van den Heuvel (eds.), *Medical Sociology Research on Chronic Illness*. Bonn: Informationszentrum Sozialwissenschaften.

Blaxter, Mildred. 1989. "A Comparison of Measures of Inequality in Morbidity." In A. J. Fox (ed.), *Health Inequalities in European Countries*. Aldershot: Gower, 199–230.

——. 1997. "Whose Fault is it? People's Own Conceptions of the Reasons for Health Inequalities." *Social Science & Medicine* 44: 747–56.

Bobak, Martin, Hinek Pikhart, Clyde Hertzman, R. Rose, and Michael Marmot. 1998. "Socio-Economic Factors, Perceived Control and Self-Reported Health in Russia." *Social Science & Medicine* 47: 269–79

Bowling, Ann. 1991. *Measuring Health: A Review of Quality of Life Measurement Scales*. Buckingham: Open University Press.

——. 1995. *Measuring Disease: A Review of Disease-Specific Quality of Life Measurement Scales*. Buckingham: Open University Press.

de Bruin, A., H. S. J. Pichavet, and Anatoly Nossikov. 1996. *Health Interview Surveys: Towards International Harmonization of Methods and Instruments*. Copenhagen: WHO Regional Publications.

Cavelaars, Adriënne, Anton Kunst, José Geurts, Uwe Helmert, Eero Lahelma, Olle Lundberg, Jill Matheson, Andreas Mielck, and Johan Mackenbach. 1998a. "Differences in Self-Reported Morbidity by Income Level in Six European Countries." In A. Cavelaars (ed.), *Cross-National Comparisons of Socio-Economic Differences in Health Indicators*. Erasmus University Rotterdam: 49–66.

Cavelaars, Adriënne, Anton Kunst, José Geurts, Rita Crialesi, Liv Grötvedt, Uwe Helmert, Eero Lahelma, Olle Lundberg, Andreas Mielck, Jill Matheson, An. Mizrahi, Ar. Mizrahi, Niels K. Rasmussen, Enrico Redigor, Thomas Spuler, and Johan Mackenbach. 1998b. "Differences in Self-Reported Morbidity by Educational Level: A Comparison of 11 Western European Countries." *Journal of Epidemiology and Community Health* 52: 219–27.

Cavelaars, Adriënne, Anton Kunst, José Geurts, Uwe Helmert, Olle Lundberg, Jill Matheson, Andreas Mielck, An. Mizrahi, Ar. Mizrahi, Thomas Spuler, and John Mackenbach. 1998c. "Morbidity Differences by Occupational Class Among Men in Seven European Countries: An Application of the Erikson-Goldthorpe Social Class Scheme." *International Journal of Epidemiology* 27: 222–30.

Cavelaars, Adriënne, Anton Kunst, José Geurts, Rita Crialesi, Liv Grötvedt, Uwe Helmert, Eero Lahelma, Olle Lundberg, Jill Matheson, Andreas Mielck, An. Mizrahi, Ar. Mizrahi, Niels K. Rasmussen, Enrico Redigor, Maria do Rosario-Giraldez, T. Spuler, and Johan Mackenbach. 2000. "Educational differences in smoking: an international comparison." *British Medical Journal* 320: 1102–07.

Chadwick, Edwin. 1842. "Report on an Inquiry into the Sanitary Conditions of Labouring Population of Great Britain." London: HMSO.

Claus, Lisbeth. 1983. "The Development of Medical Sociology in Europe." *Social Science & Medicine* 17: 1591–7.

Cockerham, William. 1997. "The Social Determinants of the Decline of Life Expectancy in Russia and Eastern Europe: A Lifestyle Explanation." *Journal of Health and Social Behavior* 38: 117–30.

Dahl, Espen, and Gunn E. Birkelund. 1999. "Sysselsettning, klasse og helse 1980–1995. En analyse av fem norske levekårsunderskelser" [Employment Status, Class and Health 1980–1995. An Analysis of Five Norwegian Surveys on Living Conditions]. *Tidskrift for samfunnsforskning* 40: 3–32.

Dahlgren, Göran, and Margaret Whitehead. 1991. *Policies and Strategies to Promote Social Equity in Health.* Stockholm: Institute of Future Studies.

Davey Smith, George, Mel Bartley, and David Blane. 1990. "The Black Report on Socio-Economic Inequalities in Health 10 Years on." *British Medical Journal* 301: 373–7.

Drever, Frances, and Margaret Whitehead (eds.). 1997. *Health Inequalities: Decennial Supplement.* Office for National Statistics Series DS, no. 15. London: HMSO.

Elstad, Jon Ivar. 1996. "How Large are the Differences – Really? Self-Reported Long-Standing Illness Among Working-Class and Middle-Class Men." *Sociology of Health and Illness* 18: 475–98.

Erikson, Robert, and Hannu Uusitalo. 1987. "The Scandinavian Approach to Welfare Research." In R. Erikson, E. J. Hansen, S. Ringen, and H. Uusitalo (eds.), *The Scandinavian Model: Welfare States and Welfare Research.* Armonk, NY: M. E. Sharpe, 177–93.

Fox, John (ed.). 1989. *Health Inequalities in European Countries.* Aldershot: Gower.

Fritzell, Johan. 1999. "Changes in the Social Patterning of Living Conditions." In M. Heikkilä, B. Hvinden, M. Kautto, S. Marklund, S. and N. Ploug (eds.), *Scandinavian Social Policy.* London: Routledge.

Fritzell, Johan, and Olle Lundberg. 1994. "Välfärdsförändringar 1968–1991" [Changes in Welfare 1968–1991]. In J. Fritzell and O. Lundberg (eds.), *Vardagens villkor. Välfärdsförhållanden i Sverige under'tre decennier.* Stockholm: Brombergs, 235–59.

Gerhardt, Uta. 1989. *Ideas About Illness. An Intellectual and Political History of Medical Sociology.* London: Macmillan.

Hamlin, Christopher. 1995. "Could you Starve to Death in England in 1839? The Chadwick–Farr Controversy and the Loss of the Social in Public Health." *American Journal of Public Health* 85: 856–66.

Harding, Seeromanie, Ann Bethune, Roy Maxwell, and Joanna Brown. 1997. "Mortality Trends Using the Longitudinal Study." In F. Drever and M. Whitehead (eds.), *Health Inequalities: Decennial Supplement.* Office for National Statistics Series DS, no. 15. London: HMSO, 143–55.

Hunt, Kate, and Ellen Annandale. 1993. "Just the Job? Is the Relationship Between Health and Domestic and Paid Work Gender Specific?" *Sociology of Health and Illness* 15: 632–64.

Illsley, Raymond, and Per-Gunnar Svensson (eds.). 1990. "Health Inequities in Europe." Special issue, *Social Science & Medicine* 27(3): 223–430.

"Independent Inquiry into Inequalities in Health." 1998. London: The Stationery Office.

Johansson, Sten. 1979. "Mot en teori för social rapportering" [Towards a theory of social reporting]. *Rapport nr 2 från levnadsnivåprojektet.* Stockholm: Institutet för social forskning.

Kadushin, Charles. 1964. "Social Class and the Experience of Ill Health." *Sociological Inquiry* 534: 67–80.

Kaplan, George, Elsie Pamuk, John Lynch, Richard Cohen, and Jennifer Balfour. 1996. "Inequality in Income in the United States: Analysis of Mortality and Potential Pathways." *British Medical Journal* 312: 999–1003.

Karisto, Antti, Veijo Notkola, and Tapani Valkonen. 1978. "Socio-Economic Status and Health in Finland and the Other Scandinavian Countries." *Social Science & Medicine* 12C: 83–8.

Kennedy, Bruce, Ichiro Kawachi, Roberta Glass, and Deborah Prothrow-Stith. 1998. "Income Distribution, Socioeconomic Status and Self-Rated Health." *British Medical Journal* 317: 917–21.

Keskimäki, Ilmo. 1997. "Social Equity in the Use of Hospital Inpatient Care in Finland." *Research Reports 84.* Stakes: Jyväskylä.

Krieger, Nancy, and Elizabeth Fee. 1996. "Measuring Social Inequalities in Health in the United States: An Historical Review; 1900–1950." *International Journal of Health Services* 26: 391–418.

Krieger, Nancy, David Williams, and Nancy Moss. 1997. "Measuring Social Class in US Public Health Research." *Annual Review of Public Health* 18: 341–78.

Lahelma, Eero, Sara Arber, Ossi Rahkonen, and Karri Silventoinen. 2000. "Widening or Narrowing Inequalities of Health? Comparing Britain and Finland from the 1980s to 1990s." *Sociology of Health and Illness* 22: 110–36.

Lahelma, Eero, Antti Karisto, and Ossi Rahkonen. 1996. "Analysing Inequalities: The Tradition of Socioeconomic Health Research in Finland." *European Journal of Public Health* 6: 87–93.

Lahelma, Eero, and Ossi Rahkonen (eds.). 1997. "Health Inequalities in Modern Societies and Beyond." Special issue, *Social Science & Medicine* 44(6): 721–910.

Lahelma, Eero, Ossi Rahkonen, and Minna Huuhka. 1997. "Changes in the Social Patterning of Health? The Case of Finland." *Social Science & Medicine* 44: 789–99.

Lee, David J. and Brian S. Turner. 1996. "Introduction: Myths of Classlessness and the Death of Class Analysis." In D. J. Lee and B. S. Turner (eds.), *Conflicts about Class. Debating Inequality in Late Industrialism.* London: Longman, 1–25.

Liberatos, Penny, Bruce Link, and Jennifer Kelsey. 1988. "The Measurement of Social Class in Epidemiology." *Epidemiological Review* 10: 87–121.

Lundberg, Olle. 1991. "Causal Explanations for Class Inequality in Health: An Empirical Analysis." *Social Science & Medicine* 32: 385–93.

——. 1993. "The Impact of Childhood Living Conditions on Illness and Mortality in Adulthood." *Social Science & Medicine* 36: 1047–52.

——. 1998. "... däruti få af de förmögnare sjukna – Om ohälsans ojämlika fördelning i dagens Sverige" ("... in this respect few of the more wealthy fall ill – On the unequal distribution of health in contemporary Sweden"). *En god hälsa ett socialt privilegium?* Stockholm: Nationella folkhälsokommittén: 7–46.

Lundberg, Olle, Finn Diderichsen, and Monica berg. 1999. *Changing Health Inequalities in a Changing Society: Sweden in the mid-1980s and the mid-1990s.* (manuscript).

Macintyre, Sally. 1997. "The Black Report and Beyond: What are the Issues?" *Social Science & Medicine* 44: 723–45.

Macintyre, Sally, Graeme Ford, and Kate Hunt. 1999. "Do Women Over-Report? Men's and Women's Responses to Structured Prompting on a Standard Question on Long-Standing Illness." *Social Science & Medicine* 48: 89–98.

Mackenbach, Johan, Anton Kunst, Adriënne Cavelaars, Feikje Groenhof, Jose Geurts, and the EU Working Group on Socio-economic Inequalities in Health. 1997. "Socio-economic Inequalities in Morbidity and Mortality in Western Europe." *Lancet* 349: 1655–9.

Mackenbach, Johan, and Anton Kunst. 1997. "Measuring the Magnitude of Socio-Economic Inequalities in Health: An Overview of Available Measures Illustrated with Two Examples from Europe." *Social Science & Medicine* 44: 757–71.

Mäkelä, Pia, Tapani Valkonen, and Tuija Martelin. 1997. "Contribution of Deaths Related to Alcohol Use to Socio-Economic Variation in Mortality: Register Based Follow-up Study." *British Medical Journal* 315: 211–16.

Marmot, Michael, Martin Shipley, and Geoffrey Rose. 1984. "Inequalities in Death-Specific Explanations of a General Pattern?" *Lancet* 1: 1003.

Marmot, Michael, and M. Dowall. 1986. "Mortality Decline and Widening Social Inequalities." *Lancet* 2: 274–6

Marmot, Michael, George Davey Smith, Stephen Stansfeld, Chandra Patel, Fiona North, Jenny Head, Ian White, Eric Brunner, and Amanda Feeney. 1991. "Health Inequalities Among British Civil Servants: The Whitehall II Study." *Lancet* 337: 1387–93.

Marmot, Michael, and Richard Wilkinson. 1999. *Social Determinants of Health.* Oxford: Oxford University Press.

Martikainen, Pekka, and Tapani Valkonen. 1995. *Lama ja ennenaikainen kuolleisuus* [Recession and premature mortality]. Helsinki: Statistics Finland, Population 1995, 11.

Najman, Jake M. 1993. "Health and Poverty: Past, Present and Prospects for the Future." *Social Science & Medicine* 36: 157–66.

Palosuo, Hannele, Antti Uutela, Irina Zhuraleva, and Nina Lakomova. 1998. "Social Patterning of Ill Health in Helsinki and Moscow." *Social Science & Medicine* 46: 1121–36.

Pekkanen, Juha, Jaakko Tuomilehto, Antti Uutela, Erkki Vartiainen, and Aulikki Nissinen. 1995. "Social Class, Health Behaviour, and Mortality Among Men and Women in Eastern Finland." *British Medical Journal* 311: 589–93.

Rahkonen, Ossi, Eero Lahelma, Kristiina Manderbacka, and Antti Karisto. 1994. "Persisting Health Inequalities: Social Class Differentials in Self-Reported Illness in the Scandinavian Countries." *Journal of Public Health Policy* 13: 95–110.

Rahkonen, Ossi, Eero Lahelma, and Minna Huuhka. 1997a. "Past or Present? Childhood Living Conditions and Current Socio-Economic Status as Determinants of Adult Health." *Social Science & Medicine* 44: 327–36.

Rahkonen, Ossi, Sara Arber, and Eero Lahelma. 1997b. "Health and Social Mobility in Britain and Finland." *Scandinavian Journal of Social Medicine* 25: 83–92.

Rahkonen, Ossi, Sara Arber, Eero Lahelma, Pekka Martikainen, and Karri Silventoinen. 2000. "Understanding Income Inequalities in Health Among Men and Women in Britain and Finland." *International Journal of Health Services* 30: 27–47.

Roos, Eva, Eero Lahelma, Mikko Virtanen, Ritva Prättälä, and Pirjo Pietinen. 1998. "Gender, Socioeconomic Status and Family Status as Determinants of Recommended Food Behaviour." *Social Science & Medicine* 46: 1519–29.

Rose, Geoffrey. 1992. *The Strategy of Preventive Medicine*. Oxford: Oxford University Press.

Rose, D., and K. O'Reilly (eds.). 1997. *Constructing Classes: Towards a New Social Classification for the UK*. Swindon: Office for National Statistics.

Rosen, George. 1993. *A History of Public Health* (Expanded Edition). Baltimore: Johns Hopkins University Press.

Scambler, Graham, and Paul Higgs. 1999. "Stratification, Class and Health: Class Relations and Health Inequalities in High Modernity." *Sociology* 33: 275–96.

Titmuss, Richard. 1943. *Birth, Poverty and Wealth*. London: Hamish Hamilton Medical Books.

Townsend, Peter, and Nick Davidson. 1982. *Inequalities in Health: The Black Report*. London: Penguin.

Townsend, Peter, Nick Davidson, and Margaret Whitehead. 1990. *Inequalities in Health: The Black Report and the Health Divide*. London: Penguin.

Vågerö, Denny, and Raymond Illsley (eds.). 1992. "Inequality, Health and Policy in East and West Europe." *International Journal of Health Sciences* 3: 225–39.

Valkonen, Tapani. 1989. "Adult Mortality and Level of Education: A Comparison of Six Countries." In A. J. Fox (ed.), *Health Inequalities in European Countries*. Aldershot: Gower, 142–60.

Valkonen, Tapani, and Tuija Martelin. 1999. "Social Inequality in the Face of Death – Linked Registers in Mortality Research." In J. Alho (ed.), *Statistics, Registers, Science*. Helsinki: Statistics Finland: 213–26.

Warr, Peter. 1987. *Work, Unemployment and Mental Health*. Oxford: Oxford University Press.

West, Patrick. 1991. "Rethinking the Health Selection Explanation for Health Inequalities." *Social Science & Medicine* 32: 373–84.

Whitehead, Margaret. 1997. "Life and Death Over the Millennium." In F. Drever and M. Whitehead (eds.), *Health Inequalities: Decennial Supplement*. Office for National Statistics Series DS, no. 15. London: HMSO, 7–28.

Whitehead, Margaret, and Finn Diderichsen. 1997. "International Evidence on Social Inequalities in Health." In F. Drever and M. Whitehead (eds.), *Health Inequalities: Decennial Supplement*. Office for National Statistics Series DS, no. 15. London: HMSO, 44–68.

WHO. 1985. *Targets for Health for All*. Copenhagen: WHO Regional Office for Europe.

Wilkinson, Richard. 1996. *Unhealthy Societies: The Afflictions of Inequality*. London: Routledge.

5

From Women's Health to a Gender Analysis of Health

SARA ARBER AND HILARY THOMAS

The health experiences of women differ from those of men. These differences primarily reflect gender roles relating to the social, cultural, and economic circumstances of women's and men's lives. This chapter explores how gender roles and relationships affect health, and points to some of the ways in which changes in gender roles over time and between societies influence gender differences in health. Gender is one important dimension of social life which intersects with others, especially social class, ethnicity, and age. Thus, the chapter also examines health divisions among women and among men.

Gender roles are socially constructed and therefore change over time and vary between societies. The cultural and religious norms of a society have a profound influence on the roles, attitudes, and behavior of men and women within that society. Gender ideology prescribes and circumscribes the social behavior of men and women, and of different age or ethnic groups of men and women. Social myths and stereotypes about appropriate or supposedly "natural" behavior for women and men impact on their health and well-being, such as body image and weight control. Gender permeates all aspects of life. Lorber (1997: 3) summarizes the importance of gender roles for health:

> Because gender is embedded in the major social organizations of society, such as the economy, the family, politics, and the medical and legal systems, it has a major impact on how the women and men of different social groups are treated in all sectors of life, including health and illness, getting born and dying. Gender is thus one of the most significant factors in the transformation of physical bodies into social bodies.

The chapter begins by noting that whilst greater attention is paid to women's reproductive health, much of women's other health issues are masked by the assumption that white, male bodies are the norm for human health. Recently there has been a shift to a gender analysis of health, which emphasizes the social relations between men and women and their consequences for health. The chapter considers the evidence for, and explanations of, differences in mortality and morbidity between men and women. Finally, the chapter addresses to what extent cross-cutting social structures, such as class, family structure, and age, have a similar influence on health inequalities among women and men.

WOMEN'S HEALTH

In the 1970s and early 1980s, the primary focus of interest within medical sociology was on women's health rather than a gender analysis of health. This mirrored the provision of health services based on biological differences, linked to women's distinctive reproductive systems, and resulting in extensive specialized services for childbirth, contraception, abortion, and infertility.

The relationship between biological sex and gendered social roles is most marked in the area of reproductive health. A major gender-specific cause of death in the past has been maternal mortality, and in many developing countries reduction in the maternal mortality rate remains a central aim of national health care programs. The medical domination of health care programs in these countries, and the dominant role of acute hospital medical care, has often led to a lack of expenditure on community health care and the training of traditional birth attendants (Doyal 1995, 1999). However, in western countries, maternal mortality is now at a very low level and other concerns are paramount for medical sociologists interested in reproductive health, particularly issues associated with medicalization.

Criticism of midwifery services has centered on the medicalization of reproduction at the expense of women's experiences and preferences. Maternity care is seen as organized around a search for pathology rather than women's experience of birth and parenthood. There is tension between sexual and reproductive experiences as normal, social events and the provision of care framed by professional agendas and often provided in clinical settings (Thomas 1998).

Women's sexual and reproductive health and behavior is both a private matter and a subject of public and social concern. This is rendered more complex by the tension between responsibility and power. For example, women are expected to take responsibility for using contraception, making changes in health behavior during pregnancy, and attending for cervical screening, yet their ability to affect these actions is constrained by their relative powerlessness in heterosexual relationships and in interactions with health professionals (Thomas 1998). Women's needs for safe, effective contraception may be at odds with their male partners' wishes. Women who are lesbian, or who live in poverty, or who experience racist stereotyping may experience additional constraints on the achievement of their fertility aspirations and on the willingness of services to meet their requirements.

Many women in developed countries expect pregnancy and birth to be a normal event and are primarily concerned with the social context. However, their experience of maternity care is of a medicalized search for pathology (Graham and Oakley 1981). Women's dissatisfaction with the maternity services has a long history, much of which has been concerned with the place and circumstances of birth (Garcia 1982). Research in the late 1970s and 1980s focused on women's experiences of maternity care (Graham and McKee 1979; Oakley 1979), while others contrasted user and provider perspectives (Graham and Oakley 1981), and described conflicts concerning the image of pregnancy presented by the providers (Comaroff 1977; Graham 1977).

Women's postnatal health is the least recognized, least glamorous aspect of pregnancy and birth. Once the drama of the birth is over, a woman's own health appears to take second place in the eyes of health professionals (Thomas 1998). Surveys paint a dismal picture including physical trauma arising from the birth, continuing gynaecological problems, exhaustion from interrupted sleep, and mental health problems, particularly postnatal depression (MacArthur et al. 1991).

Medicalization in other areas of women's lives has received less attention from sociologists compared with maternity care. There are rising rates of hysterectomy, whilst the menopause provides a new stage of the female life course for medical intervention. It is estimated that one in five women in Britain will have a hysterectomy by the age of 75 (Teo 1990), although few hysterectomies are performed for life-threatening conditions. Teo suggests that the large increase in the number of hysterectomies performed for menstrual problems could be due to an increase in menstrual problems, to changes in social acceptance of such problems, or to a greater willingness to use hysterectomy as a treatment. There are marked international and regional variations in the frequency with which hysterectomy is performed, which demonstrates how social and economic factors influence the decision to operate (McPherson et al. 1981).

Much research on women's reproductive health has tended to neglect differences among women in relation to the effects of poverty, class, race and ethnicity, and sexual orientation. It is important to examine how gender divisions intersect with wider social inequalities which put some women at greater risk during the "normal" processes of pregnancy and childbirth. The impact of gender roles on reproductive health needs to take center stage. For example, women's capacity to control their fertility through contraception and abortion is influenced by partners, other family members, governments, religious and other social institutions.

Women and the Male "Standard" Patient

The focus on women and reproductive health has led to a lack of attention to women as patients within mainstream areas of health. This stems from treating men as the "norm" and basing standards of health care and medical research mainly on the "male patient." The bio-medical or scientific model of disease assumes that disease is a deviation from normal biological functioning. However, what is regarded as normal depends on who is being compared to whom, and in many cases men are considered the "norm" and women compared to this standard (Lorber 1997). Medical norms have primarily been based on white, male, middle-class, working-age bodies. Definitions of health are often related to muscular strength and aerobic capacity, which are superior in men, and not to metabolic and digestive efficiency, stamina, and pain endurance, which may be superior in women.

Epidemiological research and clinical trials have often failed to include women in sufficient numbers or women have been excluded altogether (Rosser 1994), for example, in research on coronary heart disease (Sharp 1994) and on AIDs (Doyal 1995, 1999). It is important to consider the implications of this exclusion. The lack of research on whether men and women with the same medical condition present symptoms differently means that less is known about the effects of drug or surgical treatment regimes for women with heart disease (Sharp 1994).

McKinlay (1996) points out that differences in men's and women's reported illness rates may be the result of gender differences in the process of seeking care – "illness behavior" – as well as in the receipt of a diagnosis and treatment by physicians. Both are likely to occur for heart disease. The reported gender difference in coronary heart disease may partly reflect doctor's behavior. There is evidence in the US of referral bias, with women significantly less likely than men to be diagnosed as having heart disease or undergo coronary angiography or bypass surgery (McKinlay 1996; Sharp 1998). In addition, twice as many women as men aged 45–64 have undetected or "silent" myocardial infarctions (McKinlay 1996). Thus, the rates of illness measured in health services research may differ from the "true" social patterning of ill health in systematic and gender related ways.

The image of heart disease as predominantly affecting men is prevalent in the media, medical advertising, and among the medical profession. There is less publicity and discussion about the risk of CHD for women than for men, which contrasts with the high public profile of breast cancer. This contradicts reality, since coronary heart disease is the most common cause of death for women. Similarly, there is a high public concern with female-specific cancers, such as breast cancer and cervical cancer, and less publicity and research attention on other cancers, such as stomach and lung cancer among women. However, almost as many women in the UK die of lung cancer each year as of breast cancer (ONS 1998).

THE EMERGENCE OF MEN'S HEALTH

There is an imbalance between the greater amount of literature on women's health and the relative invisibility of work on men's health, which has its origins in a number of interrelated areas. Sociologists, whilst ostensibly addressing gender and health, have highlighted the experience of women at the hands of the medical profession and drawn attention to the centrality of health matters, particularly reproductive issues, for women's lives. However, as Annandale (1998) has pointed out, this empirical work is often not located clearly with reference to patriarchy, power, or social class. She argues:

This neglect can partly be explained by feminists' insistence that women's *subjective* experience should always be put at the centre of research in order to highlight the very real suffering that they have experienced in attempting to care for their own health and the health of others. However, while recourse to subjective experience is crucial, by itself it is an insufficient challenge to patriarchy. (Annandale 1998: 62)

The root of the problem is seen as the modernist legacy of a binary division between male and female, men and women. Women's position is thus defined in relation to that of men.

As a fundamental opposition, gendered difference underwrites (i.e. supports) other oppositions which attach to it, for example men are rational, women are irrational; women are caring, men are uncaring, and so on. It is by this process that the positively valued "health" attaches to men, while the negatively valued "illness" becomes the province of women. (Annandale 1998: 78)

Annandale argues that such contrasts have consequences for the way in which women and men are seen in relation to health and illness. Women are not easily seen as healthy and men are not easily viewed as ill. As such men's ill health has remained a largely neglected area. Assumptions that women are sicker than men have been challenged (Macintyre et al. 1996) and will be discussed later, but the enduring impression from the literature is of women with more symptom episodes, a greater number of visits to health care practitioners, and the overwhelming responsibility for health care in domestic settings. An additional problem is that men have consequently been cast as a homogeneous group (Cameron and Bernardes 1998).

Cameron and Bernardes (1998) have considered other possible reasons for the neglect of men's health. They point out that in Britain men's health was not an area of concern for health policy until the 1990s (Department of Health 1992). Whilst some conditions often associated with men, such as heart disease and lung cancer, have been highlighted, other areas, such as prostate problems or mental health, have been given little priority until recently.

Empirical work on ill-health conditions specific to men reveal a variety of problems which stem from the social invisibility of men's illness. Cameron and Bernardes (1998), in a study of prostate problems, reported that men of all ages regarded health as women's responsibility, knew little about men's health, and tended not to talk to others about any prostatic health problems they had experienced. Prostate problems appeared to represent a threat to the men's sense of masculine self. Amongst the younger men, there was a view that prostate disease was an old man's disease, and they had usually delayed seeking help for the problem. Cameron and Bernardes noted that the men's experiences could usefully be explored within a framework of concepts of masculinities and negotiated gender.

In all societies, whether symptoms and pains are perceived as illness by individuals is influenced by cultural values, gender roles, and family interactions. Health professionals also play a key role in defining presented symptoms as "sickness," sanctioning entry into the "sick role," and decisions about treatment, all of which may be influenced by gendered norms and assumptions.

In summary, medical sociologists should seek to follow Lorber's (1997: 2) injunction:

> to show how gender, in conjunction with the socially constructed categories of race, ethnicity, class, and sexual orientation, creates different risks and protections for physical illnesses, produces different behavior when ill, elicits different responses in health care personnel, affects the social worth of patients, and influences priorities of treatment, research, and financing.

A shift to a gender analysis of health implies a move away from a concern with women's health to one which examines both women's and men's health, and one which critically assesses to what extent similar or different factors are associated with the health of women and men.

Gender Analysis of Health

The social and economic relationships between women and men affect both women's and men's health. In patriarchal societies, women on average have less power, status, and financial resources than men, as well as less autonomy and independence. Women are more likely to be unpaid carers for their families, providing both domestic labor and health care for partners, children, and parents, when required.

Care-giving for frail or disabled family members is gendered. Women provide the majority of care for chronically sick children and for frail or disabled relatives (Green 1988; Arber and Ginn 1991). Care-giving places a major burden on carers, results in opportunities foregone, and has both physical and mental health consequences (Braithwaite 1990). The role of unpaid carers in the community is becoming increasingly significant within health care provision, as length of stay in hospital becomes shorter, shifting the costs of care to the private domain of the home. The political rhetoric of community care and deinstitutionalization has therefore had gendered impacts, resulting in greater adverse effects on women, who form the majority of carers.

Many women perform the "double shift" of household work and paid labor, so it is important to assess how combining paid and unpaid work affects their health, and how this varies with socioeconomic circumstances (Doyal 1995). Men's health may benefit from the unpaid labor of their wife in providing domestic services and health care; there is substantial evidence that married men have better health and health behaviors than never married or previously married men (Morgan 1980; Wyke and Ford 1992; Cooper et al. 1999). Therefore, a gender analysis of health needs to take into account the effects of gender roles for both women and men.

In all societies, women experience violence at the hands of men, mainly their male partners, but the extent and nature of that violence varies among and within societies (Heise 1993; Doyal 1995). Domestic violence was accepted in the past in western societies and is still often condoned today. The health consequences of domestic violence are enormous. In the US, wife battery accounts for more injury to women than car accidents, muggings, and rape combined, as well as leading to psychiatric problems (Heise 1993).

Violence is more common where men's masculinity is defined in terms of dominance, and women are relatively powerless economically and socially. It is more common in many developing societies, especially in Asia, the Middle East, and Africa (Counts et al. 1992). In India, dowry-related murder is the most visible symbol of a continuum of violence against women. Rape, child sexual abuse, and forced prostitution have profound physical and mental health consequences for women. Rape may have even greater negative consequences in societies where it is seen as a crime against the honor of a woman's family or her husband (Heise 1993), and is particularly devastating in Asian cultures which equate a young woman's worth with her virginity, leading to raped women becoming outcasts or killed because of the "dishonor" that rape has brought on their families.

Another form of culturally-sanctioned violence against women, which has serious health consequences, is female circumcision. In many parts of Africa and the Middle East, female circumcision, which removes all or part of the clitoris and other external genitalia, is life threatening (Heise 1993; Doyal 1999). It results in deaths, as well as pain, chronic urinary problems, higher levels of maternal and child mortality, and sexual problems. Although female genital mutilation has been made illegal in some countries, it is embedded in patriarchal cultural practices and continues to be a widespread practice in middle Africa and Egypt.

A gender analysis is needed which sees both women's and men's health within the wider context of relations between women and men. It requires recognition of women's disadvantage in terms of power and economic resources and the implications of gender inequalities for both men's and women's health.

Gender Roles and the Life Course

Gender roles, responsibilities, and norms about culturally acceptable behavior are socially constructed, and vary across the life course and for different birth cohorts (Arber and Ginn 1995). During this century there have been radical changes in actual and expected gender roles, especially related to women's participation in paid work and in the political sphere. We may therefore expect the nature of gender inequalities in health to vary between age groups and over time.

The health and other characteristics of women and men are influenced by their prior life course (Wadsworth 1997). For example, the extent to which women forego paid employment to raise children will lead to financial penalties both during their working life and in retirement because of lower private pension contributions (Ginn and Arber 1996, 1998), but the extent of these penalties is likely to vary by social class and according to the woman's marital relationship, with lone mothers suffering the greatest financial penalties of parenthood.

Gender inequalities in health within one life stage may be predicated on gender inequalities in another.

For women in mid-life their health and well-being is influenced by their history of childbearing and their role as parents. Increasingly, health during working life is structured according to position in the labor market, which itself is closely linked to earlier success in the educational sphere (Lahelma and Rahkonen 1997). Thus, a life course approach is advocated which "emphasizes the inter-linkage between phases of the life course, rather than seeing each phase in isolation" (Arber and Evandrou 1993: 9). The following sections examine gender differences in mortality and morbidity, highlighting how these relate to gender roles and relationships.

GENDER INEQUALITIES IN MORTALITY

In nearly all countries women outlive men. Four broad patterns of sex differences in mortality rates can be identified, each of which is related to gender roles:

1   *Women outlive men by 5–7 years*. This pattern is exemplified by western countries in the late twentieth century. For example, in the UK in 1995, the expectation of life for women was 79.4 years and for men 74.1, women outliving men by 5.3 years (ONS 1998). The comparable figures for the US are 78.9 for women and 72.5 for men, a female excess of 6.4 years. In Sweden, women outlive men by 5 years (expectation of life of 81.5 and 76.5 respectively), and in Japan by 6.6 years (83.6 and 77 years respectively) (UN 1999). Many Asian and South American societies have also achieved this pattern, e.g. Brazil, Peru, and Korea.

The "norm" of women having a 5–7 year longer life expectancy than men is the product of women's biological advantage and of men's greater mortality from occupational hazards and risky behaviors, such as smoking, drinking, dangerous sports, fast driving, and violence (Hart 1988). As women in western countries have entered the work force in larger numbers over the last 30 years and the male excess in smoking is now very small, there has been a reduction in the gender disparity of mortality (Hemstrom 1999). For example, in the UK, the sex difference in expectation of life was 6.2 years in 1971 falling to 5.3 years by 1995 (ONS 1998). This trend is expected to continue, as lifestyles of women and men converge and women undertake more risky health behaviors (Hemstrom 1999).

2   *Women outlive men by 2–4 years*. This pattern is exemplified by European countries in the mid-nineteenth century (Hart 1988), and is now typical of many developing societies, particularly in Africa and much of Asia. For example, in Kenya the expectation of life of women is 61.4 and men is 57.5 (a 3.9 year difference), and in China is 52.9 for women and 50.1 for men (UN 1999). This pattern of a modest female mortality advantage is typical of transitional societies, where the previously high maternal mortality rate is falling, and where women occupy a disadvantageous structural position with adverse effects on

their health. As countries move toward greater economic development and more education for women, there is a trend to an increased sex gap in mortality.

3 *No gender difference or men outlive women.* In some developing countries, there is very little gender difference or men outlive women. Bangladesh is one of the few countries where men outlive women, with an expectation of life of .58.6 for men and 58.2 for women, and in Nepal, men outlive women by 2 years (although the most recent data is for 1981 – UN 1999). In Pakistan and India the sexes have almost equal life expectancy (in Pakistan, life expectancy is 59.0 for men and 59.2 for women, and in India, 59 for men and 59.7 for women), while in Algeria and in Afghanistan, women outlive men by only a year (Algeria, 65.7 for men and 66.3 for women, and in Afghanistan, 43 for men and 44 for women) (UN 1999).

This pattern of approximate gender equality in mortality or excess female mortality is found in countries where women's social status is very low (Santow 1995). In these societies, women are more likely to have poor nutrition, less access to health care, are subject to frequent births, and have high maternal mortality (Doyal 1995). In some states in India, the higher mortality of women has resulted in a sex ratio which favors men. Sen (1990) examined sex ratios of men and women in different countries, and concluded that societies where the sex ratio is in balance or is favorable to men discriminate against women, especially India. He argues that this is the result of gender-related practices which disadvantage women, in particular female foeticide and infanticide, selective malnourishment of girls, lack of investment in women's health care, and various forms of violence against women.

4 *Women outlive men by 8 or more years.* This final pattern is exemplified by countries in the former Soviet Union as well as blacks in the US, and partly reflects a deterioration in life expectancy of men since 1980. In the US, the life expectancy of black men has fallen to 64.7 and for women is 73.7, a gender gap of 9 years (Kranczer 1995). In Russia, the expectation of life is only 58.3 for men and 71.7 for women (a startling 13 year female mortality advantage), with the respective figures for Latvia, 63.9 and 75.6 (UN 1999).

In some eastern European countries and the former Soviet Union mortality rates have risen for men over the past 20 years, but have fallen or remained stable for women across the age range (Leon et al. 1997). This shows how men and women can be affected differently by social and economic changes (Hemstrom 1999). There have been greater threats to the economic and psychosocial well-being of men in these societies, many of whom have lost a secure "breadwinning" role. The fall in life expectancy of black men in the US relates to socioeconomic disadvantages, unemployment, alienation, drug abuse, and violence (Lorber 1997). Parallel patterns are beginning to be evident among young men in the UK, where despite the decline in overall mortality, there has been a recent increase in the mortality rate of men aged 25–40 (Dunnell 1991; Tickle 1996).

Gender differences in mortality vary between stages of the life course. In the UK, men have a higher mortality rate than women at all ages across the life course, particularly in youth and early adulthood. For example, the death rate is

2.8 times higher for men than women aged 20–24 (Tickle 1996). Gender differences in mortality vary by cause of death, with the largest gender difference for accidents and violence. Cause-specific mortality rates show that men aged 15–45 have four times higher mortality rate than women from motor accidents, other accidents, and suicide (Tickle 1996; Dunnell et al. 1999). Thus, gender differences in mortality in youth and early adulthood relate to social and cultural roles, and risk-taking behavior of young men.

A gender-related cause of ill health and mortality is AIDS, which in western countries has hitherto mainly affected men. However, in less developed countries, especially sub-Saharan Africa, the rates are far higher and there is little gender difference unlike in developed countries (Doyal 1995, 1999). Women have been relatively neglected in AIDS research, with the result that women who contract AIDS in the US receive less treatment and have a higher death rate. Already, AIDS is the third largest cause of death for women aged 25–44 in the US, after cancer and unintentional injuries (Doyal 1999). There is increasing evidence that women have a greater biological vulnerability than men to contracting AIDS through unprotected sexual intercourse (Doyal 1999). Therefore the current gender difference in AIDS deaths may become more equal over time or result in a female excess. The prevalence of AIDS and of AIDS deaths varies enormously between countries. For example AIDS deaths are low in the UK; accounting for under 5 percent of male deaths aged 30–34 in 1992 and a smaller proportion for other age groups, and under 1 percent for women in all age groups (Tickle 1996).

EXPLAINING GENDER DIFFERENCES

Before examining gender differences in morbidity, we will review the kinds of explanations put forward to account for gender differences in mortality and in health.

1 *Biological.* Associated with genetic or hormonal differences between women and men. The range of gender differences in mortality identified above clearly demonstrates the importance of factors other than biology.

2 *Psychosocial differences.* Related to gender differences in personality, coping behaviors and self-efficacy, which influence the experience and reporting of symptoms. Emslie et al. (1999) analyze orientation to gender roles and health, showing that high "femininity" scores are associated with poor health.

3 *Risk behaviors.* Epidemiologists are particularly concerned with gender differences in health promoting and health-damaging behaviors. The higher levels of smoking and drinking among men are emphasized, including the adverse effects of binge drinking. In western countries women have a better diet (Cooper et al. 1999), and participate more in preventive health measures such as screening. The growing trend for women to engage in smoking, drinking, and more risky behaviors has been termed the "female emancipation hypothesis" (Hemström 1999).

4　*Occupational and work-related factors.* There are health hazards associated with both paid work and unpaid domestic work. Working-class men have traditionally been employed in more dangerous occupations with greater industrial hazards (Hart 1988). Less attention has been paid to the repetitive nature and lack of autonomy of much women's work, which may create greater stress and repetitive strain injuries (Doyal 1995). Bartley et al. (1992) discuss the health hazards of women's unpaid work in Britain, and in developing countries women are often involved in very hard physical work, such as carrying water long distances and heavy agricultural production (Doyal 1995).

5　*Social roles and relationships* differ between women and men and may impact on health (Fuhrer et al. 1999). Women in western countries often have better social networks than men, and can more easily rely on contact with close friends and relatives in times of crisis and stress. Marriage may provide a major source of social support, but in a differential way for men and women and across societies. In terms of social support, marriage may be good for men but less so for women. Men tend to rely more on their wife for social support and a confiding relationship, with divorced and widowed men reporting particularly poor health.

6　*Power and resources within the home.* Patriarchical control within the family and domestic settings may lead to exploitation of women and violence against them. Women's lack of power and influence in the home, and lack of access to valued resources (of food, opportunities for leisure, income), may have adverse health consequences.

7　*Social structural differences within society.* Women in most societies are more likely than men to be poor, have less education, and live in disadvantaged material circumstances, all of which are likely to impact on gender differences in health. Kawachi et al. (1999) report lower levels of women's mortality in states with higher levels of women's economic autonomy, higher levels of labor market participation, and higher political participation.

Gender inequality in the domestic setting may vary with class and ethnicity and may coexist with greater equality in the wider society (as in many western societies today). Alternatively, inequality in the domestic sphere may be predicated on and influenced by wider social, cultural, and economic inequalities at the societal level, as in India and Bangladesh. Women's health and well-being is jeopardized by women's unequal status both within the family and within society.

Gender Differences in Morbidity

It has become accepted wisdom that "women are sicker, but men die quicker" (Lahelma et al. 1999). The higher morbidity rate but lower death rate of women was characterized by Nathanson (1975) as a "contradiction" which required explanation. Other US authors in the 1970s and 1980s repeatedly demonstrated that "females have higher rates of illness than males" (Verbrugge 1979: 61), and examined reasons for "the discrepancy between the male excess of mortality and the female excess for some morbidity measures" (Waldron 1983: 1107). A number of the explanations put forward related to gender roles, for example, that women tend to over-report morbidity more frequently than men, and that women are more predisposed than men to rate their health as poor (Waldron 1983).

Survey data in Europe in the 1990s, however, suggests that gender differences in global measures of health and well-being are relatively modest, and of much less importance than the previous orthodoxy suggested (Macintyre 1993; Macintyre et al. 1996; Macintyre et al. 1999). Macintyre et al. (1996) examined different measures of health using various data sets and found a lack of consistency between health measures in whether there was a female excess in morbidity. In Finland, Lahelma et al. (1999) used eight measures of health and found no gender difference in self-assessed general health, but women reported more mental and more physical symptoms.

Despite the lack of gender difference in global measures of ill health, there are major gender differences in mental health (Macintyre et al. 1996). Women are more likely to report a range of neurotic disorders, e.g. anxiety and depressive disorders. However, Dunnell et al. (1999) show that when men's higher rates of alcohol and drug dependence are included, there is only a small gender difference in the prevalence of psychiatric disorders within five-year age groups.

Macintyre et al. (1996) show that gender differences in health vary according to the health measure used and stage of the life course. Therefore it is necessary to conduct studies of different age groups, rather than assume that the same relationships remain constant throughout the life course. A US study analyzed men and women aged 53 and showed that women had better self-assessed health than men, but women reported higher levels of functional limitation and symptom discomfort than men (Marks 1996). Lahelma et al. (1999) found a 20 percent higher level of disability among women than men over age 50.

Older women are more likely than older men to suffer from conditions which are non-fatal but result in chronic and disabling illnesses hindering their activities of daily living (Arber and Cooper 1999). In Britain in 1994, nearly twice as many women as men over 65 suffered from functional impairments sufficient to require help on a daily basis to remain living in the community – 15 percent of women and 8.5 percent of men (Arber and Cooper 1999). This gender difference in functional disability occurs for each age group of older people, but is particularly stark at ages above 85 among whom nearly 40 percent of women and 21 percent of men suffer from severe impairment. The findings of Marks (1996), Lahelma et al. (1999), and Arber and Cooper (1999) suggest a lack of gender difference in self-assessed health among older people, which co-exists with older women being much more likely than older men to experience severe disability.

A key concern is the extent of gender difference in "healthy life expectancy," that is the period of life without disability or chronic ill health (Valkonen et al. 1997). Because of women's higher level of disability, there is a smaller gender difference in "healthy life expectancy" than in mortality.

GENDER DIFFERENCES IN ACCESS TO LONG-TERM AND SOCIAL CARE

The greatest threat to a person's autonomy and independence is generally considered to be entry into a nursing or residential home. The UK 1991 census showed that twice as many women as men over 65 lived in communal establishments, 3 percent of men and 6.4 percent of women (OPCS 1993). This gender differential is particularly pronounced over age 85, when 26 percent of women and 15 percent of men are residents (Ginn and Arber 1996).

Gender differences in residential living do not exist because of gender *per se*, but are influenced by social variables such as marital status, which acts as a proxy for the availability of informal carers. Two-thirds of older men are married whereas half of older women are widowed (ONS 1998), so older women are less likely to have a spouse to provide care should they become disabled, increasing their likelihood of entering residential care. Despite the higher level of functional disability of older women than men, men who are not married are more likely than women of an equivalent age and marital status to live in residential homes (Arber 1998).

Although older women have a longer expectation of life than men, they also have a longer period in which they can expect to be disabled or live in a residential setting. The gender differential in disability means that older women are more likely to require both care from relatives and from state health and welfare services (Arber and Ginn 1991). In Britain, nearly half of disabled older women live alone, which means they are heavily dependent on the unpaid work of relatives and other unpaid carers, as well as on state domiciliary services, mainly home care services and community nurses. Older women's disadvantage is compounded by their lower average income.

Changes in community-care policies in Britain in the 1990s have made it more difficult for older people to obtain state-funded residential care and state-provided home care (Walker 1993). Although such policies are put forward as gender-neutral, they have had greater adverse effects on older women. Older men not only have more financial resources to pay for care, but are more likely to have a wife who can provide care should they need it, whereas older women tend to live alone (Arber and Ginn 1991). Thus a gender analysis of health in any society needs to consider the gendered nature of access to caring resources and the gendered effects of social policies.

STRUCTURAL INEQUALITIES IN HEALTH AMONG WOMEN AND MEN

In the late 1970s, many researchers moved away from examining gender differences in health toward a more explicit focus on differences in health *among* women. Early work was cast in a role analytic framework, examining to what extent additional roles, such as the parental role and paid employment, had beneficial or adverse consequences for women's health (Nathanson 1980; Verbrugge 1983; Arber et al. 1985). Predating and alongside this strand of work was the growing body of research on inequalities in men's health, stimulated by the publication in Britain of the Black Report (Townsend and Davidson 1982). During the late 1980s and 1990s, feminist researchers have examined to what extent similar structural factors, associated with social class and material disadvantage, were associated with women's and men's health (Arber 1991, 1997; Macran et al. 1996; Lahelma and Rahkonen 1997; Bartley et al. 1999). Researchers stressed the importance of examining women both in terms of their structural position within society and their family roles.

This approach emphasized the need to examine how socioeconomic circumstances, together with marital and parental roles, influence health and assess any differences for women and men (Arber 1997). The key structural variables which influence an individual's health are related to labor-market position, i.e. occupational class and employment status, both of which are influenced by the individual's level of educational qualifications. Family roles are likely to influence health. However, whether a woman becomes a lone parent and her age at childbearing may also be influenced by her class and educational attainment. These relationships between family roles and structural variables are likely to be greater for women than for men. The effect of women's family roles on health must be seen within the context of the material resources available to her household and for bringing up children (Arber et al. 1985; Arber 1997).

Early research on marital status and health (Verbrugge 1979; Morgan 1980; Wyke and Ford 1992) found that the divorced and separated had poorer health than the married, and that single men, but not single women, report poorer health than the married. However, recent British research (Arber and Cooper 2000) shows that married men and women have better health than the never married, and the previously married have the worst health. The previous orthodoxy that married women have poorer health than single women no longer holds, possibly reflecting changes in the meaning of marriage in the late twentieth century and career opportunities for married women which 30 years ago were only viable for single women.

There has been less research on parental roles and health, especially in relation to lone parenthood. In the UK, a major change over the past 20 years has been the increasing number of lone mothers (ONS 1999). Arber and Cooper (2000) show that parenthood in disadvantaged material circumstances is associated with poor health, especially for single mothers. Single, divorced, and separated mothers in the 1990s report particularly poor health, which can be explained largely by their disadvantaged structural circumstances.

Among working-age men and women, educational qualifications and social class, based on the individual's own occupation, are closely associated with self-assessed health (Arber and Cooper 2000). Those whose current (or last) job is in a lower class occupation and who have less educational qualifications are most likely to report poor health. These patterns are broadly similar for men and women, although the class gradient is weaker for women, whereas the health gradient with educational qualifications is comparable for women and men. Matthews et al. (1999) also found no gender difference in the magnitude of health inequalities by social class at age 33 in Britain.

Among older women and men, occupational class continues to structure health inequalities in Britain (Arber and Ginn 1993; Arber and Cooper 1999) and in Norway (Dahl and Birkelund 1997). There are strong class inequalities, showing the continued influence on health of occupational position in the labor market during working life, which is somewhat stronger for older men than for older women.

A gender analysis requires consideration of differences in the power and structural position of women and men within societies. Women and men occupy different structural locations within society; there is occupational sex segregation (see Emslie et al. 1999), and women are more likely to have low incomes and to be lone parents than men (ONS 1999). It is therefore essential to examine the extent to which gender differences in health may at least in part be explained by women's social disadvantage in terms of education, income, and political influence. For example, Verbrugge (1989) analyzed how sex differences in over 40 measures of health for adults in Detroit changed when a range of factors were statistically controlled, including role statuses, role satisfaction, lifestyle (smoking, drinking, obesity, and physical activity), stress and health attitudes. Her multivariate analyses showed that the female excess of ill health diminished for most health measures and in some cases was reversed (although the resulting male excess was non-significant).

In later life, the concentration of poverty among women is particularly marked (Arber and Ginn 1991; Ginn and Arber 1996). On average, women are older than men, they are more likely to be widowed, have worked in lower social class occupations, and have less income. Therefore, any gender differences in health in later life may reflect the socioeconomic disadvantages of older women. For older people, there is no gender difference in self-assessed health once socioeconomic and demographic characteristics are controlled, but the disadvantage of older women in terms of functional disability remains substantial (Arber and Cooper 2000). This research revealed a "new paradox" that older women have a more positive self-assessment of their health status than men, once age, class, income, and women's higher level of functional disability were taken into account.

Conclusion

Medical sociologists up until the 1980s paid particular attention to women's reproductive health and the medicalization of women's health. Broader issues associated with women's health were masked by the assumption that white, male bodies are the norm for human health. Parallel to this was a neglect of issues associated with men's ill health

A gender analysis of health needs to be sensitive to the ways in which social, economic, and political factors affect gender roles and relationships, and the consequences of these for health. The chapter considered gender differences in mortality and morbidity, including how the gendered nature of social roles and relationships impact on health inequalities.

In the quarter of a century since Nathanson (1975) published her article on "the contradiction" between sex differences in mortality and morbidity rates there have been far-reaching structural changes in women's lives in western societies. Major changes in gender roles over that period of time lead to the expectation that previous sex differences in morbidity will also have changed. Women have entered the paid labor force in increasing numbers, have gained greater financial independence and few women remain full-time housewives for more than a few years when their children are young. Because of these gender role changes it is unsurprising that the orthodoxy of women being "sicker" than men has increasingly been questioned (Hunt and Annandale 1999).

Women in most societies are more likely than men to be poor, have less education, and live in disadvantaged material circumstances. The feminization of poverty in the US and UK has been widely acknowledged, and is particularly associated with lone motherhood and older women. Gender differences in health in western societies, therefore, partly reflect these disadvantages which women are more likely to face. The chapter also examined to what extent cross-cutting social structures, such as class, family roles, and age, have a similar influence on the nature of health inequalities among women and men. We conclude that the nature of inequalities in women's and men's health is likely to differ over time and between societies in concert with the way in which gender roles and relationships vary historically and cross-nationally.

Acknowledgment

We are very grateful to Jay Ginn for her helpful comments on an earlier version of this chapter.

References

Annandale, Ellen. 1998. *The Sociology of Health and Medicine: A Critical Introduction.* Cambridge: Polity Press.

Arber, Sara. 1991. "Class, Paid Employment and Family Roles: Making Sense of Structural Disadvantage, Gender and Health Status." *Social Science and Medicine* 32: 425–36.

——. 1997. "Comparing Inequalities in Women's and Men's Health: Britain in the 1990s." *Social Science and Medicine* 44: 773–87.

——. 1998. "Health, Aging and Older Women." Pp. 54–68 in L. Doyal (ed.), *Women and Health Services: An Agenda for Change.* Buckingham: Open University Press.

Arber, Sara and Helen Cooper. 1999. "Gender Differences in Health in Later Life: A New Paradox?" *Social Science and Medicine* 48: 63–78.

——. 2000. "Gender and Inequalities in Health across the Life Course." Pp. 123–49 in E. Annandale and K. Hunt (eds.), *Gender Inequalities in Health.* Buckingham: Open University Press.

Arber, Sara and Maria Evandrou (eds.). 1993. *Ageing Independence and the Life Course.* London: Jessica Kingsley.

Arber, Sara Nigel Gilbert, and Angela Dale. 1985. "Paid Employment and Women's Health: A Benefit or a Source of Role Strain?" *Sociology of Health and Illness* 7: 377–400.

Arber, Sara and Jay Ginn. 1991. *Gender and Later Life: A Sociological Analysis of Resources and Constraints*. London: Sage.

——. 1993. "Gender and Inequalities in Health in Later Life." *Social Science and Medicine* 36: 33–46.

——. 1995. *Connecting Gender and Aging: A Sociological Approach*. Buckingham: Open University Press.

Bartley, Mel, Jenny Popay, and Ian Plewis. 1992. "Domestic Conditions, Paid Employment and Women's Experience of Ill-Health." *Sociology of Health and Illness* 14: 313–43.

Bartley, Mel, A. Sacker, D. Firth, and Ray Fitzpatrick. 1999. "Social Position, Social Roles and Women's Health in England: Changing Relationships 1984–1993." *Social Science and Medicine* 48: 99–115.

Braithwaite, Valerie. 1990. *Bound to Care*. Sydney: Allen and Unwin.

Cameron, Elaine and Jon Bernardes. 1998. "Gender and Disadvantage in Health: Men's Health for a Change." *Sociology of Health and Illness* 20: 673–93.

Comaroff, Jean. 1977. "Conflicting Paradigms of Pregnancy: Managing Ambiguity in Antenatal Encounters." Pp. 115–34 in A. Davis and G. Horobin (eds.), *Medical Encounters*. London: Croom Helm.

Cooper, Helen, Jay Ginn, and Sara Arber. 1999. *Health-Related Behaviour and Attitudes of Older People: A Secondary Analysis of National Datasets*. London: Health Education Authority.

Counts, Dorothy Ayers, Judith Brown, and Jacqueline Campbell. 1992. *Sanctions and Sanctuary: Cultural Perspectives on the Beating of Wives*, Boulder, CO: Westview Press.

Dahl, Espen and G. E. Birkelund. 1997. "Health Inequalities in Later Life in a Social Democratic Welfare State." *Social Science and Medicine* 44: 859–970.

Department of Health. 1992. *The Annual Report of the Chief Medical Officer*. London: Department of Health.

Doyal, Lesley. 1995. *What Makes Women Sick: Gender and the Political Economy of Health*. London: Macmillan.

——. 1999. "Sex, Gender and Health: A New Approach." Pp. 30–51 in S. Watson and L. Doyal (eds.), *Engendering Social Policy*. Buckingham: Open University Press.

Dunnell, Karen. 1991. "Deaths Among 15–44 Year Olds." *Population Trends 64*, London: HMSO, pp. 38–43.

Dunnell, Karen, Justine Fitzpatrick, and Julie Bunting. 1999. "Making Use of Official Statistics in Research on Gender and Health Status: Recent British Data." *Social Science and Medicine* 48: 117–27.

Emslie, Carol, Kate Hunt, and Sally Macintyre. 1999. "Problematizing Gender, Work, and Health: The Relationship Between Gender, Occupational Grade, Working Conditions, and Minor Morbidity in Full-time Employees." *Social Science and Medicine* 48: 33–48.

Fuhrer, Rebecca, Stephen Stansfeld, J. Chemali, and M. J. Shipley. 1999. "Gender, Social Relations, and Mental Health: Prospective Findings from an Occupational Cohort (Whitehall II Study)." *Social Science and Medicine* 48: 77–87.

Garcia, Jo. 1982. "Women's Views of Antenatal Care." Pp. 81–91 in M. Enkin and I. Chalmers (eds.), *Effectiveness and Satisfaction in Antenatal Care*. London: Heinemann Medical.

Ginn, Jay and Sara Arber. 1996. "Patterns of Employment, Pensions, and Gender: The Effect of Work History on Older Women's Non-state Pensions." *Work, Employment, and Society* 10: 469–90.

——. 1998. "How Does Part-time Work Lead to Low Pension Income?" Pp. 156–73 in J. O'Reilly and C. Fagan (eds.), *Part-Time Prospects: An International Comparison of Part-time Work in Europe, North America and the Pacific Rim.* London: Routledge.

Graham, Hilary. 1977. "Images of Pregnancy in Antenatal Literature." Pp. 15–37 in R. Dingwall, C. Heath, M. Reid, and M. Stacey (eds.), *Health Care and Health Knowledge.* London: Croom Helm.

Graham, Hilary, and Lorna McKee. 1979. *The First Months of Motherhood.* London: Health Education Council.

Graham, Hilary, and Ann Oakley. 1981. "Competing Ideologies of Reproduction: Medical and Maternal Perspectives on Pregnancy." Pp. 50–74 in H. Roberts (ed.), *Women, Health, and Reproduction.* London: Routledge.

Green, Hazel. 1998. *Informal Careers.* OPCS Series GHS, no. 15, Supplement A. London: HMSO.

Hart, Nicky. 1988. "Sex, Gender, and Survival: Inequalities of Life Chances Between European Men and Women." Pp. 104–41 in A. J. Fox (ed.), *Inequalities in Health within Europe.* Aldershot: Gower.

Heise, Lori. 1993. "Violence Against Women: The Missing Agenda." Pp. 171–96 in M. Koblinsky, J. Timyan, and J. Gay (eds.), *The Health of Women: A Global Perspective.* Boulder, CO: Westview Press Inc.

Hemström, Örjan. 1999. "Explaining Differential Rates of Mortality Decline for Swedish Men and Women: A Time Series Analysis, 1945–1992." *Social Science and Medicine* 48: 1759–77.

Hunt, Kate and Ellen Annandale. 1999. "Relocating Gender and Morbidity: Examining Men's and Women's Health in Contemporary Western Societies." Introduction to Special Issue on Gender and Health. *Social Science and Medicine* 48: 1–5.

Kawachi, Ichiro, Bruce Kenndy, Vanita Gupta, and Deborah Prothrow-Stith. 1999. "Women's Status and the Health of Women and Men: A View from the States." *Social Science and Medicine* 48: 21–32.

Kranczer, Stanley. 1995. "U.S. Longevity Unchanged." *Statistical Bulletin* 76: 12–20.

Lahelma, Eero and Ossi Rahkonen. 1997. "Health Inequalities in Modern Societies and Beyond." Special Issue of *Social Science and Medicine* 44: 721–910.

Lahelma, Eero, Pekka Martikainen, Rahkonen Ossi, and Karri Silventoinen. 1999. "Gender Differences in Ill Health in Finland: Patterns, Magnitude, and Change." *Social Science and Medicine* 48: 7–19.

Leon, David, L. Chenet, and V. Shkolnikov. 1997. "Huge Variation in Russian Mortality Rates 1984–1994: Artifact, Alcohol, or What?" *The Lancet* 350: 383–8.

Lorber, Judith. 1997. *Gender and the Social Construction of Illness.* Thousand Oaks, Calif.: Sage.

MacArthur, C., M. Lewis, and E. G. Know. 1991. *Health after Childbirth.* London: HMSO.

Macintyre, Sally. 1993. "Gender Differences in the Perception of Common Cold Symptoms." *Social Science and Medicine* 36: 15–20.

Macintyre, Sally, Kate Hunt, and Helen Sweeting. 1996. "Gender Differences in Health: Are Things Really as Simple as They Seem?" *Social Science and Medicine* 42: 617–24.

Macintyre, Sally, Graham Ford, and Kate Hunt. 1999. "Do Women 'Over-Report' Morbidity? Men's and Women's Responses to Structured Prompting on a Standard Question on Long Standing Illness." *Social Science and Medicine* 48: 89–98.

Macran, Susan, Lynda Clarke, and Heather Joshi. 1996. "Women's Health: Dimensions and Differentials." *Social Science and Medicine* 42: 1203–16.

Marks, N. F. 1996. "Socioeconomic Status, Gender, and Health at Midlife: Evidence from the Wisconsin Longitudinal Study." *Research in the Sociology of Health Care* 13: 133–50.

Matthews, Sharon, Orly Manor, and Chris Power. 1999. "Social Inequalities in Health: Are There Gender Differences?" *Social Science and Medicine* 48: 49–60.

McKinlay, John. 1996. "Some Contributions from the Social System to Gender Inequalities in Heart Disease." *Journal of Health and Social Behavior* 37: 1–26.

McPherson, Klim, Phil Strong, A. Epstein, and L. Jones. 1981. "Regional Variations in the Use of Common Surgical Procedures Within and Between England and Wales, Canada, and the United States." *Social Science and Medicine* 15A: 273–88.

Morgan, Myfanwy. 1980. "Marital Status, Health, Illness, and Service Use." *Social Science and Medicine* 14: 633–43.

Nathanson, Constance. 1975. "Illness and the Feminine Role: A Theoretical Review." *Social Science and Medicine* 9: 57–62.

——. 1980. "Social Roles and Health Status among Women: The Significance of Employment." *Social Science and Medicine* 14A: 463–71.

Oakley, Ann. 1979. *Becoming a Mother*. Oxford: Martin Robertson.

Office of National Statistics. 1998. *Population Trends 94*. London: HMSO.

ONS. 1999. *Social Trends 29, 1999 Edition*, Office of National Statistics. London: HMSO.

OPCS. 1993. *Communal Establishments, 1991 Population Census*. London: HMSO.

Rosser, Sue. 1994. "Gender Bias in Clinical Research: The Difference it Makes." Pp. 253–65 in A. J. Dan (ed.), *Reframing Women's Health: Multidisciplinary Research and Practice*. London: Sage.

Santow, Gigi. 1995. "Social Roles and Physical Health: The Case of Female Disadvantage in Poor Countries." *Social Science and Medicine* 40: 147–61.

Sen, Amartya. 1990. "More than 100 Million Women are Missing." *The New York Review of Books*, 20 December, pp. 61–6.

Sharp, Imogen. 1994. *Coronary Heart Disease: Are Women Special?* London: National Heart Forum.

——. 1998. "Gender Issues in the Prevention and Treatment of Coronary Heart Disease." Pp. 100–12 in L. Doyal (ed.), *Women and Health Services: An Agenda for Change*. Buckingham: Open University Press.

Teo, Philip. 1990. "Hysterectomy: A Change of Trend or a Change of Heart?" Pp. 113–46 in L. Doyal (ed.), *Women's Health Counts*. London: Routledge.

Thomas, Hilary. 1998. "Reproductive Health Needs Across the Lifespan." Pp. 39–53 in L. Doyal (ed.), *Women and Health Services: An Agenda for Change*. Buckingham: Open University Press.

Tickle, L. 1996. "Mortality Trends in the United Kingdom, 1982 to 1992." *Population Trends 86*. London: HMSO, ONS.

Townsend, Peter, and Nick Davidson. 1982. *Inequalities in Health: The Black Report*. Harmondsworth: Penguin.

United Nations. 1999. *1997 Demographic Yearbook*. New York: United Nations.

Valkonen, Tapani, A. Sihvonen, and Eero Lahelma. 1997. "Health Expectancy by Level of Education in Finland." *Social Science and Medicine* 44: 801–8.

Verbrugge, Lois. 1979. "Marital Status and Health." *Journal of Marriage and the Family* 41: 267–85.

——. 1983. "Multiple Roles and Physical Health of Women and Men." *Journal of Health and Social Behaviour* 24: 16–30.

——. 1989. "The Twain Meet: Empirical Explanations of Sex Differences in Health and Mortality." *Journal of Health and Social Behaviour* 30: 282–304.

Wadsworth, Michael. 1997. "Health Inequalities in the Life Course Perspective." *Social Science and Medicine* 44: 859–70.

Waldron, Ingrid. 1983. "Sex Differences in Illness Incidence, Prognosis and Mortality: Issues and Evidence." *Social Science and Medicine* 17: 1107–23.

Walker, Alan. 1993. "Community Care Policy: From Consensus to Conflict." Pp. 204–26 in J. Bornat, C. Pereira, D. Pilgrim, and F. Williams (eds.), *Community Care: A Reader.* London: Macmillan.

Wyke, Sally and Graham Ford. 1992. "Competing Explanations for Associations Between Marital Status and Health." *Social Science and Medicine* 34: 525–32.

6

Work Stress and Health

Johannes Siegrist

The nature of work has changed considerably over the past several decades in economically advanced societies. Industrial mass production no longer dominates the labor market. This is due, in part, to technological progress, and in part to a growing number of jobs available in the service sector. Many jobs are confined to information processing, controlling, and coordination. Sedentary rather than physically strenuous work is becoming more and more dominant. New management techniques, including quality management, are introduced, and economic constraints produce work pressure, rationalization, and cut-down in personnel. These changes go along with changes in the structure of the labor market. More employees are likely to work on temporary contracts, on fixed term, or in flexible job arrangements. Many instrumental activities that qualify as work are no longer confined to the conventional type of workplace located within an enterprise or organization, particularly with the advent of advanced communications technology (Cooper 1998). The workforce is getting older, and an increasing proportion of women enter the labor market, with an increase of double exposure among women with children or, more generally, in dual career families. Most importantly, over-employment in some segments of the workforce is paralleled by under-employment, job instability, or structural unemployment in other segments. This latter trend currently hits the economically most advanced societies as well as economies that lag behind. Overall, a substantial part of the economically active population is confined to insecure jobs, to premature retirement, or job loss.

THE CHANGING NATURE OF WORK AND THE ROLE OF COMPARATIVE MEDICAL SOCIOLOGY

Why is work so important for human well-being, and how does work contribute to the burden of stress and its adverse effects on health? In all advanced societies work and occupation in adult life are accorded primacy for the following reasons. First, having a job is a principal prerequisite for continuous income and, thus, for independence from traditional support systems (family, community welfare, etc.). Increasingly, level of income determines a wide range of life chances. Secondly, training for a job and achievement of occupational status are the most important goals of socialization. It is through education, job training, and status acquisition that personal growth and development are realized, that a core social identity outside the family is acquired, and that goal-directed activity in human life is shaped. Thirdly, occupation defines an important criterion of social stratification. Amount of esteem in interpersonal life largely depends on type of job and level of occupational achievement. Furthermore, type and quality of occupation, and especially the degree of self-direction at work, strongly influence personal attitudes and behavioral patterns in areas that are not directly related to work, such as leisure or family life (Kohn and Schooler 1983). Finally, occupational settings produce the most pervasive continuous demands during one's lifetime, and they absorb the largest amount of active time in adult life, thus providing a source of recurrent negative or positive emotions. It is for these reasons that stress research in organizations where paid work takes place is of particular relevance.

It is important to recognize that traditional occupational hazards, such as exposure to toxic substances, heat, cold, or noise, are no longer the dominant challenges of health at work. Rather, distinct psychological and emotional demands and threats are becoming highly prevalent in modern working life. There has been a recognition that the importance of work goes beyond traditional occupational diseases and, indeed, it is likely that work makes a greater contribution to diseases not thought of as "occupational" in conventional terms. At a descriptive level, recent reports find that, for instance, almost half of the workforce is exposed to monotonous tasks or lack of task rotation. Fifty percent work at a very high speed or to tight deadlines. Thus, over- and under-load at work are highly prevalent. Every third employee has no influence on work rhythm, and every fifth is exposed to shiftwork (Paoli 1997). There is now growing awareness among all parties of the labor market that psychosocial stress at work produces considerable costs, most importantly a high level of absenteeism, reduced productivity, compensation claims, health insurance, and direct medical expenses. Permanent disability and loss of productive life years due to premature death add to this burden. In the European Union, the costs of stress to organizations and countries are estimated to be between 5 to 10 percent of GNP per annum (Cooper 1998). At the same time scientific evidence on associations between psychosocial stress at work and health is growing rapidly.

What is the role of comparative medical sociology in this process? To start, sociological theory offers basic concepts to analyze work-related activities in terms of social role, social status, power, social exchange, and social identity. Based on these concepts more refined theoretical models can be developed to identify those specific sociological aspects of working life that have a direct impact on health. The next two paragraphs briefly summarize three such sociological theories and they give a selective overview of empirical evidence on adverse effects on health produced by stressful work.

Essentially, comparative medical sociology in this field is confronted with two tasks: first, to apply these concepts, most importantly in the frame of social-epidemiological studies, in different countries to assess the health burden produced by stressful work. Comparative research in this perspective provides essential information on socioeconomic and sociocultural determinants of the relationship between workplace stress and health. This also implies a comparative test of the theoretical models themselves to study their similarities and differences, and to explore whether their combined effects on health are much stronger compared to the separate effect of each model.

A second task of comparative medical sociology in this field concerns policy implications of these research findings. What are the consequences of these results for worksite stress prevention and health promotion? What intervention strategies have been developed and implemented in different countries? What are the determinants of success and failure in this policy area? It is hoped that by coping with these two tasks future medical sociology may be able to further strengthen its case, including its impact on theoretical and methodological developments in general sociology.

THEORETICAL MODELS OF WORK STRESS

Before describing some prominent theoretical models of occupational stress the basic terminology needs to be clarified. Much critique has been raised about the ambiguity of the term "stress." To avoid this, the following terms were suggested: "*stressor*," which is defined as an environmental demand or threat that taxes or exceeds a person's ability to meet the challenge. Stressors, in particular novel or dangerous ones, are appraised and evaluated by the person, and as long as there is some perception of agency on the part of the exposed person efforts are mobilized to reverse the threat or to meet the demands. Such efforts are termed "*coping*," and they occur at the behavioral (even interpersonal), cognitive, affective, and motivational level. "*Strain*" is defined as the person's response to an unmet stressor in psychological and physiological terms. Psychological responses relate to negative emotions (e.g. anger, frustration, anxiety, helplessness) whereas physiological responses concern the activation of the autonomic nervous system and related neuro-hormonal and immune reactions. Clearly, when judging strain, the quality and intensity of a stressor as well as the duration of exposure have to be taken into account, as well as individual differences in coping and in vulnerability to strain reactions. Recent research indicates that only part of human strain reactions are subject to conscious information processing whereas a large amount bypasses awareness. The term "*stressful experience*" is introduced to delineate that part of affective processing that reaches consciousness. Stressful experiences at work are often attributed to adverse working conditions created by exposed people themselves. While they usually refer to some common sense notions of "*stress*" it is crucial to note that these attributions differ from the explanatory constructs of stressful experience at work that have been identified by science.

Medical sociological research on work-related stress differs from traditional biomedical occupational health research because of the fact that stressors cannot be identified by direct physical or chemical measurements. Rather, theoretical models are needed to analyze the particular nature of the psychosocial work environment. A theoretical model is best understood as a heuristic device that selectively reduces complex reality to meaningful components. Components are meaningful to the extent that they provide the material from which the researcher can deduce explanations and, thus, produce new knowledge. Ideally, a theoretical model of psychosocial stress at work with relevance to health should encompass a wide variety of different occupations and should not be restricted to a specific time or space.

Person–Environment Fit

The first significant sociological contribution to modern occupational stress research dates back to studies conducted more than 30 years at the Institute for Social Research at the University of Michigan. They were guided by a theoretical concept termed "person–environment fit" (Caplan et al. 1980). Stressful experience at work, in this model, is conceptualized in two ways: first, as an experience where the work environment does not provide adequate supplies to meet the person's needs; secondly, as an experience where the abilities of the person fall short of demands that are prerequisite to receiving supplies. In both conditions stressful experience results from a misfit between needs or abilities on the part of the working person and demands or opportunities on the part of the work environment. In particular, this is the case if job opportunities fail to fulfill the person's needs as a consequence of unmet demands. As an example, a worker with limited skills is excluded from any promotion prospects even though he would badly need better pay to meet his level of living.

This approach represents a type of theorizing that is termed process theory. As such, it offers opportunities to be applied to a wide range of work but does not specify the particular content dimensions on which person and environment should be examined (Edwards, Caplan, and van Harrison 1998). As its basic terms are rather broad, it may be difficult to reach a consensus on how to measure core constructs. Nevertheless, person–environment fit offers an elaborate set of propositions of how critical constellations of work-related environmental and personal characteristics contribute to the development of stressful experience.

Demand, Support, and Control

A second, highly influential sociological model was introduced by Karasek (1979). This model is based upon the premise that strain occurs when there is high psychological work demand in combination with a low degree of task control. Low control at work is defined in terms of low level of decision latitude (authority over decisions) and a low level of skill utilization. While high demand/ low control jobs are assumed to produce strain in those exposed ("job strain"), this two-dimensional model offers a "salutogenic" in addition to a "pathogenic" perspective: jobs defined by high demands and a high level of decision latitude and skill utilization ("active jobs," see Karasek and Theorell 1990) promote personal growth and feelings of mastery or self-efficacy. This part of the model is rooted in health-psychological and stress-physiological research on personal control and well-being that has attracted wide attention from several scientific disciplines (Steptoe and Appels 1989; Skinner 1996; Spector 1998). More recently, the two-dimensional demand–control model was modified to include a third dimension, social support at work. The instrumental, cognitive, and emotional change at work was shown to buffer strain reactions (House 1981; Johnson and Hall 1988). Accordingly, highest level of strain – and strongest effects on health – are expected in jobs defined by high demands, low control, and low social support (Karasek and Theorell 1990).

Demand–control theory offers a sociological conceptualization of work stress that is restricted to the situational aspects of the psychosocial work environment, without taking into account aspects of individual coping. In terms of policy implications this restriction has the advantage of pointing to the structural level of measures of stress prevention at work (see below).

Effort–Reward Imbalance

A third, more recently developed model, the model of effort–reward imbalance, is concerned with distributive justice, that is with deviations from a basic "grammar" of social exchange rooted in the notions of reciprocity and fairness (Siegrist, Siegrist, and Weber 1986; see also Cosmides and Tooby 1992). This model assumes that effort at work is spent as part of a socially organized exchange process to which society at large contributes in terms of rewards. Rewards are distributed by three transmitter systems: money, esteem, and career opportunities including job security. The model of effort–reward imbalance claims that lack of reciprocity between costs and gains (i.e. high "cost"/low "gain" conditions) elicits sustained strain reactions. For instance, having a demanding but unstable job, achieving at a high level without being offered any promotion prospects, are examples of high cost/low gain conditions at work. In terms of current developments of the labor market in a global economy, the emphasis on occupational rewards including job security reflects the growing importance of fragmented job careers, of job instability, under-employment, redundancy, and forced occupational mobility, including their financial consequences.

According to this model, strain reactions are most intense and long-lasting under the following conditions: (a) lack of alternative choice in the labor market may prevent people from giving up even unfavorable jobs, as the anticipated costs of disengagement (e.g. the risk of being laid-off) outweigh costs of accepting inadequate benefits; (b) unfair job arrangements may be accepted for a certain period of one's occupational trajectory for strategic reasons – by doing so employees tend to improve their chances for career promotion at a later stage; (c) a specific personal pattern of coping with demands and of eliciting rewards characterized by overcommitment may prevent people from accurately assessing cost–gain relations. "Overcommitment" defines a set of attitudes, behaviors, and emotions reflecting excessive striving in combination with a strong desire of being approved and esteemed (Siegrist 1996). At the psychological level, experience of effort–reward imbalance is often paralleled by feelings of impaired self-esteem, whereas a balance experienced is assumed to promote "salutogenic" feelings of satisfaction, enhanced self-worth, and success. While specific individual coping characteristics (overcommitment) are included in this model it nevertheless offers a clear distinction of the extrinsic and the intrinsic component both at the conceptual and at the operational level.

A final comment on this model concerns its measurement. As stated above, a distinction is made between "strain" and "stressful experience" as evidence obtained from neuroscience tells that only part of strain reactions reach the level of conscious stressful experience (LeDoux 1996). This information to some extent contradicts the currently dominant cognitive stress theory that claims that strain experience is contingent upon conscious appraisal (Lazarus 1991). According to this new evidence, the effort–reward imbalance model attempts to include both types of information, "stressful experience" and "strain": although relying on the respondent's subjective judgments of stressful experience related to the efforts and rewards at work the researcher transforms this information into summary measures of strain according to a theory-based algorithm (see Peter, Geiler, and Siegrist 1998).

WORK STRESS AND HEALTH: SELECTED EMPIRICAL EVIDENCE

The majority of published medical sociological studies on associations of work stress and physical health (most importantly cardiovascular health) are based on the demand–control model or the effort–reward imbalance model. Therefore, this selective review of empirical evidence is restricted to these two models (for a recent review of person–environment fit research see Edwards, Caplan, and van Harrison 1998).

Demand–Control Model

A large number of prospective and cross-sectional studies were conducted to test the job strain model with respect to health outcomes. Almost thirty studies, the majority of which yielded positive results, at least as far as the control dimension of the model is concerned, were related to coronary heart disease or cardiovascular risk factors such as hypertension. Other investigations demonstrated associations with musculoskeletal disorders and mild psychiatric disorders, among others (for summary see Theorell and Karasek 1996; Schnall et al. 1998; Marmot et al. 1999). Two sets of findings deserve particular attention; the cohort studies exploring new manifestations of coronary heart disease, and the studies measuring ambulatory blood pressure on and off work.

Of the ten prospective investigations six documented positive findings with regard to low job control or the combined effect of high demand and low control. Odds ratios ranged from 1.4 to 2.6. Most of these large-scale studies were conducted in Sweden or in the United States, and one in the United Kingdom. In multivariate statistical analysis effects of potential confounders were controlled. It should also be mentioned that a few studies revealed no effects in the expected direction, but some of these used inappropriate measures of job strain.

Whereas prospective epidemiological investigations provide a powerful argument in favor of a "causal" relationship between work stress and heart disease, other study designs are needed to elucidate underlying mechanisms. One such study design is 24-hour ambulatory blood pressure monitoring. In fact, five carefully executed studies revealed a significant positive effect of exposure to job strain upon ambulatory systolic blood pressure recorded during work, and blood pressure was also found to be significantly elevated during leisure non-work time, among those exposed to job strain. In one study with a three-year follow-up it was found that exposure to job strain at baseline and three years later showed a 11.1 mm Hg effect on workplace and home systolic blood pressure compared to those unexposed at both times. Furthermore, those men who reported being exposed to job strain at baseline but not three years later showed a significant drop in blood pressure three years later (Schnall et al. 1998).

In addition to the stress physiological mechanisms and increased illness susceptibility among people suffering from stress at work may be mediated by unhealthy behaviors such as increased cigarette smoking or unhealthy diet. Several studies found evidence along these lines (Karasek and Theorell 1990). In conclusion, a body of literature has accumulated that strongly suggests a "causal" association between job strain and cardiovascular risk and disease. Less evidence is currently available on other disease outcomes. It should also be mentioned that most consistent effects are observed in middle aged blue-collar men, as opposed to white-collar men and to economically active women.

Effort–Reward Imbalance Model

Twelve independent investigations have tested the effort–reward imbalance model so far by applying either prospective or cross-sectional epidemiological study designs. Major health outcomes were incident coronary heart disease, prevalence of cardiovascular risk factors, measures of subjective health, and functioning or mild psychiatric disorders. Not all studies used identical (i.e. the originally designed) measures, but all tested the core theoretical assumption that a co-manifestation of indicators of high effort *and* indicators of low reward was required to produce the strongest health effects. A brief summary of these major findings is given here. First, based on current evidence and according to the occupation under study, between 10 percent and 40 percent of the workforce suffer from some degree of effort–reward imbalance at work, and at least a third of them are characterized by sustained intense strain reactions following exposure to effort–reward imbalance.

Secondly, with regard to future incident coronary heart disease, effort–reward imbalance at work was associated with a 2.7 to 6.1 fold elevated relative risk compared to those who were free from chronic strain at work. This excess risk could not be explained by established biomedical and behavioral risk factors, as these variables were taken into account in multivariate statistical analysis (Siegrist et al. 1990; Lynch et al. 1997; Bosma et al. 1998). Thus, the psychosocial work environment as measured by this model is associated with at least a moderate relative risk of incident coronary heart disease that is independent of established biomedical and behavioral cardiovascular risk factors. However, restricting the analysis to this association would result in an underestimation of the total burden on cardiovascular health produced by adverse psychosocial work conditions. This is due to the fact that chronic psychosocial strain at work in terms of effort–reward imbalance is also associated with relevant cardiovascular risk factors, e.g. high blood pressure (hypertension), high levels of blood lipids, or a co-manifestation of these two risk factors (Peter and Siegrist 1997; Siegrist et al. 1997; Peter, Geiler, and Siegrist 1998). These findings demonstrate that the explanatory power of the model goes beyond disease manifestation by enabling a more comprehensive definition of people at risk at an earlier stage of disease development.

Thirdly, effort–reward imbalance was associated with moderately elevated risks of impaired physical, mental, and social functioning (odds ratios ranging from 1.40 to 1.78 in men and from 1.81 to 2.33 in women; Stansfeld et al. 1998) and with moderately elevated risks of newly reported mild psychiatric disorders (odds ratios ranging from 1.67 in women to 2.57 in men; Stansfeld et al. 1999) in the Whitehall II study. Additional evidence along these lines comes from cross-sectional studies, confirming that the explanatory power of the model covers more than some specific physical diseases and biomedical risk factors; it also includes aspects of mental health and of physical, mental, and social functioning (Peter et al. 1998). In other words, an estimation of the total burden of health produced by occupational strain, as measured by this model, by far exceeds the amount identified by studies that focus on one single outcome measure.

Comparative Studies

Comparative studies across countries using identical measures of work-related strain are now underway. So far, most investigations were conducted in northern Europe, in the United States, Canada, or Japan; few are available from rapidly developing countries or even from countries that lag behind in economic terms (Karasek et al. 1998). Overall, preliminary findings confirm that substantial similarity in the amount of job stress is found across countries. Yet, the prevalence of work-related stress, as measured by both models, is higher among lower socioeconomic groups, thus pointing to a possible contribution of these models toward explaining part of the increased health burden observed among economically active populations with low socioeconomic status (Marmot et al. 1999).

Gender is another important determinant of the associations between work-related stress and health. In a majority of studies effects were substantially stronger in men than in women. The complexities of gender (role)-specific effects are still poorly understood, but part of the explanation can be attributed to inadequate conceptualization of the strain evolving from work/non-work interface including double exposure to work and family in women (Ort-Gomer and Chesney 1997).

Cross-cultural research in this area holds promise for further knowledge on social determinants of the ways in which work affects health. For instance, in Europe, a clear north–south differentiation is seen with respect to work characteristics where physical working conditions are less favorable in the south, but psychosocial job demands are highest in northern countries (Kompier and Cooper 1999).

Along these lines comparative tests of the work stress models are desirable. Such tests provide an opportunity to study their separate and combined effects on health outcome. In addition, these models might be extended beyond the work role to include other core social roles in adult life such as family and marital roles. In fact, preliminary evidence from a large-scale study in Sweden indicates that combined effects on cardiovascular health produced by the job strain model and the effort–reward imbalance model are stronger compared to the separate effects of each model (Peter et al. 1999). Moreover, in a British study mentioned (Bosma et al. 1998) it was found that the demand–control model (the control dimension only) and the effort–reward imbalance model were equally strong, independent predictors of reports of incident coronary heart disease when appropriate statistical controls were performed.

POLICY IMPLICATIONS IN A COMPARATIVE PERSPECTIVE

Overall, worksite health promotion activities are realized with little concern about scientific advances obtained in the field of occupational stress research. By and large they are focused on changes in individual health behavior or in traditional occupational health concerns (e.g. toxic agents or technical safety), ignoring the powerful effects of work organization and labor-market conditions on health. Eventually this may change in the future as all three models described above (as well as additional models not mentioned in detail, for summary see Cooper 1998) provide a rationale for evidence-based preventive activity.

Person–environment fit theory concludes that work demands need to be tailored according to the worker's abilities. This involves both specific measures of organizational development and of person development. Moreover, organizational interventions must suit the needs of affected individuals that are closely linked to the work role (e.g. motivation, learning, satisfaction; Edwards et al. 1998). In the demand–support–control model, special emphasis is put on autonomy, skill discretion, and personal growth. Measures of work reorganization include job enlargement, job enrichment, skill training, enhanced participation and teamwork (Karasek and Theorell 1990). Practical implications of the effort–reward imbalance model concern the development of compensatory wagesystems, the provision of models of gain sharing, and the strengthening of non-monetary gratifications. Moreover, ways of improving promotional opportunities and job security need to be explored. Supplementary measures are interpersonal training and skill development, in particular leadership behavior.

A sociological perspective of innovations in this field must take into account the political, legal, economic, and cultural constraints operating in individual countries. For instance, a recent comparative analysis of strategies of work stress prevention in eleven European countries identified three separate clusters of countries (Kompier and Cooper 1999). A first cluster, consisting of Sweden, Finland, and the Netherlands, already pays a lot of attention to the topic by incorporating the psychosocial factors at work into their legal framework on working conditions. Moreover, systematic data on these aspects is collected and intervention measures are promoted. In a second cluster, consisting of Belgium, Denmark, United Kingdom, Germany, and Ireland, the issue of work stress and health is on the political agenda, but decisive steps concerning legislation, monitoring, and intervention have not yet taken place. The third cluster is composed of southern European countries (Italy, Greece, and Portugal). In these countries work stress is not yet recognized as an important policy issue.

In addition to describing the global situation in the 11 European countries the study of Kompier and Cooper (1999) analyzed key factors of successful implementation of this social innovation, e.g. in leading enterprises in most advanced countries. These factors were: (1) a stepwise and systematic approach to the problem including adequate risk analysis (in this step, scientific evidence and skills obtained from medical sociology and social epidemiology are most useful); (2) a combination of situational (work-directed) and personal/interpersonal (worker-directed) measures; (3) a participative approach involving both employees and (middle) management; (4) top-management support by incorporating preventive activities into regular company management.

In conclusion, medical sociological research on work stress and health has witnessed substantial progress in recent past. Its theoretical concepts and empirical results contribute to the accumulation of an impressive body of knowledge, whose impact on policy, in terms of implementing worksite stress prevention programs, is now growing. Despite these advances, the discipline is confronted with important challenges, both at the scientific and policy level.

References

Bosma, H., R. Peter, J. Siegrist, and M. G. Marmot. 1998. "Two Alternative Job Stress Models and the Risk of Coronary Heart Disease." *American Journal of Public Health* 88: 68–74.

Caplan, R. D., S. Cobb, J. R. P. French, R. V. Harrison, and S. R. Pinneau. 1980. *Job Demand and Worker Health: Main Effects and Occupational Differences*. Ann Arbor, MI: Institute for Social Research.

Cooper, C. L. (ed.). 1998. *Theories of Organizational Stress*. Oxford: Oxford University Press.

Cosmides, L. and J. Tooby. 1992. "Cognitive Adaptations for Social Exchange." Pp. 163–228 in J. H. Barkow, L. Cosmides, and J. Tooby (eds.), *The Adapted Mind: Evolutionary Psychology and the Generation of Culture*. New York: Oxford University Press.

Edwards, J. R., R. D. Caplan, and R. van Harrison. 1998. "Person-environment fit." Pp. 28–67 in C. Cooper (ed.), *Theories of Organizational Stress*. Oxford: Oxford University Press.

House, J. 1981. *Work, Stress, and Social Support*. Reading, MA: Addison-Wesley.

Johnson, J. V. and E. Hall. 1988. "Job Strain, Work Place, Social Support, and Cardiovascular Disease." *American Journal of Public Health* 78: 1336–42.

Karasek, R. 1979. "Job Demands, Job Decision Latitude, and Mental Strain: Implications for a Job Re-Design." *Administration Science Quarterly* 24: 285–307.

Karasek, R. and T. Theorell. 1990. *Healthy Work: Stress, Productivity, and the Reconstruction of Working Life*. New York: Basic Books.

Karasek, R., C. Brisson, N. Kawakami, I. Houtman, P. Bongers, and B. Amick. 1998. "The Job Content Questionnaire (JCQ): An Instrument for Internationally Comparative Assessments of Psychosocial Job Characteristics." *Journal of Occupational Health Psychology* 4: 322–55.

Kohn, M. and C. Schooler. 1983. *Work and Personality: An Inquiry into the Impact of Social Stratification*. Norwood, NJ: Ablex.

Kompier, M. and C. L. Cooper. 1999. *Preventing Stress, Improving Productivity*. London: Routledge.

Lazarus, R. S. 1991. *Emotion and Adaptation*. New York: Oxford University Press.

LeDoux, J. 1996. *The Emotional Brain*. New York: Simon & Schuster.

Lynch, J., N. Krause, G. A. Kaplan, J. Tuomilehto, and J. T. Salonen. 1997. "Work Place Conditions, Socioeconomic Status, and the Risk of Mortality and Acute Myocardial Infarction: The Kuopio Ischemic Heart Disease Risk Factor Study." *American Journal of Public Health* 87: 617–22.

Marmot, M., J. Siegrist, T. Theorell, and A. Feeney. 1999. "Health and the Psychosocial Environment at Work." In M. G. Marmot and R. Wilkinson (eds.), *Social Determinants of Health*. Oxford University Press (in press).

Ort-Gomer, K. and M. A. Chesney. 1997. "Social Stress/Strain in Heart Disease in Women." Pp. 407–20 in G. J. Desmond and N. K. Wenger (eds.), *Women and Heart Disease*.

Paoli, P. 1997. *Working Conditions in Europe. The Second European Survey on Working Conditions*. Dublin: European Foundation.

Peter, R., and J. Siegrist. 1997. "Chronic Work Stress, Sickness Absence, and Hypertension in Middle Managers: General or Specific Sociological Explanations?" *Social Science & Medicine* 45: 1111–20.

Peter, R., H. Geiler, and J. Siegrist. 1998. "Associations of Effort–Reward Imbalance at Work and Reported Symptoms in Different Groups of Male and Female Public Transport Workers." *Stress Medicine* 14: 175–82.

Peter, R., J. Siegrist, J. Hallqvist, C. Reuterwall, T. Theorell, and The SHEEP Study Group. 1999. Psychosocial Work Environment and Myocardial Infarction: Improving Risk Estimation by Combining Two Alternative Job Stress Models in the SHEEP Study (submitted).

Schnall, P., J. E. Schwartz, P. A. Landsbergis, K. Warren, and T. G. Pickering. 1998. "A Longitudinal Study of Job Strain and Ambulatory Blood Pressure: Results from a Three-Year Follow-Up." *Psychosomatic Medicine* 6: 697–706.

Siegrist, J., R. Peter, A. Junge, P. Cremer, and D. Seidel. 1990. "Low Status Control, High Effort at Work, and Ischemic Heart Disease: Prospective Evidence from Blue Collar Men." *Social Science & Medicine* 31: 1127–34.

Siegrist, J., R. Peter, P. Cremer, and D. Seidel. 1997. "Chronic Work Stress is Associated with Atherogenic Lipids and Elevated Fibrinogen in Middle Aged Men." *Journal of Internal Medicine* 242: 149–156.

Siegrist, J., K. Siegrist, and I. Weber. 1986. "Sociological Concepts in the Etiology of Chronic Disease: The Case of Ischemic Heart Disease." *Social Science & Medicine* 22: 247–53.

Skinner, E. A. 1996. "A Guide to Constructs of Control." *Journal of Personality and Social Psychology* 71: 549–70.

Spector, P. E. 1998. "A Control Theory of the Job Stress Process." Pp. 153–69 in C. E. Cooper (ed.), *Theories of Organizational Stress*. Oxford: Oxford University Press.

Stansfeld, S., H. Bosma, H. Hemingway, and M. Marmot. 1998. "Psychosocial Work Characteristics and Social Support as Predictors of SF-36 Functioning: The Whitehall II Study." *Psychosomatic Medicine* 60: 247–55.

——. 1999. "Work Characteristics Predict Psychiatric Disorders: Prospective Results from the Whitehall II Study." *Occupational and Environmental Medicine* 56: 303–7.

Steptoe, A. and A. Appels (eds.). 1989. *Stress, Personal Control, and Health*. Chichester: Wiley.

Theorell, T. and R. Karasek. 1996. "Current Issues Relating to Psychosocial Job Strain and Cardiovascular Disease Research." *Journal of Occupational Health Psychology* 1: 9–26.

7

Migration, Health, and Stress

Judith T. Shuval

Until the 1980s and 1990s most migration theory was based on the widespread "individual relocation" approach which emphasized push–pull factors and focused on rational decision-making, transitions, and adaptation processes. These early theories were largely ahistorical and referred to tendencies to move from densely to sparsely populated areas, from low- to high-income areas, or in response to fluctuations in the business cycle. Political and religious threats or overt persecution generated populations of "refugees" which were distinguished from the category of "migrant." Early migration theory emphasized economic factors, social order and equilibrium, and focused on the inability of countries of origin to fulfill expectations. In considering the consequences of migration they tended to concentrate almost entirely on the countries of destination and assumed unilinear processes of acculturation and assimilation. Conflict was seen as a temporary expression of dislocation in the normal ordered state of host societies (Price 1969; Rose 1969; Mangalam and Schwarzweller 1970; Richmond 1984).

MIGRATION IN POSTMODERN SOCIETIES

With structural changes that have taken place in contemporary societies, more recent theoretical approaches to migration have taken the view that, in its broadest context, migration in the 1980s and 1990s can be been viewed as a stable, international phenomenon with a structure over space and time. It is widely believed that the massive dimensions of migration in the late 1990s will continue in future years, although the origins and destinations of the streams may change in accordance with shifts in economic and social conditions. Population pressures, environmental deterioration, poverty, wars, persecution, and human rights abuses are among the ongoing causes of population movement. The continued disadvantages of the Third World and the end of the cold war, which opened the boundaries of East European countries, have exacerbated ethnic and national conflicts. These have combined to generate vast numbers of refugees and immense populations seeking to move. In 1995 the United Nations High Commissioner for Refugees estimated that 14.4 million persons are considered refugees, which means that they are outside their country of citizenship and are unable to return for fear of political persecution; another 36 million, who are not formally defined as refugees, have been displaced from their homes but remain within the boundaries of their countries. Thus it is clear that streams of international migration are ongoing and respond to political, social, and economic changes in an expanding global economy (Zolberg 1989; Heisler 1992; Castles and Miller 1993; Massey et al. 1993).

Recent thinking has referred to "international migration systems" theory, which proposes a dynamic, historically-based, globalist view in which many states are interdependent in the migration process (Zolberg 1989; Massey et al. 1993). Migration is driven by structural characteristics of societies and tends to generate its own dynamics. The principal structural issues that drive migration in the 1990s are global inequality, the refugee crisis in many parts of the world, use of cheap foreign labor, and liberalization of exit from the eastern European countries. The nation-state is a prime actor in contemporary migration theory, especially with regard to its role in policy formation and control of the flow (O'Brien 1992).

Migration theories can be roughly categorized into two groups: those that refer to the *initial* motivation for migration and those that refer to the ongoing nature of the migration process (Heisler 1992). In the former category there is an emphasis on globalization processes which are seen in the political and economic context of an expanding global economy. Migration is viewed as a response to the flow of capital, technology, institutional forms, and cultural innovations in an interactive process across the globe. In the second category are theories referring to the linkage of countries by flows and counter-flows of people in sets of networks which are both interdependent and independent of each other. These processes reflect the historical context of the links between origins and destinations which are based on earlier colonization, political influence, trade, investment, or cultural ties – as well as the present economic, social, and political contexts. The inherent social – rather than predominantly economic – quality of the process is emphasized by a focus on networks which are microstructures viewed by some theorists as the core of the process because of their role in providing assistance at the destination in job location, financial support, practical information, and a base for the migration of additional persons. The ongoing nature of the process is seen in the fact that the larger the number of people who migrate, the thicker the social networks at the destinations and the consequent amount of available help; this tends to decrease the costs and risks of migration for others from the same origin. Widespread policies of "family reunification" reinforce these networks. The "culture of migration" has made the process increasingly acceptable and cumulative in many parts of the world where the notion of migration is more and more of a community value (Fawcett

1989; Hammar 1989; Portes 1989; Salt 1989; Heisler 1992; Kritz and Zlotnik 1992; O'Brien 1992; Castles and Miller 1993; Massey et al. 1993; Teitlelbaum and Weiner 1995).

Postmodern migration is distinguished by its extreme diversification in terms of the many *types* of contemporary immigrants. These include a wide variety of cross-cutting categories and people may shift over time from one type to another. Some of the most prominent categories of migrants are: permanent settlers; temporary workers and seasonal workers; refugees and asylum seekers; legal and illegal immigrants; persons who come for purposes of family reunion; skilled and unskilled persons of varying social class backgrounds; professionals and managerial workers; persons of urban and rural origins; wage earners and entrepreneurs; many varieties of ethnic groups. In addition to the above types, there has been reference to immigrants from diasporas seeking to return to their homelands (Portes 1989; Shuval 1995, 1998; Carmon 1996).

With minor exceptions, host countries admit migrants selectively in terms of policies that consider unemployment rates, labor shortages or surpluses in specific sectors of the economy, potential social conflict, security issues, and family reunion needs. However, despite the fact that no country is obligated to accept refugees or migrants, many developed countries have recognized a moral, humanitarian responsibility to do so, within the limits of their self-interest.

Within this context, extensive illegal immigration characterizes many of the receiving societies. This phenomenon poses a major threat to the authority and power of the state since it represents a loss of control in the flow of people and goods over borders. The permeability of borders has become a major political issue in Germany, France, the United States, and Israel and is expressed in heated political debate. Efforts to control illegals have included penalties on employers who provide jobs for illegals as well as limitations on such benefits as welfare payments, tax and housing assistance, family support, student loans, and medical care. However, as long as there is widespread deprivation and unemployment in the sending countries and the demand for cheap labor continues in the formal and informal markets of the receiving countries, it is extremely difficult to contain or control illegal immigration (Baldwin-Edwards and Schain 1994; Center for Immigration Statistics 1995; Carmon 1996).

Illegals take the least desired jobs on the market, make their living in the "informal" sector and satisfy employers' demand for cheap labor. In western Europe, where there has been high unemployment during the 1980s and 1990s, there is fear that immigrants pose a job threat; there is also concern with rising Islamic fundamentalism and increasing crime rates. Humanitarian concerns have been compromised for security considerations by seeking to impose tighter controls on the entry of illegal immigrants while at the same time seeking measures to encourage policies in the countries of origin that will curtail the initial causes of the flow. It is widely believed that illegal immigrants are a source of narcotics trafficking, terrorism, prostitution, and crime. Fearing cultural differences, job competition at low wages, sky-rocketing costs for schools, welfare, health, and police, wide segments of the public in many countries do not distinguish between legal and illegal migrants, and express increasing hostility and reluctance to admit all forms of migrants (Zolberg 1989; Teitelbaum and Weiner 1995).

Teitelbaum and Weiner (1995) note that in the long run a high proportion of temporary migrants become permanent settlers. Despite a system of fines on air companies which bring persons without entry visas to European points of entry, once a person manages to reach Europe he can be fairly confident that, with legal advocacy and civil rights protection, the sluggish process of asylum adjudication in democratic countries can last almost indefinitely (Massey et al. 1993; Teitelbaum and Weiner 1995).

When there are barriers to entry but large numbers of people seek to migrate, a lucrative niche is created for the establishment of special institutions relating to migration. These include private entrepreneurs who provide a variety of services and supports for legal and illegal migrants. They encompass business enterprises and humanitarian organizations but also an array of black market enterprises. These offer a variety of counseling, legal advice, social services, and protection to immigrants; such bodies provide labor contracts between employers and migrants, counterfeit documents and visas, arranged marriages, housing and credit for legal and illegal immigrants (O'Brien 1992).

If there are large numbers of immigrants, they may themselves constitute a political power in the host country. Their interests may dictate that they lobby for the admission of groups from specific countries of origin or for limitations in the numbers of immigrants. Large numbers make for influence and power on other public issues as well (Horowitz 1994).

What is Stress?

The stress model that appears to be most useful in the present context is the one developed in the 1970s by Levine and Scotch (1970). House (1974) has noted that "stress occurs when an individual confronts a situation where his or her usual modes of behavior are insufficient and the consequences of not adapting are serious." Stated most generally, this theory proposes a multi-linked chain among potential stressor situations, subjectively determined perception variables, and the availability and usability of personal and social coping mechanisms (Scott and Howard 1970; French, Rodgers, and Cobb 1974). Thus, homeostasis on the individual level will be disrupted when a person perceives a given situation to be disturbing, alarming, or threatening. If he or she is unable to mobilize personal or social resources to cope with the situation in such a manner as to restore homeostasis, that person's energy will be bound up dealing with this perceived disturbance; this preoccupation defines a stressful condition (Scott and Howard 1970).

Levine and Scotch's (1970) approach emphasizes the subjective definition of stress by making it clear that situations are not objectively stressful but are socially or psychologically constructed as such by individuals in terms of social and cultural norms. Thus, bereavement or divorce may be subjectively defined as extremely disturbing but also, under certain circumstances, as a relief or even as a positive challenge (House 1974). The conditional quality of the stress model also emphasizes the importance of coping mechanisms. These may be individual (personal skills, personality traits, intelligence, knowledge) or social (formal institutions, informal groups, social norms and values). The availability and usability of coping mechanisms constitute the link that determines whether a situation that is perceived as disturbing will in fact result in stress for the individual. Indeed there is considerable evidence for the stress-mediating and stress-buffering roles of coping resources (Pearlin and Schooler 1978; Pearlin 1989; Ensel and Lin 1991).

Mechanic (1978) distinguished between two types of coping: defense processes, which are psychological mechanisms to redefine, deny, repress, or possibly distort a disturbing reality, and instrumental coping behavior, which utilizes skills and knowledge for problem-solving in an effort to change or ameliorate the stressful situation. Defense processes may enable the individual to live with a difficult situation, e.g. chronic illness, but in the long run neurotic or more serious consequences may result from this form of coping. On the other hand, instrumental coping seeks to alter or modify a disturbing situation. Coping skills are a function of early socialization and prior experiences with the given situation or with settings perceived as similar.

Antonovsky's Salutogenic Model (1993) derives directly from the above theoreticians but makes a unique contribution in its focus on the "Sense of Coherence" as a critical coping mechanism. He has argued that a strong Sense of Coherence (SOC) is crucial to successful coping with the ubiquitous stressors of living and hence for effective health maintenance. Antonovsky defined the SOC as a global orientation that expresses the extent to which one has a pervasive, enduring, dynamic feeling of confidence that: (a) the stimuli deriving from one's external and internal environments are structured, predictable, and explicable; (b) resources are available to meet the demands posed by these stimuli; (c) these demands are viewed as challenging and as worthy of energy and emotional engagement.

The strength of an individual's SOC is shaped by life experiences of consistency, by underload–overload balance as well as by participation in socially meaningful decision-making. Some of these issues have been explored by Ben-David in relation to the migration process (Antonovsky 1979, 1987: 19, 1993; Ben-David 1996).

In sum, stress is said to exist to the extent that an individual defines a salient situation as disturbing for himself or herself and is unable to recruit effective coping mechanisms to remove or reduce the disturbance. Two simultaneous conditions are necessary for stress to be present or to increase: a subjective definition of a situation as disturbing and an inability – for whatever reason – to cope with the condition. The centrality of social and psychological factors in determining stress is seen in the fact that both these conditions are largely socially constructed.

Migration and Stress

The relationship between migration and stress may be considered on two levels that differ analytically in terms of the assumed direction of cause and effect. On the one hand, stress of various sorts may be said to cause migration; on the other, stress may be viewed as an outcome of migration. As noted, this distinction is essentially analytical since both processes may in fact occur with regard to any specific stream of migration.

Change is inherent in migration and may be considered a structural characteristic of the process. Such change may, under the circumstances proposed in the model above, be viewed as a potential stressor. Three forms of change characterize the migration process: physical, social, and cultural.

Physical Change

Migration involves movement from one geographical location to another. Such movement differs in magnitude depending on the distance of the destination from the origin. The migrant may experience changes in climate, level of sanitation, and dietary habits, as well as exposure to pollution, new pathogens, and endemic diseases. Changes in climate, in conjunction with the new culture, may induce changes in lifestyle that express themselves in patterns of sleep, nutrition, timing of meals (e.g. when the main meal of the day is taken), clothing, housing, or general pace of activity. All these physical changes may, under certain circumstances, serve as stressors (Wessen 1971; Hull 1977).

Social Change

All migrants disengage from a network of social relations in the society they are leaving. In the case of migration of whole kin groups, disengagement may be minimal, but in other cases there are numerous breaks in social relationships. Disruption of long-standing ties may or may not be perceived as disturbing by the migrant; accordingly, disengagement will cause the migrant to feel isolated and unsupported, or relieved and unencumbered. Separation may be viewed as permanent (e.g. when leaving aged parents behind in a society to which access is closed), or as temporary when the person left behind can come to visit the migrant in his or her new residence or the migrant himself can revisit his original home. In some cases, the disengagement may be perceived as disturbing only after a lapse of time: a young migrant, initially exhilarated by the freedom from ties of parents and other kin, may begin to feel disturbed by their absence after a period of separation. Experiences in the host society – difficulties in establishing new social networks, employment problems, or other frustrations – may sharpen the sense of loneliness at a later stage (Laffrey et al. 1989; MacCarthy and Craissati 1989).

The relevant coping mechanism for this feeling is a new social network that serves as a functional alternative to the earlier one. Immigrants experience different levels of difficulty in developing such alternative relations in their new location. When entire kin groups or whole communities migrate, membership within such groups provides considerable support (Kuo and Tsai 1986; Mavreas and Bebbington 1989), but meaningful primary relations with veterans in a new social context generally develop slowly (Gordon 1964; Haour-Knipe 1989). In many cases, social relations develop among migrants of the same origin, either because of residential proximity or because of deliberate choice.

But when migrants seek to move into the larger social context of the host society, their success will be determined by its receptiveness to newcomers (Rose 1969).

Cultural Change

All migrants need to learn new norms and values and to abandon or adapt their old ones. However, the extent of the culture gap between the places of origin and destination determines the amount of learning and relearning that must be undergone. But even when the gap is minimal, the sensitive migrant will nevertheless feel subtle culture changes. Learning skills, youth, flexibility, and readiness for change serve as individual coping mechanisms for this need. Individual coping by immigrants is mediated by attitudes and behavior of the host population, which may range from acceptance, tolerance, and encouragement to disdain, ridicule, or hostility toward immigrants' efforts to learn the new language, norms, and values. Some host societies in which the culture gap is large may provide formal institutions for instruction in the local language and culture, but most acculturation takes place informally (Baider et al. 1996).

An immigrant's entry into a new society is a gradual process. The length of the time span that is relevant depends on the parameters being considered. At what point in time does an immigrant turn into a veteran? The critical time span may be defined in terms of months, years, or even generations. What seems to be important is the dynamic quality of the process.

Different stages in the process have different characteristics, so that issues that are important at one stage may disappear at another. For example, knowledge of a new language has differential meaning in terms of behavior and interaction with others when an immigrant is in a new country 6 months, 5 years, or 20 years. The same is true for primary relations between immigrants and veteran members of the host society: these generally develop relatively late in the integration process (Gordon 1964). Even unemployment, downward mobility, and poverty may be perceived for a short period as transitional stages in the immigration process and therefore as acceptable (Munroe-Blum et al. 1989). Although the orderly progression described by Park and Burgess in their pioneering classic (1921), from contact to competition and conflict and finally to accommodation, does not seem to characterize all situations, the migrant's experience undoubtedly varies by stages (Hertz 1988).

There are a variety of approaches with regard to the conceptual definition of integration in a new social system (Richmond 1984). Terms such as socialization, resocialization, acculturation, accommodation, and normative behavior have been widely used but, in most cases, inadequately spelled out either conceptually or empirically (Bar-Yosef 1968; Price 1969). Does the term "integration" refer to the dispersal of immigrants in the institutional structure? To their conformity to the prevalent norms of the society? To an absence of pathological behavior among them? To their feelings of identification, well-being, familiarity, acceptance, hopefulness? To their interaction on a primary level with other members of the society? To lack of conflict between them and other groups? These issues refer to a variety of contents of the integration concept.

It is essential to establish which point of view is being considered with regard to the integration of immigrants. Several are undoubtedly relevant. One salient point of view is, of course, that of the immigrants themselves: How do they feel about the new society? Do they see it as their permanent home or is it more of a way-station in a series of moves? Do they feel at home? Do they have a sense of marginality? Another point of view is that of veteran residents: Do they accept newcomers or do they view them with hostility – as potential competitors or disrupters of the status quo? Are they apathetic? Finally, one may consider the viewpoint of the society as a whole in terms of its dominant values and their relationship to the issue of immigration. These values have both manifest and latent components expressed by more and less formal mechanisms.

It would seem essential to view integration into a new society as a multi-dimensional process which can be considered in terms of a variety of subprocesses, each focusing on a different aspect of life in the new society. Thus, there are many pathways and mechanisms by means of which immigrants enter a new social system. At any point in time integration in one life area is not necessarily correlated with integration in others: some areas are more highly correlated with each other than are others, but there seems to be no consistency across populations or situations to permit one to establish necessary correlations (Shuval, Markus, and Dotan 1975).

The implication of such a multidimensional approach is that little is to be gained from seeking one overall measure of integration. The problem is to establish which points of view are to be considered, which content areas are deemed relevant for understanding the process and to seek the empirical relationships among them at various points in time. Composite indexes of integration, such as the one used by Rose (1969), involve arbitrary weighting of the measures from which the composite is derived. They are, therefore, of limited use. It would seem preferable to focus on different meanings and factors depending on the temporal stage in a group's process of entry into the social system. Focusing on one specific area, for example, the occupational sphere, is legitimate provided one bears in mind that, despite its centrality, it is only one of several life areas that could be considered. While behavior and feelings in the occupational sphere are not positively correlated with behavior in *all* other areas, they are generally highly correlated with morale, identification, and feelings about the new society, which gives special salience to employment in the overall process of migration (Shuval, Markus, and Dotan 1975; Shuval and Bernstein 1997).

The integration process in all its dimensions may involve conflict no less than solidarity. The process does not necessarily re-establish an earlier equilibrium but may result in a re-definition of the social situation in terms quite different from those initially characterizing the society. Indeed, the differing interests and values that inhere in the meeting of groups and subgroups suggest that the process is unlikely to be smooth. One can assume that various groups are characterized by different interests and goals as a result of their differential position in the social system and these may not always be complementary. No less important are value conflicts inherent in the orientation of any one group.

Immigrants are just as likely – or even more likely – to come into contact with the problems and pathologies of the institutional structure of the host society as they are to encounter its more stable elements. Chronic problems to which veterans have accommodated often plague newcomers during their initial stages in the society. It has even been suggested that acceptance of certain chronic pathologies of a society be used as one index of integration! Furthermore, weak or imperfectly functioning institutional structures may be strained by the arrival of an immigrant population, so that the group itself may contribute further to that institution's dysfunction. An example of this would be a social service that was over-utilized before the arrival of an immigrant group and is under even greater pressure as a result of an influx of additional clients. This phenomenon has been noted with regard to the health services in Israel (Shuval 1992). However, high utilization rates of immigrants tend to taper off after they have been in the new society for a period of time (Ben-Noun 1994, 1996).

In a rapidly changing society, newcomers are not always presented with a coherent set of norms to which conformity is expected. Differentiation of the host society in terms of ethnic, social class, regional, occupational, or political subgroups results in a variety of norms to which immigrants are differentially exposed depending on the groups with which they come into contact.

By channeling newcomers into specific subgroups or locations, a pluralistic-ally structured society allows immigrants to learn the norms of one group but remain ignorant of the norms of others or of those held in common by all members of the society. If that subgroup happens to consist of other immigrants from the same place of origin, the familiarity and intimacy may provide a positive cushioning effect for some period but separation from broader segments of the host society may intensify feelings of isolation or conflict (Mavreas and Bebbington 1989).

Styles of interpersonal relations are culturally constructed and often require a process of readjustment. For example, expected levels of intimacy among friends, relations with officials in bureaucratic settings, and styles of politeness vary widely from society to society and may require migrants to change many patterns of behavior. An immigrant from the Soviet Union stated the issue poignantly with regard to the expected level of intimacy in his new home in the United States.

> [In the Soviet Union] life is hopeless and dark. So the relationship among people, relations of the "soul", is very developed and this adorns (ykrashchaet) the life of the individual. In America a man is free but alone in his little corner. In Russia there is no freedom, so in order to escape the influence of the environment, people hide in groups of two or twenty or thirty people.... When life became unbearable we banded together in groups and such strong friendships developed in these groups and there was so much self-sacrifice that spiritual contact was stronger than in family relations. This was the natural defense of the soul against tyranny. This cannot be repeated in a free country.... Here life is too multi-faceted (mnogo-granna), but that's the price you pay for freedom in the West... (quoted in Gitelman 1982: 215)

In considering the relation between stress and migration, it should be noted that in some cases coping resources and mechanisms that were effective in the countries of origin are also effective in the new society; in other cases such resources are absent, reduced, or less effective in the new society. The transformation of prior coping mechanism to meet new needs or the development of alternative ones geared to address unfamiliar situations, takes time and skill. It may therefore be assumed that many immigrants are characterized by stress for varying periods of time (Antonovsky 1979; Shuval 1992).

Certain subgroups among immigrants are at a relatively high risk. These include persons migrating on their own, children and adolescents, especially those unaccompanied by adults, mentally handicapped, elderly, single parent families, large families. Women, especially pregnant women and those who have recently given birth, are especially vulnerable (Hattar-Pollara and Meleis 1995; Carballo et al. 1996). Refugees who have suffered major traumas before migrating and during the transition are a high-risk group. It has been shown that asylum-seekers report severe stress because of their fear of repatriation to threatening places, barriers to work and social services, separation from family, and the complicated, frustrating process of pursuing refugee claims (Clinton-Davis and Fassil 1992; Muecke 1992; Sinnerbrink et al. 1997).

Refugees and others who have suffered traumas or torture carry scars of persecution for undefined periods of time. These people cannot quickly slough off the impact of their earlier experiences, the effects of which may be immediate or may become visible at a later date. Among such persons, earlier, traumatic experiences have weakened their coping skills and the ensuing stress makes them more vulnerable than others to local diseases and new stressors. For example: there is some evidence in Israel that the traumatic impact of the Gulf War was greater on Holocaust survivors than on others, despite the fact that many years had passed since the World War II (Hantman et al. 1992; Shuval 1992).With regard to post-traumatic stress disorders, in some cases the passage of time makes the situation worse.

Migration and Health

The link between stress and migration, makes clear the potential for disease as an outcome of the migration process. While inability to cope with stressors can have many results, one of the most direct is somatization and psychological distress. Indirect results include a variety of behaviors characterized by health risks such as smoking, alcohol consumption, drug use, and eating disorders.

Minority status or marginality can be viewed as stressor situations. The health status and behavior of immigrant populations is expressed in patterns of disease, health behavior, and utilization of health care services. Furthermore the response of the health care system to special needs of immigrant populations needs to be considered.

One of the most useful conceptual frameworks for the study of the relationship of the acculturative process to mental health has been developed by Berry and his colleagues (Berry and Kim 1988; Williams and Berry 1991). They have noted the role of social support found by immigrants in the host society and the importance of socioeconomic variables; pre-migration variables such as adaptive functioning (self-esteem, coping ability, psychiatric status), knowledge of the new language and culture and motives for the move (voluntary or involuntary); cognitive variables such as attitudes toward the acculturative process and future expectations. They have also emphasized the degree of tolerance and acceptance of cultural diversity in the host society. All of these variables are viewed as "buffers" in the reduction of acculturative stress.

Studies of psychological well-being among recently arrived immigrants from the former Soviet Union in Israel show them to be characterized by more symptoms of anxiety, depression, and somatization than a comparable sample of veterans. They also show higher rates of somatization on the above symptoms than a comparable group of immigrants to the United States, even though the latter reported a greater improvement in their standard of living than the Israeli immigrants. A similar pattern of somatization has been shown among Korean immigrants (Flaherty et al. 1988; Kohn et al. 1989; Lerner et al. 1992; Koh 1998).

Most countries that accept immigrants pose health criteria for admission. These range from exacting requirements to lax prerequisites and are in many cases checked at the point of origin to avoid the complications of deportation of those not qualified for admission. The principal purpose of health criteria for admission is to prevent the spread of infectious diseases in the host society and to avoid increased burdens on the health care and social welfare systems which could result from both infectious and chronic disease. However it is not always possible to maintain the full gamut of health standards for admission because of the proliferation of illegal entries as well as the legal and humanitarian difficulties of deportation (Massey et al. 1993; Teitelbaum and Weiner, eds., 1995).

Despite formal health criteria for admission, refugees, illegals, and diaspora immigrants may import infectious and chronic diseases that were endemic in their countries of origin. Upon arrival in refugee camps and in urban areas where migrants tend to be located, living conditions are often conducive to the spread of infectious diseases as a result of crowding, poor sanitary facilities, contaminated water and food, and malnutrition. These may cause a breakdown of the health services and result in epidemics as well as long-term effects on mental health. Societies which have in the past successfully eradicated such diseases as tuberculosis, malaria, and measles have found that these (and others) have been imported by immigrants and are in danger of spreading to the local population. The spread of AIDS as a result of migration is one of the most critical contemporary issues (Kalipeni and Oppong 1998).

The extent of importation of chronic diseases is determined in major part by the age of immigrants and by the quality of health care in the countries of origin. High proportions of older persons among the immigrants result in a high frequency of chronic diseases. When treatment facilities in the countries of origin were deficient or did not reach major segments of the population, immigrants bring with them a variety of health problems that were inadequately treated for prolonged periods before they left (Field 1990; Garbe and Garbe 1990; Rowland and Telyukov 1991; Ben-Noun 1994).

Styles of life and environmental conditions in the countries of origin play a role in the health status of immigrants causing health problems that may not be evident at the time they arrive but emerge over time. Among these are dental practices and oral health. Widespread use of abortion and ignorance of other means of birth control pose health problems for women immigrants from countries where family planning practices were not generally known or practiced; if alternative methods are available in the host society, it takes time for women to become acquainted with them and learn the procedures to gain access (Sabatello 1995). Norms and behavior regarding alcohol consumption, smoking, and drug use are also imported when they were endemic in countries of origin but may be intensified in new, stress-ladened settings. This phenomenon has been reported among Cambodian refugee women (D'Avanzo 1994).

Illegal immigrants are a high-risk group with respect to health. In many cases they are not covered by the prevailing health insurance systems. Their precarious status in the host society prevents their seeking health care through publicly sponsored or even private agencies because of fear of deportation. Furthermore their location in deprived, poorly serviced, or slum areas increases the likelihood of infectious disease among them. Children of illegals are especially vulnerable if they are not formally registered and attending schools in the host society.

There are cases in which immigrants underutilize the health care system. This occurs when they are not covered by health insurance and the charges are beyond their reach. This can result in delay of care for acute problems or of use of the emergency services rather than the appropriate community services. Immigrant women have been found to be more likely than non-newcomers to have ill infants with a high risk for infectious diseases. Mental health services may be underutilized because of the stigma felt by some immigrants; in such cases rates of utilization do not accurately reflect the mental health status of immigrants (Zambrana et al. 1994; Guendelman et al. 1995; Noh and Avison 1996).

Some Policy Issues Regarding Migration and Health

If the health care system is to be geared to meet needs and identify at-risk groups, a full assessment of the health problems imported by newcomers is essential. In addition to basic demographic data, this involves background information with regard to health practices and health care in the countries of origin. Immigrants are vulnerable to endemic diseases to which the host population has developed immunity. They also include high-risk groups – e.g. the elderly, childbearing women, persons with a background of psychiatric problems, individuals previously exposed to environmental hazards such as Chernobyl.

High-level policy decisions are required so that the host society can realign its resources to deal with these problems. In societies where there is ambivalence or resentment with regard to the desirability of immigration, a sense of deprivation is likely to be felt in the veteran population because of competition for scarce resources, e.g. housing, jobs, health care. Xenophobia accompanied by overt violence has been seen recently (1999/2000) in Germany and in other European countries against such a background and can only be controlled by stringent, unambiguous law enforcement.

The prevailing dominance of the medical profession has resulted in a bio-medical definition of the health problems of immigrants. The first concern of host countries is to protect their own population from imported diseases and epidemics. Health care providers are therefore most concerned to provide patients with physical assessment, diagnosis, and treatment. Preoccupation with disease has resulted in a *medical* definition of immigrants' problems. Failure to utilize a bio-psychosocial model (Engel 1977) has resulted in a focus on repair of parts of physical bodies rather than a concern with the whole person or attention to mental and emotional problems. There is concern with emergencies and immediate survival issues but little interest in long-term effects of migration or rehabilitation. Ongoing medicalization has transformed many immigrants and refugees into "patients."

The ethnic heterogeneity of immigrants raises issues of meaningful communication between health care providers and immigrant patients. Health care, both preventive and curative, inevitably involves ongoing interaction between providers and receivers. Cultural distance results in problems of verbalizing the nature of health problems, of describing and explaining symptoms so that the full meaning of the illness experience can be transmitted from client to provider. Experience indicates that the provider–recipient relationship in health care is a sensitive one which requires indepth understanding of the nuances and meaning of cultural symbols, traditions, and body language (Pliskin 1987). There is a danger of elitist assumptions by providers regarding the "appropriateness" of health behavior of groups stemming from different cultural origins and a tendency on the part of health practitioners to denigrate what may appear to them to be "primitive" behavior. Indeed the patient role differs from society to society and migrants may be unfamiliar with the norms and expectations of providers.

The universalistic, culture-blind approach of western medicine has prevented particularistic orientations to the needs of specific ethnic groups. However there is more and more evidence that equality is not equity and this approach has resulted in less effective treatment to newly arrived groups with cultural patterns that differ from those of the providers. Karmi and Horton (1993) report that the British National Health Service, realizing that a "color-blind" approach results in failure to meet the needs of major parts of a multicultural population, offers patients the option to indicate their ethnic origin when they contact the health care services in an effort to assign them to a provider who speaks their language and can relate to their needs. Similarly, in Australia major segments of the health care services are structured to include practitioners from ethnic origins that match those of their clients. Such structures permit health policy makers to monitor how services are provided for different immigrant groups so as to set priorities and policies accordingly (Lerner et al. 1992; Karmi and Horton 1993).

The more general policy issue relates to questions of separatism of the health care services along ethnic lines as contrasting to a universal service which includes outreach programs focusing on specific groups. The latter carries the latent function of reinforcing a sense of identity and belongingness by means of a universal health care system which services the entire population, immigrants and veterans alike; the former – while it may provide effective services – promotes a sense of social separatism among newly arrived immigrants.

In addition to its culture-blindness, biomedicine tends also to be gender-blind. This is expressed in an "obstetrical definition" of womens' needs – a focusing on reproductive roles and "women's diseases" and an ignoring of the impact of gender as a more general organizing principle of life. Needless to say, this issue is not limited to the migration context; however, since migration poses special problems with health implications for women, gender blindness blocks attention to a variety of gender linked needs exacerbated or generated by the migration process: e.g. vulnerability to torture and sexual exploitation, malnutrition, single motherhood, exploitative employment conditions and discriminatory pay. In the context of a biomedical model, these issues are not perceived to be directly relevant to health while in the context of a bio-psychological-social model of health their relevance is self-evident.

As noted above, within the immigrant populations there are millions of illegal immigrants in numerous countries and their health status poses critical policy issues. Governments have found it extremely difficult to control the entry and ongoing presence of illegal immigrants who are protected by other immigrants and by local employers who are interested in exploiting them at low wage standards. In their efforts to avoid the authorities many "illegals" live in socially isolated, slum conditions in crowded, sub-standard housing often lacking basic amenities and services, with minimal access to social or health benefits. Some come from countries in which serious health problems including AIDS are endemic. One of the means utilized by governments to control illegal immigrants is to deny them access to public services including health care. The moral and ethical issues involved in such policies are extremely serious.

Health care providers are often characterized by "health oriented ethnocentrism," i.e. a conviction that there is only one way to care for health and that their own way is the "correct" one. There is not always sufficient awareness that alternative practices may be functional in the immigrants' cultural context even though they are different from the ones defined as acceptable in the host society. What is more, many traditional health practices and behaviors show remarkable tenacity over time. These include food preferences, patterns of nutrition, response to and expressiveness with regard to pain, traditions of infant and child care, personal health behavior, reliance on traditional and home remedies, patterns of solidarity and social support among family members, levels of dependency, occupational and gender roles, and others. Differential use of contraceptives and family planning is associated with religious orthodoxy and level of education but also with ethnic origin. Health educators who have sought to change patterns which are viewed by them as unhealthy, have frequently met with resistance and lack of success largely because some of these patterns are rooted in meaningful traditional culture contexts that remain viable in the host society.

In conclusion, I would like to refer again to the work of Aaron Antonovsky who emphasized issues of *salutogenisis* (1979, 1987). Indeed much of the discussion above has been a "litany of lament" which has focused on problems and pathologies. Antonovsky has turned our attention to the remarkable *resilience* of most migrants and to the need to learn more about the sources of that resilience which tends to promote health. In societies which have been admitting large numbers of immigrants in recent years, analysts cannot help but be struck by the ability of these newcomers to restructure their lives in a new social context and, despite losses and stressors, to show high levels of social competence and functional adequacy. Rather than focusing entirely on pathologies, we would do well to consider the social construction of the immigrants' reality in terms of the meanings they attribute to change and their ensuing capacity to transform social roles. Research to elucidate these issues would undoubtedly contribute to our understanding of the relationship between migration and health.

References

Antonovsky, A. 1979. *Health, Stress, and Coping*. San Francisco: Jossey-Bass.

——. 1987. *Unraveling the Mystery of Health*. San Francisco: Jossey-Bass.

——. 1993. "The Structure and Property of the Sense of Coherence Scale." *Social Science and Medicine* 36: 725–33.

Baider, L., P. Ever-Hadani, and A. Kaplan. 1996. "Crossing New Bridges: The Process of Adaptation and Psychological Distress of Russian Immigrants in Israel." *Psychiatry* 59: 175–83.

Baldwin-Edwards, M., and M. A. Schain. 1994. "The Politics of Immigration." *West European Politics* 17: 1–16.

Bar-Yosef, R. 1968. "Desocialization and Resocialization – The Adjustment Process of Immigrants." *International Migration Review* 2: 27–42.

Ben-David, Amith, 1996. "Cross-Cultural Differences between Russian Immigrants and Israeli College Students: The Effect of the Family on the Sense of Coherence." *Israel Journal of Psychiatry and Related Sciences* 33: 13–20.

Ben-Noun, L. L. 1994. "Chronic Diseases in Immigrants from Russia (CIS) at a Primary Care Clinic and their Sociodemographic Characteristics." *Harefuah* 127: 441–5 (Hebrew).

——. 1996. "Pattern of Visits to a Primary Care Clinic by Recent Russian Immigrants." *Harefuah* 130: 308–10 (Hebrew).

Berry, J. W., and U. Kim. 1988. "Acculturation and Mental Health." Pp. 207–306 in P. Dasen, J. W. Berry, and N. Sartorius (eds.), *Health and Cross Cultural Psychology: Towards Application*. London: Sage.

Carballo, M., M. Grocutt, and A. Hadzihasanovic. 1996. "Women and Migration: A Public Health Issue." *World Health Statistics Quarterly* 49: 158–64.

Carmon, N. (ed.). 1996. *Immigration and Integration in Post Industrial Societies*. Houndmills: Macmillan Press.

Castles, S., and M. J. Miller. 1993. *The Age of Migration*. New York: Guilford Press.

Center for Immigration Statistics. 1995. *Immigration-Related Statistics 1995*. Washington, DC.

Clinton, Davis, and Yohannes Fassil. 1992. "Health and Social Problems of Refugees." *Social Science and Medicine* 35: 507–13.

D'Avanzo, C. E., B. Frye, and R. Froman. 1994. "Culture, Stress, and Substance Use in Cambodian Refugee Women." *Journal of Studies on Alcohol* 55: 420–6.

Engel, G. L. 1977. "The Need for a New Bio-Medical Model." *Science* 196: 129–36.

Ensel, W. M., and N. Lin. 1991. "The Life Stress Paradigm and Psychological Distress." *Journal of Health and Social Behavior* 32: 321–42.

Fawcett, J. T. 1989. "Networks, Linkages, and Migration Systems." *International Migration Review* 23: 671–80.

Field, M. G. 1990. "Noble Purpose, Grand Design, Failing Execution, Mixed Results – Soviet Socialized Medicine after Seventy Years." *American Journal Of Public Health* 80: 144–5.

Flaherty, J. A., R. Kohn, I. Levav, and S. Birz, 1988. "Demoralization in Soviet-Jewish Immigrants to the United States and Israel." *Comprehensive Psychiatry* 29: 588–97.

French, J. P. R. Jr., W. Rodgers, and S. Cobb. 1974. "Adjustment as Person–Environment Fit." Pp. 315–33 in G. V. Coelho, D. A. Hamburg, and J. E. Adams (eds.), *Coping and Adaptation: Interdisciplinary Perspectives*. New York: Basic Books.

Garbe, S., and E. Garbe. 1990. "La Santé en URSS à l'heure de la Peristroika." *Cahiers De Sociologie Et De La Demographie Medicales* 30: 6–45.

Gitelman, Z. 1982. *Becoming Israeli: Political Resocialization of Soviet and American Immigrants in Israel*. New York: Praeger.

Gordon, M. 1964. *Assimilation in American Life*. New York: Oxford University Press.

Guendelman, S., P. English, and G. Chavez. 1995. "Infants of Mexican Immigrants: Health Status of an Emerging Population." *Medical Care* 33: 41–52.

Hammar, Thomas. 1989. "Comparing European and North American Immigration." *International Migration Review* 23: 631–7.

Hantman, S., Z. Solomon, and A. Prager. 1992. "The Effect of Previous Exposure to Traumatic Stress on the Reactions of the Elderly During the Gulf War." Paper presented at the 10th Congress of the Israeli Association of Gerontology, Tel Aviv, December, 1992.

Haour-Knipe, M. 1989. "International Employment and Children: Geographical Mobility and Mental Health among Children of Professionals." *Social Science and Medicine* 28: 197–205.

Hattar-Pollara, M., and A. I. Meleis. 1995. "The Stress of Immigration and the Daily Lived Experiences of Jordanian Immigrant Women in the United States." *Social Science and Medicine* 41: 261–6.

Heisler, B. S. 1992. "The Future of Immigrant Incorporation: Which Models? Which Concepts?" *International Migration Review* 26: 623–45.

Hertz, D. G. 1988. "Identity Lost and Found: Patterns of Migration and Psychological and Psychosocial Adjustment of Migrants." *Acta Psychiatrica Scandinavica*, Supplement 344: 159–65.

Horowitz, T. 1994. "The Influence of Soviet Political Culture on Immigrant Voters in Israel: The Elections of 1992." *Jews in Eastern Europe* 1: 5–22.

House, J. S. 1974. "Occupational Stress and Heart Disease: A Review." *Journal of Health and Social Behavior* 15: 12–27.

Hull, D. 1977. "Migration, Adaptation, and Illness: A Review." *Social Science and Medicine* 13A: 25–36.

Kalipeni, E., and J. Oppong. 1998. "The Refugee Crisis in Africa and Implications for Health and Disease: A Political Ecology Approach." *Social Science and Medicine* 46: 1637–53.

Karmi, G., and C. Horton. 1993. "Ethnic Monitoring in Health Service Provision." *Migration And Health* 12: 1–2. Quarterly Newsletter of the International Organization for Migration, Geneva.

Koh, K. B. 1998. "Perceived Stress, Psychopathology, and Family Support in Korean Immigrants and Non-Immigrants." *Yonsei Medical Journal* 39: 214–21.

Kohn, R., J. A. Flaherty, and I. Levav. 1989. "Somatic Symptoms Among Older Soviet Immigrants: An Exploratory Study." *International Journal of Social Psychiatry* 35: 350–60.

Kritz, M. M., and H. Zlotnik. 1992. "Global Interactions: Migration Systems, Processes, and Policies." Pp. 1–16 in M. M. Kritz, C. B. Keely, and S. M. Tomasi (eds.), *International Migrations Systems: A Global Approach*. New York: Oxford University Press.

Kuo, W. H., and Y. M. Tsai. 1986. "Social Networking, Hardiness, and Immigrants' Mental Health." *Journal of Health and Social Behavior* 27: 133–49.

Laffrey, S. C., A. I. Meleis, J. G. Lipson, M. Solomon, and P. A. Omidian. 1989. "Assessing Arab–American Health Care Needs." *Social Science and Medicine* 29: 877–83.

Lerner, Y., J. Mirsky, and M. Barasch. 1992. *New Beginnings in an Old Land: The Mental Health Challenge in Israel*. Jerusalem: JDC-Falk Institute for Mental Health and Behavioral Studies.

Levine, S., and N. A. Scotch. 1970. *Social Stress*. Chicago: Aldine.

MacCarthy, B., and J. Craissati. 1989. "Ethnic Differences in Response to Adversity: A Community Sample of Bangladeshis and their Indigenous Neighbors." *Social Psychiatry and Psychiatric Epidemiology* 24: 196–201.

Mangalam, J., and H. Schwarzweller. 1970. "Some Theoretical Guidelines toward a Sociology of Migration." *International Migration Review* 4: 5–21.

Massey, D. S., J. Arango, G. Hugo, A. Kouaouci, A. Pellegrino, and J. E. Taylor. 1993. "Theories of International Migration: A Review and Appraisal." *Population and Development Review* 19: 431–66.

Mavreas, V., and P. Bebbington. 1989. "Does the Act of Migration Provoke Psychiatric Breakdown? A Study of Greek Cypriot Immigrants." *Acta Psychiatrica Scandinavica* 80: 469–73.

Mechanic, David. 1978. *Medical Sociology*. New York: Free Press.

Muecke, Marjorie A. 1992. "New Paradigms for Refugee Health Problems." *Social Science and Medicine* 35: 507–13.

Munroe-Blum, H., M. H. Boyle, D. R. Offord, and N. Kates. 1989. "Immigrant Children: Psychiatric Disorder, School Performance, and Service Utilization." *American Journal of Orthopsychiatry* 59: 510–19.

Noh, S., and W. R. Avison. 1996. "Asian Immigrants and the Stress Process: A Study of Koreans in Canada." *Journal of Health and Social Behavior* 37: 192–206.

O'Brien, P. 1992. "German-Polish Migration: The Elusive Search for a German Nation-State." *International Migration Review* 26: 373–87.

Park, R., and E. Burgess. 1921. *Introduction to the Science of Sociology*. Chicago: University of Chicago Press.

Pearlin, L. I., and Carmin Schooler. 1978. "The Structure of Coping." *Journal of Health and Social Behavior* 23: 2–17.

Pearlin, L. I. 1989. "The Sociological Study of Stress." *Journal of Health and Social Behavior* 30: 241–56.

Pliskin, K. L. 1987. *Silent Boundaries: Cultural Constraints on Sickness and Diagnosis in Israel*. New Haven: Yale University Press.

Portes, A. 1989. "Contemporary Immigration: Theoretical Perspectives on its Determinants and Modes of Incorporation." *International Migration Review* 23: 606–30.

Price, C. 1969. "The Study of Assimilation." In J. A. Jackson (ed.), *Migration*. New York: Cambridge University Press.

Richmond, A. 1984. "Socio-Cultural Adaptation and Conflict in Immigrant-Receiving Countries." *International Social Science Journal* 36: 519–36.

Rose, A. 1969. *Migrants in Europe*. Minneapolis: University of Minnesota Press.

Rowland, D., and A. V. Telyukov. 1991. "Soviet Health Care from Two Perspectives." *Health Affairs* 10: 71–86.

Sabatello, E. 1995. "Continuity and Change in Reproductive and Abortion Patterns of the Soviet Immigrants in Israel." *Social Science and Medicine* 40: 117–24.

Salt, John. 1989. "A Comparative Overview of International Trends and Types: 1950–80." *International Migration Review* 23: 431–56.

Scott, R., and A. Howard. 1970. "Models of Stress." Pp. 259–78 in S. Levine and N. A. Scotch (eds.), *Social Stress*. Chicago: Aldine.

Shuval, J. T., E. J. Markus, and J. Dotan. 1975. *Patterns of Adjustment of Soviet Immigrants to Israel*. Jerusalem: Israel Institute of Applied Social Research.

Shuval, J. T., 1992. *Social Dimensions of Health: The Israeli Experience*. Westport: Praeger.

——. 1995. "Migrants, Refugees, and Health: Some Policy Implications of Israel's Experience." Pp. 198–212 in G. Gallagher and J. Subedi, *Global Perspectives on Health Care*. Englewood Cliffs, NJ: Prentice-Hall.

——. 1998. "Migration to Israel: The Mythology of 'Uniqueness.'" *International Migration* 36: 3–26.

Shuval, J. T., and J. H. Bernstein. 1997. *Immigrant Physicians: Former Soviet Doctors in Israel, Canada, and the United States*. Westport: Praeger-Greenwood.

Sinnerbrink, I., D. Silove, A. Field, Z. Steel, and V. Manicavasagar. 1997. "Compounding of Pre-migration Trauma and Post-Migration Stress in Asylum Seekers." *Journal of Psychology* 131: 463–70.

Teitelbaum, M. S., and M. Weiner (eds.). 1995. *Threatened Peoples, Threatened Borders*. New York: W.W. Norton.

Wessen, A. E. 1971. "The Role of Migrant Studies in Epidemiological Research." *Israel Journal of Medical Sciences* 7: 1584–91.

Williams, C. L. and J. W. Berry. 1991. "Primary Prevention of Acculturative Stress Among Refugees: Application of Psychological Theory and Practice." *American Psychologist* 46: 632–41.

Zambrana, R. E., K. Ell, C. Dorrington, L. Wachsman, and D. Hodge. 1994. "The Relationship Between Psychosocial Status of Immigrant Latino Mothers and Use of Emergency Pediatric Services." *Health and Social Work* 19: 93–102.

Zolberg, A. R. 1989. "The Next Waves: Migration Theory for a Changing World." *International Migration Review* 23: 403–30.

8

Health Professions and Occupations

Elianne Riska

Over the past 30 years, sociologists have debated the state and future of the health professions. While the theoretical discussion in the 1960s was characterized by a belief in the future of powerful professions, the debate in the field since the mid-1980s has predicted the demise of such groups. It has even been argued that the distinction between health professions and occupations is an artifact of the vocabulary of sociologists. In fact some languages, such as French, make no distinction between a profession and an occupation and have but one word for both concepts.

Here the theoretical discussion in the field of the past decades is reviewed. First, the classics that focused on the medical profession are described, followed by an overview of the theoretical reinvigoration of the field that took place during the ten-year period between about 1975 and 1985. Finally, the main strands of research on health professions and occupations in the 1990s are presented.

PHYSICIAN-CENTERED THEORIES: HEALTH CARE AS THE CARE OF AND TRUST IN THE PHYSICIAN

The sociology of professions is a rather narrow field of research despite its vast literature. It covers economic restructuring and changes in knowledge and service delivery by trained experts. There is a clearly identifiable scholarly debate in the field. In fact, few other fields in sociology present such a linear development of the theoretical discussion as in the sociology of the professions. Each decade has been characterized by a dominant theoretical perspective that has first been gradually challenged and then superseded by alternative interpretations. These have subsequently become dominant in the field and have served as the interpretative frameworks for empirical research. The focus of this review will therefore be on the theoretical perspectives rather than the ensuing empirical studies where single health professions or occupations have served as case studies.

Seven theoretical perspectives on the power and structure of health professions and occupations will be reviewed: the functionalist, interactionist, neo-Weberian, neo-Marxist, feminist, social constructionist, and neo-system theories. A summary of the characteristics of these theoretical frameworks is presented in figure 8.1 that lists each perspective by level of analysis, the assumptions about the structure underlying the power of various health professions, and the characteristics of the internal structure of health professions and their relations to each other.

The classical theory on professions in sociology derives from a functionalist sociological approach represented by Emile Durkheim and Talcott Parsons. For Durkheim, the role of intermediary organizations and the organic solidarity, growing out of the modern division of labor, signaled the rise of the functions that professions and occupations would come to occupy in modern society. A functionalist perspective on professions was also the interpretative framework used by the American sociologist Talcott Parsons (1949, 1951) in his work on professions. Parsons saw in the profession of law, but especially in the medical profession, the prototype of occupations based on expertise in modern society. The role of the professions was based on expert knowledge, a service- and collective-orientation that guaranteed the kind of expertise and trust that individuals needed to handle their intimate problems. The professions harbored a particular relationship of trust *vis-à-vis* the client compared to the morality of the businessmen whose interest in profit was the underlying motive for a different kind of behavior. Hence, Parsons distinguished the "professional man" from the "business man." He viewed the former as an altruistic servant of his clients, whereas the latter pursued his own self-interest (Parsons 1949: 186). Although a consensual view of society and a view of professions based on mutual trust between the client and the professional has been attributed to Parsons, Parsons was not unaware of the special character of the American medical profession. He pointed to the growth of the American industrial economy characterized by giant corporations and mass commodity production, while at the same time the medical profession was acting outside of this industrial economy and even defending the entrepreneurial character of American medicine and its ties to the private character of the family and the residential community (Parsons 1963: 26).

The functionalist theory of professions became the dominant perspective for studying the medical profession in the 1950s and 1960s. Yet it is important to remember that another perspective was also launched during those years, representing a social interactionist perspective. Everett Hughes's (1958) collection of essays *Men and their Work* offered an alternative interpretation of work, occupations, and professions. For Hughes (1958: 53), the focus of a study of any kind of occupations was the "social drama of work." In his view, most occupations bring together people in definable roles and it is in the interaction that the content of work and status are defined. An occupation is not a priori by means of its expertise and knowledge a profession but a social status that is socially constructed (Hughes 1958: 44–5). According to Hughes (1958: 48), the aim of the study of work of occupations and professions should therefore be "to *penetrate more deeply* into the personal and social drama of work, to understand the social and social-psychological arrangements and devices by which men make their work tolerable, or even glorious to themselves and others."

The dramaturgical approach to health care as work was also represented by Erving Goffman (1961). He viewed an occupation as a service relation between the server and the served. Similarly to Hughes, Goffman (1961: 325–6) did not view professions as intrinsically distinct from occupations but rather as a particular type of personal-service occupation based on expertise. An expert provided a special type of "tinkering service," a service that Goffman defined in the following way: "the ideals underlying expert servicing in our society are rooted in the case where the server has a complex physical system to repair, construct, or tinker with – the system here being the client's personal object or possession." Tinkering services contain a series of distinct phases, which constitute the "repair cycle" (Goffman 1961: 330). The medical version of the tinkering-services model confronts, however, a major problem – the body. It is a possession of the served that cannot be left under the care of the server while the client goes about his or her other business. A large part of the medical encounter contains therefore "non-person treatment" or ways of handling the patient/the body as "a possession someone has left behind" (Goffman 1961: 341). Furthermore, the verbal part of the server's exchange contains three components: a technical part that contains the relevant repair information, a contractual part that specifies the terms of the repair task, and the sociable part that involves courtesies, civilities, and signs of deference (Goffman 1961: 328–9). During the past decade, the dilemma of the presence of the body in medical encounters and the physician's preference to focus on the technical part while being oblivious to the social part of the verbal exchange have been in focus of a whole new genre of research. Based on the interactionist framework, several studies have examined the interaction between clients and health care experts. A new method – conversational analysis – has been one of the outcomes of this research (Atkinson and Heritage 1984; Silverman 1987; Peräkylä 1995; 1997; Psathas 1995).

While Goffman has continued to inspire sociologists interested in the dynamics of the patient–physician relationship, Hughes's work seems to have been less referred to in the 1970s and 1980s. Those were the decades of rebuttals of the functionalist view of professions, much of it inspired by Hughes's work. The initial challenge came from Eliot Freidson's book *The Profession of Medicine* (1970). Freidson challenged the basic assumptions of the Parsonian model of the physician's behavior, that is, its normative basis. For Freidson and the approaches that were to follow, the assumption was that the medical profession's power was based on its appeal to its service orientation and scientific expertise that legitimated its mandate and autonomy. Yet the profession was also seen as a group acting to preserve and confirm this position.

Later critics have argued that Freidson's theoretical foundation is diffuse (Coburn 1992) and even inconsistent, not to mention that it completely lacks an empirical foundation. Such criticism seems to miss the point about the role of *The Profession of Medicine* (Freidson 1970) and its path-breaking influence in the field. At the time it was published, it offered a fresh look at an old theme and showed a way forward from the theoretical stand-still that had characterized the field for well over a decade. Freidson's book sparked a debate in American research on health professions that went on for over two decades. The positive aspect of this debate was the ensuing alternative interpretations of the power of the medical profession and a mushrooming of case studies of the development and power of the medical profession in various countries. The drawback of this debate was that it retained the focus on only one health profession – physicians – and postponed in this way the exploration of the character, clientele, and function of other health professions and alternative health occupations.

The intense phase of research on the American medical profession that followed between 1975 and 1985 was in retrospect related to the dramatic change of the American health care system that began during those years. There were two main trends in this research: one approach focused on the extraordinary power that the medical profession had acquired in the American health care system, and the other projected the demise of this power as a sign of a structural change of American health care characterized by a bureaucratic and consumer-challenging structure. The neo-Weberian perspective became the major theoretical framework for those who tried to explain the united power of the medical profession and the challenges or professional projects pursued by other health professions and occupations. Larson's (1977) work was influential in starting this genre of research, and the concepts professional projects and social closure were used to describe the jurisdictions, mandates, licensure, and power of professions *vis-à-vis* occupations (see figure 8.1). This theoretical framework has been the one most used in empirical studies of the history of the (allopathic) medical profession and of how it succeeded in becoming a united professional body among competing medical sects in various national contexts. It has also been applied in studies on how certain types of physicians managed to achieve a specialty status, and on the professionalization of a variety of health occupations and the steps they had to take to achieve a professional status. Furthermore, this framework has been used by American and European scholars to explain the division of labor within their health care systems (e.g. Wilsford 1991; Hafferty and McKinlay 1993; Moran and Wood 1993; Johnson et al. 1995).

The neo-Marxist perspective on the power of the medical profession, introduced by McKinlay and his colleagues (McKinlay and Arches 1985; McKinlay and Stoeckle 1988; McKinlay and Marceau 1998), foresaw the gradual decline of the professional dominance of the American medical profession due to the growing corporate and bureaucratic structure of American medicine. American physicians, they argued, were increasingly becoming salaried and the power was no longer in the hands of the profession but in those of large health care corporations that composed the expanding medical industrial complex (see figure 8.1). This process was not an isolated American event but a more global development or as they argued "no country or health care system can be considered immune. Indeed US experience may be instructive for doctors and

Perspective	Underlying structure	Focus of analysis	Structure of the profession
Functionalist: Parsons	Normative consensus	Professional role of physicians	United body
Interactionist:			
Hughes	Social drama of work	Occupational culture	Contractual and relational power
Goffman		Tinkering service	
Freidson	Professional knowledge	Medical work	Professional dominance of physicians
Neo-Weberian	Modern society and rationalization	Professional projects	United profession due to professional closure
Neo-Marxist	Capitalist economy	Corporate and bureaucratic structure of health care	Corporate control of health care and proletarianization of physicians
Feminist	Patriarchy/gendered structures	Gendered organization of health care	Gendered Professional projects
Postmodern/social constructionist	The medical discourse/the medical gaze	Discursive practices/strategies	Fragmented character of power
Neo-system theories	Marketization of medicine	Jurisdictions and allies	Pluralist notion of power

Figure 8.1   Theoretical perspectives on the power of health professions

health care researchers in other national settings as to what they may expect" (McKinlay and Stoeckle 1988: 191).

This debate originated in the responses to Freidson's (1984, 1985) addendum to his original monopolization or professional dominance thesis. In his addendum – the so-called restratification thesis – Freidson proposed that despite changes, the American medical profession would be able to maintain its dominance because it had adapted by differentiating into three segments, each with its specific task: an administrative segment, a knowledge elite, and a rank-and-file group. This internal differentiation would guarantee a status quo of the profession's traditional power position. Although such an internal differentiation indeed has taken place, critics have argued that the managerial positions are no longer filled by physicians and that the knowledge elite itself is internally differentiated into small expert circles, with their own associations and little affinity to advance the interests of the profession as a whole. Furthermore, the statistical facts have added strong evidence to McKinlay's argument: The growth of corporatized medical care and the proportion of salaried physicians have increased dramatically in American health care during the past 15 years. For example, in 1983, only 23 percent of American physicians practiced as salaried employees but in 1994 the figure had already reached 42 percent and it is steadily increasing among the younger physicians, the majority of whom now practice as salaried employees (Kletke et al. 1996: 557).

A more general theory of professions was introduced by Abbott (1988) in *The System of Professions*. According to Abbott, the power of a profession lies in its jurisdiction and the profession is linked to other professions through a system of professions, where boundaries are constantly negotiated (Abbott 1988: 33). This approach is exemplified by three case studies: a presentation of the historical roots of the jurisdiction of information professions, law, and experts on personal problems. In his more recent work, Abbott (1999) has tended to move even further into a neo-functionalist framework by viewing the "system" as an "ecology" with fluid boundaries between interacting groups and audiences. Abbott's model seems to have been more used in studies of service occupations than in studies of health professions or occupations that have tended to be well organized and strive for professional recognition and status (Benoit 1994). As MacDonald (1995: 14–17) suggests, Abbott's concept of system is a theoretical hybrid, suggesting partly an interdependence (systems theory) and partly a market model of actors (Weberian theory). A similar hybrid is Light's concept of "countervailing powers" which he, by references, locates in the neo-Marxist tradition of professional theory (e.g. Light 1995: 26), even though his own theoretical arguments suggest a pluralist perception of power in the area of health care. In this respect, both Abbott and Light fall into the category of neo-system theories listed in figure 8.1.

GENDER AND HEALTH CARE WORK

All the theoretical perspectives mentioned above have been gender-neutral or tacitly gendered in the sense that physicians have been viewed as men and subordinated health professions as composed of women (which until recently has been a statistical fact in most countries). Yet this gendered division of labor was not problematized and explained but taken as a given in mainstream theories on medical work. Already in the 1970s, feminist scholars began to challenge the gendered character of medical work and to portray medicine as a patriarchal institution (e.g. Ehrenreich and English 1978; Oakley 1980) and the medical profession as composed of men (figure 8.1). Furthermore, nursing has not only been portrayed as a caring profession but also as a subordinated female profession (Abbott and Wallace 1990; Witz 1992; Davies 1995). The identification by British sociologists (e.g. Witz 1992; Davies 1996) of the gendered structure of medicine, the gendered character of professional projects in health care, and the gendering of profession, has constituted a significant new addition in the otherwise gender-neutral literature on health professions and occupations. According to Davies (1996: 623), "acknowledging that what contemporary professions profess is masculine gender may then prove to mark an altogether new stage in the sociology of professions."

Yet the increasing number of women in the medical profession in most countries has constituted a welcomed statistical figure (see table 8.1) for many feminists, but also a complex question in feminist terms. Will medicine remain a masculine culture, as propagated by the patriarchal theorists, despite women's presence at various levels in the medical profession, or will women constitute a vanguard that will change the culture of the profession as a whole? These issues have been raised over the past decade by many women's health advocates and researchers alike. Empirical studies on women physicians in various countries tend to confirm a drastic increase of women in medicine since 1970, but marked gender segregation of medical specialization and type of practice is still found in the United States, Great Britain, and the Nordic countries (Lorber 1984, 1993; Riska 1993; Pringle 1998). Women physicians tend to practice in specialties that fit their assumed, traditional female-gender qualities: they tend to work in primary-care areas that are high-interaction fields and other fields that cater to children and elderly, such as pediatrics, child psychiatry, and geriatrics. By contrast, low-interaction fields and fields associated with heroic medicine tend to be male-dominated, such as surgery, sports medicine, and internal medicine.

Two types of explanation have been given for the gender-segregated character of medical work: a structural and a voluntaristic. The structural explanation points to barriers that prevent women from advancing in medicine, e.g. lack of mentors (Lorber 1993). The voluntaristic interpretation covers a broad range of frameworks, including the socialization theory and essentialist explanations. According to the former, women are socialized to follow stereotypic gender expectations and tend therefore to make occupational choices that fit these expectations. According to the latter, women are essentially different from men – more empathic, less interested in the heroic aspects of medicine than men – and tend therefore to choose specialties that provide them opportunities to practice the kind of medicine that they prefer and in areas where they can use their gender-specific skills (Altecruse and McDermott 1987: 85).

Table 8.1 Percentage of women physicians in various countries

Country	Percentage of women physicians	Year
Nordic countries		
Denmark	35	1999
Finland	49	1999
Iceland	20	1999
Norway	30	1999
Sweden	38	1999
Great Britain	28	1990
Italy	20	1990
France	31	1990
Germany	26	1990
Spain	41	1990
Soviet Union	68	1990
United States	17	1994

Source: Nordic Medical Associations 1996: 44; 1999; Bickel and Kopriva 1993: 142; Kauppinen et al. 1996: 166.

THE DIVISION OF LABOR IN HEALTH CARE AND ALTERNATIVE MEDICINE

The feminist research on health professions has raised the issue of the broader underlying power structures in health care. While the American theorizing and research has almost exclusively focused on the medical profession, it is characteristic of British research that it has covered a broad range of health care practitioners. In the British context, Freidson's work did not have as much influence as other representatives of the power approach: Johnson (1972) and Parkin (1979). Parkin's development of the Weberian notion of closure became a framework for studying intra-and inter-professional competition and control and a useful analytical tool for the empirical study of a variety of health professions and occupations. The broader division of labor in health care seems to characterize most British research on health professions and occupations and includes even lay carers as health workers (Stacey 1988). This broader view of the division of labor in health care has been evident in studies that have covered single professions. Dingwall's studies on health visitors (1979) and nursing (Dingwall et al. 1988) were suggestive of such a framework. Furthermore, traditional views of nurses as a passive and homogeneous group have been challenged by British sociologists, who have pointed out the social class and race divisions within nursing (Carpenter 1993) and reconceptualized nurses as actors dealing with their subordinated status as a group of women (Porter 1992; Witz 1992; Davies 1995).

The specific feature of British sociological research on health professions and occupations is, however, its coverage of alternative medicine and its practitioners – homeopaths, chiropractors, acupuncturists, osteopaths (e.g. Saks 1992, 1995; Sharma 1995) – compared to the American focus on predominantly the practitioners of bio-medicine. Studies on alternative practitioners tend to remind its readers of the power structure of regular medicine and its specific therapy tradition in western societies compared to developing societies. Even in western societies, regular medicine has become more tolerant of the coexistence of alternative therapies and most European societies have allowed some of these therapies to be reimbursed/delivered within the the national health system/ insurance schemes.

THE SOCIAL CONSTRUCTION OF MEDICINE

The social constructionist perspective on medical work is not primarily focused on the medical profession but rather on medicine as an institution of social control and the medical profession as its agent (figure 8.1). Some perceive the central task to be the identification of the cultural basis of contemporary medical knowledge (bio-medicine) and practice, while others take an interactionist stance and suggest that the sociological inquiry should focus on how medicine is constructed and confirmed in the interaction between the patient and the physician. In the 1990s, these approaches have found a common denominator.

The body is seen as the site and contested terrain where the cultural conceptions of illness and disease, the lay and professional knowledge, the taken-for-granted character of biology and culture, and the readings of signs of symptoms and experience of illness are projected and negotiated.

In the literature on medical/health sociology, the social constructionist view traces back to the Brandeis school of medical sociology represented by the concept of medicalization and medicine as an institution of social control (Zola 1972; Conrad 1992, 1999). The medicalization thesis is based on the notion of the power of the medical profession to define and even expand its jurisdiction to include phenomena that are social rather than biological. A refurbished version of this thesis is Conrad's (1999) gene theory, by means of which he denotes a trend in society to present a new reductionist explanation for illnesses and behaviors supplanting the germ theory: the media and public discourse present genes as the cause not only for diseases but also for a variety of behaviors, such as alcoholism, mental illness, homosexuality.

As Lupton (1998) points out, there is a clear difference between the social constructionist perspective and its medicalization argument and the Foucauldian notion of medical knowledge and the power of medicine and the medical profession. While the medicalization thesis presents medical knowledge as a form of ideology, there is a tacit assumption that lay and experiential knowledge represents a more "authentic" medical knowledge, at least as represented in the works of Illich (1976), Fisher (1986), and Martin (1989) to mention a few. In these works, the medical profession is viewed as an all-powerful body and patients as almost the "victims" of the practice of the physicians' abstract medical knowledge (Atkinson 1995: 33). Current society, characterized as "late modernity," is predicted to provide a fertile ground for a process of demedicalization, whereby a lay "reskilling" – viewed as the reappropriation of the skills and knowledge about health and the body – is going to take place (Williams and Calnan 1996: 1616).

The Foucauldian view, deriving from the works of the French philosopher Michel Foucault (1975), presents medical knowledge as a discourse, a way of seeing and reading the body. The medical profession is the applier of a medical discourse, which in the age of bio-medicine is a certain medical gaze that constructs the body as a body of organs and tissues. The task of the physician is to read the signs of the disease and thereby read the body and the disease within it. The power of the medical profession and the way that it has organized medicine around this medical discourse have been in focus of a number of sociological studies. For example, Armstrong (1983) has used the Foucauldian framework to explain the rise of the British medical profession, the public health orientation within the British national health system, and the more recent preventive and lifestyle orientation of medicine that he calls "surveillance medicine" (Armstrong 1995). Others have looked at how certain groups of specialist physicians, for example surgeons (Fox 1992) and haematologists (Atkinson 1995) construct their work by means of certain discourses and discursive strategies. The power of the medical expert is perceived as embedded in the medical context, a characteristic that Atkinson (1995) calls the "liturgy of the clinic."

The Foucauldian view of the power of the medical profession seems at first sight similar to the medicalization thesis. Yet, in the Foucauldian approach the concept of power is seen as fragmented: power is a relationship that is localized, dispersed, and operates through various practices (Lupton 1998). There exist competing discourses, even if the medical discourse is the dominant one. Furthermore, practices cannot merely be conceptualized as expansive and exploitative characteristics of the medical profession since they operate as disciplinary regimes at different levels, including self-regulatory practices in constructing the self. In this regard, the patient is not primarily an object of a medical discourse. The status of patienthood presupposes an internalization of the concepts and the gaze of medicine but entails also its contestation. As Lupton (1998: 107) notes, according to the Foucauldian perspective, so-called de-medicalization does not lead to more "authentic" modes of subjectivity and embodiment but merely to a different frame of reference.

CONCLUSIONS

This chapter has reviewed seven theoretical perspectives on the power and structure of health professions and occupations: the functionalist, the interactionist, the neo-Weberian, the neo-Marxist, the feminist, the social constructionist perspectives, and neo-system theories. A summary of the characteristics of these theoretical frameworks, shown in figure 8.1, lists each perspective by level and focus of analysis, the assumptions about the structure underlying the power of various health professions, and the characteristics of the internal structure of health professions and their relations to each other. The advent of this field of sociological research was based on the functionalist framework, which saw the institutionalization and authority of the medical profession as based on the trust in the profession. These assumptions were, and continue to be, challenged by alternative theoretical frameworks. The issues of the benevolence of and the trust in the medical profession continue to characterize the debate.

American research in this field has been heavily focused on the medical profession. The concept of "medicalization" was introduced early as an analytical tool to describe the unique power of the medical profession not only in its own domain but also in its expansionist endeavors to integrate many aspects of life and behavior under its jurisdiction, as, for example, birth, adolescence, aging, alcoholism, and PMS. Feminist researchers have shown that these expansionist endeavors have primarily been directed at women's bodies and therefore perceive medicalization as evidence that medicine is a patriarchal institution. Empowerment of women as patients and the care by other health professions – midwives and nurses – and practitioners of alternative medicine became a central theme in the non-physician-oriented research.

British research on health professions and occupations has been less physician-centered than American research and has presented a broad view of the division of labor between various health professions, which even included lay carers as health workers. Furthermore, European, Canadian, and Latin American research has given the state a central role in shaping the conditions of health professions (see Jones 1991; Hafferty and McKinlay 1993; Johnson et al. 1995) and for obvious reasons: health care systems with publicly financed and run medical care, with a large fraction of physicians being salaried employees, and public health nurses and general practioners working at local health centers constitute a different arena for the relationships between various health professions than the market-oriented American health care context. This research has also illustrated how external economic and political conditions have influenced the internal divisions within the medical profession in, for example, Spain, Israel, Belgium, and the Netherlands (Rodriguez 1995; Shuval 1995; Schepers and Casparie 1997).

There are, however, a number of issues that have been but sparsely covered in current research on health professions and occupations. There are, for example, only a few sociological studies of work pursued in the hospital setting. A number of sociological classics on the hospital as a social organization – studies on work done at the ward and on the external ties of hospitals to the community – were done in the 1960s, but presently this institutional setting of medical work seems mostly to be a research field of health services researchers. While clinics and office-based practice have been in the focus of sociologists using an ethnographic and symbolic-interactionist approach, the hospital setting has received less attention. The changing nature of the hospital (Armstrong 1998) might partly explain this void.

Another area related to hospital medicine is the vast array of health professionals, who do work that does not entail any caring. Laboratory medicine, medical research, and health care managers include a variety of occupational groups that have diverse educational backgrounds and occupational loyalties (Nettleton 1995). These groups have so far been largely ignored in the sociology of health professions and occupations. Furthermore, efforts to control and regulate the therapy traditions of physicians by means of evidence-based data sources constitute a new feature of public health policy. In many countries (e.g. Sweden and Canada), evidence-based medicine and its emphasis on clinical guidelines and rules for "good practice" represents a professional reform movement, which is composed of an interesting coalition of various health professionals. But to what extent these endeavors constitute a symbolic or real control over the clinical and professional autonomy of the medical profession is an issue that needs further sociological study. Obviously, more studies on the occupational culture of specialist physicians and other health professions will provide a greater understanding of how health workers construct the content of their work, and how they accommodate with or overrun the effects of the large structural changes that are currently taking place in most health care systems. Here the work by Hughes, Goffman, and Foucault provide useful theoretical frameworks for understanding the workplace, the larger institutional settings, and the cultural arrangements and practices embedded in health care work.

The interactionist and phenomenological accounts of the work conducted in health care settings provide a much needed understanding of what Hughes and Goffman called the social drama of work. In these days of the revival of the micro-level analysis of health care work, it is, however, important to continue the examination of two powerful macro-level systems – the market-driven economic system and the gender system. Both systems shape the broader structural framework within which the members of health professions and occupations conduct their everyday work.

References

Abbott, Andrew. 1988. *The System of Professions*. Chicago: University of Chicago Press.
——. 1999. "System Revised: A New View of the Ecology of Professions." Paper presented at the 94th annual meeting of the American Sociological Association in Chicago, August 6–10.
Abbott, Pamela and Claire Wallace (eds.). 1990. *The Sociology of the Caring Professions*. London: Falmer Press.
Altecruse, Joan M. and Susanne W. McDermott. 1987. "Contemporary Concerns of Women in Medicine." Pp. 65–88 in S. V. Rosser (ed.), *Feminism within Science and Health Professions: Overcoming Resistance*. Oxford: Pergamon Press.
Armstrong, David. 1983. *The Political Anatomy of the Body: Medical Knowledge in Britain in the Twentieth Century*. Cambridge: Cambridge University Press.
——. 1995. "The Rise of Surveillance Medicine." *Sociology of Health and Illness* 17: 393–404.
——. 1998. "Decline of the Hospital: Reconstructing Institutional Dangers." *Sociology of Health and Illness* 20: 445–57.
Atkinson, J. Maxwell and John Heritage (eds.). 1984. *Structures of Social Action: Studies of Conversation Analysis*. Cambridge: Cambridge University Press.
Atkinson, Paul. 1995. *Medical Talk and Medical Work: The Liturgy of the Clinic*. Thousand Oaks, CA: Sage.
Benoit, Cecilia. 1994. "Paradigm Conflict in the Sociology of Service Professions: Midwifery as a Case Study." *Canadian Journal of Sociology* 19: 303–29.
Bickel, Janet and Phyllis R. Kopriva. 1993. "A Statistical Perspective on Gender in Medicine." *Journal of the American Medical Women's Association* 48: 141–4.
Carpenter, Mick. 1993. "The Subordination of Nurses in Health Care: Towards a Social Divisions Approach." Pp. 95–130 in E. Riska and K. Wegar (eds.), *Gender, Work and Medicine: Women and the Medical Division of Labour*. London: Sage.
Coburn, David. 1992. "Freidson Then and Now: An 'Internalist' Critique of Freidson's Past and Present Views of the Medical Profession." *International Journal of Health Services* 22: 492–512.
Conrad, Peter. 1992. "Medicalization and Social Control." *Annual Review of Sociology* 18: 209–32.
——. 1999. "A Mirage of Genes." *Sociology of Health and Illness* 21: 228–41.
Davies, Celia. 1995. *Gender and the Professional Predicament in Nursing*. Buckingham: Open University Press.
——. 1996. "The Sociology of Professions and the Profession of Gender." *Sociology* 30: 661–78.
Dingwall, Robert. 1979. *The Social Organization of Health Visiting*. Beckenham: Croom Helm.
Dingwall, Robert, Anne M. Rafferty, and Charles Webster. 1988. *An Introduction to the Social History of Nursing*. London: Routledge.
Ehrenreich, Barbara and Deirdre English. 1978. *For Her Own Good: 150 Years of Experts' Advice to Women*. New York: Anchor Press.

Fisher, Sue. 1986. *In the Patient's Best Interest: Women and the Politics of Medical Decisions.* New Brunswick, NJ: Rutgers University Press.

Foucault, Michel. 1975. *The Birth of the Clinic: An Archaelogy of Medical Perception.* New York: Vintage Books.

Fox, Nicholas J. 1992. *The Social Meaning of Surgery.* Milton Keynes: Open University Press.

Freidson, Eliot. 1970. *The Profession of Medicine.* New York: Mead and Company.

——. 1984. "The Changing Nature of Professional Control." *Annual Review of Sociology* 10: 1–20.

——. 1985. "The Reorganization of the Medical Profession." *Medical Care Review* 42: 11–35.

Goffman 1961. *Asylums.* Garden City, NY: Anchor Books.

Hafferty, Frederic W. and John B. McKinlay (eds.). 1993. *The Changing Medical Profession: An International Perspective.* New York: Oxford University Press.

Hughes, Everett C. 1958. *Men and their Work.* Glencoe, IL: Free Press.

Illich, Ivan. 1976. *Medical Nemesis.* New York: Pantheon Books.

Johnson, Terry. 1972 . *Professions and Power.* London: Macmillan.

Johnson, Terry, Gerry Larkin, and Mike Saks (eds.). 1995. *Health Professions and the State in Europe.* London: Routledge.

Jones, Anthony (ed.). 1991. *Professions and the State: Expertise and Autonomy in the Soviet Union and Eastern Europe.* Philadelphia: Temple University Press.

Kauppinen, Kaisa, Lyudmila Yasnaya, and Irja Kandolin. 1996. "Medical Doctors in Moscow – Their Work, Family, and Well-being." Pp. 164–74 in A. Rotkirch and E. Haavio-Mannila (eds.), *Women's Voices in Russia Today.* Aldershot: Dartmouth.

Kletke, Philip R., David W. Emmons, and Kurt D. Gillis. 1996. "Physicians' Practice Arrangements: From Owners to Employees." *Journal of the American Medical Association* 276: 555–60.

Larson, Magali Sarfatti. 1977. *The Rise of Professionalism.* Berkeley: University of California Press.

Light, Donald. 1995. "Countervailing Powers: A Framework for Professions in Transition." Pp. 25–41 in T. Johnson, G. Larkin, and M. Saks (eds.), *Health Professions and the State in Europe.* London: Routledge.

Lorber, Judith. 1984. *Women Physicians.* London: Tavistock.

——. 1993. "Why Women will Never be True Equals in the American Medical Profession." Pp. 62–76 in E. Riska and K. Wegar (eds.), *Gender, Work and Medicine: Women and the Medical Division of Labour.* London: Sage.

Lupton, Deborah. 1998. "Foucault and the Medicalization Critique." Pp. 94–110 in A. Petersen and R. Bunton (eds.), *Foucault: Health and Medicine.* London: Routledge.

MacDonald, Keith. 1995. *The Sociology of the Professions.* London: Sage.

Martin, Emily. 1989. *The Woman in the Body: A Cultural Analysis of Reproduction.* Boston: Beacon Press.

McKinlay, John B. and Joan Arches. 1985. "Towards the Proletarianization of Physicians." *International Journal of Health Services* 15: 161–95.

McKinlay, John B. and John D. Stoeckle. 1988. "Corporatization and the Social Transformation of Doctoring." *International Journal of Health Services* 18: 191–205.

McKinlay, John B. and Lisa D. Marceau. 1998. "The End of the Golden Age of Doctoring." Paper presented at the annual meeting of the American Public Health Association, Washington, DC, November 1998.

Moran, Michael and Bruce Wood. 1993. *States, Regulation and the Medical Profession.* Buckingham: Open University Press.

Nettleton, Sarah. 1995. *Sociology of Health and Illness.* Cambridge: Polity Press.

Nordic Medical Associations. 1996. *Den Framtida Läkararbetsmarknaden i Norden.* Stockholm: Norstedts tryckeri.

——. 1999. *Physicians in the Nordic Countries.* Leaflet.

Oakley, Ann. 1980. *Women Confined. Towards a Sociology of Childbirth.* Oxford: Martin Robertson.

Parkin, Frank. 1979. *Marxism and Class Theory: A Bourgeois Critique.* London: Tavistock.

Parsons, Talcott. 1949. *Essays in Sociological Theory: Pure and Applied.* Glencoe, IL: Free Press.

——. 1951. *The Social System.* New York: Free Press.

——. 1963. "Social Change and Medical Organization in the United States: A Sociological Perspective." *Annals of the American Academy of Political and Social Sciences* 346: 21–33.

Peräkylä, Anssi. 1995. *AIDS Counselling: Institutional Interaction and Clinical Practice.* Cambridge: Cambridge University Press.

——. 1997. "Conversational Analysis: A New Model of Research in the Doctor–Patient Communication." *Journal of the Royal Society of Medicine* 90: 205–8.

Porter, Sam. 1992. "Women in a Woman's Job: The Gendered Experience of Nurses." *Sociology of Health and Illness* 14: 510–27.

Pringle, Rosemary. 1998. *Sex and Medicine: Gender, Power and Authority in the Medical Profession.* Cambridge: Cambridge University Press.

Psathas, George. 1995. *Conversation Analysis: The Study of Talk in Interaction.* Sage: London.

Riska, Elianne. 1993. "The Medical Profession in the Nordic Countries." Pp. 150–61 in F. W. Hafferty and J. B. McKinlay (eds.), *The Changing Medical Profession: An International Perspective.* New York: Oxford University.

Rodriguez, Joseph. 1995. "The Politics of the Spanish Medical Profession: Democratization and the Construction of the National System." Pp. 141–61 in T. Johnson, G. Larkin, and M. Saks (eds.), *Health Professions and the State in Europe.* London: Routledge.

Saks, Mike (ed.). 1992. *Alternative Medicine in Britain.* Oxford: Claredon Press.

——. 1995. *Professions and the Public Interest: Medical Power, Altruism, and Alternative Medicine.* London: Routledge.

Schepers, Rita M. and Anton F. Casparie. 1997. "Continuity or Discontinuity in the Self-Regulation of the Belgian and Dutch Medical Professions." *Sociology of Health and Illness* 19: 580–600.

Sharma, Ursula. 1995. *Complementary Medicine Today. Practitioners and Patients.* London: Routledge.

Shuval, Judith. 1995. "Elitism and Professional Control in a Saturated Market: Immigrant Physicians in Israel." *Sociology of Health and Illness* 17: 550–65.

Silverman, David. 1987. *Communication and Medical Practice: Social Relations in the Clinic.* Sage: London.

Stacey, Margaret. 1988. *The Sociology of Health and Healing.* London: Unwin Hyman.

Williams, Simon J. and Michael Calnan. 1996. "The 'Limits' of Medicalization? Modern Medicine and the Lay Populace in 'Late' Modernity." *Social Science and Medicine* 42: 1609–20.

Wilsford, David. 1991. *Doctors and the State: The Politics of Health Care in France and the United States.* Durham: Duke University Press.

Witz, Anne. 1992. *Professions and Patriarchy.* London: Routledge.

Zola, Irving K. 1972. "Medicine as an Institution of Social Control." *Sociological Review* 20: 487–503.

9

The Convergence and Divergence of Modern Health Care Systems

Fred Stevens

Do countries at about the same stage of industrial development adopt the same approach to the organization and management of their health care system? Or are cultural heritages distinctive enough that each society fashions its own political and administrative structure? And to what extent do national and international policies affect and determine the organizational structures located in and emerging from the institution of health care?

A widespread view in reflections on modern health care systems is that they are becoming increasingly similar. This view is based on the fact that modern societies are faced with analogue problems impinging their health care organization. Most importantly are an aging population, technological developments, and rising costs of health care. The percentage of very old people will continue to rise. With this, we see a shift in disease patterns from acute to chronic illnesses. When people are getting older, the chance that they will age in good health decreases. Combined with the growth of science and medical technology, these factors influence public expectations and demands for health care, and consequently result in higher expenditures on health care.

The scope of this chapter is to review developments in health care organization of industrialized societies in the context of the current debate on health care reform, with a specific focus on the structural and cultural context of health services. We argue that the organization of health care in modern societies reflects a wide range of convergencies and divergences. This is illuminated by discussing international trends in health care, and some of the basic health care organization models in three regions: Europe, North America, and Asia.

INTERNATIONAL TRENDS IN HEALTH CARE ORGANIZATION

During the last decades industrialized nations have felt an increasing need to reform health care. This need is due to a general dissatisfaction with overall performance, evidence of inefficiencies in the use of resources, and a lack of responsiveness of services to users. The latter is particularly reflected in attempts to increase patient choice and in demands for more public accountability and participation in the organization and management of services. More and more nations are seeking ways to increase the choices of patients in selecting their general practitioner, specialists, and hospital.

Dissatisfaction is further manifested in attempts to change the balance between public health, prevention, and primary health care on the one side, and secondary care at the other. It has been recognized that in the past too much priority has been given to hospital care at the expense of the development of primary care, community care, and public health. By means of budgetary incentives, health care services are refashioned, for example, with regard to the relation between primary and secondary care provision and with regard to measures to improve continuity of care. New professions come into existence at the interface of nurse and physician, while the content of nursing practice is changing. Particularly in primary health care the role of nursing is expanding.

Another general trend is that the future role of the hospital in health care is increasingly being questioned (Ginzberg 1996). Epidemiological and demographic changes, and new technological developments in the field of diagnosis and treatment have a tremendous impact on the delivery of services. Many services that, until recently, were only delivered in hospitals have found their ways to the home of patients. Typical examples are renal dialysis and diabetes care, where patients and their relatives are taught to deal with low- and high-tech medical equipment (Gallagher 1999). The number of acute beds in hospitals and the average length of stay have dropped substantially in almost all industrialized countries (OECD 2002). This is a direct result of changes in treatment procedures, new diagnostic techniques, the changing role of primary health care, early discharge procedures, and overall cost-containment measures.

With the changing role of hospitals in health care we see that the involvement of health professionals in the management of health services is also changing. By making health professionals responsible for management in health care, professional accountability and cost containment will benefit. It results in a shift of focus of professional norms exclusively aiming at the quality of professional care, to one also focusing on issues of cost containment and service reduction (Leicht and Fennell 1997). A variety of initiatives have been launched. One example is the recent purchaser – provider split in the UK, where groups of general practitioners are held responsible for purchasing hospital services. Groups of primary care physicians receive the allocation for their patients' health care to purchase all services, including hospital care. In other countries, for example in the Netherlands, experiments are going on by giving doctors a greater role in the management of services, notably with regard to the management of hospitals. In the US, shifts in decision-making are taking place as a result of contract relationships and reimbursement policies. For example, physicians are forming associations to negotiate managed care contracts. But also, as was predicted almost two decades ago, medical work is becoming more and more under bureaucratic control (Starr 1982). The overall impact of these developments on professional autonomy is not clear. Indeed, professionals will lose some of their professional control. But then again, professionals are moving into managerial positions which create new opportunities for control and satisfaction (Zeitz 1984; Stevens, Diederiks, and Philipsen 1992; Warren, Weitz, and Kulis 1998).

The thread through all these developments is a continuing debate on the financing of health care. Dependent on the country under consideration, these debates focus on overall expenditures (for example in the US), on the role of the government in cost containment (for example in Sweden and Canada), and on policies regarding health care coverage restrictions (for example in Germany and the Netherlands). In most countries an increasing interest has been shown in the introduction of competition between providers. This is considered as a reform strategy to tackle inefficiencies and to enlarge the responsiveness of providers to users. Policy makers are trying to find a position in the middle between competition on the one hand and managed care on the other. Countries where competition lies at the heart of service provision, as is the case in the US, are moving toward more regulated and managed care. In countries with a long tradition of governmental planning and regulation like, for example, in Sweden or in the UK, we see a movement in the opposite direction toward more competition on the basis of market mechanisms. Not surprisingly, the overall trend in health care reform is managed competition, being a mixture of competition on the one side and management on the other. But as Saltman and Figueras (1998: 87–8) recently noted in their overview of health care reforms in Europe: "There is no single concept of a market that can be adopted for use within a health care system. Rather, market-style mechanisms include a number of different specific instruments such as consumer sovereignty (patient choice), negotiated contracts and open bidding, which can be introduced on the funding, allocation, or production sub-sectors of the system."

Because of these congruent cross-national patterns and policies seeking an optimal mix of public and individual responsibility, there is a growing interest in the comparison of health care systems. Countries in the process of health care reform seek to adopt suitable financial and organizational solutions, but also try to learn from each other's mistakes. The necessity of making health care available and accessible for whole populations within certain budget restrictions gives rise to dilemmas in priority setting and rationing. Making choices about the allocation of resources has traditionally been considered an almost exclusive part of the jurisdiction of the medical profession. What we see now, however, is that priority setting and rationing are becoming part of the public debate.

Priority setting and rationing are not pure technical operations. The course and direction of these activities are influenced by the dominant belief system of a nation. Many European countries try to find ways to combine the values of equity, efficiency, and autonomy. Equity implies that health care should be accessible for everyone who is in need of it. It reflects a *collectivist* approach with regard to the equal distribution of health care resources among all strata of the population. The contrasting value of individual autonomy reflects the ability of self-determination and independence in health care. It signifies that people should have a free choice, and preferably would have the means to decide for themselves what they would need from health care, irrespective of the distribution of resources. Efficiency indicates that resources for health care should be spent as economically as possible. In their priority setting, all modern nations try to combine these three values in one way or another. Some nations, however, put more emphasis on the collectivist approach (equity), others on individual autonomy. But for all modern nations efficiency has become the more dominant orientation in the light of the increasing costs of health care.

A major dilemma is whether values of efficiency and self-determination can be sustained without losing principles of equity and solidarity. But as priority setting and rationing in health care have become important policy issues in many countries, the outcomes of the political debate are not spectacular. As Mossialos and King (1999: 131) noted: "Greater relative awareness of rationing and priority setting issues in countries such as the Netherlands, Sweden and the UK, is accompanied by some ambivalence about the actual need for rationing or priority setting." Indeed, in Scandinavian countries and in countries like Israel and the Netherlands, with their long tradition of equity and solidarity principles, governments are rather reluctant to introduce measures to restrict the payment for services (Saltman and Figueras 1997).

HEALTH CARE AS A SOCIETAL SECTOR

While the comparison of health care systems has grown in popularity during recent years, some may have wondered at the quasi-absence of studies relating health care and health care organization to the broader societal and institutional environment. The literature on the comparison of health care systems has strongly been influenced by (neoclassical) economic, managerial, and policy perspectives. These focus on issues of macro-and micro-efficiency, on organizational arrangements conducive to effectiveness, on quality of services, and on measures to improve the continuity and accessibility of care. Many studies try to answer the question how, in the context of changing circumstances, goals and priorities in health care can be reached within the limits of political and legislative boundaries, and using resources economically. In essence, this question regards the *effectiveness* of health care.

For their survival and continuity, however, health care systems also must be assessed on their *legitimacy*. Societies have to solve the problem of how health care goals and priorities can be set and achieved in such a way, that the actions of health care actors and the effects of these actions, intentionally or unintentionally, will be judged as socially acceptable. To evaluate the effectiveness of health care, but in particular its legitimacy, it is important to envisage health care as a societal sector, and to take its societal and institutional environment into consideration.

Societal sectors are defined as collections of actors who are functionally interconnected, who operate in the same domain (for example, health, education, economics, or welfare), and who have a set of similar or interrelated functions (Powell and DiMaggio 1991; Scott and Meyer 1991). Defining health care as a societal sector would imply a focus on the collectivity of actors working within the context of that specific institution. In other words, it comprises of focal organizations, services and functions delivering specific products, but also includes all other organizations, providers, facilities, and services that directly or indirectly influence the core actors. This includes facilities such as hospitals, medical practices, nursing homes, and the health professions (medical and non-medical), their clients, client organizations, funding sources on a national, federal, regional level, local governmental bodies, suppliers of facilities such as the pharmaceutical industry, and so on.

Societal sectors have their primary orientation on one societal core function, in this case, health and illness (Lammers 1993: 321–39). They further have a (social) structure, and a specific pattern of relationships between actors in super/subordinate or egalitarian positions. Societal sectors also have their specific institutional culture. This includes a dominant belief system, a specific system of routines, norms, and values, and specific notions of their "bond." In some sectors, for example in economy, these bindings will be primarily competitive. In health care they are more cooperative.

Analyzing health care systems as societal sectors would also imply the recognition of their distinctive history over time, their specific values and value patterns that go beyond technological requirements, and their commitment to a set of normative standards (Parsons 1951; Selznick 1957). In the comparison of health care systems across nations it may seem that goals do not vary much, but that, over time, variations are primarily found in the implementation of technologies used to reach these goals. Where health care systems vary is in their emphasis on goals and priorities; this is mainly due to long-term cultural and structural developments. Consequently, it can be argued that every health care system is typified by its structure of relations of actors and organizations. Every health care system is typified by its unique pattern of underlying norms, values, and value orientations.

THE STRUCTURE OF HEALTH CARE SYSTEMS

To conceptualize health care systems as societal sectors indicates a high degree of specialization and vertical integration of system elements (Scott and Meyer 1991). Vertical integration denotes that in a production chain activities are controlled at both ends. The health economist Robert Evans, however, argues that because of their distinctive structure, health care systems are characterized by incomplete vertical integration (Evans 1981). As relative independent subsections are involved, such as hospitals, medical services, drugs prescribers, and so forth, vertical integration is difficult to achieve.

Vertical integration is further complicated by the fact that regulatory authority is for the major part delegated by the government to the suppliers. Also, the provision of health insurance is directly linked to one or more of the other transactors in health care (Evans 1981). Consumers permit providers to act as their agents. But professional organizations enjoy, to a substantial degree, independence from other actors, which indicates that the integration between first-line providers and consumers is far from complete. This incompleteness also regards the physician – hospital relations. In general, physicians do not own or manage hospitals, although in some countries, like for example in Japan, this is different.

Also the role of the government in health care can vary considerably. In some countries the state has only very limited control of the insurance activities, as is the case, for example, in the US. In other countries, for example in Canada and in the UK, the state is in control of insurance by means of taxation.

Health care systems vary in structural relationships and in formal interactions between system elements. A traditional market structure presupposes bilateral relations between buyers and suppliers. The health care sector differs essentially from the market sector, because interactions between the actors are not organized in bi-directional relations of pairs of producers and consumers. In contrast to these typical market structures, the exchange relations between the actors in health care are much more complex (Evans 1981). Multilateral transactions involve many participants who have limited independence and jurisdictions. The organization of health care, therefore, consists of multidirectional relations within an interacting system of five principle actors. These are the consumers, first-line providers (general practitioners), second-line providers (hospitals), governments, and insurers (Evans 1981). How these five actors are connected reflects the basic structure of a system.

HEALTH CARE MODELS OF EUROPEAN HEALTH CARE SYSTEMS

Although health care systems diverge in their methods of financing, organization, and regulation, certain organizational configurations dominate, dependent on the role and position of the respective (trans)actors. From the relations between these transactors typical health care systems can be modeled: the social insurance system, the centralized system of (former) communist countries, and the UK national health care system (Evans 1981; Hurst 1992; Marrée and Groenewegen 1997). These are found in eastern and western Europe, as well as in America and Asia.

The Bismarck model. The first model is the social insurance or Bismarck model, named after its founder. Typical for the social insurance system, or "Bismarck" model, is that patients pay an insurance premium to the sick fund which has a contract with first-line and second-line providers. The role of the state is limited and is confined to setting the overall conditions of the contracts between patients, providers, and insurers. The social insurance system is funded by premiums paid and controlled by employers and labor unions. These, however, have little inference with the provision of services. This is left to the professions, specifically the medical profession, and to charity organizations (e.g. home nursing, home help). For people with lower-and middle-class salaried incomes, collective and enforced arrangements are available. This social security model was founded in Germany at the end of the last century, and then almost immediately adopted by Czechoslovakia during the Austrian–Hungarian rule, Austria, Hungary, and Poland. During World War II it was enforced on the Netherlands (1941), and later also adopted by Belgium and France. The social insurance system survived two world wars and national socialism, and essentially still exists in Germany, the Netherlands, Belgium, France, Austria, Switzerland, and Luxembourg (Saltman and Figueras 1997).

The Semashko model. Founded in 1918, the second major European health care model is the centralized communist model or "Semashko model." This model is characterized by a strong position of the state, who guarantees free access to health care for everyone. This is realized by state ownership of health care facilities, by funding from the state budget, and by geographical distribution of services throughout the country. The state dominated Semashko model is funded by taxation. Health services are hierarchically organized. They are provided by state employees, planned by hierarchical provision, and organized as a hierarchy of hospitals, with outpatient clinics (polyclinics) as the lowest levels of entrance. Among the nations that still have a health care system based on the Semashko model are Russia, Belarus, the central-Asian republics of the former USSR, and some countries in central and eastern Europe. Many former soviet republics, however, are now in a process of transition toward a social insurance-based system.

The Beveridge model. The third European model is the UK National Health Services (NHS) or "Beveridge" model. The basic model is virtually similar to the Semashko model. It is also centralized, funded by means of taxation, while the state is responsible for the provision of institution-based care (hospitals). The major difference between the Beveridge model and the Semashko model, however, is that in the former model the medical profession has a more independent position. Further, self-employed general practitioners have an important role as the gatekeepers in primary health care. This implies that before visiting the hospital or a medical specialist it is obligatory to have a referral from a general practitioner. Another difference is that the NHS model has less government regulation, and leaves more room for private medicine.

Through processes of diffusion and adaptation, the Beveridge model was first adopted in Sweden, and then by the other Nordic countries: Denmark, Norway, and Finland. At present, the Beveridge model applies to the United Kingdom, Ireland, Denmark, Norway, Sweden, Finland, and Iceland. Four southern European countries have adopted, or are in the process of adopting the tax-based model. These countries are Spain, Italy, Portugal, and Greece (Saltman and Figueras 1997).

NORTH AMERICAN HEALTH CARE SYSTEMS: CANADA AND THE UNITED STATES

It has been argued that a crucial element of ways in which health care systems are structured, in essence, depends on the relationship between three principal actors: the medical profession, the state, and the insurers (Johnson, Larkin, and Saks 1995; Tuohy 1999). There is a mix of mechanisms of social control systemizing and legitimizing between these actors. The first is by the market, characterized by voluntary exchange relationships. The second is through a hierarchy, based on a chain of command and on obedience to rules. The third is characterized by collegiality, based on common norms and values and on a common knowledge base. While the National Health Service in the UK is a typical example of the hierarchy model (strong position of the state; rules), the US and Canada reflect the market and the collegiality models (Tuohy 1999). In the United States the logic of the market and enterpreneuralism dominates. Canada relies more on collegial mechanisms.

While during past decades many health care systems underwent major structural reforms, the Canadian health care system remained remarkably stable. There has been continuing public and political support for maintaining a system that provides universal access to medical services, regardless of economic position. In the late sixties, Canada adopted universal hospital and medical care insurance, based on tax financing, while the provision of professional services remained in private hands. Most physicians (about two-thirds) are in private, self-employed, fee-for-service practice. Provincial governments were the exclusive payers for most services, and the allocation of services was negotiated with the medical profession. Prior to the introduction of universal public programs, the financing of hospital and medical care occurred in a mixture of funding modalities. State-provider negotiations promoted enormous discretion for the profession, which explains, in part, why the Canadian health care system ranked among the high-spenders of publicly financed systems. Physicians' fees tended to rise faster than the general income level. In the early seventies Canada broke with this previous trend.

As Evans (1985) notes, the Canadian health care system is quite clearly not "socialized medicine," despite the rhetorics. Only the insurance can be typified as socialized, because it is exclusive, without competition, and superimposed by the government upon a delivery system that is virtually private. For a long period, with this model Canada succeeded in complying to the effectiveness and legitimacy criterion in health care, in providing all the citizens access to all the medically necessary hospital and medical services, without financial barriers, and at a reasonable and acceptable price in terms of share of the national income.

Just like everywhere in the world, however, Canadian physicians favor the use of the power of the state to ensure their professional monopoly without being publicly accountable. Consequently, continuing profession–government tensions and public concerns on rising costs and limited access resulted in several modifications of the Canadian health care system. According to most recent figures (2002), the Canadians spent 9 percent of their Gross Domestic Product (GDP) on health care, which is again quite high. It ranks them among the highest spenders among 29 OECD countries. One of the questions in Canada is whether market competition should be introduced, by permitting private entrepreneurs to provide for-profit services, next to the well-established Canadian Medicare model. On this issue, the Canadian medical profession is divided, whether to continue to accommodate with the state, or to press for more entrepreneurial freedom. On a provincial level, the accommodation of the state with the medical profession, serving purposes on both sides for more than two decades, has become more and more of an uneasy relationship in the nineties (Tuohy 1999).

While Medicare and Medicaid provide services to the poor and to the elderly, the basic model of the United States health care system is a voluntary reimbursement model, with four actors playing a key role (Hurst 1992). First-level (general practitioners) and second-level providers (hospitals) deliver services to patients who will be reimbursed for their medical bill, in part or in whole. Patients pay a voluntary risk-related premium to voluntary insurers, who reimburse them for medical expenses. In principle, there is no, or minimal interaction between insurer and provider. Only the patient interacts with both parties.

This private reimbursement model has two major drawbacks (Hurst 1992). One is that it does not have built-in incentives to restrict demand and, therefore, is often accompanied by cost sharing. Another drawback is that it does not have built-in mechanisms to prevent inequities. For reasons of profit maximization, private insurers have an incentive to select against poor risks. Moreover, access to voluntary insurance is only open to those who are willing, or can afford to pay. This has enormous consequences for health care insurance coverage in the US. While most OECD countries achieved universal coverage, with only 33 percent the United States had the largest percentage of citizens without government-assured health insurance. According to the most recent estimates, 43 million Americans are uninsured which is about one out of every seven people (US Census 1998; Anderson and Poullier 1999).

US health care spending per capita grew more rapidly in the 1990s, compared to the average industrialized country. From 1990 to 1997 US spending per capita increased 4.3 percent per year, compared to 3.8 percent of the OECD median. In this period, the increase in Canada was only 2.7 percent, and actually leveled off (Anderson and Poullier 1999). In spite of managed care initiatives and of attempts of government regulation, costs kept increasing in the US (Anderson 1997; Anderson and Poullier 1999).

Just like in other industrial societies, health care reforms in the US are essentially focusing on cost containment. Managed care initiatives, for example Health Maintenance Organizations (HMOs) were developed to increase competition, to change methods of payment for medical services, and to curb the power of the medical profession. The fundamental model of the Health Maintenance Organization is to be typified as a voluntary contract model (Hurst 1992). It involves contractual relationships between insurers and independent providers, which give these providers an exclusive right to supply complete services, mainly free of charge. Patients pay a voluntary, risk-related premium to voluntary insurers who have contracts with providers. The difference with the voluntary reimbursement model is that insurers now have contractual relationships with providers. Variations on this voluntary contract model are the Individual Practice Organizations, where insurers are controlled by providers. These managed care models are all aimed at controlling the costs of health care by monitoring the work of doctors and hospitals, and by limiting the visit to second-level hospital care. In practice, this is often done by means of a "case manager," who, on behalf of the insurer, is authorized to decide whether the care to be rendered is effective and efficient. Another feature is that patients are only allowed to see a specialist after they have visited a general practitioner. This gatekeeper role of the primary care physician to the use of specialist care is similar to the role of GPs in European countries like in Denmark, Norway, Italy, the Netherlands, Portugal, Spain, and the UK (Boerma, Van der Zee, and Fleming 1997).

At present, almost 90 percent of practicing physicians in the US participate in at least one or more managed care organizations (Tuohy 1999). Its share in patient enrollment rose from 12 percent in 1981 to 62 percent in 1997. Therefore, managed care is the most significant development in the US health care arena in the 1990s. But as Tuohy explains, the "competition revolution" in US health care in the 1990s was more driven by the increasing activism of purchasers, than by the supply side (Tuohy 1999). As a result of government efforts to introduce more tight payment schemes under Medicare, hospital providers sought to shift some of their costs from public to private payers. Within the context of changing economic circumstances, this alerted purchasers, and provoked them to play a more substantial role in the organization and management of the use of services. For the medical profession, the increasing importance of bargaining relationships and the contracting with entrepreneurs ultimately led to a dramatic decline of their influence in the private-market-oriented US health care arena.

HEALTH CARE SYSTEMS IN ASIA: THE CASE OF JAPAN

Conceptually, the Japanese health care system can be typified as a social insurance model with mixed public and private providers (Abell-Smith 1996). Japan adopted the Bismarckian health care model of Germany in 1927. It has achieved universal health insurance coverage since 1961, with one insurance program for employees and their dependents (paid by employers and employees), and one national program for all others (paid by taxes). Japan has one of the most equitable health care systems in the world (Ikegami 1991; Ikegami and Campbell 1999). An insured person is free to go to any hospital or clinic, with no differences in costs.

Despite this nationwide insurance scheme, the delivery of services is highly privatized with an overwhelming amount of physicians in solo practices working on a fee-for-service basis (Nakahara 1997). These physicians are essentially general practitioners, similar to European GPs, but prefer to see themselves as more specialized (Nakahara 1997).

The Japanese health care system would benefit from more differentiation and vertical integration. Private practitioners are not allowed to practice medicine in the hospital, just as is the case in several European countries (Garland 1995). But, different from the situation in other countries, there is no referral relation between first-level services of these office-based physicians and second-level services provided in hospitals. As a consequence of the fee structure, office-based physicians compete with hospitals for patients, and try to keep them in their own practice as much as possible. Hospitals do the same, because they are in the main owned by physicians, who also serve as prescribers and dispensers of medications (Ikegami and Campbell 1999). Also long-term care for the elderly is burdened by the absence of a differentiated and vertical integrated health care system. While the rate of institutionalized elderly does not deviate from figures in other industrialized societies, care is provided in hospitals rather than in nursing homes. A consequence is the extremely high average hospital length of stay (OECD 2002).

Incomplete vertical integration of Japanese health care services is, for an important part, due to the high degree of autonomy of the medical profession in medical practice and in capital expenditures. This is evident in the availability of medical equipment. Japan has the highest rate of CT scanners and MRI equipment in the world, because not only hospitals but also private clinics are allowed to purchase expensive equipment (Anderson and Poullier 1999).

The Japanese medical profession is divided between physicians employed in hospitals and those working in private practice (Nakahara 1997). This weakens their position in relation to the state and other health care actors. The office-based physicians, however, have always been the mainstay of the Japanese Medical Association (Ikegami and Campbell 1999).

While having adopted a basic European health care model, Japan kept many of its typical cultural peculiarities. Traditional medicine continues to be widely practiced in Japan (Anderson, Oscarson, and Yu 1995; Garland 1995). As Anderson et al. have noted, since western medicine was introduced in Japan it has been shaped and molded to fit into the cultural context of East Asian medicine (Anderson, Oscarson, and Yu 1995). Despite the long average intra-mural length of stay, Japan has the lowest rate of hospital admissions in the world. One reason is the cultural antipathy for invasive procedures and a preference for more conservative treatments. Another is that invasive procedures are discouraged by low fees for physicians to conduct surgery (Ikegami and Campbell 1999).

In recent years, the Japanese health care system has been faced with rising costs, an aging population, and growing consumer consciousness. This has led the government to initiate proposals to reform the system, similar to those in other industrialized countries. However, the necessity of health care reform in Japan should be considered in the circumstance that its health spending is still among the lowest in industrialized societies. There may be more reason to reform because of organizational problems than of financial ones (Ikegami and Campbell 1999).

CULTURE AND VALUE ORIENTATIONS IN HEALTH CARE

Anthropologists have argued that differences between health care systems are imbedded in the values and social structure of the societies involved (Helman 2003). Based on specific histories, traditions, customs, and so on, differences in health care organization reflects the way in which societies define and deal with issues of health and illness. Health and health care are imbedded in value systems which give explanations why and how, in specific cultures, health problems are handled. For example, in some societies health care is considered as a collective good for the benefit of all citizens. In others, health care is considered more a "commodity" that can be bought or sold on a free market. As Gallagher (1988: 65) notes, "The concept of health care as a calculable resource is an essential feature in its role as a carrier of modernity." The notion of health care as a commodity, however, has not been rooted everywhere. It appears that it has been more established in the essentially market-oriented organization of health care in the US than in Europe or Asia. Nowhere in Europe has it become part of health policy objectives, notwithstanding a wide range of health care reforms in recent years introducing market-oriented approaches with incentives to introduce more competition between providers and to use resources more economically (Saltman and Figueras 1997).

Cultures or nations can vary in value orientations to a considerable degree. For example, values of equity, solidarity, and autonomy may have different significance (Hofstede 1984). As will be discussed, emphasis on hospital care versus home care or care for the elderly, on individual responsibilities or on solidarity between people, reflects general value orientations that have priority in a society (Philipsen 1980; Hofstede 1984; Stevens and Diederiks 1995). The cultural embeddedness of health care in industrialized societies, however, is an often discussed, but rather under-researched topic (Saltman and Figueras 1997; Stevens and Diederiks 1995). There is little research on core values underlying the organization of health care systems in modern societies.

One notable exception is Lynn Payer's *Medicine and Culture* (Payer 1990). She compared medical culture and health practices in Germany, Great Britain, France, and the United States on the basis of her own observations, literature study, and interviews with key persons. Not unexpectedly, she found the largest differences between the US and the European systems. For example, the dominant attitude of doctors in the US is described by her as "aggressive" and "action oriented," in accordance with a kind of "frontier mentality." American doctors appear to favor surgery above drug therapy. But when drug therapy is used, they do it more aggressively than in Europe. European doctors were found to prefer less radical approaches, although the differences between Germany, France, and Great Britain were also substantial, in particular with regard to procedures in diagnosis and treatment (Payer 1990).

Another study is Hofstede's research on international differences in value orientations. For his *Culture's Consequences: International Differences in Work Related Values*, Hofstede (1984) surveyed employees of IBM plants in 40 different nations. He found that national cultures could be classified along four different value orientations: (a) individualism versus collectivism, (b) large versus small power distance, (c) strong versus weak uncertainty avoidance, and (d) masculinity versus femininity.

Individualism/Collectivism refers to whether, in a particular society, the individual opinion and the individual interest is considered as more important than collective opinions and collective interest, or vice versa. It indicates the weight of our own interests versus the weight of the public good. The second dimension,

Power Distance, indicates the extent to which the less powerful members in a society expect and accept that power is unequally distributed. Power distance, therefore, points to the degree of inequality in a society. The third dimension, *Uncertainty Avoidance*, reflects the extent to which members of a society feel threatened by uncertain or unknown situations, and whether people can cope with this. It also indicates whether people are willing to take certain risks in life. Finally, *Masculinity/Femininity* refers to the division of social roles between the sexes and indicates whether achievement, competitiveness (masculine behavior), prevails above "tender" relations and care for others (feminine behavior).

Hofstede's study was not designed to analyze health care systems. But his work goes beyond the settings that were subject to his research, and indeed applies to the organization of health care services (Hofstede 1991). For example, in health care the masculinity/femininity dimension would indicate the importance of rationality, efficiency, justice, and so forth on the one side (masculinity), and solidarity, continuity, importance of care and caring relationships, on the other (femininity). Uncertainty avoidance has been related to the nurse–physician ratio in a country (Hofstede 1984; 1991). When people in a society would have difficulty in dealing with uncertain situations, they will be more likely to consult the doctor (the "expert") rather than a nurse. Consequently, work of physicians is considered as more important than that of nurses. Comparing doctor–nurse ratios in different European countries gives some support for Hofstede's hypothesis. The group of *northern* European countries, consisting of Sweden, Norway, Finland, Denmark, and also the Netherlands, share high scores on femininity and low scores on uncertainty avoidance. These countries are characterized by their long-standing tradition of social democratic policies, and their well-developed systems of social security and health insurance coverage. All have a well-established system of "care" provision with regard to the delivery of home care, mental health care services, and care for the elderly. All these countries also have many more nurses than physicians (Saltman and Figueras 1997: 240; WHO 2001). Alternatively, in the *southern* European countries with high scores on masculinity and on uncertainty avoidance, specifically in Italy and Greece, there are more physicians than nurses.

But there is another inference to be made from these data, which regards the development of professional home care nursing. Because doctors and nurses have different work, it is likely that in countries where the medical profession dominates health care, professional home care provided by the nursing profession is less in existence. Philipsen (1988) hypothesizes that in societies typified by a high degree of *uncertainty avoidance* and a *masculinity* orientation, it is more likely that: (a) "cure" (medical intervention) instead of "care" will prevail; (b) the physician has a dominant position in the health care system; (c) social positions are ascribed according to traditional sex roles.

Philipsen's hypothesis is also consistent with a north–south division in Europe, whereby in southern regions priority would be given to the cure and treatment of health care problems, while care activities would be dealt with more in family relations than by professional nursing (Philipsen 1980; Giarchi 1996). This is supported in an OECD study of the early nineties, showing that the lowest percentages of institutionalized care (nursing home care) were found in southern Europe (Greece, Italy, Portugal, Spain, Turkey). Most institutional care for the elderly was found in northern Europe (the Netherlands, Finland, Norway, Luxembourg) and in Canada.

However, the absence of institutional care for the elderly is not compensated for by professional home care everywhere. For example, this is the case in the US, Canada, Austria, Germany, Ireland, and Japan. All these countries are considered as masculine societies, but divide on the uncertainty avoidance dimension.

High levels of institutional and professional home care were found in Denmark, Finland, and Norway, while low levels of both types of care were found in southern Europe (Italy, Spain, Portugal). Other countries were somewhat in the middle (Belgium, France, Sweden, UK, the Netherlands). From these data it appears that there is indeed evidence of a north–south division in Europe, whereby institutional care for the elderly in the north is not paralleled by professional home care in the south, but more by family care (Mossialos and Le Grand 1999: 56). This latter conclusion also applies to Japan, that has the highest masculinity score among countries that were under consideration (Hofstede 1984). Also Canada and the US are considered masculine societies, but in contrast to Japan they are low on uncertainty avoidance.

Conclusions: The Convergence and Divergence of Health Care Systems

In this chapter, models of health care organization have been presented within the context of their cultural environment. While these models are the major ones that can be found in industrialized countries in Europe, America, and Asia, since the nineties there is no system that fully complies to one of these. Because of financing problems necessitating cost containment, and through processes of adaptation and diffusion, national health care systems vary. For example, Bismarckian health care systems and the enterpreneurial system of the US were confronted with problems of rising costs in the sixties and seventies. The NHS systems and Semashko-like systems of eastern Europe had problems of neglect, underfunding, and extensive bureaucracy. In some countries this led to more state regulation to curb the costs of health care. In other countries it resulted in less state intervention and in the introduction of experiments with different forms of managed competition. For example, in eastern Europe, after the fall of the Berlin wall, we see the demise of state funding and state provision because of economic deficits. In the countries that have adopted the Bismarck model we see more state regulation in order to introduce more planning and to curb the rising costs of health care. One of the results has been a stronger position of hospitals. In the United Kingdom we have seen a movement toward more decentralization, which was realized by the earlier noted split between purchasers and providers (Saltman and Figueras 1997; Tuohy 1999).

Health care organization, however, is also influenced by cultural circumstances. For example, nations with a strong collective orientation have more state intervention, a small private sector, have a preference for tax rather than insurance funding, and prefer a comprehensive coverage with universal entitlement based on the notion of rights. In contrast, societies steeped in individualism prefer private enterprise and insurance funding with selective coverage and high responsiveness to consumer demand. In societies which have equity as an important root we see explicit attempts to avoid discrimination and to facilitate public participation.

We have started this chapter with the question whether countries at the same stage of industrial development have the same approach to the organization and management of health care services. Indeed, institutional patterns are converging. There is ample evidence that contingencies like increasing health care costs, an aging population, changing disease patterns, technological developments, growing public demand, and so forth, impose a common logic in terms of institutional performance and in the structuring of modern health care systems. In the literature a wide range of convergencies in health policy and health care organization have been listed (Field 1989; Mechanic and Rochefort 1996; Raffel 1997; Saltman and Figueras 1997). These include (a) the concern of governments to control health care costs while at the same time improving the effectiveness and efficiency of the system; (b) the increasing attention for health promotion and healthy lifestyles such as abstinence from substance use (alcohol, smoking, drugs), and healthy behavior; (c) reduction of health care inequalities and differences in access; (d) the stimulation of primary health care at the expense of cutting-back further medical specialization; (e) the promotion of patient participation and improving patient satisfaction; (f) the reduction of fragmentation of services and the promotion of continuity of care.

The convergence of modern health care systems, however, is not undisputed. Even if societies are faced with similar contingencies, their societal structures have to be consonant with culturally-derived expectations (Lammers and Hickson 1979). Consequently, while there is substantial evidence that modern societies are evolving in the same direction with efficiency equity and utilitarian individualism as core value orientations, differences exist in degree and similarity of these developments. Modern societies still vary considerably in the way they deal with issues of health and illness (Anderson, Oscarson, and Yu 1995). Moreover, while nations may have similar goals, alternative options are available to reach these. National health systems are the outcome of a dialectical tension between universal aspects of technology and medicine on the one hand, and particularistic cultural characteristics of each nation on the other (Field 1989). These particularistic cultural characteristics refer to the historical foundations of health care systems, to the societal and national context, and to specific values and value orientations of societies and health care systems under consideration. According to Pomey and Poullier (1997), health care institutions are still largely country-specific. Such country-specific elements would include the social, economic, institutional, and ideological structures, the dominant belief system, the role of the state versus the market, patterns of health care coverage, and centralization or decentralization of political authority (Saltman and Figueras 1997, 1998). As Saltman and Figueras (1998: 105) note, "Given unbridgeable conceptual differences and divergence in organizational principles, suggestions of convergence among the health care systems of industrialized countries seem to be misplaced." Whether health care systems and not only policy objectives will converge remains to be seen.

Acknowledgment

The author wishes to thank Tatiana Maiorova for her assistance in literature research.

References

Abell-Smith, Brian. 1996. "The Reform of Health Care Systems. A Review of Seventeen OECD Countries." Paris: Organization for Economic Co-operation and Development.

Anderson, Gerard F. 1997. "In Search of Value: An International Comparison of Cost, Access, and Outcomes." *Health Affairs* 16: 163–71.

Anderson, Gerard F. and Jean-Pierre Poullier. 1999. "Health Spending, Access, and Outcomes: Trends in Industrialized Countries." *Health Affairs* 18: 178–92.

Anderson, James G., Renee Oscarson, and Yan Yu. 1995. "Japan's Health Care System. Western and East Asian Influences." Pp. 32–44 in E. Gallagher and J. Subedi (eds.), *Global Perspectives on Health Care*. Englewood Cliffs, NJ: Prentice-Hall.

Boerma, W. G., J. Van der Zee, and D. M. Fleming. 1997. "Service Profiles of General Practitioners in Europe." *British Journal of General Practice* 47: 481–6.

Evans, Robert G. 1981. "Incomplete Vertical Integration: The Distinctive Structure of the Health-Care Industry." Pp. 329–54 in J. Van der Gaag and M. Perlman (eds.), *Health, Economics, and Health Economics. Proceedings of the World Congress on Health Economics, Leiden, The Netherlands, September 1980*. Amsterdam: North-Holland.

Evans, Robert G. 1985. "The Grass on Our Side is Actually Quite Green . . . Health Care Funding in Canada." *Gezondheid and Samenleving* 6: 245–55.

Field, Mark. 1989. "The Comparative Evolution of Health Systems: Convergence, Diversity and Cross-Cutting Issues." Pp. 15–30 in G. Lüschen, W. Cockerham, and G. Kunz (eds.), *Health and Illness in America and Germany*. München: Oldenbourg.

Gallagher, Eugene. 1988. "Modernization and Medical Care." *Sociological Perspectives* 31: 59–87.

——. 1999. "'Hi-Tech' Home Treatment for Patients with Serious Chronic Illness: Sociological Questions." Paper presented to the *International Conference on Socio-Cultural and Policy Dimensions of Health Care*. Singapore.

Garland, Neal T. 1995. "Major Orientations in Japanese Health Care." Pp. 255–67 in E. Gallagher and J. Subedi (eds.), *Global Perspectives on Health Care*. Englewood Cliffs, NJ: Prentice-Hall.

Giarchi, George Giacinto. 1996. *Caring for Older Europeans. Comparative Studies in Twenty-Nine Countries*. Aldershot: Arena.

Ginzberg, Eli. 1996. *Tomorrow's Hospital. A Look to the Twenty-First Century*. New Haven: Yale University Press.

Helman, Cecil G. 2000. *Culture, Health and Illness*, 4th edition. London: Hodder Arnold.

Hofstede, Geert. 1984. *Culture's Consequences. International Differences in Work-Related Values*. London, Beverly Hills: Sage.

——. 1991. *Cultures and Organizations. Software of the Mind*. London: McGraw-Hill.

Hurst, Jeremy. 1992. "The Reform of Health Care. A Comparative Analysis of Seven OECD Countries." Paris: Organization for Economic Co-Operation and Development.

Ikegami, Naoki. 1991. "Japanese Health Care: Low Cost Through Regulated Fees." *Health Affairs* 10: 87–109.

Ikegami, Naoki and John Creighton Campbell. 1999. "Health Care Reform in Japan: the Virtues of Muddling Through." *Health Affairs* 18: 56–75.

Johnson, Terry, Gerry Larkin, and Mike Saks. 1995. *Health Professions and the State in Europe*. London and New York: Routledge.

Lammers, Cornelius J. 1993. *Organiseren van Bovenaf en Onderop* [Organizations in Comparison]. Utrecht: Het Spectrum.

Lammers, Cornelis J. and David J. Hickson. 1979. "Organizations Alike and Unlike. International and Inter-Institutional Studies in the Sociology of Organizations." London: Routledge and Kegan Paul.

Leicht, Kevin T. and Mary Fennell. 1997. "The Changing Organizational Context of Professional Work." *Annual Review of Sociology* 23: 215–31.

Marrée, Jorgen and Peter P. Groenewegen. 1997. *Back to Bismarck: Eastern European Health Care in Transition*. Aldershot: Avebury.

Mechanic, David and David A. Rochefort. 1996. "Comparative Medical Systems." *Annual Review of Sociology* 22: 239–70.

Mossialos, Elias and Derek King. 1999. "Citizens and Rationing: Analysis of a European Survey." *Health Policy* 49: 75–135.

Mossialos, Elias and Julian Le Grand. 1999. "Health Care and Cost Containment in the European Union." Aldershot: Ashgate.

Nakahara, Toshitaka. 1997. "The Health System of Japan." In M. Raffel (ed.), *Health Care and Reform in Industrialized Countries*. University Park, PA: Pennsylvania State University Press.

OECD. 2000. "OECD Health Data: A Comparative Analysis of Twenty-Nine Countries." Paris: Organization for Economic Cooperation and Development.

Parsons, Talcott. 1951. *The Social System*. New York: The Free Press.

Payer, Lynn. 1990. *Medicine and Culture. Notions of Health and Sickness in Britain, the U.S., France and West Germany*. London: Gollancz.

Philipsen, H. 1980. "Internationale vergelijking van welvaart, gezondheidszorg en levensduur: het probleem van Galton" ["International Comparisons of Prosperity, Health Care, and Life Expectancy: Galton's Problem"]. *Gezondheid en Samenleving* 1: 5–17.

———. 1988. *Gezondheidszorg als project en bejegening. Waarden ten aanzien van ziekte, gezondheid en samenleving* [Health Care as a Project and Attitude. Values in Illness, Health, and Society]. Maastricht: Rijksuniversiteit Limburg.

Pomey, Marie-Pascal and Jean-Pierre Poullier. 1997. "France." In M. Raffel (ed.), *Health Care and Reform in Industrialized Countries*. University Park, PA: Pennsylvania State University Press.

Powell, Walter W. and Paul J. DiMaggio. 1991. "The New Institutionalism in Organizational Analysis." Chicago: University of Chicago Press.

Raffel, Marshall W. 1997. "Dominant Issues: Convergence, Decentralization, Competition, Health Services." Pp. 291–303 in M. Raffel (ed.), *Health Care and Reform in Industrialized Countries*. University Park, PA: Pennsylvania State University Press.

Saltman, Richard B. and Josep Figueras. 1997. "European Health Care Reform." In *WHO Regional Publications, European series*. Copenhagen: World Health Organization, Regional Office for Europe.

Saltman, Richard B. and Josep Figueras. 1998. "Analyzing the Evidence on European Health Care Reforms." *Health Affairs* 17: 85–105.

Scott, W. Richard and John W. Meyer. 1991. "The Organization of Societal Sectors: Propositions and Early Evidence." Pp. 108–40 in W. Powell and P. DiMaggio (eds.), *The New Institutionalism in Organizational Analysis*. Chicago: University of Chicago Press.

Selznick, Philip. 1957. *Leadership in Administration*. New York: Harper and Row.

Starr, Paul. 1982. *The Social Transformation of American Medicine*. New York: Basic Books.

Stevens, Fred C. J. and Joseph P. M. Diederiks. 1995. "Health Culture: An Exploration of National and Social Differences in Health-Related Values." Pp. 137–44 in G. Lüschen, W. Cockerham, and J. Van der Zee (eds.), *Health Systems in the European Union. Diversity, Convergence, and Integration*. München: Oldenbourg.

Stevens, Fred C. J., Joseph P. M. Diederiks, and Hans Philipsen. 1992. "Physician Satisfaction, Professional Characteristics, and Behavior Formalization in Hospitals." *Social Science and Medicine* 35: 295–303.

Tuohy, Carolyn Hughes. 1999. "Dynamics of a Changing Health Sphere: The United State, Britain, and Canada." *Health Affairs* 18: 114–31.

U.S. Bureau of the Census. 1998. "Current Population Reports." Washington DC.

Warren, Mary Guptill, Rose Weitz, and Stephen Kulis. 1998. "Physician Satisfaction in a Changing Health Care Environment: The Impact of Challenges to Professional Autonomy, Authority, and Dominance." *Journal of Health and Social Behavior* 39: 356–67.

World Health Organization. 2001. *World Health Indicators*. CD-ROM.

Zeitz, Gerald. 1984. "Bureaucratic Role Characteristics and Member Affective Response in Organizations." *The Sociological Quarterly* 25: 301–18.

Part II
Regional Perspectives

The Americas

10

The American Health Care System: Entering the Twenty-first Century with High Risk, Major Challenges, and Great Opportunities

BERNICE A. PESCOSOLIDO AND CAROL A. BOYER

At the end of the nineteenth century, the medical profession stood in the midst of great change in America. The coming of the industrial revolution coupled with new scientific theories for the practice and training of physicians produced the modern system of medicine. Given that great "social transformation" of American medicine (Starr 1982), there was little doubt in the minds of the leaders of the new scientific profession that the American health care system would be substantially different from the one at the beginning of the nineteenth century or even at mid-century. As it evolved during the twentieth century, the modern health care system in the United States took a very different form from many of its European counterparts, building a mixed private and public system of care with powerful physician direction.

What has been less anticipated but equally remarkable is the contrast between the health care system at the end of the twentieth century and its predecessor at the beginning of the 1990s. Escalating costs, the newer burden of chronic and degenerative diseases, the increasing number of Americans not covered by any form of health insurance, and only a modest relationship between health care spending and some important markers of "success" (e.g. the infant mortality rate) compared to other countries led to a major federal government effort to restructure the American health care system. Its failure led to the private health insurance market launching initiatives that greatly transformed the structure and financing of health services. As a result, the richest country in the world, with almost 274 million people, is undergoing a massive social experiment in the form of a new organization of health care.

The purpose of this chapter is to briefly describe the different eras of health care in the United States, concentrating on the challenges and opportunities in this radical, contemporary change. We begin with a review of the eras in the evolution of the American health care system, focusing on the power of its major practitioners, physicians, and the limits of their power in determining the recent arrangements by which health care is provided. We then discuss the issues that figure prominently in today's debate about how the newly emerging organization of American health care assure access and quality care in a cost effective manner.

THE RISE OF A HEALTH CARE "SYSTEM" IN THE UNITED STATES

Historians and sociologists alike have argued that the discovery that a bacillus caused anthrax, the routine use of antiseptics, and the introduction of anesthesia combined to produce the "great break" between medicine of the past and the modern form of science-based practice. While different societies embraced the new science in different ways in how it shaped their health care system, the industrializing countries of the United States and Europe all used political, social, and economic mechanisms to place the "scientific" physician at the center of the modern health care systems. Figure 10.1 provides a simple heuristic device charting the relative power of physicians in the American health care system over time. As figure 10.1 indicates, the power and reach of the modern physician grew dramatically from 1860 to 1910. The release of the Flexner Report reinforced physician authority with its indictment of the status of medical training in the United States and a recommendation that only medical schools following the German model of scientific training should receive financial assistance and public support. Suppressed were the itinerant medicine men delivering "elixers" that either were laced with opium or alcohol or that "purged" disease by "cleansing" the body through vomiting or elimination. Gone also was the standard practice of "regular" physicians (i.e. the precursors of the scientific physician such as Benjamin Rush) of "bleeding" the ill person to remove tainted blood. "Granny" midwives who delivered babies at home and female and minority physicians who had learned medicine through apprenticeships were eliminated as well through the establishment of licensing laws.

These laws required all those wishing to practice medicine to take state examinations which were, in practice, written by physicians at the newly established, science-based medical schools like The Johns Hopkins University in Baltimore. Both aspiring and practicing medical providers not trained at these medical schools failed the examinations and were prohibited from practicing medicine in the United States (Brown 1979). Even the well-established chiropractors of the midwest and homeopathists who were the preferred providers of the upper classes in the United States found themselves without substantial support (i.e. health insurance unwilling to cover their services), even though they were not barred from practice. The scientific medical profession became, in essence, a successful if not total monopoly (Berlant 1975; Collins 1979; Starr 1982).

The medical profession's role in building the American health care system looms large and substantial. The American Medical Association, formed in 1847, became extremely powerful and helped direct the use of resources generated by wealthy industrialists in the United States. But these corporate interests, while backing the large infusion of wealth into the emerging system of modern

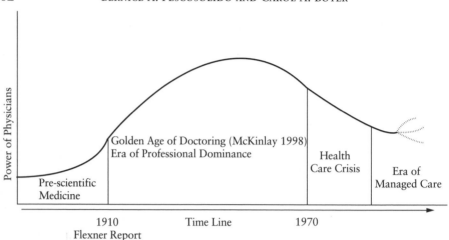

Figure 10.1   Eras in the American health care system

medicine, did it indirectly through their newly established philanthropic foundations. The government, whether federal or state, played a minimal early role in the design of the American health care system. This differed substantially from the European experience in Germany, for example, where the federal government played an early and active role in directing general and employer taxes to cover the services of scientific medical practice (Rosen 1963; Berlant 1975).

Medical care in the United States could only loosely be referred to as a "system" of health care financed by private sources, including patient fees. It was, and still is at best, a patchwork of providers in the private sector including solo-practitioners; incorporated groups of physicians; voluntary, community hospitals; and some early Health Maintenance Organizations such as Kaiser Permanente in California that arose from the lack of physicians to serve the workers in important industries which were developing outside urban centers (e.g. railroads, mining). This private sector is supplemented by a weak public sector that includes city and county hospitals; long-term care facilities (e.g. mental hospitals, TB sanitariums), a Veterans Administration System established at the end of the Civil War in the 1860s, public health nursing, and specialized community clinics (e.g. the Community Mental Health Centers or CMHCs that were established in the face of the decision to "deinstitutionalize" the treatment of mental illness). Only in the 1960s did the federal government develop programs to provide limited health insurance coverage for the elderly (Medicare) or develop a partnership with the states to offer coverage for the poor (Medicaid).

The period from 1910 through 1970 represented an era of great growth, success, and power of the medical profession. The US health care system, aided after World War II by large federal support for research and development as well as hospital building, became one of the most prominent in the world. It was, according to McKinlay and Marceau (1998), the "Golden Age of Doctoring," or drawing from Eliot Freidson's (1970) terms, "An Era of Professional Dominance" (see figure 10.1). Physicians in a primarily private health care system determined both the nature of medical care and the arrangements under which it was provided. Physicians set their prices, worked from predominantly solo-practices, and joined the American Medical Association. For the most part, patients could choose who they wanted to visit for their problems and they purchased private health insurance to do so, starting in the 1940s. Even the Great Depression of the 1930s, which established unemployment, public works, and other federal welfare programs, did not extend to the public provision of health care in a systematic form characteristic of the health insurance or health systems of Europe.

THE END OF UNQUESTIONED DOMINANCE

In 1970 President Richard Nixon announced the existence of a "health care crisis" in the United States (see figure 10.1). The number of uninsured Americans and those with limited access to medical care was growing. Even the introduction of Medicare and Medicaid were decried as inadequate, the cause of increasing spending, and the source of a "two-tiered" or "two-class" system of health care in the United States. Scientific medicine's limits on a number of fronts were coming to the fore as cancer, heart disease, and other chronic and degenerative illnesses did not appear to be understood under the "germ theory" so central to modern, scientific medicine. While medicine offered more sophisticated, technological solutions to diagnosis and treatment, people began to question a quick resort to surgery for problems (e.g. prostate surgery), the extension of life through artificial means (e.g. life support in hopeless cases), and the spiraling costs of medical care. Simultaneously, it seemed that there was a growing interest in both older and newer forms of complementary and alternative medicine including midwifery, acupuncture, chiropractic, and homeopathy. Scholars began to write about scientific medicine's "deprofessionalization"and "deskilling"; about patients' rights and a growing consumer movement; and about the need for "holistic" approaches to health care (see Pescosolido and Kronenfeld 1995; Pescosolido, McLeod, and Alegría 2000). As health care insurance began to cover "alternative" medicines, albeit on a very limited basis (e.g. chiropractic) and greater numbers of physicians declined to join the American Medical Association, professional dominance was unraveling. Sociologists shifted their discussion from issues of "professional dominance" to notions of "deprofessionalization," "corporatization," "proletarianization," and "countervailing powers"; anthropologists talked about alternative medical systems being "complementary" rather than "competing" and discussed the potential for the integration among different systems of medical care (Unschuld 1976; Light and Levine 1988; Light 1995).

These disillusionments were not exclusive to modern medicine and, perhaps, reflected larger changes in modern society (Pescosolido and Rubin 2000). Rubin (1996) has argued that the social and economic bases of modern society "tarnished" in the early 1970s, marked a turning point. The postwar growth that had fueled prosperity in all sectors, including medicine, stopped. A long decline in expansion resulted in downsizing of corporations and displacement of large numbers of workers. While new jobs continued to be created, they were also increasingly part-time, temporary, low wage, and without important benefits like health insurance (Kronick and Gilmer 1999). The costs of medical care in the United States continued to rise at rates higher than inflation in other sectors at the same time that individuals experienced greater barriers to access and faced substantial medical problems. Old problems, thought to have been solved, returned (e.g. the resurgence of tuberculosis), new ones that perplexed medical researchers and strained the limits of scientific medicine arose (e.g. HIV/AIDS, antibiotic-resistant bacterial infection), and persistent failures plagued the country that continued to spend the most on health care in the world (e.g. the relatively higher infant mortality rate compared with countries like Japan, Poland, Italy, or Sweden with lower national spending rates for health care).

ENTER HEALTH CARE REFORM

For the first time in a century, health care became a central political issue in national, political debates in the 1990s (see figure 10.1). In the presidential elections of 1990, Democratic candidates Bob Kerry and, later, Bill Clinton focused on the crisis in health care as a central issue. To the surprise of many, this issue became a lightening rod among the American people. When he was later elected, Clinton sought major reform in the health care system. He appointed his wife, Hillary Clinton, to chair a Task Force that, between 1992 and 1994, deliberated and crafted the Clinton Health Security Act. Based on the triad of "managed competition," "global budget," and "universal coverage," it sought to achieve improved access to health care through privately provided health insurance and to control costs simultaneously (see Zelman 1996).

The original ideas about *managed competition* focused on the creation of "health alliances," a group of individuals who would enroll in a health insurance plan together and purchase insurance from a private group (see Enthoven 1978). The system would be employer-based, which would allow the "invisible hand of the market" to set a competition in motion among plans to provide the best and widest range of coverage at the lowest prices. A public agency would be established to certify these managed care plans, monitor quality, and guarantee yearly enrollment. The *global budget* provision would essentially move the United States to a single payer system where the federal government would cap the overall health care budget, develop and receive the paperwork (i.e. reimbursement forms), and cut the checks in order to reduce the high costs of administration. Finally, with the goal of *universal coverage*, health alliances would be created for all citizens. Through various provisions (e.g. Medicaid would no longer exist; Medicare would be folded into a health alliance), the Clinton Plan proposed for the first time that health care in America was a right and not a privilege based on ability to pay. In essence, the Clinton Plan essentially preserved the private nature of health care in the United States while ensuring it as a public good.

While scholars, politicians, and policy makers debated the merits of the approach (e.g. Relman 1993) the Clinton Health Reform Act was gutted after the lengthy report recommendations were issued. Very soon after release of the report, the latter two provisions were dropped and the entire plan was abandoned by 1994 (see Domhoff 1996; Skocpol 1997). However, in its demise the private health insurance market transformed the structure and financing of health services and increased the complexity of the health care system. Facing total health benefit costs increasing more than 20 percent each year (Higgins 1991), fiscal constraints resulting from a mounting federal budget deficit, and more skepticism about the value of health care given its costs under a fee-for-service system, private employers sought and achieved substantial changes in their health benefit "designs."

The last decade of the twentieth century represents an historic turn in the American health care system with the expansion of managed care and the privatization of health care markets. No longer is managed care the alternative health care delivery model that it once was, but is increasingly becoming the dominant model in the private sector and a growing one among the public programs of Medicare and Medicaid (Jensen et al. 1997; Gold 1998). And, despite the claims of a "backlash" against managed care and controversy about its impact and growth, two-thirds of Americans report that they are relatively satisfied with their own managed care plan (Blendon et al. 1998).

It is not accurate to talk about "managed care" as a single entity. Managed care refers to a number of diverse insurance options and organizations that integrate the financing and delivery of care (Gold 1998). In fact, there are so many forms of managed care that the term, according to some, has become relatively meaningless. What they share are the goals of increasing efficiency and higher quality of care. Managed care also shares key features including: (1) the use of a fixed prepayment, capitated, or negotiated fee for a defined set of services for a specified population of enrollees; (2) the assumption of insurance risk shared by the managed care organization (MCO) and/or providers to provide necessary services; (3) selective contracting where enrollees are limited to a panel of providers; (4) the use of primary care gatekeepers to coordinate care and control the use of services; (5) utilization review to assess the appropriateness of care and provider decisions before services are provided, including pre-certification, concurrent review, and high-cost case management; (6) the managing of quality of care through the use of clinical practice standards or guidelines; and (7) the tracking of patient and organizational "outcomes," referred to as "performance monitoring," that are to be used to ferret out poor quality plans, care, and providers.

Only a small portion of the insurance market retains the traditional indemnity plan where the insurer pays for the costs of services included in the benefit package after they are delivered, without any pre-negotiation of fees or oversight. Health care insurers achieved this transition to managed care in many ways but all placed limits on type, amount, and providers who can deliver services. For example, pressures were exerted on traditional indemnity insurers who had previously offered limited participation in health maintenance organizations (HMOs) to increase their HMO options and other "products." These other "products" have taken the form of preferred provider organizations (PPOs), independent practice associations (IPAs), or point-of-service (POS) designs, all of which allow employers to purchase services at lower costs than traditional indemnity insurance and manage care in some way (Gabel et al. 1989; 1990; see Zelman 1996 for a discussion of these different models). While more choice was given to individuals by most employers than the traditional HMO, the clear intent was to limit the growth in both insurance premiums and health services costs.

THE CURRENT SYSTEM

The arrangements in American society between the people, medical care providers, health insurers, and the government have been fundamentally reconfigured. There is little doubt that we have entered into a second "social contract" regarding the provision of medical care in the United States (Pescosolido, McLeod, and Alegría 2000). The growing "penetration'" of managed care, as this shift is routinely called, especially in the private sector during the 1990s, has been quite significant. By 1998, 86 percent of employees in large firms (more than 200 employees) were enrolled in some form of managed care plan (Gabel and Hurst 1998). More growth has occurred in the less tightly managed PPOs, IPAs, and POS designs than in the traditional HMOs. These newer managed care models offer more choice in providers and more flexibility (e.g. co-payments for the use of specialists). Even among the traditional plans, various forms of utilization review are being used. Further, there has been substantial growth of managed care among the large public programs for the elderly, disabled, and low income population. For example, among the Medicaid population enrollment in managed care has grown from 3 percent of beneficiaries in 1983 to more than one-half (53.6 percent) by 1998 (Health Care Financing Administration 1992, 1998).

In adopting managed care, states have not only set goals to control costs and improve access for Medicaid beneficiaries, but also to expand coverage to the uninsured (Gold 1997). Many states have taken advantage of this larger shift to the new financing and organization of care to move from being a provider of services to a manager of services (e.g. in the mental health sector). Managed care has grown more slowly in the federal government's Medicare program for the elderly and disabled, although enrollment varies markedly across geographical areas. As of 1999, approximately 17 percent of all Medicare beneficiaries nationally were participating in HMOs, but 52 percent were in "risk contracts" (i.e. arrangements that lay out who is responsible for costs exceeding the capitation fee) in Portland, Oregon compared to 17 percent in New York City (Brown and Gold 1999; Iglehart 1999).

The nature of the second social contract has dramatically altered the powerful position of physicians, making them more subject to limitations set by those who fund their services and the demands of those employers who purchase managed care plans. It has reconfigured the power and position of many stakeholders of America's health care system. But it is also the case that, in the end, this reform has been primarily economic in nature. It has not fundamentally altered the patchwork system of care in the United States nor has it attempted to resolve the great disparities in health and health care access that have always characterized social class and race/ethnic differences in the United States. The second social contract, to date, has neither been guided by nor addressed the social, moral, and political dilemmas facing the American population. In essence, the current reconfiguration of the American health care system has targeted "financial risk" which now may be shared among the organizations that decide on which package to offer employees, the MCO, physicians, hospitals, and health care organizations that provide services (Gold et al. 1998).

The system that has emerged over the past decade is considerably more complex than in the past with changed and complicated relationships among diverse actors. It is a health care system in flux, but one that is no longer centrally focused on the traditional relationship between patients and physicians, with insurance provision as simply a means to an end. People are now "clients" or "consumers." Physicians, along with nurses, technicians, physicians assistants, counselors, are now a generic category of "providers." Limiting the costs of medical care has translated into the growth and use of non-physician providers as a first contact. Often choice by client over their providers is limited and both client and provider must seek permission to engage in certain activities of care (e.g. tests, types of medications, experimental treatments). It is the government and employer "purchasers" of health care services, subject to regulatory constraints, who negotiate with health care plans and managed care organizations (MCOs) about the products and services to be offered to their clients in the health care system. Health plans not only pay for services, but define how and which services are delivered. Access to specialty providers is defined by the benefit plan and subject to a "gatekeeping" role with financial incentives affecting primary care providers. For example, many plans require a visit to a primary care physician before any specialty care can be offered. Providers, themselves, must respond to professional and government regulatory statutes that define the content of their work and, along with utilization review processes, that define standards of "medical necessity." Many insurance companies, MCOs, and providers have merged, creating local, regional, and sometimes national medical networks designed to achieve both economies of scale and more bargaining power (Thorpe 1997). Finally, while the clients' support system of family, friends, and consumer groups may act as advocates in their interactions with providers and MCOs, managed care has also shifted much of the burden from the medical care system to the community (Pescosolido and Kronenfeld 1995). Families may be the recipients of services as well as be required to provide greater levels of informal support services as allowable days of hospitalization have decreased and outpatient surgery increased.

The greater complexity of arrangements means that multiple perspectives of many key stakeholders, beyond the traditional physician – patient relationship, must be taken into account in health outcomes, professional norms, and behaviors. The interests of these multiple actors may be compatible, but they are more likely to result in increased tensions and conflicts in the provision of medical care. Physicians, patients, and the courts are struggling with denied request for treatment and grievance procedures following from them (Rodwin 1995). There are also increasing concerns about offering financial incentives to physicians or MCOs that may result in conflicts of interest that can compromise care. Under a capitated system, for example, physicians have a financial incentive to minimize expensive services, and yet to provide high quality care that may require the use of costly treatments. Referrals to specialty providers may be costly to a provider network, but may offer more appropriate and effective care to clients (Schlesinger and Mechanic 1996).

EMERGING ISSUES IN THE CONTEMPORARY AMERICAN HEALTH CARE SYSTEM

Coupled with the explosive growth of managed care are serious concerns about the increasing uninsured population, the future control of health expenditures, caring for individuals with chronic illnesses and disabilities under a managed care environment, the changing nature of the medical profession and how new relationships among providers, insurance plans, and consumers will best serve the delivery of care. In moving from a predominantly fee-for-service system controlled by physicians to a corporatized system dominated by financial and industrial interests, McKinlay and Marceau (1998) contend that the federal government has abandoned its role in protecting public health or producing any significant change in America's health care system. Among the major concerns that have arisen, two issues are likely to dominate the policy agenda of both state and federal governments: (1) the impact on Medicaid and Medicare, and (2) the public reaction to experiences in managed care.

First, the only groups in America served by government-sponsored insurance programs may be at risk. Medicaid beneficiaries are especially vulnerable to the new financing and delivery arrangements because they are more likely to have special health care needs that require a complex array of social and rehabilitative services in addition to medical treatment (Gold, Sparer, and Chu 1996). The medical necessity criteria used by MCOs have been narrow, failing to encompass the ongoing services and care that persons with chronic illnesses and disabilities may require. Second, there may be a "fraying national safety net" (Zelman 1996), that results in a decrease in care for the uninsured population as Medicaid managed care programs expand. Under managed care, hospitals and other community health centers face reduced revenues from capitated or negotiated fees to cross-subsidize the care for the uninsured. Under prior rate regulation, hospitals received enhanced rates from private insurers to finance charity care. Improving access, but not universally, through managed care plans may paradoxically occur at the expense of the uninsured and the public hospitals that can no longer shift the costs from "profit-making" services to those that routinely serve the uninsured (Gold, Sparer, and Chu 1996). Similarly, at the state government level, policymakers use funding sources for eligibility expansion under their managed care plans that in the past were used to finance uncompensated care.

Further, despite enrollment gains, the Medicare program has also faced 28 percent of their HMO contracts terminating coverage or reducing services in selected unprofitable areas in 1998 with additional withdrawals occurring in 1999 and others expected in 2000 (Laschober et al. 1999). These withdrawals have been more likely to affect beneficiaries enrolled in for-profit managed care plans, those in HMOs with lower Medicare payment rates, and those whose plans had significant financial losses (Neuman and Langwell 1999). This retrenchment in HMOs serving Medicare beneficiaries results in the elderly and disabled having to switch to another managed care plan or return to a fee-for-service option. In addition to the disruption in their care, beneficiaries face higher premium costs and the loss of some benefits not currently covered by the Medicare program, notably outpatient prescription drugs and vision care, that may not be available in another plan or only with much higher premiums.

Similar to Medicaid beneficiaries, the Medicare population has subgroups whose care is expensive because of chronic illnesses and catastrophic events. A fundamental, yet unresolved issue, is adjusting for health risks for "sicker-than-average" enrollees in order that plans are not unfairly penalized and those plans with healthier enrollees are not too generously reimbursed. At the present time, providers with a good reputation in providing care for the most seriously ill are disadvantaged (i.e. referred to as "unfavorable risk selection") and incur large income losses forcing their withdrawal from managed care plans. With the financial incentive under a capitated fee to minimize services to control costs, quality of care is threatened for the most vulnerable beneficiaries with poor health status and complex needs.

Under the 1997 federal government's Balanced Budget Act (BBA), wide-ranging changes occurred in the Medicare program. Changes made in the pay-ment "methodology" resulted in tighter restraints on rates, beneficiaries were allowed expanded choice in managed health plans, and risk adjustment mechan-isms based on health status are to be implemented in 2000. The new payment rates to MCOs and providers are to be based on the "expected relative health status of each enrollee." Because of the "imperfect nature" of risk adjustment, a partial capitation approach has been recommended with both the capitated rate and a payment based on the actual services used. This strategy could reduce risk selection in managed care plans and lessen the incentives to minimize services for the most seriously and chronically ill persons (Newhouse 1998; Wilensky and Newhouse 1999).

Second, the rapid growth of managed care over the past decade has not occurred without considerable controversy and consumer backlash evidenced in the courts, the media, and public opinion surveys. A series of class action lawsuits are underway, more than one thousand bills have been introduced in state legislatures and the Congress to address consumer protection, and a pre-sidential commission was created to consider future guidelines for the managed care industry (Blendon et al. 1998). Surveys show that under managed care the public has concerns about the quality of health care, the denial of services when sick, difficulty in getting referrals to specialists, and that health plans value cost control over the best medical care. The public also seems to regard possibly rare events, such as the denial of cancer treatment for a child, as a common occur-rence among managed care plans (Blendon et al. 1998). For the first time, at the end of 1999, a plan in one state (New Jersey) announced its intention to cover experimental cancer treatments. Still, most Americans remain relatively satisfied with their own health insurance plan whether it is managed or not

(Blendon et al. 1998). This contradictory finding of individuals being satisfied with their own managed care plan, yet skeptical of managed care generally fits with a long tradition of research that similarly showed Americans as being satisfied with their own physician but critical of the larger system of health care.

CHALLENGES AND OPPORTUNITIES IN THE AMERICAN HEALTH CARE SYSTEM

Ultimately the success of the current system of health care in the United States will be measured by its ability to achieve cost control while enhancing access, outcomes, and satisfaction among the public. Broadly speaking, most research shows mixed results and few significant differences in how patients fare in managed care compared to the more traditional fee-for-service arrangements. But few studies are currently available which compare various forms and arrangements of managed care to fee-for-service plans, so little is known about which financing strategies work most effectively to ensure quality of care. There are some studies showing that the poor, elderly, and others with chronic illnesses receive less appropriate treatments under managed care (Miller and Luft 1994; Ware et al. 1996). For children and adolescents, there is some indication that managed care may compromise quality of care, but insufficient data exist to be fully certain about its impact. For example, one large study of utilization management in a managed fee-for-service health plan showed that concurrent review reduced inpatient days, but also significantly increased the risk of readmissions within 60 days after discharge (Wickizer, Lessler, and Boyd-Wickizer 1999). Enrollees in HMOs and other managed care plans are more likely to receive preventive services (e.g. mammograms), but the long-term benefits of these services across populations with different risks is unknown. Finally, the expectation that managed care, in general, will lead to better integrated systems and promote continuity of care has yet to be demonstrated.

These concerns set the agenda for three basic challenges for those in the health care system, those who study it, those responsible for the public's health, and those who live under its arrangements. We detail these below.

CHALLENGE 1: THE RISING UNINSURED POPULATION

One of the most pressing issues facing policy makers, state administrators, and providers today is the rising numbers of uninsured individuals in the United States. The most recent estimate from the Census Bureau was that 44.3 million people or 16.3 percent of the population had no health insurance in 1998, an increase of about one million people since 1997 (United States Department of Commerce 1999). Over the past ten years alone, the number of uninsured has grown by 35 percent or by 11.6 million people.

Using a comparison with national census data, it appears that several characteristics influence the risk of not having health insurance coverage. The number of uninsured children in 1998 was 11.1 million or 15.4 percent of all children less than 18 years of age (United States Department of Commerce 1999). Individuals aged 18 to 24 years old are more likely than other age groups to lack coverage (30 percent). Those of Hispanic origin have the highest rate of being uninsured (35.3 percent) within racial and ethnic groups. Among the poor, Hispanics also have the highest rates of being uninsured (44 percent). In general, not having insurance declined as educational level increased; but among the poor, no differences in uninsurance rates existed across educational levels. Further, among the poor, workers were less likely to be insured than non-workers creating a growing pool of uninsured workers (i.e. approximately one-half or 47.5 percent of poor, full-time workers in 1998). Workers employed by smaller firms (with fewer than 25 employees) were least likely to be insured (Cooper and Schone 1997; Ginsburg, Gabel, and Hunt 1998; Kronick and Gilmer 1999).

Paradoxically, the uninsured population has increased at a time of fairly robust economic growth and relatively low unemployment levels. However, the sharp decline in the number of Americans with health insurance appears to be linked to increases in health care spending relative to real family income (Custer 1999; Kronick and Gilmer 1999). As personal health care costs consumed a larger portion of personal and family budgets, health insurance premiums and the proportion of premiums paid by employees became less affordable.

The most recent major legislation to address the growing number of uninsured is directed to children, the Children's Health Insurance Program (CHIP), enacted as part of the Balanced Budget Act of 1997. The program is a federal/state government partnership initiative that gives considerable discretion to the states in implementing the program. CHIP provides three options for increasing affordable insurance coverage to low income, uninsured children in working families who earn too much to be insured through the Medicaid program but whose income is insufficient to afford private coverage. The options include designing a new children's health insurance program, expanding the current state Medicaid programs, or introducing a combination of both strategies. Ambiguities in the legislation and conflicting policy agendas at the state level have hampered initial enrollment and implementation, but it is too early to document CHIP's impact (Rosenbaum 1998; Halfon et al. 1999).

CHALLENGE 2: DOES MANAGED CARE CONTROL COSTS? HEALTH SPENDING IN A COMPARATIVE PERSPECTIVE

Given the major transformations in the American health care sector during the past decade, a key indicator of success is how well health expenditures have been controlled. An unprecedented slowing in the growth of health expenditures occurred between 1993 and 1997 in the United States. Health care's share of the gross domestic product (GDP) fluctuated between 13.5 and 13.7 percent, an unexpected plateau given the previous trend and predictions at the start of the decade (Smith et al. 1999). The decline in health expenditure growth as a share of GDP was also accompanied by increases in the GDP.

Between 1993 and 1997 the average annual growth in health spending was 3.3 percent for the private sector and 7.1 percent for public spending. For the Medicaid program the average annual growth was limited to 5.6 percent, a record decline since 1960 and a sharp comparison to the 21.7 percent steep growth between 1990 and 1993. For Medicare, only a slight decline in average annual growth (9.6 percent) occurred between 1993 and 1997 compared to the 10.1 percent growth in the three previous years. Tighter constraints on Medicare payment rates associated with the Balanced Budget Act of 1997 may result in sharper, recent declines in the rate of growth of spending in the Medicare program (Smith et al. 1999).

All industrialized countries have encountered escalating health care costs, and various forms of rationing, however openly discussed, have helped to slow health expenditure growth cross-nationally (Mechanic 1999). The percent of GDP spent on health care between 1990 and 1997 appeared to be relatively stable cross-nationally, even declining in 10 of the 29 countries that are members of the Organization for Economic Cooperation and Development (OECD). The United States still continues to spend a substantially greater share of its GDP on health than the median (7.5 percent) for the OECD countries (OECD 1998). The historical trend showed the percent of GDP spent on health care in the United States increasing from 5.2 percent to 13.5 percent from 1960 to 1997 compared to the median levels of 3.8 percent to 7.5 percent in the OECD countries. Further, in comparison with these countries, per capita health spending also continued to diverge substantially between the United States and the OECD countries during that same time period (i.e. from $141 to $3,925 compared to the median increase of $66 to $1,728).

The question at the center of the current controversy is whether managed care has resulted in a one time reduction in the growth of health expenditures or whether some permanent control of spending can be sustained. Some analysts project that the slowing of health spending will not continue as national health expenditures are projected to reach $2.2 trillion (16.2 percent of the GDP) by 2008 (Smith et al. 1998). Enrollment in less restricted forms of managed care; a loosening of constraints on access to treatments and services under managed care given consumer backlash and patient protection legislation; appropriate risk adjustment for seriously and chronically ill individuals; the aging of the population and increasing technological innovation stand at the heart of these projections. However, the growth of managed care in the Medicaid and Medicare programs should also moderate the growth of health spending to some extent given payment reductions from the Balanced Budget Act.

CHALLENGE 3: HOW WILL MANAGED CARE AFFECT THE PHYSICIAN–PATIENT RELATIONSHIP?

As the organization and financing of health care have changed in the United States, so has the practice of medicine been transformed in significant ways. Starr (1982) predicted that the coming of corporate medicine and the financial behavior of large corporations in the 1980s would threaten the autonomy and power of the medical profession. As figure 10.1 indicates, the relative power of physicians has declined in the era of managed care but we have yet to know whether, how, and if this will level off, be reversed, or continue downward (see dotted lines). The continuing frustration and dissatisfaction among physicians about their loss of authority in clinical decision-making, the ethical dilemmas faced in balancing financial incentives with good care, and their inability to refer to specialists and prescribe optimal drugs are invariably associated with the expansive presence of managed care in medical practices (Grumbach et al. 1998; Hadley et al. 1999).

The significant change has not been the introduction of financial considerations in client/physician relationships. Financial incentives have always existed for physicians in their medical work even beyond the early forms of pre-paid practices where physicians were paid a salary or a capitated fee to provide necessary medical services. Though the medical profession has portrayed itself as having erected a wall between money and medicine, and the professional ideology has been that "doctors' decisions and recommendations were dictated by the best interests of the patient and by science and distinctly not by the pecuniary interests of the doctor" (Stone 1997), the reality of medical practice has been much more complicated and different from this idealized conception of professional practice.

The fee-for-service payment system prompted physicians and other practitioners to provide more services for their clients without the pressing consideration of their cost-effectiveness nor financial risk to themselves. Under managed care arrangements, the financial incentives are reversed. Physicians and other providers are to care for their clients with fewer services to attain high quality care. But the more significant changes in the practice of medicine have been in the social and cultural depiction of the physician and the medical profession where physicians are seen as "subordinated to financiers" (Stone 1997).

In essence, the explicit linking of the financing and delivery of services under managed care has changed the locus of decision-making in medical practice. Representatives in organizations beyond the physician dictate the process of referrals, certify admission and discharge decisions, profile the services that physicians use, and recommend types of services. Managed care organizations establish the networks in which physicians operate and to which clients seek care. Treatment guidelines have been established in an effort to standardize care and reduce variations in practice that can limit the independent decision-making of physicians. Physicians may be dropped from networks and health plans if they are not performing to standards set by the MCO. Some treatments that were previously performed by physicians are now delegated to other health professionals. All of these changes remove the power over medical care from the physician and transfer it to others.

The call for a "responsive medical professionalism" (Frankford and Konrad 1998) brings attention to the potential of physicians to recapture levels of leadership, albeit in different ways than under the era of professional dominance. A united effort between physicians and community programs can lessen the long-standing resistance of physicians to public health efforts and serve the profession, the public, and MCOs (Mechanic 1998). Further, since one of the most troublesome issues under managed care is the potential for the denial of treatment, physicians may become effective advocates for their clients. In representing their clients' interests to MCOs and others, physicians can preserve the trust that is an essential component of the physician – patient relationship (Mechanic and Schlesinger 1996). However, the shift to managed care requires that these new organizations *also* inspire trust and "prove" their trustworthiness, in part, by assuring their enrollees that they will not interfere with the trust that patients can put in their physicians (Flood 1998; Sleeper et al. 1998). In a national study of utilization review firms, about one-third of the firms reported successful appeal rates of 2 percent or less which might suggest that this low rate results, at least in part, from physicians failing to take a strong advocacy role (Schlesinger, Gray, and Perreira 1997).

CONCLUSION: WHERE TO NOW?

The now dominant payment system of managed care in the United States continues to expand, and yet considerable flux exists in its various organizational and financial arrangements. Changes are ongoing as evidenced by the recent decision by the United Health Group (UHG), one of the nation's largest MCOs, to return decision-making about admissions and other treatments to physicians. That is, upon documenting that utilization review was costing more than it saved, they eliminated the practice and dismissed employees engaged in that process. Prior approval about certain treatment decisions will no longer be necessary. While UHG will continue to monitor physicians' use of hospitalization and other services, this landmark decision represents the return of some discretion to physicians (New York Times 1999). Aside from the financial issue, this decision responds to patients' rights laws, the potential of litigation, and physician dissatisfaction. These forces are shaping the American medical care system of the future.

From a comparative perspective the United States, as well as other countries with very different health care systems, continue to search for strategies to contain costs, manage the care for chronic illnesses and disabilities, and develop new and better services. A study of reform in seventeen OECD countries noted the "emerging convergence" of strategies "pioneered earlier in other countries" (OECD 1998). The Diagnostic Related Group (DRG) prospective payment methodology has been implemented in several Australian state governments to decrease inpatient length of stay (Davis 1999). Canada has adopted model community-based programs for caring for the seriously mentally ill that have been used in the United States (Rochefort and Goering 1998). Britain considered, but found unworkable, a plan to compile a list of procedures that would not be covered by the National Health Service (Klein 1994). In the United States, physician associations are negotiating capitated managed care contracts not unlike the general practitioner fundholding in Great Britain and the physician groups in New Zealand who plan to operate under risk-based contracts (Davis 1999). Although the various health care systems operate under different organizing principles and evolve from unique political and social cultures, economic climates, and the roles of the medical profession, many common problems exist cross-nationally. The American health care system can benefit greatly from sharing strategies and learning from what is happening beyond its borders.

References

Berlant, J. 1975. *Profession and Monopoly: A Study of Medicine in the United States and Great Britain*. Berkeley, CA: University of California Press.

Blendon, R. J., M. Brodie, J. M. Benson, D. E. Altman, L. Levitt, T. Hoff, and L. Hugick. 1998. "Understanding the Managed Care Backlash." *Health Affairs* 17: 80–94.

Brown, E. R. 1979. *Rockefeller Medicine Men: Medicine and Capitalism in America*. Berkeley, CA: University of California Press.

Brown, R. S. and M. R. Gold. 1999. "What Drives Medicare Managed Care Growth?" *Health Affairs* 18: 140–9.

Collins, R. 1979. *The Credential Society*. New York: Academic Press.

Cooper, P. F. and B. S. Schone. 1997. "More Offers, Fewer Takers for Employment-Based Health Insurance: 1987 and 1996." *Health Affairs* 16: 103–10.

Custer, W. S. 1999. "Health Insurance Coverage and the Uninsured." A Report to the Health Insurance Association of America. Washington, DC: Health Insurance Association of America.

Davis, K. 1999. "International Health Policy: Common Problems, Alternative Strategies." *Health Affairs* 18: 135–43.

Domhoff, W. G. 1996. *State Autonomy or Class Dominance? Case Studies on Policy Making in America*. New York: Aldine.

Enthoven, A. C. 1978. "Consumer-choice Health Plan: Inflation and Inequity in Health Care Today: Alternatives for Cost Control and an Analysis of Proposals for National Health Insurance." *New England Journal of Medicine* 298: 650–85.

Flood, A. B. 1998. "Risk, Trust, and the HMO: An Editorial." *Journal of Health and Social Behavior* 39: 187–8.

Frankford, D. M. and T. R. Konrad. 1998. "Responsive Medical Professionalism: Integrating Education, Practice and Community in a Market-Driven Era." *Academic Medicine* 73: 138–45.

Freidson, E. 1970. *Professional Dominance*. New York: Atherton Press.

Freudenheim, M. 1999. "Big HMO to Give Decisions on Care Back to Doctors." *New York Times*. November 9: A1, C8.

Gabel, J., S. DiCarlo, S. Fink, and G. deLissovoy. 1989. "Employer-Sponsored Health Insurance in America." *Health Affairs* 8: 116–128.

Gabel, J., S. DiCarlo, C. Sullivan, and T. Rice. 1990. "Employer-Sponsored Health Insurance in America 1989." *Health Affairs* 9: 161–175.

Gabel, J. R. and K. Hurst. 1998. *Health Benefits in 1998: Executive Summary*. Washington, DC: KPMG Peat Marwick.

Ginsburg, P. B., J. R. Gabel, and K. A. Hunt. 1998. "Tracking Small-Firm Coverage, 1989–1996." *Health Affairs* 17: 167–71.

Gold, M. R. 1997. "Markets and Public Programs: Insights from Oregon and Tennessee." *Journal of Health Politics, Policy, and Law* 22: 633–66.

——. 1998. "Understanding the Roots: Health Maintenance Organizations in Historical Context." Pp. 7–16 in M. R. Gold (ed.), *Contemporary Managed Care: Readings in Structure, Operations, and Public Policy*. Chicago: Health Administration Press.

Gold, M. R., M. Sparer, and K. Chu. 1996. "Medicaid Managed Care: Lessons from Five States." *Health Affairs* 15: 153–66.

Gold, M. R., L. Nelson, T. Lake, R. Hurley, and R. Berenson. 1998. "Behind the Curve: A Critical Assessment of How Little is Known about Arrangements between Managed Care Plans and Physicians." Pp. 67–100 in M. R. Gold (ed.), *Contemporary Managed Care: Reading in Structure, Operations, and Public Policy.* Chicago: Health Administration Press.

Grumbach, K., D. Osmond, K. Vranizan, D. Jaffe, and A. B. Bindman. 1998. "Primary Care Physicians' Experience of Financial Incentives in Managed-Care Systems." *New England Journal of Medicine* 339: 1516–21.

Hadley, J., J. M. Mitchell, D. P. Sulmasy, and M. G. Bloche. 1999. "Perceived Financial Incentives, HMO Market Penetration, and Physicians' Practice Styles and Satisfaction." *Health Services Research* 34: 307–19.

Halfon, N., M. Inkelas, H. DuPlessis, and P. W. Newacheck. 1999. "Challenges in Securing Access to Care for Children." *Health Affairs* 18: 48–63.

Health Care Financing Administration, Medicaid Bureau. 1992. *Medicaid Coordinated Care Enrollment Report: Summary Statistics as of June 30, 1992.* Baltimore: US Department of Health and Human Services.

Health Care Financing Administration, Office of Managed Care. 1998. *National Summary of Medicaid Managed Care Programs and Enrollment as of June 30, 1998.* Baltimore: US Department of Health and Human Services.

Higgins, A. F. 1991. *Health Care Benefits Survey*, vol. 1. NJ: Health Care Benefits Survey.

Iglehart, J. K. 1999. "Bringing Forth Medicare + Choice: HCFA's Robert A. Berenson." *Health Affairs* 18: 144–9.

Jensen, G. A., M. Morrisey, S. Gaffney, and D. K. Listin. 1997. "The New Dominance of Managed Care: Insurance Trends in the 1990s." *Health Affairs* 16: 125–36.

Klein, R. 1994. "Can we Restrict the Health Care Menu?" *Health Policy* 27: 103–12.

Kronick, R. and T. Gilmer. 1999. "Explaining the Decline in Health Insurance Coverage, 1979–1995." *Health Affairs* 18: 30–47.

Laschober, M. A., P. Neuman, M. S. Kitchman, L. Meyer, and K. M. Langwell. 1999. "Medicare HMO Withdrawals: What Happens to Beneficiaries?" *Health Affairs* 18: 150–7.

Light, D. 1995. "Countervailing Powers: A Framework for Professions in Transition." Pp. 25–41 in T. Johnson, G. Larking, and M. Saks (eds.) *Health Professions and the State in Europe.* London: Routledge.

Light, D. and S. Levine. 1988. "The Changing Character of the Medical Profession: A Theoretical Overview." *Milbank Quarterly* 66 (supplement): 10–32.

McKinlay, J. B. and L. D. Marceau. 1998. "The End of the Golden Age of Doctoring." Presented at the American Public Health Association, Washington, DC, November.

Mechanic, D. 1998. "Topics for Our Times: Managed Care and Public Health Opportunities." *American Journal of Public Health* 88: 874–5.

——. 1999. "Lessons from Abroad: A Comparative Perspective." Pp. 25–34 in F. Powell and A. Wesson (eds.), *Health Care Systems in Transition: An International Perspective.* Newbury Park, CA: Sage.

Mechanic, D. and M. Schlesinger. 1996. "The Impact of Managed Care on Patients' Trust in Medical Care and Their Physicians." *Journal of the American Medical Association* 275: 1693–7.

Miller, R. H. and H. S. Luft. 1994. "Managed Care Plan Performance Since 1980: A Literature Analysis." *Journal of the American Medical Association* 271: 1512–19.

Neuman, P. and K. M. Langwell. 1999. "Medicare's Choice Explosion? Implications for Beneficiaries." *Health Affairs* 18: 150–60.

Newhouse, J. P. 1998. "Risk Adjustment: Where Are We Now?" *Inquiry* 35: 122–31.

Organization for Economic Cooperation and Development. 1994. *The Reform of*

Health Care Systems: A Review of Seventeen OECD Countries. Paris: Organization for Economic Cooperation and Development.

——. 1998. *OECD Health Data 98: A Comparative Analysis of Twenty-Nine Countries.* Paris: Organization for Economic Cooperation and Development.

Pescosolido, Bernice A. and J. J. Kronenfeld. 1995. "Sociological Understandings of Health, Illness, and Healing: the Challenge From and For Medical Sociology." *Journal of Health and Social Behavior* (Extra Issue): 5–33.

Pescosolido, Bernice A., J. McLeod, and M. Alegría. 2000. "Confronting the Second Social Contract: The Place of Medical Sociology in Research and Policy for the 21st Century." Pp. 411–26 in C. Bird, P. Conrad, and A. Fremont (eds.), *The Handbook of Medical Sociology*, 5th edn. Upper Saddle River, NJ: Prentice-Hall.

Pescosolido, Bernice A. and B. A. Rubin. 2000. "The Web of Group Affiliations Revisited: Social Life, Postmodernism and Sociology." *American Sociological Review*: 65: 52–76.

Relman, A. S. 1993. "Controlling Costs by 'Managed Competition' – Would It Work?" *New England Journal of Medicine* 328: 133–5.

Rochefort, D. and P. Goering. 1998. "More a Link than a Division: How Canada Has Learned from U.S. Mental Health Policy." *Health Affairs* 16: 110–27.

Rodwin, M. A. 1995. "Conflicts in Managed Care." *New England Journal of Medicine* 332: 604–7.

Rosen, G. 1963. "The Hospital." Pp. 1–36 in E. Freidson (ed.), *The Hospital in Modern Society*. New York: Free Press.

Rosenbaum, S. 1998. "The Children's Hour: The State Children's Health Insurance Program." *Health Affairs* 17: 75–89.

Rubin, B. A. 1996. *Shifts in the Social Contract*. Thousand Oaks, CA: Pine Forge Press.

Schlesinger, M. and D. Mechanic. 1996. "An Integrated National Study of Relationships and Outcomes in Managed Mental Health Care." Proposal submitted to the National Institute of Mental Health. New Brunswick, NJ: Rutgers University.

Schlesinger, M. J., B. H. Gray, and K. M. Perreira. 1997. "Medical Professionalism under Managed Care: The Pros and Cons of Utilization Review." *Health Affairs* 16: 106–24.

Skocpol, T. 1997. *Boomerang – Health Care Reform and the Turn Against Government*. New York: North and Co.

Sleeper, S., D. R. Wholey, R. Hamer, S. Schwartz, and V. Inoferio. 1998. "Trust Me: Technical and Institutional Determinants of Health Maintenance Organizations Shifting Risk to Physicians." *Journal of Health and Social Behavior* 36: 189–200.

Smith, S., S. Heffler, M. Freeland, and the National Health Expenditures Projection Team. 1999. "The Next Decade of Health Spending: A New Outlook." *Health Affairs* 18: 86–95.

Smith, S., M. Freeland, S. Heffler, D. McKusick, and the Health Expenditures Projection Team. 1998. "The Next Ten Years of Health Spending: What Does the Future Hold?" *Health Affairs* 17: 128–40.

Starr, P. 1982. *The Social Transformation of American Medicine*. New York: Basic Books, Inc.

Stone, D. A. 1997. "The Doctor as Businessman: The Changing Politics of a Cultural Icon." *Journal of Health Politics, Policy and Law* 22: 533–56.

Thorpe, K. 1997. "The Health System in Transition: Care, Cost and Coverage." *Journal of Health Politics, Policy, and Law* 22: 339–61.

United States Department of Commerce, Bureau of the Census. 1999. *Current Population Survey*. Washington, DC: Department of Commerce.

Unschuld, P. 1976. "Western Medicine and Traditional Healing Systems: Competition, Cooperation, or Integration?" *Ethics in Science and Medicine* 3: 1–20.

Ware, J. E., M. S. Bayliss, W. H. Rogers, M. Kosinski, and A. R. Tarlov. 1996. "Differences in 4–Year Health Outcomes for Elderly and Poor Chronically Ill Patients Treated in HMO and Fee-for-Service Systems." *Journal of the American Medical Association* 276: 1039–47.

Wickizer, T. M., D. Lessler, and J. Boyd-Wickizer. 1999. "Readmissions among Children and Adolescents." *American Journal of Public Health* 89: 1353–8.

Wilensky, G. R. and J. P. Newhouse. 1999. "Medicare: What's Right? What's Wrong? What's Next?" *Health Affairs* 18: 92–106.

Zelman, W. A. 1996. *The Changing Health Care Marketplace*. San Francisco: Jossey-Bass.

11

The Evolution of Health Care in Canada: Toward Community or Corporate Control?

HARLEY D. DICKINSON AND B. SINGH BOLARIA

Health policy in Canada oscillates between preventative and curative approaches. In general, prevention and promotion are subordinate to treatment and cure, but the balance is historically variable. Policy shifts in one direction or the other are accompanied by shifts in the nature of control over, and the distribution of power within, the health care system. In the late nineteenth century, for example, we saw the professionalization, scientization, and institutionalization of the curative approach in health care. More recently, in the last decades of the twentieth century, we have begun to see a reassertion of preventative approaches and various other challenges to the dominance of modern medicine.

In this chapter we outline key dimensions of the nature and organization of the Canadian health care system. We review the literature on the introduction of state hospitalization and medical care insurance programs (Medicare). We then look at current reforms initiatives and argue that they are manifestations of the struggle both for, and against, medical dominance.

HEALTH CARE AND HEALTH CARE POLICY IN CANADA

Canada does not have a single health care system. Under the Canadian constitution health is an area of provincial jurisdiction. As a result, there are ten provincial and three territorial health care systems. The main policy tools available to the Federal government, to influence health care policy and service delivery, are rather blunt fiscal and budgetary mechanisms combined with whatever influence it can exert on the formation of public opinion.

The federal – provincial jurisdictional split has meant, historically, that health care reforms occur at the provincial or sub-provincial levels of government. Examples include the Saskatchewan Municipal Doctor Plans, Union Hospital arrang-

ements, regionalized forms of health policy planning and service delivery, community clinics, as well as various hospital and medical care insurance plans (Douglas
1946; Mott 1947; Roth and Defries 1958; Wolfe 1964; Mombourquette 1991).

Health care insurance was an issue that was variously on and off the national
and provincial political agendas. By the 1940s, failure of the market to ensure
adequate access to necessary medical and hospital care, combined with limitations of the various locally developed collectivist solutions, had generated
renewed interest in state medical care and hospitalization insurance. This was
given added impetus by experiences with war time military and industrial
recruitment where it was discovered that an alarming proportion of recruits
were too sickly for military or industrial service (Fuller 1998: 27). As a result of
this experience, and other statistics that demonstrated the poor health status of
the Canadian population, health insurance was firmly established as a key
component in government plans for postwar reconstruction.

Thus, in 1945, the Federal government put forward a plan for a universal
health care insurance program cost shared by the federal and provincial governments. The general rationale for state intervention in this area was the belief that
improved access to hospital and physician services would result in improved
health status. This in turn was seen to translate directly into increased productivity and national prosperity. A more particular motivation for proposing a
state financed, universal, and comprehensive health insurance program was
concern that the proposed alternatives were inadequate.

By the end of the war there was a political consensus that health care could not
be left to the market. Beyond that, however, there was little agreement. The
medical profession favored a hospital and medical care insurance system that
was based on voluntary participation in physician-sponsored or commercial
insurance plans. The state's role would be limited to providing coverage on a
means-tested basis to the medically indigent. The private insurance industry was
in favor of a similar arrangement. Business organizations in general also
favoured such an arrangement because of concerns about creeping socialism,
as were several provincial governments. Even the organized trade-union movement was somewhat ambivalent about universal, compulsory state health insurance because they had largely secured coverage for their membership through
various voluntary, private plans (Walters 1982). Among the strongest supporters
of state insurance were the various farmer organizations, especially in western
Canada. It is not surprising then that the first compulsory, universal, state
financed and administered hospitalization insurance plan was introduced in
Saskatchewan by a newly elected political party dominated by farmer interests
(Dickinson 1993).

The federal government was convinced of the necessity to introduce a similar
plan on a national scale for the reasons cited above. Thus, in 1945, at the
Federal-Provincial Conference on Reconstruction, it introduced draft legislation.
Key features of the legislation were the establishment of health regions, patient
registration with physicians, a capitation mode of payment, additional financial
incentives for physicians who adopted preventative approaches, and the administration of the system by commissions consisting of both physicians and consumers (Taylor 1978; Vayda and Deber 1992: 126).

The proposed plan was not implemented, however, because of provincial government concerns about Federal incursion into areas of provincial jurisdiction, and failure to reach agreement on taxation issues (Taylor 1960). As federal–provincial discussions bogged down and the prospects of implementation receded into the future, a new consensus emerged around the adoption of an incremental approach to the introduction of state health insurance.

The first major step in this regard was taken at the provincial level by the government of Saskatchewan when, in 1946, it introduced the country's first universal, comprehensive system of tax-paid hospitalization insurance. For its part the Federal government contented itself with introducing the National Health Grants program in 1948. This program was uncontentious from the perspective of the provinces and the organized medical profession because its main purpose was to increase hospital bed capacity across the country. The rationale behind this was that increased and equalized hospital bed capacity would result in increased access to needed hospital services and, as a result of that, equalized health status and increased productivity and economic prosperity. From a purely political perspective the National Health Grants program was seen as an important dimension of national building.

The 1946 Saskatchewan hospitalization insurance program was designed to be eligible for federal cost-sharing once agreement was reached between the rest of the provinces and the Federal government. Before that happened, however, four more provinces introduced hospitalization insurance plans. These five provinces increased pressure on the Federal government to introduce the long-promised cost-sharing arrangements. This was done in 1956 with passage of the Hospital Insurance and Diagnostic Services (HIDS) Act. By 1961, the remaining five provinces had introduced hospitalization insurance plans. The medical profession, although wary of this development, were not opposed to it, largely because it served to increase their incomes and posed no real threat to their autonomy.

Hospitalization insurance encouraged both physicians and patients to think of hospitalization as a treatment of first resort. This ensured high occupancy rates and rising costs. This inflationary feature of hospitalization insurance plans was reproduced and amplified in the medical care insurance plans that followed.

Although the introduction of state hospitalization was largely uncontentious, the introduction of medical care insurance was accompanied by bitter struggles. Analytical approaches to understanding the nature and consequences of those struggles vary (Tollefson 1963; Thompson 1964; Badgley and Wolfe 1967; Taylor 1978; Naylor 1986). A common theme, however, is medical autonomy and dominance, and its consequences for the nature and organization of health care delivery (Taylor 1960; Blishen 1969; Swartz 1977; Walters 1982; Coburn, Torrance, and Kaufert 1983; White 1984; Tuohy 1994;).

Walters (1982), for example, analyzes the introduction of Medicare in terms of the state's contribution to capital accumulation and political legitimation. Relative to capital accumulation, she sees Medicare as an attempt by the state to ensure the reproduction of a healthy and productive working class. Access to health care services, particularly hospital and physician services, is assumed to result in improved health status among the working population. The prevailing decentralized system of hospital and physician services was seen to be in need of rationalization and reform. Medical autonomy and the self-interest of the private insurance industry were seen as inadequate foundations for national health policy. From this perspective medical autonomy and professional monopoly were seen as barriers both to the rationalization of the health care system and to improved population health status.

Swartz (1977), in contrast to Walters, argues that the introduction of Medicare is best understood as a concession wrung from the capitalist class and its state through the struggles of a militant working class and its political allies. He maintains that Medicare was part of an effort to appease the working class by increasing the social wage. Swartz's analysis draws attention to the ways in which the resistance of the medical profession resulted in modifications to the form and content of the original proposals for socialized medicine. These concessions had the effect of entrenching the interests and dominance of the medical profession (Weller and Manga 1983; Naylor 1986).

Coburn, Torrance, and Kaufert (1983) argue that the introduction of Medicare is best understood both as a response to working class agitation, and as an attempt to supply the capitalist class with adequate quantities of healthy labor. In contrast to Swartz (1977) and others, however, they argue that the introduction of Medicare marked the beginning of the end of medical autonomy and dominance, not its entrenchment.

Thus, debate over whether Medicare entrenched or undermined medical autonomy and dominance continues, and the evidence is contradictory. What is clear, however, is that the organized medical profession was afraid for its autonomy (Badgley and Wolfe 1967). Although the organized medical profession was unable to thwart the introduction of Medicare they were able to force the governments of the day to make significant compromises.

The main compromises made by the government of Saskatchewan, which eventually came to characterize medical care insurance programs throughout all of Canada, were retention of the fee-for-service system of remuneration and professional control over fee setting. From the perspective of the profession, fee-for-service, as opposed to the alternatives of a salaried physician service or a capitation scheme, was seen as a bulwark against even greater erosion of their professional autonomy. It was well known that a consequence of this compromise would be rising medical care and hospital costs.

At the time there was an awareness of the fiscal effects of these decisions. This, however, was not seen to be a particular problem. Partly because fee-for-service remuneration was seen as a necessary compromise with the profession, and partly because it was still widely held that unrestricted access to physician and hospital services was the major factor in improving population health status. This assumption quickly came to be challenged. At the same time various cost-containment strategies were deployed.

MEDICARE AND COST CONTAINMENT

Following the lead of Saskatchewan, and the recommendations of the 1964 Royal Commission on Health Services, the Federal government introduced

Medicare in 1966. By 1972 all provinces and territories had opted into the program. The five principles upon which Medicare was founded are universality of eligibility, comprehensiveness of coverage, portability between provinces, accessibility achieved by prepayment through taxation, and public administration on a non-profit basis. Provinces that established medical care insurance programs in accordance with these principles were eligible for a fifty-fifty cost sharing arrangement with the Federal government.

A core structural feature of the federal–provincial cost-sharing agreement established in 1966 was that only physician provided services, either outpatient or inpatient, were included. This discouraged the provinces from developing non-physician, non-hospital services because they were not eligible for federal funds. It did, however, encourage the provinces to try various cost-control strategies (Dickinson 1994).

In this regard efforts were made to reduce the number and duration of contacts with the health care system during an episode of illness, and to reduce the cost per contact. Even these efforts were discouraged, however, because each dollar in savings achieved by provincial governments resulted in a one dollar reduction in federal government transfers. Not surprisingly, the provincial governments quickly came to be dissatisfied with this funding arrangement. The Federal government was also dissatisfied because its health care expenditures were determined directly by the level of provincial expenditures. Consequently, it had no control over the level of its expenditures. Thus, both federal and provincial governments were interested in changing the terms and conditions of the cost-sharing arrangement (Soderstrom 1978).

This was done in 1977 with enactment of the Federal – Provincial Arrangements and Established Programs Financing Act (EPF) by the Federal government. The EPF had a number of effects: it provided a $20 per capita incentive for provinces to put more of its resources into community care; it reduced the Federal government's share of Medicare cost from approximately 50 percent to approximately 25 percent; it uncoupled federal costs from provincial expenditures; and it limited the growth in direct federal government increases to the rate of growth of the gross national product (GNP). Provincial health care expenditures above that were ineligible for federal cost sharing (Vayda, Evans, and Mindell 1979; Crichton, Robertson, Gordon, and Farrant 1997). The motivation for the provinces to accept the terms of the EPF was an increased capacity to tax incomes as a means to offset reduced federal cash transfers.

The ascendancy of fiscal conservatism in the 1980s resulted in further federal cost cutting initiatives. In the mid-1980s federal transfers to the provinces were reduced to 2 percent *below* the rate of growth in the GNP. In the early 1990s further reductions in federal government transfers to the provinces were introduced. Under that formula federal transfers were frozen for a period of two years at 1989–90 levels. In 1992–3 they were allowed to increase at a rate 3 percent *less* than the rate of increase in the GNP.

These changes resulted in decreased total health expenditures expressed as a proportion of GDP. In 1994, for example, they were 9.7 percent of GDP, down from 10.1 percent in both 1992 and 1993. Despite this proportional decrease total health spending increased to $72.5 billion in 1994, up from $71.8 billion the previous year. This represented a 1 percent rate of increase for 1994, down from 2.5 percent in 1993 and 5.6 percent in 1992 (Health Canada 1996: 3).

Federal government reductions in transfer payments initiated a series of cost-cutting measures at the provincial level. These included budget reductions, reductions in the number of hospital beds, efforts to control medical services fee increases, the deinsuring of some types of services, limits on the number of certain types of services for which physicians could bill, and increased monitoring and disciplinary powers for regulatory bodies (Vayda et al. 1979: 226; ACPH 1996).

Government cost-cutting efforts were also associated with changes in the types and location of health care services – a reduction in hospital services and an increase in various community-based and home care services – and an increased use of drug and alternative therapies. In addition, these developments corresponded to increased private expenditure on health care services (Health Canada 1996).

Not surprisingly, physicians, and other health care providers, responded critically, and in some cases militantly, to these initiatives. There were, throughout the 1980s, a number of nurses and doctor's strikes, as well as increases in the use of user fees and extra-billing to offset the effects of various cost-control initiatives (Northcott 1994).

Thus, cost control and various reforms were not popular with health care providers. Nor were they popular with health care service users. Reforms are generally claimed to have resulted in crowded hospital emergency rooms, and longer waiting lists for various diagnostic and therapeutic services. This has resulted in growing concerns that contemporary health reforms are really a strategy to dismantle Medicare by stealth. To counter these concerns, and to deflect the political consequences of being seen to violate a sacred political trust, politicians at all levels of government have reasserted their commitment to the five principles of Medicare.

The first retaking of vows came in the form of the Canada Health Act (CHA) in 1984. The CHA effectively banned extra-billing by physicians by imposing dollar-for-dollar reductions in federal transfers to the provinces for each dollar in extra-billing or user fees they allowed. One response of the organized medical profession and its political allies was to mobilize for the reprivatization of health care in Canada (Weller and Manga 1983; Stevenson, Williams, and Vayda 1988; Armstrong 1997; Fuller 1998).

In 1997, all levels of government reaffirmed their commitment to the principles of Medicare in the form of a joint statement. This was accompanied by a $1.5 billion increase (from $11 to $12.5 billion) in federal cash transfers to the provinces for health care. In 1999, the federal budget announced a further increase in health care funding through the Canada Health and Social Transfer (CHST). This amounts to an additional $11.5 billion targeted specifically for health care to be distributed to the provinces and territories on an equal per capita basis over the next three years. In addition to the increased cash transfer, the 1999 Federal budget announced increased tax transfers to the provinces with the understanding that new revenues will be used for health care.

The nature and organization of the contemporary health care system is much different than it was when Medicare was first introduced. It is also the case that

Medicare increasingly is seen as an inadequate response to the health needs of Canadians.

THE DETERMINANTS OF HEALTH AND HEALTH PROMOTION

In addition to the general efforts to directly control costs in the health care system discussed above, efforts in the area of health promotion have also increased since the early 1970s. In particular, thinking about the relationship between enhanced access to hospital and medical care services and improved population health status changed dramatically. In the immediate post-World War II period, as we have seen, the primary goal of health policy was to optimize access to medical and hospital services. That is, health policy was really health care policy narrowly conceived. There was, however, widespread optimism that this in itself would have a substantial impact on the health status of the population. By the early 1970s, however, this optimism already had faded. The first official indication of this was the publication of a White Paper by the Federal Minister of National Health and Welfare, Marc Lalonde, entitled *A New Perspective on the Health of Canadians*.

This document put forward the Health Field Concept. This concept expressed the idea that health status is the result of several determinants, not simply, or even primarily, access to medical and hospital services. The main determinants of population health were identified as human biology, self-imposed risks associated with individual lifestyle choices, environmental factors, and health care services. The Lalonde report noted that "there is little doubt that improvements in the level of health of Canadians lie mainly in improving the environment, moderating self-imposed risks and adding to our knowledge of human biology" (Lalonde 1974: 18). There is no mention here of increased access to medical services as a means to increase population health status.

Reaction to, and assessment of, this initial statement of the determinants of health framework was mixed. Some, like Renaud (n.d.: 230), saw it as nothing but a few broad statements of little policy significance. Others saw the health field concept, particularly its emphasis on individual lifestyle choices, as a potentially harmful form of victim-blaming and potential abandonment of the sick (Bolaria 1988).

Evans and Stoddart (1998: 561), on the other hand, suggested that the health field concept, or the determinants of health framework, results in a proliferation of outreach and screening programs in which increased numbers of people are placed on continuing regimes of drug therapies and regular monitoring. Thus, the determinants of health policy framework, given its focus on individual lifestyle choices, was seen by some to perpetuate and expand the individually oriented, professionally dominated, clinical approach to health care and injury and illness prevention (Evans and Stoddart 1998).

Others saw in the determinants of health /health promotion framework opportunities for the empowerment of the marginalized and the democratization of a wide array of social institutions (Dickinson 1996; VanderPlaat 1998). This optimism was tempered by a healthy dose of realism. Simply because a potential exists for health promotion to contribute to greater equality of health status through democratic empowerment there is no guarantee that potential will be realized. There are powerful vested interests who may actively or passively resist the sweeping changes in power associated with health promotion. The history of health care reform is replete with such struggles.

At about the same time that the determinants of health/health promotion framework was being articulated, others were arguing that modern, scientific medicine had a direct, negative impact on health (Illich 1976). The notion of iatrogenic disease was quite influential in critical social science circles. This notion was given increased credence with the publication of empirical studies which showed that some proportion of physicians' services – from drug prescriptions to surgical procedures – were medically unjustified (Swartz 1987).

Concerns about the iatrogenic effects of medicine, and mounting evidence showing that many health care services were unnecessary, motivated a movement to assess the effectiveness of clinical interventions known as Evidence-based Medicine (EBM). The EBM movement can be understood as having two contradictory origins. On the one hand, it is part of an effort to rationalize medical and hospital care. As such, it is part of contemporary efforts to micromanage the practice of medicine and to erode medical autonomy and dominance in determining the form and content of the health care system (Naylor 1993). On the other hand, it is part of the response of the organized medical profession, particularly university-based researchers, to bolster claims that the clinical practice of medicine is more science than art. These contradictory origins of EBM are reflected in the contradictory responses to it by practicing physicians (Dickinson 1998).

In their analysis of the Health Field Concept, Vayda, Evans, and Mindell (1979: 226) noted that if medical and hospital services contributed only a small and decreasing amount toward increased population health status, there was no justification for continually increasing health care expenditures. Given this, several analysts saw the determinants of health policy framework as the first serious effort to dismantle Medicare (Swartz 1987; Armstrong 1997).

Proponents of the determinants of health framework responded to criticisms of it by refining and refocusing the health field concept (Epp 1986; Mustard and Frank 1991; ACPH 1994; Evans, Barer, and Marmor 1994; Hamilton and Bhatti 1996; Report of the Roundtable 1996; Evans and Stoddart 1998). In an effort to allay these fears, and to clarify the concept of health promotion, an influential Federal government policy paper stated that it was "an approach that complements and strengthens the existing system of health care" (Epp 1986: 2).

Despite the controversy over the effects it has had for Medicare, the determinants of health/health promotion policy framework has focused attention on a number of important issues. First, it highlights the fact that access to medical and hospital services has not eliminated inequalities in health status. Disadvantaged groups are consistently shown to have lower life expectancy, poorer health, and a higher prevalence of disability than others (Epp 1986; Bolaria 1994; Frideres 1994; D'Arcy 1998; Wilkins and Sherman 1998; ACPH 1994). It has also been shown that this health effect is on a gradient within all socioeconomic groups

(Marmot, Rose, Shipley, and Hamilton 1978; Hertzman, Frank, and Evans 1998).

Second, the injury and illness prevention dimension of health promotion has focused attention on a wide array of preventable injuries and illnesses that differentially characterize social groups. These include, *inter alia*, youth suicide, disease associated with tobacco use, sexually-transmitted diseases, and injuries associated with impaired driving.

Third, the health care needs of the population are changing. Whereas it used to be the case that the main sources of morbidity and mortality were infectious diseases, currently chronic conditions and disabilities predominate. This has significant implications for the nature of health care needs and, consequently, for the nature and organization of health care services.

Many chronic conditions currently are not amenable to medical or hospital treatment. Modern medicine has no cures for chronic conditions like arthritis or diabetes. The aging of the Canadian population has added urgency to efforts to find appropriate and affordable means to deal with a wide range of chronic conditions that are often associated with the elderly. What is required is long-term support in the management of these conditions. Although medicine often has a role to play in the management of many chronic conditions, it need not always be a dominant role.

Adoption of the determinants of health/health promotion policy framework, along with various cost-control strategies, has been accompanied by a variety of changes in the nature and organization of health care services. Not since the introduction of Medicare itself have such dramatic changes occurred.

REGIONALIZATION: FROM INSTITUTIONAL TO COMMUNITY CARE

The most recent and dramatic reform of the health care system has been regionalization. Regionalization emerged in the late 1980s and early 1990s as a means to accomplish several health policy objectives, including cost control, improved health outcomes, increased responsiveness to health care needs, flexibility in care delivery, better integration and coordination of services, and greater citizen awareness of, and participation in, health care planning and service delivery (Angus 1991; Angus, Auer, Cloutier, and Albert 1995; Crichton et al. 1997; Lomas 1996; Lomas, Woods, and Veenstra 1997; Lewis 1997; Mhatre and Deber 1998).

How are we to understand these changes and their consequences? There is general agreement that regionalization marks an important shift in the model of health care governance and service delivery. The main direction of the change is away from collegial control and medical domination of health policy-making and service delivery toward either some form of communal or corporatist control.

Blishen (1991: 145), for example, sees regionalization as the emergence of a system of control in which "a community, or a community organization such as a consumer's group, rather than an occupational group, such as physicians, or a third party such as the government, seeks to define the needs of members and the manner in which they are satisfied." He is cautious in his early assessment of regionalization. Although he recognizes that it has redefined the relations between the state, the medical profession, and consumers in the direction of increased consumer control, there currently is no evidence to show that it is a more effective way to organize and deliver health care.

Crichton et al. (1997) also see regionalization as a shift in the nature and organization of health care planning and service delivery. Unlike Blishen, however, they see it as a manifestation of neo-corporatism which, following Pleiger (1990), they term emergence of the Welfare Society. The key features of the Welfare Society are the decentralization and involvement of key stakeholders in partnerships as a means of reaching policy consensus. This is distinct from the centralized, bureaucratic and professionally dominated mode of decision-making associated with the Welfare State. As Crichton et al. (1997: 40) observe, in a Welfare Society, "the former power holders have to share their power with other groups of corporate decision makers."

Enthusiasm for a corporatist model of policy-making emerged from a 1980 OECD conference. At that conference it was argued that a corporatist model of policy-making was more likely to enable policy makers "to contain the bargaining power of physicians and other provider groups and thereby move the system toward real health outputs" (Wilensky 1981: 194). Britain, Canada, and the US were identified as countries that were least likely to accomplish this because of the nature of their policy-making processes. The Canadian Federal government did, however, over the 1980s, adopt more of a corporatist approach to policy-making (Crichton et al. 1997).

Picking up on this theme Lomas (1997) sees the new Regional Health Authorities (RHAs) as both allies and fall-guys for provincial governments in their struggle for control of the health care system. As allies the RHAs are intended to increase community participation and empowerment relative to policy-making and health system governance. The putative goal is to generate the critical mass of political power needed to break the so-called Medicare Pact. That is, the particular structural features of Medicare that entrenched medical dominance, inflationary cost increases, and a curative approach to health problems. As fall-guys, he suggests, the new RHAs are intended to deflect criticism from provincial governments as budgets are cut and the health care system is rationalized.

At this time it seems unlikely that regional health authorities are designed to break the "Medicare Pact." No provincial government has given the RHAs control over medical care or pharmaceutical budgets. Without such control RHAs have no capacity to adopt a "command and control strategy" relative to non-hospital medical care services. The exclusion of control over medical care and pharmaceutical budgets is not an oversight. Medical resistance to any organizational reform seen as a threat to professional autonomy and collegial control is fierce. Indeed, the profession effectively scuttled earlier attempts at regionalization because of the threat to medical autonomy (Taylor 1978).

Like earlier health reform initiatives provincial governments have taken an incrementalist approach. The first step is the rationalization of institutional, particularly hospital, services; the second is the vertical and horizontal coordination and integration of institutional and community services. The provinces have differential priorities in this regard. Some, like Saskatchewan and New Brunswick, rationalized hospital services prior to regionalization. In Saskatchewan, for example, this entailed closing or converting to community health centers 53 small rural hospitals. Other provincial governments left this task to the newly created RHAs.

The consequences of these differing strategies relative to the goal of creating new political allies remains to be seen. In part it will depend both on how various interest groups respond to the boards and how the boards themselves respond to the provincial governments. If local citizenry perceive the boards as empowering them and giving them effective control over the best way to satisfy local health needs, particularly their health care needs, then the regionalization might be considered a successful experiment in democratic corporatism.

On the other hand, if RHAs join forces with disgruntled citizens and health care providers against provincial government cutbacks, then it might also be seen as a successful experiment in community empowerment, but a failure as a means to wrest control over health policy and health care service delivery from providers. Aware of this possibility, some provinces have prohibited health care providers from serving on RHAs. Others that had announced intentions to institute elected boards have backed away from that commitment.

If this second scenario comes to pass it will likely herald the end of the regionalization experiment, and the beginning of a search for a new means to break the "Medicare Pact." The coalition for the privatization of health care is ever ready to extol the virtues of the market and modern management techniques as a panacea for all that ails a public health care system like Medicare.

Despite repeated assurances to the contrary, concerns remain that current health reforms are simply paving the way for the reprivatization of health care (Tsalikis 1989; Armstrong 1997; Fuller 1998; O'Neill, 1998). In one sense, as we have just seen, this is the case. Government is trying to limit medical autonomy and dominance relative both to health policy and health care services. In itself, reduced medical autonomy and dominance is not a threat to Medicare.

There is, however, a more serious threat to Medicare related to its structure. Currently, medical and hospital based services are covered by Medicare. Other services, in general, are not. As the system shifts the locus of treatment from hospital to community, and as service providers other than medically trained physicians come to play a larger role in health care delivery, there also is occurring a *de facto* privatization of health care.

Pressures also are mounting for privatization of the medical and hospital care sector of the health care system. Leading the charge in this regard is the medical profession, private sector health care corporations, many of which are US-based, and provincial governments ideologically committed to the market as a social policy tool. Pressure to adopt market solutions to social policy problems is given added impetus through various trade liberalization agreements and organizations.

Conclusion

In this chapter we have examined the changing goals of health policy and their relationship to the changing nature and organization of the health care system. A central theme in analyses of health care in Canada has been, and is, the nature and locus of control. More specifically, health care policy and service delivery has been greatly influenced, if not dominated, by the medical profession. We have argued that current reform initiatives, including the adoption of the determinants of health policy framework and the regionalization of health care decision-making and service delivery, is the most recent manifestation of the struggle to control the health care sector and improve population health status.

We have also shown that the outcome of these efforts is, at this time, indeterminant. It is not certain what the future holds. There is a potential for a more needs-based, publicly funded, and democratically controlled health care system to emerge. There is evidence to suggest that this possibility is real. There is also, however, the potential for an increasingly privatized, corporate controlled health care system to develop. There is, perhaps, even more evidence to suggest that this is the future of health care in Canada.

References

Advisory Committee on Population Health. 1994. *Strategies for Population Health: Investing in the Health of Canadians*. Ottawa: Health Canada.

———. 1996. *Toward a Healthy Future: Second Report on the Health of Canadians*. Ottawa: Health Canada.

Angus, Douglas E. 1991. *Review of Significant Health Care Commissions and Task Forces in Canada Since 1983–84*. Ottawa: Canadian Hospital Association/Canadian Medical Association/Canadian Nurses Association.

Angus, Douglas E., L. Auer, J. Eden Cloutier, and T. Albert. 1995. *Sustainable Health Care for Canada*. Ottawa: University of Ottawa Press.

Armstrong, Pat. 1997. "Privatizing Care." Pp. 11–30 in P. Armstrong, H. Armstrong, J. Choiniere, E. Mykhalovskiy, and J. P. White (eds.), *Medical Alert: New Work Organizations in Health Care*. Toronto: Garamond Press.

Badgley, Robin F. and Samuel Wolfe. 1967. *Doctors' Strike: Medical Care and Conflict in Saskatchewan*. Toronto: MacMillan of Canada.

Blishen, Bernard. 1969. *Doctors and Doctrines: The Ideology of Medical Care in Canada*. Toronto: University of Toronto Press.

———. 1991. *Doctors in Canada: The Changing World of Medical Practice*. Toronto: The University of Toronto Press in association with Statistics Canada.

Bolaria, B. Singh. 1988. "The Politics and Ideology of Self-Care and Lifestyles." Pp. 537–49 in B. S. Bolaria and H. D. Dickinson (eds.), *Sociology of Health Care in Canada*. Toronto: Harcourt Brace Jovanovich.

———. 1994. "Income Inequality: Food Banks and Health." Pp. 245–54 in B. S. Bolaria and H. D. Dickinson (eds.), *Health, Illness and Health Care in Canada, Second Edition*. Toronto: W. B. Saunders.

Coburn, David, George M. Torrance, and Joseph M. Kaufert. 1983. "Medical Dominance in Canada in Historical Perspective: The Rise and Fall of Medicine?" *International Journal of Health Services* 13: 407–32.

Crichton, Anne, Ann Robertson, Christine Gordon, and Wendy Farrant. 1997. *Health Care A Community Concern? Developments in the Organization of Canadian Health Services.* Calgary: University of Calgary Press.

D'Arcy, Carl. 1998. "Social Distribution of Health Among Canadians." Pp. 73–101 in D. Coburn, C. D'Arcy, and G. Torrance (eds.), *Health and Canadian Society: Critical Perspectives, Third Edition.* Toronto: University of Toronto.

Dickinson, Harley D. 1993. "The Struggle for State Health Insurance: Reconsidering the Role of Saskatchewan Farmers." *Studies in Political Economy* 41: 133–56.

——. 1994. "The Changing Health Care System: Controlling Costs and Promoting Health." Pp. 106–29 in B. S. Bolaria and H. D. Dickinson (eds.), *Health, Illness and Health Care in Canada, Second Edition.* Toronto: W. B. Saunders.

——. 1996. "Health Reforms, Empowerment and the Democratization of Society." Pp. 179–90 in M. Stingl and D. Wilson (eds.), *Efficiency vs. Equality: Heath Reform in Canada.* Halifax: Fernwood.

——. 1998. "Evidence-Based Decision-Making: An Argumentative Approach." *International Journal of Medical Informatics* 51: 71–81.

Douglas, T. C. 1946. "Saskatchewan Plans for Health." *Health* (December): 1–3.

Epp, Jake. 1986. *Achieving Health for All: A Framework for Health Promotion.* Ottawa: Health and Welfare Canada.

Evans, Robert G., Morris L. Barer, and Theodore R. Marmor. 1994. *Why are Some People Healthy and Others Not? The Determinants of Health of Populations.* New York: Aldine De Gruyter.

Evans, Robert G. and Gregory L. Stoddart. 1998. "Producing Health, Consuming Health Care." Pp. 549–79 in D. Coburn, C. D'Arcy, and G. Torrance (eds.), *Health and Canadian Society: Critical Perspectives, Third Edition.* Toronto: University of Toronto.

Frideres, James S. 1994. "Racism and Health: The Case of the Native People." Pp. 202–10 in B. S. Bolaria and H. D. Dickinson (eds.), *Health, Illness and Health Care in Canada, Second Edition.* Toronto: W. B. Saunders.

Fuller, Colleen. 1998. *Caring for Profit: How Corporations are Taking Over Canada's Health Care System.* Vancouver/Ottawa: New Star Books/The Canadian Center for Policy Alternatives.

Hamilton, Nancy and Tariq Bhatti. 1996. *Population Health Promotion: An Integrated Model of Population Health and Health Promotion.* Ottawa: Health Canada.

Health Canada. 1996. *National Health Expenditures in Canada, 1975–1994: Summary Report.* Ottawa: Health Canada.

Hertzman, C., John Frank, and Robert G. Evans. 1998. "Heterogeneities in Health Status and the Determinants of Population Health." Pp. 67–92 in R. G. Evans, M. L. Barer, and T. R. Marmor (eds.), *Why Are Some People Healthy and Others Not?: The Determinants of Health of Populations.* New York: Aldine De Gruyter.

Illich, Ivan. 1976. *Limits to Medicine, Medical Nemesis: The Expropriation of Health.* Toronto and London: McClelland and Stewart Limited in association with Marion Boyars.

Lalonde, Marc. 1974. *A New Perspective on the Health of Canadians: A Working Document.* Ottawa: National Health and Welfare.

Lewis, Steven. 1997. *Regionalization and Devolution: Transforming Health, Reshaping Politics?* HEALNet Regional Health Planning Theme, Occasional Paper no. 2. Saskatoon.

Lomas, Jonathon. 1996. "Devolved Authorities in Canada: The New Site of Health-Care System Conflict." Pp. 26–34 in J. L. Dorland and S. M. Davis (eds.), *How Many*

Roads?: Regionalization and Decentralization in Health Care. Kingston: Queens University, School of Policy Studies.

——. 1997. "Devolving Authority for Health Care in Canada's Provinces: 4. Emerging Issues and Prospects." Canadian Medical Association Journal 156: 817–23.

Lomas, Jonathon, John Woods, and Gerry Venstra. 1997. "Devolving Authority for Health Care in Canada's Provinces: 1. An Introduction to the Issues." Canadian Medical Association Journal 156: 371–7.

Marmot, Michael G., G. Rose, M. J. Shipley, and P. J. S. Hamilton. 1978. "Employment Grade and Coronary Heart Disease in British Civil Servants." Journal of Epidemiology and Community Health 32: 244–9.

Mhatre, Sharmila L. and Raisa B. Deber. 1998. "From Equal Access to Health Care to Equitable Access to Health: A Review of Canadian Health Commissions and Reports." Pp. 459–84 in D. Coburn, C. D'Arcy, and G. Torrance (eds.), Health and Canadian Society: Critical Perspectives, Third Edition. Toronto: University of Toronto.

Mombourquette, Duane. 1991. "'An Inalienable Right': The CCF and Rapid Health Care Reform." Saskatchewan History 43: 101–16.

Mott, Frederick D. 1947. "Hospital Relations: Hospital Services in Saskatchewan." American Journal of Public Health 37: 1539–44.

Mustard, Fraser and John Frank. 1991. The Determinants of Health. CIAR Publication no. 5. Toronto: Canadian Institute for Advanced Research.

Naylor, C. David. 1986. Private Practice, Public Payment: Canadian Medicine and the Politics of Health Insurance, 1911–1966. Montreal–Kingston: McGill–Queens University Press.

——. 1993. "The Canadian Health Care System: A Model for America to Emulate?" Pp. 25–66 in A. King, T. Hyclack, R. Thornton, and S. McMahon (eds.), North American Health Care Policy in the 1990s. Chichester: John Wiley and Sons.

Northcott, Herbert A. 1994. "Threats to Medicare: The Financing, Allocation, and Utilization of Health Care in Canada." Pp. 65–82 in B. S. Bolaria and H. D. Dickinson (eds.), Health, Illness and Health Care in Canada, Second Edition. Toronto: W. B. Saunders.

O'Neill, Michael. 1998. "Community Participation in Quebec's Health System." Pp. 517–30 in D. Coburn, C. D'Arcy, and G. Torrance (eds.), Health and Canadian Society: Critical Perspectives, Third Edition. Toronto: University of Toronto.

Pleiger, Doris. 1990. "Policy Networks and the Decentralization of Policy Making." Bulletin European Social Security 55–6: 37–9.

Renaud, Marc. n.d. "Social Sciences and Medicine: Hygeia vs. Panakeia." Health and Canadian Society 1: 229–47.

Report of the Round Table. 1996. Report of the Round Table on Population Health and Health Promotion. Ottawa: Health Canada.

Roth, F. B. and R. D. Defries. 1958. "The Saskatchewan Department of Public Health." Canadian Journal of Public Health 49: 276–85.

Soderstrom, Lee. 1978. The Canadian Health System. London: Croom Helm.

Stevenson, Michael, A. Paul Williams, and Eugene Vayda. 1988. "Medical Politics and Canadian Medicare: Professional Response to the Canada Health Act." The Millbank Quarterly 66: 65–104.

Swartz, Donald. 1977. "The Politics of Reform: Conflict and Accommodation in Canadian Health Policy." Pp. 311–43 in L. Panitch (ed.), The Canadian State: Political Economy and Political Power. Toronto and Buffalo: University of Toronto Press.

——. 1987. "The Limits of Health Insurance." Pp. 255–70 in A. Moscovitch and J. Albert (eds.), The Benevolent State: The Growth of Welfare in Canada. Toronto: Garamond Press.

Taylor, Malcolm G. 1960. "The Role of the Medical Profession in the Formation and Execution of Public Policy." *Canadian Journal of Economics and Political Studies* 25: 108–27.

——. 1978. *Health Insurance and Canadian Public Policy: The Seven Decisions that Created the Canadian Health Insurance System*. Montreal–Kingston: McGill–Queens University Press.

Thompson, W. P. 1964. *Medical Care: Programs and Issues*. Toronto: Clarke, Irwin, and Company.

Tollefson, E. A. 1963. *Bitter Medicine: The Saskatchewan Medicare Feud*. Saskatoon: Modern Press.

Tsalikis, G. 1989. "The Political Economy of Decentralization of Health and Social Services in Canada". *International Journal of Health Planning and Management* 4: 293–309.

Tuohy, Carolyn. 1994. "Health Policy and Fiscal Federalism." Pp. 189–212 in Keith G. Banting (ed.), *The Future of Fiscal Federalism*. Kingston: Queen's University School of Policy Studies.

VanderPlaat, Madine. 1998. "Empowerment, Emancipation and Health Promotion Policy." *Canadian Journal of Sociology* 23: 71–90.

Vayda, Eugene, Robert G. Evans, and William R. Mindell. 1979. "Universal Health Insurance in Canada: History, Problems, Trends." *Journal of Community Health* 4: 217–31.

Vayda, Eugene and Raisa B. Deber. 1992. "The Canadian Health Care System: A Developmental Overview." Pp. 125–40 in C. D. Naylor (ed.), *Canadian Health Care and the State: A Century of Evolution*. Montreal–Kingston: McGill–Queen's University Press.

Walters, Vivienne. 1982. "State, Capital, and Labour: The Introduction of Federal-Provincial Insurance for Physician Care in Canada." *Canadian Review of Sociology and Anthropology* 19: 157–72.

Weller, Geoffrey R. and Pranlal Manga. 1983. "The Push for Reprivatization of Health Care Services in Canada, Britain, and the United States." *Journal of Health Politics and Law* 8: 495–518.

White, Rodney F. 1984. "The Professions and Collective Action: Responses to State Control and Public Criticism." Pp. 469–86 in A. Wipper (ed.), *The Sociology of Work: Papers in Honour of Oswald Hall*. Ottawa: Carlton University Press.

Wilensky, Harold L. 1981. "Democratic Corporatism, Consensus, and Social Policy: Reflections on Changing Values and the 'Crisis' of the Welfare State." Pp. 185–95 in OECD (ed.), *The Welfare State in Crisis: An Account of the Conference on Social Policies in the 1980s*. Paris: OECD.

Wilkins, Russell and Gregory Sherman. 1998. "Low Income and Child Health in Canada". Pp. 102–9 in D. Coburn, C. D'Arcy, and G. Torrance (eds.), *Health and Canadian Society: Critical Perspectives, Third Edition*. Toronto: University of Toronto.

Wolfe, Samuel. 1964. "Saskatchewan's Community Clinics." *Canadian Medical Association Journal* 91: 225–9.

12

Medical Sociology in Mexico

ROBERTO CASTRO

The reflection on health problems from a social perspective constitutes an academic practice that has been present in Mexico for several decades. In regards to the study of such problems, various papers have credited the existence of a tradition, which is both sociological (Laurell 1975; Almada 1986) and anthropological in nature (Aguirre Beltrán 1986; Campos 1992) that has manifested itself very strongly, at least from the 1960s, in spite of having started in an irregular, heterogeneous manner. Currently, it is possible to identify several "traditions" or schools within the social thought of health in Mexico. These schools are substantially different among one another, not only due to the theoretical frameworks they have chosen to conceptualize the problems they study, but also because of the political positions they have adopted in their scientific undertaking. These differences have led to intense debates concerning the origin of the health inequalities in this country and on the public policies that are to be implemented to resolve them.

This chapter will discuss some of the main developments of medical sociology in Mexico over the last 25 years. This study does not pretend to be exhaustive in matters of all that has been produced in this field in this period. On the contrary, I will solely concentrate on the main authors and the most relevant contributions. This implies acknowledging in principle the injustice that, due to omission or simplification, I will have to do to the numerous researchers that currently carry out, directly or indirectly, social research in health. The first part of this chapter presents a brief description of the focus of the different social scientists specializing in the health of Mexico, namely, the health conditions in the country, the health system, and the public policies that regulate that system. In the second part, I will present the main theoretical and methodological developments that have resulted from their studies, differentiating between the main trends and schools and emphasizing the most relevant debates. Finally, in the third part of this chapter, I will seek to make a brief characterization of the current situation of medical sociology in Mexico, pointing out some of its latest and most important developments and stressing some of the significant contributions of the social sciences to the study of health problems and disease among the population.

To facilitate the understanding of what follows, it is important to consider one of the distinctive traits of contemporary medical sociology in Mexico: its eminently Latin American character. This attribute results from the fact that Mexico shares the same mother tongue (Spanish) with almost all the countries in the region (exception made of Brazil) and very similar historical antecedents in that every country is a former colony of Spain and Portugal. Similarly, it is also a consequence of the military repression that took place in many countries in the southern part of the continent, in the 1970s and the 1980s, as many researchers of those countries emigrated to Mexico, seeking to preserve their academic careers. Social sciences applied to health were particularly enriched with this migration. The Latin American character of the Mexican medical sociology accounts in turn for the fact that many authors prefer to publish their papers in books and scientific journals in Mexico, Brazil, Argentina, or Chile, rather than in American or European publications. This may explain the relative lack of knowledge that prevails in those countries, regarding the socioscientific undertaking in health in places like Mexico.

HEALTH AND HEALTH SERVICES IN MEXICO

Evolution of Health Conditions

Due to a variety of reasons related to the backwardness in the development of the country, Mexico has lacked, for a long time, a reliable system for recording morbidity statistics. Only until recently has this problem begun to be solved. General mortality is only an indirect indicator of health conditions. Nonetheless, it is a useful tool to approach a description of the evolution of health and disease in Mexico. The first indicator of the transition in matters of health that this country has experienced is reflected in the advancement of life expectancy at birth: in 1950 it was 46.9 years, in 1994 it increased to 71.6 (Frenk 1997). However, in 1994, the states with the lowest life expectancy at birth showed the same rate that the states with the highest life expectancy had 20 years before. This serves to illustrate the marked contrasts that still prevail in Mexico in matters of health.

Table 12.1 shows the main causes of mortality in Mexico, at three different moments (1940, 1970, and 1997), that is, at intervals of almost 30 years. I would like to emphasize, above other considerations, the changing nature of the mortality profile. The main causes of mortality in 1940 were essentially attributable to infectious diseases. In 1997, in turn, the main causes of mortality were chronic-degenerative diseases and accidents, which in the 1940s were completely irrelevant. In addition to this fact I would like to note that the various diseases that in 1940 constituted the main causes of mortality in Mexico virtually disappeared in 1997.

Table 12.1 Evolution of the main causes of mortality in Mexico, 1940, 1970, and 1997

Causes	1997		1970		1940	
	Rate per 100,000	Order of importance	Rate per 100,000	Order of importance	Rate per 100,000	Order of importance
Heart diseases	71.8	1	68.3	3	54.3	8
Malignant tumors	54.1	2	37.6	5	23.2	13
Diabetes Mellitus	38.0	3	15.3	12	4.2	17
Accidents	37.9	4	71.0	6	51.6	9
Cerebrovascular disease	26.1	5	24.7	7	18.9	15
Cirrhosis and other chronic liver diseases	24.1	6				
Pneumonia and influenza	24.1	7	170.8	1	365.3	2
Perinatal ailments	20.9	8				
Homicide	14.3	9	18.0	10	67.0	6
Nephritis	10.8	10				
Nutrition deficiencies	10.7	11				
Congenital anomalies	10.1	12				
Chronic bronchitis, emphysema and asthma	9.0	13	16.7	11	66.8	7
Infectious intestinal diseases	7.8	14				
AIDS	4.4	15				
Anemia	4.1	16				
Tuberculosis	3.9	17	19.9	9	47.9	10
Gastroenteritis and colitis			141.7	2	490.2	1
Malaria			0.6	16	121.7	3
Perinatal mortality			51.5	4	100.7	4
Measles			24.3	8	91.2	5
Pertussis			7.1	13	42.4	11
Typhoid			5.8	14	31.9	12
Syphilis			0.8	15	19.2	14
Smallpox					6.8	16

Sources: for the 1940 and 1970 statistics: Laurell 1982; for the 1997 statistics: SSA 1999.

The aforementioned trend is an indirect reflection of the epidemiological transition that this country has experienced in this century, which has been characterized by the gradual disappearance or decline in the importance of infectious diseases and their concomitant replacement with chronic-degenerative diseases, accidents, and cases of violence.

As mentioned before, Mexico is not a homogeneous country as it comprises distinctly different regions. A recent study (Frenk 1997) classified the 32 Mexican states as per their epidemiological lag (measured through child mortality) and its relationship with emerging changes (measured through adult mortality). The combination of such indicators (whether below or above the national average) produced five regions classified as follows: (a) of advanced transition, (b) of intermediate transition, (c) of incipient transition, (d) of child lag, and (e) of extreme lag. I would like to note that this classification is pursuant to an approximate geographic pattern, where the northern states of the country (those closest to the United States) are the entities with the best indicators. Conversely, the states in the southeast (those closest to Central America) are those that lag the most.

In 1994, the second national health survey was carried out in the country, which provided more updated information on the prevalence of diseases reported by the population, as well as on the differences that in that regard are found among the various social groups. Table 12.2 shows the main causes reported as health problems within 15 days before the survey, by socioeconomic index. This table shows that individuals from the low socioeconomic level reported infectious diseases more frequently, while individuals from the high socioeconomic level more commonly reported chronic diseases. Such differences, as reported by the survey (SSA 1994) may be the result of both the differential perception that the various groups have of their health and the different lifestyles of the social classes.

Table 12.2 Main causes reported as health problems within 15 days previous to the survey, by socioeconomic index (in percentages)

	Low	Middle-Low	Middle-High	High
Upper airway	27.2	24.7	26.8	22.3
Musculoskeletal diseases	15.2	13.7	12.0	10.5
Gastrointestinal diseases	12.6	12.4	9.2	8.8
Headache	5.7	5.2	2.9	2.1
Hypertension	2.7	3.9	4.5	3.9
Diabetes	1.0	2.1	2.7	2.1

Source: II National Health Survey 1994.

Lastly, table 12.3 presents a priorization of health needs in Mexico, based on three indicators. As is well known, disability-adjusted life years or DALYs is an indicator developed by the World Bank, the World Health Organization, and Harvard University, and it is a measure of the healthy years lost due to both premature death and disability. This table serves also to illustrate the complexity of the current epidemiological profile in Mexico: the identification of the main health needs is based on the type of indicator that is used.

Table 12.3   Priority health needs using three indicators – Mexico, 1994

Causes	Mortality adjusted for age	Potential disability-adjusted life years	Disability-adjusted life years
Ischemic Cardiopathy	1	9	6
Diabetes Mellitus	2	8	4
Pneumonia	3	1	3
Cerebrovascular disease	4	11	11
Cirrhosis	5	4	8
Homicide and third-party injuries	6	2	1
Chronic Obstructive Pulmonary disease	7	17	19
Acute Diarrhea	8	3	7
Protein-Energy malnutrition	9	6	9
Nephritis and nephrosis	10	12	14
Motor vehicle accidents (occupants)	11	5	2
Hypertensive Cardio-pathy	12	27	21

Source: taken from Lozano 1997.

Summarizing, health conditions in Mexico have significantly changed throughout this century. However, this change has not been homogeneous for either the social groups or the regions in the country. As herein below discussed, a sophisticated explanation of these differences – based on variables such as social class, gender, region, ethnicity, and age, among others – constitutes one of the goals of Mexican social scientists and one of the axes around which one of the most important debates of the contemporary, medical sociology in Mexico, revolves.

Evolution of Health Policies and Services

From the beginning of this century to the early 1980s, as a result of the Mexican Revolution, the various Mexican administrations fostered a set of social policies that sought, with lesser or greater efficacy, to balance the socioeconomic inequalities and the poverty in the country. Health and education policies in principle, and to a lesser degree housing, employment, and food provision policies, among others, had throughout those years a relatively popular orientation and the intention of reaching broader layers of the population.

This accounts for the creation of the Mexican health system in 1943. That year, the Mexican Social Security Institute (in Spanish, IMSS) and the Ministry of Health (in Spanish, SSA) were created. The former was constituted to provide health and social security services to the workers of Mexican private companies and is funded with the fees paid by the workers of this sector, the employers, and the government. As from 1977, the IMSS broadened its coverage to include the poorest zones in the country (a program known today as IMSS-Solidaridad), thereby providing free services to the most marginalized populations in the country.

The SSA, in turn, had the objective of providing basic health services to that segment of the population that was left on the margin of social security, mainly peasants and individuals of the poorest sectors in the country. Over many years, the services provided by the SSA, however insufficient and of poor quality, were free.

In 1959, the Institute of Social Security and Services for Public Employees (in Spanish, ISSSTE) was created to provide health services and retirement pensions for state workers. As from that year, some of the larger state-owned companies, like Petróleos Mexicanos (Mexican Petroleum), Ferrocarilles Nacionales (National Railways) and Comisión Federal de Electricidad (Federal Electricity Commission), among others, developed their own institutes for the provision of health and social security services for their employees. Finally, although developed parallel to the above-mentioned institutions, private medicine has gained importance only recently.

As a whole, social security health services serve slightly over 50 percent of the Mexican population, which is constituted essentially by employees of the private and public sectors of the country. Neither the SSA nor private medicine have the capacity to cover the rest of the population, thus, 10 million Mexicans lack access to health services (SSA 1999). This phenomenon derives, among other things, from the logic to which health policies have been subject in Mexico, and that, summarizing, have privileged the urban proletariat – work force of the capitalist industry – to the detriment of those sectors of the population that have been left on the margin of development of this mode of production in Mexico. This accounts for the simultaneous existence of two broad sectors of the population: one with access to several sorts of health services, and the other with no access whatsoever to any service (Hernández Llamas 1982; López Acuña 1986).

In the 1980s, the Mexican government adopted a neo-liberal orientation, pursuant to the recommendations of the International Monetary Fund and the World Bank. This action led to a reduction in social policies that the various sectors had been fostering hitherto, as well as to the promotion of the privatization of State institutions and their services. Health did not escape this trend. Recently, a law that allows private institutions to administer the retirement funds of the workers was passed, thus breaking with one of the fundamental principles that the Mexican State had previously endorsed: the possibility of implementing mechanisms of solidary assistance to help those in greater need. Currently, one of the central elements of the state-held policy refers to what is denominated the "Health Sector Reform," which consists mainly of the inclusion of the private sector in the service provision and the reduction or elimination of free services.

The present orientation of the health policy, evidently influenced by the World Bank's recommendations, constitutes the other pole around which the main debates of the Mexican medical sociology revolve. Consequently, carrying out a further analysis of the recent evolution of this discipline in Mexico is appropriate.

Trends of Medical Sociology in Mexico

Social thought in matters of health in Mexico has constituted for many years a very dynamic expanding field, where a number of leaders and trends can be noticed, though not without the risk of schematization. To that end, it is suitable to divide this analysis into specific topics.

Basic Trends

In the mid-1970s, the Master's in Social Medicine was established at the Metropolitan Autonomous University, at Xochimilco. Together with researchers from other Latin American countries, this institution has fostered the so-called Social Medicine trend (Laurell 1989). This trend represents one of the best examples, at the international level, of the contributions that Marxist analysis can make in matters of health. A well-known study by Laurell (1975) established that the objective of Latin American social medicine does not rest as heavily on the notion that the capitalist system determines the nature of the diseases of the populations, as pointed out by Navarro in the United States (Navarro 1976), among others. Rather, it is the specific manner in which such determination takes place that supports said objective. The author maintains that a disease cannot be considered merely a biological state or the mechanical consequence of poverty. Health and disease, as she argues, cannot be considered two separate entities; they have to be understood as two moments (dialectally united) of the same phenomenon. This concept leads to one of the main notions of the trend of Latin American social medicine: rather than discussing health and disease separately, the object of study of this school is the *health–disease process*.[1]

Due to its critical approach, social medicine favors the study of social inequality and how such inequality determines the health–disease processes in the populations. Another work, renowned throughout Latin America (Bronfman and Tuirán 1983; Bronfman, Lombardi, and Victora 1998), showed that it was empirically possible to achieve a sophisticated operationalization of the Marxist concept of social class and its utilization both to illustrate and account for child mortality differentials among the various social classes in Mexico. Such study became a model, which a number of researchers applied to their studies on social inequality and health (see, for example, Battellino and Bennun 1991; Salcedo and Prado 1993; Ortales 1996). The concept as such, however, was highly complex, which resulted in the reluctance by specialists to implement it. Consequently, some years later, Bronfman (Bronfman et al. 1988) proposed a simpler strategy for the classification of the population into differentiated socioeconomic groups, which has been widely accepted in the region (see, for example, Engstrom and Anjos 1996; Santos 1996; Tellez 1997).

Social medicine has also sought to problematize the health–work linkage in Mexico (Noriega 1989). In so doing, various authors have pointed out the importance of studying the "work process" itself (Laurell 1979) and understanding it as a source of the "wearing down" of the worker (Laurell and Marquez 1983) with direct consequences on the health–disease process. Based on concrete, empirical results, the studies by Laurell have demonstrated that concepts like the "wearing down" of the worker and "specific patterns of wearing down" are more precise and pertinent than those of "absolute expropriation" and "relative expropriation" of health that other theoreticians of the Marxist medical sociology had proposed in the United States (Navarro 1982).

A second core of theoretical and empirical production of great importance is the Center for Research and Higher Studies in Social Anthropology that has promoted the development of medical anthropology from a critical perspective, since the beginning of the 1980s. Its main author (Menéndez 1978) surmised the concept of the "Hegemonic Medical Model" to characterize the prevailing model of medicine at the beginning of the nineteenth century under capitalism and that, apart from juridically laying the foundations of its exclusive appropriation of disease, privileged an outlook that was biologistic, individualistic, ahistorical, asocial, mercantilistic, and pragmatic in nature. The development of this concept fostered a series of studies on how the various institutions that act on health and disease are articulated, whether from a position of subordination (Menéndez 1984) or from the situation of "crisis" that the hegemonic medical model experiences (Menéndez 1985a). Similarly, as per this perspective, several studies on alcoholization (Menéndez 1985b), self-care in health (Menéndez 1983), and how professional medicine coexists with alternative (traditional and domestic) medical practices (Módena 1990) emerged.

Together with these approaches, which are rather structural and critical in nature, another school of thought in medical sociology that is more directly linked with public health has existed in Mexico. Since the early 1980s, Frenk has studied the behavior of the medical work market in an effort to link the characteristics of the phenomenon with the doctors' social class of origin (Frenk and Bashshur 1983; Frenk 1988a). To that end, the author first formulated a conceptualization that allowed him to differentiate the general determinants of the medical work market, among which he included the economic structure of the country, the State's policies, forms of social organization, social institutions, and ideology. Secondly, he was able to distinguish specific determinants, such as medical service supply and demand, and medical education. Afterwards, the author engaged in a historical reconstruction of the evolution of health services in this country, as well as of the influence of this factor on the medical work market (Frenk, Hernández, and Alvarez 1980). Frenk showed that the socio-economic origins of doctors are closely associated with the type of university they attend, the specialization they choose, and the institution that finally hires them (Frenk 1984; Frenk 1985). These pioneering studies encouraged the development of a line of empirical research on the characteristics of the medical work market in Mexico, which allowed documenting the existence of grave contradictions in the sector – sub or unemployed doctors, on the one hand, broad sectors of the population lacking access to health services, on the other. Furthermore, these studies explored the various alternative solutions to such imbalance (Nigenda et al. 1990; Frenk et al. 1991).

By founding the National Institute of Public Health, Frenk contributed significantly to the legitimization of research studies that were no less sociological than those promoted by authors like Laurell or Menéndez. This allowed the exploration of problems through different theoretical approaches tied to the structural, critical perspectives that these authors advocate. Frenk's new proposals emerged within the framework of a series of important, highly-politized debates he held with representatives of social medicine during the second half of the 1980s. These debates determined that it was of crucial importance to prepare theoretical and methodological frameworks that would avoid a rigid economicism when accounting for health problems and policies (Fragoso, Velázquez, and Hermida 1986; González-Block and Frenk 1986a, 1986b). Additionally, these debates highlighted that theoretical perspectives, such as public health and social medicine, which were so different from one another, had to be mutually enriched with their respective contributions and analytical capacities, or run the risk of working from the perspective of academic traditions interested in the health problems of the population, but having very little or nothing to say to one another (Frenk 1988b, 1988c; Eisbenschutz 1988a, 1988b).

New Developments

The debates held between social medicine representatives and public medical sociologists have continued up to the present decade. When the North American Free Trade Agreement (NAFTA) was signed by Mexico, the United States, and Canada in 1994, the discussion about the possibilities of including health services among the goods to be exchanged by these three countries began. While public health sociologists deemed NAFTA a beneficial opportunity for health services in Mexico (Frenk et al. 1994; Gómez-Dantéz et al. 1997), social medicine representatives noticed that such treaty showed an evident sign of a privatization trend of the Mexican State that would consolidate the disarticulation of the social policies in effect in former decades (Laurell and Ortega 1992).

Additionally, upon the release of the World Bank's 1993 Report (Banco Mundial 1993), the official health policy in Mexico adopted the proposals issued by that institution and started advocating the "reform" of the health sector and the privatization of services, or at least the participation of private capital for health service provision and the administration of the employees' retirement funds. These changes led to one of the most important debates in matters of health in which the various social sectors in the country have participated. Among the contributing academics were once more, on the one hand, the public health sociologists with their proposals on how such privatization could be carried out without detriment to the ideals of justice and equity (Frenk and González-Block 1992; Londoño and Frenk 1997). On the other hand, there were those that criticized the methodology and utilization of DALYs (López and Blanco 1996) and maintained that such a reform sought to benefit, mainly, the big-capital holders to the detriment of the least protected sectors of the population, seriously damaging, in the social sense, the State policies in matters of health fostered in previous decades (López Arellano 1994; Tetelboin 1994; Laurell 1999).

Simultaneously, without necessarily participating in those important debates, a second generation of studies on social sciences applied to health has been appearing in Mexico during the 1990s. Some of the authors of these studies have been directly or indirectly formed in one of the three above-mentioned foundational poles, and a number of them have benefited from the contributions of these trends, apart from having been able to study at universities in the United States, Canada, Spain, England, or France, with highly specialized academics in the field. This has favored a sort of "oxygenation" of the contemporary debate, in that new theoretical perspectives and methodological approaches have appeared in a setting that was previously characterized almost exclusively by both the structural perspective and the public health approaches.

Therefore, it is adequate to devote this last part of the chapter to a summarized revision of some of the main contributions of this new generation of research studies. To that end, the analysis will be divided into three brief sections. The first will refer to some of the main theoretical or conceptual studies that have appeared in the last years. The second will follow suit, focusing on methodological research; and the third will center on substantive research that, as will be discussed, refers to various health and service utilization problems that are appealing to the attention of medical sociologists in this country.

In regards to *theoretical production*, in the early 1990s, a series of reflections that sought to review the prevalence – and the excesses – of structural approaches in health began to appear (Almada Bay 1990) and analyze the possibilities of the theoretical frameworks that privileged the analysis of those phenomena that are better observed at the "micro" level of analysis. In one of his best studies, Menéndez (1992) pointed out that the depletion of large ideological systems is linked with the inability of substantial theoretical paradigms when attempting to give a satisfactory account of the various levels of reality. As he maintains, this has driven the growing trend to seek the explanations of the phenomena of health–disease in social action (practices, strategies, transactions, etc.), rather than in macro-social structures. However, the author warns that unless this level of analysis is linked with the great social determinations, we will run the risk of not transcending the level of psychologism when accounting for problems of our interest.

In that regard, there have been very suggestive studies on the concepts of "quality of life" (Blanco et al. 1997), "lifestyles" and "risks" (Martínez 1993; Menéndez 1998), and "social support" (Castro et al. 1997). This research suggests that as long as the sociological character of such concepts – and consequently, the effort to elucidate its association with more general social processes – is preserved, these concepts will continue to be useful for the study on the determination of health and disease in society.

Other theoretical papers that were released in this decade updated the contribution of feminist theory in regards to the study of health problems, not only in North America and Europe, but also in Latin America (Castro and Bronfman 1993; Cardaci 1998). At the *methodological* level, within the context of medical sociology in Mexico, several studies with innovating proposals for the social study on the health and disease phenomena have been published in the last few years. In the mid-1980s, as per the thought of social medicine, the perspective of the "working-class model," originally developed in Italy, was adopted for the execution of research into the workers' health. At the beginning of this decade, the validation of such strategy was published in a modified version for Latin

America. This is a research strategy, whose foundation lies on the application of collective, not individual, interviews among the workers in the industry, with the triple purpose of generating information about health hazards derived from work conditions, promoting an awareness in that regard among those thereby affected, and formulating collective solution proposals among the workers (Laurell et al. 1990).

A second theoretical and methodological development has emerged in the field of social inequality in the presence of disease. Bronfman (1992) showed first that conventional explanations on the relationship between socio-demographic variables (i.e. the mother's education) and child mortality face very clear limits and leave a large part of the phenomenon unexplained. Afterwards, this author showed that the most powerful explanations of the problem could be reached by skillfully articulating quantitative and qualitative approaches. The author successfully tested an explanation that linked the structural determinations of child mortality (mainly the social class) with the interactional elements of the actors (such as family structure, family dynamics, and the operation of social networks). Additionally, he showed that the latter play a central role in both the generation and manner of solving the problems that lead to child mortality (Bronfman 1999).

Actually, in the 1990s, qualitative methods applied to social research on health (Langer and Nigenda 1995; Sasz and Lerner 1996) have become important, while some papers on epistemological reflection and ethics said that the articulation between qualitative and quantitative methods presents a series of yet unsolved problems. Furthermore, this research declares that such articulation would not be correctly achieved unless researchers remained anchored to the most relevant sociological theories and abandoned the mere empiricism and atheoretical approaches that flood this field (Castro and Bronfman 1999).

The level of *substantive studies* is the one that presents a higher degree of difficulty when attempting a synthesis, not only because of its including a large number of papers and topics, but also because it comprises both studies that utilize the theory and methods of the social sciences, and research that superficially alludes to these matters. In practice, many of the latter are largely public health research weakly supported by social sciences, which can hardly be considered medical sociology papers. Consequently, the rest of this brief review will focus on some of the most remarkable studies with an evident sociological orientation that have appeared in the last few years.

Such studies refer to various priority health problems in this country. AIDS is one of such problems. Recently, significant research has been carried out on the change in sexual habits experienced by Mexican workers who migrate to the United States, which translates into increased risk practices (Bronfman and Minello 1995). Other studies have explored in detail the social construction of both solidarity and family and community rejection regarding those infected with HIV/AIDS (Castro et al. 1998a, 1998b), and the social construction of AIDS and sexuality among the youth in this country (Rodríguez et al. 1995). Such research is qualitative in nature and explores the subjectivity of the individuals in regards to this matter.

Additionally, along the line of subjectivity, a group of papers has explored the illness experience and how such experience is articulated with the more general social structure and gender inequality (Castro 1995; Castro and Eroza 1998). In other instances, research on the subjective experience has focused on chronic ailments (Mercado 1996), the negotiation of sexuality and the meaning of virginity (Amuchástegui 1999), as well as on the meaning of pregnancy for adolescents (Stern 1996; Tuñón and Guillén 1999), among others.

Reproductive health has gained great importance for medical sociologists in this country (González 1995; Pérez-Gil, Ramírez, and Ravelo 1995; Langer and Tolbert 1996). As of late, several studies that explore the relationship between the perceived social support and the experience of labor (Campero et al. 1998) have been published, together with sociological studies on contraception (Castro and Bronfman 1991; Lerner and Quesnel 1994), the dimensions of masculinity, and the role of men in reproduction processes (Figueroa 1998; Rodríguez and de Keijzer 1998). Other courses of research have centered on the situation of female occupational health (Garduño and Rodríguez 1990; Denman, Balcázar, and Lara 1995; Lara 1995), and the relationship between the occupational condition of women and child health (Bronfman and Gómez-Dantés 1998). Similarly, the problem of violence against women has gradually gained importance among scientists (Bedregal, Saucedo, and Ríquer 1991; Ríquer, Saucedo, and Bedolla 1996; Saucedo 1996), even though there is still much to do regarding the socio-logical explanation of this issue.

Lastly, a set of sociological research courses has referred to a variety of aspects of the utilization of health services and medication. In some instances, they have explored the linkage social networks-service utilization (Infante 1990). Others in turn have carried out qualitative studies to determine the perception of health service users (Bronfman et al. 1997a) and health providers (Bronfman et al. 1997b) in regards to the problem of the utilization of services or to determine the type of cultural barriers that hinder utilization (Lazcano et al. 1999). Still others have researched into the consumption patterns of unsafe medication without prescription, in private pharmacies (Leyva et al. 1999).

CONCLUSION

Medical sociology in Mexico is a discipline that has been enriched through the contributions of many social scientists that have carried out research in this country in the last 25 years. At the Latin American level, the Mexican leadership can be appreciated in the first edition of the recent compilation entitled *Salud, cambio social y política: perspectivas desde América Latina* (Health, Social Change and Policy: Latin American Perspectives), which having been dissemi-nated throughout the subcontinent, sold out in less than six months (Bronfman and Castro 1999). Lately, the almost absolute predominance that the critical structural perspective had in the 1980s has begun to decline. This field has benefited by new interpretative approaches and discussions on the scope and implications of the various theoretical and methodological approaches. What these studies as a whole have contributed toward understanding health problems has already reached a critical peak: nowadays, a great deal of research into public health in Mexico is based on the most important concepts and methods developed by the social sciences.

It is possible to state that, to some extent, Mexican medical sociology is on the frontiers of knowledge, especially at the global level. This is reflected in several studies – like the successful operationalization in the past decade of the Marxist concept of social class and its application to the study of various health problems and the development of a qualitative perspective incorporating variables, such as family structure and the operation of social networks, to further explore the role of social inequality in the face of child mortality – which constitute true, unparalleled innovations in the international literature.

Lastly, a final question upon which it is worth reflecting is that, in spite of its dynamism and productivity, Mexican medical sociology is practically unknown in North America and Europe. Consequently, the researchers in this country should seek to better disseminate their work in these settings. Nonetheless, does it not also mean that scientists in those places should make greater efforts to approach the scientific production of countries like Mexico, which due to natural reasons is mainly disseminated in Spanish and through Latin American journals?

Note

1 Years later, Menéndez maintains that the behaviors of the individuals in the presence of disease are also an integral part of the health–disease concept, hence inferring a concept of *health–disease-care process* (Menéndez, 1985b).

References

Aguirre Berltrán, Gonzalo. 1986. *Antropología Médica*. [Medical Anthropology]. Mexico City: CIESAS.

Almada Bay, Ignacio. 1986. "Las Ciencias Sociales en Salud en México." ["Social Sciences in Health in Mexico"]. Pp. 133–42 in E. Duarte Nuñes (ed.), *Ciencias Sociales y Salud en América Latina*. Montevideo: Organización Panamericana de la Salud.

——. 1990. "Siete Tesis Equivocadas Sobre Salud y Sociedad." ["Seven Wrong Theses on Health and Society"]. *Cuadernos Médico-Sociales* 52: 15–25.

Amuchástegui, Ana. 1999. "Dialogue and the Negotiation of Meaning: Constructions of Virginity in Mexico." *Culture, Health and Sexuality* 1: 79–93.

Banco Mundial. 1993. *Informe sobre el Desarrollo Mundial 1993. Invertir en Salud*. Washington: Banco Mundial.

Battellino, Luis José, and Fernando Rubén Bennun. 1991. "Niveles, Tendencias y Estructura de la Mortalidad Infantil en la Provincia de Córdoba (Argentina)." ["Levels, Trends, and Structure of Infant Mortality in the Province of Cordova, (Argentina)"]. *Cuadernos Médico Sociales* 56: 45–58.

Bedregal, Ximena, Irma Saucedo, and Florinda Ríquer. 1991. *Hilos, Nudos y Colores en la Lucha Contra la Violencia Hacia las Mujeres*. Mexico City: Ediciones CICAM.

Blanco Gil, José, Olivia López, José Alberto Rivera, and Fabiola Rueda. 1997. "Una Aproximación a la Calidad de Vida. Límites Conceptuales y Metodológicos." ["An Approximation to the Concept of Quality of Life. Conceptual and Methodological Limits"]. *Estudios en Antropología Biológica* 8: 433–48.

Bronfman, Mario. 1992. "Infant Mortality and Crisis in Mexico." *International Journal of Health Services* 22: 157–67.

——. 1999. *Como se Vive se Muere. Familia, Redes Sociales y Mortalidad Infantil.* Cuernavaca: CRIM/UNAM.

Bronfman, Mario, and Roberto Castro (eds.). 1999. *Salud, Cambio Social y Política: Perspectivas Desde América Latina.* Mexico City: EDAMEX.

Bronfman, Mario, Roberto Castro, Elena Zúñiga, Carlos Miranda, and Jorge Oviedo. 1997a. "Del 'Cuánto' al 'Por Qué': La Utilización de los Servicios de Salud Desde la Perspectiva de los Usuarios." ["From 'How Many' to 'Why': Health Services Utilization from the Users' Perspective"]. *Salud Pública de México* 39: 442–50.

——. 1997b. "'Hacemos Lo Que Podemos': Los Prestadores de Servicios Frente al Problema de la Utilización." ["We Do What We Can: Health Service Providers Facing the Service Utilization Problem"]. *Salud Pública de México* 39: 546–53.

Bronfman, Mario, Castro Victoria, Guiscafré Héctor, Castro Roberto, and Gonzalo Gutiérrez. 1988. "La Medición de la Desigualdad: Una Estrategia Metodológica. Análisis de las Características Socioeconómicas de la Muestra." ["Measuring Social Inequality: A Methodological Strategy"]. *Archivos de Investigación Médica* (Instituto Mexicano del Seguro Social), 19: 351–60.

Bronfman, Mario, and Héctor Gómez-Dantés. 1998. "La Condición de la Mujer y la Salud Infantil." ["Women's Condition and Infant Health"]. Pp. 89–125 in J. G. Figueroa (ed.), *La Condición de la Mujer en el Espacio de la Salud.* Mexico City: El Colegio de México.

Bronfman, Mario, Cintia Lombardi, and César G. Victora. 1988. "Operacionalizacao de Conceito de Classe Social em Estudos Epidemiologicos." ["The Operation of the Concept of Social Class in Epidemiological Studies"]. *Revista de Saúde Pública* (Sao Paulo) 22: 253–65.

Bronfman, Mario, and Nelson Minello. 1995. "Hábitos Sexuales de los Migrantes Temporales Mexicanos a los Estados Unidos de América. Prácticas de Riesgo para la Infección por VIH." ["Sexual Habits among Temporal Mexican Migrants in the USA. Risk Practises for HIV Infection"]. Pp. 3–89 in M. Bronfman, A. Amuchástegui, R. M. Martina, N. Minello, M. Rivas, and G. Rodríguez (eds.), *SIDA en México. Migración, Adolescencia y Género.* Mexico City: Información Profesional Especializada.

Bronfman, Mario, and Tuirán Rodolfo. 1983. "La Desigualdad Social ante la Muerte: Clases Sociales y Mortalidad en la Niñez." ["Social Inequality before Death: Social Classes and Infant Mortality"]. *Cuadernos Médico Sociales* 29: 53–75.

Campero, Lourdes, Cecilia García, Carmen Díaz, Olivia Ortíz, Sofia Reynoso, and Ana Langer. 1998. "'Alone I Wouldn't Have Known What to Do': A Qualitative Study on Social Support during Labor and Delivery in Mexico." *Social Science and Medicine* 47: 395–403.

Campos, Roberto (ed.). 1992. *La Antropología Médica en México.* Mexico City: Instituto Mora y Universidad Autónoma Metropolitana.

Cardaci, Dora. 1998. "Nuevos Entramados: Familia, Salud y Organizaciones de Mujeres." ["New Networks: Family, Health and Women's Organizations"]. Pp. 243–65 in J. G. Figueroa (ed.), *La Condición de la Mujer en el Espacio de la Salud.* Mexico City: El Colegio de México.

Castro, Roberto. 1995. "The Subjective Experience of Health and Illness in Ocuituco: A Case Study." *Social Science and Medicine* 41: 1005–21.

Castro, Roberto, and Mario Bronfman. 1991. "Embarazo y Parto Entre la Tradición y la Modernidad: El Caso de Ocuituco." ["Between Tradition and Modernity: Pregnancy and Childbirth in Ocuituco"]. *Estudios Sociológicos* 9: 583–606.

——. 1993. "Teoría Feminista y Sociología Médica: Bases para una Discusión." ["Feminist Theory and Medical Sociology: Basis for a Discussion"]. *Cadernos de Saúde Pública* 9: 375–94.

——. 1999. "Problemas No Resueltos en la Integración de Métodos Cualitativos y Cuantitativos en la Investigación Social en Salud." ["Unsolved Problems in the Integration between Quantitative and Qualitative Methods in Social Research on Health"]. Pp. 49–64 in M. Bronfman and R. Castro (eds.), *Salud, Cambio Social y Política. Perspectivas desde América Latina.* Mexico City: EDAMEX.

Castro, Roberto, Lourdes Campero, and Bernardo Hernández. 1997. "La Investigación Sobre *Apoyo Social* en Salud: Situación Actual y Nuevos Desafíos." ["Research on Social Support and Health: Current Situation and New Challenges"]. *Revista de Saúde Pública* 31: 425–35.

Castro, Roberto, and Enrique Eroza. 1998. "Research Notes on Social Order and Subjectivity: Individuals' Experience of *Susto* and *Fallen Fontanelle* in Central Mexico." *Culture, Medicine and Psychiatry* 22: 203–30.

Castro, Roberto, Emanuel Orozco, Enrique Eroza, María Cristina Manca, Juan Jacobo Hernández, and Peter Aggleton. 1998a. "AIDS-Related Illness Trajectories in Mexico: Results from a Qualitative Study in Two Marginalized Communities." *AIDS Care: Psychological and Socio-medical Aspects of AIDS/HIV* 10: 583–98.

Castro, Roberto, Enrique Eroza, Emanuel Orozco, Juan Jacobo Hernández, and Peter Aggleton. 1998b. Family Responses to HIV/AIDS in Mexico. *Social Science and Medicine* 47: 1473–84.

Denman, Catalina, Héctor Balcázar, and Francisco Lara. 1995. "Factors Associated with Work-Related Accidents and Sickness of Maquiladora Workers: The Case of Nogales, Sonora, Mexico." *International Journal of Health Services* 25: 489–502.

Eibenschutz, Catalina. 1988a. "¿Qué Tan Moderna es la Salud Pública Moderna?" ["How Modern is the Modern Public Health?"]. *Nexos* 123: 74–5.

——. 1988b. "(Dónde está la Polémica?" ["Where is the Debate?"]. *Nexos* 126: 78–9.

Engstrom, Elyne, and Luiz Anjos. 1996. "Relationship between Maternal Nutritional-Status and Overweight in Brazilian Children." *Revista de Saúde Pública* (Brasil) 30: 233–9.

Figueroa, Juan Guillermo. 1998. "Algunos Elementos para Interpretar la Presencia de los Varones en los Procesos de Salud Reproductiva." ["Some Elements to Interpreting Men's Role in Reproductive Health Processes"]. *Cadernos de Saúde Pública* 15 (Supl. 1): 87–96.

Fragoso, Ana, Sergio Velázquez, and Juan Hermida. 1986. "El Contrahorizonte de la Salud." ["Health's Counter-Horizon"]. *Nexos* 104: 46–7.

Frenk, Julio. 1984. "La Estratificación Social en la Educación Médica Mexicana." ["Social Stratification in Mexican Medical Education"]. *Salud Pública de México* 26: 484–91.

——. 1985. "Efectos del Origen Social y de la Socialización Profesional Sobre las Preferencias Vocacionales de los Internos de Medicina en México." ["Social Class Origin and Professional Socialization's Effects on the Career Preferences among Medical Interns in Mexico"]. *Educación Médica y Salud* 19: 426–51.

——. 1988a. *Social Origin, Professional Socialization and Labor Market Dynamics: The Determinants of Career Preferences among Medical Interns in Mexico.* Mexico City: Serie Perspecivas en Salud Pública, Instituto Nacional de Salud Pública.

——. 1988b. "La Modernización de la Salud Pública." ["The Public Health Modernization"]. *Nexos* 122: 57–8.

——. 1988c. "De la Autonomía al Autismo." ["From Autonomy to Autism"]. *Nexos* 124: 75–6.

——(ed.). 1997. *Observatorio de la Salud. Necesidades, Servicios, Políticas.* Mexico City: Fundación Mexicana para la Salud.

Frenk, Julio, and R. Bashshur. 1983. "Career Preferences and Perceptions of the Medical Labor Market among Mexican Interns." *Social Science and Medicine* 17: 693–704.

Frenk, Julio, Héctor Hernández Llamas, and Lourdes Alvarez Klein. 1980. "El Mercado de Trabajo Médico." ["The Medical Labor Market"] . *Gaceta Médica de México* 116: 187–95.

Frenk, Julio, Javier Alagón, Gustavo Nigenda, Alejandro Muñoz del Río, Cecilia Robledo, Luis Alonso Vázquez, and Catalina Ramírez. 1991. "Patterns of Medical Employment: A Survey of Imbalances in Urban Mexico." *American Journal of Public Health* 81: 23–9.

Frenk, Julio and Miguel Angel González-Block. 1992. "Primary Care and Reform of Health Systems: A Framework for the Analysis of Latin American Experiences." *Health Services Management Research* 5: 32–43.

Frenk, Julio, Octavio Gómez-Dantés, Carlos Cruz, Fernando Chacón, Patricia Hernández, and Peter Freeman. 1994. "Consequences of the North American Free Trade Agreement for Health Services: A Perspective from Mexico." *American Journal of Public Health* 84: 1591–7.

Garduño, María de los Angeles, and Julia del Carmen Rodríguez. 1990. "Salud y Doble Jornada: Taquilleras del Metro." ["Health and Double Working-Day: The Subways' Female Workers"]. *Salud-Problema* 20: 41–5.

Gómez-Dantéz, Octavio, Julio Frenk, and Carlos Cruz. 1997. "Commerce in Health Services in North America within the Context of the North American Free Trade Agreement." *Revista Panamericana de Salud Pública* 1: 460–5.

González, Soledad (ed.). 1995. *Las mujeres y la salud.* Mexico City: El Colegio de México.

González-Block, Miguel Angel and Julio Frenk. 1986a. "El Horizonte de la Salud." ["The Health's Horizon"]. *Nexos* 100: 59–61.

——. 1986b. "El Contrahorizonte del Economicismo." ["The Economicism's Counter-Horizon"]. *Nexos* 106: 41–2.

Hernández Llamas, Héctor. 1982. "Historia de la Participación del Estado en las Instituciones de Atención Médica en México 1935–1980." ["A History of the State's Participation in Medical Care Institutions in Mexico 1935–1980"]. Pp. 49–96 in F. Ortíz Quesada (ed.), *Vida y Muerte del Mexicano*, vol. 2. México: Folios Ediciones.

Infante, Claudia. 1990. "Utilización de Servicios de Atención Prenatal: Influencia de la Morbilidad Percibida y de las Redes Sociales de Ayuda." ["Use of Prenatal Health Services: The Influence of Perceived Morbidity and Social Networks"]. *Salud Pública de México* 32: 419–29.

Langer, Ana, and Gustavo Nigenda (eds.). 1995. *Métodos Cualitativos para la Investigación en Salud Pública.* Cuernavaca: Instituto Nacional de Salud Pública, serie: "Perspectivas en Salud Pública" 20.

Langer, Ana, and Kathryn Tolbert (eds.). 1996. *Mujer, Sexualidad y Salud Reproductiva en México.* Mexico City: The Population Council–EDAMEX.

Lara, María Asunción. 1995. "Incorporación de la Mujer al Trabajo Remunerado: Repercusiones para su Salud Reproductiva." ["Women's Incorporation to Paid Work: Reproductive Health Consequences"]. Pp. 243–58 in S. E. Pérez-Gil, J. C. Ramírez, and P. Ravelo (eds.), *Género y Salud Femenina. Experiencias de Investigación en México.* Mexico City: CIESAS-UG-INN.

Laurell, Asa Cristina. 1974. "Sociología Médica: Una Bibliografía Comentada." ["Medical Sociology: An Annotated Bibliography"]. *Revista Mexicana de Ciencia Política* 75: 105–11.

———. 1975. "Medicina y Capitalismo en México." ["Medicine and Capitalism in Mexico"]. *Cuadernos Políticos* 5: 80–93.

———. 1979. "Work and Health in Mexico." *International Journal of Health Services* 9: 543–68.

———. 1982. "La Salud-Enfermedad Como Proceso Social." ["Health–Illness as a Social Process"]. *Revista Latinoamericana de Salud* 2: 7–25.

———. 1989. "Social Analysis of Collective Health in Latin America." *Social Science and Medicine* 28: 1183–91.

———. 1999. "The Mexican Social Security Counterreform: Pensions for Profit." *International Journal of Health Services* 29: 371–91.

Laurell, Asa Cristina, and Margarita Márquez. 1983. *El Desgaste Obrero en México. Proceso de Producción y Salud*. Mexico City: Era.

Laurell, Asa Cristina, Mariano Noriega, Olivia López, and Víctor Ríos. 1990. "La Experiencia Obrera como Fuente de Conocimiento. Confrontación de Resultados de la Encuesta Colectiva e Individual." ["Workers' Experience as a Source of Knowledge. A Validation of a Collective and Individual Survey"]. *Cuadernos Médico Sociales* 51: 5–26.

Laurell, Asa Cristina, and M. Ortega. 1992. "The Free Trade Agreement and the Mexican Health Sector." *International Journal of Health Services* 22: 331–7.

Lazcano-Ponce, Eduardo, Roberto Castro, Betania Allen, Patricia Nájera, Patricia Alonso de Ruíz, and Mauricio Hernández-Avila. 1999. "Barriers to Early Detection of Cervical-Uterine Cancer in Mexico." *Journal of Women's Health* 8: 399–408.

Lerner, Susana, and André Quesnel. 1994. "Las Transacciones Institucionales y la Pluralidad de Trayectorias Reproductivas." ["Institutional Transactions and Reproductive Trajectories' Plurality"]. *Estudios Demográficos y de Desarrollo Urbano* 9: 543–78.

Leyva, René, Joaquina Erviti, Mario Bronfman, and Nadine Gasman. 1999. "Consumo de Medicamentos en Farmacias Privadas: Los Medicamentos Inseguros." ["Drug Consumption in Private Drugstores: The Case of Unsafe Drugs"]. Pp. 493–508 in M. Bronfman and R. Castro (eds.), *Salud, Cambio Social y Política: Perspectivas desde América Latina*. Mexico City: EDAMEX.

Londoño, J. L., and Julio Frenk. 1997. "Structured Pluralism: Towards an Innovative Model for Health System Reform in Latin America." *Health Policy* 41: 1–36.

López Acuña, Daniel. 1986. *La Salud Desigual en México*. México: Siglo XXI editores.

López Arellano, Oliva, 1994. "La Selectividad en la Política de Salud." ["Health Policy Selectivity"]. Pp. 33–60 in A. C. Laurell (ed.), *Nuevas Tendencias y Alternativas en el Sector Salud*. Mexico City: Universidad Autónoma Metropolitana-Xochimilco.

López Arellano, Olivia, and José Blanco Gil. 1996. "Las Necesidades de Salud y las Propuestas de Solución. Notas Para la Discusión." ["Health Needs and Proposed Solutions. Notes for a Discussion"]. Pp. 79–97 in C. García and H. Hernández (eds.), *Mortalidad, Salud y Discurso Demográfico*. Cuernavaca: Centro Regional de Investigaciones Multidisciplinarias (UNAM).

Lozano, Rafael. 1997. "El Peso de la Enfermedad en México: Avances y Desafíos." ["Disease's Weight in Mexico: Achievements and Challenges"]. Pp. 23–61 in J. Frenk (ed.), *Observatorio de la Salud: Necesidades, Servicios, Políticas*. México: Fundación Mexicana para la Salud.

Martínez, Carolina. 1993. *Sobrevivir en Malinalco. La Salud al Margen de la Medicina*. México: El Colegio de México, Universidad Autónoma Metropolitana-Xochimilco.

Menéndez, Eduardo. 1978. "El Modelo Médico y la Salud de los Trabajadores." ["The Hegemonic Medical Model and the Workers' Health"]. Pp. 11–53 in *La Salud de los Trabajadores*, by Franco Basaglia. Mexico City: Ed. Nueva Imagen.

———. 1983. "Hacia Una Práctica Médica Alternativa. Hegemonía y Autoatención (Gestión) en Salud." ["Towards an Alternative Medical Practice. Hegemony and Self-Care in Health"]. Mexico City: Cuadernos de la Casa Chata # 86.

———. 1984. "Estructura y Relaciones de Clase y la Función de los Modelos Médicos." ["Class Structure and the Medical Models' Functions"]. *Nueva Antropología* 6: 71–102.

———. 1985a. "El Modelo Médico Dominante y las Limitaciones y Posibilidades de los Modelos Antropológicos." ["The Dominant Medical Model and the Limits and Possibilities of the Anthropological Models"]. *Desarrollo Económico* 24: 593–604.

———. 1985b. "Saber 'Médico' y Saber 'Popular': El Modelo Médico Hegemónico y su Función Ideológica en el Proceso de Alcoholización." ["'Medical' Knowledge and 'Lay' Knowledge: The Hegemonic Medical Model and its Ideological Function in the Process of Alcoholism"]. *Estudios Sociológicos* 3: 263–96.

———. 1992. "Grupo Doméstico y Proceso Salud/Enfermedad/Atención. Del 'Teoricismo' al Movimiento Continuo." ["Domestic Group and Health/Illness/Care Process. From 'Teoricism' to Permanent Movement"]. *Cuadernos Médico Sociales* 59: 3–18.

———. 1998. "Estilos de Vida, Riesgos y Construcción Social. Conceptos Similares y Significados Diferentes." ["Life-Style, Risk and Social Construction. Similar Concepts and Different Meanings"]. *Estudios Sociológicos* 16: 37–67.

Mercado, Francisco Javier. 1996. *Entre el Infierno y la Gloria. La Experiencia de la Enfermedad Crónica en un Barrio Urbano.* Guadalajara: Universidad de Guadalajara.

Modena, María Eugenia (1990). "Madres, médicos y curanderos: diferencia cultural e identidad ideológica" ["Mothers, physicians, and curers: cultural difference and ideological identity"]. Mexico City: Ediciones de la Casa Chata, # 37.

Navarro, Vicente. 1976. *Medicine Under Capitalism.* New York: Prodist.

———. 1982. "The Labor Process and Health: A Historical Materialist Interpretation." *International Journal of Health Services* 12: 5–29.

Nigenda, Gustavo, Julio Frenk, Cecilia Robledo-Vera, Luis Alonso Vázquez, and Catalina Ramírez. 1990. "Los Sistemas Locales de Salud y el Mercado de Trabajo Médico: Resultados de un Estudio de Preferencias de Ubicación Geográfica." ["Local Health Systems and Medical Labor Market. Results from a Study on Geographic Work Preferences"]. *Educación Médica y Salud* 24: 115–35.

Noriega, Mariano. 1989. "Problemas Teórico-Metodológicos de la Investigación Sobre Salud en el Trabajo." ["Theoretical and Methodological Problems in Research on Work and Health"]. *Salud-Problema* 17: 9–13.

Ortales, Sergio. 1996. "Infant Malnutrition: A Biocultural Study in Urban Areas of Provincia de Buenos Aires, Argentina." *Archivos Latinoamericanos de Nutrición* 46: 136–42.

Pérez-Gil, Sara Elena, Juan Carlos Ramírez, and Patricia Ravelo (eds.). 1995. *Género y Salud Femenina. Experiencias de Investigación en México.* Mexico City: CIESAS-UG-INN.

Ríquer, Florinda, Irma Saucedo, and Patricia Bedolla. 1996. "Agresión y Violencia Contra el Género Femenino: Un Asunto de Salud Pública." ["Violence Against Women: A Public Health Issue"]. Pp. 247–87 in A. Langer and K. Tolbert (eds.), *Mujer: Sexualidad y Salud Reproductiva en México.* México: The Population Council–EDAMEX.

Rodríguez, G., A. Amuchástegui, M. Rivas, and M. Bronfman. 1995. "Mitos y Dilemas de los Jóvenes en Tiempos del SIDA." ["Youths' Myths and Dilemmas in Times of AIDS"]. Pp. 91–200 in M. Bronfman, A. Amuchástegui, R. M. Martina, N. Minello, M. Rivas, and G. Rodríguez (eds.), in *SIDA en México. Migración, Adolescencia y Género.* Mexico City: Información Profesional Especializada.

Rodríguez, Gabriela, and Benno de Keijzer. 1998. "La Noche se Hizo Para los Hombres: Las Regulaciones Sexuales del Cortejo en una Comunidad Cañera." ["Nights were

Made for Men: Sexual Regulations of Courtship in a Rural Community"]. *Debate Feminista* 9: 237–66.

Salcedo, Ana Leticia, and Carlos Alberto Prado. 1993. "Proceso Migratorio Familiar como Factor de Riesgo en la Desnutrición del Preescolar Migrante en los Cañeros de Jalisco." ["Family Migration as Risk Factor of Malnutrition Among Cane Workers' Children in Jalisco"]. Pp. 353–82 in C. Denman, A. Escobar, C. Infante, F. J. Mercado, and L. Robles (eds.), *Familia, Salud y Sociedad. Experiencias de Investigación en México*. Guadalajara: Universidad de Guadalajara.

Santos, Raúl. 1996. "Socioeconomic Differentiation and Body Morphology in the Surui of Southwestern Amazonia." Current Anthropology 37: 851–6.

Saucedo, Irma. 1996. "Violencia Doméstica y Salud: Conceptualización y Datos que Existen en México." ["Domestic Violence and Health: Existing Concepts and Data in Mexico"]. *Revista Perinatología y Reproducción Humana* 10: 100–10.

Sasz, Ivonne, and Susana Lerner (eds.). 1992. *Para Comprender la Subjetividad. Investigación Cualitativa en Salud Reproductiva y Sexualidad*. Mexico City: El Colegio de México.

SSA. 1994. *Encuesta Nacional de Salud II*. México: Secretaría de Salud.

——. 1999. *Programa de Reforma del Sector Salud*, 1995–2000. México: Secretaría de Salud.

Stern, Claudio. 1996. "El Embarazo en Adolescentes como Problema Público: Una Visión Crítica." ["Pregnancy among Adolescents as a Public Problem: A Critical View"]. *Salud Pública de México* 39: 137–43.

Tellez, Alberto. 1997. "Prevalence of Intestinal Parasites in the Human Population of Leon, Nicaragua." Acta Trópica (Switzerland) 66: 119–25.

Tetelboin, Carolina. 1994. "El Problema de los Recursos Humanos." ["The Problem of Human Resources in Health Services"]. Pp. 89–110 in A. C. Laurell (ed.), *Nuevas Tendencias y Alternativas en el Sector Salud*. México: Universidad Autónoma Metropolitana-Xochimilco.

Tuñón, Esperanza, and Claudia Guillén. 1999. "Embarazo Adolescente en dos Generaciones de Madres Tabasqueñas: Una Exploración a sus Vivencias." ["Adolescence Pregnancy in Two Generations of Mothers from Tabasco: An Exploration of their Lived-Experiences"]. In E. Tuñón (ed.), *Género y Salud en el Sureste de México*. San Cristóbal de las Casas: UADY-Ecosur (in press).

13

Social Science and Health in Brazil

Everardo Duarte Nuñes

This chapter presents the principal aspects of the origin and development of medical sociology in Brazil, along with a short discussion of the country's health situation. I will also provide an overview of the discipline's antecedents in Brazil, along with the relationship between medical sociology's origin and the pedagogic practices that resulted from the Latin American Preventive Project. Finally, the main theoretical formulations that have been favored in Brazil and the recent interests of Brazilian researchers will also be introduced. In prior studies, I have characterized the significant aspects of the trajectory of Brazilian social science in health (Nunes 1986, 1991, 1997) and in this paper I have tried to place this trajectory in its context while focusing more specifically on the development of medical sociology.

GENERAL HEALTH CHARACTERISTICS OF BRAZIL

Located in the central portion of South America, Brazil is a Federative Republic comprised of 26 states plus a federal district. The country was discovered by the Portuguese in 1500 and existed as a colony until independence in 1822, followed by its establishment as a republic in 1899. Brazil is a multi-racial society whose population in 1996 consisted of the following population groups: whites (55.2%), blacks (6%), mulatto or mixed race (38.2%), Asian (0.7%), and local Indian (0.2%). It is the fifth largest country in the world in area, with 8,547,404 square kilometers, and has a population of 157,079,573 (as of the 1996 census). Nine urban areas, considered together, hold about 30 percent of the country's total population. The first census carried out in 1872 showed a population of only 9,993,478 inhabitants. The birth rate has been steadily dropping, from an average of 6 children per woman of childbearing age in 1950, to 4 in the mid-seventies, and then to 2.5 in 1990. This decrease probably stems from changes in the lifestyle of the population, including rapid urbanization, widespread use of contraceptives, and, in certain areas of the country, sterilization. In 1930, infectious and parasitic diseases caused 45.7 percent of the total deaths in Brazil, and 11.8 percent of the total deaths were caused by cardiovascular diseases. More recently, between 1990 and 1994, cardiovascular diseases jumped to 34 percent of total deaths, traumatic injuries made up 14.8 percent, cancer caused 13 percent of the deaths, and transmissible diseases were only 11 percent of the total.

Although the nation has many accomplishments in the health area, serious health problems remain. In the rich, industrialized countries of the world, there was a gradual and progressive diminishing of infectious and parasitic illnesses and the rise of chronic-degenerative diseases, especially ailments of the cardiovascular system. In developing countries, like Brazil, there has also been a transition in morbidity profiles in the last 40 years that are similar, but not identical, to those of core nations. These transformations became evident in the 1960s and have progressed to the point today that Brazil has a polarized epidemiological profile: the simultaneous existence of a high incidence and prevalence of morbidity from chronic illnesses combined with a much higher incidence of infectious and parasitic diseases than that of developed countries (Araujo 1992).

The modern Brazilian health delivery system is characterized by two distinct periods: prior to the health reform that took place in 1988 and afterwards. There were many problems in the provision of health care by the government sector. During the first period, there were at least three parallel systems operating health delivery facilities. The first was the National Social Security Institute (INAMPS) that was responsible for curative care. It operated its own hospitals and health centers, as well as contracting services from private hospitals, clinics, and laboratories. The second system was the Ministry of Health, which was primarily responsible for preventive care. However, the State Secretary of Health carried out most of this system's activities at the state level. The third system was the various municipal networks of health facilities.

With these three different systems at work, many problems in the provision of health care arose; these were finally addressed in the 1980s by health reform. The 8th National Health Conference in 1986 produced a series of recommendations that were incorporated into the Federal Constitution of 1988. These recommendations, named the Unified Health System (SUS), included two main directives: (1) decentralization, with dedicated administration in each government sphere; and (2) priority to preventive activities, without loss to individual medical attention and community participation. Today, public health services, complemented by private services contracted under SUS's responsibility, cover about 75 percent of the Brazilian population.

There is also a private sector of health care that is paid directly by private insurance plans that fall into four categories: (1) privately owned insurance companies (*medicina de grupo*), which is a pre-payment system representing 47 percent of the private medical industry market; (2) physician cooperatives (physician-owned groups), which is also a prepayment system and represents 25 percent of the market; (3) self-health insurance, which is an association of self-insurance and third- party out-sourcing that represents 20 percent of the market; and finally (4) reimbursement health insurance, which repays either the insured person or a third party and represents 8 percent of the private market. These private types of insurance were used by 20 percent of the Brazilian population in 1995 and involved about 6.4 billion dollars worth of investments.

The majority of the SUS hospitals are privately owned but under contract with SUS. However, 75 percent of the ambulatory- care facilities are purely governmental institutions. Since 1994, the Ministry of Health has been developing a Family Health Program in order to give attention to the health of the family as a whole. In 1996 this program was extended to 226 municipalities, which also involved the institution of community agents that reached a total of 45,000 individuals in that one year.

Brazil's regional differences in health are significant. Many analyses (Lampreia 1995; Barreto et al. 1997; OPAS 1998) have shown evidence that Brazil is one of the countries with the most pronounced socioeconomic inequalities. Naturally, these socioeconomic inequalities have a strong impact on the living conditions of the population, and therefore on its health. Brazilian life expectancy in 1960 averaged 51.3 years and the infant mortality rate was 105.2 deaths per 1,000 life births. In 1995, life expectancy at birth was 66.6 years, and it reached 67.6 in 1996. The reader must remember the fact that women's average life expectancy surpasses that of men by about seven years. Looking at the accentuated differences between the various regions in Brazil, one can see that the South and Southeast regions have the highest average life expectancy, at 70.2 and 68.8 years respectively. The West-Central and Northern regions are next with 68.5 and 67.4 years, respectively. Finally, the Northeast region had the lowest life expectancy with an average of only 64.5 years (IBGE 1998).

The infant mortality rate in 1995 was 48.0 per one thousand live births for male and 36.4 per thousand for female babies. When broken down by region, this figure also illustrates the dramatic differences in living conditions and health. The best regional results, again, are in the South, with 25.2 per thousand for live male births and 14.8 per thousand for live female births, and the Southeast, with 27.7 per thousand for males and 17.2 per thousand for females. The West-Central region is again third, with 29.5 and 19.3 per thousand for male and female births, respectively. The urban Northern region has about 45.2 deaths per thousand males and 34.6 deaths per thousand for females. Again falling far behind the other regions is the Northeast, with 71.7 and 60.8 per thousand live male and female births, respectively (IBGE 1998).

Both life expectancy and infant mortality rates illustrate the regional differences found in Brazil, showing a certain "hierarchy of the poor, a pyramid at the base of which we find the poorer states – all belonging to the Northeast Region – and at the top the state of São Paulo, followed by the country's extreme south (Rio Grande do Sul and Santa Catarina)" (OPAS 1998: 8). Another striking statistic in Brazil is that in 1990 the truly poor represented 30.2 percent of the total population, and 54.1 percent of these poor were located in the Northeast (OPAS 1998: 9). The document from OPAS points out that in Brazil, two critical poles of poverty may be identified completely opposite in their characteristics. One of these is the Northeast (especially the rural part), with poverty typical of traditional societies at the margin of industrial urban growth. The other is the Southeast metropolis with 23 percent of individuals below the poverty line, which is associated, socially and economically, with the participation of this region as the dynamic center of the national economy.

ANTECEDENTS TO MEDICAL SOCIOLOGY IN BRAZIL

In North America, research and teaching in the social sciences in the health area go back over a period of 50 years, while in the case of Latin America, the beginning was only 30 years ago. Furthermore, researchers have highlighted the lack of a classical tradition in health social sciences, especially medical sociology. As Cockerham (1988: 576) observed: "The notion that medical sociology has an aberrant character stems not only from its neglect by sociology's founders, but, more important, from the fact that it matured in an intellectual climate far different from sociology's traditional specialties, with direct roots in nineteenth- and early twentieth-century social thought." There were some minor developments in medical sociology in the United States in the first half of the twentieth century, obviously with different characteristic from those assumed later. But the reference point for the development of sociology as applied to health, both in Europe and the United States, without any doubt, is the end of World War II. It was only in the 1950s, however, that the United States advanced in the direction of the regular production of medical sociology with the seminal work of Parsons (1951).

The author agrees with Menéndez (1992) that a global revision of a discipline takes place not only in relation to a structural crisis, but can also occur because of restricted or unavailable paradigms and the discipline's own hegemonic tendencies. Both of these latter situations need not necessarily coincide and the growth and transformation of each area has an historical origin as well as internal and external determining factors. In the case of the United States, the federal government stimulated the development of medical sociology through funding for research intended to address the relationship between health and social conditions. In Latin America, it was the local middle classes who showed the first signs of concern regarding the relationship between the 1930s and 1950s as they made an effort towards industrialization, free-market capitalism, and social modernization.

Though there were no projects in the area of medical sociology as such during the 1940s, there are some forerunners to the discipline that should be noted. In 1942, there was a great deal of interest in the area of health when bilateral agreements were reached between the United States and several Latin American countries. As a result, the Health and Sanitary Division of the Institute of American Affairs had the following objectives: (1) from a military viewpoint – to improve health conditions, especially in relation to the demands of the army; (2) from a political viewpoint – to fulfill the government's obligations of sanitary programs promised during the 30th Resolution at the Rio de Janeiro Conference (1942); (3) from an industrial viewpoint – to increase the production of essential materials in areas with poor health conditions; and (4) from a moralistic point of view – to use facts and not just words to show the tangible benefits of the democracy which was in progress and to obtain the support of the civilian population (García 1989).

Another antecedent is the establishment of medical anthropology in Latin America. Beginning in the early 1940s, the first medical anthropology programs were sponsored by the Pan American Sanitary Department, an international division of the Rockefeller Foundation, and the Inter-American Cooperative Public Health Service. Also important was the emergence of general sociology. Sociology began in Brazil with the School of Sociology and Politics in São Paulo in 1933 and the Faculty of Philosophy, Sciences, and Arts of the University of São Paulo in 1934. Elsewhere in Latin America, sociology had been institutionalized much earlier when faculties were established in Colombia (1882), Argentina (1897), Mexico (1900), and Ecuador (1906). An emphasis on positivism, with roots in European ideas, which had dominated much of Latin American social thinking prior to World War II, gave way in the middle of the twentieth century to new lines of thinking promoting empirical research and adoption of modernization theory. This development was strongly influenced by the empirical style of sociology practiced at this time in the United States.

Later during the mid-1960s, after the failure of many government-sponsored economic projects in Latin America, a period of sociological criticism arose. According to Pablo González Casanova, in 1966, the distinctive direction of sociology during this period in Mexico and the rest of the continent was to investigate "'the dynamics of inequality' – conditions including demography, food and nutrition, work and employment, consumption and economy, transport, domicile, clothing, leisure and entertainment, health and social security, and human rights (especially women's right to vote and participate)." These studies were part of what Sefchovich (1989: 29) had in mind when he encouraged "a social and political interpretation of conditions as a criticism of the State." In general, the primary topic of study for Latin America was to determine the social reality of each country within a Marxist focus. According to some analysts, during the period 1966–82, Latin American sociologists developed an original theory – the theory of dependence based on relations between the center and the periphery of the world capitalist economy (Cardoso and Falleto 1970). However, these theories disappeared after 1982 because they were "unable to predict the future of the region's political regime and even less so the character of the political forces that contributed toward these changes" (Garza Toledo 1989: 126).

THE EARLY STAGES OF MEDICAL SOCIOLOGY (1960s)

The precedents set by medical anthropological research in the 1940s were important, but the systematic incorporation of sociology and other social sciences in health took place only in the 1960s when there was a great deal of criticism regarding the bio-medically-oriented model of medicine. This criticism occurred particularly in Brazil, Ecuador, Mexico, and Venezuela (Nunes 1986). About the same time, there was a major reformulation of medical education in the region associated with the Latin American Preventive Project.

In order to provide a more complete vision of the individual and his or her illness, medical courses were expanded to include other disciplines and themes linked to epidemiology, behavioral science, the administration of health services, and biostatistics. Two important aspects of the new pedagogical practices were the success of the biopsychosocial integration of the individual and a new "comprehensive medicine" focused on integrated family medicine within the community.

The functionalist view and systemic theories developed by Talcott Parsons, Samuel Bloom, David Mechanic, and other North American researchers were predominant among the theoretical perspectives introduced in schools teaching medical sociology. One of the original proposals of this period in Latin American medical schools was the teaching of sociology based on the natural history of disease perspective adapted by García (1971).

BRAZIL'S MEDICAL SOCIOLOGY DEVELOPS FURTHER (1970S AND 1980S)

Some very important events in the area of medical sociology took place at the beginning of the 1970s. There was again clear dissatisfaction with the teaching models and references used in the discipline. Criticism arose particularly in response to the use of the natural history of diseases and atheoretical literature (whose possibilities were therefore limited), especially with regard to the literature's understanding of underdeveloped societies (Gaete and Tapia 1970). Because of this, sociologists and other social scientists found it very important to reevaluate other epistemological categories. The Pan American Health Organization organized seminars to deal with such concerns, such as the one held in Cuenca (Ecuador), in 1972. This seminar proposed an alternative model for sociological research that would analyze societal changes and include theoretical elements that would allow a better understanding of social reality and its internal contradictions at the specific structural levels (OPAS/OMS 1974).

Researchers conducted many discussions at this point regarding an alternative model that would (1) take into consideration the relation between concepts of health and actions as well as the modes of production and the socioeconomic structure; (2) conduct historical research about health practices and medical education; and (3) define the relationship between biological science and social science from an epistemological viewpoint. Emphasis on a theoretical approach based in historic materialism began in the seventies and is a distinct milestone for medical sociology in Latin America. According to Mercer (1986: 226), from the mid-seventies to 1980, medical sociology went through a period of "identification and legitimization." It was a period of acute theoretical turmoil and, alongside the traditional Marxism, there was also structuralism by Michel Foucault and Claude Lévi-Strauss. These perspectives, without doubt, influenced the objectives of many graduate courses in medicine that aimed at "a double target: theoretical formation and political criticism" (Bezerra and Sayd 1993). The courses' emphasis on sociology resulted in the production of several important dissertations and theses.

From a political viewpoint, the main objective during this time period was to guarantee health as an inalienable right of the citizen through State intervention. Although located within a critical financial context, the rationalization of resources and the expansion of services were deemed fundamental by the government. Brazilian sociologists conducted many of the important studies that marked this period, dealing with medicine and society, state medicine, historical analyses and health programs. In Latin America, during the period 1970–9, the production of scientific papers in the health service area made up 35.7 percent of the total paper production. For example, in 1975, Donnangelo conducted a study on the medical profession and its articulation with social practice. Later, the same author carried out an analysis to try to establish the relationship of medicine with the social structure in political, ideological, and economic plans in which the economy is the determining factor and politics the mediating variable (Donnangelo and Pereira 1976). Another example is Arouca (1975), who elaborated a critical aspect of preventive medicine using Foucaultian analytical methodology. His research also raised important questions regarding medical care as a work process. Nogueira (1977) and Gonçalves (1979) agreed that the topic was worth further research, as proven by their study of the characteristics and practices of medicine in a society with capitalist production.

Toward the end of the 1970s there was an acute economic recession in Latin American countries because of inflation, increase in international debt, unemployment, and fiscal deficit. This had an overwhelmingly negative effect on the health of Brazil, so changes in health care became necessary. The country directed primary attention toward health on an international level; on the national front the government took a stronger position regarding sanitary problems, preventive medicine, social medicine, and public health. In addition to the changes to medical education discussed earlier, two organizations were created which were important for the further organization of academic and political health movements. ABRASCO (the Brazilian Graduate Association in Collective Health) was founded in 1979 and the CEBES (the Brazilian Centre for Health Studies) originated in 1976. According to ABRASCO (1982) graduate courses in health-related studies should be oriented "by a critical analysis of the health sector within its social reality and should have the capacity to influence the teaching, research and services rendered."

Besides structural and political factors, which undoubtedly were important in reevaluating the health system, the financial factor positively influenced the development of research. This can be seen in the role played by FINEP (the financier for research studies), which provided "a scientific and technological infrastructure for research in health not subject to biomedicine" (Costa 1992: 129). During the seventies, it can be briefly stated that health became the main theme of the social sciences, particularly sociology, as seen by the concern given to theory, the institutionalization of new graduate health-related courses, and the finance provided for research.

A review of this period cannot fail to mention the importance given to methodology, especially qualitative, and its applications in the area of health (Minayo 1989). At the beginning of the eighties, a preoccupation with the methodology and theory of medical sociology was evident in a pioneer study by Pereira (1983) in which he analyzed the manner in which functionalism, comprehensive and dialectic, was introduced when researching the social organization of health practices. Later Luz (1988) analyzed the socio-historical development of modern scientific rationality using strategies that were common in both medicine and sociology.

RECENT THEORETICAL PERSPECTIVES

The vitality of medical sociology is evidenced not only by its many publications in recent years, which includes the establishment of two journals – *Health and Society* and *Science and Collective Health* – but also by the manner in which social scientists have addressed certain theoretical questions. As mentioned earlier, there was a preoccupation with methodology and theory in research during the seventies. It was present when attempting to better understand the health/ illness process, as well as the social organization of health practices. Significantly, all of this took place in a context that favors debate. The following decades have continued these interests, resulting in important new perspectives on medical sociology. The diversity of theoretical reference, in particular, became evident during the eighties. The concept of "habitus" developed by Pierre Bordieu, the perspective of communicative action by Jurgen Habermas, and Michel Foucault's discourse analysis have been applied in recent studies. Clifford Geertz has served as a reference for research on symbolic and cultural aspects of medical practice. Agnes Heller's work on individual–community relations have also been influential, as well as Felix Guattari's ideas on subjectivism and territorialities as applied to mental health studies. Other studies have used Cornelius Castoriadis's concept of the construction of subjectivity, or Alain Touraine's ideas on the formation of new actors and actions, which are based on rules of collective life. Theoretical positions on the state, democracy, and modernity derive from authors such as Paul Evans, N. Lechner, and Guillermo O'Donnell. Finally, Claudine Herlizch's studies on social representations have been important, along with many other social scientists and philosophers.

There are three approaches that I feel define the present direction of medical sociology. The first deals with politics in the area of health – a field that has shown notable development. Many specialists have noted a crisis of the classical models. For example, Bodstein (1992) criticizes the predominance of structural-functionalist Marxism in the study of the state's health policies. According to the author, these analyses were extremely limited because they were highly generalized and abstract. One of the main problems lies in finding how the macro and micro social dimensions relate to the significance of collective agents and to the new identities that are created during the process. According to Bodstein (1997), social science since the mid-seventies has been heading toward "a questioning of the subject, the meaning of its actions, its various roles, complex categories that construct socio-political expectations and representations." The author emphasizes that "what is central in the sociological dimension today generally follows the Weberian tradition of obtaining an explanation of the social processes in two ways: starting from the exterior aspect, beyond the intentions of the social

agents, but without abandoning dimensions of human participation in the formation and transformation of social institutions and relationships" (Bodstein
1992). The author criticizes studies that give more importance to the functional
character of social politics in health in order to guarantee the legitimacy of the
system by establishing the clear subjugation of politics to economy. A reinter-
pretation of politics in health means the recovery of the relationship between
social agents.

A second direction of Brazilian medical sociology is the health/disease
approach, which shows the necessity of analyzing "the appropriation of the
health concept by infirm social agents" (Chammé 1993). According to Minayo
(1989), research regarding the field of social representations of health and
disease could be better conducted through attention to three orientations: (1)
health/disease as a social and individual expression; (2) health/disease as an
expression of social contradictions; and (3) health as a political battlefield. The
1990s has witnessed the progressive advance of sociological studies on disease,
with the use of qualitative methodologies and a focus on distinct pathologies like
AIDS (Loyola 1994; Uchoa 1997: 94).

The third example that illustrates the recent (and future) direction of researchers is criticism regarding the use of macro theories. According to Ferreira (1993),
in the face of an "explanation crisis" researchers adopted theoretical references
that emphasized the constitution of identities and valued subjectivity, the ima-
ginary and cultural phenomenon in themselves or as mediators between structures and systems and social action.

CONCLUSION

This paper shows that in Latin America and Brazil, the field of medical sociology
not only reflects intellectual traditions but also the fact that the living conditions
of the population are marked by deep social inequalities. According to Stavenhagen (1966: 20–1) there is no doubt that Latin American medical sociology was
politically impregnated by reform and revolution. In the case of Brazil, the
confirmation of the importance of sociology took place in the area of health –
through the Faculties of Medicine and Public Health courses and not through the
Faculties of Social Science and Philosophy. It is clear that during its development,
medical sociology was strengthened and became more important. There are
many problems and challenges to be overcome but it has achieved institutionalization. This is demonstrated by the fact that 44.1 percent of the subject matter
in the Master's degree of Public Health/Collective Health is in the area of social
sciences. For the Doctorate degree, this figure goes up to 44.9 percent of the
coursework (Nunes and Costa 1997).

This study is a general review and it is therefore impossible to comprehens-
ively list all of the research that has taken place during the last few years. Many
developments have taken place only recently. The direct involvement of health
professionals in discussing and critically evaluating health reform favored a
political approach to health using a theoretical perspective. There has been
a renewal of interest in historical research on diseases and public health organi-

zation. Also, basic theories of health planning have been reevaluated, and discussion has taken place regarding workers' health in relation to the new problems of economic globalization and technological progress. Finally, studies on biomedical practices and on bioethics have become very important.

References

ABRASCO. 1982. "Documento Preliminar de Princípios Básicos." ["Preliminary Document of Basic Principles"]. Pp. 100–17 in *Ensino da Saúde Pública, Medicina Preventiva e Social no Brasil* [Teaching of Public Health, Preventive and Social Medicine in Brazil]. Rio de Janeiro: ABRASCO.

Araujo, Jose Duarte de. 1992. "Polarizacao Epidemiologica no Brasil." ["Polarization of Epidemiology in Brazil"]. Informe Epidemiologico do SUS 1: 5–16.

Arouca, A. S. da S. 1975. "O dilema preventivista: contribuição para a compreensão e crítica da Medicina Preventiva." ["The Preventivist Dilemma: A Contribution to the Comprehension and Criticism of Preventive Medicine"]. Ph.D. Thesis. Campinas: Faculdade de Ciências Médicas.

Barreto, Maurício, Eduardo Hage Carmo, Carlos Antonio de S. T. Santos, and L. D. A. Ferreira. 1997. "Saúde da População Brasileira: Mudanças, Superposição de Padrões e Desigualdade." ["Health of the Brazilian Population: Change, Social Class and Patterns of Inequality"]. Pp. 45–60 in S. Fleury (ed.), *Saúde e Democracia: A Luta do CEBES*. São Paulo: Lemos Editorial.

Bezerra Jr., B. and J. D. Sayd. 1993. "Um mestrado para um momento preciso. Estudos em Saúde Coletiva." ["Master's Degree for a Precise Moment"]. *Studies in Collective Health* 47.

Bodstein, R. C. A. 1992. "Ciências Sociais e Saúde Coletiva: novas questões, novas abordagens." ["Social Sciences and Collective Health: New Issues, New Approaches"]. *Cadernos de Saúde Pública* 8: 140–9.

——. 1997. "Políticas de serviços de saúde na perspectiva sociológica (notas metodológicas)." ["Policies of Health Services in the Sociological Perspective (Methodological Notes)"]. Pp. 219–26 in A. M. Canesqui (ed.), *Ciências Sociais e Saúde*. [Social Sciences and Health]. São Paulo, Rio de Janeiro: HUCITEC/ABRASCO.

Cardoso, F. H. and E. Falleto. 1970. *Dependência e Desenvolimento na América Latina: Ensaio de Interpreta ç ã o Sociológica.* [Dependency and Development in Latin America: A Study of Sociological Interpretation]. Rio de Janeiro: Editora Guanabara.

Chammé, S. J. 1993. "Os problemas de saúde e as contribuições das Ciências Sociais." ["Health Problems and Contributions of Social Sciences"]. I Encontro Brasileiro de Ciências Sociais em Saúde, Belo Horizonte, MG (mimeo).

Cockerham, William C. 1988. "Medical Sociology." Pp. 575–99 in N. Smelser (ed.), *Handbook of Sociology.* London: Sage.

Costa, N. R. 1992. *Política e projeto acadêmico: notas sobre a gênese do campo da Saúde Coletiva.* [Politics and Academic Project: Notes on the Genesis of the Field of Collective Health]. Cadernos de História e Saúde 2: 125–36.

Donnangelo, M. C. F. and L. Pereira. 1976. *Saúde e sociedade.* [Health and Society]. São Paulo: Duas Cidades.

Ferreira, M. A. F. 1993. "Notas sobre a contribuição dos cientistas sociais ao campo da saúde." ["Notes on Contribution of Social Scientists to the Health Field"]. Encontro Brasileiro de Ciências Sociais em Saúde, Belo Horizonte, MG (mimeo).

Ferreira-Santos, C. A. 1973. *A enfermagem como profissão.* [Nursing as a Profession]. São Paulo: Pioneira/EDUSP.

Gaete, J. E., and I. Tapia. 1970. "Ciencias Sociales: una discusión acerca de su enfoque en medicina" ["Social Sciences: A Discussion on its Focus on Medicine"]. *Cuadernos Medico-Sociales* 9: 32–7.

García, J. C. 1971. "Paradigmas para la enseñanza de las Ciencias Sociales en las escuelas de medicina." ["Paradigms for Teaching Social Sciences in Medical Schools"]. *Educación Médica y Salud* 5: 130–48.

——. 1975. "Las Ciencias Sociales en América Latina: alcances políticos y ciencia política." ["Social Sciences in Latin America: Political Scope and Political Science"]. *Revista Mexicana de Ciencias Políticas y Sociales* 82: 49–55.

——.1989. "A articulação da medicina e da educação na estrutura social." ["Articulation of Medicine and Education in Social Structure"]. Pp. 189–92 in E. D. Nunes (ed.), *Juan César García: O pensamento social em saúde na América Latina* [Social Thinking in Health in Latin America]. São Paulo: Global.

Garza Toledo, E. de 1989. "La história de la epistemologia, la metodologia y las tecnicas de investigación en la Sociología mexicana." ["The History of Epistemology, Methodology and Investigation Techniques in Mexican Sociology"]. *Revista Mexicana de Sociologia* 1: 103–33.

Gonçalves, R. B. M. 1979. "Medicina e história: raízes sociais do trabalho médico." ["Medicine and History: Social Roots of the Medical Work"]. São Paulo, MS Diss. Faculdade de Medicina/USP.

Hardy, E. 1992 "Ciencias Sociales y Medicina: una experiencia personal." ["Social Sciences and Medicine: A Personal Experience"]. Pp. 15–20 in F. L. Stepke, R. Florenzano, G. E. Gyarmati, and C. E Trejo (eds.), *Ciencias Sociales y Medicina: Perspectivas latino americanas* [Social Sciences and Medicine: Latin American Perspectives]. Santiago do Chile: Editorial Universitária.

IBGE. 1998. "Pesquisa Nacional por Amostra de Domiciílios 1996." Rio de Janeiro.

Lampreia, Luiz Felips. 1995. "Relatório Brasileiro sobre Desenvolvimento Social." *Estudos Avançados* 9: 9–74.

Loyola, M. A. (ed.). 1994. *AIDS e sexualidade. Oponto de vista das ciências Humanas.* [AIDS and Sexuality: The View of the Human Sciences]. Rio de Janeiro: Relume – Dumará/UERJ.

Luz, M. T. 1988. *As instituições de saúde no Brasil: Instituição e estratégia de hegemonia* [Health Institutions in Brazil: Institution and Hegemony Strategy]. Rio de Janeiro: Graal.

Menendez, E. L. 1992. "Salud Pública: sector estatal, ciencia aplicada o ideologia del posible." ["Public Health: State Sector, Applied Science or Ideology of Possible"]. Pp. 103–22 in *La crisis de la Salud Pública: reflexiones para el debate* [The Crisis in Public Health: Reflections for Debate]. Washington, DC: OPS.

Mercer, H. 1986. "Las contribuciones de la Sociología a la investigación en salud." ["Contributions of Sociology to the Investigation on Health"]. Pp. 231–42 in E. D. Nunes (ed.), *Ciencias Sociales y salud en América Latina: tendencias y perspectivas* [Social Sciences and Health in Latin America: Trends and Perspectives]. Washington: OPS, Montevideo: CIESU.

Minayo, M. C. de S. 1989. "O desafio do conhecimento: Metodologia de pesquisa social (qualitativa) em saúde." ["Challenge in Knowledge: Methodology of Social Research (Qualitative) in Health"]. Ph.D. thesis, Rio de Janeiro: Escola Nacional de Saúde Pública/FIOCRUZ.

Nogueira, R. P. 1977. "Medicina Interna e Cirurgia: a formação social da prática médica. Dissertação de Mestrado." ["Internal Medicine and Surgery: Social Formation of Medical Practice"]. MS.Diss., Rio de Janeiro: Instituto de Medicina Social/UERJ.

Nuñes, E. D. 1986. "Tendencias y perspectivas de las investigaciones en Ciencias Sociales en la América Latina: una visión general." ["Trends and Perspectives of Investigations in Social Sciences in Latin America: An Overview"]. Pp. 33–83 in E. D Nunes (ed.), *Ciencias Sociales y salud en América Latina: tendencias y perspectivas* [Social Sciences and Health in Latin America: Trends and Perspectives]. Washington, DC: OPS, Montevideo: CIESU.

——. 1991. "As Ciências Sociais em Saúde: reflexões sobre as origens e a construção de um campo do conhecimento." ["Social Sciences in Health: Reflections on the Origins and Construction of a Field of Knowledge"]. *Saúde e Sociedade* 1: 59–84.

——. 1997. "Las Ciencias Sociales en salud en América Latina: una historia singular." ["Social Sciences in Health in Latin America: A Unique Story"]. *Espacio Abierto – Cuaderno Venezolano de Sociología* 6: 215–36

Nuñes, E. D. and P. S. da Costa. 1997. "Os cursos de Saúde Coletiva no Brasil – Mestrado e Doutorado: um estudo sobre as disciplinas básicas." ["Courses on Collective Health in Brazil – Master and Ph.D. A Study on Basic Subjects"]. *Ciência e Saúde Coletiva* 2: 72–90.

OPAS/OMS. 1974. "Aspectos teóricos de las Ciencias Sociales aplicadas a la Medicina." ["Theoretical Aspects of Social Sciences Applied to Medicine"]. *Educación Médica y Salud* 8: 354–9.

Organização Pan-Americana de Saúde – OPAS/OMS. 1998. "A Saúde no Brasil." ["Health in Brazil"].

Parsons, Talcott. 1951. *The Social System*. New York: Free Press.

Pereira, J. C. de M. 1983. "A explicação sociológica na Medicina Social." ["The Sociological Explanation in Social Medicine"]. Thesis, Ribeirão Preto: Faculdade de Medicina/USP.

Sefchovich, A. 1989. "Los caminos de la Sociología en el laberinto de la Revista Mexicana de Sociología." ["The Paths of Sociology in the Labyrinth of the Mexican Review of Sociology"]. *Revista Mexicana de Sociología* 1/89: 5–101

Stavenhagen, R. 1966. "Las Ciencias de la Conducta en la América Latina." ["Behaviour Sciences in Latin America"]. In R. F. Badgley (ed.), *Ciencias de la Conducta y enseñanza médica en América Latina* [Behaviour Sciences and Medical Teaching in Latin America]. New York: Fundación Milbanl Memorial 44: 19–29.

Uchoa, E. 1997. "Epidemiologia e Antropologia: Contribuições para uma abordagem dos aspectos transculturais da depressão." ["Epidemiology and Anthropology : Contributions to an Approach of Cross-Cultural Aspects of Depression"]. Pp. 87–109 in A. M Canesqui (ed.), *Ciências Sociais e Saúde* [Social Sciences and Health]. São Paulo, Rio de Janeiro: HUCITEC/ABRASCO.

Western Europe

14

Medical Sociology in Great Britain

ELLEN ANNANDALE AND DAVID FIELD

Medical sociology[1] is now firmly established as an academic discipline in Britain. In this chapter we reflect upon more than 30 years of scholarship, focusing upon the academic and policy issues that have concerned those working in the field. In particular, we consider the interplay of medical sociology's relationship with the theoretical concerns of its parent discipline of sociology and its strong empirical engagement with issues of health policy and practice. We argue that it is the shifting nature of this interplay, notably the ongoing tension between academic and practical policy concerns, that has defined the parameters of both theoretical and empirical research since the development of medical sociology in Britain in the late 1960s.

An enduring feature of medical sociology in Britain is that scholars work in diverse settings such as university social science departments (notably sociology and social policy), medical schools, departments of nursing, research units with very specific foci, and the National Health Service. This diversity enables the subdiscipline to respond very successfully to emerging policy agendas and to funding agencies (such as the Research Councils and the Department of Health). The subdiscipline, however, has been less successful in directing wider sociological debates, a concern which has exercised many commentators over the last three decades (e.g. Williams et al. 1998). However, its contribution in this respect has notably strengthened since the early 1990s, reflecting a heightened concern with health issues within both academic sociology and wider society. This concern is part of sociology's response to the large-scale shift from collectivism to individualism, which characterized the second half of twentieth-century Britain and continues into the new millennium. The impetus for this shift lies in changes in the economy, notably the decline in industrial production, the rise in service-sector employment, and the move away from the production of mass-market goods toward commodities tailored for highly specialized, and ever changing, consumer markets. Related changes have taken place in the public sector which, increasingly, is directed less toward meeting mass universal need through monolithic bureaucratic structures and more toward responding to a diversity of need through "welfare pluralism, quasi-markets, reorganized welfare work and consumer-sovereignty" (F. Williams 1994: 49).

These shifts from collectivism to individualism at the structural level have occurred alongside fast-paced changes in what medical sociologists once rather simplistically called "the biomedical model," such as the emergence of the "new genetics" and concerns about the health-related risks of living (e.g. Beck 1992). These changes have implications for both the social patterning of health and the experience of health and illness. Under these social conditions, a new socio-logical sensitivity has drawn attention away from a hitherto "disembodied" conceptualization of the rational individual bounded by collectivities such as social class, "race" and ethnicity, toward a self-reflexive individual making an array of life-style choices (e.g. in family formation, living arrangements, patterns of work and leisure). Since the body has been central to this new reflexivity (e.g. Giddens 1991), health concerns have begun to move, if not center stage, at least out of the wings and into the spotlight of wider sociology.

We begin the chapter with a discussion of the institutional context within which medical sociology developed in Britain and the research agenda of the early years. We then explore the shift from collectivism to individualism within British society, firstly as it is reflected within the National Health Service (NHS), and secondly in terms of its impact upon research in two areas of enduring interest to British medical sociology – health inequalities and the experience of illness.

THE DEVELOPMENT OF MEDICAL SOCIOLOGY IN BRITAIN

The Institutional Context

The development of medical sociology in Britain parallels that of sociology generally. Sociology was established as an academic discipline in the 1960s during a period of rapid expansion in higher education (HE) which lasted until the early 1970s. Over this period entrants to HE increased from around 60 percent of the 18–19 year-old population in 1961, to 14 percent in 1973 (CVCP 1997: 20). Three particular events mark the development of medical sociology during this period: the first conference gathering of around 60 medical socio-logists in the city of York in 1969 which signalled the birth of the British Sociological Association's (BSA) Medical Sociology Group;[2] the publication of the first edition of *Medical Sociology in Britain: A Register of Research and Teaching* in 1970 (hereafter referred to as the Register); and the publication of the Group's newsletter, *Medical Sociology News*, in 1973. Despite these signific-ant developments, the struggle of the fledgling subdiscipline to define its disciplinary boundaries was an enduring theme of the 1970s. Medical sociology's "minority" relationship to medicine, the appropriate balance of the Medical Sociology Group's academic and political activities, and the consequences of the vagaries of funding and "changing fashions of what is worth being researched," exercised the Group's convenor in the late 1970s (Stimson 1978). When reflecting on the Group's activities between 1974 and 1978 he raised what appears to have been an enduring concern since the late 1960s: "so each year one is inclined to ask – 'how long can it last' – yet each year the interest in the sociology of medicine continues" (Stimson 1978: xiv).

Concerns about the status of medical sociology persisted into the early 1980s, overlain with fears about financial cutbacks in HE in Britain (Murcott 1982) and their consequences for the employment of research and teaching staff in universities and polytechnics (Homans 1986). This echoed wider concerns as HE experienced a period of stagnation involving a retrenchment in employment, minimal growth in undergraduate student numbers, and the beginning of a downward spiral in public funding. The late 1980s were the beginning of a period of renewed growth, but in a context of fiscal constraint. There was a rapid upturn in undergraduate students from 1988 as government funding became more closely linked to student numbers even though funding per student continued to decline. By 1994, 34 percent of the 18–19 year-old population entered HE (CVCP 1997: 20).[3] This expansion of the university sector from an elite to a mass system of higher education was accompanied by a change of status of the polytechnics which became universities in 1992.

Sociology matured during this period of significant change in HE and medical sociology grew rapidly to become the largest section of the BSA with an annual conference attracting well over 300 delegates. Its scholarship was consolidated through the UK-based journal *Sociology of Health and Illness*, first published in 1979 and now recognized as a major international journal in the field. By the end of the twentieth century the institutional foundations of medical sociology were firmly established and the discipline was confident in its contribution to both academic and policy debates. Medical sociologists who, like many of their contemporaries in other branches of sociology were first employed in the 1960s and early 1970s, began to attain senior academic positions. The Registers of the 1980s listed only ten full professors, by the mid-1990s this had risen to 38, and by the close of the decade, to 47 (Field et al. 1982; Field and Platt 1986; Field and Woodman 1990; Barbour and van Teijlingen 1994, 1998). Over this period, medical sociology/the sociology of health and illness became part of the curriculum of most sociology departments although then, as today, this was typically as an option for upper-level undergraduates rather than as a core course, or part of a core course, for those majoring in sociology. This perception of medical sociology as a specialist area is reflected in introductory sociology textbooks in Britain which have only very recently included health and illness as a topic.

In addition to expansion at undergraduate level, HE has seen a rapid growth in postgraduate students over the last 30 years, more than doubling as a percentage of total student numbers from just 6 percent in 1962/3 to 14 percent in 1995/6 (Burgess 1997; CVCP 1997: 19). Within medical sociology, a range of Masters programs has developed to accommodate both the training needs of contract researchers and students planning to register for a doctorate. In addition, the movement of nursing into HE (UKCC 1987) alongside a professionalizing strategy within the professions allied to medicine which stressed research-based practice, has encouraged many senior health practitioners and nurse educators to pursue a Masters-level qualification with sociology as its basis.

The Research Agenda

The political context into which the subdiscipline was born, and within which it began to mature, significantly influenced the type of research that was undertaken. "Medico-centrism," that is, the tendency of sociologists to adopt their ideas of what is problematic, and thereby worthy of study, from medicine was high on the agenda in the 1970s (e.g. Murcott 1977). This echoed concerns voiced for some time in the United States, reflected, for example, in Straus's (1957) discussion of medical sociology as either *in* or *of* medicine. Concerns about medico-centrism also inaugurated a long-standing debate over whether the field should be titled "medical sociology" (which some see as medico-centric and constraining the research agenda) or whether the "sociology of health and illness" and related titles with a broader remit are more appropriate. In Britain worries about medico-centrism have been exacerbated not only by the exigencies of government funding, but also by the employment of a significant number of medical sociologists in medical schools and health service settings (for a recent discussion, see Jefferys 1996). Medical sociology became part of undergraduate medical education in Britain in the 1970s (Field 1988) and around one-fifth of people who placed entries in the Registers between 1978 and 1998 worked in medical school or related settings. A further quarter to almost one-third worked in a range of research centers, many with a strong health service focus, with others employed in various positions in the National Health Service, and to a lesser extent, nursing. Over the same period, between one-third to one-half of people worked in academic social science departments.[4] The diversity which has characterized British medical sociology is therefore at the core of its relationship with medicine/the health service, and sociology. Horobin (1985: 95) captured this well, and signalled a clear power relationship when he referred to medical sociologists inhabiting the "interstices between the citadel of medicine and the suburb of sociology." Carrying these concerns into the 1990s, consecutive editors of the Registers remarked upon the very applied nature of many research projects and their lack of attention to wider sociological issues (Field and Woodman 1990; Barbour and van Teijlingen 1994).

The topic areas that have defined the field reflect very clearly British medical sociology's relationship with both academic sociology, medicine, and health policy. Although there have been ebbs and flows of interest and the particular foci and conceptual approaches to issues have changed considerably over the decades, there is an enduring core built around analyses of the experience of health and illness, health inequalities (notably as they relate to social class and, more recently, gender, "race," and age), and the provision of health care (both formal and informal). In each of these broad areas different issues came to the fore in response to developments within medical science, sociology, and social theory, new national policy agendas, and the emergence of new diseases and changes in the social patterning of health and illness characterized the 1990s (DOH 1997,

2000). For example, in terms of conceptual developments in social science, "risk" appears as a topic area for the first time in the 1994 Register (Barbour and van Teijlingen 1994). With respect to new disease patterns, research on AIDS and HIV was proliferate in the early 1990s accounting for the majority of all funding listed in the 1990 Register (Field and Woodman 1990). By 1994 its absolute level of funding remained the same, but its place in the league table of funded areas had been superseded by research into primary care/general practice and studies of chronic illness (Barbour and van Teijlingen 1994). The 1998 Register does not list AIDS/HIV as a separate category (Barbour and van Teijlingen 1998).

Research on genetics, though only commanding 3 percent of funding listed in the most recent 1998 Register (and listed as a topic area for the first time in the 1994 Register (Barbour and van Teijlingen 1994, 1998)), seems likely to move ever more to the fore in the new century (e.g. Conrad and Gabe 1999). Topic area rankings also provide an insight into the impact of government policy upon the nature of research. The increased prominence of health services research in recent years probably reflects the direction of funds toward evaluation of the national health service (NHS) from the mid-1990s following a virtual moratorium during the Conservative government's sweeping reforms of the early 1990s (DoH 1989). The specific attention to primary care undoubtedly reflects the intensification of moves toward a "primary care-led" health service that characterized the 1990s (DoH 1997).[5]

Even though broad areas of research have endured since the 1970s, emphases have changed and new research directions have emerged. Examples are legion, but by way of illustration, research on gender and health which was until the mid-1990s virtually synonymous with women's health, now gives increasing attention to the health of men. Here, and in other topic areas, theoretical developments within sociology have been crucial. Thus, developments in the sociology of gender and within feminism have sparked new approaches to the analysis of gender inequalities in health (Annandale and Hunt 2000) and the sociology of the body has had a major impact upon research on chronic illness (Bury 1997). Moreover, new empirical foci within the wider discipline, such as the increased emphasis upon the life course, have influenced medical sociologists' conceptualization of health issues. For example, child health developed significantly as a research area during the 1990s (Mayall 1998).

A final issue that needs to be raised in respect of topic areas that define medical sociology in Britain is what is excluded. Here the most problematic feature of the discipline is its parochialism. Although British medical sociologists have both drawn from and contributed to international debates on key empirical and conceptual issues (e.g. health inequalities and the sociology of the body), this has largely been used to inform domestic concerns with relatively little attention to comparative research. Moreover, many research areas to which medical sociology could make an important contribution such as the impact upon physical and mental health of ethno-nationalisms, violence, and warfare, remain largely unexplored. Not only is contemporary British medical sociology inward looking, but the previous emphasis upon historical sociology, which produced high-calibre work on the development of modern medicine (e.g. Jewson 1974; Waddington 1984) has virtually disappeared.

MEDICAL SOCIOLOGY FOR THE NEW CENTURY: THEMES AND ISSUES

At the beginning of the twenty-first century the anxieties of the 1970s about medical sociology's future, indeed if it even *had* a future, and where its allegiances should lie have been replaced by a new optimism about the subdiscipline's contribution to health policy and practice, and to academic sociology. We suggested earlier that this optimism reflects the increased prominence of health issues both within academic sociology and within society prompted by wider-scale changes in the economic and social structure of late modernity, summarized in the shift from a collectivist to an individualist social ethos. This section begins by discussing this shift through a consideration of British health policy, particularly in relation to the NHS. We then discuss two enduring themes of British medical sociology; research on health inequalities, and on the experience of illness, illustrating the increasingly symbiotic relationship between medical sociology and its parent discipline in the course of the discussion.

There is wide-scale recognition that, along with most other western societies, post-World War II Britain witnessed a significant period of economic and social restructuring. There are many competing theories about whether we are witnessing a maturing of modernity, albeit in a manner that is radically different from its traditional form (e.g. Bauman 1987; Giddens 1991; Beck 1992; Lash and Urry 1994), or whether this has been superseded by postmodernity (e.g. Baudrillard 1983; Lyotard 1986). These theories have a common interest in the declining relevance of the traditional structures of class, gender and, to a lesser extent, "race," for the actions of individuals. Differences in interpretation, simply put, turn upon whether new social parameters of late modernity such as risk and uncertainty invite, or even mandate, individuals to actively construct identities, or whether the postmodern condition signals a "loss of meaning," as the barrage of information that confronts individuals means that they are no longer able to grasp what is happening in society. Although to date postmodern perspectives have received little attention within British medical sociology (although see Fox 1993), writings which can be considered under the umbrella of theories of "late modernity" have been influential within both academic and political circles. Foremost in this regard has been the work of the sociologist Anthony Giddens who has both contributed to and intervened in center–left political debates (Driver and Martell 1998).

At the center of Giddens' project (e.g. 1994a, 1994b) is the premise that far from confirming the Enlightenment expectation that over time more and more areas of social life will become subject to prediction and control, late modernity has witnessed a contrary development – namely, a "run-away world" characterized by "dislocation and uncertainty" (Giddens 1994b: 21). Two related processes lie behind this. First, intensifying globalization which forces existing traditions, such as the gender order, into the open and makes them subject to ongoing justification. Second, an enhanced need for self-reflexivity which means that the self needs to be made "amid a puzzling diversity of options and possibilities" (Giddens 1991: 3).

This social reflexivity is now firmly embedded in contemporary British welfare politics. Giddens (1994b: 29) stresses that under conditions of "high reflexivity" people must "achieve a certain amount of autonomy" in order to "survive and forge a life." Autonomy does not equate with egoism, but implies reciprocity and interdependence. Thus "reconciling autonomy and interdependence" is crucial to social life as reflected in Giddens' proposed model of "positive welfare." In contrast to the old welfare state of the postwar period which "picked up the pieces in the aftermath of misfortune," this model "places much greater emphasis upon the mobilising of life-political measures, aimed . . . at connecting autonomy with personal and collective responsibilities" (Giddens 1994b: 35). Such intentions are very evident in the policies of the New Labor government (elected with a 179 seat majority in May 1997 after 18 years in political opposition). Characterized as enjoining democratic socialism and liberalism in a "third way" which moves beyond the Old political Left and New political Right (Blair 1998), New Labor policy "is simply that citizens have certain responsibilities toward their fellow citizens and that the state has a legitimate, indeed essential, role in cultivating the disposition to act on these obligations and, in some cases, in directly enforcing them" (White 1999: 167). As White explains, a doctrine of civic responsibility, that is, a balance of individual rights and responsibilities, is at the heart of New Labour. Current social policy agendas therefore construe the "reflexive" individual as the "responsible" individual. This vision of people making choices, while taking account of others and holding others to account is at the heart of changes in the British NHS (DoH 1997).

The NHS and the Welfare State

The NHS has been subject to major change and intense political debate over the last three decades following a period of relative consensus during the 1950s and 1960s (Baggott 1998). As one commentator put it, the NHS is "an institution which is constantly reinventing itself [like] a car that is being re-engineered even while it is roaring round the test track" (Klein 1995, quoted in Ranade 1998: 117). The early 1990s saw the replacement of a centralized health service system with the introduction of an internal market. "Purchasers" (general practitioners[6] and health authorities) placed contracts to buy care for their patients from a range of "providers" such as community care services and hospitals which had taken on self-governing trust status (see DoH 1989). Criticisms were made about transaction costs, the impact of contracting upon the health care workforce (e.g. short-term contracts for nurses and the increased use of agency staff), and the emergence of a two-tier system of care which favored the patients of general practices which held their own funds (fundholders) (Audit Commission 1996). Moreover, it was argued that the "contract culture" was fostering a climate of low trust both between health care providers and between providers and their patients (e.g. Flynn et al. 1996). However, despite strong initial criticism from the Labor party in opposition and later in government, there is now a moving political consensus in health care (Baggott 1998; Ranade 1998) and the main elements of the Conservative government reforms, namely the purchaser–provider split, contracts, public–private partnerships, NHS trusts, the emphasis on primary care and "evidence-based medicine" remain (Ranade 1998: 116). Thus, the internal market is intact despite a rhetoric of its abolition (DoH 1997: 12), as the division between fundholding and non-fundholding general practices is replaced by local Primary Care Groups consisting of local networks of GPs and community nurses (which commission most of the services for their patients on a longer term basis from a delegated share of health authority budgets (DoH 1997)).

These changes in the NHS reflect those in society generally. Quasi-contractual relationships between individuals dominate the provision of care in the context of a public no longer so ready to passively accept what is offered to them. The consumerist ethos which began in the 1970s was fostered by the Patient's Charter (first introduced in 1992 and in existence in revised form today) and active encouragement of health authorities by government to take the views of local people into account (NHSME 1992; NHSE 1995; Milewa et al. 1999). Medical sociologists have made a significant contribution to analyses of the ethos of individualism embedded in contract culture (e.g. Flynn et al.'s (1996) study of community care) and the consumerist mood in health care (e.g. Allsop and Mulcahy's (1996) consideration of professional regulation in analyses of the health care system).

One contribution of social science to health policy and practice that requires special mention is research on informal or unwaged carers. From the 1980s, British feminists have pointed to the ways in which patterns of informal care reflect and reinforce gender divisions in society (e.g. Graham 1993; Thomas 1993). Alongside this, empirical work (e.g. Parker and Lawton 1990) has documented just how common informal care in the community is in Britain. Some 3.7 million people report that they are the main carers for relatives, friends, and neighbors who are sick, disabled, or elderly. Crucially, 1.7 million people provide an average of 20 hours unpaid work a week (ONS 1998), a figure which exceeds the whole NHS workforce (James 1998), providing a resource worth between £15 billion to £24 billion to the state (N. Kohner 1993 cited in Barnes 1997).

In the context of our discussion of the shift from collectivism to individualism as reflected in health policy, governmental recognition of the existence of large numbers of informal carers and their incorporation into health care policy underscores the ethos of individual and family responsibility and self-care (Barnes 1997; James 1998). Taking this point further in the wider context of welfare provision, Bauman argues that the *universal* (collectivist) founding principles of the NHS (in 1946) – a free, comprehensive, and equitable service for all citizens – are out of tune with a culture which elevates *selective* values of difference and choice. Consumerism and the welfare state are at cross-purposes, and, since a universal welfare state cannot deliver true consumer choice, its existence is under threat as selective practices (such as means-tested benefits) are increasingly accepted by a self-reliant "contented majority" confident that they can control their own lives (Bauman 1998).

Health Status and Health Inequalities

Evidence of the "new individualism" can also be found within wider public health policy. Expectations of individual responsibility for health which have been part of both government and public consciousness since the 1970s, have taken on a new dimension in recent years. For example, exercise and dietary practices and advances in medical science (such as plastic surgery, transplantation and genetic engineering) have expanded what were once seen as the limits of the corporeal body (Williams et al. 1998). Sociologists have conceptualized this in terms of the emphasis on the body as a social project to be made and remade (Turner 1984, 1992) which is drawn ever more into the reflexive organization of social life (Giddens 1991: 98). However, this stress upon the individual as the orchestrator of her or his own health exists alongside an enduring concern for the wider social patterning of health within Britain.

Interest in the social patterning of health and illness dates back to the mid-1880s and Engels' (1993 [1845]) writing on the conditions of the English working class. It gained particular momentum in the 1980s after the publication of *The Black Report* in 1979 (Townsend and Davidson 1988). This drew together existing evidence within a sociologically informed explanatory framework which stressed the significant role of socioeconomic factors in explaining the relatively poor health of working-class people. The recent *Independent Inquiry into Inequalities in Health* (Acheson 1998) which was overseen by a five-member Scientific Advisory Group, three of whom were leading British social scientists, also strongly argues that "the weight of scientific evidence supports a socioeconomic explanation of health inequalities." The Report highlights that even though average death rates have fallen and life expectancy has risen, health inequalities between social class groups have widened in Britain. For example, using the Registrar General's Classification of social class based on occupation, "in the late 1970s, death rates were 53 percent higher among men in classes IV and V compared with those in classes I and II. In the late 1980s, they were 68 percent higher. Among women, the differential increased from 50 to 55 percent" (Acheson 1998: 11). Moreover, despite increases in life expectancy, there is little evidence that the physical and mental health of the nation has improved over the last 10 to 20 years and, again, class gradients are evident. These class differences in health have been accompanied by widening differentials in the economic circumstances of Britons. Despite a period of substantial economic growth since the 1980s, income differentials have widened "to a degree not seen since the World War II" (Acheson 1998: 32).

Government enquiries into matters of health take place within a highly politicized arena. For example, it seems likely that during the late 1970s, the authors of the Black Report felt it expedient to present cultural/behavioral, health selection, artefact, and material/economic explanations as alternative rather than as interacting explanations for health inequalities in order that the first three could not be used to "explain away" the fourth, and preferred, economic explanation (Macintyre 1997). The Acheson Report (1998) still seems sensitive to the political context even though it is able to welcome the current government's concern to improve the health of the worse off in society and to narrow the health gap (as expressed in *Our Healthier Nation* (DoH 1998)). Social scientists, however, appear to have felt freer to explore the interacting role of a range of socioeconomic and lifestyle factors as well as to consider the combined effects of class, "race," gender, and age upon health (e.g. Macintyre 1997; Bartley et al. 1998; Marmot and Wilkinson 1999; Annandale and Hunt 2000).[7]

As well as a strong empirical research agenda, British sociologists have recently begun to raise questions about the theoretical underpinnings of health inequalities research. It has been argued that researchers have stuck rather steadfastly to conventional approaches to social divisions of class, "race," and gender, failing to appreciate that the social changes of late modernity that we outlined earlier invite new theoretical and methodological approaches to inequality (Annandale 1998; Bartley et al. 1998; Scambler and Higgs 1999; Popay and Groves 2000). There is a need to reflect more critically upon sociologically constructed social positions to take account of human agency in the construction of social class, ethnic, gender, and age-related identities and their significance for health status. In contrast to most research on health inequalities, work on the experience of illness which we now turn to consider, has given significant attention to the active construction of self-identity both in and through illness.

The Experience of Illness

Along with other areas of sociology, such as crime and deviance (e.g. Taylor 1971; Young 1971), the initial theoretical underpinnings of research on the experience of illness derive from the growing interest in action theories, particularly symbolic interactionism, in Britain during the 1960s. Certainly, the concerns with self and reflexivity which we have discussed can be traced back to this strand of research work and interest. However, as we will see in the course of the discussion, recent developments in social theory, such as the sociology of the body, the sociology of emotions, and Foucauldian social constructionism, have fostered different approaches to the self and the experience of illness. In the 1970s, British work was strongly influenced by the work of US interactionists such as Davis (1963), Goffman (1963), Roth (1963), and Zola (1966, 1973) as can be clearly seen in the early textbooks produced by British medical sociologists (e.g. Robinson 1973; Field 1976). Early research informed by this seminal work tended to focus upon the crisis created by chronic illness or major disability and the fundamental alteration of the meaning of social life and personal identities. Examples of such work are Locker's (1981) analysis of the lay construction of the symptoms and meaning of chronic illness and Voysey's (1975) research on the difficult reconstitution of social life by parents of disabled children.

Research on chronic illness was complemented by the development of a broader body of work on lay perceptions and constructions of illness. For example, Cornwell's (1984) influential ethnographic study of "Eastenders" in London, explored the ways in which health beliefs and illness behaviors were firmly embedded within working-class age and gender relations, limited autonomy and control over life, and "fatalistic" beliefs and attitudes. During the 1980s researchers also began for the first time to consider the relationship between ethnicity and health within a qualitative framework, for example Donovan's (1988) study of Afro-Caribbeans and South Asians in London (see Kelleher and Hillier (eds.) 1996 for more recent work). Interactionism also influenced studies of health behavior during the mid-to-late 1970s and early 1980s (Dingwall 1976; Morgan et al. 1985: ch. 3) which mounted a forceful critique of earlier research which tended to ignore the active role of individuals in interpreting and responding to symptoms. Finally, interactionism provided the foundation for a large body of research on the interaction of patients and health care providers and the social construction of illness in various formal health care settings (e.g. Stimson and Webb 1975; McIntosh 1976; Strong 1979; A. Davis 1982).

This early work set a firm foundation for a substantial and growing body of research on the experience of illness. From the mid-1980s data on morbidity (rather than simply mortality) became more readily available as a resource for researchers working in the area of health status and the experience of illness. This shows, as noted earlier, that there is little evidence of general improvement in morbidity in Britain in recent years, despite increases in life expectancy. The prevalence of limiting long-standing illness, which is often used as a measure of disability, fluctuated over the 1980s and 1990s. Between 1980 and 1994 approximately 17 to 22 percent of British women and 16 to 19 percent of British men reported a limited long-standing illness (OPCS 1995). By the early 1990s this body of information as well as the many criticisms that were being levied against interactionism and new theoretical developments in European social theory led to new directions in work on the experience of illness. Critical debates arose about the tendency of much early research to ignore the impact of economic and political realities upon the experience of illness and disability. Sociologists of the body and of the emotions also highlighted the "cognitive bias" of work in the field. Together, these criticisms (e.g. Freund 1990; S. Williams and Bendelow 1996) prompted researchers to develop stronger conceptualizations of the relationship between the individual and society, and between self and body, in illness.

As we discussed in the context of health inequalities, the politics of health and illness have been central to British medical sociology. Perhaps because of the long-recognized neglect of issues of power in interactionism, early research tended to gloss over the impact of relations of domination and subordination upon the experience of illness. These were brought strongly to the fore in the late 1980s through the work of disability activists (e.g. Oliver 1990) and feminists (e.g. Morris 1991). Most recently, this realist approach to power has been contested by social scientists influenced by postmodern approaches to the body (e.g. Seymour 1998). Gareth Williams (1999) uses the metaphor of a battlefield to depict the contesting approaches within British social science to disability at present:

> while body theorists emphasize, and often celebrate, differentiation in embodied experience by impairment, gender, sexuality, and race, disability theorists are more likely to stress the common factors disabled people face in a world built by and for

people with able bodies – two hostile camps facing each other: oppressor and oppressed, able-bodied and disabled. (1999: 243)

The nature and experience of health and illness has also become highly contested as the interactionist orthodoxy of the 1970s and 1980s has given way to a range of competing approaches. By the late 1990s, realist (e.g. Kelly and Field 1996), social constructionist (e.g. Petersen and Bunton 1997) and, to a lesser extent, postmodern (Fox 1993) approaches existed side by side. Within this corpus of research and conceptualization, the body has been a central theme. Significantly influenced by social constructionism and the groundbreaking work of Turner (1984), the sociology of the body has been a major resource for British medical sociologists seeking theoretically to locate the relationship between self and society in the context of illness. In this regard Simon Williams and Bendelow (1996, 1998) argue that taking account of emotions in illness provides a link between self and society, mind and body. This link has been explored through an increasing body of international work which draws upon the narrative method (e.g. Kleinman 1988; Frank 1995). Building upon this and earlier British work on "biographical disruption" (Bury 1982) and "narrative reconstruction" (Williams, G. 1984), narrative accounts of illness "illuminate the subjectively experienced relationship between identity (people's sense of who they are), agency (an individual's capacity for action) and social structures (macro mechanisms and processes by which power and control are socially distributed and utilized) which impinge on the ways in which individuals negotiate their lives" (Popay and Groves 2000: 76).

CONCLUSION

In this chapter we have outlined the development of medical sociology in Britain from its early and uncertain beginnings in the 1960s to its present status of a self-assured and substantial subdiscipline within British sociology. We have attempted to locate this development within the wider context of British society, especially with reference to the move from collectivism toward the individualistic ethos of "late modern" Britain. We have also sketched in the varying influences of conceptual developments within sociology as a discipline and the practical concerns of health policy and attempted to indicate new trends and emerging topics. At the start of the twenty-first century, as in the 1960s, British medical sociologists remain strongly influenced by the sometimes competing demands of applied research driven by policy agendas and the desire to contribute to the development of more adequate sociological conceptualizations of health and illness.

Notes

1 We use the term "medical sociology" throughout the chapter. However, in Britain, as elsewhere, there has been a long-standing debate over whether more inclusive definitions of the field, such as the sociology of health and illness, are more appropriate.

2 Further details on the current activities of the BSA Medical Sociology Group can be found on its website: http://medsocbsa.swan.ac.uk. The Group's archives for 1969–1982 are deposited in The Modern Records Center, University of Warwick, Coventry CV4 7AL, UK.

3 It should also be noted that the 1980s and early 1990s also saw a significant increase in the entry of mature applicants (i.e. those over the age of 21) to higher education, many studying part-time.

4 Despite some fluctuations, these divisions have remained fairly stable over the 1978 to 1998 period. We cannot necessarily assume that these figures accurately represent the employment of medical sociologists in Britain since they include only those who chose to place an entry in the various Registers (the number of entrants ranges from between just under 200 to almost 300 at various points over the period).

5 It needs to be borne in mind that data on funding from the Medical Sociology Registers are simply based on information provided by researchers. Although the national picture is likely to be similar, we do not assume that the data presented here are representative.

6 Within the NHS in Britain, 95 percent of the population are registered with general practitioners who act as gatekeepers to a range of services.

7 The ESRC (Economic and Social Research Council) has funded the Health Variations Programme, details of which can be found at http://www.lancs.ac.uk/users/apsocsci/hvp.htm

References

Acheson, Donald. 1998. *Report of the Independent Inquiry into Inequalities in Health*. London: Stationery Office.

Allsop, Judith, and Linda Mulcahy. 1996. *Regulating Medical Work*. Buckingham: Open University Press.

Annandale, Ellen. 1998. *The Sociology of Health and Medicine*. Cambridge: Polity Press.

Annandale, Ellen and Kate Hunt (eds.). 2000. *Gender Inequalities in Health*. Buckingham: Open University Press.

Audit Commission. 1996. *What the Doctor Ordered: A Study of GP Fundholders in England and Wales*. London: HMSO.

Baggott, Rob. 1998. "The Politics of Health Care Reform in Britain: A Moving Consensus?" Pp. 155–73 in D. Field and S. Taylor (eds.), *Sociological Perspectives on Health, Illness and Health Care*. Oxford: Blackwell Science.

Barbour, Rosaline and Edwin van Teijlingen (eds.). 1994. *Medical Sociology in Britain* (7th edition). British Sociological Association.

——. 1998. *Medical Sociology in Britain* (8th edition). British Sociological Association.

Barnes, Marian. 1997. *Care, Communities and Citizens*. London: Longman.

Bartley, Mel, David Blane, and George Davey Smith. 1998. *The Sociology of Health Inequalities*. Oxford: Blackwell.

Baudrillard, Jean. 1983. *Simulations*. New York: Semiotext(e).

Bauman, Zygmunt. 1987. *Legislators and Interpreters: On Modernity, Post-modernity and Intellectuals*. Cambridge: Polity Press.

——. 1998. *Work, Consumerism and the New Poor*. Buckingham: Open University Press.

Beck, Ulrich. 1992. *Risk Society*. London: Sage.

Blair, Tony. 1998. *The Third Way. New Politics for the New Century*. Fabian Pamphlet 588. London: The Fabian Society.

Burgess, Robert. (ed.). 1997. *Beyond the First Degree*. Buckingham: Open University Press.

Bury, Michael. 1982. "Chronic Illness as Biographical Disruption." *Sociology of Health and Illness* 5: 168–95.

——. 1997. *Health and Illness in a Changing Society*. London: Routledge.

CVCP (Committee of Vice-Chancellors and Principles). 1997. *The National Committee of Enquiry into Higher Education* (The Dearing Report).

Conrad, Peter and Jonathan Gabe (eds.). 1999. *Sociological Perspectives on the New Genetics*. Oxford: Blackwell.

Cornwell, Jocelyn. 1984. *Hard Earned Lives*. London: Tavistock.

Davis, Alan. 1982. *Children in Clinics*. London: Tavistock.

Davis, Fred. 1963. *Passage through Crisis: Polio Victims and their Families*. Indianapolis: Bobbs-Merrill,

Department of Health. 1989. *Working for Patients*. London: HMSO, Cmnd 555.

——. 1997. *The New NHS: Modern, Dependable*. London: Stationery Office. Cmnd 3807.

——. 1998. *Our Healthier Nation: A Contract for Health*. London: Stationery Office. Cmnd 3852.

——. 2000. *The NHS Plan*. London: Stationery Office.

Dingwall, Robert. 1976. *Aspects of Illness*. London: Martin Robertson.

Donovan, Jenny. 1988. *We Don't Buy Sickness, It Just Comes*. Aldershot: Gower.

Driver, Stephen and Luke Martell. 1998. *New Labour. Politics after Thatcherism*. Cambridge: Polity Press.

Engels, Frederick. 1993 [1845]. *The Condition of the Working Class in England*. Oxford: Oxford University Press.

Field, David. 1976. "The Social Definition of Illness." Pp. 334–66 in D. Tuckett (ed.), *An Introduction to Medical Sociology*. London: Tavistock.

——. 1988. "Teaching Sociology in UK Medical Schools." *Medical Education* 22: 294–300.

Field, David and Stephen Platt (eds.). 1986. *Medical Sociology in Britain* (5th edition). British Sociological Association.

Field, David and David Woodman (eds.). 1990. *Medical Sociology in Britain* (6th edition). British Sociological Association.

Field, David, Brian Clarke, and Nigel Goldie (eds.). 1982. *Medical Sociology in Britain* (4th edition). British Sociological Association.

Flynn, Rob, Gareth Williams, and Susan Pickard. 1996. *Markets and Networks*. Buckingham: Open University Press.

Fox, Nicholas. 1993. *Postmodernism, Sociology and Health*. Buckingham: Open University Press.

Frank, Arthur W. 1995. *The Wounded Story Teller: Body, Illness and Ethics*. Chicago: University of Chicago Press.

Freund, Peter. 1990. "The Expressive Body: A Common Ground for the Sociology of Emotions and Health and Illness." *Sociology of Health and Illness* 12: 452–77.

Giddens, Anthony. 1991. *Modernity and Self Identity*. Cambridge: Polity Press.

——. 1994a. *Beyond Left and Right: The Future of Radical Politics*. Cambridge: Polity Press.

——. 1994b. "Brave New World: The New Context of Politics." Pp. 21–38 in D. Miliband (ed.), *Reinventing the Left*. Cambridge: Polity Press.

Goffman, Erving. 1963. *Stigma: Notes on the Management of Spoiled Identity*. Englewood Cliffs, NJ: Prentice-Hall.

Graham, Hilary. 1993. "Social Divisions in Caring." *Women's Studies International Forum* 16: 461–70.

Homans, Hilary. 1986. "Introduction." Pp. 1–3 in D. Field and D. Woodman (eds.), *Medical Sociology in Britain* (6th edition). British Sociological Association.

Horobin, Gordon. 1985. "Medical Sociology in Britain: True Confessions of an Empiricist." *Sociology of Health and Illness* 7: 94–107.

James, Veronica. 1998. "Unwaged Carers and the Provision of Health Care." Pp. 211–29 in D. Field and S. Taylor (eds.), *Sociological Perspectives on Health, Illness and Health Care*. Oxford: Blackwell Science.

Jefferys, Margot. 1996. "The Development of Medical Sociology in Theory and Practice in Western Europe 1950–1990." *European Journal of Public Health* 6: 94–8.

Jewson, Nick. 1974. "The Disappearance of the Sick-Man from Medical Cosmology, 1770–1780." *Sociology* 10: 225–44.

Kelleher, David and Sheila Hillier (eds.). 1996. *Researching Cultural Differences in Health*. London: Routledge.

Kelly, Michael and David Field. 1996. "Medical Sociology, Chronic Illness, and the Body." *Sociology of Health and Illness* 18: 241–57.

Kleinman, Arthur. 1988. *The Illness Narratives*. New York: Basic Books.

Lash, Scott and John Urry. 1994. *Economies of Signs and Space*. London: Sage.

Locker, David. 1981. *Symptoms and Illness: The Cognitive Organisation of Disorder*. London: Tavistock.

Lyotard, J. 1986. *The Postmodern Condition: A Report on Knowledge*. Manchester: Manchester University Press.

McIntosh, Jim. 1976. *Communication and Awareness in a Cancer Ward*. London: Croom Helm.

Macintyre, Sally. 1997. "The Black Report and Beyond: What are the Issues?" *Social Science and Medicine* 23: 393–415.

Marmot, Michael and Richard Wilkinson (eds.). 1999. *Social Determinants of Health*. Oxford: Oxford University Press.

Mayall, Berry. 1998. "Towards a Sociology of Child Health." *Sociology of Health and Illness* 20: 269–88.

Milewa, Timothy, Justin Valentine, and Michael Calnan. 1999. "Community Participation and Citizenship in British Health Care Planning: Narratives of Power and Involvement in the Changing Welfare State." *Sociology of Health and Illness* 21: 445–65.

Morgan, Myfanwy, Michael Calnan, and Nick Manning. 1985. *Sociological Approaches to Health and Illness*. London: Routledge.

Morris, Jenny. 1991. *Pride and Prejudice: Transforming Attitudes Towards Disability*. London: Women's Press.

Murcott, Anne. 1977. "Blind Alleys and Blinkers: The Scope of Medical Sociology." *Scottish Journal of Sociology* 1: 155–71.

——. 1982. "Introduction." Pp. 1–3 in D. Field, B. Clarke, and N. Goldie (eds.), *Medical Sociology in Britain* (4th edition). British Sociological Association.

NHSE (National Health Service Executive). 1995. *Priorities and Planning Guidance, 1996–97*. Leeds: NHSE.

NHSME (National Health Service Management Executive). 1992. *Local Voices*. Leeds: NHSME.

Oliver, Mike. 1990. *The Politics of Disablement*. London: Macmillan.

ONS (Office of National Statistics). 1998. *Informal Carers*. London: Stationery Office.

OPCS (Office of Population Censuses and Surveys). 1995. *Living in Britain: Results from the 1994 General Household Survey*. London: HMSO.

Parker, Gillian and Dot Lawton. 1990. *Different Types of Care. Different Types of Carer: Evidence from the GHS*. London: HMSO.

Petersen, Alan and Robin Bunton. 1997. *Foucault, Health and Medicine*. London: Routledge.

Popay, Jennie and Keleigh Groves. 2000. "'Narrative' in Research on Gender Inequalities in Health." Pp. 64–89 in E. Annandale and K. Hunt (eds.), *Gender Inequalities in Health*. Buckingham: Open University Press.

Ranade, Wendy. 1998. "Reforming the British National Health Service: All Change, No Change?" Pp. 101–21 in W. Ranade (ed.), *Markets and Health Care*. London: Longman.

Robinson, David. 1973. *Patients, Practitioners and Medicine*. London: Heineman Medical Books.

Roth, Julius A. 1963. *Timetables: Structuring the Passage of Time in Hospital Treatment and Other Careers*. Indianapolis: Bobbs-Merrill.

Scambler, Graham and Paul Higgs. 1999. "Stratification, Class, and Health: Class Relations and Health Inequalities." *Sociology* 33: 275–96.

Seymour, Wendy. 1998. *Remaking the Body: Rehabilitation and Change*. London: Routledge.

Stimson, Gerry. 1978. "The Activities of the Medical Sociology Group, 1974–1978." Pp. xi–xv in S. Arber (ed.), *Medical Sociology in Britain* (3rd edition). British Sociological Association.

Stimson, Gerry and Barbara Webb. 1975. *Going to see the Doctor*. London: Routledge and Kegan Paul.

Straus, Robert. 1957. "The Nature and Status of Medical Sociology." *American Sociological Review* 22: 200–4.

Strong, Philip. 1979. *The Ceremonial Order of the Clinic*. London: Routledge & Kegan Paul.

Taylor, Laurie. 1971. *Deviance and Society*. London: Joseph.

Thomas, Carol. 1993. "De-Constructing Concepts of Care." *Sociology* 27: 649–69.

Townsend, Peter and Nick Davidson. 1988. *Inequalities in Health: The Black Report*. Harmondsworth: Penguin.

Turner, Bryan. 1984. *The Body and Society*. Oxford: Blackwell.

——. 1992. *Regulating Bodies*. London: Routledge.

UKCC (United Kingdom Central Council). 1987. *Project 2000. The Final Proposals*. Project Paper 9. London: UKCC.

Voysey, Margaret. 1975. *A Constant Burden: The Reconstitution of Family Life*. London: Routledge and Kegan Paul.

Waddington, Ivan. 1984. *The Medical Profession in the Industrial Revolution*. Dublin: Gill and Macmillan.

White, Stuart. 1999. "'Rights and Responsibilities': A Social Democratic Perspective." Pp. 166–79 in A. Gamble and S. White (eds.), *The New Social Democracy*. Oxford: Blackwell.

Williams, Fiona. 1994. "Social Relations, Welfare, and the Post-Fordist Debate." Pp. 49–73 in R. Burrows and B. Loader (eds.), *Towards a Post-Fordist Welfare State?* London: Routledge.

Williams, Gareth. 1984. "The Genesis of Illness. Narrative Re-Construction." *Sociology of Health and Illness* 6: 175–200.

——. 1999. "Review Article: Bodies on a Battlefield. The Dialectics of Disability." *Sociology of Health and Illness*. 21: 242–52.

Williams, Simon J. and Gillian Bendelow. 1996. "Emotions, Health and Illness: The 'Missing Link' in Medical Sociology?" Pp. 25–54 in V. James and J. Gabe (eds.), *Health and the Sociology of Emotions*. Oxford: Blackwell.

——. 1998. *The Lived Body: Sociological Themes and Issues*. London: Routledge.

Williams, Simon, Ellen Annandale, and Jonathan Tritter. 1998. "The Sociology of Health and Illness at the Turn of the Century: Back to the Future?" *Sociological Research Online*, 3 (4). http://www.socresonline.org.uk/socresonline/3/4/1.html

Young, Jock. 1971. *The Drug Takers*. London: MacGibbon and Kee.

Zola, Irving K. 1966. "Culture and Symptoms: Analysis of Patient's Presenting Complaints." *American Sociological Review* 31: 615–30.

——. 1973. "Pathways to the Doctor: From Person to Patient." *Social Science and Medicine* 7: 677–89.

15

The French Paradoxes

KRISTINA ORFALI

Ever since its first appearance in 1979 in the highly respected journal *The Lancet*, the famous "French paradox" has kept the health media in an uproar (Renaud et al. 1992; Criqui et al. 1994; Goldberg 1995, etc.). In 1991, the renowned American television program "60 Minutes" focused on this surprising French statistic: a country famous for its rich diet not to mention its smokers and alcoholics (in 1991, there were 11,910 deaths directly related to alcohol), comes out on top in studies on cardiac health, with the lowest rates of coronary vascular incidents (infarction). In fact, 4.2 times fewer coronary bypasses are performed in France than in the United States, and 2.1 times fewer than in Canada – and France in general experiences a low incidence of ischemic cardiac disease (including not only myocardial infarction, but angina).[1] And the hubbub shows no signs of abating: *Time* magazine published yet another article on this strange French phenomenon in its July 19, 1999 issue (Lemonick 1999).

Media accounts such as these leave one with the impression that the so-called "French paradox" is the single dominant characteristic of the health situation in France. It is true that alcohol consumption provides protection against a French diet rich in fats, a known risk factor in arteriosclerosis. However, despite this diet, a large proportion of women are underweight (12.1% of 18- to 24-year-olds). In the 55 to 74 age group, only 6.1 percent of men and 6.8 percent of women are considered seriously overweight (Enquête Santé 1992; SESI 1998). From a general point of view, the average life expectancy for a French man in 1991 was 74.2, and for a French woman 82.1. To be French and female in the 1990s is to be at the top of the list in the European Union in terms of life expectancy.[2] France has known one of the most phenomenal gains in life expectancy in the western world: from 1980 to 1994, average life expectancy increased by 2.2 years for men and 2.4 years for women. The picture is the same for active life expectancy[3] or EVSI (life expectancy without being incapacitated), which, from 1981 to 1991, increased by more than 3 years for men and more than 2.6 years for women. By 1995, infant mortality had dropped significantly as well, hovering today at around 5.1 per thousand (1997).

The general health of the French population thus appears to be satisfactory, both in comparison to other western countries and in terms of progress made. These figures cannot be explained simply by health care expenditures per capita. At about 1,870 dollars per person per year, France compares favorably to both Germany and Quebec, but remains well below the 3,600 dollars per capita spent in the US in 1994[4] – although, as elsewhere, debates on how to control health care costs are a perennial item on the French political agenda, and recent reforms in this area (1996) have met with limited success. Prof. R. Curtis Ellison, at Boston University School of Medicine, cites three factors behind the "French secret" – "wine, food and lifestyle." But even though medical literature has already publicized the chemistry of both wine and food, there have been few studies in France on health lifestyle participation (Corbett 1994; Lüschen et al. 1995; Cockerham 1998). How do the French as a population perceive their own health condition? And all clichés aside, what is the statistical and sociological reality of the health situation in France?

In fact, there are several "French paradoxes." Take the situation of public health policy. In the eyes of a public stunned by the recent scandals over contaminated blood, growth hormones, and the infamous "mad cow" disease, French public health policy appears in many ways to be a failure. Its too-recent development has been handicapped not only by an insufficient institutional infrastructure (Murard and Sylberman 1997), but also by surprisingly limited financial resources (de Kervasdoué 1996; Johanet 1998) and apparent lack of political will. What exactly is at stake here then? Why should the native country of Louis Pasteur be so slow to develop a working public health policy?

Another French paradox: the slow emergence (1970s) of the field of medical sociology, a fact which is surprising in the context of the nation that gave birth not only to sociology (Durkheim) but also to the clinic.[5] It is curious that the France of Bichat, Laennec, and Claude Bernard did not play a more innovative role in making "illness" and "medicine" the objects of sociological study. In fact, modern hospital medicine, which originated in Paris at the turn of the century (Ackerknecht 1967), did not generate interest among sociologists until the 1970s (Herzlich 1973; Steudler 1974; Chauvenet 1978). Since then the topic of hospitals, however hot it may be politically, has received relatively little attention on the part of the French (or European) sociologists in general. While far from the only paradox to be found upon examining the French public health situation, this characteristic in particular merits closer analysis.

THE SOCIAL DEMOGRAPHY OF HEALTH

The Perception of Health Problems

First of all, how do the French themselves perceive their health? According to studies done by the Research Center for the Study and Observation of Life

Conditions (CREDOC), since 1992 the French population as a whole has rated its health as relatively satisfactory, a finding reconfirmed at the end of 1997 by 89 percent of respondents.[6] This opinion (Le Quéau et al. 1998) varies mainly in relationship to the age of the person queried: 95 percent of those aged 20 to 34 reported themselves to be satisfied overall, while only 76 percent of those over 70 felt themselves satisfied with their general state of health. Two-thirds of those questioned thought that the general health of the French population had improved over the last ten years.

On the other hand, when evaluating the future health of the population the figures are clearly less optimistic: only one out of eight people interviewed thought that the overall health of the population will improve in the next ten years. The perception of environmental risks seems to be an important new factor behind this pessimism about the future: 81 percent of individuals interviewed believed that the population is increasingly being exposed to multiple risks. While age did not seem to be a factor in the opinions held by the people interviewed on this point, men remained slightly more optimistic than women. In addition, it is worth noting a strong correlation observed between an optimistic view of the future health of the population and a positive perception of one's own health.

Socioeconomic factors obviously play a key role in individual perception, as has been widely shown in medical sociology literature, but these factors are not always easy to identify. The notion of social causality remains complex (Adam and Herzlich 1994). One social variable that clearly has a significant impact on the health of the individual is unemployment. This is particularly obvious in France because of its high unemployment rate (currently above 10% – as high as 12.4% in 1996). While unemployment can occasionally have a positive impact on the health of the worker by reducing exposure to occupational hazards and eliminating the specific stresses of the work environment, it can also have a pathogenic effect, including anxiety, loss of social status, and instability. Oddly enough, according to Bungener and Pierret in 1994, the unemployed were more likely than those employed to describe themselves in good health, even though a significant number of them suffered a higher incidence of multiple pathologies than individuals in the employed population. But by 1997 CREDOC found that the unemployed were half as likely as the employed population to describe themselves as "very satisfied" with their current state of health, and three times more likely to describe themselves as dissatisfied (17% as opposed to 6%). Even those who had a positive perception of their individual health expressed a more negative view of the evolution of the general health of the population. Among those employed, 33 percent of executives and professionals rated themselves "very satisfied," as opposed to 24 percent of clerks and manual laborers.

Lifestyle issues also appear to be perceived as a determining factor in health. More and more people in France acknowledge the importance of moderating alcohol and tobacco consumption, with 81 percent of respondents agreeing strongly, 14 percent agreeing, and 5 percent disagreeing with this proposition. While young people, and young males in particular, remain more reticent, this reticence decreases with age.

The most striking development since the 1992 CREDOC survey concerns the perception of instability (for example, unemployment or lack of money) as a determining factor in a person's health. By 1997, 73 percent of those interviewed agreed that unemployment had a major effect on health, and 67 percent thought that lack of money also has an impact. Furthermore, we can see a homogenization of responses according to social group, for it is among executives and those with the highest incomes that the greatest shift in opinion took place (+ 15%). This evolution is evidently linked to the increase in unemployment, affecting more than one million people between 1990 and 1996, the year in which unemployment reached a record 3,160,000 people, e.g. 12.4 percent of the active population. If these figures have improved somewhat as a result of the current economic recovery, the fact remains that as of September 1999, over 11 percent of the French labor force remained unemployed.

Finally, the proportion of people believing in the effectiveness of public health campaigns and research for prevention went from 56 percent in 1992 to 75 percent in 1997. But little connection was made between the total number of physicians and the health of the population. In fact, more than 67 percent of people surveyed thought that it would be useless to increase the number of physicians as a way of improving health. Despite a stronger belief in the impact of external factors – both social and environmental – on the health of the population, a majority expressed the opinion that maintaining good health is the responsibility of the individual: in 1997, 69 percent strongly agreed, and 27 percent agreed somewhat. Consistent with the 1992 results, the population in 1997 was split in two on the question of whether or not the government should single out groups with special needs as part of its public health policy. Among those to agree, women over the age of 35 figured most prominently. Those lowest on the socioeconomic ladder were given the highest priority, while the elderly received very little support. Despite 1996 reforms in the health care system stressing the role of regional control – holding regional health conferences, setting up regional hospitalization agencies, etc. – only 10 percent of the population surveyed continued to view the region as a significant locus of public health policy. In a new development, the French have begun to view the emerging European Community as a significant factor in public health policy, despite the fact that its role is still limited in both legal and financial scope. International health crises such as the "mad cow" disease have likely served to reinforce this opinion.

Altogether, it appears that the French hold simultaneously a very individualized view of health as being linked to lifestyle, and an acute awareness of the role of larger factors in the equation, such as "environment, instability, and the need for community." In the final analysis, manual workers were those who were most concerned with the concept of "good health," expressed in terms of longevity (a fact which probably reflects their true disadvantage in this regard). By 1997, autonomy ("being able to do what you want" and "not suffer") had become a major concern compared to in 1992, as had certain ethical debates involving issues such as euthanasia, palliative care, and end-of-life decisions. Fear of illness, which was a major concern for 63 percent of respondents in 1992, is even more so today as expressed by 82 percent. Lastly, the 1997 CREDOC study indicates more clearly than before, how the French population's increased preoccupation with illness is now associated with the fear of unemployment.

Statistical Reality

But are these fears borne out by statistics? What are the indicators of the general state of health of the French population, and what are the known determinants of the current health situation?

High-Risk Behavior

France indeed tops the charts in terms of life expectancy, especially for women, though there remains a gap of eight years in life expectancy between the sexes. The French also enjoy low infant mortality rates, as well as low rates of cardiovascular illness, (though the latter remains the principal cause of death: 32% of the total in 1996).

However, this excellent global performance should not hide several important problems. Among the 60,000 annual deaths considered to be "avoidable," 40,000 are (according to the HCSP) directly related to lifestyle, such as reckless driving and/or the consumption of tobacco or alcohol. While the average alcohol consumption per adult has been dropping since the 1960s, the opposite is true for young people of both sexes. Even more troublesome are recent changes in adolescent drinking habits, with an increase in periodic binge drinking, especially on weekends, sometimes mixed with psychotropic medications or illicit drugs. As a result, alcohol is now being considered by the health authorities as almost a psychoactive substance along with tobacco and illegal drugs.

In a broader context, these changes represent what could almost be called a cultural revolution at the heart of the French public health situation, as shown in Roques' 1998 report. On the one hand, the statistics demonstrate the serious consequences of excessive alcohol consumption for public health. On the other hand (as has even been noted by the HCSP itself) traditional French denial in the face of the disease combined with the importance of alcohol to the nation's economy represents an enormous obstacle to any overt political action against alcoholism, despite numerous warnings about its dangers. Just as in the case of gun control in the USA, the problem of alcohol consumption in France is not only a public health problem, but a larger social issue with roots deeply embedded in French culture.

Worse, alcohol is not alone on the public health docket. In 1996 it was estimated that there were approximately 13.5 million smokers in France. Despite the Evin law of 1993, which banished all advertising for tobacco and prohibited smoking in public places, the current trends in tobacco consumption are alarming. More women and more young people are smoking than ever before. As for men, the blue-collar workers top the list in cigarette consumption, followed by white-collar workers and executives. Conversely, among women it is office employees and the intermediate professions who smoke the most, followed by blue-collar workers. Nicotine addiction during the third trimester of pregnancy has increased as well, going from 15 percent in 1981 to 25 percent in 1996. Investigations in six different sites aimed at evaluating the enforcement of the Evin law revealed what can only be called indifference toward the new regulations concerning smoking; fully half of the companies surveyed did not take them into account in any way (ORS 1995). Not only that, but in the case of public education, 45 percent of students, 40 percent of supervisors and 20 percent of teachers had been caught with a lit cigarette inside the school buildings

High-risk behavior is not exclusively defined by the consumption of alcohol or other substances – reckless driving is also high on the list. Ninety percent of automobile accidents in France are estimated, in one way or another, to be the fault of the driver. Though (at 48%) alcohol-related accidents are responsible for nearly half of all traffic fatalities, reckless driving is cited as the primary culprit in 30 percent of traffic fatalities, and not wearing a seat belt (mandatory since 1975) comes in third at 24 percent.

Ever since the advent of the AIDS epidemic, sexual behavior has been added to the list of high-risk behaviors. This has aroused the interest both of public authorities (in terms of research funding, particularly for the study of sexual behavior) and of sociologists. As a result, KAPB-style (Knowledge, Attitudes, Beliefs and Practices) investigations sought to make the connection between the perception of risk and subsequent behavioral modifications. However, while the population appears to be remarkably well-informed about the risks of contracting AIDS, this knowledge does not seem to have had a strong impact on changes in sexual behavior (Moatti, Dab, and Pollack 1990).

In addition to investigating specific populations at risk (D. Carricaburu's 1993 study on hemophiliacs, the 1994 KAPB studies of teenagers, of populations in the Antilles and Guyane, and the homosexual community), larger cross-sections of society were polled (Spira and Bajos 1993) in an attempt to measure modifications in sexual behavior since the last global investigation in 1972 ("*Enquête Simon*"). Results show that the average age of first sexual encounter is 17 for men and 18 for women, (though it must be noted that these figures are lower amongst the lower classes). Condoms were used by more than three-quarters of the young people surveyed in 1994 compared with only 56 percent in 1989 (1994 KAPB Survey on teenagers). Teen pregnancy was at 3.3 percent; with 72 percent of these pregnancies ending in termination. With regard to the risk of sexually-transmitted diseases, the most radical changes appear to have taken place in the homosexual community, with a strong increase in the number of participants surveyed who rely on the tracking test; 65 percent of homosexuals surveyed in 1995 are tested several times a year, versus 48 percent in 1993.

Ever since the outbreak of the AIDS epidemic, sexuality, more than any other category of high-risk behavior, has been the chief object of scrutiny of numerous sociological studies related to the concept of "social representation" (Herzlich 1973), a well-developed trend in French medical sociology. Thus, from the moment of its appearance, the discourse on AIDS has been analyzed as the very "essence of evil" (Augé and Herzlich 1984) in modern society. These sociological studies have doubtless contributed to the definition of AIDS as a *social* problem rather than an epidemiological problem, a definition specific to the French health policy approach.

The link between unemployment and health perceived by the French as a problem is a statistical reality too, with unskilled workers suffering the most. In 1997, 15.8 percent of blue-collar workers were without employment, compared with only 5.1 percent for white-collar workers. While little work has been done on the impact of stress linked to unemployment on the individual (Le Disert 1985; Bungener and Pierret 1994), we do know that the risk of mortality among the unemployed in 1982 was almost triple that of those employed between 1982 and 1987. Not only that, but between 1990 and that in 1995 it was fully 90 percent higher – a disparity present across all social groups regardless of class or education (Mesrine 1998).

Gender Disparities

In 1998 a comparative study of Europe and America (Badeyan et al., INSEE 1998) revealed the curious fact that France has one of the highest death rates from cancer among men, and one of the lowest among women. Women are more likely to suffer from cardiovascular illnesses (36% of deaths) than from cancer (23%). On the other hand, France holds the negative distinction of having a high rate of traumas and violent deaths (suicides, traffic accidents, etc.), with over 10 percent of deaths among men and 7 percent of deaths among women falling into this category.

France thus has a disproportionately high "premature" male mortality rate (defined as death occurring before age 65) in comparison with other European countries (cf. table 15.1). It is interesting to note that the greatest gap between the sexes occurs between the ages of 25 and 74, (when the risk of death for men is 2.5 times higher than that for women), while after age 74 the male mortality rate drops to only 1.5 times as high as the female rate. France's premature death rate among "young" men (a category spanning ages 25 to 44) is twice as high as that in Great Britain, the Netherlands, and Sweden. The greatest gap between male and female mortality rates occurs in the incidence of cancer of the upper gastro-intestinal tract and in lung cancer. For these pathologies, the mortality rate for men remains striking: the risk of death among males multiplies by a factor of 9 and 7 respectively overall, and for deaths before age 65, by a factor of 11 and 7. Next in line, with double the risk for men in each case: AIDS,[7] suicide, alcoholism, traffic accidents, stomach cancer, infarction, and respiratory illness.

Table 15.1   Male surmortality by age, 1996 and 1991 (ratio male/female)

	1996	1991
Total	1.83	1.81
< 25 years	1.87	1.86
25–44 years	2.40	2.64
45–64 years	2.50	2.58
65–74 years	2.42	2.39
> 75 years	1.57	1.53

Source: Inserm SC8.

Statistics also corroborate a general tendency already observed previously (Cockerham 1998), – the greater incidence of high-risk behavior among men, such as tobacco and alcohol use (accounting for 6% of premature deaths in 1995) and reckless driving. Deaths labeled "avoidable" (those linked to high-risk behaviors) were thus shown to be four times as significant for French men as deaths related to failures in the quality of health care – e.g. deaths that could have been averted through better preventative care and management.[8] By contrast, deficiencies in the health care system (and particularly early detection) were shown to affect women more frequently. As a result, breast cancer represents 12.2 percent of premature deaths among females out of 4.2 percent of total deaths in 1996. However, differences between the sexes in terms of high-risk behaviors are beginning to blur. The rate of cancers linked to alcohol and tobacco consumption among young, French women has shown a marked increase. It is feared that France is following in the footsteps of the United States in this respect – French female mortality rates from tobacco are currently comparable to those seen in the United States in the mid-1960s.

In the area of mental health, suicide rates in France – as in most countries – are higher among males (3.1%) than females (1.3%). Moreover, from 1991 to 1996, there was an increase in the number of suicides among men between the ages of 15 and 44. On the other hand, depression, especially so-called major depression, known to be a characteristically female trait (Cockerham 1996; Kessler et al. 1994) remains so even in France. A recent study (Lépine et al. 1997) ranks France, along with the United Kingdom, as the European leader in terms of overall rates of depression. Regarding psychotropic drugs sales, France shows 3 to 4 times higher rates than elsewhere.

Gender as well as social class plays a role in who benefits the most from available health care. Statistically, women consult a doctor more frequently than do men, as well as being more likely to consult a specialist (62% against 56%). Since 1970, this gap in health care between the sexes has increased in nearly every domain. On the other hand, men seek medical care for accidents twice as often as women do. French medical demography thus follows the same general tendencies as have already been observed elsewhere, both on the statistical level and on the level of individual behavior (Cockerham 1997). Still, behavioral differences, while gradually diminishing, remain more exaggerated in France than elsewhere, in particular with regard to high-risk behavior.

Social and Regional Disparities

Just as typical of the French situation are differences between regions. Infant mortality rates vary widely from region to region, ranging from 7 to 7.5 percent in northern France to 5.4 to 5.7 percent in the southeast and the west. The respective ranking of the regions has changed very little in recent years. Similarly, overall mortality (generally on the decline) varies greatly by region, and these discrepancies show no sign of narrowing. In 1996, Pas-de-Calais remained the region with the highest overall mortality in France, a statistic that has remained constant ever since World War II. A 1998 study conducted by INSEE found that the life expectancy for men in North Pas-de-Calais was only 71, with 27 percent of deaths occurring before the age of 65. This region maintains records for most pathologies: deaths from cardiovascular illness, illnesses of the respiratory and digestive systems, and alcoholism. Before the age of 65, alcohol causes twice as many deaths as would normally occur – in fact, among women between the ages of 35 and 64, cirrhoses of the liver represented the number one cause of death, ranking even higher than breast cancer! These regional disparities, of which Pas-de-Calais is only one example, are not related solely to socioeconomic hardship, but also to a lack of medical facilities.

There are a great many well-known studies in both Europe (Fox 1989; Leclerc 1989; Lahelma and Valkonen 1990) and the USA linking significant variation in mortality rates among social and economic groups to unfavorable socioeconomic conditions. However, in a recent European study (Kunst 1997), France was shown to have a wider statistical variation in this respect than the majority of other European countries. In France, the risk of death for men between 35 and 60 years of age varies from 10 percent for white-collar workers to 20 percent for blue-collar workers. Those at greatest risk are agricultural employees, manual laborers, and service industry employees. Not only do the differences between the different categories not average out evenly, but they become even more exaggerated as the population moves into old age, as the more "privileged" categories (such as executives and liberal professions) are the most likely to profit from increased life expectancy. Interestingly enough, the largest discrepancies in life expectancy among social and economic groups were found with relation to pathologies involving alcoholism. One can see why the "French paradox," linking lowered risks of ischaemic cardiopathies to the (moderate) consumption of alcohol, could hardly be a widespread notion in French public health policies!

Although few disparities exist between various social groups with respect to the availability of medical care (Mormiche 1995), the exact nature of these visits differs markedly according to both age and social class. Members of the upper classes are more likely to practice preventative health care, while members of the lower classes often do not consult a doctor until their condition is serious enough to require hospitalization.

Finally, throughout the 1990s the French infant mortality rate declined dramatically, from 7.3 percent in 1990 to 5.1 percent in 1997, a positive change that can be attributed to a combination of increased prenatal care and educational programs (such as the campaign against Sudden Infant Death Syndrome). From 1981 to 1995 the percentage of women undergoing seven or more prenatal checkups increased from 43 to 73 percent. In addition, ultrasound monitoring has become more common since 1981: in 1987, half of all pregnant women had at least two or three ultrasounds, and 48.5 percent had more. Between 1981 and 1995, hospitalization rates for high-risk pregnancies rose from 16 to 20 percent. However, while the proportion of unmonitored pregnancies remained very low (estimated at less than 0.2%), other factors besides prenatal care are at work in the premature birth rates. 13.5 percent of women claiming to have no support had a premature baby, as opposed to 7.5 percent of those with a variety of available resources, and 5.5 percent of those with their own income (Badeyan et al. 1998). Socially disadvantaged women are thus at greater risk of having a premature birth. In addition, compared to the statistics for the Scandinavian countries or the United Kingdom, the number of maternal deaths in France remains high (linked perhaps to higher average age at time of pregnancy?), despite generally favorable indicators for prenatal health.

Despite undeniable progress (including a 21% reduction in avoidable premature mortality of either sex due to high-risk behavior), the French situation can thus be characterized by serious inequalities in general health, not only between social and economic groups but also between the sexes (particularly amongst young people), and finally between geographic regions. As a result, and despite the government's proclamation in 1998 guaranteeing access to health care for all, the rising poverty and exclusion levels remain the top priorities of the HCSP (High Committee on Public Health), the organization responsible for monitoring the French health situation since 1994.

THE SYSTEM OF HEALTH COVERAGE

The Organization of the French Health Care System

GENERAL STRUCTURE

Overall, France devotes 10 percent of its national wealth to financing health care (versus 7% in 1970). Despite this increase, the French system is characterized by fragmented management of health policies and a multiplication of regulatory channels (Stasse 1999). It is only since the introduction of the global health care budget in 1983[9] as well as the health care reform of 1996, that the central role of the State in the French Social Security system has finally been recognized.

The structure of the French Health Care system was initially dictated by a sort of compromise between employers and unions. The difficulty arose from the fact that health care, as an institution, was caught between two opposing poles. While in one sense control of the system lay entirely in the hands of doctors and their patients, the financing was controlled by employers and unions. As if this weren't complicated enough, the State, originally intended to remain a neutral third party in this dynamic, proved unable to maintain this intermediary position. The tension between these three factors lies at the heart of the genesis of the French institutional configuration.

In fact, the French health system, unlike the British nationalized system or the German system of regional and professional co-administration, continues to combine the participation of employers, government regulation, and health care professionals. Financing is assured primarily by the "Social Security system," created in 1945 out of roughly 15 different branches of health insurance, each offering different degrees of coverage. Health insurance is consequently managed by the various branches according to the occupation of the individual.

In addition to the "general plan," which covers employees in commerce and industry and represents the most significant portion of the insured population, there are also a great many occupational groups, such as miners and railroad employees and so forth. Furthermore, a significant percentage of the population holds some form of complementary coverage through mutual and insurance companies. The French Social Security system has fixed prices for most forms of standard medical care, paid directly to the care provider. While it is common practice to exceed these fixed prices, the patient is still liable for all additional costs. Even within the context of covered expenditures, a portion of the cost for certain procedures, called "*ticket modérateur,*" remains the responsibility of the patient, in an effort on the part of the system to discourage policy-holders from incurring frivolous expense. There are exceptions in which the patient is completely covered; these generally fall into one of three categories: serious pathology (cancer, AIDS, etc.), certain medical procedures and treatments (such as fertility treatments), or finally certain specific situations (disability or childbirth, etc.). Lastly, the State has always theoretically taken under its wing those uninsured or without resources (free medical care existing in principle since 1905) as is reaffirmed and stated more clearly in the law of 1992.

The French have the freedom to choose their own doctors and can directly consult any specialist without the intermediary of a primary care physician. They can also choose either a private or a public care facility (Duriez et al. 1996) without affecting their financial liability for care received. For outpatient care, professional and medical infrastructures remain primarily in the private sector. The public sector dominates, however, in the arena of hospitalization and collective programs (such as public health education and prevention).

In addition to allowing free access to specialists, the French system distinguishes itself from its European neighbors with regard to the distribution of goods and medical services. Not only do the majority of specialists have private practices in urban centers rather than working in hospitals, but also an important fraction of hospitals are privately run for profit. As a result, the role of the general practitioner in screening and controlling access to specialized care is thereby greatly reduced compared to that of his or her counterpart in other western countries.

Additionally, alternative forms of medical care, a common resource in French society, enjoy quasi-institutional recognition. For example, 65 percent of costs for homeopathic treatment are reimbursed by the public system. It should be noted that in France, it is the doctors who prescribe homeopathic drugs, thereby simultaneously controlling access to both clinical medicine and alternative medicines.

RECENT REFORMS

As of 1996, the Parliament (which previously held no direct authority over the health care system except insofar as it controlled the national budget), directly controls the entire public health budget. It is now the responsibility of the Parliament to fix the rate of inflation of health care costs each year. This rate constitutes a fiscal ceiling that is binding for all participants to the health insurance system. While the new budgetary laws concerning the French Social Security system have brought these participants closer to political decision-makers at the national level, compartmentalization remains a major problem. In 1993 an attempt was made to modernize the system by creating a series of organizations comparable to those already existing in the United States (a French equivalent to the Food and Drug Administration is one example). An entire program built around both cost management and standardization of care is thus under development, at the regional as well as the local level (for example the creation of ANAES, or National Agency for the Evaluation and Accreditation of Health Care Institutions). However, one must be careful not to mistake this reinforcement of regional responsibilities for a move toward decentralization. In spite of recent reforms, the French health care system (particularly in comparison to its immediate neighbors in the West) suffers from an accumulation of different institutional strategies, some structural and some procedural. This multiplication of strategies often paralyzes health care providers in the performance of their duties and renders even more difficult the implementation of any coherent and logical system on a large scale. The reasons of such poorly planned institutional health environment are probably due to the relatively late development of the concept of "public health" in France, compared to other countries.

Which Public Health Policy?

A LONG-OVERDUE CHANGE

According to certain historians (Murard and Sylberman 1996), the question of public health, and consequently of collective management of disease and health, has long attracted little attention. Public health and sanitation have been devalued in relationship to the "clinic" (Foucault 1963), which to this day enjoys an unrivaled level of prestige. In fact, up until World War II, unlike Great Britain or Germany, public health and sanitation remained primarily a local affair, existing within only a very precarious institutional framework.

The reticence demonstrated by the State when it came to intervening on the local level in health matters (except in the event of epidemic) stemmed partly from political considerations. Local authorities were little inclined to participate in any move which might be construed as a remnant of authoritarianism (in part for electoral reasons). The hesitation on the part of the local authorities also stemmed from a simultaneous desire to safeguard private property while still protecting individual liberties (hence the difficulty in getting any intervention accepted). For a long time no social support in matters of public health existed to compensate for the failure of the authorities – neither from the political parties, nor from the doctors, however Pasteurian.

The particular nature of the French public health system stems from the combination of all these factors – administrative impotence born of a lack of means, the fragmentation of authority (and thus responsibility), and the devalorization of·the most basic components of public health medicine, as well as of prevention programs (De Kervasdoué 1996; Johanet 1998). It seems that the State has great difficulty knowing how its own health care system functions and evolves. In fact, up until the recent creation of the ANAES, no means of evaluating and monitoring the quality of care in hospitals were in place. It is only since 1994 that a true diagnosis of the situation has been established (by the HCSP),[10] with the creation of programs for disease control such as the "*veille sanitaire*," and for identifying sources of pollution. However, while this would indicate that "public health care had thus finally achieved citizenship," or full validity in the eyes of the State, the HCSP was still deploring the weakness of public health policies in terms of environmental risks (for example in the case of asbestos), and lack of statistical data as recently as 1998.

This evolution is astonishingly late in coming for a country that is by tradition both solidly Jacobean and strongly centralized. In fact, it is only in the aftermath of the recent avalanche of scandals – contaminated blood in 1991, growth hormone, and Creutzfeldt-Jakob's disease, etc. – that the medical bankruptcy of a country lacking any real public health policy has finally become apparent (Setbon 1993). The multiple deficiencies of the system are reflected by the statistics, as in the case of posttransfusion contamination, 3.2 times higher in France than the European average, and 7.8 times higher in France than in Germany (Morelle 1996). The limited action of the State in combination with the lack of accountability demonstrated by those responsible in the medical profession will eventually expose the failure of the French health system to the public, as well as question the very legitimacy of the political, administrative, and medical institutions responsible. It will also reveal another characteristic of the French system; the autonomy of the medical field and its influence on the State (Fassin 1996).

THE POWER STRUCTURE OF FRENCH MEDICINE

While the majority of developed countries (and in particular the United States) are currently experiencing a decline of the power of the medical establishment, France continues to follow its own path. "*L'Ordre des médecins*,"[11] well-known for its conservative stance, and even the French medical profession in general, have been very opposed to all attempts at reform (witness for example their resistance to patient access to medical charts (1995), their struggle against any form of collective sanction (1996), or the medical specialists' strike of 1998). Among health professionals of all sorts, physicians today still hold a central position. In fact, the power held by hospital physician unions is all the more remarkable given that it is in no way founded in law (Stasse 1999). Unions of independent doctors, on the other hand, have the legal right to contract with health insurance organizations.

Finally, the medical standpoint has always held priority in France in the chain of any health policy decision-making, possibly even at the expense of other social factors. In fact, the very nature of the French health care system has been determined much more by the medical and institutional side of the system than by the patient. One cannot therefore truly speak of the same decline in the power of the medical establishment in France as has been observed elsewhere (Hassenteufel 1997). In fact, rather than a simple loss of influence on the part of the medical establishment, what is really at stake is a profound reconfiguration of the power structure combined with a search for new modes of legitimization (Aïach and Fassin 1996). The indignation expressed by the patients – first with the cancer survey[12] in November of 1998 and then more recently with the *États*

Généraux de la Santé of 1999 – testifies to the lack of transparency of the whole health care system combined with a typically French taste for secrecy in the medical profession.

The remarkable significance of the professional medical power shows up in the legislative domain as well. "Patients' rights" as a legal term doesn't even appear until 1991 (Evin 1999) and indicates a level of reticence still present in the profession to this day. It is true that the Huriet law (1988), protecting patients undergoing experimental therapies and requiring their consent, has been in place for some time, and informed consent (art. 36 of the French Medical Deontology Code) is now admissible in a court of law. Nevertheless in a recent case (June 9, 1998) a Jehovah's Witness, though he had clearly expressed in advance his refusal to have a blood transfusion, was subsequently given a blood transfusion in a situation of medical emergency. When the case went before a judge, the court prioritized the "physician's respect of the obligation to protect life and health." In similar fashion, even though the physician has, under recent legislation, the obligation not only to inform the patient but also to provide proof that the patient has been so informed (Decision by the French Court of "Cassation" on February 25, 1997), he or she can nevertheless, in the name of "the apeutic justification" (art. 35 of the "*Code de déontologie*"), choose not to inform the patient of a serious diagnosis or risks related to treatment if he or she believes that such a revelation would be harmful to the patient. In cases of terminating life support, while the family of the patient is informed as a general rule, they are not the ones who make the decision. In France this decision remains in the hands of the physicians, as shown in a recent investigation.[13]

Within the context of the French health care system, the patient is thus far from having any real autonomy, in spite of recent (though limited) changes. In addition, even though the National Advisory Committee on Medical Ethics recommends getting the proxy's consent when the patient is incapable of consent, this consent is not required, thereby depriving the family of any direct control. While it is true that confidentiality cannot legally be maintained to the detriment of the patient, the definition of what constitutes "detriment" nevertheless seem to remain in the hands of the physician. The issues surrounding informed consent and confidentiality thus remain, along with the issue of individual access to one's medical charts and records (accessible in theory following the hospital reform law of 1991), the subject of constant debate among patients and more generally health care consumers in France today.

THE EMERGENCE OF CLAIMS AND THE HEALTH CARE CONSUMER

However, one of the more remarkable recent developments in the French health world is the emergence of a new factor, hitherto forsaken and rarely consulted: the patient, or rather the health care consumer. In a country characterized until very recently by the weakness of any patients' organizations, and by a paternalistic model of the doctor–patient relationship as well as by a highly medicalized vision of social problems, some notable changes have taken place.

The ways in which the French health care system has chosen to deal with the AIDS epidemic represent a veritable revolution in the manner in which the health care institution assumes responsibility for a patient. For a variety of reasons (ranging from social control to the epidemiological threat), this approach was instituted in an exemplary way. Admittedly, many of the institutional transformations that have been taking place as a result of the AIDS epidemic borrow from devices already in place and from previously tested initiatives (palliative care, pain management, psychological support, home medical care, and so forth). But they were readapted, reorganized in record time to respond to the needs of patients suffering from HIV. The acceleration of these transformations is undoubtedly one of the major facts of this epidemic[14] in the French case.

Beyond these institutional modifications, we are also witnessing a true ideological revolution. Two factors – the obligation to tell the patient the truth in the case of AIDS, and the lack of any real therapeutic solution in the early days of the epidemic – abruptly modified the traditional doctor–patient relationship by imposing a new transparency of communication. The law of silence rooted in a paternalistic model of doctor–patient relationship was suddenly not acceptable; the AIDS patient was right away "socialized" within the medical sphere (contrary to the standard clinical vision, which typically gives precedence to the pathological over the social). It is in this way that the AIDS patient assumes the role of a true "social reformer" (Defert 1989). The specific mobilization around AIDS, in particular the efforts of patients' groups (Pollak 1992) and the institution of a "politics of compassion" in spite of shortages (Barbot 1998), thus contributed to these radical transformations on the level of the social representation of disease.

The situation of the AIDS patient went a long ways toward breaking up what was, up until that point, an extremely powerful identification between a person's professional situation (and health coverage) and his or her degree of social integration.[15] In addition it has provided the nucleus for a movement of genuine solidarity (unlike the sometimes only rhetorical solidarity expressed toward the unemployed), as was amply demonstrated by the outcry surrounding the affair of the tri-therapies in 1996.[16] The AIDS patient is henceforth the focal point of all forms of tolerance, thus justifying both institutional solicitude and national solidarity. This is particularly true since the 1991 scandal over contaminated blood, which finally succeeded in separating AIDS as a disease from the context of "sin," so pervasive up until that point. From that point on, the patient was perceived as the innocent victim, both of the disease and of institutional malpractice.

Where the plight of the AIDS patient is unique is the manner in which it has transformed a public health problem into a social issue. For the first time in French public health policy, a uniquely patient-centered approach was formulated in response to an epidemiological problem. This is in marked contrast to viewing epidemiological problems as strictly sanitary or medical issues, as has so often been the case in the past. The AIDS patient has never (contrary to other pathologies), been objectified or treated like a "disease," but rather has always been treated like an individual. Within the political as well as the institutional domain, the methods for assuming responsibility have now acquired a new "ethical" reference. This new-found importance of individual over collective interests represents a true break with the traditional model of public health policies (Orfali 1997).

And yet, in spite of the exemplary approach that has been taken to the issue of AIDS (an issue which has reverberated strongly throughout a public opinion already sensitized to the serious institutional deficiencies by the recent scandals), has anything really changed on the level of medical and hospital practices? Is there any evidence of a genuine shift toward a more patient-centered care?

Nothing could be less certain, as was most emphatically revealed in the most recent national surveys on health care (*États Généraux de la santé*), a system of surveys that was originally established in an attempt to promote a "medical democracy." In fact, it would seem that the transformations that took place in response to the AIDS epidemic have remained specific to the epidemic and have not extended to the rest of the health care system. Not only were the medical and institutional adaptations resulting from the AIDS epidemic not applied to other pathologies, they weren't really extended to the rest of hospital care either, thereby creating even greater institutional disparities in quality and type of patient care. In the final analysis, despite a number of indirect repercussions, the impact of the revolutionary policies surrounding AIDS on French health care remains rather limited when seen in the context of the system as a whole.

The French health care system's tardiness in addressing the needs and the role of its patients[17] (as well as in developing an efficient public health policy) undoubtedly reflects the separation between the medical and the social spheres so characteristic of the French system. From this point of view, the current demand for the patient to take control of and to participate in his or her own health care (a field heretofore strictly limited to the medical profession and neglected by the State) is all the more interesting. This desire originates in an increased general social demand to participate in a society whose institutions' very legitimacy is being called into question. This movement is not limited to the health sector, but also relates to other spheres of social life, such as education, labor market, etc. That people's personal experiences no longer match the normative goals of institutions such as school, family, or medicine, etc. has become a more clearly accepted perception, but one that has been in fact more developed by general sociology (Dubet 1987, 1994; Lapeyronnie et al. 1992) than by medical sociology in particular, at least in France.

Where Does French Medical Sociology Stand Now?

Not only is public health in France a new concept, but medical sociology as well is a relatively recent development (dating from the 1970s). That both should develop so relatively late in the game is perhaps not simply the result of chance – the two aspects are in fact more strongly linked than may initially be apparent. Admittedly, medical sociology has finally come into its own, and medical sociologists are called upon more and more to intervene at the institutional level. However, this same medical sociology still has few ties with medical schools, in contrast with the situation in America and in neighboring European countries (Cockerham 1983). In an academic community that remains largely unreceptive to any discipline still in search of legitimization, this lack of support from medical schools has very likely restricted the development of medical sociology as a field (Claus 1983). The limiting nature of specific training, especially one in which the vast majority of existing literature is in English,[18] is undoubtedly another factor which has slowed its development, as is demonstrated by the fact that the first French Medical Sociology textbook was published as recently as 1994 (Adam and Herzlich).[19]

How is it that the country which saw the simultaneous birth of both sociology (Durkheim) and the clinic (Bichat; Laennec; Corvisart) can be so slow to make advances in medical sociology and public health? Paradoxically, it is perhaps this very coincidence which explains the later divorce. Widespread reservations about studying social determinism in a field apparently governed exclusively by biological mechanisms have played an important role in the late development of medical sociology. In addition, in France the "founding fathers of sociology" in particular manifest an aversion to biological explanations, or to any kind of "social Darwinism." Durkheim is a particularly good example of this phenomenon, despite his study on suicide. Also, it should be noted that sociology developed at a time when medicine did not yet occupy a solid institutional and professional position, but was still in the process of defining itself as such. While sociology affirmed the autonomy of the social sphere, at the same time, the medical realm was defining itself exclusively on the basis of the opposite assertion, the autonomy of the pathological sphere. These two worlds thus appeared to be in direct and irreparable opposition from the beginning. After all, the development of the clinic (Foucault 1963) may very well have sounded the death-knell for the socialized conception of the individual in medicine, thereby eliminating from its field of investigation this social element, this subjectivity which only confused the objectivity of "pathological fact." This fundamental conception of the nature of medicine has its roots in the very heart of the Parisian hospital (Ackernecht 1967). And in France it is the *clinic* which will triumph (to a certain extent) to the detriment of the *hygiene* and a more lay-referral type of medicine.

This opposition and these tensions are still present in today's medical profession and in the French health system (Brémond 1999). They inform many of the reservations on the part of the medical profession with respect to managed care/ medicine or to any social organization of coverage not necessarily based on strictly medical expertise (including the problem of the rising cost of health care). Moreover, the governing vision in France (except in the case of AIDS) is clearly one of a medicalization of all social problems. Initially responsible for determining the strictly pathological, physicians are now in the position of defining what is ethical as well (Orfali 1997; Paillet 1997), even if the profession has prudently begun to borrow from other disciplines (law, economics, or psychology, etc.). Decision-making in health care (at least in France) remains still largely dominated by the medical expertise.

It is certainly not our intention within the limits of this discussion to analyze the specific development of French medical sociology. At most we will try first to formulate a few hypotheses based on the paradoxes we have observed up to this point. Dominant from the moment of its inception, the clinical vision gained further strength on the basis of its own prestige (Claude Bernard). In this context, medical sociology was slow to emerge, finally appearing in the 1970s in conjunction with the first controversies over medical power and the first hospital and medical studies reforms (Herzlich 1973; Steudler 1974; Chauvenet 1978). More than elsewhere, to borrow the expression of A. Touraine, "all of the elements that go to make up a society were not immediately recognized as belonging to the social sphere,"[20] in a context so heavily dominated not only by the medical, but also by the very "clinical gaze."

In addition, while the United States was developing a more empirical school of sociology, often quantitative, French sociology at that time initially favored a more general, theoretical approach. But what most clearly differentiates French medical sociology is the prioritization of discourse over practices as a source of information for analysis. It is here that Foucault's heritage becomes apparent. The analysis of discourse surrounding disease and health, as well as of medical discourse in general are the dominant themes of medical sociology "*à la française.*" Who speaks? What makes sense? The means of enunciation, production, and legitimization of discourse as well as the power dynamics of it are thus at the heart of these approaches, often inspired either by contemporary trends in Bourdieu's sociology of social reproduction[21] (Boltanski 1971), or, from a more anthropological and psychosocial perspective, by work on social representations – of disease in the case of Herzlich (1973) or Chauvenet (1978), and more precisely of cancer in the case of Pinell (1992).

Today, medical sociology in France represents a much more diverse field. Many studies borrow from the dominant paradigms of medical sociology (interactionism, ethnomethodology, etc.). What these studies have in common overall is a greater focus on fieldwork. During recent decades, several ethnographic studies, most often inspired by the model of the "negotiated order" (Strauss 1963; Strauss et al. 1985), have been carried out on the experience of illness across various social strata, involving various types of patient (Baszanger 1986; Pollak and Schiltz 1987; Dodier 1993). There also exist a great many studies on specific populations – the elderly (Guillemard 1986), the handicapped, substance abusers, etc. Health care organizations such as hospitals, are either addressed by so-called "strategic analysis" (Crozier 1963, 1986), or more practical studies (Gonnet 1992), or else analyzed along more ethnographic lines (Peneff 1992).

Lastly, the inception within what constitutes "medical" sociology is perhaps not as clear in France as it is elsewhere, and on purpose; questions of health are now considered as "social" problems just as issues surrounding education, social marginalization, suburban violence, etc., and are assumed to originate in general sociology. The transformations which take place in the world of health and medicine today are seen thus to have social implications which exceed the simple limited field of the hospital, the disease or the medical institution.

The temptation for the French sociology is undoubtedly (and even more so than elsewhere) to connect health issues to some sort of broader "ultimate" conception of society.

Notes

1   Source: La Documentation française, 1998.
2   Source: Insee, statistiques de l'état civil.

3 Active life expectancy: A global indicator of the health of a population, consisting of the number of years out of the total life span of the individual that are lived without illness or handicap resulting in incapacitation of the individual. Two levels of incapacity are distinguished – moderate and severe.

4 Source: indicateurs sociosanitaires, comparaisons internationales, évolution 1980–1994, Sesi et Diris. *La Documentation française*, 1998.

5 See Foucault (1963).

6 It must be noted that as this was a telephone survey certain sectors of the population were not contacted for their opinion, specifically those in nursing homes and the homeless.

7 Since 1996, France has experienced a dramatic drop in the number of AIDS cases; while in 1995 there were 5,208 new cases and 3,876 deaths by AIDS in France, in 1997 this had dropped to 2,289 new cases diagnosed and 1,311 deaths.

8 *La santé en France*, September 1998.

9 This reform, which has succeeded in slowing the growth of expenditure in public hospitals (from 15% per annum to 4% in 1996), consists of financing the hospitals through an annual budget instead of individually reimbursing the hospital according to each patient's care.

10 Report *"Health in France" (La santé en France)* by the High Committee of Public Health, 1994.

11 All 182,000 French doctors are required to register with the "Ordre des Médecins," the French equivalent of a kind of AMA, created under the Vichy government to control access to the profession and maintain a certain standard of medical ethics.

12 Organized by the government, the "Etats Généraux" are a vast survey of the health care system throughout the country. Two surveys of this type have taken place to date, one on cancer, the other on health.

13 Survey by the French Association of Intensive Care (Société de réanimation de langue française), in *Réanimation urgences*, vol. 6, 1998.

14 Creation in record time of the ATU (temporary authorization of the use of certain drugs for human use) in 1994; creation of the CISIH (Center of information and care for human immune-deficiency) since 1987, with the aim "of closely associating patient care facilities and medical technology services and research in order to offer a better quality of care and services to the patients"; creation of the City-Hospital networks in 1991 etc.

15 Admittedly, unemployment had already started this separation, but in spite of its prevalence, it only very recently acquired a "positive" definition within the social sphere.

16 In February 1996, the national Council of AIDS proposed to determine access to these therapies (in case of a shortage) by drawing lots. It resulted in a nationwide outcry.

17 For example, the various hospital boards of directors were only opened up to patient advocates in 1996.

18 The first translations date back to 1970 with an anthology of texts published by C. Herzlich, *Médecines, maladie et société*, Paris–La Hague: Mouton.

19 By comparison the first handbook in German language dates back to 1974 (Siegrist 1974) as mentioned by Cockerham (1983).

20 Preface of A. Touraine (Steudler 1974).

21 Even if this particular sociologist never worked in the field of medical sociology.

References

Ackerknecht, Erwin Heinz. 1967. *Medicine at the Paris Hospital (1794–1848)*. Baltimore: Johns Hopkins University Press.

Adam, Paul and Claudine Herzlich. 1994. *Sociologie de la maladie et de la Medecine*. [Sociology of Illness and Medicine]. Paris: Nathan.

Aïach, Pierre and Daniel Delanoe. 1998. *L'ère de la médicalisation. Ecce homo sanitas*. [The Era of Medicalization]. Paris: Anthropos, Collection Sociologiques.

Aïach, Pierre and Didier Fassin. 1994. *Les métiers de la santé: enjeux de pouvoir et quête de légitimité*. [Health Care Professions: Power Issues and Search for New Modes of Legitimization]. Paris: Anthropos.

Augé, Marc and Claudine Herzlich. 1984. *Le Sens du mal. Anthropologie, histoire, sociologie de la maladie*. [The Meaning of Evil. Anthropology, History, and Sociology of Illness]. Paris: Archives Contemporaines.

Badeyan, Gerard, Daniel Foulon, Jacqueline Gottely, Pierre Gottely, and Patrick Pauriche. 1998. *La Santé comparée en Europe et en Amérique*. [Comparing Health in Europe and in USA]. In *Données Sociales, La Société française, INSEE, 1998*.

Barbot, Jeanine. 1998. *Science, marche et compassion. L'intervention des associations de lutte contre le sida dans la circulation des nouvelles molecules*. [Science, Market and Compassion. How Associations Fighting Against AIDS are Involved in Helping to Put New Molecules into Circulation]. *Sciences Sociales et Sante*, 16: 67–93.

Baszanger, Isabelle. 1986. *Douleur et Medecine, la fin d'un oubli*. [Inventing Pain Medicine: From the Laboratory to the Clinic]. Paris and New Brunswick, NJ: Seuil and Rutgers University Press.

Boltanski, Luc. 1971. "Les usages sociaux du corps." ["Social Uses of the Body"]. *Annales, Economies, Societes et Civilisations* (Jan.–Feb.): 205–31.

Boltanski, Luc. 1993. *La souffrance a distance*. [Suffering at a Distance]. Paris: Metaillie.

Bremond, Marc. 1999. *Les syndicats de medecins contre l'organisation de la protection sociale, tout contre*. [The Physicians' Professional Associations and Health Care Coverage]. In *Le Pouvoir Medical, Revue Pouvoirs*. Paris: Seuil.

Bungener, Martine and Jeanine Pierret. 1994. "De l'influence du chomage sur l'état de santé." ["The Impact of Unemployment on Health"]. In MIRE/INSEE (eds.), *Trajectoires Sociales, Inegalites et Conditions de Vie*. Paris: Editions Eres.

Carricaburu, Daniele. 1993. *L'Association française des hémophiles face au danger de contamination par le virus du sida*. [The French Association of Hemophilia Patients and the Danger of Contamination by HIV Virus]. *Sciences sociales et santé* 11.

Castel, Robert. 1976. *L'Ordre psychiatrique, l'âge d'or de l'aliénisme*. [The Psychiatric Order, the Golden Age of Madness]. Paris: Editions de Minuit.

Chauvenet, Antoinette. 1978. *Medecines au choix, médecine de classe*. [Choice Medicine, Class Medicine]. Paris: PUF.

Chiappori, Pierre-Andre and Kristina Orfali. 1997. *Préferences et Interactions; une mise en perspective*. [Preference and Interaction: Placed in Perspective]. *Revue française de sociologie* 38: 429–64.

Claus, Lisbeth M. 1983. "The Development of Medical Sociology in Europe." *Social Science and Medicine* 17: 1591–7.

Cockerham, William. 1983. "The State of Medical Sociology in the United States, Great Britain, West Germany, and Austria: Applied vs. Pure Theory." *Social Science and Medicine* 17: 1513–27.

——. 1996. *Sociology of Mental Disorder*, 4th edition. Upper Saddle River, NJ: Prentice-Hall.

——. 1997. *This Aging Society*, 2nd edition. Upper Saddle River, NJ: Prentice-Hall.

——. 1998. *Medical Sociology*, 7th edition. Upper Saddle River, NJ: Prentice-Hall.

Corbett, James. 1994. *Through French Windows*. Anne Arbor: University of Michigan Press.

CREDOC. 1992. *Enquête Santé* [Health Survey]. Paris: Centre de Recherche pour l'étude et l'observation des conditions de vie.

——. 1997. *Enquête Santé* [Health Survey]. Paris: Centre de Recherche pour l'étude et l'observation des conditions de vie.

Criqui, M. H. and B. L. Ringel. 1994. "Does Diet or Alcohol Explain the French Paradox?" *Lancet* 34: 1719–23.

Crozier, Michel. 1963. *Le phenomene bureaucratique*. [The Bureaucratic Phenomena]. Paris: Seuil.

——. 1986. "L'analyse strategique appliquée en milieu hospiltalier: pertinence et methodologie." ["Strategic Analysis Applied to Hospitals: Pertinence and Methodology"]. *Gestion Hospitalière* 261: 787–92.

Crozier, Michel and Erhard Friednerg. 1977. *L'acteur et le systeme*. [The Actor and the System]. Paris: Seuil.

Defert, Daniel. 1989. *Journal Liberation*. Paris.

Dodier, Nicolas. 1993. *L'Expertise médicale. Essai de sociologie du jugement*. [Medical Expertise. An Essay on the Sociology of Judgment]. Paris: A. M. Métailié.

Données sur la situation santaire et sociale en France [Data on Health and the Social Situation in France]. 1998. Paris : SESI, *Ministère de l'Emploi et de la Solidarité*.

Dubet, Francois. 1987. *La Galère* [The Gallery]. Paris: Fayard.

——. 1994. *Sociologie de l'experience*. [Sociology of Experience]. Paris: Seuil.

Duriez, Marc, Pierre-Jean Lancry, Diane Lequet-Slama, and Simone Sandier. 1996. *Le système de santé en France*. [The Health System in France]. Paris: PUF.

Evin, Claude. 1999. "Les Droits des Malades." [The Patients' Rights]. Pp. 15–30 in *Le Pouvoir Medical-Revue Pouvoirs*. Paris: Seuil.

Fassin, Didier. 1996. *L'espace politique de la santé*. [The Politics of Health]. Paris: PUF.

Foucault, Michel. 1963. *Naissance de la Clinique*. [The Birth of Clinic]. Paris: Quadrige/Presses Universitaires de France.

Fox, A. J. (ed.). 1989. *Health Inequalities in European Countries*. Aldershot: Gower.

Goldberg, David M. 1995. "Does Wine Work?" *Clinical Chemistry* 41: 14–16.

Gonnet, Francoise. 1992. *L'Hôpital en question(s). Un diagnostic pour améliorer les relations de travail*. [Issues on Hospital. A Diagnosis for Improving Working Relationships]. Paris: Lamarre.

Guillemard, Anne-Marie. 1986. *Le déclin du social*. [The Decline of the Social]. Paris: PUF.

——. 1996. "State, Society, and Old-Age Policy in France: From 1945 to the Current Crisis." *Social Science and Medicine* 23: 1319–26.

Haut Comité de la Santé Publique. 1994. *La Santé en France* [Health in France]. Paris: La Documentation Française.

Hamon, Herve. 1994. *Nos médecins*. [Our Doctors]. Paris: Seuil.

Hassenteufel, Pierre. 1997. *Les Médecins face à l'Etat, une comparaison européenne*. [Physicians and State: A European Comparison]. Paris: Presses de la FNSP.

Herzlich, Claudine. 1973a. *Health and Illness*. London: Academic Press.

——. 1973b. *Types de clientèle et fonctionnement de l'institution hospitalière*. [Types of Clientele and the Functioning of Hospital Institutions]. *Revue française de Sociologie* 14: 41–59.

Herzlich, Claudine, Martine Bungener, and Genevieve Paicheler. 1993. *Cinquante Ans d'exercice de la medecine en France. Carrières et pratiques des médecins français, 1930–1980*. [Fifty Years of Medical Practice in France. Careers and Practices of French Physicians, 1930–1980]. Paris: Doin-INSERM .

Herzlich, Claudine and Jeanine Pierret. 1987. *Illness and Self in Society*. Baltimore, MD: Johns Hopkins University Press.

———. 1988. *Une maladie dans l'espace public. Le sida dans six quotidiens français.* [Illness in the Public Sphere. AIDS in Six Daily Newspapers]. *Annales ESC.*

Johanet, Gilles. 1998. *Sécurité Sociale: L' Echec et le Défi.* [French Public Healthcare: Failures and Challenges]. Paris: Seuil.

KAPB Enquête Nationale. [National Knowlege, Attitudes, Beliefs, and Practices Model Survey]. 1994. Paris: ANRS (Agence Nationale de Recherche sur le SIDA) and DGS (Direction Generale de la Santé).

De Kervasdoué, Jean. 1996. *La Santé intouchable.* [Untouchable Health]. Paris: J. C. Lattès.

Kessler, Ronald C., K. A. McGonagle, S. Zhao, C. Nelson, M. Hughes, S. Eshleman, H. Witchen, and K. S. Kendler. 1994. "Life-Time and 12-month Prevalence of DSM-III-R Psychiatric Disorders in the United States." *Archives of General Psychiatry* 51: 8–19.

Kunst, A. E. 1997. *Cross National Comparisons of Socio-Economic Differences in Mortality.* Rotterdam: Erasmus University.

Lahelma, Eero and Valkonen Tapani. 1990. "Health and Social Inequities in Finland and Elsewhere." *Social Science and Medicine* 31: 257–66.

Lapeyronnie, Didier and Jean-Louis Marie. 1992. *Campus-Blues: les etudiants face a leurs etudes.* [Campus-Blues: Students Facing their Curriculum]. Paris: Seuil.

La Santé en France 1994–1998. [Health in France 1994–1998]. 1998. Paris: HCR, La Documentation Française.

Leclerc, Annette. 1989. "Differential Mortality by Cause of Death: Comparison Between Selected European Countries." Pp. 92–108 in J. Fox (ed.), *Health Inequalities in European Countries.* Aldershot: Gower.

Le Disert, Dominique. 1985. *La Maladie; la part du social* [Sickness: The Social Part]. Paris: CNRS, CDSH.

Lemonick, Michael D. 1999. "Eating Smart for Your Heart." *Time* (July 19): 40–9.

Lépine, Jean-Pierre, Michel Mendlewicz Gatspar, and Tylee Andre Jean. 1997. "Depression in the Community: The First Pan European Study of Depression." *Psychopharmacology* 12: 19–29.

Le Quéau, Paul and Christian Olm. 1998. *La perception de la santé en France.* [Health Perception in France]. Paris: *Etude réalisée à la demande du Haut Comité de la santé publique, CREDOC.*

Lüschen, Günther, W. Cockerham, J. Van der Zee, F. Stevens, J. Dideriks, M. G. Ferrando, A. D'Houtaud, P. Ruud, T. Abel, and S. Niemann. 1995. *Health Systems in the European Union : Diversity, Convergence, and Integration.* Munich: Oldenbourg.

Mesrine, Annie. 1998. "Les differences de mortalité par milieu social restent fortes." [Mortality Differences by Social Background Remain Important]. Pp. 228–35 in *Donées Sociales, La Societé Française.* Paris: INSEE.

Moatti, Jean-Paul, William Dab, and Michael Pollack. 1990. *Les attitudes et comportements des Francais face au sida.* [French People's Attitudes and Behaviors Regarding AIDS]. *La Recherche* 223: 888–95.

Morelle, Aquilino. 1996. *La Défaite de la santé publique.* [The Failure of Public Health]. Paris: Flammarion.

Mormiche, Paul. 1995. *Les disparités de recours aux aux soins* [Disparities in Health Consumption]. *Economie et statistique* 265: 45.

Murard, Lion and P. Sylberman. 1996. *L'Hygiène dans la République, La santé publique en France, une utopie contrariée, 1870–1918.* [Hygiene in the Republic. The Public Health in France, a Failed Utopia, 1870–1918]. Paris: Fayard.

Orfali, Kristina. 1993. *Construction de l'identité du malade à l'hôpital,* in *Maladie, médecine et société.* [Construction of Patient's Identity in Hospital Settings in Illness, Medicine, and Society]. Tome II, Paris: L'Harmattan (Histoire du Présent).

——. 1997. *L'Hopital ou la Critique de la Raison Instrumentale, Essai sur l'expérience hospitalière des malades.* [The Hospital: The Critique of Instrumental Reason, Essay on Patient's Hospital Experience]. Thèse, EHESS (Ecole des Hautes Etudes en Sciences Sociales), Paris.

ORS Bourgogne, Centre, Champagne-Ardenne, Limousin, Haute-Normandie, Poitou-Charentes. 1995. *Evaluation de l'application de la législation relative à la protection des non-fumeurs.* [Evaluation of the Implementation of Law Protecting Non-Smokers].

Paillet, Anne.1997. *Ethique et Pratiques quotidiennes a l'hopital: approche sociologique des decisions d'arret, d'abstention et de poursuite therapeutique.* [Ethics and Everyday Medical Practices in Hospitals: A Sociological Approach on Withdrawing, Withholding, or Continuing Treatment]. Paris: MIRE.

Payer, Lynn. 1988. *Medicine and Culture.* London: Penguin.

Peneff, Jean. 1992. *L'Hôpital en urgence.* [Emergency in Hospital]. Paris: Métaillié.

Peter, Jean-Pierre. 1989. *Dimension mythique des épidémies et sida, in Sida, le défi social.* [Mythical Dimensions in Epidemics and AIDS, in AIDS, the Social Challenge]. *Actions et Recherches Sociales* 3–4.

Pinell, Patrice. 1992. *Naissance d'un fléau: histoire de la lutte contre le cancer en France (1840–1940).* [The Birth of a Scourge: The Fight Against Cancer in France, an Historical Approach]. Paris: A. M. Métailié.

Pollak, Michael. 1988. *Les Homosexuels et le sida, sociologie d'une épidémie.* [Homosexuals and AIDS, the Sociology of an Epidemic]. Paris: A. M. Métailié.

——. 1992. "Organizing the Fight against AIDS." In Michael Pollak with Genevieve Paicheler and Anne-Marie Schiltz, 1987. *Identite sociale et gestion d'un risque de sante: les homosexuels face au sida.* [Social Identity and Health Risk Management: Gays Facing AIDS]. *Actes de la Recherche en Sciences Sociales* 68: 77–102.

Renaud, Serge and Michel de Lorgeril. 1992. "Wine, Alcohol, Platelets, and the French Paradox for Coronary Heart Disease." *Lancet* 339: 1523–6.

Roques, Bertrand. 1998. *Problèmes posés par la dangérosité des "drogues."* [Problems Linked to Addiction Dangers]. Paris: Rapport au sécrétaire d'Etat à la Santé.

St. Léger, A. S., A. L. Cochrane, and F. Moore. 1979. "Factors Associated with Cardiac Mortality in Developed Countries with Particular Reference to the Consumption of Wine. " *Lancet* 326: 1017–20.

Setbon, Michel. 1993. *Pouvoirs contre sida. De la transfusion sanguine au dépistage: décisions et pratiques en France,Grande-Bretagne et Suède.* [Powers Against AIDS. From Blood Transfusion to Testing: Decision-Making and Practices in France, Great-Britain, and Sweden]. Paris: Seuil.

Spira, A. and N. Bajos, Groupe ACSF [Analyse des Comportements Sexuels des Français]. 1993. *Les Comportements Sexuels en France.* [Sexual Behaviors in France]. Paris: Rapports Officiels.

Stasse, Francois. 1999. *Les acteurs de la politique de santé, in Le Pouvoir Medical.* [Health Policy Agents, in The Medical Power]. *Revue Pouvoirs* 89: 65–78.

Steudler, Francois. 1974. *L'Hôpital en observation.* [Hospital Under Scrutiny]. Paris: A. Colin.

Strauss, Anselm, Leonard Schatzman, Danuta Ehrlich, Rue Bucher, and Melvin Sabshin. 1963. "The Hospital and Its Negotiated Order." Pp. 147–89 in E. Freidson (ed.), *"The Hospital in Modern Society".* New York: Free Press.

Strauss, Anselm, Fagerhaugh Shizuko, and Barabara Suczek. 1985. *Social Organization of Medical Work.* Chicago: University of Chicago Press.

Touraine, Alain. 1995. *The Critique of Modernity.* Oxford: Blackwell.

Veil, C. Veil-Barat. 1994. "Sida et cancer." In *Des infirmiers face au sida.* [AIDS and Cancer in Nurses Facing AIDS]. Paris: Inserm.

16

Medical Sociology in Germany

OLAF VON DEM KNESEBECK AND JOHANNES SIEGRIST

The German health care system represents an approach that is located between a national health care system like the United Kingdom at one end of the spectrum and a market system at the other end (e.g. the United States). Germany is characterized by decentralized care delivered by social security agencies, and it is influenced to a large extent by two structural features, federalism and corporatism. By federalism, we mean that competencies and regulations with regard to health care are divided between the national, state, and community levels. By corporatism, we mean that health care providers and financing institutions act as self-administrative public institutions, most importantly the sickness funds and the physicians' associations. In this system, the government has delegated important monopolies and rights to these corporate associations (Alber 1992).

Statutory sickness funds, or "Gesetzliche Krankenversicherung," are the most important financing institutions in the German health care system. Almost 90 percent of the population is covered by statutory sickness funds. Federal regulations prescribe the range and modalities of health care provision and health financing. Health care financing is regulated in a rather complicated way. Its main contribution comes from economically active insured members and their employers (50% each). The amount of social security deduction depends on the income level of the legally insured members. Prices and modalities of health care provision in ambulatory and hospital care are negotiated between statutory sickness funds and physicians' associations.

In Germany, the Association of the Free Practicing Physicians ("Kassenärztliche Vereinigungen") was successful in establishing a treatment monopoly as early as 1955. Hospital admissions largely depend on free practicing physicians' decisions as to which patients released from hospitals have to return for continued treatment. Thus, there is a clear-cut cleavage between the ambulatory and the hospital health care sector that produces many dysfunctional, cost-expanding consequences. While half of free practicing physicians are general practitioners, the other half are specialists. It is probably unique for a health care system to provide two categories of specialist physicians, with one category exclusively in the ambulatory sector, and the other category exclusively in hospital services.

The health care industry in Germany represents a strong economic force. More than two million employees total are involved in health care. The direct costs of the German health care system were about 380 billion DEM in 1998, which is equal to 10.4 percent of the gross domestic product. The hospital sector is still the largest cost-producing sector since Germany has an unusually high number of hospital beds and, in international comparisons, also has a rather high mean duration of hospital stay (Schneider et al. 1998). In addition, health care expenditure for drugs is high in Germany, a fact that recently motivated the government to introduce a highly restrictive legal regulation on drug administration.

Despite high economic significance, the German health care system has little information available on the efficacy of its performance. Quality assurance and control, health economic evaluations, and the application of evidence-based medicine are still in beginning stages. Because there is no consensus on prioritization of health goals or on long-term strategies, and because of the lack of coordination (OECD 1997), the health care system in Germany in its current shape must be considered ready for far-reaching reformation. In the discussion about strategies to rationalize health care, especially in the ambulatory sector, elements of the managed care models often play an important role (Kongstvedt 1996; Arnold et al. 1997). Hopefully, medical sociology will make a more substantial contribution to the reformation process of the health care system than it did in the past.

HEALTH STATUS OF THE GERMAN POPULATION

As part of the reformation process, and as a measure for a rational health policy in Germany, efforts increase to improve health reporting. Recently Germany published its first health report that includes information about the health status and health-related behavior of the population, as well as about prevalence of diseases and risk factors, and the utilization of health care services (Statistisches Bundesamt 1998). To provide an overview of the health status of the German population, we present some basic data on life expectancy, causes of mortality, and absence from work.

Like all other industrial nations, the life expectancy in Germany has increased considerably this century. Life expectancy at the beginning of this century for men was 44.8 years, and it was 48.3 years for women. By 1995, it had reached 73.3 years for men and 79.8 years for women. The main reasons for this development are the decline of infant mortality and infectious diseases due to improved medical care and standard of living. There is still a remarkable difference in life expectancy between East and West Germany: almost 3 years for men and about 1.5 years for women in favor of West Germany (Schneider et al. 1998). The smaller difference in women's life expectancy indicates that East German women have come closer to West German standards since the reunification than have East German men. This is largely due to an increased number of young East German men who were killed in road accidents right after the reunification in 1990 and 1991. From a comparative perspective, Germany still has one year below the mean life expectancy in the European Union (77.3 years).

The main causes of death are cardiovascular disease and cancer, with a proportion of almost 75 percent in 1995. Although mortality caused by cardiovascular diseases has decreased since 1980, it is still the most important single cause of death. Almost 50 percent of all deaths were caused by cardiovascular disease (43.5% in men and 52.9% in women with the mean standardized age of death being 76.9 and 80.2 years respectively). The higher mortality in East Germany is mainly due to a higher prevalence of ischemic heart diseases (Statistisches Bundesamt 1998).

Interestingly in 1991, one year after reunification, the number of working days lost through absenteeism in East Germany was very low, like in the times of the former GDR (9.8 days per member of the statutory sickness funds). Within four years, absence from work for health reasons increased dramatically to 19.4 days in 1995, which is about the same number as it was in West Germany. This development indicates that absence from work should always be interpreted in the light of the political and economical frame of reference. Musculoskeletal diseases or symptoms are most significant causes of people's inability to work.

MEDICAL SOCIOLOGY IN GERMANY – ITS CONTRIBUTION TO TEACHING AND RESEARCH

Teaching

Before 1970 "medical sociology" as a distinct discipline was nonexistent in Germany. While a few scholarly studies on the sociology of hospitals (Rohde 1962) and on the social role of physicians (Kaupen-Haas 1969) were published in the sixties, the major writings were critical appraisals of the role of medicine in capitalist societies (Haug 1973). The professional expansion of academic sociology at that time by-passed medicine, unlike the situation in other European countries such as the United Kingdom (Claus 1982). In fact, in 1970 the first decisive step was taken to develop medical sociology as a teaching activity and, later, as a research activity within medical faculties of German universities. This was a major reform of the medical curriculum, in which medical sociology, together with medical psychology, became part of a new centralized, written medical examination system in the pre-clinical term of medical education. Unfortunately, medical sociology was not accorded a mandatory course within this new curriculum, unlike medical psychology. Therefore, there was no real pressure to establish new professorships and departments for this discipline within medical faculties (Pflanz and Siegrist 1978). As a consequence, only about one-third of all medical faculties opened positions for a professor of medical sociology and offered a small, modest department to this aim. In a way, this was appropriate because academic sociology at that time did not provide a substantial number of well-trained specialists in this field. During the early years, no more than half of the 14 newly-created posts were occupied by trained sociologists whereas physicians took the other half. This situation persisted until recently. Some years ago, schools developed a new medical curriculum that accords much more weight and significance to the content of medical sociology. However, although approved by the medical faculties, this innovation has not yet passed federal legislation, due to financial and political constraints.

In summary, the institutional basis of medical sociology within medical faculties has been – and continues to be – rather weak. Moreover, academic sociology has not supported this special discipline nor has it created any significant development within its own faculties. Despite this critical structural basis, medical sociologists have accomplished some remarkable activities in teaching and research. For instance, one widely-used medical sociology textbook, first published in 1974, is currently in its fifth edition (Siegrist 1995). Teaching activities have also been expanded beyond the basic medical curriculum to include postgraduate training programs in medicine and nursing education.

During the early nineties a new initiative was started in Germany that aimed at establishing public health research and teaching within universities. A substantial federal research grant was made available to this end. Some five or six research networks evolved subsequently, all of them related to a new postgraduate training program in public health (Schwartz et al. 1998). Medical or "health" sociology became part of this new curriculum and plays a central role in this research program, along with epidemiology and health economics. Programs established a few new chairs with a specific sociological orientation. The next section briefly describes some major research contributions of medical sociologists in the past ten or fifteen years.

Research

German medical sociology's major research activities focused on what are internationally recognized as core topics of medical sociology. In particular, these researchers contributed over the past two decades to the following areas: (1) the social determinants of health and health-related behavior; (2) chronic illness, patient–physician interaction, and evaluation of treatment; (3) analyses of health care and health systems research.

SOCIAL DETERMINANTS OF HEALTH AND HEALTH-RELATED BEHAVIOR

Social inequalities in health define one of the most urgent concerns of the discipline. One might argue that the German health care system prevents the development of substantial health inequalities because it offers almost equal provision of medical care to the whole population. However, this view greatly overemphasizes the contribution of medical care to population health. It is not surprising, therefore, that the first large-scale epidemiologic studies that explored socioeconomic variations in health confirmed the internationally established trends. The so-called German Cardiovascular Prevention Study documented elevated odds by two- to four-fold in the ratio of important cardiovascular risk factors in members of the lowest as compared to the highest socioeconomic status group (Helmert et al. 1990, 1995). Moreover, researchers observed a decline in cardiovascular risk over time among higher, but not lower status groups (Forschungsverbund DHP 1998; von Troschke et al. 1991). In another large investigation, the so-called MONICA study of the World Health Organization, found that men and women with a lower educational level exhibited higher cardiovascular risks (Härtel et al. 1993).

The social gradient in health is not restricted to cardiovascular diseases. Additional studies revealed similar effects with respect to smoking and smoking-related diseases (Brenner et al. 1997), colorectal cancer (Brenner et al. 1991), severity of disease in Type I diabetes patients (Mühlhauser et al. 1998) and all cause-mortality (Geyer and Peter 1999). Recently, some researchers attempted to compare the magnitude of differences in health inequalities between several European countries including Germany. Due to selective data available from German health statistics this comparison had to be restricted to chronic illness and long-standing handicaps. Again, a clear social gradient was evident, leaving those at the bottom with the highest burden of illness (Mackenbach et al. 1997; Cavelaars et al. 1998).

Three further lines of research are of interest in this context. First, the issue of excess morbidity and mortality of groups that are exposed to social deprivation has been explored (Mielck 1994). Among these studies are ones that explore unemployment (Elkeles and Seifert 1993), immigration (Elkeles and Seifert 1996), poverty (Helmert et al. 1997), and people suffering from severe chronic illness such as schizophrenia (Müller et al. 1998). A second, rapidly expanding line of research is devoted to health-related lifestyles, their measurement and the study of their sociocultural and socioeconomic determinants (Abel 1991; Lüschen et al. 1995; Abel et al. 1999). Interestingly, distinct patterns of health-related lifestyles can be identified that vary with the availability of social resources, as expected in a Weberian perspective (Cockerham et al. 1997). Finally, while research on social determinants of health in the past was largely restricted to men, more recent investigations explored gender differences in illness susceptibility with particular emphasis on psychosocial and sociocultural influences (Härtel 1996; Maschewsky-Schneider et al. 1998).

Additional contributions to medical sociological research on social determinants of health and illness aimed at explaining the documented variations in terms of sociogenic models. As transdisciplinary stress research witnessed rapid progress during the seventies and eighties the sociological study of psycho–biological bases of physical and mental diseases gained considerable attraction (Weiner 1992). One area of research concerns sociogenic models as related to the working life. One such model, effort–reward imbalance at work, was developed and widely tested at the Universities of Marburg and, later, Düsseldorf (Siegrist

1996, see also chapter "Work stress and health"). A second area to which several studies made a relevant contribution was research on social support and social isolation (Siegrist 1986; Pfaff 1989; Waltz 1994). A third area, life event research, largely followed the pioneering approach of British medical sociologist George W. Brown (Brown and Harris 1989), and found evidence of a socially patterned prevalence of severe life events (Geyer 1999). A further study along these lines documented indirect effects of lower social status on poor subjective health that were mediated by increased levels of stressful experience and decreased coping resources, at least among elderly males (Knesebeck 1998).

Chronic Illness, Patient–Physician Interaction, and Evaluation of Treatment

Two further prominent contributions of German medical sociology are related to the sick role and the psycho-social sequelae of chronic illness. Uta Gerhardt reanalyzed Parsons' seminal concept of the sick role (Gerhardt 1989, 1990a) and tested a series of hypotheses related to the social construction of chronic illness and the re-normalization processes in patients and their partners (Gerhardt 1990c). In particular, it was shown that "dual career"-couples where both the chronically ill and the healthy partner had employment experience were best suited to cope with the burden of illness. These studies also contributed to qualitative research methodology (Gerhardt 1990b). A second investigation by Bernhard Badura and his group consisted of a longitudinal study on some 1,000 cardiac patients to be followed over a mean 5.5 years (Badura et al. 1987; Waltz 1994). Of the many findings the following two deserve special attention: first, it was shown that a return to work was of crucial importance to well-being and adjustment to chronic illness; secondly, the two types of provision of medical rehabilitation care available in Germany, inpatient care in special rehabilitation clinics and outpatient ambulatory care by local teams, showed no significant differences in treatment outcomes (Badura et al. 1995). Additional research focused on predictors of early retirement and rehabilitation (Biefang et al. 1998), on the sociological analysis of communication and information between physicians and chronic patients in hospitals (Siegrist 1978; Raspe 1983; Trojan and Nickel 1999), and on the contribution of lay-people to health care and coping (von Ferber 1987).

Special attention was focused on a problem of growing concern in psychiatric sociology, which is the social discrimination and stigmatization of psychiatric patients, and schizophrenics in particular. Matthias Angermeyer and his group conducted several studies on this topic showing that stereotypes against and social distance from mentally ill people are still rather high among the general public in Germany. This was especially the case following selective media reporting of violent attacks conducted by schizophrenic patients against prominent personalities (Angermeyer and Matschinger 1996).

More recently, the international movement of outcome research influenced medical sociology. This research proved to be valuable to physicians, health administrators, and health policy makers. A number of clinical trials and more comprehensive intervention studies were conducted with emphasis on psycho-social parameters (e.g. measures of functioning, of health-related quality of life). In at least two of the newly established public health research networks, evaluation research became an explicit focus (Badura and Siegrist 1999; Manz and Kirch 1999). Distinct prevention programs, in particular work-site health promotion programs, further substantiate this trend toward applied medical sociological research where sociological researchers play an active role (Slesina et al. 1988; Müller and Rosenbrock 1998; Slesina et al. 1998; Aust 1999).

HEALTH CARE AND HEALTH SYSTEMS RESEARCH

From a comparative perspective German medical sociological research, until recently, has been biased toward a "sociology in medicine" approach (Claus 1982). This bias is largely due to the researcher's institutional base within medical faculties and available resources of research funding. Due to a lack of independent inquiries from outside (i.e. due to a lack of genuine sociological research as applied to medicine and health care) these latter topics have not received adequate attention. This is particularly troublesome in a country whose health care system is characterized by overregulation and corporatism, by resistance against structural innovations, and by poorly developed information on treatment efficacy and health gain. Only a few research teams contributed to a sociological analysis of the current German health care system, its roots and dynamics. Hans Ulrich Deppe has probably been one of the most active researchers in this regard (Deppe 1987, 1989). After the re-unification process in 1990, there were some contributions that addressed the differences between and integration of the former eastern and western German health care systems (Deppe et al. 1993; Lüschen et al. 1997). Besides a few other works by Deppe and colleagues (Deppe and Oreskovic 1996; Iliffe and Deppe 1996), the field of comparative health systems research has been left to health economists almost exclusively (as an exception see Lüschen et al. 1989, 1995). This tends to leave the theoretical and methodological opportunities and challenges of comparative sociology to professional colleagues in other countries.

CONCLUSION

This chapter has documented some strong and weak points of the development of medical sociology in Germany. Its strong points are (1) the development and diffusion of a sociological curriculum for health professions, most importantly medical students, nursing students, and, more recently, public health students at the postgraduate level; (2) distinct advances in basic and applied research on social determinants of health and on chronic illness, including client–professional exchange; (3) a strengthening of the outcome research movement in terms of content and measurement, both with regard to health care delivery and, more recently, with regard to public health activities. The weak points are (1) the still-fragile institutional basis of the profession within medicine and the almost nonexisting structural and intellectual support from academic mainstream sociology; (2) the poor development of health care research and of comparative health systems research; (3) the lack of professional impact on health policy at the regional and at the national level. This latter point is particularly troublesome as sociological expertise could be helpful in a health care system that needs innovation and rational decision-making. It is to be hoped that medical sociology in concert with the newly established public health movement will be allowed to contribute to future medicine and health care in a more visible and influential way.

References

Abel, Thomas. 1991. "Measuring Health Lifestyles in a Comparative Analysis: Theoretical Issues and Empirical Findings." *Social Science and Medicine* 32: 899–908.

Abel, Thomas., E. Walter, S. Niemann, and R. Weitkunat 1999. "The Berne-Munich Lifestyle Panel. Background and Baseline Results from a Longitudinal Health Lifestyle Survey." *Sozial- und Präventivmedizin* 44: 91–106.

Alber, J. 1992. *Das Gesundheitswesen in der Bundesrepublik Deutschland.* [The German Health Care System]. Frankfurt am Main: Campus.

Angermeyer, M. C. and H. Matschinger. 1996. "The Effects of Violent Attacks by Schizophrenic Persons on the Attitude of the Public towards Mentally Ill." *Social Science and Medicine* 43: 1721–8.

Arnold, M., K. W. Lauterbach, and K. J. Preua. 1997. *Managed Care.* Stuttgart: Schattauer.

Aust, B. 1999. *Gesundheitsförderung in der Arbeitswelt.* [Health Promotion at the Work Place]. Ph.D. Thesis, University of Bielefeld.

Badura, B., G. Kaufhold, H. Lehmann, H. Pfaff, T. Schott, and M. Waltz. 1987. *Leben mit dem Herzinfarkt. Eine sozialepidemiologische Studie.* [Life with Heart Attacks. A Social Epidemiological Study]. Berlin: Springer.

Badura, B., G. Grande, H. Janaen, and T. Schott. 1995. *Qualitätsforschung im Gesundheitswesen. Ein Vergleich ambulanter und stationärer kardiologischer Rehabilitation.* [Quality Research in the Health Care System. A Comparison between In-Patient and Out-Patient Cardiological Rehabilation Care]. Weinheim: Juventa.

Badura, B. and J. Siegrist (eds.). 1999. *Evaluation im Gesundheitswesen.* [Evaluating the Health Care System]. Weinheim: Juventa.

Biefang, S., P. Potthoff, B. M. Bellach, and R. Buschmann-Steinhage. 1998. "Predictors of Early Retirement and Rehabilitation for Use in a Screening to Detect Workers in Need of Rehabilitation." *International Journal of Rehabilitation Research* 21: 13–27.

Brenner, H., A. Mielck, R. Klein, and H. Zeigler. 1991. "The Role of Socioeconomic Factors in Survival of Patients with Colorectal Cancer in Saarland/ W-Germany." *Journal of Clinical Epidemiology* 44: 807–15.

Brenner, H., J. Born, P. Novak, and V. Wanek. 1997. "Smoking Behavior and Attitude Towards Smoking Regulations and Passive Smoking in the Workplan." *Preventive Medicine* 26: 138–43.

Brown, G. and T. Harris (eds.). 1989. *Life Events and Illness.* London: Unwin Hyman.

Cavelaars, A., A. E. Kunst, J. J. Geurts, U. Helmert, O. Lundberg, A. Mielck, J. Matheson, A. Mizrahi, N. Rasmussen, T. Spuhler, and J. P. Mackenbach. 1998. "Morbidity Differences by Occupational Class Among Men in Seven European Countries." *International Journal of Epidemiology* 27: 222–30.

Claus, L. M. 1982. *The Growth of a Sociological Discipline. On the Development of Medical Sociology in Europe*, 2 vols. Leuven: Sociological Research Institute.

Cockerham, William C., A. Rütten, and T. Abel. 1997. "Conceptualizing Contemporary Health Lifestyles: Moving beyond Weber." *Sociological Quarterly* 38: 321–42.

Deppe, H.-U. 1987. *Krankheit ist ohne Politik nicht heilbar.* [Illness is not Curable without Politics]. Frankfurt am Main : Suhrkamp.

——. 1989. "State and Health." *Social Science and Medicine* 28: 1159–64.

Deppe, H.-U., H. Friedrich, and R. Müller (eds.). 1993. *Gesundheitssystem im Umbruch: Von der DDR zur BRD.* [Health Care System in Transformation: From GDR to FRG]. Frankfurt am Main: Campus.

Deppe, H.-U. and S. Oreskovic. 1996. "Back to Europe – Back to Bismarck?" *International Journal of Health Services* 26: 777–802.

Elkeles, T. and W. Seifert. 1993. "Unemployment and Health- Impairments: Longitudinal Analyses from the Federal Republic of Germany." *European Journal of Public Health* 3: 28–37.

——. 1996. "Immigrants and Health". *Social Science and Medicine* 43: 1035–47.

Forschungsverbund DHP (ed.).1998. *Die deutsche Herz-Kreislauf- Präventionsstudie.* [The German Cardiovascular Prevention Study]. Bern: Huber.

Gerhardt, U. 1989. *Ideas About Illness. An Intellectual and Political History of Medical Sociology.* London: Macmillan.

——. 1990a. "Models of Illness and the Theory of Society: Parsons' Contribution to the Early History of Medical Sociology." *International Sociology* 5: 337–55.

——. 1990b. "Qualitative Research on Chronic Illness." *Social Science and Medicine* 30 (Special Issue).

——. 1990c. "Patient Careers in End-Stage Renal Failure." *Social Science and Medicine* 30: 1211–24.

Geyer, S. 1999. *Macht Unglück krank? Lebenskrisen und die Entwicklung von Krankheiten.* [Does Misfortune Lead to Disease? Life Crises and the Development of Diseases]. Weinheim: Juventa.

Geyer, S. and R. Peter. 1999. "Occupational Status and All-Cause Mortality: A Study with Health Insurance Data from Nordrhein-Westfalen, Germany." *European Journal of Public Health* 9: 115–21.

Härtel, U. 1996. "Frauen und Herz-Kreislauf-Erkrankungen" [Women and Cardiovascular Diseases]. Pp. 112–24 in G. Kaiser, J. Siegrist, E. Rosenfeld, and K. Wetzel-Vandai (eds.), *Die Zukunft der Medizin* [The Future of Medicine]. Frankfurt: Campus.

Härtel, U., U. Keil, U. Helmert, E. Greiser, S. Dai, F. Gutzwiller, A. R. Folsom, M. Szklo, A. D. White, J. Schreinber, and H. A. Tyroler. 1993. "The Association of Coronary Risk Factors with Educational Achievement. Results of the ARIC-MONICA Collaborative Studies." *Annals of Epidemiology* 3 (Supplement): S55–S61.

Haug, W. F. 1973. "Argumente für eine soziale Medizin IV." [Arguments for a Social Medicine IV]. *Das Argument* 78 15 (1–3).

Helmert, U., S. Shea, B. Herman, and E. Greiser. 1990. "Relationship of Social Class Characteristics and Risk Factors for Coronary Heart Disease in West Germany." *Public Health* 104: 399–416.

Helmert, U., A. Mielck, and S. Shea. 1997. "Poverty and Health in West Germany." *Sozial-und Präventivmedizin* 42: 276–85.

Helmert, U., S. Shea, and U. Maschewsky-Schneider 1995. "Social Class and Cardiovascular Disease Risk Factor Changes in West-Germany from 1984 to 1991." *European Journal of Public Health* 2: 103–8.

Iliffe, S. and H.-U. Deppe 1996. *Health Care in Europe: Competition or Solidarity?* Frankfurt am Main: Campus.

Kaupen-Haas, H. 1969. *Stabilität und Wandel ärztlicher Autorität* [Stability and Change of Medical Authority]. Stuttgart: Enke.

Knesebeck, O.v.d. 1998. *Subjektive Gesundheit im Alter. Soziale, psychische und somatische Einflüsse* [Subjective Health Among the Aged. The Impact of Social, Psychological, and Somatic Factors]. Münster: LIT.

Kongstvedt, P. R. 1996. *The Managed Health Care Handbook*. Gaithersburg/Maryland: Aspen.

Lüschen, Guenther, William C. Cockerham, and Gerhard Kunz (eds.). 1989. *Health and Illness in America and Germany*. München: Oldenbourg.

Lüschen, Guenther, William C. Cockerham, J. van der Zee, F. Stevens, J. Diedericks, M. Ferrando, A. d'Houtaud, R. Peters, T. Abel, and S. Niemann (eds.). 1995. *Health Systems in the European Union: Diversity, Convergence and Integration*. München: Oldenbourg.

Lüschen, Guenther, S. Niemann, and P. Apelt 1997. "The Integration of Two Health Systems: Social Stratification, Work and Health in East and West Germany." *Social Science and Medicine* 44: 883–99.

Mackenbach, J. P., A. E. Kunst, A. E. Cavelaars, F. Groenhof, and J. J. Geurts 1997. "Socioeconomic Inequalities in Morbidity and Mortality in Western Europe." *Lancet* 349: 1655–9.

Manz, R. and W. Kirch (eds.). 1999. *Public Health Research and Practice: Report of the Public Health Research Association Saxony 1993–1998*. Regensburg: Roderer.

Maschewsky-Schneider, U., B. Babitsch, and A. Ducki. 1998. "Geschlecht und Gesundheit." ["Gender and Health"]. Pp. 357–70 in K. Hurrelmann and U. Laaser (eds.), *Handbuch Gesundheitswissenschaften* [Handbook of Public Health]. Weinheim: Juventa.

Mielck, A. (ed.). 1994. *Krankheit und soziale Ungleichheit. Ergebnisse der sozialepidemio-logischen Forschung in Deutschland*. [Illness and Social Inequality: Results of Research in Social Epidemiology in Germany]. Opladen: Leske & Budrich.

Mühlhauser, I., H. Overmann, R. Bender, U. Bott, V. Jörgens, C. Trautner, J. Siegrist, and M. Berger. 1998. "Social Status and the Quality of Care for Adult People with Type 1 Diabetes – A Population Based Study." *Diabetologia* 41: 1139–50.

Müller, P., W. Gaebal, B. Bandelow, W. Kopcke, M. Linden, F. Müller-Spahn, A. Pietzcker, and J. Tegeler 1998. "Zur sozialen Situation schizophrener Patienten." ["The Social Status of Schizophrenic Patients"]. *Nervenarzt* 69: 204–9.

Müller, R. and R. Rosenbrock (eds.). 1998. *Betriebliches Gesundheitsmanagement, Arbeitsschutz und Gesundheitsförderung – Bilanz und Perspektiven*. [Occupational Health Management, Worker Protection, and Health Promotion]. St.Augustin: Asgard.

Organisation for Economic Cooperation and Development (OECD) (ed.). 1997. *Länderberichte. Deutschland*. Paris: OECD-Publications.

Pfaff, H. 1989. *Streabewältigung und soziale Unterstützung. Zur sozialen Regulierung individuellen Wohlbefindens*. [Coping and Social Support]. Weinheim: Deutscher Studien Verlag.

Pflanz, M. and J. Siegrist 1978. "Basic Assumptions in Teaching Medical Sociology in Medical Schools. The Case of West- Germany." Pp. 107–17 in Y. Nuyens and J. Vansteekiste (eds.), *Teaching Medical Sociology*. Leiden: Nijhoff, Social Science Division.

Raspe, H. H. 1983. *Aufklärung und Information im Krankenhaus*. [Information and Communication in Hospitals]. Göttingen: Vandenhoek & Ruprecht.

Rohde, J. J. 1962. *Soziologie des Krankenhauses*. [Sociology of Hospitals]. Stuttgart: Enke.

Schneider, M. 1998. *Gesundheitssysteme im internationalen Vergleich*. [International Comparison of Health Care Systems]. Augsburg: BASYS.

Schwartz, F. W., Badura, R. Leidl, H. Raspe, and J. Siegrist (eds.). 1998. *Das Public Health Buch*. [The Public Health Book]. München: Urban & Schwarzenberg.

Siegrist, J. 1978. *Arbeit und Interaktion im Krankenhaus*. [Work and Interaction in the Hospital]. Stuttgart: Enke.

——. 1995. *Medizinische Soziologie*. [Medical Sociology]. München: Urban & Schwarzenberg.

——. 1996. *Soziale Krisen und Gesundheit*. [Social Crises and Health]. Göttingen: Hogrefe.

Siegrist, K. 1986. *Sozialer Rückhalt und kardiovaskuläres Risiko*. [Social Support and Cardiovascular Risk]. München: Minerva.

Slesina, W., A. Schroer, and C. von Ferber. 1988. "Soziologie und menschengerechte Arbeits gestaltung." ["Sociology and Human Working Conditions"]. *Soziale Welt* 39: 205–23.

Slesina, W., F. R. Beuels, and R. Sochert. 1998. *Betriebliche Gesundheitsförderung*. [Occupational Health Promotion]. Weinheim: Juventa.

Statistisches Bundesamt (ed.). 1998. *Gesundheitsbericht für Deutschland*. [Health Report on Germany]. Stuttgart: Metzler-Poeschel.

Trojan, A. and S. Nickel. 1999. "Wiederholte Patientenbefragungen als Instrument zur Evaluation von qualitätsverbessernden Interventionen im Krankenhaus" ["Patients' Surveys as a Measure to Evaluate Interventions in Hospitals"]. In R. Buck and H. Raspe (eds.), *Patienten zufriedenheit in stationären Einrichtungen* [Patient Satisfaction in Patient Facilities], (in print).

von Ferber, C. (ed.). 1987. *Forschungsverbund: Laienpotential, Patientenaktivierung, Gesundheitsselbsthilfe und professionelle Dienstleistungen* [Research Network: Lay Potential, Activating Patients, Self-Help and Professional Services]. Berlin. Springer.

von Troschke, J., L. Klaes, and U. Maschewsky-Schneider (eds.). 1991. *Erfolge gemeindebezogener Prävention*. [Success of Prevention Measures at the Community Level]. St. Augustin: Asgard.

Waltz, M. 1994. *Social Isolation and Social Mediators of Stress and Illness*. Münster: LIT.

Weiner, H. 1992. *Perturbing the Organism. The Biology of Stressful Experience*. Chicago: University of Chicago Press.

17

Society, Health, and Health Care in Sweden

Örjan Hemström

The epidemiologist Geoffrey Rose (1985: 34) argued that if we are to understand the incidence and prevalence of disease in a society, "we need to study characteristics of populations, not characteristics of individuals." There are probably three major social determinants of population health, namely material wealth, social structure (i.e. political climate, occupational structure, social networks, health care organization), and lifestyles (behaviors), which are intimately related. In order to determine which factors may cause or prevent disease and illness, historical changes are important. Blau (1977) argued that the size and number of different population groups are important constituents of a society or a collectivity as are, changes in numbers; size also changes the social relations between groups of people. We may hypothesize that changes in social indicators may change population health, and that the share of such indicators in the population contribute to health differences between populations. Notions of "healthy" and "unhealthy" societies are relevant in this respect (Qvarsell 1994; Wilkinson 1996). I will attempt a brief analysis in this area by comparing some population characteristics of Sweden with those of other countries. This will include a description of the development of socioeconomic differences in health in Sweden, as well as a basic description of Swedish health care organization. Equality topics have been central in Swedish (and Nordic) medical sociology, and the description below is tilted toward such research (sociology in medicine).[1]

Sweden has been recognized as having lower mortality than most other affluent countries (Thom et al. 1985). In 1996, Swedish men can expect to live 76.5 years, and only the male population in Japan has a higher life expectancy (77 years). The life expectancy for women in Sweden is five years above that of men (81.5 years) – less than half a year shorter than that of women in Switzerland, France, and Hong Kong, and two years shorter than in Japan, as shown in table 17.1. Life expectancy may be a crude indicator of population health,

Table 17.1 Sex-specific life expectancy at birth for a selection of primarily low mortality countries in descending order

Country and year(s)	Women	Country and year(s)	Men
Japan (1996)	83.59	Japan (1996)	77.01
Switzerland (1995–6)	81.90	**Sweden (1996)**	**76.51**
France (1995)	81.86	Hong Kong (1996)	76.34
Hong Kong (1996)	81.82	Iceland (1995–6)	76.20
Sweden (1996)	**81.53**	Switzerland (1995–6)	75.70
Norway (1996)	81.07	Israel (1994)	75.49
Australia (1994–6)	81.05	Norway (1996)	75.37
Canada (1992)	80.89	Cyprus (1994–5)	75.31
Italy (1994)	80.74	Australia (1994–6)	75.22
Belgium (1994)	80.61	Greece (1995)	75.02
Iceland (1995–96)	80.59	Singapore (1997)	75.00
Finland (1996)	80.52	Malta (1996)	74.94
Spain (1990–1)	80.49	Canada (1992)	74.55
Greece (1995)	80.20	The Netherlands (1995–6)	74.52
The Netherlands (1995–6)	80.20	Italy (1994)	74.34
Austria (1996)	80.19	United Kingdom (1996)	74.31
Malta (1996)	79.81	Maccau (1990–5)	74.30
Cyprus (1994–5)	79.75	Austria (1996)	73.93
Germany (1994–5)	79.72	France (1995)	73.92
United Kingdom (1996)	79.48	Belgium (1994)	73.88
Israel (1994)	79.38	Cuba (1990–5)	73.50
Maccau (1990–5)	79.30	New Zealand (1992–4)	73.44
Singapore (1997)	79.20	Spain (1990–91)	73.40
New Zealand (1992–4)	79.11	Germany (1994–5)	73.29
Luxembourg (1990–5)	79.00	Finland (1996)	73.02
USA (1995)	78.90	United Arab Emirates (1990–5)	72.90
Portugal (1995–6)	78.57	Costa Rica (1990–5)	72.89
Puerto Rico (1990–2)	78.50	Denmark (1994–5)	72.62
Slovenia (1995–6)	78.25	USA (1995)	72.50
Chile (1997)	78.10	Brunei (1990–5)	72.40
Ireland (1990–2)	77.87	Ireland (1990–2)	72.30
Denmark (1994–5)	77.82	Chile (1997)	72.13
Costa Rica (1990–5)	77.60	Luxembourg (1990–5)	72.10
Cuba (1990–5)	77.30	Panama (1995)	71.78
Czech Rep. (1996)	77.27	Portugal (1995–6)	71.27
Brunei (1990–5)	77.10	Slovenia (1995–6)	70.79
Poland (1996)	76.57	Czech Rep. (1996)	70.37
Panama (1995)	76.35	Sri Lanka (1990–5)	69.70
Slovakia (1995)	76.33	Puerto Rico (1990–2)	69.60
United Arab Emirates (1990–5)	75.30	Bosnia-Herzegovina (1990–5)	69.50
Bosnia-Herzegovina (1990–5)	75.10	Slovakia (1995)	68.40
Sri Lanka (1990–5)	74.20	Poland (1996)	68.12
Russia (1995)	71.70	Russia (1995)	58.27

Source: Demographic Yearbook 1997, table 22. New York: United Nations 1999.

nevertheless it is often used to compare the health situation between countries (e.g. Preston 1975; Wilkinson 1996). So by this health measure, Sweden seems to be one of the healthiest societies; only Japan is clearly healthier than Sweden in this respect. In the list of countries in table 17.1, one could note that some developing countries (Cuba, Costa Rica, Chile) have as long or longer life expectancy than a number of more affluent countries (USA, Denmark, Finland, Ireland), indicating that economic prosperity only partly explains population health.[2]

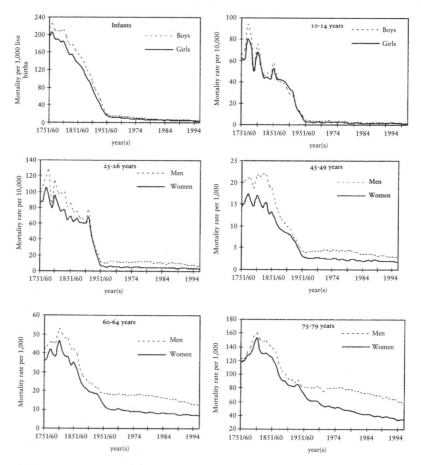

Figure 17.1 Long-term development of sex-specific mortality in Sweden in sex selected age groups. For the period 1751–60/1951–60 data are ten-year averages; for 1961/5 five-year average and for 1966–96 annual data are given

Sources: Historical statistics of Sweden. Part 1: Population (second edition). Stockholm: Statistics Sweden, 1969 [for the period 1751/60–1967]. Causes of death 1968–96. Annual reports, published by Statistics Sweden for the years 1968–93, and by The National Board of Health and Welfare for the years 1994–6.

TRENDS IN MORTALITY AND ILLNESS IN SWEDEN

The long-term development of mortality in Sweden is shown in figure 17.1. In all age groups there was a steep mortality decline in the century from 1850 to 1950 (the exception to this was a mortality increase among young adults in 1910–20). For older persons the decline started around 1800, and for infants already in the eighteenth century. In the age span of 10–50 years there were rather strong fluctuations during most of the period before 1850. After 1950, Swedish women of all adult age groups experienced a continuation of the declining trend, and for women in the age group 75–79 years the decline was only slightly less steep than in the period before 1950. Middle-aged men experienced a slight increase, and older men a stagnation, in the 1960s and 1970s.

There are no data on long-term trends in ill health. From 1975 there are annual national surveys including a number of components of social living conditions and ill health indicators. Self-perceived general health is a good indicator of an individual's health status, probably less biased by propensity to seek contact with health care professionals than most other health indicators. Nearly all groups reported better health in 1995 as compared with 1975 as seen in figure 17.2. The only exception to this was for women aged 25–44, although the prevalence of self-reported illness is very low (<3%) before 45 years of age, and changes therefore are indeed small. Women and men report ill health roughly to the same extent. We should note that 45–64 year-old men had an excess in ill health over women in 1975 which had disappeared 20 years later. This corresponds well with the development of male mortality in these ages in the period. In fact, this was the only age group where there has been any notable narrowing of the mortality gender gap in Sweden (Hemström 1998: 19). In sum, declining mortality and improved health has characterized the development in Sweden in the last two decades.

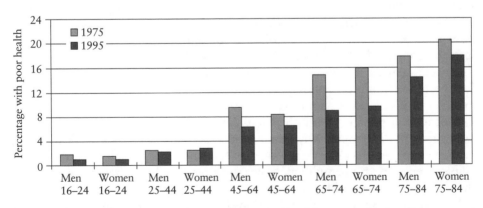

Figure 17.2 Proportion with self-perceived general health as poor for Swedish men and women in five age groups in 1975 and 1995

Source: Statistics Sweden 1997a. Data from Swedish Surveys of Living Conditions (ULF).

ARE SOCIAL STRUCTURES AND LIFESTYLES HEALTHY IN SWEDEN?

Occupational Structure, Poverty, and Social Cohesion

The proportional size of socioeconomic classes are plausible explanations of health variation across time and countries. The replacement of manual by non-manual work probably is a major force of secular mortality decline. In Sweden, changes in the proportion of non-manual workers in manufacturing industry was related to men's as well as to women's mortality decline after 1945 (Hemström 1999a). By European standards, Sweden seems to have a relatively healthy class structure. Data from Kunst (1997: 94), for men aged 45–59 years,[3] show that Denmark, Sweden, Switzerland, Norway, and Italy had about 50 percent non-manual workers around 1980. The corresponding figures were about 45 percent for France and United Kingdom, 36 to 39 percent for Ireland and Finland, and 31 to 33 percent for Portugal and Spain.[4] For Sweden, and a number of European countries, the term "service" or "non-manual society" was relevant already in the 1980s. The average skill level of jobs has increased since then. The corresponding proportion of non-manual workers were 55 percent in Sweden in 1990.[5]

The social class structure should be related to the educational level of the population. Survey data from 11 European countries show that the proportion of the population that have completed more than a basic education was clearly largest in Switzerland[6] (Cavelaars et al. 1998). Sweden was somewhere in the middle, although Norway, France, Italy, and Spain have clearly lower proportions of people above basic educational levels (ranging 14–46%) than has Sweden (55% among men and 54% among women) in ages 25–69 years.

From national surveys it has been observed that, no matter the type of poverty measured, poor people more often report ill health than others. In Sweden, the proportion of poor people has increased in the 1990s (Halleröd 1999). Halleröd found that those defined as materially poor (by household consumption characteristics) report particularly poor health in Sweden. In comparative research poor people in Sweden tend less often to be old people or single parents, but instead young adults (Halleröd 1999; Saunders, Halleröd, and Matheson 1994). The rapid increase in youth unemployment in the period 1991–3 is one reason for the concentration of poor people among young adults. Social policy may explain why old people and families with children make up relatively low proportions of poor people in Sweden (Halleröd 1999).[7] Shortcomings in this policy may partly explain why young adults often are poor today. For instance, most welfare revenues are based on the "income-loss" principle and previous employment. Youth unemployment has until recently been low in Sweden, and the shortcomings not widely recognized.

Nevertheless, Sweden (and other Nordic countries) has among the lowest proportions of poor people in western Europe, around 6 percent by a European standard (Vogel 1997: 634). Southern European countries, United Kingdom, and Ireland have considerably higher proportions of poor people (15–47%). Thus, Sweden still has a low proportion of poor people, which may contribute to its internationally low mortality rates. The situation seems to be particularly favorable among old people. Poverty decreased by three different measures in the age group 65–74 years between 1986/7 and 1994/5 (Halleröd 1999).

Income inequality and social cohesion are also thought to be related to population mortality rates and life expectancy (Wilkinson 1996). The issue of income inequality and health is far from unproblematic, since different measures could lead to different conclusions (Judge et al. 1998). Whether income inequality is an important determinant of population health or not, Sweden belongs to one of the five countries in Europe (Denmark, Norway, Finland, Sweden, and Belgium) with the lowest such inequality in the early 1990s (Björklund 1998).[8] There was a trend toward greater income inequality in Sweden between the 1980s and 1990s, which seems to have been more of a general trend in many countries, although reduced income inequality occurred in Italy, Belgium, and Norway (ibid.).

It has been shown that the degree to which people are members of voluntary associations (as one example of how social cohesion can be measured) are related to health status both at individual and aggregate level (Carlson 1998). The greater the proportion of members in civil associations (excluding religious and political ones),[9] the better the health tends to be. Carlson observed that especially the Nordic countries and the Netherlands have high proportions of people in such associations (ibid.: 1360). This measure of social cohesion and low income inequality may both contribute to relatively favorable survival in Sweden. This should apply equally to the Netherlands and Norway – which also have been found to have low mortality for long periods (Thom et al. 1985). Denmark were among these until the 1980s, but the development of Danish survival has been less favorable in recent times, probably due to increased alcohol consumption, high prevalence of smoking, and increased relative poverty and social isolation (Chenet et al. 1996; Osler 1999).

The indicators presented above should be viewed as the beginning of a more detailed large-scale analysis. Obviously, there are unfavorable social indicators for Sweden also, such as relatively high proportions of immigrants and social isolation. Social isolation increased from 16 to 21 percent between 1975 and 1995 (Vogel 1997). Immigrants have poorer health than other Swedes, and their social situation, compared with native Swedes, is unfavorable for indicators such as unemployment, poor social network, and financial difficulties (Emami 1997; Vogel 1997). Vogel observes that immigrants, young adults, and lone parents are the groups who have experienced the greatest decline in social conditions in the 1990s.

Lifestyle Factors

A number of lifestyle indicators show a change toward healthier behavior in Sweden in the period 1975–85, especially cigarette consumption which is related to cardiovascular diseases, certain cancers, and respiratory diseases. As shown in figure 17.3a, per capita alcohol consumption was reduced between 1975 and 1985, but has been relatively stable after that year. Dietary changes may be more complex, although at least fat and butter consumption show a decreasing trend after 1984 in figure 17.3b. The decline in cigarette smoking has clearly contributed to the narrowing of the gender gap in mortality after 1980. This is especially the case for the rapid decline in mortality from ischemic heart disease among men (Hemström 1998, 1999a).

Differences in per capita cigarette and alcohol consumption may help to explain part of country differences in health and survival. Data on per capita alcohol consumption for 38 countries showed that the only countries in Europe having lower consumption than Sweden were Norway, Iceland, and Turkey (FHI and CAN 1997). France, Portugal, and Hungary are examples of high

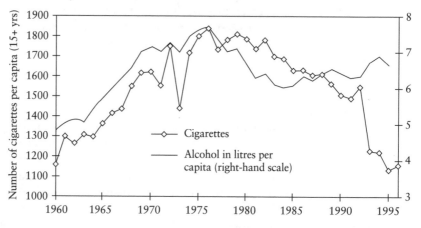

Figure 17.3a Trends in cigarette and alcohol consumption in Sweden, 1960–95
Source: Swedish Statistical Yearbooks (cigarette consumption) and FHI and CAN (1997).

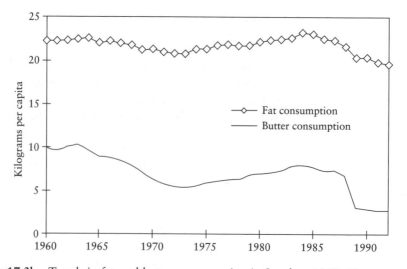

Figure 17.3b Trends in fat and butter consumption in Sweden, 1960–92
Source: Own calculations from data given in Swedish statistical yearbooks, published by Statistics Sweden (butter consumption was used in Hemström 1999a).

consumption countries.[10] For a number of European countries, recent data on gender-specific smoking prevalence by country is given in figure 17.4. Data are from national surveys during the period 1991–5. Sweden has the lowest prevalence of smoking for men (22%). For women, the lowest smoking prevalence is found in Italy (17%). Swedish women had a higher smoking prevalence than men (24%). This however, is a lower prevalence than for men in all other countries and clearly lower than for women in Denmark, Norway, and the Netherlands (above 30% female smokers).

Thus, for smoking and alcohol indicators, Sweden tends to be among the healthier populations in terms of prevalence rates and per capita consumption. This holds true particularly for Swedish men (when compared to men in other countries). There may be other lifestyle indicators which may not have developed in a similar favorable direction in Sweden, such as increased urbanization and more sedentary lifestyles.

Development of Socioeconomic Differences in Health

It is believed that social and health policy in Sweden has substantially narrowed health and survival differences between population groups. For instance, in the Black report it was suggested (without any statistical facts) that inequalities in health had disappeared in Sweden (Townsend and Davidson 1992). Considerable Swedish research has now demonstrated that socioeconomic differences in mortality (and excess mortality among manual workers) exists in infancy, childhood (Östberg 1996), throughout adulthood to old age (Diderichsen 1991; Otterblad-Olausson 1991; Vågerö 1992) and for men and women (Vågerö and Lundberg 1995). Morbidity measures – physical as well as mental – point in a similar direction (e.g. Lundberg 1990, 1992). Trends indicate a widening of mortality differences from the 1960s until the first half of the 1980s (Vågerö and Lundberg 1995). Industrial workers' mortality rate increased among men aged 45–69 years during the 1970s when women and men in non-manual occupations experienced a continued mortality decline (Diderichsen and Hallq-

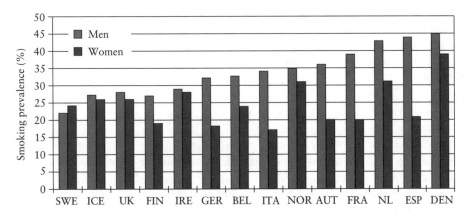

Figure 17.4   Gender-specific prevalence of smoking in a number of European countries
Source: Statistics Sweden 1997b.

vist 1997, 1998). In the latter half of the 1980s however, differences between manual and non-manual occupational groups did not grow (Gullberg and Vågerö 1996). Recent data show that unskilled female workers have not experienced any reduction in mortality from the 1980s to the 1990s, so that occupational class differences tend to increase among women while these have not changed among men (Lundberg 1998a).

In comparative research, the relative mortality difference between manual and non-manual workers is the same in Sweden as in most other western European countries, that is around 1.4 times excess mortality among male manual workers (Mackenbach et al. 1997). Comparing the mortality rates, it becomes clear that both manual and non-manual Swedish workers have low absolute mortality in relation to other countries (Vågerö and Erikson 1997).

Sweden seems to have some of the largest health inequalities by educational level, both among men and women (Cavelaars et al. 1998). In comparison to mortality, prevalence rates of ill health show greater variation between western European countries which might be due to methodological inconsistencies, including differences in non-response patterns in different surveys. However, since excess mortality among manual workers exists in all countries for which data are available, no matter the cause of death structure (Kunst 1997: 117), and from infancy to old age (Vågerö 1992), it is suggested that explanations are embedded in the social structure of society (Lundberg 1998a).

Lundberg (1990, 1992) found three important explanations to social class differences in morbidity in Sweden: the physical work environment, health behaviors like smoking and alcohol consumption, and childhood living conditions. In a later article, he notes that the contribution from health behaviors tend to increase relative to the work environment and childhood conditions (Lundberg 1998a). Lifestyle factors (e.g. alcohol drinking habits, smoking, and risk taking) are probably more important predictors of mortality than of morbidity, while working conditions may be more important determinants of morbidity (Hemström 1998). The widening mortality differences between socioeconomic groups and between men and women in Sweden during the period 1960–80 may have changes in alcohol and cigarette consumption as common explanations. After the 1960s, alcohol-related mortality has become more common among manual workers in Sweden – also relative to non-manual workers (Leifman 1998). A similar class-shift applies to smoking behavior.

Women's Employment and Health

International comparisons of occupational classes have a severe gender bias in that women may be incorrectly classified. It is debatable how women should be classified; on their own, by a household, or by a husband's class (Erikson 1984). Because traditionally there has been a relationship between family status and employment status for women (few wage-earning married mothers), we may postulate that the gender system cut across other measures of socioeconomic position for women. One outcome is the smaller class differences in health among women than among men that are widely reported (Koskinen and Martelin 1994; Vågerö and Lundberg 1995; Vallin 1995; Lundberg 1998a). Professional women may more often be unmarried and childless relative to professional men (Emslie, Hunt, and Macintyre 1999).[11] European comparisons of women show that educational differences in illness are relatively larger in Scandinavian countries than in the Netherlands, Switzerland, Germany, and Spain (Cavelaars 1998: 22). This is not surprising because Scandinavian countries have high proportions of employed women, in particular among women aged 55–64 years (Vågerö and Lahelma 1998: 75). If we recall that differences in work environments are important explanations to socioeconomic differences in ill health (Lundberg 1992), we should find larger health inequalities among women when labor force participation is high. When labor force participation is low, a large proportion of women have relatively similar (unpaid) work environments in the home, which cannot cause any great variation in illness among women.

Sweden is a suitable case for analyzing the health effects of increased female employment. It has been debated whether paid work is beneficial or harmful for women's health, although most evidence points at prolonged lives for employed women (Vågerö and Lahelma 1998). When the increase in women's employment was the greatest in the 1970s (from 54% to 72% employed women), women to a large extent entered relatively "healthy jobs," that is jobs characterized by low mortality rates (Hemström 1999b). Although Swedish women's mortality declined throughout the 1970s and 1980s, high rates of female smoking may have counteracted any survival benefits from increased employment rates (Nathanson 1995). Danish women, for instance, had nearly 40 percent smokers in the 1990s (figure 17.3a), and they had little improvement in survival during the 1980s (Chenet et al. 1996).

In the period 1981–91 structural changes may have disproportionately hit traditional female jobs in the public sector with increased job stress and job insecurity (Szulkin and Tåhlin 1994). Health care work, care for the elderly, and teaching work are among these occupational groups.

THE SWEDISH HEALTH CARE SYSTEM IN TRANSITION

Roemer (1985: 31) distinguished five components used to describe a country's health care system, which I will partly follow below: organization of programs (governmental, voluntary, private), production of resources (e.g. manpower, facilities), economic support (charity, voluntary, or social insurance, governmental revenues), management (planning, regulation, evaluation), and delivery of services (primary, secondary, tertiary).

Organization of Programs

In 1968, health and social issues were integrated under the Ministry of Social Affairs (National Board of Health and Welfare [NBHW] 1977). It is stated that "Swedish health care has a decentralized organization. By law the national parliament (Riksdagen) sets goals and demands for health care"[12] (NBHW 1998: 73). Typical goals are equal access to health care and universal inclusion of all citizens. The latter is a common feature of many European countries, although in the US only about 40 percent of the population are covered by insurance for hospital care (Jönsson 1990).

Decentralization refers to the relatively independent role played by the county councils in Sweden (23 today) which are responsible for health care delivery in their geographical areas (NBHW 1998), including the right to collect regional taxes. Each county council has at least one major hospital. The health care act of 1982 clearly gives the prime responsibility for health care within the county councils (Lindgren 1990). Within the county councils there are a number of primary care centers ("Vårdcentraler"). After a reform in 1994 individuals in a catchment-area of a primary care center could choose their own family physician (Andersen, Smedby, and Vågerö 1999).

The vast majority of health care is provided by the public sector in Sweden (Lindgren 1990), although the number of private hospitals (often small-scale) has increased greatly in the 1990s (280). Today, they outnumber large-scale public hospitals (86) (NBHW 1998). About 20 percent of hospital beds are now in the private sector (Diderichsen 1999). It is particularly nursing homes and ambulatory home care facilities that are now privately run in Sweden, while 95 percent of beds in emergency units are still found in public hospitals (Andersen et al. 1999).

Some important changes that have occurred in Sweden are the transfer of the responsibility for mental health care from the state to county councils in 1963 (Lindgren 1990), while in 1992 municipalities took on the responsibility of long-term health care for the elderly ("Ädelreformen"). Another reform was implemented in 1995, when municipalities were given more responsibility to serve and support people with certain long-term mental illnesses (NBHW 1999). Thus, much health care is now statistically regarded as social care. In 1995, municipalities employed 9 percent of physicians and more than one-fifth of registered nurses (NBHW 1998). Recent changes are in the direction of increased decentralization and privatization of health care.

Resources, Management, and Financing

Health care facilities available for the Swedish population have changed greatly in the last 20 years. There has been a steady increase in the number of physicians per inhabitant (from 124 per 100,000 persons in 1968 to 305 in 1995). This is partly true also for registered nurses, although in the 1990s there were approximately 1,050 registered nurses per 100,000 persons. For other personnel involved in patient treatment (e.g. psychologists, assistant nurses, auxiliary nurses, physiotherapists, etc.) there has been a reduction in the 1990s (figure 17.5). Many auxiliary nurses lost their jobs in this period (Diderichsen 1999). In 1975 there were 880 hospitals and 680 primary care centers (NBHW 1977). Twenty years later there were only 366 hospitals, but the number of primary care centers had increased to 905 (NBHW 1998).

Regulation and evaluation of health care is a central responsibility of the National Board of Health and Welfare. It regulates and controls professional health care personnel. The follow-up of the 1995 mental health care reform is an example of the evaluations performed by the NBHW (1999). Follow-ups of how communities have managed their increased obligations in recent years, due to the decentralization of health care, is likely to be a major task for NBHW in the near future.

About 73 percent of the Swedish health care system is financed by county councils' income taxes, 16 percent is from user charges, and 11 percent is financed by grants from the national government (Diderichsen 1999). The grants from the national government are meant to compensate poorer counties and counties with differential need (such as a large proportion of old people) to ensure some equality on a national level. Patient charges have increased in the 1990s, including reduced state subsidies for prescribed medical goods.

Sweden has decreased its relative spending on health services from 9.5 percent of the gross domestic product in 1981 to 7.2 percent in 1995 (NBHW 1998). Such reduction in spending on health care has not been observed in other countries, and a number of countries, such as the US, spend more than 10 percent of GDP on health care (Andersen et al. 1999). Also, considering that a substantial part of health care (for the elderly) was transferred to municipalities in 1992 (about 1% of GDP), there has been a "true" decrease in health care expenditure that began as early as the 1980s (ibid.; Diderichsen 1999). Some argue that we should also look at the proportion of people employed in health care in order to better estimate the relative weight of health care resources in a country (Anell and Persson 1998). Such data show that the proportion of people employed in the health care sector was stable in the years 1988 to 1993 (slightly above 10%), but fell to 8.5 percent in 1996 (NBHW 1998).

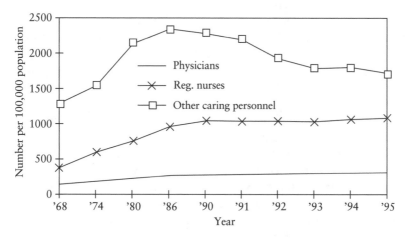

Figure 17.5 Development of the number of health care personnel with patient contacts in Sweden 1968–95

Source: National Board of Health and Welfare 1998.

Delivery of Services

It used to be that Swedish health care was heavily focused on hospital inpatient care (Diderichsen et al. 1992: 110). One indicator of this fact is that three-quarters of physicians used to be employed in inpatient care. Although a relatively large share of outpatient health care has been provided by hospitals in Sweden (i.e. Lindgren 1990), primary health care probably has had less importance in Sweden than in other comparable countries, such as in Norway or Britain.[13] There were numerous political suggestions that primary health care ought to be extended in Sweden, but it seems that it was not until the 1980s that health care provided at primary care centers clearly increased relative to hospital care (Diderichsen et al. 1992).

Some forms of preventive care have had a special status in Sweden and are still provided free of charge. These are maternal care and care for infants and pre-school children, as well as medical and dental examinations of school children. A recent comparative analysis notes that infant mortality in the most privileged areas of London is higher than in the most unprivileged areas of Stockholm. The authors interpret this as being partly caused by preventive care at maternal and child care centers in Sweden (Kallner, Gilljam, and Sandstedt 1999).[14]

Effects of the Recent Health Care Transition in Sweden

The major components of the recent transition of health care in Sweden are decentralization, increased physician supply, reduction in hospital facilities, increased share of privately run health care, and increased user charges. In addition, there has been a slight decline in health care expenditure as measured by percent of GDP, as well as by percent of health care personnel in the employed population. Much of the changes are referred to as cost containment due to the economic recession in Sweden in the early 1990s (Andersen et al. 1999). Due to the relatively rapid transformations of the health care system, Sweden may be sociologically analyzed as an instance of natural experimentation. How have the working conditions changed for physicians and other health care personnel? What has happened to equal access to care? How are the growing numbers of old people affected? It seems obvious that changes have led to social and health consequences, and not only positive consequences.

The clearest instance of negative effects is working conditions within the health care sector. Many auxiliary nurses have gone on unemployment (Diderichsen 1999). Of those still employed, many have experienced deteriorating working conditions such as decreased job security (temporary job contracts) and time pressure (Ahlberg-Hultén 1999). The shortage of personnel and increased charges may also have caused social inequalities in health care use. In the mid-1990s social inequalities in health service use appear in a way not observed for at least three previous decades in Sweden (Whitehead et al. 1997). No such inequalities are present in Britain.[15]

There may have been negative consequences for old people (and their close relatives) as well. Charges for nursing homes and ambulatory home care have increased, and the availability of such help has decreased as well. Usually, this means that the contribution of help from close relatives has to replace public assistance. It has been noted that informal health care, most often provided by an adult daughter or a wife (less often a husband or a son), has increased in the 1990s (Gustafsson and Szebehely 1996). It is likely that the transition of health care in Sweden affected women more than men, by increasing pressure on them as professional caregivers but also by increasing the pressure to be informal care-givers.

PRIMARY PREVENTION

Three main strategies to increase public health were distinguished by Carlsson and Arvidsson (1994): (1) juridical legislation and collective decision-making toward well-defined threats to health; (2) information about healthy and unhealthy behaviors ("health education"); and (3) general social changes or transitions. Carlsson and Arvidsson mention that collective efforts in areas 1 and 2 have characterized the history of Swedish public health policy. In legislative sources it is suggested that public health efforts should focus on diseases which (1) take life and health from the expected length of life, (2) are unequally distributed between socioeconomic groups and between men and women, and (3) are possible to prevent.

Primary prevention can be traced to efforts to reduce infant mortality as early as the eighteenth century. It was also part of investments in the water and sewage systems in the nineteenth century, and campaigns about personal hygiene in the early twentieth century (Palmblad 1990; Sundin 1992; Qvarsell 1994). From a historical summary, it is noted that trained midwives contributed to the rapid decline in infant mortality from the early nineteenth century with "conscious campaigns for better child care" (Sundin 1992: 520).[16] Qvarsell (1994) mentions that the idea of reducing poverty in order to improve health was politically debated in the first three decades of the twentieth century, indicating that social factors may have already been recognized as contributors to ill health at this time. Health issues may also have been prioritized politically. Lundberg (1998b) quoted Bäck from 1765, that poverty and misery in disadvantaged groups cause much poor health. Thus, there may have been a long tradition linking social factors to health in Sweden, as well as a belief in the possibility to change such factors in order to improve health.

Swedish alcohol policy is known to be restrictive (Carlsson and Arvidsson 1994). At present, middle- and strong-beer (>2.8% alcohol by weight), all wine, and all spirits are sold only at special shops (closed on Saturdays and Sundays). The restriction has its origin in a strong temperance movement in the early twentieth century which led to the implementation of a rationing system of alcohol in the period 1915 to 1920, and to 1955, and alcohol policy has remained restrictive (Leifman 1995). Similar alcohol policies are found in Norway, Iceland, and Finland. In recent years, restrictions on alcohol have been seriously questioned in Sweden. Harmonization with other countries of the European Union is supposed to take place in the nearest future (Leifman

1996). Whether changes in Swedish alcohol policy will lead to more alcohol-related problems is the main question in present political debates.

In an historical–sociological analysis, it was found that attempts to reduce health risks in the work environment have been relatively useless in Sweden, although in a few areas, such as chemical exposures, preventive efforts have sometimes been successful (Gustafsson 1994). Frick (1994) concludes that work environment reforms in the 1970s did not reduce occupational accidents and illnesses. It seems that it was not until the mid-1980s that work-related injuries clearly decreased in Sweden (Nationella folkhälsokommittén 1999: 23). No similar decline has been reported for work-related diseases, which in fact increased steadily in the 1980s. In 1993, discussion increased as to what should be considered a work-related disease (ibid.). The policy change, rather than actual change in the indicators of improved working conditions, probably caused the "statistical decline" in work-related diseases after 1993. An evaluation of changes in the work environment due to prevention efforts seems to be positive for some indicators (chemical exposures, accidents) but not for others.

In the 1970s there was a growing emphasis on prevention in the form of anti-smoking campaigns, but also on advice concerning diets and physical exercise.[17] In 1992, the National Public Health Institute was introduced to help strengthen primary prevention in Sweden, focusing on areas such as alcohol and drugs, allergies, injuries, tobacco, diet, and physical exercise. An earlier Swedish study suggested that people in general are likely to respond slowly to advice given in prevention campaigns (Carlsson et al. 1979: 158–62).

DISCUSSION

In Sweden, prevention has been dominated by health information directed toward the whole population. Primary prevention ought to have partly influenced the fact that both smoking and alcohol consumption show a healthier profile in Sweden than in most other affluent countries.[18] Moreover, Sweden may have a relatively healthy society with regard to the social structure. The country has a high proportion of non-manual workers and low levels of poverty and income inequality.

The Swedish health care system was transformed in the 1990s, partly because of reduced resources allocated to health care, both as measured by percent of GDP and by percent of all workers employed within health care. Still, the forefront goal in Swedish health policy is that there should be equal access to care and attempts to reduce health inequalities.

Nevertheless, socioeconomic health inequalities in Sweden have been found to be similar to neighboring countries. An evaluation of primary prevention aimed at change in individual behaviors may demonstrate why the goal of reducing health inequalities has come to a halt in Sweden (and elsewhere). It is generally known that educated and affluent people are more responsive to health information (Vågerö and Illsley 1992: 230). A relevant example is given by a multi-level heart disease intervention program in Sweden (Norsjö). Those who had high levels of education improved their health behaviors (e.g. smoking, dietary habits, and physical exercise) more than others (Brännström et al. 1993). Therefore, an unintended consequence of health campaigns is increased relative health inequalities. People most in need of behavioral change to prevent later illness may be those who are least likely to "improve" their lifestyles (Brännström 1994).[19] Thus, do we need to implement unequal prevention to reduce health inequalities (Carlsson and Arvidsson 1994)? Primary prevention aimed at the whole population may well improve the whole population's health (in terms of life expectancy for instance), but prevention in the form of social change (such as reorganization of working conditions in a fundamental sense), is probably necessary to reduce health inequalities. This area of prevention involves more ideological and political conflicts than traditional areas of public health, and consequently is less likely to be established.

Recent changes in the health care sector probably have increased inequalities in health care use in Sweden. Whether or not such inequalities also influence inequalities in health and survival is unclear. Macintyre (1989) concluded that differences in health service use have no substantial influence on inequalities in health. As noted earlier, there were widening health inequalities in mortality among women (but not among men) between the 1980s and 1990s. The rapid transformation of the health care system is not a satisfactory explanation of the stagnation in unskilled female workers' survival. It is more important to elucidate the fact that these women are the most frequent smokers in Sweden today and that their work environments have developed in a negative, stressful direction.

On the positive side of the social and health situation for a number of subgroups, it is my impression that especially old people have benefited from the development of social welfare.[20] Simultaneously however, improved material resources in this group may have gone straight to pay for increased charges for health care, medical goods, and home care facilities. It seems that there has been continued improvements in social conditions for some subgroups also during the economic recession of the 1990s, while for others, such as young adults, female manual workers, immigrants, and single parents, social changes have been in the opposite direction. It might be that those who experienced unemployment during young adulthood in the 1990s will later develop disease, but it is still too early to be certain of this. From an international perspective, social changes in the 1990s have not substantially affected the general picture that Sweden is a relatively healthy society with relatively healthy people.

Acknowledgment

The author acknowledges his co-workers who contributed valuable comments on an earlier draft of this chapter, namely Per Carlsson, Marit Dahlén, Carolina Johansson, Carin Lennartsson, Bitte Modin, and Denny Vågerö.

Notes

1   Sociology of medicine, in particular in the area of health care organization and evaluations of health care, is also an important part of Swedish medical sociology.

2   In a demographic study of a large number of countries, it was concluded that (referring to the increase in life expectancy) "economic advance was not a major factor in that increase" (Preston 1975: 244).

3   The age and sex group with best country comparability.

4   Countries with low proportions of non-manual workers (e.g. Ireland, Finland, Portugal, Spain) have relatively large proportions of people in agricultural classes.

5   Own calculations of 1990 census data, for men aged 45–59 years in 1990. Those not gainfully working were excluded, as was made by Kunst. The social class measure was the Swedish socioeconomic classification which is slightly different from the EGP scheme applied by Kunst (1997). Nevertheless, data show an increase in non-manual work carried out also after 1980, which has been described elsewhere (Szulkin and Tåhlin 1994).

6   Approximately 85 percent of men and 75 percent of women.

7   Lone mothers receive benefits such as housing allowance, subsidized daycare charges, and social assistance (Hobson and Takahashi 1997).

8   Measured by the Gini coefficient. Other measures given by Björklund do not alter this picture. The same countries tend to be in the same end of the income inequality ladder, regardless of measurement type.

9   In some countries membership in political associations may be due to oppression (e.g. the former Soviet Union), and in others, membership in religious associations may be due to severe conflicts between religious parties (Northern Ireland).

10   All these countries have above 10 liters per capita alcohol consumption.

11   Thus, holding advantageous social statuses is somewhat less advantageous for women than for men since women often have to sacrifice marriage and childbearing which are related to improved survival.

12   Own translation.

13   Roemer (1985) described both Norway and Britain.

14   A note on this may be the drop in infant mortality in Sweden in the mid-1990s which is believed to stem from the advice to lay the infant on the back.

15   This is perhaps particularly interesting since Britain widely is seen as a more unequal society than Sweden.

16   A look at figure 17.1 indicates that there was a steeper mortality decline in infant mortality that began in the first decades of the nineteenth century.

17   All are lifestyle factors known to be related to cardiovascular disease.

18   Prevention in child and maternal care centers may also have contributed to low infant mortality in Sweden.

19   Brännström mentions working-class men, although I would like to especially point at such men unmarried.

20   Data on self-reported illness in figure 17.1 also point at substantial improvements in health in ages above 65.

References

Ahlberg-Hultén, Gunnel. 1999. *Psychological Demands and Decision Latitude Within Health Care Work*. Stockholm: Stockholm University, Department of Psychology.

Andersen, Ronald, Björn Smedby, and Denny Vågerö. 1999. "Cost Containment, Solidarity, and Cautious Experimentation: Swedish Dilemmas." Paper presented at the American Sociological Association Meetings, Toronto, August, 1997.

Anell, A. and M. Persson. 1998. "International Comparisons of Health Care Resources: Expenditure Shared the GNP is Inadequate; Complementary Real Measures are Necessary." *Läkartidningen* 95: 3315–18.

Björklund, Anders. 1998. "Income Distribution in Sweden: What is the Achievement of the Welfare State?" *Swedish Economic Review* 5: 39–80.

Blau, Peter M. 1977. *Inequality and Heterogeniety: A Primitive Theory of Social Structure.* New York: Free Press.

Brännström, Inger. 1994. "Livsvillkor, kulturella normer och levnadsvanor." ["Living Conditions, Cultural Norms, and Lifestyles"]. *Socialmedicinsk tidskrift* : 171–4.

Brännström, Inger, L. Weinhall, L. Å. Persson, P. O. Wester, and S. Wall. 1993. "Changing Social Patterns of Risk Factors for Cardiovascular Disease in a Swedish Community Intervention Programme." *International Journal of Epidemiology* 22: 1026–37.

Carlson, Per. 1998. "Self-Perceived Health in East and West Europe: Another European Health Divide." *Social Science & Medicine* 46: 1355–66.

Carlsson, Gösta and Ola Arvidsson. 1994. "Inledning." ["Introduction"]. Pp. 11–32 in G. Carlsson and O. Arvidsson (eds.), *Kampen för folkhälsan: Prevention i historia och nutid.* Stockholm: Natur och Kultur.

Carlsson, Gösta, Ola Arvidsson, Lars-Olov Bygren, and Lars Werkö. 1979. *Liv och hälsa: En kartläggning av hälsoutvecklingen i Sverige.* [Life and Health: A Mapping of Health Development in Sweden]. Stockholm: Liber Förlag.

Cavelaars, Adriënne. 1998. *Cross-National Comparisons of Socio-Economic Differences in Health Indicators.* Rotterdam: Department of Public Health, Erasmus University.

Cavelaars, Adriënne, Anton Kunst, J. J. M. Geurts, R. Crialesi, L. Grötvedt, U. Helmert et al. 1998. *Journal of Epidemiology and Community Health* 52: 219–27.

Chenet, Laurent, Merete Osler, Martin McKee, and Allan Krasnik. 1996. "Changing Life Expectancy in the 1980s: Why Was Denmark Different from Sweden?" *Journal of Epidemiology and Community Health* 50: 404–7.

Diderichsen, Finn. 1991. "Health and Social Inequities in Sweden." *Social Science & Medicine* 31: 359–67.

———. 1999. "Devolution in Swedish Health Care: Local Government Isn't Powerful Enough to Control Costs or Stop Privatisation." *British Medical Journal* 318: 1156–7.;

Diderichsen, Finn and Johan Hallqvist. 1997. "Trends in Occupational Mortality Among Middle-Aged Men in Sweden 1961–1990." *International Journal of Epidemiology* 26: 782–7.

———. 1998. "Social Inequalities in Health: Some Methodological Considerations for the Study of Social Position and Social Context." Pp. 25–39 in *Inequality in Health: A Swedish Perspective.* Stockholm: Swedish Council for Social Research.

Diderichsen, Finn, Rosmari Eliasson, Rolf Å. Gustafsson, Urban Janlert, and Pär Nygren. 1992. *Samhällsvetenskap, vård och omsorg,* second edition. Stockholm: Almqvist & Wiksell Förlag.

Emami, Abbas. 1997. "Invandrarnas hälsotillstånd i Sverige." [The Health Status of Immigrants in Sweden]. *Socialmedicinsk tidskrift* 74: 252–7.

Emslie, Carol, Kate Hunt, and Sally Macintyre. 1999. "Gender Differences in Minor Morbidity Among Full-Time Employees of a British University." *Journal of Epidemiology and Community Health* 53: 465–75.

Erikson, Robert. 1984. "Social Class of Men, Women, and Families." *Sociology* 18: 500–14.

FHI and CAN. 1997. *Alkohol- och narkotikautvecklingen i Sverige.* [Alcohol and Drug Development in Sweden]. Stockholm: Folkhälsoinstitutet (FHI) and Centralförbundet för alkohol- och narktikaupplysning (CAN).

Frick, Kaj. 1994. *From "Sidecar" to Integrated Health and Safety Work.* Stockholm: Föreningen för arbetsskydd.

Gullberg, Anders and Denny Vågerö. 1996. *Yrke och dödlighet under 1980-talet.* [Occupation and Mortality During the 1980s]. Stockholm: National Board of Health and Welfare and Stockholm University, Department of Sociology.

Gustafsson, Rolf Å. 1994. "'Traditionernas ok' inom arbetsmiljöpreventionen." ["The Tradition's Yoke." in Work Environment Prevention]. Pp. 263–320 in G. Carlsson and O. Arvidsson (eds.), *Kampen för folkhälsan: Prevention i historia och nutid.* Stockholm: Natur och Kultur.

Gustafsson, Rolf Å. and Marta Szebehely. 1996. "Äldreomsorgens förändringar och kvinnors hälsa." [Changes in Care for the Elderly and Women's Health]. Pp. 255–80 in P. Östlin, M. Danielsson, F. Diderchsen, A. Härenstam, and G. Lindberg (eds.), *Kön och ohälsa.* Lund, Sweden: Studentlitteratur.

Halleröd, Björn. 1999. *Fattigdom i Sverige.* [Poverty in Sweden]. Stockholm: Nationella folkhälsokommittén.

Hemström, Örjan. 1998. *Male Susceptibility and Female Emancipation: Studies on the Gender Difference in Mortality.* Stockholm: Almqvist & Wiksell International. Doctoral thesis.

——. 1999a. "Explaining Differential Rates of Mortality Decline for Swedish Men and Women: A Time-Series Analysis, 1945–1992." *Social Science & Medicine* 48: 1759–77.

——. 1999b. "Does the Work Environment Contribute to Excess Male Mortality?" *Social Science & Medicine* 49: 879–94.

Hobson, Barbara and Mieko Takahashi. 1997. "The Parent-Worker Model: Lone Mothers in Sweden." Pp. 121–39 in J. Lewis (ed.), *Lone Mothers in European Welfare Regimes: Shifting Policy Logics.* London and Philadelphia: Kingsley.

Jönsson, Bengt. 1990. "What Can Americans Learn From Europeans?" Pp. 87–101 in *Health Care Systems in Transitions: The Search for Efficiency.* Paris: OECD.

Judge, Ken, Jo-Ann Mulligan, and Michaela Benzeval. 1998. "Income Inequality and Population Health." *Social Science & Medicine* 46: 567–79.

Kallner, Mora, Hans Gilljam, and Birgitta Sandstedt. 1999. "Storstad bäst för barn." *Dagens Nyheter,* DN debatt, p. A4, 31 July.

Koskinen, Seppo and Tuija Martelin. 1994. "Why are Socioeconomic Mortality Differentials Smaller Among Women than Among Men?" *Social Science & Medicine* 38: 1385–96.

Kunst, Anton. 1997. *Cross-National Comparisons of Socio-Economic Differences in Mortality.* Rotterdam: Department of Public Health, Erasmus University.

Leifman, Håkan. 1995. "Alcohol and Primary Prevention in Scotland and Sweden: A Comparative Study." *Nordisk Alkoholtidskrift* 12: 31–60, *English Supplement.*

——. 1996. *Perspectives on Alcohol Prevention.* Stockholm: Almqvist & Wiksell International. Doctoral thesis.

——. 1998. *Socialklass och alkoholvanor.* [Social Class and Alcohol Habits]. Stockholm: The Swedish Institute for Public Health.

Lindgren, Björn. 1990. Untitled Response to A. C. Enthoven. Pp. 74–9 in *Health Care Systems in Transitions: The Search for Efficiency.* Paris: OECD.

Lundberg, Olle. 1990. *Den ojämlika ohälsan: Om klass- och könsskillnader i sjuklighet.* [Inequality in Ill Health in Sweden]. Stockholm: Almqvist & Wiksell International. Doctoral thesis.

——. 1992. "Health Inequalities in Sweden: Levels and Trends." *International Journal of Health Sciences* 3: 167–74.

——. 1998a. "Om ohälsans ojämlika fördelning i dagens Sverige." [About Unequal Distribution of Ill Health in Sweden Today]." Pp. 7–46 in *En god hälsa – ett socialt privilegium?* Stockholm: Nationella folkhälsokommittén.

——. 1998b. "Exploring Causal Mechanisms that Generate Health Inequalities." Pp. 169–84 in *Inequality in Health: A Swedish Perspective.* Stockholm: Swedish Council for Social Research.

Macintyre, Sally. 1989. "The Role of Health Services in Relation to Inequalities in Health in Europe." Pp. 317–32 in J. Fox (ed.), *Health Inequalities in European Countries.* Aldershot: Gower.

Mackenbach, Johan P., A. E. Kunst, A. E. J. M. Cavelaars, F. Groenhof, J. J. M. Geurts, and the EU Working Group on Socioeconomic Inequalities in Health. 1997. "Socioeconomic Inequalities in Morbidity and Mortality in Western Europe." *The Lancet* 349: 1655–9.

Nathanson, Constance. A. 1995. "Mortality and the Position of Women in Developed Countries." Pp. 135–57 in A. D. Lopez, G. Caselli, and T. Valkonen (eds.), *Adult Mortality in Developed Countries: From Description to Explanation.* Oxford: Clarendon Press.

National Board of Health and Welfare. 1977. *Public Health in Sweden.* Official Statistics of Sweden. Stockholm: Liber Förlag/Allmänna Förlaget.

——. 1998. *Yearbook of Health and Medical Care 1998.* Official Statistics of Sweden. Stockholm: National Board of Health and Welfare.

——. 1999. *Welfare and Freedom of Choice? Final Report From the Evaluation of the 1995 Psychiatric Care Reform.* Stockholm: National Board of Health and Welfare, Report 1999: 1.

Nationella folkhälsokommittén. 1999. *Arbetslivsfaktorer.* [Work Life Factors]. Stockholm: Nationella folkhälsokommittén, underlagsrapport nr 1.

Osler, Merete. 1999. "Editorial: Why Has Health in Denmark Failed to Improve?" *European Journal of Public Health* 9: 6–7.

Östberg, Viveca. 1996. *Social Structure and Children's Life Chances: An Analysis of Child Mortality in Sweden.* Stockholm: Stockholm University, Swedish Institute for Social Research.

Otterblad-Olausson, Petra. 1991. "Mortality Among the Elderly in Sweden by Social Class." *Social Science & Medicine* 32: 437–40.

Palmblad, Eva. 1990. *Medicinen som samhällslära.* [Medicine as Societal Knowledge]. Göteborg: Daidalos.

Preston, Samuel H. 1975. "The Changing Relation Between Mortality and Level of Economic Development." *Population Studies* 29: 231–48.

Qvarsell, Roger. 1994. "Ett sunt folk i ett sunt samhälle." [Healthy People in a Healthy Society]. Pp. 76–108 in G. Carlsson and O. Arvidsson (eds.), *Kampen för folkhälsan: Prevention i historia och nutid.* Stockholm: Natur och Kultur.

Roemer, Milton I. 1985. *National Strategies for Health Care Organization.* Ann Arbor, Michigan: Health Administration Press.

Rose, Geoffrey. 1985. "Sick Individuals and Sick Populations." *International Journal of Epidemiology* 14: 32–8.

Saunders, Peter, Björn Halleröd, and George Matheson. 1994. "Making Ends Meet in Australia and Sweden: A Comparative Analysis Using the Subjective Poverty Line Methodology." *Acta Sociologica* 37: 3–22.

Statistics Sweden. 1997a. *Välfärd och ojämlikhet i 20-årsperspektiv 1975–1995.* [Living Conditions and Inequality in Sweden – A 20-Year Perspective 1975–1995], edited by J. Vogel and L. Häll. Stockholm: Official statistics of Sweden, Statistics Sweden, Report 91.

——. 1997b. *Tobacco Consumption 1970–1994 in the Member States of the European Union and in Norway and Iceland.* Stockholm: Statistics Sweden.

Sundin, Jan. 1992. "Surveys of the Developments in the Social History of Medicine: IV. The History of Public Health Prevention: Current Swedish Research." *Social History of Medicine* 5: 517–24.

Szulkin, Ryszard and Michael Tåhlin. 1994. "Arbetets utveckling." [The Development of Work]. Pp. 87–116 in J. Fritzell and O. Lundberg (eds.), *Vardagens villkor: Levnadsförhållanden i Sverige under tre decennier.* Stockholm: Brombergs.

Thom, Thomas J., Frederick H. Epstein, Jacob J. Feldman, and Paul E. Leaverton. 1985. "Trends in Total Mortality and Mortality from Heart Disease in 26 Countries from 1950 to 1978." *International Journal of Epidemiology* 14: 510–20.

Townsend, Peter and N. Davisson. 1992. "The Black Report." Pp. 1–213 in P. Townsend, M. Whitehead, and N. Davidson (eds.), *Inequality in Health: The Black Report and Health Divide.* London: Penguin.

Vågerö, Denny. 1992. "Health Inequalities from the Cradle to the Grave? Hypotheses on Health Policy." *International Journal of Health Sciences* 3: 175–83.

Vågerö, Denny and Robert Erikson. 1997. "Correspondence: Socioeconomic Inequalities in Morbidity and Mortality in Western Europe." *The Lancet* 350: 516.

Vågerö, Denny and Raymond Illsley. 1992. "Inequality, Health, and Policy in East and West Europe." *International Journal of Health Sciences* 3: 225–39.

Vågerö, Denny and Eero Lahelma. 1998. "Women, Work, and Mortality: An Analysis of Female Labor Participation." Pp. 73–85 in K. Orth-Gomér, M. Chesney, and N. K. Wenger (eds.), *Women, Stress, and Heart Disease.* Hillsdale, NJ: Lawrence Erlbaum.

Vågerö, Denny and Olle Lundberg. 1995. "Socio-Economic Mortality Differentials Among Adults in Sweden." Pp. 223–42 in A. D. Lopez, G. Caselli, and T. Valkonen (eds.), *Adult Mortality in Developed Countries: From Description to Explanation.* Oxford: Clarendon Press.

Vallin, Jaques. "Can Sex Differentials in Mortality be Explained by Socioeconomic Differentials?" 1995. Pp. 179–200 in A. D. Lopez, G. Caselli, and T. Valkonen (eds.), *Adult Mortality in Developed Countries: From Description to Explanation.* Oxford: Clarendon Press.

Vogel, Joachim. 1997. "Living Conditions and Inequality 1975–1995." Pp. 627–51 in J. Vogel and L. Häll (eds.), *Välfärd och ojämlikhet i 20-års perspektiv 1975–1995.* Stockholm: Statistics Sweden, Report 91.

Whitehead, Margaret, Maria Evandrou, Bengt Haglund, and Finn Diderichsen. 1997. "As the Health Divide Widens in Sweden and Britain, What's Happening to Access to Care?" *British Medical Journal* 315: 1006–9.

Wilkinson, Richard G. 1996. *Unhealthy Societies: The Afflictions of Inequality.* London and New York: Routledge.

Russia and Eastern Europe

18

The Russian Health Care Experiment: Transition of the Health Care System and Rethinking Medical Sociology

ELENA DMITRIEVA

The health situation in Russia has become crucially important after the massive social, political, and economic changes that have taken place since the 1980s. High morbidity, epidemics of infectious diseases, and high rates of heart disease mortality have caused concern about the state of health in contemporary Russia. In the 1990s, for the first time since World War II, the country faces the problem of depopulation as mortality rates exceed birth rates (Gorbachova 1999). The birth rate, for example, fell from 12.1 births per 1,000 in 1991 to 8.6 in 1997; however, the 1997 mortality rate was 13.8 deaths per 1,000 persons indicating a net decrease in population. Likewise, there has been an unprecedented decline of life expectancy from 65.1 (1987) to 60.7 years (1997) for men and from 73.1 (1987) to 72.9 years (1997) for women in Russia (Goskomstat 1998). There is also a steadily growing number of poor people, who constituted 62 percent of the total population in 1996 (Kara-Murza 1997).

As a result of living conditions, deterioration of the immune system of many individuals has weakened and infectious diseases increased by two fold (Gorbachova 1999). For instance, tuberculosis morbidity is steadily growing and increased 9.5 percent for the adult population and 11.4 percent among children in 1997 (State Report on Health of the Citizens of the Russian Federation 1997). As of January 1, 1999, there were 10,758 HIV-positive persons, of whom 449 were children (Aloyan and Nikolay 1999), while the number of HIV-positive persons in 1988 was only 69. There has also been a dramatic increase in the number of individuals with sexually-transmitted diseases, with more than 2 million people registered annually with these diseases in the late 1990s compared to 640,000 in 1989 (State Report on Health of the Citizens of the Russian Federation 1997). Most of these diseases are socially determined and they, along with Russia's other health problems, require serious sociological analysis.

THE HISTORICAL BACKGROUND OF MEDICAL SOCIOLOGY IN RUSSIA

The first studies of health, illness, and morbidity were conducted in Moscow and later extended elsewhere in Russia. Studies done by P. I. Kurkina and E. A. Osipova date back to the nineteenth century (Zhuravleva 1989). Russian scientist A. Shingarev was one of the first to investigate the population's health in rural regions using such variables as household, income, food variety, and mortality. He established a correlation between health and the social economic situation of peasants (Shingarev 1907). At the beginning of the twentieth century, the most significant medical–sociological research using a sampling method were carried out by N. Semashko. At the beginning of the 1920s most of the research shifted to social hygiene and medical demography. Between that time and the 1960s, the development of medical sociology in the USSR was restricted, because Stalin ordered the replacement of sociology by historic materialism. Sociology was proclaimed as a "bourgeois" science opposed to Marxist–Leninist theory; the word "sociology" was illegal, and all fundamental research was halted (Osipov et al. 1995).

In the 1960s, after Stalin's death, some initial attempts were taken to develop theoretical and applied sociology, and to distinguish medical sociology from social hygiene and medical demography (Chikin 1966; Izutkin 1967; Tzaregorodtzev 1968). One of the first definitions was provided by N. Dobronravov in 1970, who described medical sociology "as a integral part of the sociology studying the social problems correlated with health, illness, health care, and the role of health and working ability of the population in social development" (Dobronravov 1970). In a handbook on medical sociology, its main subject was defined as the study of the correlation between medicine as a social phenomenon with society and different social institutions (Izutkin et al. 1981). In the 1970s and 1980s, there were a number of works devoted to the methodology and techniques of sociological research in medical sociology (Bedniy 1979; Dmitriev 1983) and developing basic concepts (Ivanov and Lupandin 1984). It is worth mentioning that up until the present, quantitative methodology dominates the field and very few studies of health have been done using qualitative techniques.

RESEARCH IN THE SOVIET UNION AND POST-SOVIET RUSSIA

Up to the 1990s there were few sociological studies of health representative of the entire Russian population, rather they were limited to different social and professional groups (Alexandrova 1984) or geographical regions. In the meantime, there were studies covering health issues conducted by Soviet demographers (Bedniy 1979) and social hygienists (Lisitzin 1998; Sadvokasova 1969). However, these studies were predominantly based on data from medical screenings, filled in by medical professionals instead of respondents. They focused on patients and ignored critical assessments of the health care system and the role of medicine in society.

Most of the research at that time was guided by Marxist–Leninist ideology. It was stated that "historic materialism as well as Marxist–Leninist philosophy gave an important perspective of great methodological importance for medicine and other sciences including medicine, biology and social sciences . . . The object of these sciences is health and the health care of communities in general with respect to social relations" (Izutkin et al. 1981). Theoretically, Soviet society was described as a classless society, without class oppression, private property, or health inequalities. Considerable attention has been paid to studies of the socialist system and small groups ("collectives"). In some sociological works, the authors pointed out that a good psychological climate within a group could raise work effectiveness and even compensate for negative factors influencing individual health (Alexandrov and Sluchevsky 1984). Research conducted in 1982–3 stated that a strong association was found "between the rise of individual weariness and a decrease of the 'collectivism' index in the observed groups" (Tolmachov and Karaga 1984). It is apparent that during the Soviet period the role of kinship, neighborhood, and community in health maintenance was overestimated and exaggerated.

Medical sociology was not institutionalized in the Soviet Union. There were no departments or chairs of medical sociology. This discipline was not taught to either sociologists or medical professionals. A few conferences on health were held in the Ukraine (1984), Novosibirsk (1986), and Lithuania (1987). The fact that those conferences were not held in Moscow demonstrates that health issues were not the focus of social scientists and not supported by the official ideology.

Sociological accounts of health issues were initiated in the 1980s. The value of health was studied in research about the lifestyle of Soviet citizens, while the Department of Social Issues of Health was organized in the Institute of Sociology of the Russian Academy of Science at the beginning of the 1980s. The Institute of Sociology participated in the projects "Health of the Population" (1985) and "Your Health" (1987, 1989). Comparative studies of Finns and Russians in 1991 examined attitudes about life expectancy, and individual estimates of health (Palosuo et al. 1998). MONICA research that was part of the WHO project on health examined the role of risk factors in mortality and morbidity (1985–6), while Shilova (1989) elaborated on the concept of self-protective behavior as a "system of actions and attitudes influencing health and individual life expectancy."

The theme of the Soviet citizens' health was covered in a case study of the Russian city Taganrog entitled "Taganrog." The panel research conducted by the Institute for Socio-Economic Problems of Population consisted of four stages. The first was conducted in 1968–9 with focus on the reaction of the Soviet people to Khrushchev's reforms. The second study was carried out in 1978–9 during Brezhnev's stagnation period and it was followed by "Taganrog-3" (1988–9) during Gorbachov's *perestroika*. "Taganrog-3.5" (1993–4) was aimed at studying the public's reaction to economic reforms. The most recent part of this study dates to 1998–9. As a whole, the research has revealed health deterioration over time, along with an intensive decrease of living standards. One researcher pointed out that the focus on the health decline of retired people has shifted to the poor health of children and youth

(Rimachevskaya 1998). "As a result the upcoming generation with poor health couldn't reproduce a healthy new generation... This might be explained by the drastic worsening of children's health, and particularly newborn's health" (Rimachevskaya 1997).

SOCIOLOGICAL ACCOUNTS OF HEALTH EVALUATION

Health as a Value and Real Behavior

At the beginning of the 1990s a number of research projects were begun by sociologists. Among them were studies of social adaptation by the handicapped (Ellansky and Peshkov 1995); families of children with chronic diseases (Silaste 1997; Smirnova 1997); doctors' research and their values (Lavrikova 1999), the transition of the health care system (Kucherenko 1995; Malachova 1995; Boikov 1999) and others. Some projects had a unique character, like one study of the health and living conditions of the population persecuted by Nazis during World War II in the former Soviet Union (Knazev 1996).

It is hard to find comprehensive research on health and health behavior in the former Soviet Union, because sociologists were limited by Marxist–Leninist theory that dominated Soviet society. In a representative research of Soviet citizens' lifestyle, a majority of the respondents (87%) put a priority on "health," choosing it from among 16 main values (such as talent, education, and money) important for the achievement of the success in life (Shilova 1989). There were, however, a number of inconsistencies between a person's declared value of health and actual behavior.

Evidence supporting this fact is seen in the data. For example, in Nizniy Novgorod, only 16 percent of the students took meals regularly (3 times per day). Most of them (40%) didn't seek physicians in case of illness. In Moscow, only 28 percent of respondents said they followed their physician's prescriptions. Others (24%) undergo their own medical treatment and continue to work in case of disease (28%) (Aktualnie medico-sozialnie aspecti propagandi zdorovogo obraza zhizni 1986). Research from 1987 in Kamchatskaya oblast has demonstrated that three-fourths of Russians recognized the importance of physical exercise for people of their age, but in fact less than 40 percent exercise. Half of the respondents realized the harm in smoking and drinking, but less than one-third stopped these behaviors (Adametz 1990). Visiting a general practitioner if required is one of the indicators of self-protective behavior. However, 60 percent of respondents see a general practitioner only if they need a document confirming their illness for their employer (Shilova 1999).

Since the introduction of the free market economy in Russia, attitudes toward work have changed. As a result of restricted work opportunities, people place a higher priority on work and less on health. Fewer people in all age groups have been to a hospital or stay home because of illness than in past years (Nazarova 1998). This situation may possibly be due to high competition in the labor market and fear of unemployment, even in the case of illness.

Health Evaluation

An important measure of health status is self-reported health. In research conducted in 1978 in seven cities of the former Soviet Union, the majority (66.7%) evaluated their health as "normal," 21.1 percent as "good," and 13.2 percent as "bad." For a decade this distribution did not change significantly, and in 1988 most Russians (59.6%) evaluated their health as "normal," 24.6 percent as "good," and 8.4 percent as "bad" (Kogan 1993). There were also observed geographical differences in attitudes toward health. Self-esteem and health were found to worsen from the west to the east, with the lowest self-esteem in the Permskaya region. "With equal proportions of 'normal' self-esteem (54–6%) in all three groups, the proportion of 'bad' increased from 13 to 17 percent, while 'good' decreased from 33 to 36 percent from Latvia to the Urals or from west to the east" (Kogan 1993).

Evaluations of health are also correlated with gender. In the former Soviet Union, men evaluated health more pessimistically than women: 30 percent of men think their health is "good" compared to 48 percent of women, and 10 percent evaluate their health as "bad" compared to 4 percent of women (Zhuravleva 1988). Women, however, have higher rates of morbidity and Bedniy (1984) accounts for this situation by pointing out that: "Women address a general practitioner more often than men because they take health more seriously and not because of their poor health. As a result women's illnesses are registered more often then men's."

Social changes that have occurred in Russia since *perestroika* (1985) likewise influenced health perception and health behavior. In 1991, one study found that most of the respondents evaluated their health as "normal" (68% of men and 60% of women), while others (14% of men, 7% of women) chose "very good" and "fairly good" to describe their health. Noticeably, the situation with women's evaluation of health has reversed. Thus one-third of women (34%) qualified their health as "bad" compared to 17 percent of men (Palosuo and Zhuravleva 1998). A negative perception of health among women has to do with unfair working opportunities for men and women in contemporary Russia. Women's choices are restricted and most of the unemployed are women. The proportion of women going to work with different illnesses has increased. In the meantime, fewer men in 1995 said they "frequently go to work in case of illness" compared to 1988 (Shilova 1999).

The monitoring of the Russian population from 1994 to 1996 demonstrated that men evaluated their health higher than women in all age categories: more men (37.6%) have "good" and "very good" health compared to women (25.4%). More women reported that they feel "bad" and "very bad" (18.8%) than did the men (13.8%) (Nazarova 1998). Russian adolescents have also shown low self-esteem about health. Most Russian young people (45.4%) aged 13–16 thought of their health as normal; 22.2 percent had problems with their health (choosing "very bad" and "satisfactory"), and only one-third of all respondents considered their health as "fairly good" and "very good" (Zhuravleva 1997).

Morbidity of the Russian Population

To describe the health situation accurately, it is necessary to correlate health perception with morbidity. Data confirmed the fact that Russians tend to think more optimistically about their health than in fact they feel. Among those who evaluated their health as "good rather then bad," 50.3 percent have chronic illnesses. Correlation between professional groups and morbidity in Russia has shown that highest morbidity registered among low-qualified workers (63.8%) and among directors of big enterprises (62.5%) (Adametz 1990). The most frequent morbidity factors experienced by Soviet people were colds (47.9%), chronic illness (38.6%), and accidents (13.4%) (Shilova 1989).

Health in post-Soviet Russia has deteriorated noticeably. A high proportion of people (77.8%) have health problems. More specifically, 15.4 percent have serious diseases, more than one-third have at least two diseases, and still others have more than two chronic illnesses (McKeehan et al. 1993). Russians see doctors most often in case of intestinal diseases (18% of men and 16% of women) and back injuries (14% of men and 18% of women). Women also tend to be concerned about abnormal blood pressure (27%) (Palosuo and Zhuravleva 1998). Poor health has been reported particularly in certain regions of Russia. In the Tumenskaya region, for instance, only 16.5 percent consider themselves healthy, and most citizens (83.5%) think that they have some disease (Gubin 1999).

Lifestyle Factors Influencing Health

Any sociological account of health requires an analysis of the factors influencing it. Research shows that self-protective health behavior and healthy lifestyles are not prevalent in the Russian population. Middle-age, working-class males, in particular show especially high levels of alcohol consumption, smoking, fatty diets, and little or no participation in leisure-time exercises (Cockerham 1999). Furthermore, social, economic, and political changes have imposed significant stress on the Russian population. Russians experienced more stress in 1991 than any year after *perestroika*, but later research shows an adjustment to the stress factor (Shilova 1999).

"Life conditions" are increasingly recognized as important for health since the early 1990s as noted by Palosuo and Zhuravleva (1998). In 1991, 45 percent of the respondents in a Moscow study considered their nourishment "fairly unhealthy" or "very unhealthy," and less than one-third could claim a healthy diet (Palosuo and Zhuravleva 1998). In fact, most people in the former Soviet Union (48.9%) could not participate in a healthy lifestyle for social and economic reasons and more than half of Russians could not take a rest after work since they have to work at more than one job to earn money (Adametz 1990).

In the period 1995–6 the proportion of Russians playing sports did not change and constituted only 8 percent of the population, mostly males (Nazarova 1998). This indicator will not increase in the near future because of the high costs of sports facilities in Russia. Currently, only 15.4 percent of the population exercise at least three times a week and only 1.1 percent more then three times a week (Nazarova 1998). Smoking behavior is very stable among Russians as there were 44 percent of men smoking daily in Moscow in 1986 compared to 46 percent in 1991. Smoking in 1991 was considered a method of "coping with stress" for 61 percent of women smokers and 47 percent of the men (Palosuo and Zhuravleva 1998). However, in some parts of Russia, like Siberia, nearly 70 percent of the men have been found to smoke and in some industrial areas the figures may be even higher (Hurt 1995). Russian males also have the highest per capita rate of alcohol consumption in the world and excessive alcohol use is the singly most important determinant of the premature mortality among males (Shkolnikov and Nemtsov 1994). Russian men exercise more than women, but women show healthier overall lifestyle than men in that they drink and smoke much less, and eat more fruits and vegetables, while consuming less fat (Cockerham 1999).

Only the deterioration of their health causes Russians to consider their health behaviors. Most people say that they would start taking care of their health after its worsening (57.4%); special medical information (10.9%) or other peoples' behavior influences (15.2%) are not taken seriously as factors to incite change (Kogan 1993). Health perception is also influenced by the images of age that dominate in a society. Both Russian men and women correlate women's aging with biological age and men's aging with changes in their social and professional status and appearance. Women start feeling "old" earlier then men. Respondents marked the age of being "elderly" as 48.1 years for men and 43.3 years for women (Shilova 1989).

Individuals appear to largely rely on doctors and their own willingness to take prescription drugs for their health outcomes. Research in Rostov showed that almost all cancer patients (94%) expected favorable conditions after surgery and did not plan on doing anything themselves to promote their health. The patients were "alienated somatically and morally from the active treatment of their own health, relying purely on medical professionals" (Sidorenko and Maksimov 1988). A large proportion of people (38.6%) in the Tumenskaya region indicate that their health depends primarily on the health care system rather than themselves (Gubin 1999).

Consequently, we may state that Russian citizens' health has deteriorated over time, health esteem is declining, and the morbidity level is growing. This happened because self-protective behavior is not typical for Russians and health is considered to be a functional characteristic and not a value. Moreover, the main factor influencing health perception in Russia is its deterioration, which can be defined as the expected or real decline of health. Most people rely on external factors like state support and the provision of health and diagnostic services. Also, they consider deterioration of life conditions to be a key factor in health status and do not believe in individual abilities. The lack of self-protective culture in Russia is a result of Soviet times that neglected the individual, its life, and, consequently its health. Certain types of health care systems and a dominating model of doctor–patient relations have also contributed to the neglect of health.

TRANSITION OF THE HEALTH CARE SYSTEM

Health Care System in Russia

The history of the Russian health care system up to 1917 was ignored in Soviet textbooks, and its importance in the contemporary state of medicine was underestimated. The health care system introduced in 1864 by the Zemskaya reform made medical care available for rural areas that sometimes was free of charge and included a hospital for each administrative district (Lisitzin 1998). In 1910, for the first time in Russian history, a Ministry of Health was established. In the early 1900s Russia ranked fourth in Europe in the number of physicians. Russia had 13,475 physicians, compared to 22,105 in England, 16,270 in Germany, and 14,380 in France (Samoilov 1997). More than 7,000 students studied at the medical departments of nine Russian universities. St. Petersburg and Moscow established new refresher training institutes for doctors (Samoilov 1997).

After 1917, the Soviet government set up a new concept of health care guided by the Marxist–Leninist theory. Soviet medicine was based on the principal of universal, free access to all levels of care as a fundamental human right. It became possible within the new system to stop epidemics like the typhus epidemic of 1907–17. Also, from 1926 to 1927 life expectancy increased to 44 years (Lisitzin 1998) and in 1965 it increased to 64 years for males and 72.1 years for females (Shkolnikov 1995). A network of local "polyclinics" provided primary care. As of 1995, there were 38 physicians and 95 nurses per 10,000 people. At the current time these figures vary largely throughout Russia: from 67.7 per 10,000 physicians in Moscow to 20.8 per 10,000 in Ingushetia (Ministry of Health Care of the Russian Federation 1996). The former Soviet Union declared the importance of preventive medicine and health promotion. From the mid-1980s a costly campaign of annual mandatory population screening was introduced. In fact, this campaign is not really effective because of the medical bureaucracy, and a lack of motivation in general practitioners.

Since 1991 Russia has been undergoing a reform in the health care system. Currently, it is changing from being financed by the state budget to a system of combined finance from the state budget and insurance system. Health care in Russia consists of a state health care system, a municipal health care system, and a private system. The Russian constitution guarantees health care free of charge within the state and municipal health care system. But the most profitable services (such as dental, diagnostic, gynecological, and obstetric services) have shifted to the private sector and are not covered by the compulsory medical insurance provided by the state.

Private medicine was a new phenomenon for Russians who were used to the free health care system. At the very beginning of reforms, people were positive about private medicine. According to a 1991 telephone survey in Moscow, most of the respondents (83.6%) stated that they would be ready to pay for the right to choose a physician and clinic instead of going to the "polyclinic" to which they were assigned (McKeehan et al. 1993). Most of the clients at that time had to give bribes in state clinics for better medical care or pay illegally for the medicine. Physicians sometimes asked for under-the-table money, gifts, or services from their patients in exchange for medical care. The dynamic over time has shown that attitudes toward the privatization of medicine and paid services have changed and Russian citizens tend to visit state clinics instead of private ones. The percentage of clients visiting private polyclinics was the following: 3 percent of patients (compared to 88.6% visiting a state polyclinic) in 1994; 2.7 percent (as to 88.5%) in 1995 and 2.9 percent (as to 88.5%) in 1996 (Nazarova 1998). The relatively small proportion of clients who went to private clinics is explained by the high cost charged for medical services compared to the average salary, not because the bureaucratic attitude of medical professionals changed over time.

Russian attitudes about the health care system are ambivalent. On one hand, they distrust it and on the other totally rely on it. At the beginning of the 1980s, 20 percent of the respondents preferred to stay at home rather than visiting a general practitioner; 6 percent waited until the disease ended on its own (Dmitriev 1983). In rural regions access to the health care system was more complicated compared to metropolitan areas. One-third of rural residents didn't see a physician because of difficulties in finding one near their residence. Other reasons that patients didn't see a general practitioner were because medical professionals were rude toward them (0.7%), lack of time (22%), fear of having to go to a hospital (9%), and distrust of the general practitioner (0.9%) (Usachev 1988). Most residents of small cities said that health care was bad (58%). About one-third were satisfied with it and only 1.8 percent of the respondents thought of it as "good" or "excellent" (Zibzev and Dolzhanskiy 1990). Because of the distrust about the quality of health services, Russians tend to see doctors only if they need to be registered as sick and stay at home. Most people visit medical professionals very rarely (62.7%) and one-fifth never go to the doctor if they catch a cold. With respect to chronic illnesses, one-fourth of the respondents still don't see a doctor (Adametz 1990). This distrust of the health care system was aroused by a medical bureaucracy that "judged a physician's work mainly by quantitative indicators of care (numbers of visits and procedures) while the quality was rarely considered" (Remennick and Shtarkshall 1997). Physicians and nurses had low salaries, so that their work motivation steadily diminished over time.

As a result of distrust of the official health care system, Russians establish informal contacts with general practitioners. Thus about half of surveyed people (46.9%) answered positively the question: "Do you have someone among your relatives and friends who work in the health care system, or do you have access to a health care system that helps to resolve your health problems?" Most of those aged 18–40 years who have informal contacts have a high level of education. This variable doesn't correlate with income, and this group consists of those who have an income higher then average as well as students and women having children up to 3 years who receive state welfare insufficient for food coverage (Rusinova and Brown 1997). Although most people distrust it, they also tend to rely on the state provision of health services. This mode of behavior is more typical for people over 40 years of age. Reliance on the health care system and distrust in individual abilities might be explained in terms of strong state support of individuals' health and ideology that existed in Soviet times.

The transition of the health care system was followed by social inequalities in health (Field and Twigg 2000). Analysis of health distribution is one of the key aspects of medical sociology, but issues of social inequality in health were not studied by the social sciences in the former Soviet Union because of ideological reasons. According to Marx and Lenin, the existence of inequality in a capitalist society was a result of the relationships within the sphere of production where one class subordinated another class. After eliminating antagonism among the classes in 1917, the Soviet Union destroyed the conditions required for social inequality. As a result, health inequalities were ignored. Some differences in access to health were supposed to be eliminated over the time. For a long time Soviet society was described as a community with equal access of all the citizens to the health services. In the meantime the resources were distributed unevenly giving a priority to big cities versus small ones and rural regions. The general health network available for the majority of the population differs from the medical institutions serving certain professional groups, the Communist Party, and state functionaries. The system of elite clinics ignored such at-risk groups as children, adolescents, retired people, and invalids. Therefore, any research on differentiation and inequality in care were prohibited and prosecuted.

Sociological research carried out in the early 1990s demonstrated differences in health access among observed groups. Significant differences were found between the highly professional group ("stable intelligentsia") and the group of "less qualified" workers. Respondents from the first group are characterized by a low level of chronic illness and morbidity in general compared to the "less qualified" group in which 51 percent of respondents have "poor health," or at least one chronic illness and abnormal blood pressure. In the first group only 5.5 percent required external assistance because of their health compared to 33 percent in the latter group (Rusinova and Brown 1997). Health inequalities affect the elderly in particular. Most eyesight problems (77.6%) happen mostly to people aged 55 years and older. Many of these patients have only an average income and a high proportion (81.3%) have a below average income. This type of medical service is quite expensive (US $950) when compared to the average person's salary of $103.90 (in 1994), who is not covered by compulsory medical insurance. As a result, retired people often cannot afford to have eye care (Tankovsky and Shamshurina 1997). The issue of health inequalities is shifting into the focus of Russian sociologists.

CONCLUSION

In conclusion, medical sociology in Russia has faced an intriguing situation with health. One could observe unprecedented deterioration of health in an industrialized nation: a decline of life expectancy, a low birth rate, a revival of epidemics, an increase of the number of HIV-positive people, a high mortality rate among the working population, and a high proportion of people with chronic illness, which shifted to the younger groups in the population.

The theoretical foundation of medical sociology in Russia is fairly poor as a result of the previous dominance of Marxist–Leninist theory. Western theories, methodology, and techniques are not incorporated in the theoretical body. Russian sociology is positivistically oriented and its interpretive tradition is very weak. Therefore, quantitative methods dominate in medical sociology and very few qualitative techniques are being used in the field. Theories of inter-actionism, phenomenology, ethnomethodology approaches, and postmodernism are underrepresented in Russian medical sociology.

Since health research shifted in the early 1920s to social hygiene and medical demography, sociological indicators were replaced by environmental and ecological factors. Moreover, social hygiene as a part of medicine was focused on the patients, ignoring critical analysis of the health care system, doctor–patient relations, and interpretation of the role of medicine in the society. There were very few sociological studies of health since sociology was prohibited up to the 1960s. Health in Russia has been studied using the concept of health-protective behavior. However, in using this concept, researchers discovered that a health-protective mode is not typical for Russians and that their concern for health is usually stimulated only by its deterioration. This attitude might be considered a result of the neglect of the individual during Soviet times. Since Russian society has faced a market economy, the health care system has changed from state-provided health care to a combination of state and private provision. The introduction of private medicine caused significant inequalities in health care distribution in Russian society. All of these issues require sociological analysis and new research to explain the health of Russians.

References

Adametz, S. V. 1990. "Ob otzenkakh zdorovia naselenia i realizatzii potrebnosti v ego ukreplenii i profilktike zabolevaniy." ["On Evaluation of Populations' Health and Exercising Need in Mainaining Health and Prevention of Diseases"]. Pp. 49–62 in *Demographiceskoe povedenie. Opit soziologicheskogo izuchenia*. Moscow: Institute of Sociology.

Alexandrov, O. A. and I. I. Sluchevsky. 1984. *NTR, zdorovie i zdravookhranenie*. [NTR, Health and Health Care System]. Moscow: Nauka.

Alexandrova, V. Y. 1984. "Metodologicheskie aspecti problemi vozniknovenia i rasprostranenia kurenia sredi podrostkov." ["Methodological Aspects of Studying Smoking Behavior of Adolescents"]. Pp. 134–6 in *Sozialno-philosophskie i mirovozzrencheskie problemi zdorovia cheloveka*. Lvov, Ukraine.

Aloyan, V. and Kolesnikov Nikolay. 1999. "Get rid of AIDS!" *Komsomolskava Pravda* (May 21):1-2.

Bedniy, M. S. 1979. *Medico-demographicheskoye izuchenie narodonaselenia*. [Medical and Demographic Studies of Population]. Moscow: Statistika

——. 1984. *Demographicheskie factori zdorovia*. [Demographic Factors of Health]. Moscow: Nauka.

Boikov, V. 1999. "Raskhodi na meditzinu: soziologichesky aspekt." ["Expenses for Medicine: Sociological Analysis"]. *SOZIS* 7: 100–2.

Chikin, S. 1966. *Obshestvo i Zdorovie Naroda*. [Society and Health of Population]. Moscow: Znanie.

Cockerham, William C. 1999. *Health and Social Change in Russia and Eastern Europe*. London: Routledge.

Dimov, V. 1998. *Philosophia i Sociologia zdorovia*. [Philosophy and Sociology of Health]. Almaty, Kazakhstan.

Dmitriev, Vitaliy. 1983. *Medico-soziologisheskye issledovania v zdravoohranenii*. [Medical and Sociological Studies in the Health Care]. Moscow: Nauka.

Dobronravov, Nikolai. 1970. "Soziologia medizini." ["Sociology of Medicine"]. Pp. 5–98 in *Philosophskaya enziklopedia*, vol. 5. Moscow.

Ellansky, Yuri and Sergei Peshkov. 1995. "Kontzepsia sozialnoi nezavisimosti invalidov." ["Concept of Social Independence of Invalids"]. *SOZIS* 12: 123–5.

Field, Mark G. and Judith L. Twigg (eds.). 2000. *Russia's Torn Safety Nets*. New York: St. Martin's Press.

Gubin, Alexey. 1999. "Sostoyanie zdorovia naselenia Tumenskoy oblasti." ["Social Health of the Population in Tumenskaya Region"]. *SOZIS* 7: 93–5.

Gorbacheva, Ada. 1999. "Kak my chuvstvuem." ["How We Feel"]. *Nazavisimaya Gazetta* (December 12): 1–2.

Goskomstat. 1998. *The Demographic Yearbook of Russia*. Moscow.

Hurt, Richard D. 1995. "Smoking in Russia: What Do Stalin and Western Tobacco Companies Have in Common?" *Mayo Clinic Proceedings* 70: 1007–11.

Ivanov, V. N. and V. M. Lupandin. 1984. "Issledovaniy problem zdravookhranenia – soziologichesky podkhod." ["Sociological Approach to Studies of Health Care System Problems"]. *Communist Ukraini* 11: 72–7.

Izutkin, Anatoliy. 1967. *Soziologia i Zdravookhranenie*. [Sociology and Health Care System]. Gorky, Russia: Volgo-Vyatskoye izdatelstvo.

Izutkin, Anatoliy, Victor Petlenko, and Gennady Tzaregorodtzev. 1981. *Soziologia meditziny*. [Sociology of Medicine]. Kiev, Ukraine: Zdorovya.

Kara-Murza, S. 1997. "Reforma i zdorovie naroda Rossii." ["Reform and Health of Russian Population"]. Pp. 36–47 in N. Belyakov (ed.), *Zdorovie obshestva i budushee Rossii*. Moscow: Klub Realisti.

Knazev, Victor. 1996. "Uslovia zhizni i zdorovie liz presledovavshihsia pri nazismi." ["Life Conditions and Health of People Prosecuted by Nazists"]. *SOZIS* 3: 134–40. *soziologicheskogo izuchenia*. Moscow: Institute of Sociology.

Kogan, V. 1978. "Izuchenie motivov gigienicheskogo povedenia i viavlenie tipov otnoshenia cheloveka k zdoroviu." ["Study of the Motives of the Hygienic Behavior and Identification of types of Individuals' Attitudes Towards Health"]. Moscow: Health Care Ministry.

——. 1993. "Pshcologisheskie factori zdorovia." ["Psycological Factors of Health"]. Pp. 77–100 in *Otnoshenie naselenia k zdoroviu*. Moscow: Institute of Sociology.

Kopina, O. S. and A. E. Korolkov. 1990. "Informirovannost po voprosam zdorovia u liz s razlichnim urovnem obrazovania." ["Awareness on Health Issues Among Different Educational Groups of Population"]. Pp. 73–8 in *Demographiceskoe povedenie*.

Kucherenko, Vladimir. 1995. "Reformi zdravookhranenia." ["Reforms of the Health Care System"]. *SOZIS* 12: 106–8.

Lavrikova, Irina. 1999. "Tverskie vratchi: otnoshenie k evtanazii." ["GP in Tver: Attitudes to Euthanasia"]. *SOZIS* 7: 95–8.

Lisitzin, Yuri. 1998. "Obshaia chast." ["Essentials"]. Pp. 3–185 in Y. Lisitzin (ed.), *Sozialnaya gigiena i organizatsia zdravookhranenia*. Kazan: Medicoservice.

Malachova, Natalia. 1995. "Rinok uslug zdravookhranenia." ["Market of Health Care System Services"]. *SOZIS* 12: 115–18.

McKeehan, Irina, Roy Campbell, and Sergei Tumanov. 1993. "Obraz zhizni, privichki vliyauchie na zdorovie moscvichei i zakon o medizinskom strachovanii 1991–1993."

["Life-Style, Habits Influencing Health of Moscovites, and Law on Medical Insurance"]. *SOZIS* 3: 45–9.

Ministry of Health of the Russian Federation. 1996. "*Gosudarstvennyi Doklad o Sostoyanii Zdorovia Naselenia Rossiskoi Federatzii v 1995.*" ["State Report on Health of the Russian Federation Population"]. Moscow: Ministry of Health.

Naselenie i obshestvennoe razvitie. [Population and Social Development]. 1988. Edited by T. Ivanova. Moscow: Institute of Sociology.

Nazarova, Inna. 1998. "Subectivnie i obectivnie ozenki zdorovia naseleniya." ["Subjective and Objective Evaluations of Population's Health"]. *Soziologichesky Journal* 3–4: 246–9.

Nemtzov, Alexandr. 1997. "Potreblenie alcogolia i smertnost v Rossii." ["Alchohol Consumption and Mortality in Russia"]. *SOZIS* 9: 113–16.

Osipov, Geenady, Moisey Tulchinsky, and Adolf Kabisha. 1995. *Sociology: A Handbook.* Moscow: Nauka.

Palosuo, Hannele, Antti Uutele, Irvina Zhuravleva, and Nina Lakomava. 1998. "Social Patterning of Ill Health in Helsinki and Moscow: Results from a Comparative Survey in 1991." *Social Science and Medicine* 46: 1121–36.

Palosuo, Hannele and Irina Zhuravleva. 1998. *Vospriatie zdorovia i svzaizanniy s nim privichek i ustanovok.* [Health Perception and Attitudes Connected with It]. Moscow: Institute of Sociology.

Remennick, Larisa and Ronny Shtarkshall. 1997. "Technology versus Responsibility: Immigrant Physicians from the Former Soviet Union Reflect on Israeli Health Care." *Journal of Health and Social Behavior* 38: 191–202.

Rimachevskaya, Natalia. 1997. "Sozialniye posledstvia economicheskih transformatzi v Rossii." ["Social Consequences of the Economic Reforms in Russia"]. *SOZIS* 6: 55–65.

——. 1998. "Project 'Taganrog' (1968–1994)." Pp. 477–84 in V. Yadov (ed.), *Soziologia v Rossi.* Moscow: Institute of Sociology.

Rusinova, Nina and Julie Brown. 1997. "Sozialno-statusnie gruppi: razlichia v subectivnom Zdorovie." ["Social-Status Groups: Differences in the Subjective Health"]. *Peterburgskaya Soziologia* 1: 38–59.

Sadvokasova, E. A. 1969. *Social and Hygienic Aspects of Birth Control.* Moscow: Meditzina.

Samoilov, Vladimir. 1997. *Istoria Rossiskoi meditzini.* [The History of Russian Medicine]. Moscow: Apidavr.

Shilova, Ludmila. 1989. "Samosokhanitelnoye povedenie otdelnikch sozialno-demographicheskikh grup naselenia." ["Self-Protective Behavior of Different Social and Demographic Groups of Population"]. Pp. 54–63 in I. Zhuravleva (ed.), *Otnoshenie cheloveka k zdoroviu a prodolzhitelnosti zhizni.* Moscow: Institute of Sociology.

——. 1993. "Razlichia v samosohranitelnom povedenii muzchin i zhenshin." ["Differences in Self-Protective Behavior of Men and Women"]. Pp. 70–7 in I. Zhuravleva (ed.), *Otnoshenie naselenia k zdoroviu.* Moscow: Institute of Sociology.

——. 1999. "Transformatzia samosokhranitelnogo povedenia." ["Transformation of Self-Protective Behavior"]. *SOZIS* 7: 84–92.

Shingarev, Andrey. 1907. *Vimiraushaya derevnya. Opit sanitarno-epdimiologisheskogo issledovania dvuch seleniy Voronezhskogo uezda.* [Dying Village. The Experience of Sanitary-Epidemiological Study of Two Villages in the Voronez Region]. St. Petersburg, Russia.

Shkolnikov, Vladimir. 1995. "Recent Trends in Russian Mortality: 1993–1994." Paper presented at the USAID Conference, October. Moscow, Russia.

Shkolnikov, Vladimir and Alexander Nemtsov. 1994. "The Anti-Alcohol Campaign and Variations in Russian Mortality." Paper presented at the Workshop on Mortality and Adult Health Priorities in the New Independent States, November, Washington, DC.

Sidorenko Y. and G. Maksimov. 1988. "Ethic and Deontological Voprosi v onkologicheskom Stationari." ["Ethic and Deontological Issues in Cancer Clinics"]. *Zdravoochranenie Rossiskoy Federatzii* 1: 8–11.

Silaste, Galina. 1997. "Sozialnaya adaptazia semei s onkologisheski bolnimi detmi." ["Social Adaptation of Families with Children Having Cancer"]. *SOZIS* 1: 56–64.

Smirnova, Yelena. 1997. "Kogda v semiye rebenok-invalid." ["When the Family has a Handicapped Child"]. *SOZIS* 1: 83–9.

State Report on Health of the Citizens of the Russian Federation in 1997. 1998. Moscow: Ministry of Health of the Russian Federation.

Tankovsky, Vladimir and Nina Shamshurina. 1997. "Sozialno-economicheskiye problemi Oftalmologii." ["Social and Economic Issues of Ophthalmology"]. *SOZIS* 5: 120–3.

Tolmachov, N. T. and I. A. Karaga. 1984. "Sozialno- psychologicheskye factori zdorovia chlenov pervichnogo proizvodstvennogo collectiva." ["Socio-Psychological Factors Influencing Health of the Members of the Industry Community"]. Pp. 101–4 in *Sozialno-philosophskie i mirovozrencheskie problemi zdorovia cheloveka.* Lvov, Ukraine.

Tzargorodtzev, Gennady. 1968. *Sozialnye problemi medizini.* [Social Problems of Medicine]. Moscow.

Usachev, N. 1988 "K voprosu izuchenia medizinsoy aktivnosty selski zhiyteley." ["To the Issue of Medical Activity of People in Rural Regions"]. *Zdravoochranenie Rossiskoy Federatzii* 5: 34–7.

Zhuravleva, Irina. 1988. "Zdorovie i samosokhranitelnoye povedenie." ["Health and Self-Protective Behavior"]. Pp. 156–67 in T. Ivanova (ed.), *Naselenie i obshestvennoye razvitite.* Moscow: Institute of Sociology.

——. 1989. "Aktualnost issledovania." ["Importance of the Research"]. Pp. 5–9 in I. Zhuravleva (ed.), *Otnoshenie cheloveka k zdoroviu i prodolzhitelnosti zhizni.* Moscow: Institute of Sociology.

——. 1997. *Zdorovie podrostkov i okruzhaushi mir.* [Health of Adolescents and Environment]. Moscow: Institute of Sociology.

——. 1998. "Health of the Citizens as an Interdisciplinary Problem. Formation of the Sociology of Health." Pp. 484–9 in V. Yadov (ed.), *Soziologia v Rossii.* Moscow: Institute of Sociology.

Zibzev, Valeriy and Igor Dolzhanskiy. 1990. "Problemi zdravookhranenia glazami chitateley." ["Health Care System Problems from Reader's Perspective"]. *SOZIS* 4: 138–40.

19

In and Out of Communism: The Macrosocial Context of Health in Poland

Nina Ostrowska

Poland belongs to the group of European countries distinguished by the worst health indicators. Particularly striking is the difference in mortality indicators related to chronic diseases between Poland and the countries of western Europe. In the beginning half of the nineties, many unfavorable trends stopped or reversed. Still, many consider the present situation to be far from desirable.

Problems of bad health status, particularly the excessive mortality in eastern Europe, are the subject of numerous debates and publications. Most often, these attempts to explain eastern Europe's bad health status consider factors like lifestyle, quality of medical care, exposure to stress, environmental dangers, or the general well-being of society, and, in general, they blame the communist system for the bad health condition of the Poles. Still, it seems that the truth is more complex and requires taking into account other parameters or, at least, adopting a broader perspective that could illustrate 45 years spent under communism. Additionally, a broader perspective would require looking back to the more distant past to find the historically and culturally determined sources of the Poles' current health condition. In this article, the main focus will be on those macrosocial (i.e. political and economic) factors, which in the last half of the century have determined individual choices for better health in Poland and shaped the context in which styles of life, value systems, aspirations, and stressful experiences exist (Cockerham and Ostrowska 1999).

COMMUNISM

Poland at the beginning of the twentieth century was an economically backward country which was, for more than 100 years, deprived of its own statehood. Conquerors' policies focused on the exploitation of human and natural resources rather than on investments, with foreign capital profiting from cheap labor. The development of a modern capitalist economy and a modern social structure with a middle class as the dominant factor of social change was delayed. The respective governments took no care to develop an educational structure and cultural institutions. There was almost no health care development, and agriculture was especially unprogressive. Peasantry, the largest segment of the population, was mostly illiterate and lived in primitive and unhealthy conditions.

The Polish state was re-established in 1918 and the devastated country slowly began to return to a normal life. The government initiated new social policies and reforms. The state also made some efforts to address the problem of the country's health, which was much worse than that of other European countries, by introducing the health insurance law. The average life expectancy in 1931–2, for example, was 49.2 years while it reached 61.3 years in Germany at that time. The main cause of mortality was infectious diseases, particularly tuberculosis.

The existence of Polish independent state lasted only 20 years, and ended in 1939 with Hitler's invasion of Poland. By the time the war ended, the Polish population had suffered an enormous loss of life; out of 35 million citizens of prewar Poland, over 6 million had perished. The intelligentsia, the most educated stratum of society, lost about 35 percent of its members due to particularly severe reprisals from the hostile Nazi government. The Polish boundaries were moved from east to west and millions of Poles were forced to move from the eastern to the western territories. They abandoned their households and belongings and broke traditional local ties. Undoubtedly, these events were an enormous source of social stress on the macroscale and were not without influence on the people's health (Bejnarowicz 1994). The country was in ruins. Poland signed no peace treaty and therefore could not claim any war reparations. The cold war quickly ended aid from international organizations. The only prospect for Poland was very hard work under conditions of extreme hardship and suffering.

The changes that were of paramount importance were those in the political and economic system. Poland became a member of "The Communist Bloc." The new political order aimed at creating a new society, with the dominant role going to those social classes who had been regarded as inferior throughout Polish history (Szczepański 1970). This new social order was founded on a socialized economy that was based on nationalization and central planning.

According to the communist ideology, the main objective of a socialized economy is to provide for all segments of the population. The educational and health needs of society were particularly essential at this time, so free health care and education at all levels were introduced. Initially, the system excluded farmers who owned their farms (as opposed to other socialist countries, Poland did not carry out mass collectivization).

The peasantry constituted the largest part of population. Hence, it fell to this class to repopulate the destroyed cities and to supply the labor force necessary for industrialization and restoration of Poland. This brought about a new wave of large migrations from the countryside to the cities. For these migrating populations, which were relatively uneducated and not skilled, the migration was a challenge and an opportunity for upward mobility, a better life, better education and health care. However, the first years of this often forced migration were the source of considerable stress and social tensions. The new representatives of the working class experienced many hardships of adaptation. They were not accustomed to life in a city and work in industry. Additionally, they often left their families in the countryside deprived of basic social support. Therefore, at the moment communists started their rule, the society was devastated by war, poorly educated, socially destabilized, had no specialists or infrastructure, and was subject to poor health.

Despite this situation, the postwar years in Poland were marked by many achievements. In addition to the reconstruction of the country destroyed by the war, one can even find apparent effects of activities targeted at health and health care. Although many would raise objections to some of the political and economic decisions of the time, one cannot disregard the fact that during the years 1945–66 over 405,000 individuals completed university studies, which was five times greater than the number during the 20-year-long period between wars. The number of qualified medical professionals also grew substantially. In 1938 there were around 12,900 medical doctors; in 1946 there were only 7,700. However, in 1965 their number rose to 39,600 with the indicator of doctors per 10,000 inhabitants reaching the value of 12.6. This dynamic growth in the number of medical personnel shows the emphasis that was put on the creation of the new and effective socialist health care system, which was seen as a key to the health of the society.

Despite the fact that the development of health care was subordinated to the goal of industrialization, the first years of the socialist regime brought some measurable health results. In 1948, the average life expectancy was 58.6 years (55.6 for men and 61.5 for women). In the next two decades it increased by 12 years (67 for men and 73.5 for women). In the mid-sixties, the indicators of average life expectancy equaled those of the Federal Republic of Germany.

When interpreting this fact, one has to take into account the above-noted advance by substantial parts of the population, especially those which were previously the most vulnerable in this respect. The improvement of living and sanitary conditions, mass employment and education, and the appearance of health care that was the most universal and accessible in Polish history all had important effects. Centralized health care was particularly effective in organizing national health programs like the popularization of hygiene, health screenings, and mass vaccinations. These last two programs were particularly effective in fighting infectious diseases.

These forward-moving trends did not last long, however. They stopped in the same decade and then reversed in the mid-seventies. The average life expectancy, particularly for men, reached its lowest value (66.1 years) at the beginning of the nineties. The amount of sick leave that workers took increased by about 80 percent between the years 1970 and 1992 (Bejnarowicz 1994). This situation leads to many questions, such as: What influenced the decline of health indicators in the second half of the sixties? What happened in Polish society that could influence these changes? Was it a reaction to new situations or was it the result of processes which started much earlier and manifested later? In order to answer these questions, one needs to refer to social determinants of health on different levels of societal organization: politics and ideology, the concept of social development, living standards, functioning of institutions, and also individual behavior and lifestyle which was the consequence of all macrosocial determinants.

First, it is worth noting that the spectacular achievements of centralized socialist health care came mostly from fighting infectious diseases. After successes in this respect, it became more and more clear in the seventies that new health dangers were appearing; these were mostly so-called "civilization diseases," in particular diseases of the blood, circulatory system, and cancer, but also obesity, diabetes, rheumatism, and others. During a ten-year period (1978–88), the percent of people receiving disability benefits increased from 4.1 to 8.6. It turned out that the old mechanisms of taking care of societal health, based on mass programs effective in fighting infectious diseases, were not satisfactory. New problems required a new social policy that would focus more on molding pro-health behavior and habits in the population, as well as on more individualized health care (Kirschner and Kopczyński 1999).

Development of the health care system, which started only in the postwar period, began to stagnate and was not able to react to the changing needs of the society. At the same time, as the population was becoming more and more educated, health demands increased. Services offered to people for whom they were never before provided and for whom every contact with medical science was beneficial, ceased to be satisfactory when their general knowledge and health culture improved. It is worth adding a reflection of a more general nature here: in all countries aiming for communism, a precarious, "claiming" relationship between the individual and the state appeared. Full employment, free health care, low cost of living, and other welfare benefits began to be taken for granted as a right of citizens and an obligation of the state. Often, workers did not think about the relationship between one's productivity and the scope of services obtained. On the other hand, reliable efforts rarely were properly rewarded by the system. What resulted was a sense of hopelessness, bitterness, and a lack of perspective. Imposed egalitarianism obstructed people's aspirations and promoted mediocrity. A certain kind of fatalism developed that was also visible in the sphere of health care. This fatalism was characterized by the idea that "it is not worth it to try and strive, because in the end the results of our actions are outside our control."

At the same time in the macrosocial perspective, it was increasingly clear that many social and health problems resulted from the excessive concern of the state about the economic development of the country. Accelerated industrialization was integral to the socialist development, because socialist states fought to challenge capitalist economies. Competitive development was measured by the rate of economic growth and other economic indicators. A large proportion of the state budget was allocated to huge industrial projects. Unfortunately, the price of focusing on industry was serious underfunding of "non-productive" spheres such as health care. The priority given to economic objectives impinged on issues of a healthy living environment and occupational health (Firkowska-Mankiewicz et al. 1990). For several years, industrial enterprises preferred to pay relatively low penalties for environmental pollution rather than to adopt more costly measures that would reduce environmental pollution. In Poland, there were high rates of mortality from accidents and poisonings. Policies dictated by economic priorities also distorted the health consciousness of the population. Employees were willing to work overtime or in hazardous conditions as long as they were financially compensated.

Despite the fact that the government established a special system of industrial medicine responsible for providing health care to the working class (parallel to the national health system), the material base of health services was insufficient, and sometimes the country experienced acute shortages of basic medical equipment. The medical profession was underpaid and became gradually subject to corruption because of the scarcity of appropriate care. Still, quality health care was better assured for workers than for peasants (private farm owners) who were not covered by a national health insurance system until 1972 and who could participate without charge only in selected health programs.

The People's Republic of Poland had some spectacular health outcomes during its first postwar period. However, when evaluating the general contribution of health care to shaping the health of society during the years 1960–90, it is necessary to point out that the rate of decline in mortality related to conditions amenable to medical care was still a few times lower than in the countries of western Europe (Kirschner and Kopczyński 1999). The health care systems were not prepared, either in organization or in infrastructure, to make use of the advances of modern medicine. This was not only a result of the underinvestment of health care at the expense of the industry development; an important role was also played by the organizational structure, which preferred specialist medical centers and neglected primary care. In the first postwar period a large number of first-line physicians contributed effectively to the improvement of health. However, as Poland developed more specialization and a tendency toward spectacular and costly medical institutions, doctors were slowly losing interest in primary care medicine. They preferred instead highly specialized institutions that could guarantee more prestige and the possibility of gaining additional income from patients' informal payments.

However, these changes in health care cannot be charged with too much responsibility for the worsening health of Polish society. The structure of morbidity and mortality indicators shows that from the beginning of the seventies there were increasing risks of heart disease and cancer. Therefore, elements of a changing lifestyle must be considered. The health policy of the time must also be judged on the basis of activities that could influence the development of healthy lifestyles.

Alcohol overuse has a tradition of over one hundred years, dating back to the partition of Poland. Even at the beginning of the nineteenth century, alcohol production reached 10 liters of pure spirits per capita (Rozenowa 1961). Additionally, traditional Polish cuisine was heavy and based on high consumption of fat and carbohydrates, and low consumption of vegetables and fruits. The rural and urban poor could consume meat only on special occasions. The main diet consisted of products made of flour, potatoes, and cabbage. Physical activity was mostly related to one's job or simply to the activity of getting around.

The postwar victory of the "people's government" and the social promotion of the "working masses" set in motion for the average citizen a longing for a better life. Many understood "better" as the abundant consumption of once scarce products, such as sugar, meat, and fat. In the years 1950–90 the consumption of fat rose, on average, from 700 calories to 1100, mostly due to animal fats (Bejnarowicz 1994). With the increasing affluence of the country, consumption of these products increased. Usually, they were supplemented by alcohol, which was not in shortage and which was relatively cheap and affordable. Also, because of the stresses and scarcities resulting from war devastation in addition to migration and the cost of accelerated industrialization, society began to accept alcohol and cigarettes as popular cures for all problems. These products expanded to take root in society and became an element of everyday reality. In the years 1960 to 1991 alcohol consumption increased by two and a half times and the number of cigarettes smoked doubled. It must be added that, until recently, Polish cigarettes were characterized by a high content of toxic substances and their filters violated quality standards. Although official health policy nominally appreciated the impact of living standards on health, the government generally believed that progress in the sphere of health would take place through medical interventions. This attitude was popular among citizens as well, and they demanded a greater number of medical services.

For a long time, the government did not acknowledge officially that alcoholism and the growth of alcohol consumption were a social problem. No one published data concerning these problems, because it was not in line with the vision of a society aiming for communism. The first sign of an official anti-alcohol policy came in 1956, when the Polish Parliament passed the first anti-alcohol act. However, at that time the sinister effects of alcohol overuse were perceived as a bothersome social pathology rather than a health hazard.

When western European countries began to promote healthy lifestyles in the seventies as a result of epidemiological research pointing out the dominant role of lifestyle in determining life expectancy, Poland was still using a model of societal health that consisted of contacting health care (Ostrowska 1980). This trend prevailed until the nineties. One study undertaken in 1996 revealed that during the three months in which research was conducted, half of adults consulted a physician at least once in health-related matters. This system was not conducive to the creation of pro-health habits through taking individual responsibility for health. In particular, as mentioned earlier, securing health was seen as the duty of the state. Proper nutrition and reducing alcohol and cigarette consumption were the subject of broad educational campaigns, but the campaigns were not accompanied by activities on the part of the state that would facilitate these goals for everyday life. Vodka and cigarettes were cheap, and fresh fruits and vegetables were accessible only some parts of the year. In fact, reducing the consumption of meat was more regulated by economic problems and limited supply than by a deliberate policy of molding consumption decisions. It is noteworthy that there were unquestionable efforts to popularize physical culture and sports. However, to a great extent, they were addressed only to children and youths.

OUT OF COMMUNISM

In 1990, Poland initiated a transformation of the political and socioeconomic system, the goals of which were the introduction of democratic principles and a market economy. The first years of the transformation, long awaited and commonly expected to solve all of the country's problems, brought many disappointments. Unemployment, inflation, the sudden impoverishment of a large part of the society, and the lack of basic social security as guaranteed by the former system, were the source of new, previously unknown stresses. Public opinion polls conducted during the years 1990 to 1993 revealed decreasing feelings of security, increasing fears about the threat of poverty and, in general, decreasing optimism about both the individual's future and the future of the country. This social anxiety was also accompanied by the rise of social pathologies of all kinds, like suicide due to the inability to adapt to a new situation and economic crime committed by more "entrepreneurial" individuals who took advantage of loopholes in the still-in-flux economic system. For example, during the beginning of the nineties, there was unprecedented importation of large amounts (millions of liters) of cheap alcohol that was out of state control. Easily accessible alcohol, together with the stresses experienced by a substantial part of society, led to an abrupt growth in alcohol consumption (from about 6 liters of pure spirit annually per capita in 1988 to 10 liters in 1991 [Zatonski 1996]). The society also faced problems of drug addiction in schools, and spontaneous growth in the market for narcotics.

Increasingly poor health indicators accompanied the general anxiety experienced by citizens. The years 1990–1 were the most critical, because many health indicators reached their worst values during the postwar period. Mortality rates grew considerably in general, but particularly in men aged 15–64. The sudden change in rates was related to an increase in mortality due to sudden causes (which is associated with alcohol consumption) and circulatory system diseases, which are hypothetically related to the strength of macrostressors. The first years of the nineties were also characterized by the highest percentage of infants with a birth weight below 2,500 grams, which indicates a decline in living standards of women. During the years 1990 through 1993 an increased occurrence of tuberculosis was noted, which for many years had ceased to be a problem in Poland. Concurrently, underfunded health care, now in a state of organizational disorder, decreased the quality of its services. According to World Bank estimates, almost one-third of providing units did not meet necessary standards. Doctors' income, which in the West is higher than average, was about the same as average in Poland. Sociological research done in 1992 revealed that every seventh patient made informal payments for health care that was supposed to be still nominally free of charge (Kopczyński and Halik 1997). In this context, comprehensive reform became necessary instead of temporary measures. However, the process of reaching consensus about what the principles of reform should be and how it should be implemented lasted for almost a decade.

Official explanations for the worsening health status of Poles emphasize the price that societies must pay for abrupt and deep social changes, to which society takes time to adjust. In what had been a materially egalitarian society, the processes of polarization began and social inequalities appeared more and more clearly, especially in the sphere of health. While in the seventies and eighties there was no significant correlation between self-reported morbidity and indicators of social position, research conducted in 1991 found such an association in regard to income and general perception of one's material situation (Ostrowska 1992). The greatest cost of the economic transformation was shouldered by families with many children, the older and disabled, and workers and farmers in general. The lack of state policies concerned with the impoverishment of a substantial part of the population suggested that what was already an unfavorable health status might deteriorate.

However, against this pessimistic outlook, a decrease or at least a stabilization of many of the unfavorable health indicators appeared, starting in 1993. It was particularly visible in the case of mortality rates. For example, the infant mortality rate decreased from 17.9 per 1,000 live births in 1991 to 13.6 in 1995. There was also a sharp drop in deaths caused by circulatory diseases, the main cause of premature deaths in Poland. In this same period of time, the standardized indicators of circulatory diseases per 100 thousand inhabitants decreased from 609 to 532. A comparison of subjective health status for the years 1992 and 1995 also revealed improvement in people's evaluations, in particular where psychological frame of mind is concerned. This puzzling, "accelerated" reversal of trends in health raises questions about its underlying factors.

When analyzing the macrosocial context of Poland's change, one has to note that during this particular period of time definitive improvement in the country's situation did not yet appear. After 1992 there was an increase in GDP and industrial production and a decrease of inflation and budget deficit, unemployment was still growing in 1993 and started to decrease only in the next year. Health expenditures remained at a similar level (5 to 5.3 percent of GDP), and indicators of health risks in the work environment did not improve. Crime was increasing and the number of suicides did not decrease.

Despite this, public opinion polls in 1993 and 1994 noted a sense of social stabilization connected to people's acclimatization to the new socioeconomic reality and the principles of market economy (Marody 1996). General feelings of insecurity and uncertainty diminished as the public learned new strategies for dealing with life under new rules. One can presume that feelings of normalization combined with increasingly effective individual mechanisms of adaptation influenced and lowered what was for years a major societal health risk – social stresses. The shadow economy could also have played a certain protective role not seen in statistics. This phenomenon, difficult to estimate in numbers, is usually seen as a socioeconomic pathology. However, the existence of a shadow economy undoubtedly counteracted the impoverishment of some part of society. According to existing estimates, illegal work was an important source of income for the unemployed, narrowing the official extent of poverty (Beskid 1997).

It is worth noting that changes in the economic system, particularly the introduction of a market economy, led to important modifications of the Poles' lifestyle. The range of available food products, weakly diversified in socialist times, changed radically. Diversity, attractive packaging, and commercials appeared in the market, extending the possibility of choice. It is worth adding that commercials for food often utilized health-related arguments and cited known and respected medical professionals (one example could be arguments for changing animal fats to vegetable ones).

Because of these changes, the average Polish diet began to "Westernize" and to improve. Polish people consumed more citrus fruits, fresh vegetables, and other fruits as they became available throughout the year. Also the new price structure seemed to favor pro-health products; for example, the price of poultry is now lower than the price of either pork or beef. The average energy value (daily intake) of food consumed decreased from 3489 calories in 1989 to 3172 in 1976. The patterns of alcohol consumption changed as well. Although average consumption of alcohol did not change, the distribution did. In the years 1992 through 1995 the share of people annually drinking more than 10 liters of alcohol decreased, and the percentage of those who drink only a small amount (less than a liter) increased. This shift in drinking patterns was definitely influenced by the growing supply and commercial promotion of beer, which slowly started to appear in social situations where vodka would have previously been present. The health consequences of this fact, although not affecting all strata to the same extent, can be generally judged as positive.

Two other important factors that modified the lifestyle of Poles were the opening of eastern Europe to the West and the country's growing aspirations for joining the European Community. Stimulating new lifestyles can create the background for changing attitudes and behaviors (Cockerham and Ostrowska 1999). The growing health awareness of the society plays a role as well. Consumers increasingly check the expiration date of products, along with their chemical content or the possibility of hazardous packaging. It seems that the Polish people are coming to value health itself, and using it as an important attribute for improvement in one's life situation.

Obviously, it is hard to judge to what extent the changes presented, occurring in such a short period of time, could influence the improvement of Poland's health status (e.g. in the years 1991–7 the male life expectancy rose from 66.1 to 68.5). Even if these socioeconomic changes have not yet contributed, they are likely to have a positive impact in the long run. Still, it must be emphasized that these positive changes affect only the wealthier and better-educated part of society. There is a rising danger of increasing social inequalities in the realm of health and health care. It is also hard to predict whether health indicators will continue to improve and whether the change in trends will be merely temporary. The Polish lifestyle has generally become more rational, but it is still worse than those in western Europe. Will it improve further? At what pace?

In 1999, the long-awaited health care reform has finally come. However, it has not been a source of patients' satisfaction; rather, it deprived Polish society of the privilege of free access to medical services. Despite the fact that this privilege was never fully realized, it gave the people an elementary feeling of security in the sphere of health. According to a survey conducted after the introduction of reform, the majority of respondents awaited the new health care system with anxiety and only a few with hope. In principle, it is supposed to change the system of medical financing through the introduction of health insurance and a new institution called "Sickness Funds," which will mediate between the patient and the health care system. For most Poles, their insurance premium equals 7.5 percent of their income. It is collected from employers as a part of income tax, and it entitles insured people to a package of basic services. Regional Sickness

Funds receive premiums and contract services from providers (state-owned or private hospitals, clinics and outpatient units).

The reform prioritizes primary care, reinstates the role of family doctors, delegates authority over primary health care to local governments, and creates a system of financial incentives that are expected to prevent corruption. The government expects also that changes in health care provision will reduce the excessive use of high-cost treatments.

The reform implementation, which coincided with the reform of the administrative and pension systems of the country, was not prepared well enough and hence resulted in organizational chaos and conflicts between doctors, patients, and Sickness Funds (at least in the first few months). These conflicts were magnified by the fact that the creation of new regional bureaucracy turned out to be very costly, and the salaries of insurance managers are several times higher than the salaries of doctors. This fact causes dissatisfaction among patients (who believe that their money is being wasted) and makes the negotiations of contracts between Sickness Funds and health providers more difficult. However, because the new institutional rules have been functioning only a short time, it is impossible to evaluate their long-term effects.

SOCIOLOGY OF MEDICINE

Sociology of medicine as a separate scientific discipline has existed in Poland since the mid-1960s. In the beginning, it developed exclusively within the academic framework of sociology. It constituted a domain of knowledge about society, similar to the sociology of law, politics, or religion. From this perspective sociologists analyzed illness behavior, health culture, and the institution of medicine as a social system (Titkow 1974; Bizon 1976; Sokołowska and Kosinski 1978; Uramowska 1980). The study of health care utilization and the related attitudes and expectations of patients also has a relatively long tradition. The fact that medical services in Poland were only partially nationalized (medical cooperatives and private practice existed) allowed for analyses of different aspects of health care delivery in various sectors (Sokołowska 1969; Ostrowska 1975; Titkow 1983). During the 1980s studies of the health care system became openly critical, indicating discrepancies between medical sector capabilities and social requirements, as well as indicating organizational pathologies and growing corruption (Halik 1988).

Another area of interest in Polish medical sociology has been the emerging health problems of the population. In general, epidemiologists studied public health problems rather than sociologists. Still, there were some topics that became the subject of sociological investigations. For example, sociologists focused much attention on the problems of health inequalities, workers' health in heavy industry, and the impact of living and working conditions on health (Sokołowska et al. 1965; Sokołowska 1980; Tobiasz-Adamczyk 1984; Wnuk and Lipinski 1987; Wnuk-Lipinski, and Illsley 1990; Bejnarowicz 1994). Gender-related inequalities in health were also examined within this framework. More recently, the relationship between lifestyle and health became a subject of research interest. It has been conceptualized as a sociological category – as everyday behavior which identifies individuals' social position, aspirations and motivations, and also their structural and macrostructural determinants (Gniazdowski 1990; Ostrowska 1999).

The increasingly visible deficiencies of health care directed the attention of researchers to the family as a social system that has to compensate for insufficient medical care of the chronically-ill and disabled. Frequently, researchers studied coping mechanisms and the various consequences of illness for the functioning of families (Butrym 1987; Radochoński 1987). Another interesting concern for sociological analysis was the expansion of unconventional alternative healing methods, positioned to a greater or lesser extent against official medicine and receiving growing criticism (Piatkowski 1990a, 1990b). These studies also helped to penetrate the lay concepts of health and disease that existed in the Polish society (Puchalski 1994).

The impulse for the development of medical sociology that came from the medical side was more oriented toward concrete problem solving. It originated among psychiatry and rehabilitative medicine representatives. They tend to understand better than other doctors that the life problems of their patients are equally medical and social in nature. The alliance with psychiatrists influenced the development of community psychiatry and changed mental hospitals. The collaboration of sociologist and rehabilitative medicine specialists in 1978 helped to prepare the National Report on Disability and Rehabilitation, which became an important tool for shaping social policy. Further studies on this subject were devoted to social attitudes toward handicapped people and structural factors causing their social marginalization (Rychard 1983; Gorczycka 1992; Ostrowska and Sikorska 1996).

In the 1990s the impact of sociopolitical and economic transformation on the health and well-being of the society became a concern of medical sociologists. It particularly brought attention to the consequences of "socialist welfare state" withdrawal and to health problems associated with poverty and unemployment (Ostrowska 1992; Bejnarowicz 1994). Also, researchers investigated subjects related to planned health care reform (Włodarczyk 1995). The new trend toward public health is blooming as health promotion finds many enthusiasts among Polish medical sociologists. The scientific quarterly "Health Promotion, Social Sciences and Medicine" has been in publication since 1994.

Sociology of medicine has been inspired by general sociological theory, rather than by the specific theoretical concepts of western medical sociology. The structural-functionalist theory was most popular among researchers. This theory was especially attractive for eastern European societies. The Marxist emphasis on conflict could not be applied to the analysis of a socialist society, which was expected to be conflictless. Parsons's vision of cooperation, goodwill, and the mutually complementary components of a system met the ideological pattern of a socialist society in many respects. Paradoxically, in Poland there were very few medical sociology studies that could be directly derived from the traditions of Marxist sociological theory. In 1970s some empirical studies were inspired by symbolic interactionism, and in 1980s there were some analyses located within phenomenological and ethnomethodological traditions. However, the majority of empirical studies tended to neglect theory, or to use it only to a limited degree. Mainly due to financial reasons, in the 1990s medical sociology became increasingly institutionalized within medicine rather than sociology. Because of this, the de-theorizing of medical sociology became progressively worse.

References

Bejnarowicz, Janusz. 1994. "Zmiany stanu zdrowia i jego uwarunkowan. Wyzwania dla promocji zdrowia." ["Changes of Health Status and its Determinants. Challenges for Health Promotion"]. *Promocja Zdrowia. Nauki Społeczne i Medycyna*, 1–2.

Beskid, Lidia. 1997. "Potoczne oceny poziomu życia." ["Common Evaluations of Living Conditions"]. In H. Domański and A. Rychard (eds.), *Elementy nowego ładu*. Warsaw: IFiS PAN.

Bizon, Zdzisław. 1976. "Adaptation Patterns of the Medical System and Social Change." In M. Sokołowska, J. Holowka, and A. Ostrowska (eds.), *Health, Medicine, Society*. Warsaw, Dordrecht: PWN and D. Reider Publishing Company.

Butrym, Zofia. 1987. *Funkcjonowanie rodziny a choroba*. [Illness and Family Functioning]. Lublin: Akademia Medyczna.

Cockerham, William C. and Antonina Ostrowska. 1999. *Changes in Health Lifestyles. The Transition out of Communism in Poland*. Paper presented at the World Congress of International Institute of Sociology, Tel Aviv.

Firkowska-Mankiewicz, Anna et al. 1990. "Ideology – Politics – Health: A View from Poland." *Health Promotion International* 5.

Gniazdowski, Andrzej. 1990. *Zachowania zdrowotne*. [Health Behavior]. Lodz: Instytut Medycyny Pracy.

Gorczycka, Ewa. 1992. *Polityka społeczna wobec osółb niepelnosprawnych*. [Social Policy Towards Disabled People]. Czestochowa: Politechnika Czestochowska.

Halik, Janusz. 1988. "Rola kontaktów nieformalnychw korzystaniu ze świadczeń Warszawskiej słuzby zdrowia." ["The Role of Informal Contacts in the use of Warsaw Health Care Services"]. In J. Kostrzewski and J. Kopczyń[]ski (eds.), *Perspektywy zdrowotne Polski*. Wroclaw: Ossolineum.

Kirschner, Henryk and Janusz Kopczyński.1999. *Aktualne problemy zdrowotne. Zagrożenia i szanse*. [Present Health Problems. Threats and Chances]. Warsaw: IGNIS.

Kopczyński, Janusz and Janusz Halik. 1997. "Zdrowie ludnosci i jego ochrona." ["Health of Population and Health Care"]. In *Społeczeństwo polskie w latach 1989–96*. Warsaw: Friedrich Ebert Stiftung.

Marody, Mira. 1996. *Oswajanie rzeczywistosci. Między realnym socjalizmem a realną demokracją*. [Domesticating Reality. Between Real Socialism and Real Democracy]. Warsaw: ISS.

Ostrowska, Antonina. 1975. *Opinie społeczeństwa polskiego o lekarzach i placówkach służby zdrowia*. [Opinions of the Polish Society About Doctors and the Health Care System]. Warsaw: Ossolineum.

——. 1980. *Elementy kultury zdrowotnej społeczeństwa polskiego*. [Elements of Health Culture of the Polish Society]. Warsaw: OBOP.

——. 1992. "Sytuacja społeczno-ekonomiczna a stan zdrowia." ["Socio-Economic Conditions and Health"]. In L. Beskid (ed.), *Warunki zycia i kondycja Polaków na początku zmian systemowych*. Warsaw: IFiS PAN.

——. 1999. *Styl życia a zdrowie. Z zagadnien promocji zdrowia*. [Lifestyle and Health. From the Health Promotion Issues]. Warsaw: IFiS PAN.

Ostrowska, Antonina and Joanna Sikorska. 1996. *Syndrom niepełnosprawnosci w Polsce. Bariery integracji.* [Disability Syndrome in Poland. Barriers to Integration]. Warsaw: IFiS PAN.

Piatkowski, Włodzimierz. 1990a. *Listy do Kaszpirowskiego.* [Letters to Kashpirovsky]. Lublin: Marek Los.

——. 1990b. *Spotkania z inną medycyną.* [Meetings with Another Medicine]. Lublin: UMCS.

Puchalski, Krzysztof. 1994. "Kryteria zdrowia w potocznej świadomości." ["Health Criteria in a Common-Sense Knowledge"]. *Promocja Zdrowia. Nauki Społeczne i Medycyna* 1–2.

Radochonski, Mieczysław. 1987. *Choroba a rodzina.* [Illness and Family]. Rzeszów: Wyższa Szkoła Pedagogiczna.

Rozenowa, Helena. 1961. *Produkcja wódki i sprawa pijaństwa w Polsce.* [Production of Vodka and Drunkenness Issues in Poland]. Warsaw: PWN.

Rychard, Andrzej. 1983. *Organizacyjne ideologie instytucji rehabilitujących.* [Rehabilitating Institutions and Their Organizational Ideologies]. Warsaw: IFiS PAN

Sokołowska, Magdalena et al. 1965. *Lekarze przemysłowi.* [Industrial Physicians]. Wroclaw: Ossolineum.

——. 1980. *Granice medycyny.* [The Limits of Medicine]. Warszawa: Wiedza Powszechna.

——(ed.). 1969. *Badania socjologiczne w medycynie.* [Sociological Research in Medicine]. Warsaw: Książka i Wiedza.

Sokołowska, Magdalena and Stanisław Kosinski (eds.). 1978. *Socjologia zawodów medycznych.* [Sociology of Medical Professions]. Warsaw: IFiS PAN.

Szczepański, Jan. 1970. *Polish Society.* New York: Random House.

——. 1973. *Zmiany społeczeństwa polskiego w procesie uprzemysłowienia.* [Changes of Polish Society in the Process of Industrialization]. Warsaw: CRZZ.

Titkow, Anna. 1976. "Zachowania związane ze zdrowiem i chorobą jako element wiedzy o społeczeństwie." ["Health and Illness Related Behavior as a Component of Knowledge About Society"]. *Studia Socjologiczne* 3.

——. 1983. *Zachowania i postawy wobec zdrowia i choroby.* [Attitudes and Behavior Towards Health and Illness]. Warsaw: PWN.

Tobiasz-Adamczyk, Beata. 1984. *Absencja chorobowa i jej psychospołeczne uwarunkowania.* [Psychosocial Factors Influencing Absenteeism]. Krakow: Akademia Medyczna.

Uramowska, Barbara. 1980. *Medycyna jako wiedza i system działań.* [Medicine as a Knowledge and System of Activities]. Wroclaw: Ossolineum.

Włodarczyk, Cezary. 1995. *Projekt ustawy o powszechnym ubezpieczeniu zdrowotnym.* [National Health Insurance Project]. *Antidotum* 11 and 12.

Wnuk-Lipinski, Edmund. 1987. *Nierówności i uposledzenie w swiadomosci społecznej.* [Inequality and Inequity in Social Consciousness]. Warsaw: IFiS PAN.

Wnuk-Lipinski, Edmund and Raymond Illsley (eds.). 1990. "Non- Market Economies in Health." *Social Science and Medicine* 8.

Zatoński, Witold. 1996. *Rozwój sytuacji zdrowotnej w Polsce po roku 1988.* [Health Situation Development After the Year 1988 in Poland]. Warsaw: Centrum Onkologii.

20

Transformation of the Health Care System in the Czech Republic – A Sociological Perspective

Hana Janečková

The Czech Republic arose from the former Czechoslovakia, which was established after the disintegration of the Austrian–Hungarian Monarchy in 1918 as a democratic country with a modern industry and well-developed social and health care system. Czechoslovakia became a part of the Soviet Bloc after World War II. This merger impacted political, economic, and social life negatively. The only experience of political freedom came during the short period of the so-called "Prague Spring" which was curtailed by the Soviet occupation in 1968. Czechoslovakia finally became free after the "velvet" revolution in November 1989. In January 1993, the country was peacefully divided into two independent states – the Czech Republic and the Slovak Republic. The revolution meant the replacement of the totalitarian political model employed by the Soviet government with a modern pluralistic democracy open to political freedom, a market economy, and human rights.

MAIN DEMOGRAPHIC AND SOCIOECONOMIC CHARACTERISTICS

This small central European country, a member of NATO since 1999, occupies a territory of about 79,000 square kilometers and has about 10.3 million inhabitants with the density of population totaling 131 persons per square kilometer (Čákiová 1999). The country is politically divided into 76 districts, each with about 120,000 inhabitants with the exception of the capital Prague, which contains 1.2 million people. Historically, there has been two parts: Bohemia on the west and Moravia on the east. The socioeconomic differences between regions are increasing in connection with the restructuralization of heavy industry and with rapidly growing unemployment in some regions. In northern and western Bohemia as well as in northern Moravia where coal mines, heavy machinery, and chemical industry are traditionally concentrated, unemployment reaches 17.7 percent while in Prague it is only 2.7 percent. These regions are also characterized by a high level of social deprivation and pathology, ethnic problems, and bad environmental conditions. Also differences between big cities and the countryside increases in regard to the average wages, unemployment, and accessibility of services including public transport and health care.

According to national statistics, 24 percent of inhabitants over 15 years of age have only a basic education (8 or 9 years), 35 percent have secondary vocational education, 34 percent have full secondary education and 8 percent have university level education. With the exception of basic education, percentages of the population classified in the remaining educational categories increased during the last 10 years.

As in other European countries, the Czech population is aging. Since 1918, the number of deaths has exceeded the number of births. Also, the size of the population is expected to decline, as shown in table 20.1, and grow older at the same time. Due to prolonged life expectancy, women live 2.1 years longer and men 2.9 years longer than 4 years ago. In 1997, the proportion of the population over 65 years of age was 13.6 percent which signifies a 1.1 percent increase compared to 1987 (12 percent of 65+). Also in 1997, there were 20 people of post-productive age for every 100 people of productive age, which is a rather high level of dependency. Table 20.1 shows that the proportion of seniors over 60 years (post-productive age) will grow more than 4 percent yearly (from present 18 percent of population up to 25 percent in 2010).

Table 20.1 Demographic prognosis

| Age | Proportion of inhabitants (%) | | | |
	1995	2000	2005	2010
0–14	19.0	18.5	18.0	16.8
15–59	60.7	60.6	59.2	57.7
60+	20.3	20.9	22.8	25.5

Source: Faculty of Natural Sciences of Charles University, Prague.

The Czech Republic belonged to the highly developed countries during its modern history. In its territory, 70 percent of the economic potential of the former Austrian-Hungarian monarchy was produced. Between the first and second World Wars the Czechoslovak Republic was ranked among the 15 most developed countries of the world. The economy was terribly damaged during the communist period; however, it still stayed ahead of the other countries of the Soviet Bloc. The economic transformation was relatively successful till 1997. Since this year, indicators have shown economic crisis connected with the decrease of the GDP (–3.6 percent in 1998 comparing to 1990), increasing unemployment (8.4 percent in June 1999, which is 2.8 percent more than in the same period in 1998), deficit in the state budget, decrease in investments, and 10 percent inflation.

The Health Status of the Population

Until the 1960s, the health status of the Czech population was the best in Europe. The centralist system of health care was successful in the eradication of infectious disease through effective vaccination and better hygiene and sanitation. Since then, growth of the cardiovascular and oncological diseases started to significantly influence the health status of the population. Total standardized mortality rate (SMR) for all causes of death in the CR surpassed the EU by 16 percent in 1970, by 26 percent in 1980, and by nearly 30 percent in 1995. Specific mortality rates due to cardiovascular and oncological diseases were the highest in Europe. While in the countries of EU, the SMR continuously declined as a result of cardiovascular diseases, in the CR it was increasing through the first half of the 1980s when a mild decrease in mortality began. Since 1991, a significant decrease of the SMR due to cardiovascular diseases was observed but did not reach the European level. Previously the number of deaths related to oncological diseases had always remained higher than that in western countries. While the incidence of cancer is getting higher, a mild decrease of the SMR due to malignant neoplasms also began in the 1990s. The distribution of the causes of death is very stable in the CR: cardiovascular diseases represent 56 percent of all deaths, cancer 25 percent, external causes (injuries, poisoning) 7 percent, respiratory diseases 4 percent, diseases of the digestive system 4 percent.

Life expectancy indices showed stagnation during the 1970s and 1980s and in the case of men, it decreased compared to 1960. The 20 years of declining health concerned mainly middle and older age groups. Since 1990, the life expectancy at birth has increased 2.9 years for men and 2.1 years for women. In 1997 it reached 70.5 years for males and 77.5 years for females. It is still 6–7 years less for males and 4–5 years less for females compared to European countries with the highest rates. Analysts say that life expectancy at birth will increase, but will not reach that of the countries of EU until 2020. The only comparable decline to that of western Europe was infant mortality. In 1997 the infant mortality rate reached 5.9 per 1,000 births.

The latest documentation of life expectancy and mortality rates in the CR differs significantly from that of other postcommunist countries. Initially, it was the decline in cardiovascular mortality, particularly amongst older age groups, that caused this phenomenon. A very complex and synergic influence of more factors seems to be the most important. The fact there have been tremendous changes in the health care system, numerous investments in medical technology, improvement in the quality of care, in particular the ability to make earlier diagnoses, more effective medication, and cardiosurgery available to elderly people, has played an important role. Since 1985, the people of this particular population have shown a noticeable change in their lifestyle. This change is indicated by a decrease in fat and milk consumption and an increase in nutrition, intake of more vegetables and fruits. (Drbal 1997; Škodová et al. 1997). Smoking amongst men has also declined over the last 13 years (in 1996, 32 percent of men and 20 percent of women smoked daily).

The impact that environmental conditions had on the relative health status of the population was exaggerated at the end of the 1980s as a means for combating political forces that did not recognize the importance of environmental awareness. The negative impact of air pollution on people's health was evident but its global impact on mortality was minimal. Bobak and Feachem reported that only 2–3 percent of the global mortality in 1987 was caused by air pollution (Bobak and Feachem 1995). The decline of environmental conditions in some parts of the country (Northern and Western Bohemia, Northern Moravia) has been attributed to coal mining, energy production (power plants), heavy and chemical industries, in combination with typical socio-economical and sociopathological phenomena (low education of population, higher unemployment, lower income, ethnic minorities, criminality etc.). While the air and water pollution increased dramatically, the social structure amongst inhabitants of these regions did not change very much (high unemployment being the typical feature) and table 20.2 shows that differences between regions in the health status indices or social risk factors remained.

Table 20.2   Values of the selected demographic characteristics in different typological groups of patients

	A Districts with the most favorable environment n = 21		B Districts with the most devastated environment n = 8		C Difference B – A	
	1990	1997	1990	1997	1990	1997
Life expectancy of men	68.1	69.2	65.7	67.4[*]	−2.4	−1.8
Life expectancy of women	75.4	76.3	72.7	74.5[*]	−2.7	−1.8
Standardized mortality per 1,000 inhab.	11.5	9.8	13.9	11.0	+ 2.1	+ 1.2
Infant mortality	5.7	5.3	10.7	9.0	+ 4.4	+ 3.7
Abortions per 100 live births	83.2	53.4	108.7	74.6	+ 25.5	+ 21.4
Divorces per 1,000 inhab.	2.3	2.5	4.4	4.0	+ 2.1	+ 1.5
Suicides per 100,000 inhab.	12.2	13.6	14.0[**]	12.9[**]	+ 1.8	− 0.7

[*] 1995
[**] 1994 and 1998

Source: IHIS Praha. Typological groups according to Moldan 1990.
A = group of districts with relatively high level of environment, with favorable indicators of social environment and with favorable indicators of mortality, significantly lower than the average of the CR.
B = group of districts with extremely devastated environment, with very bad indicators of social environment and with significantly increased mortality rate.

At the end of the 1980s, the overall reduced health of the population proved to be a major issue, giving rise to a political crisis within the government. In 1990, during the beginning stages of the reformation process, the government declared that improvement of the overall health of the population would be the primary goal of health care reform. However, politicians did not take the proclaimed goal seriously. This sent health care reform in a different direction throughout the years that followed.

THE HEALTH CARE SYSTEM – RAPID TRANSFORMATION FROM CENTRALIST STATE HEALTH CARE SYSTEM TO THE GENERAL HEALTH INSURANCER AND PLURALISTIC MARKET-BASED MODEL

The Social Climate

As a result of the political changes in 1989, all areas of social life suffered major consequences. The "change" itself as well as the vision of the healing role of the market economy, privatization, diminishing state control, and increased individual responsibility, became dominating ideologies. This increased freedom brought new opportunities to all people involved with the health care system – patients, the state and health care professionals, particularly physicians. Reformation substantially impacted the entire health care system completely changing its financing, organization, and ownership. The rate of change can be explained in terms of the overall reduced health of the population. The accomplishment of this goal would be challenging, not only to policy makers but also to physicians who frequently suffered periods of frustration. However, they honestly believed that increased competition would improve the quality of care and contribute to fair evaluations of their jobs through a fee-for-service system.

Later on, doubts and criticism emerged concerning the speed of reformation. There were also arguments and concerns dealing with the efficiency of correspondence and coherence between health care reform and the processes that were actually taking place in the communities and society as a whole. Health was understood as a commodity and an individual problem, the market was supposed to distinguish between good and bad providers of health care, and also should have reflected the health needs of the population. It was believed that governmental regulation or management in health care was unnecessary (Kalina 1992). Under the influence of liberal ideology, radical changes were implemented without any serious consideration of the needs of society, without a complete evaluation of the previous existing health care system, without comparisons to foreign health care systems and without respecting any warnings from experts abroad. Shockingly, the Institute of Social Medicine in Prague (ÚSLOZ), originally the only institution where any empirical research took place, was abolished in 1993.

In this context, the latest sociological studies have shown interesting results. Health care is one area of the social system in which Czech citizens expect the state to play a strong role. In the Survey on Family and Reproduction, 70 percent of women between 15 and 44 years of age expressed the opinion that the state should bear the full responsibility in the area of health care and care for the elderly (Čákiová 1999: 87). In her latest research, Křížová reports similar results (Křížová 1999 – oral communication). Some 57 percent of respondents believed that the state would be more effective in regulating health care for the population than insurance companies. An international comparative study (Večerník and Matějů 1998) showed that in the CR only 17 percent of inhabitants were convinced that hospitals should be private property. Ninety-seven percent agreed that the government should assure health care for people, and 83 percent believed that the government should increase expenditures for health care (Večerník and Matějů 1998). Also, the Charter of Basic Human Rights, which has become a part of the Czech Constitution, says that the state guarantees every citizen the right to free health care provision on the basis of general health insurance as well as for the preservation of healthy living conditions. Contrary to the charter, major forces of the Czech health care system – particularly physicians – implemented complete change in the financing and organization of health care provisions. From their point of view, they believed that the change would fulfil the following important goals:

- improve their socioeconomic position
- extend their diagnostic and therapeutic possibilities (new drugs, technology) and thus improve the quality of care for patients
- supply more sources
- improve effectiveness and management of the health services

Later developments not only disappointed physicians but also the public.

Principle Changes in the Health Care System Organization (1989–1999)

The former health care system had a fixed organizational structure based on the Regional and District Institute of National Health, which integrated all health facilities in the given territory. The Ministry of Health (MoH) supervised the quality of care through the main specialists (central, regional, and district) in all medical branches. The MoH was also responsible for legislation, medical research, situations concerning hygiene, and drug policy. All health facilities had their catchment areas, so that patients could not select their own physicians. This system formed a dense network of basic health services, easily accessible for people, with well-developed preventive health care for younger generations, dental care, and health promotion strategies. The primary problems of the old health care system were the lack of financial sources, old and insufficient medical technology, lack of drugs, lack of motivation for professionals, black market, bribes, and animosity between health care professionals and patients. At the beginning of reformation, ethical challenges were very taxing.

The first step of the transformation (1990–2) led to the abolition of this centrally organized structure, which seemed highly ineffective. The state monopoly was unacceptable because physicians suffered from a shortage of financial resources and from a lack of clinical freedom. Individual health facilities obtained legal and economic independence. Later they were either privatized (particularly smaller health centers, i.e. primary care and special ambulatory care) or in the case of a few hospitals transferred to communities or churches. Most hospitals remained in the hands of the state controlled by the District

Authority (the Health Department) or, in the case of large or teaching hospitals, under the control of the Ministry of Health.

Though removal of state control was the dominant philosophy of most health facilities in that period (1992–3), frequently the process was unsuccessful for economic and legal reasons. For hospitals, it was very difficult to profit. Some of them fell into tremendous debt. Legislation regarding the not-for-profit sector was missing. In fact, reform of the health sector was simplified and reduced to the mere privatization taking place in industry and business. It was more an ideological affair than a reasonable, well-prepared and coordinated process, because it cost too much energy and too much money. Thousands of privatization projects were elaborated and passed through privatization commissions established in each district. The projects were assessed from many aspects (privatization design, economic effect, solvency of the proposer, etc.) but first of all the privatization of property should not have threatened the accessibility of the health care for the population. At present, process of decentralization and privatization is virtually finished. More than one-half of all physicians work in private sectors.

In 1998, there were about 25,000 individual health facilities in the CR (out of the original 142 state health organizations existing before 1990). Most of them were private practices of GPs, GPs for children, gynecologists, and dentists, who had traditionally formed the network of primary care. Practically all ambulatory specialists were private, too. Some physicians formed an association or a company and privatized a policlinic or another health facility together.

The state owned about 685 health facilities. Of those 685 facilities, 27 were large regional and university hospitals directly managed by the MoH and 82 were hospitals managed by the District Authorities. Cities or communities owned 261 health facilities. Of those 261, 43 were hospitals. Some 64 hospitals belonged to the church or to other private entities.

Health Care Financing Reform

Before reform, health care in the Czech Republic was financed exclusively through the state budget. Health care made up about 4 percent of the GDP. There was a substantial shortage of sources for expensive drugs, modern medical technology, modernization of buildings, and adequate wages. The lack of economic incentive discouraged health care professionals in their work. The population's limited access to many health care services gave way to a black market and under-the-table payments. These factors made up the principal causes of the common crisis of the Czech health care system in the 1980s. Even before 1989, some proposals were submitted to increase the functional and organizational autonomy of the Regional and District Institutes of National Health.

Czech reformists adopted the model of general health insurance as the main source for health care financing because of its tradition in this country before World War II. The corresponding legislation was prepared very quickly and passed by the Parliament in 1991–2 under significant political pressure.

Health insurance companies were built as public institutions established by law to collect and administer the resources of public health insurance. The largest one, the General Health Insurance Company (GHIC) came into existence in 1992. Shortly after the GHIC, the government also allowed other health insurance companies (HICs) for some professional groups like police, military service, miners, and bank employees. The lack of legal possibilities for cost containment under the fee-for-service system and the lack of rules for dealing with public sources led to a misuse of general insurance sources to accommodate the private interests of health care providers or pharmaceutical companies. This led to the progressive deterioration of financial stability in the insurance system.

The New Public Health Insurance Act, adopted in 1997, brought the most substantial changes in health care financing since 1992. It clearly defined the fund's ability to impose limitations in contracts with health care providers and permitted alternate payment schemes aside from the fee-for-service system. The new legislation also intensified the public's control over actions taken by HICs, so that they had to present annual reports for approval in the Parliament. Along with bankruptcy, this was another way to reduce the number of HICs. In fact, the number of HICs decreased from 27 in 1995 to the present figure of 10.

General health insurance is not the only financial source for health care in the CR. The State has also been involved. Large investments, research, postgraduate education, activities for regional and district hygienic centers, preventive activities, and health promotion programs are financed from the state budget. Districts and cities can also contribute to the development of health care from their budgets. For some procedures (unrelated to health status, such as those for cosmetic reasons, license to drive, etc.) citizens pay directly in cash.

The total proportion of the GDP that health care expenditures occupy reached 7.20 percent in 1997, which was approximately 11,500 CZK per capita ($330 US).

Health insurance is mandatory for all citizens of the country. Premium contributions are by law defined as a percentage of personal income. Employees pay 4.5 percent of their wages, while employers pay 9 percent. Combined, this figure equals 13.5 percent. Self-employed persons and those with income from capital pay premiums from 35 percent of their profit. However, there is a ceiling to contribution, which is set at about six times the average salary in the Czech Republic. The problem is that thousands of self-employed persons do not pay their contributions due to weak monitoring by the government. Also, many employers owe contributions. For example, in 1998 employers' debts to the GHIC reached more than 10 percent of the total budget, while its administrative expenditures were a mere 4.6 percent.

For those who do not have their own income, the premium is paid by the state. This category, which represents 50 percent of the population, is composed of children and students, pensioners, women on maternal leave, unemployed people, recipients of social support, and other social groups. The premium for these people is very low as derived from their minimal wages. To adjust the selection of insurees and prevent economical problems due to a disadvantageous age structure, 60 percent of the income of each insurance company is redistributed according to the number of the state insurees with special regard to the age. All insurance companies are open to insure anybody who asks. Thus, citizens are free to select their insurance company, though 76 percent of citizens are insured by the GHIC, because its solvency is guaranteed by the state.

Practically all necessary care for the population is covered by the mandatory health insurance, such as diagnostic and therapeutic care in ambulances and hospitals including room services, care for chronically ill, prevention, drugs, transport of patients, special health care and spa care. The contract between the insurance company and the health facility defines the conditions of the reimbursement. HICs can apply regulative measures, which influence economic behavior of the health care providers.

Originally (between 1993 and 1997) the health care provided by physicians and hospitals was paid for through a fee-for-service system. In this system, the number of provided services increased dramatically, which consequently increased the costs of health care. The lack of sources for reimbursement of this increased amount of services led to the introduction of a capitation system for GPs (with some services paid through fee-for-service), lump-sum payments to the special ambulatory services, and budgeting for hospitals in 1997. This step was successful because it ended "procedures hunting" and helped the system to survive. At the same time, the motivation structure for providers was changed so that the amount of care was minimized. According to statistics from HICs, the real decrease in medical procedures reached 20 percent (Jaroš 1998: 34).

Health Care Professionals

For physicians, radical organizational changes in the health care system and its financing meant also radical changes in their social position. As employees of centrally managed health organizations they had little possibility of reaching a significant professional or social position. Their wages did not differ very much from the societal average and were often lower than those of manual laborers (Vecerník 1998: 121). Thus, physicians were not motivated to improve or intensify their work. They did not have enough medical technology, foreign drugs, and experience from abroad to provide medical care that met their personal standards. Physicians' frustration was high, which was reflected in the declining medical ethic and tension in relations between professionals and patients.

Physicians wanted to use new chances as quickly as possible, so they participated very intensively in the creation of the new health policy. However, they also created many of its problems. A content analysis of the health care press (Janečková and Hnilica 1996) showed that articles regarding professional identity of physicians were a high priority. Their representative body – the Medical Chamber – was frequently discussed in the health care press. It was already an institution in 1991, embodying the ability of the professional group to exist autonomously in order to guarantee the high quality of health care and to maintain the norms of medical ethics. Later this group became a sort of trade union organization representing the economic interests of physicians.

The topic of physician wages always culminated in the health press with hopes in vain. First, shortly after the beginning of the transformation between 1991 and 1992, strong physicians lobbied in the Parliament to influence the direction and speed of the reforms. Later in 1995, the expected economic effect of the first transformation steps did not occur so physicians decided to strike. The wages of employed physicians are still not comparable with wages of similar professions in the CR but they are twice as high as the country's average wages.

The supply of physicians is frequently discussed in connection with their wages and risk of unemployment. In the CR there were 36,676 physicians in 1997, which was 36 per 10,000 inhabitants and represented 16.4 percent of health care professionals (6.3 other health personnel per one physician). The number of physicians in the CR increased in the 1960s and 1970s as compensation for the lack of imported medical technology and drugs. However, the 20 percent growth in the number of physicians during the last 10 years corresponds with the improvement of the health status of inhabitants since 1990.

Physicians in the CR continuously find themselves in a difficult plight, not only because of inadequate wages, but more generally because of the very unstable milieu in which they work. It is caused by ever-changing conditions for physicians' work reimbursement, by unsolved ownership conditions (in many cases), and finally by uncertainty about physicians' contracts with the HICs. One last frustrating situation is the difficulty in providing care of the highest quality because of a lack of resources.

Patients – Subject or Object of Health Care?

From the patients' point of view the transformation should lead to better quality health care and healthier conditions for life. Democratization and humanization of health care were the key to citizens' higher satisfaction with health provision, but citizens also need to increase their general interest and involvement in health care. In fact, the public's opinion about individual reform interventions has not been systematically studied. The politicians who were shaping the new health care system did not prioritize the empowerment of citizens in the area of health care.

The principal steps of the reform – decentralization, privatization, and health insurance – concerned health care professionals rather than patients. Patients were not supposed to recognize any change in the accessibility of services or financing. Nonetheless, there were many changes for patients during the transformation. The most important changes are the following:

Free choice. Patients received the right to health care and healthy living conditions through the Charter of Basic Human Rights. They are obliged to participate in the general insurance system. By law, the state has carried responsibility for the accessibility of health care for all citizens since 1966. The law is still valid but some amendments have been made, with one in particular regarding the right of citizens to choose their physician, health facility, and health insurance company. Only a small portion of patients took advantage of this amendment: only 5 or 10 percent changed physicians, usually patients in large towns with higher education. It is practically impossible for the average patient to decide what physician or health facility is actually the best. Free choice also enabled some patients to circulate between multiple physicians with one health problem. Thus, the psychological effect of free choice is combined with an increase of costs in health care. For the best application of free choice, it would be necessary for health insurance companies and hospitals to publish regular information about measures such as their quality assessment, accreditation, and patient satisfaction. This system has not yet been implemented in the CR.

Better relationships between professionals and patients. Patient emancipation in a democratic society is also connected with the changed role from passive consumer of the physician's instructions into a partner who can discuss his or her health problems with a physician or a nurse. This new concept of the patient's position is expressed in the Charter of Patients' Rights. Even if it is not a legal document, it was approved by the Central Ethical Commission of the MoH and is generally applied in Czech hospitals. Surveys of patient satisfaction have become a regular part of the quality improvement of health care, and they are applied at about 30 percent of Czech hospitals (Janečková 1997; Hnilicová 1998). The research also showed typically high levels of patient satisfaction in Czech hospitals (89% of patients were either satisfied or highly satisfied). Overall satisfaction with hospital care was significantly related to a high level of satisfaction with the professionalism and commitment of physicians and nurses.

Better quality of care. Between 1992 and 1995, hospitals and ambulances were continuously equipped with new medical technology and a wide supply of high-quality drugs became available. Many physicians got the opportunity to study abroad and to learn new methods of treatment. The fee-for-service system motivated physicians to offer more procedures to their patients than ever before. The higher accessibility of new medical procedures and modern drugs is the crucial factor in the health status improvement of the Czech population after 1990. Since 1997, quality care has become a priority, and a system of criteria for assessing quality has been developed (Hnilicová 1994).

Cost sharing. With expanding economic problems in the health care system a new question connected with patients has arisen. Until now, health insurance has covered more than 90 percent of all possible care. Statisticians have documented that private expenditure for health care is nearly 9 percent of total health care budget which is on average about 1,000 CZK (about $30) per capita a year and is much less than in the countries of the EU (where it is estimated to be 22 percent). The sum includes all direct payments or co-payments of patients for drugs and medical aids, above-standard dental services, cosmetic operations, abortions, and services provided for non-health reasons.

There is no legal possibility for copayment in the case of care that is fully covered by the health insurance. But there is a rather strong tendency on the part of the provider to increase co-payments of patients – either legally or illegally. Patients are often asked for "donations," especially for services where coverage from insurance companies is not sufficient according to the opinion of physicians and managers (e.g. in case of long-term care for elderly).

There is no proof that the amount of traditional bribes to physicians increased. But a renewed occurrence of waiting lists for operations and examinations due to the new prospective system of financing since 1997 (capitation and budgeting) has reopened the discussion about ways to involve patients more in the financing of health care.

Inequalities. Transformation of the whole society has brought diversification to the social structure of the society and, in connection with the transformation of health care reform, consequences for equity and equality of health care can be observed. Czech sociologists have paid considerable attention to this phenomenon since the beginning of the 1990s (Janečková 1992, 1996, 1998; Křížová 1998). Differences were studied in relation to education, age, region, sex, and ethnicity. Because of the rapidly changing health care system, with growing complexity that necessitates more information for patients who want to face the challenges of individual choice and individual responsibility, it is relevant to consider the question of decreasing accessibility for certain social groups.

An analysis of health indicators in various regions of the Czech Republic shows stable differences. For example, life expectancy at birth for men in Prague is three years longer than in Northern Bohemia, which is an industrial region with high levels of social pathology, lower education, and a high proportion of ethnic minorities. For women, the difference in life expectancy between the best and worst regions is two years. There are also interregional differences in the distribution of health services. The highest concentration of hospitals is in the capital of Prague as well as in other big cities, and also in Northern Bohemia. However, primary care is developed less in this last region.

Among social groups, seniors are worth mentioning. Elderly people were treated insufficiently until 1990, compared to their western counterparts (life expectancy at 45 was even worse than the average for East Europe). Since then, elders' life expectancy has rapidly increased and reached the European average in 1994. Their mortality rate significantly decreased. However, the assurance of institutional capacity and home care for seniors with disabilities is still a problem that has not yet been addressed. Access to this type of care, the gap between health and social care, and speculations about its financing have all been lasting problems of the Czech health reform.

With regard to women's health Křížová (1995) showed that differences between women and men are caused not only by biological factors, but also by sociocultural determinants. Women's social position at work and in the family of modern society plays an important role. Aging is mostly a woman's problem and their added years are associated with a greater rate of illness. During the period between 1989 and 1996, Czech women's life expectancy increased by only 1.87 years, while men's increased by 2.26 years. The health interventions ensuing from the transformation of the health care system seem to be less effective in the case of women. Women need health services more often, suffer from a lack of information about medical procedures, need more psychological support, and consume more medicaments. The health care system should reflect more of the specific needs of women in its financing.

Roma gypsy ethnic minority is another social group threatened by unequal chances to improve their health status. At present, data indicate this minority's worse health status (shorter life expectancy, higher infant mortality, more infectious diseases, social deprivation, alcoholism, drug addiction, diabetes, respiratory diseases, and injuries) and some peculiarities in health care consumption (insufficient use of preventive and specialized care, lack of cooperation with physicians in therapy, misuse of primary care, and delay in visiting a health center in case of serious problems). Their health status is probably worse due to the very specific lifestyle of this ethnic minority that includes many health risks connected to low education, high unemployment, and poverty. In spite of the many problems that the Roma minority has at present, it has not been politically acceptable to study specific health indicators in connection with ethnicity because this is seen as contradictory to the equal rights of all citizens. Křížová calls this praxis "alibistic" because in fact "it covers up the existing social and health inequality, not admitting it" (Křížová 1998). Finally, in 1999, the MoH provided a grant for the research of the health status of Roma under the pressure of international criticism of the Czech policy towards ethnic minorities (Nesvatbová 1998).

Patients' Associations. Shortly after the change of the political system in November 1989, citizens got the chance by law to create civic associations in the non-governmental sector. People with various diseases and handicaps began to create self-help groups. There are about 150 such associations in the field of health care at present. They can receive some financial support from the MoH and Ministry of Labor and Social Affairs as well as from international foundations. In spite of the high level of financial and legal uncertainty that they face, these associations offer a number of services which address the specific needs of their members, such as home care agencies, hospices, centers of early intervention, helplines, rehabilitation centers, and sheltered homes.

THE ROLE OF MEDICAL SOCIOLOGY IN ASSESSING HEALTH CARE REFORM IN THE CZECH REPUBLIC

Although there has not been a direct demand by politicians, some attempts have been made to analyze the ten-year transformation of the health care system in the CR. There is only a very limited institutional basis for doing complex analyses and large research projects of systematic collections of empirical data. The 1993 abolition of the Institute of Social Medicine and Health Care Organization, the only state research institution in this field, thus represented the attitude of the liberal government toward intellectual and evaluative work as a source of valid information for decision-making.

Besides the Institute of Medical Information and Statistics (ÚZIS) – a governmental organization responsible for national health information systems and yearly statistics – there are several nongovernmental initiatives, largely on the part of Czech universities. These facilities' research activities are usually based on grants from the Ministry of Health, for whom social research has not been a priority until now. The number of active sociologists with an interest in health care has also been minimal.

Sociological analyses of the transformation process occurred only recently. Křížová (1998) identifies the absence of the vision in her studies as the principal problem of Czech health care and its "oscillation between the state health care system and mixed general health insurance system." This resulted in a hybrid system, which maintained some negative features of the previous socialistic system (i.e. totally free services at the moment of consumption and ineffective use of sources) and didn't introduce certain useful elements of the national health insurance system like control mechanisms. It would have been better for the country to have adopted a clear perspective, either transition of the centrally managed system into a form of National Health Service (with complementary private sector and a strong private primary care) or its global transformation to the decentralized and pluralistic model of general health insurance. This second alternative won, but the preparation of necessary legislative and economic preconditions was underestimated.

Křížová (1999) also negatively evaluates the government's failure in the case of needed interventions into health care, its lack of a basic concept and vision, and the lack of reflection on the transformation process. Because the public interest was not well-defined both spheres – private and public – became intermixed and confused. The social and ethical dimension of private property was suppressed, so the possibility of a private not-for-profit sector in health care was underestimated and practically lost its chance in the transformation process. Finally Křížová points out the problem of poor communication by all partners in the process, which was previously stigmatized by history – the authoritarian decision-making, refusal of any criticism, and incapability of negotiation. The voice of providers in this case was stronger than that of consumers. After ten years, the process of transformation is once more at a crossroads and the same choices must be considered anew. At both times, the market must be taken into account as a complementary mechanism and the public must undertake a discussion about the consequences of any choice. Improvement of the existing system seems to be simpler than a complete change.

Patient satisfaction research represents another important topic in Czech medical sociology and provides information about the satisfaction of patients with their hospital care (Hnilicová 1998). The contribution of this activity to quality of care improvement is generally well known. Until recently, the bad economic situation did not allow hospitals to employ sociologists. It is necessary to add that some smaller sociological studies exist in the frame of various medical branches and can be characterized as sociology in medicine. This is especially the case in gerontology, with special regard to the caregivers' burden, childcare, primary medicine and health promotion, various chronic diseases, and drug abuse. Types of communication, ethical aspects, life events and hardiness, the family, and social risks were all studied in this context. Team collaboration was typical in such studies that connected sociologists, psychologists, and physicians (Matejcek 1988; Bútora 1990; Kabele 1991). As this direction of medical sociology was less politically engaged, it could exist even during the communist period and helped many sociologists to survive. After the revolution in 1989, nearly all sociologists active in medicine left the field. This is why the new, analytical, period of medical sociology had to wait till the second half of the nineties.

CONCLUSION

All sociological analyses of the transformation process until now have shown that rash solutions and inconsistent reactions to the emerging problems hindered the process. Subjective opinions of the political leaders or of the lobbying groups dominated over expert analyses and outcome-oriented evaluations of the course of transformation. The absence of rational conceptual work was repeatedly stressed as the most unfortunate feature of the Czech health care reform. Many criticized the lack of analytical reflection on the process. Two elements of the "reform culture" in the Czech Republic are underestimation of the systematic development of social research and total ignorance about measuring outcomes of the reform steps. Building institutional bases and professional capacities for evaluative studies either at universities or elsewhere represents a very important task in connection with the future reform steps.

At the present time there is another strong element of the reform – a more developed civic society with active involvement of citizens. Various associations of providers and consumers came into existence and contribute to the discussion on various aspects of the reform. They debate both with each other and with the government, and they have more opportunities to express their dissatisfaction. They even form coalitions and try to present their common proposals. This mutual balancing of different partners and forces will certainly play an important role in the process of transformation in the future.

Abbreviations

IHIS – Institute Health Information and Statistics of the Czech Republic
ŠVZ – School of Public Health
IPVZ – Institute of Postgraduate Medical Education
MoH – Ministry of Health
HIC – Health Insurance Company
GHIC – General Health Insurance Company
ÚSLOZ – Institute of Social Medicine
SMR – Standardized Mortality Rate

References

Bartlová, S. 1999. *Vybrané kapitoly ze sociologie medicíny.* [Selected Chapters of the Sociology of Medicine]. Brno: Institute for Continual Education of Medical Personnel.

Bobak, M. and R. Feachem. 1995. "Air Pollution and Mortality in Central and Eastern Europe: An estimate of the impact." *European Journal of Public Health* 5:82–6.

Butora, M. 1990. Prekrocit svuj stin. [To Overcome One's Shadow]. Praha: Avicenum.

Čákiová, E. 1999. "Šetřeni rodiny a reprodukce." [Survey of Family and Reproduction]. *Demografie* 2: 85–94.

Drbal, C. 1997. *Zdravotni stav populace ČR ajeho prognoza jako dominantni determinanta požadavkůna system peče ozdravi.* [Health Status of Population of the CR and

its Prognosis as a Dominant Determinant of Demands on the Health Care System].
Praha: Narodohospodařský ústav J. Hlávky.

Hnilicová, H. 1994. "Kvalita léčebné péče a spokojenost pacientů ve světle výsledků
dotazníkového šetření." ["Quality of Medical Care and Satisfaction of Patients in the
Light of a Survey"]. *Zdravotnické noviny* 20: 10.

——. 1998. Some Results of the Patient Satisfaction Survey at Prague University Hospitals. Pp. 75–8 in *Feasibility, Effectiveness, Quality and Sustainability of Health Promoting Hospitals Projects*, edited by J. M. Pelikan, K. Krajic, H. Lobnig. Gamburg:
Health Promoting Publications.

Hnilicová, H., and H. Janečková. 1998. "Co se pacient m v nemocnici líbí a co nikoli."
["What Patients Like and Dislike in a Hospital"]. Zdravotnické noviny 38: 6.

Hnilicová, H., H. Janečková, M. Holcát, and V. Riegl. 1998. "Trendy spokojenosti
pacientů jako soucást sledování kvality zdravotní péce. Návrh standardního dotaz-
níku." ["Trends in the Patients' Satisfaction as a Part of Quality Assessment of Health
Care. Standardized Questionnaire Proposal"]. Report of the Empirical Research Carried by the School of Public Health of the Institute of Postgraduate Medical Education.
Prague: SVZ IPVZ.

Janečková, H. 1997. *Sociologie medicíny v kontextu veřejného zdravotnictví.* [Sociology
of Medicine in the Context of Public Health]. Praha: SVZ IPVZ.

Janečková, H., and K. Hnilicová. 1992. "The Health Status of the Czechoslovak Population. It's Social and Ecological Determinants". *International Journal of Health Sciences*
3: 143–56.

——. 1996. "Priority zd razn néve zdravotnickém tisku. Souhrn výsledk obsahové
analýzy zdravotnického tisku v období 1990–1995." ["Priorities Accented in the
Health Press. Summary of Results of the Content Analysis of the Health Press in the
Period 1990–1995"]. Paper prepared for the seminar in the Parliament of the Czech
Republic, Prague, March.

——. 1998. "Průzkumy spokojenosti pacientů v nemocnicích ČR." ["Patient Satisfaction
Surveys in the Hospitals of the Czech Republic"]. *Zdravotnické noviny* 33: 5; 34: 5.

Jaros, J. and K. Kalina. 1998. Szech Health Care System: Delivery and Financing. OECD
Study. Prague: Czech Association for Health Services Research.

Kabele, J. 1991. "Chronicka nemoc jako soucast rodinneho deni" ["Chronic illness as
part of family events"]. Sociologicky casopis 5: 653–65.

Kalina, K. 1992. "Průvodce novým zdravotnictvím." ["A Guide Through New Health
Care System"]. Praha: Maxima.

Křížová, E. 1998. *Zdravontické systémy v mezinárodním srovnání.* [Health Care Systems
in an International Comparison]. Prague: Narodohospodarsky Ustav J. Hlavky.

——. 1999. Public Opinion on the Cost Sharing. Oral Communication on a Seminar on
Empirical Research in Health Care. 1st Medical Faculty of the Charles University,
Prague, May.

Křížová, E., and H. Janečková. 1997. *Lékařské, sociologické a etické aspekty zdraví žen.*
[Medical, Sociological and Ethical Aspects of the Health Status of Women]. *Zdravotnické noviny* 21: 15–16.

Matejcek, Z, Z. Dytrych, and V. Schuller. 1988. "Deti narozene y nechteneho teho-
tenstvi" ["Children Born from Unwanted Pregnancy"]. Casopis Lékařů Ceskych 127:
14–18.

Nesvatbová, L. et al. 1998. *Determinanty zdraví romské populace – pilotní studie*
[Determinants of the Health of the Roma Population – A Pilot Study]. Report of the
pilot survey. Prague: Ministry of Health.

Škodová, Z. et al. 1997. "Pokles úmrtnosti na kardiovaskulární onemocěněni v Česke
repulbice v obdobi 1984–1993 a jeho možné pričiny ["Decline of the cardiovascular

mortality rate in the Czech Republic in 1984–1993 and its possible causes"]. Casopis Lékařů Ceskych 136: 373–9.

Večerník, J., and P. Matějů. 1998. *Zpráva ovývoji české společnost; 1989–1998* [Report on the development of the Czech Society 1989–1998]. Praha: Academia.

Africa

21

Health and Health Care in South Africa Against an African Background

H. C. J. van Rensburg and Charles Ngwena

Basic to medical sociology, or the sociology of health and health care, is the premise that the health of populations is profoundly influenced and determined by society, in particular by the social, cultural, political, and economic contexts. In similar vein, health care systems closely reflect the broader societal environments in which they nestle. The opposite also holds: societies are in significant ways influenced by health and disease in their populations.

This chapter sets out to describe and explain the nature and development of health and health care in South Africa. It does so against the background of health and health care on the African continent. In particular, we focus on the main features, trends, and deformations of health and health care in Africa, as well as the underpinning historical forces. When it comes to South Africa, our focus is mainly on the current transformation of the health system, against the backdrop of inequalities, disparities and distortions entrenched in the South African health system over three and a half centuries of exposure to colonialism and apartheid. In particular we assess the current reforms of, and constraints on, the health sector. We also glance at some of the main features of morbidity and mortality in South Africa, as well as at the daunting challenges these pose to the health system and the current reform process.

HISTORICAL FORCES SHAPING HEALTH AND HEALTH CARE IN AFRICA

The Main Historical Shapers of African Health Care

Some of the earliest evidence of medical practice comes from Africa. Ancient Egyptians were known, over 5,000 years ago, for their advanced knowledge of medicine. Imhotep (3,000 BC), the "historical father of medicine," instructed

Greeks in medicine, possibly built the first hospital, and wrote about medicine and surgery. Two renowned documents reveal the achievements of the ancient Egyptians: the Code *of Hammurabi*, possibly the first code of medical practice, and the *Ebers Papyrus*, summarizing knowledge about several disease categories and offering advice on diagnosis, prognosis, and treatment (Weiss and Lonnquist 1994; Zoneraich et al. 1996; David 1997; Miller 1997). Again around 300 BC, Alexandria became the world's intellectual center where the scientific basis of modern medicine was laid. Thereafter, the African continent remained silent and did not contribute to modern medicine until the mid-twentieth century.

The spread of Islam by the Arabs in the seventh century, brought new nuances to health care on the African continent. The Arabs' intense interest in medicine is reflected in the famous teaching hospitals they built which served as links between Greek and Renaissance medicine (Weiss and Lonnquist 1994). The influence of Islam on African medicine, resulted in mixed African–Islamic medical systems, and the conversion of magico–religious African medical beliefs and practices to scientific principles fundamental to western medicine – thus paving the way for the acceptance of western biomedicine (Kirby 1993). Even in present-day Islamic Africa, there are strong influences toward the Arabization and Islamization of medicine (Kandela 1993).

Western medicine in Africa was predominantly pioneered by Christian (Protestant and Catholic) missionary societies during the last quarter of the nineteenth century and early decades of the twentieth century, mostly in advance of health services provided by colonial governments (Waite 1987; Brown 1998). Hundreds of mission hospitals and dispensaries were established, with healing eventually seen as an essential element of the missionary mandate. The nature of the missions (e.g. Protestant or Catholic) and the country of origin of the missionaries (Britain, France, Germany, Switzerland, Belgium, with smaller cadres from Italy, Spain, and Portugal) influenced the organization of health care and the orientation of health practitioners. Even today, many African countries still rely heavily on missionary hospitals and health services, with church-related health care services accounting for 25 percent to 50 percent of services (Good 1991; Fyle 1993; Banda and Walt 1995).

Though European colonization of Africa coincided to a large extent with missionary initiatives on the continent, it was only after World War I that colonial governments accepted some responsibility for the health care of indigenous populations (Van Heyningen 1990; Good 1991; Comoro 1993). Prominent among the factors affecting the shape of health systems in colonial Africa, was the relationship of domination–exploitation between imperial powers and the colonized peoples. As a result, typical structural deformations were ingrained on the emerging health systems. Among these, doctor-orientated, hospital-centred, urban-concentrated, and curatively-biased policies and systems featured most strongly. Also recognizable was the creation of segregated structures in which the colonial population was treated preferentially to its "native" counterparts (Good 1991; Fetter 1993; Alubo and Vivekanando 1995). In South Africa this "apartheid in medicine" grew to the fullest extremes (van Rensburg et al. 1992; van Rensburg and Benatar 1993). However, the benefits brought to health care in Africa by western countries should not be underestimated.

Most notable were the introduction of western allopathic medicine to the continent, control of epidemics, and strong traditions of management and administration, especially by British colonial regimes (Burrows 1958; Laidler and Gelfand 1971; Fetter 1993). In many cases, colonial powers provided the first modern health facilities.

Liberation from the colonial heel in the mid-twentieth century set in motion new trends in health care in Africa. Mass emigration of colonial personnel left a great void in postcolonial African health systems that was gradually filled by expatriate professionals, graduates from newly established local training institutions. Progressive Africanization of health systems and indigenized cadres of health personnel gave rise to less doctor-dependent models of care, especially nurse-based health services (Last and Chavunduka 1986; Alubo and Vivekananda 1995). However, to varying degrees, mother countries remained influential in sustaining western health care in the postcolonial Africa, and in the process reproduced and perpetuated the distortions inherited from the colonial period (Comoro 1993; EIU Country Profiles 1997–8).

Western Allopathic and African Traditional Health Care – A Pluralism

For centuries health care in Africa was confined to traditional medicine. The appearance of western influences on the African scene inaugurated a pluralism in health care where western allopathic medicine came to exist side by side with African traditional medicine. Colonial governments and missionaries generally despised, discouraged, and even suppressed traditional medicine. As a result, traditional medicine was relegated to an officially inferior and often covert position. Subordination of traditional medicine was carried further by organized professions in the western-scientific mold. In time, four broad varieties of relationships crystallized (Stephan 1983; Last and Chavunduka 1986; Pretorius 1995, 1999): (1) *exclusive (monopolistic) systems*, recognizing only the practising of scientific medicine; (2) *tolerant systems*, characterized by *laissez-faire* policies which virtually ignore traditional medicine, yet allow its existence; (3) *inclusive (parallel) systems*, recognizing traditional health systems alongside scientific medicine; and (4) *integrated systems*, tending to unite allopathic and traditional medicine in a combined system of training and practice.

Political emancipation and to an extent, the Alma Ata Declaration in 1978, have been instrumental in propelling governments toward strong support of traditional health care, in particular toward either parallel or integrated systems. Policies in several African countries have moved a long way toward establishing beneficial coexistence and cooperation of the two systems, and even incorporating traditional health care into modern systems. African traditional healers have also gone a long way toward organizing themselves in somewhat autonomous local and national organizations (Abdool Karim et al. 1994). However, despite such strides, an anti-traditional medicine attitude still prevails generally, with the two systems still interlocked in a relationship underpinned by mistrust, prejudice, and even antagonism (Last and Chavunduka 1986; Comoro 1993). The grounds for supporting or opposing traditional medicine in Africa are varied, ranging from political ideology and religious doctrine to scientific and practical reasons. In terms of the essential qualities of professions, African traditional medicine remains marginal and has a long way to go before it can achieve the stature of an organized profession.

The Current Shape of Health and Health Care in Africa

It is not possible to speak of one common history or one common format of African health care. Rather, health care in each country is shaped by a combination of unique historical and societal circumstances. Despite this limitation, some broad observations can be made regarding the nature and status of health care in Africa.

Africa's Population, Health, and Burden of Disease

Africa comprises 53 independent states, harboring an estimated population of over 600 million. An average annual growth rate of between 2.2 percent and 3.3 percent between 1950 and 1990, resulted in an explosive increase from 170 million to 500 million. The majority of this population can still be classified as non-urban (Sparks 1998). In the mid-1990s, life expectancy averaged 53 years; in only nine African countries it exceeds 60 years; while in many countries it is still well below 50 years (e.g. Zambia, Burundi, Guinea, Malawi, Mali, Niger, Somalia, Uganda), and even lower in Sierra Leone (35 years for females, 32 for males) (*Africa at a Glance* 1998; *EIU Country Profiles* 1997–8/1998–9).

Although infant mortality rates have fallen spectacularly during the past century – from levels exceeding 200–300/1,000 IMR – it remains high in Africa, with the highest rates recorded in Rwanda (145), Mali (156), and Sierra Leone (200), and the lowest rates in Mauritius (17), Tunisia (41), South Africa and Algeria (51). Under-5 mortality often exceeds 200/1,000, reaching exceptional heights in Mozambique (275), Sierra Leone (284), Angola (292), and Niger (320). Only in Botswana, Cape Verde, Mauritius, Namibia, South Africa, most of the northern African countries, and Seychelles, are both the infant and under-5 mortality rates below the developing world's averages of 64 and 95/1,000 respectively (compared respectively to the developed world's of 14 and 18/1,000) (Fetter 1993; Vogel 1993; World Bank 1996; UNDP 1997; *Africa at a Glance* 1998). In sub-Saharan Africa, maternal mortality amounts to 971/100,000 live births; is more than double the rate of 471/100,000 in the developing world as a whole. For the 1980–90 period, rates were highest in Ghana, Somalia, and Mali: 1,000, 1,100 and 2,000/100,000 respectively (Vogel 1993; UNDP 1997).

Africa's burden of disease is very high especially in the communicable and preventable categories. In earlier times it was smallpox, and now it is TB, measles, malaria, and HIV/AIDS, and many other infectious diseases. Tuberculosis is the leading single killer and is on the increase, aggravated by the HIV epidemic. Of the world's 30 million people infected with HIV 21 million live in sub-Saharan Africa, and of 12 million deaths 83 percent occurred in Africa

(Lachman et al. 1999). Malaria is endemic in many African countries; annually there are 300–500 million clinical cases of malaria and between 1.5 and 2.7 million deaths, 90 percent present in Africa (WHO Report 1996). A disease burden of this magnitude profoundly impacts on health and continuously taxes African health systems as well as social services to their limits. However, there have been significant achievements: Treatment for leprosy increased from 7 percent in 1987 to 27 percent in 1990 and to 63 percent in 1993, reducing the prevalence of the disease from 483,000 cases in 1990 to 159,000 in 1993. Vaccination programs have markedly reduced the incidence of neonatal tetanus in several African countries, and poliomyelitis is on the decrease. With the upsurge in malaria in recent years, and in particular the development of widespread resistance to chloroquine, malaria control programs are being given high priority through a WHO global malaria strategy which includes 17 African countries (WHO Report 1997).

Africa's health status, burden of disease, and health care needs are conspicuously shaped by poverty, malnutrition, infectious diseases, armed conflict, drought, famine, inadequate access to primary and secondary education, lack of safe water, sanitation, and a range of socioeconomic factors propelling inequitable distribution of resources. To understand the causes of this sad state of the continent requires focused attention on exploitation in the past, its continuation in the present, aggravated by the burdens imposed by the "curse of the nation-state" and progressive marginalization of Africa by the industrialized world (Gill 1986; Davidson 1992; Benatar 1995; Logie and Benatar 1997).

Economic Realities, Living Standards, and Social-Economic Well-Being

Africa has a veritable history of political instability which has dislocated large numbers of people, with devastating effects on health and health systems. The European colonial legacy left serious voids and instabilities that threatened the emerging independent nations in the 1960s. In many cases, conflicts were initiated by withdrawals of colonial powers. In others, independence triggered bitter conflict battles among contending internal factions and fuelled a sequence of ruinous wars, military regimes, and authoritarian one-party states. The establishment of a range of socialist/collectivist political power structures has molded and reformed national health systems into centralized systems, which jeopardize the already inadequate private health care sectors. Man-made catastrophes (civil wars and sporadic genocide), as well as natural disasters (droughts, floods, and famine) have dislocated millions of people, profoundly disrupting their health and health systems. Cases in point are Rwanda where the ethnic massacre in 1994 claimed the lives of 1 million people within three months, and Malawi, which in recent times has absorbed about 1 million Mozambican refugees.

On the Human Development Index (HDI – measuring human progress on a 0 to 1 scale), African countries fare dismally. According to recent grading, only three African countries (Seychelles, Mauritius, and Libya) rank in the "high category", and then only in the 52nd, 61st, and 64th positions respectively. Thirteen African countries are in the "medium category" (South Africa 90th), while the majority (35 of them) in the "low category" of the HDI – with the last 19 positions in the index filled by African countries, the very last being Niger, Rwanda, and Sierra Leone (175th) (UNDP 1997; *Africa at a Glance* 1998). Compared to Seychelles' relatively favorable score of 0.845, Sierra Leone has the most unfavourable score (0.176) on the scale – and the "worst quality of life" and the "poorest health services in the world" (Fyle 1993a: 60). Sub-Saharan Africa has the highest proportion of people in – and the fastest growth in – human poverty. The Human Poverty Index (HPI – reflecting the combined basic dimensions of poverty) is 40 percent for the whole of sub-Saharan Africa, and exceeds 50 percent in seven countries in the world, of which six (Niger, Sierra Leone, Burkina Faso, Ethiopia, Mali, and Mozambique) are in Africa. Some 220 million people in the region are poor, and it is estimated that by 2000 half the people in sub-Saharan Africa will live in poverty. Women and children, and more so those in rural areas, are disproportionately poor. However, despite the depressing performance of Africa, the HDI of sub-Saharan Africa as a whole has nevertheless improved during 1990–4 from 0.200 to 0.380 (UNDP 1997).

Economic indicators show that Africa's annual per capita GNP in 1996 ranged from a minimum of $80 in Mozambique to a maximum of $6,280 in the Seychelles, with a mean of less than $500. Africa's economic plight is further aggravated by debt-ridden economies, which are supported by almost valueless currencies. The majority of initially defined Heavily Indebted Poor Countries (HIPCS) – 33 of 41 – are in sub-Saharan Africa (Sparks 1998); the subcontinent's debt stands at $300 billion (Oxfam 1997), which is about $370 for every man woman and child on the continent (UNDP 1997; *Mail and Guardian* 1998a; Williams 1998). Niger exemplifies Africa's plight: it has a per capita GNP of $200; 92 percent of its population lives on $2 a day or less; the debt burden comprises 88 percent of the GNP; and three times more money is spent on international debt repayments than on health and education (*Mail and Guardian* 1998a). Rwanda, Burundi, Liberia, the two Congos, Sierra Leone, and Somalia grapple with similar mountainous debts in the aftermath of military conflicts. These facts have a profound effect on the nature of health care in all its dimensions.

The Variety of National Health Systems and Health Policies in Africa

Africa's national health systems are variable. They range from predominantly socialist/collectivist (Tanzania), socialized/national health service (Kenya), to strongly inclined private/free market dispensations (South Africa) (Field 1989). Although most African countries do entertain a private health sector, private health care is generally weakly developed. Western-style health care is primarily provided by the state. Many factors militate against private health care; and foremost are restrictive national economies, poor populations served by the free public health services, weakly developed insurance, the absence of large numbers of self-paying patients, and the typical disease and mortality profiles of Africa's populations. Despite these constraints, there have been significant strides toward private health care in several African countries, albeit more often the result of negative propellers such as recent economic reforms, declining health budgets accompanied by decreasing expenditure on government services, collapsing public health services, and unavailability or poor quality of drugs and medical equipment (Banda and Walt 1995).

Featuring prominently in the African context, but certainly not unique to Africa, is the regional and rural–urban maldistribution going hand in hand with absolute shortages in the health corps, leaving sizeable proportions of rural populations without access to doctor services (Comoro 1993; Fyle 1993; Alubo and Vivekananda 1995). For instance, although 85 percent of Kenya's population live in rural areas, less that 10 percent of its physicians are located in rural settings (Cockerham 1998). Country wise, doctor: population ratios vary greatly, Libya (1:962), Seychelles (1:1,064), and South Africa (1:1,500) are most favorably supplied, while Malawi (1:50,000), Chad and Mozambique (both 1:33,333) are in the least favorable situations. Generally, the provision in sub-Saharan countries is poor to very poor – an average of 1:18,514. Although there have been improvements (some impressive) during the past 20 to 25 years in many African countries (1:97,000 to 1:33,333 in Burkina Faso, 1:86,100 to 1:33,333 in Ethiopia, 1:50,000 to 1:7,692 in Guinea, 1:30,400 to 1:2,500 in Lesotho), it should be clearly noted that during the same period this ratio has deteriorated in several countries. Most notable is the worsening ratio in Uganda from 1:9,200 to 1:25,000; in Ghana from 1:14,894 to 1:22,970; in Kenya from 1:8,000 to 1:20,000, and in Mozambique from 1:18,900 to 1:33,333 (World Bank 1996; UNDP 1997; *EIU Country Profiles* 1997–8).

African countries have devised a variety of strategies to overcome the pronounced maladies in the provision and distribution of health services, especially to attract or compel staff to undeserved rural areas or disadvantaged sectors. Among these measures are the introduction of a variety of less expensive and less qualified medical and clinical auxiliary staff categories. In particular, nurses have come to constitute throughout the African continent the backbone of health services in the delivery of both ambulatory and institutional-based health care. As primary health care (PHC) is making headway, African health systems are becoming less accommodating to, and less concerned about, sophisticated medical services.

Health Reforms in Africa

Amidst worsening economic conditions and often as part of structural adjustment programs, many African countries have recently embarked on either piecemeal or major health reforms, particularly to achieve greater efficiency and equity in public health (Gilson and Mills 1995). These measures manifest in cost-cutting, curbing of government expenditure on health, strides toward privatization, and the introduction/reintroduction of user-charges and cost-recovery policies. However, they also surface in changes in health and health-seeking behavior (reduced health care, reduced clinic and hospital attendance, decline in illness episodes), changes in health outcomes (increase in malnutrition) (Bijlmakers et al. 1996), the resurgence of epidemics (yellow fever and tuberculosis), skin infections (due to the unaffordability of soap and detergents) (Alubo and Vivekananda 1995) and, in general, a negative effect on welfare (Costello et al. 1994). Such health reforms are often spear-headed or supported by a multitude of international multilaterals and bilaterals from the developed world extending technical and financial assistance for strengthening national health care systems, and with particular emphasis on PHC. In addition, health programs launched by the World Bank and the IMF often came to the rescue of many African countries, but at the same time, created dependency and subscription to the interests and agendas of these agencies (Banda and Walt 1995).

Health and Health Care in South Africa – A Study in Transition

Although South Africa's health and disease profiles, as well as its health system, in many respects resemble that of Africa at large, and perhaps more so that of sub-Saharan and southern Africa, we can in no way conclude that the South African health system and health profiles are typically African or a typical reflection of the African scene. Major differences prevail, both of qualitative and quantitative nature. Quantitatively, South Africa has more than other African countries – more health staff and health facilities, and generally a larger health budget. Qualitatively, South Africa has a different make-up of health issues, and generally a far more sophisticated health care system.

Legacy of Colonialism and Apartheid – The Need for Reform

For the greater part of the twentieth century, income, geographical location, and most importantly, race or ethnicity have been the arch determinants of the quantity and quality of health care received by South Africans. The health care system that the ANC-led government inherited in 1994 following the first democratic elections, can scarcely be described as functional and much less egalitarian. The new government came to power at the tail-end of a long period that through a combination of deliberate official policy, discriminatory legislation, and at times benign neglect had managed to firmly imprint on the country's health care system a number of structural distortions. These distortions can be subsumed under five main headings (Savage and Benatar 1990; MRC 1991; van Rensburg et al. 1992; ANC 1994b; van Rensburg and Fourie 1994; Benatar and van Rensburg 1995; van Rensburg and Harrison 1995).

First, is the dominance of curative-oriented health care. On the one hand, the exponential growth of allopathic medicine in the twentieth century has been a boon to the country and has witnessed phenomenal gains in the health of the populace, including the eradication of many infectious diseases. On the other hand, it has exerted some negative consequences. In the main, modern medicine has become a victim of its own success. It has led to overdependence on massively expensive hospital-based care at the expense of more affordable preventative and community-based care, e.g. for the 1992/3 financial year, 81 percent of public health expenditure was toward curative hospital-based care of which 44 percent was allocated to tertiary or academic hospitals (Health Systems Trust and World Bank 1995).

Second, is the intensification of racial segregation in the provision of services. Race or ethnicity rather than need has indubitably been the most important variable determining quantitative and qualitative access to health care (De Beer 1984; van Rensburg and Benatar 1993). In colonial and apartheid South Africa in particular, health care also became an instrument for maintaining white supremacy (Price 1988). At the height of apartheid, whites disproportionately enjoyed the bulk of public expenditure on health care and received four times more per capita than their African (black) counterparts, whilst Coloureds (mixed race) and Indians enjoyed a somewhat intermediate position (van Rensburg 1991). Racial fragmentation of services was taken to absurd heights under the homelands policy which began in the fifties, and since 1983 under the tricameral dispensation (van Rensburg et al. 1992).

Third is the functional fragmentation of services, which has its origins in the *Public Health Act* of 1919, which bequeathed to the country a three-tiered, uncoordinated and uncomplimentary system of organizing and dispensing health care services. It created a national Department of Public Health, provincial authorities and local authorities, each with its own domain and jurisdiction in health matters, but also leading to gross deficiencies in coordination of responsibilities and functional areas. Provincial authorities unduly concentrated on the provision of urban curative hospital-based care, while primary and community health care were grossly neglected. Despite sporadic attempts toward transforming the system in later years, the paradigm of a fragmented system lacking cohesion and a community-based care focus continued largely unmitigated (Gluckman Commission 1944; Browne Commission 1986).

Fourth, is the accentuation of rural–urban discrepancies and inequalities in the provision of services. For two reasons, urban areas have historically consumed a preponderant share of health care services, but at the expense of rural areas. One, the establishment and location of health care facilities essentially adhered to the country's pattern of urbanization, which in turn was a consequence of the development of the mining industry and industrialization. Two, successive governments were primarily preoccupied with establishing health facilities to serve and secure the health of the white population concentrated in urban areas. The "homelands" policy further deepened the chasm between rural and urban areas, as more and more resources were channelled into (white) South Africa.

Fifth, is the growth of a pluralistic structure of health care in which the private sector was repeatedly augmented at the expense of the public sector. A perverse asymmetry has for decades existed between the private and the public sector in terms of resources and health coverage (Price 1986). The private sector commands 60 percent of the resources that are spent on health care, and yet it provides coverage for a mere 20 percent of the population (van Rensburg et al. 1992). The proliferation of the private sector was particularly facilitated by the National Party government during the seventies and eighties as part of a shift from Keynesian economics to monetarism (Price 1988). Privatization was regarded as indispensable to devolving responsibility to the individual, downsizing the public sector, and reducing the state's financial burden. This resulted in a strong, competitive, and lucrative free market in the health sector, proliferation of high-tech medicine, phenomenal growth of the pharmaceutical industry, and generally inflated costs (Naylor 1988; van Rensburg and Fourie 1988).

Current health sector reforms are driven by the desire to rectify these structural distortions in the health sphere and in particular are aimed at unifying the fragmented health services into a comprehensive and integrated National Health System; reducing disparities and inequities in service delivery and health outcomes; and extending access to an improved health service (Department of Health 1996a, 1996b, 1997a, 1997c). Note however, that health sector reforms in South Africa have not only to do with internal restructuring. Reform also fits into a broader reform process in Africa and further afield – that is reform to cope with rising demand, and to render more accessible and more affordable care, especially for the deprived.

Reform of the South African Health System

CONSTITUTIONAL AND LEGAL REFORMS – THE RIGHT TO HEALTH SERVICES

The present health reforms in South Africa are not entirely the initiative of the new government. Several reforms, some anticipating those of the current government, had been introduced by the previous government. However most of these were nullified by the confines of an unchanging sociopolitical order which left little leeway for fundamental reform of the health system (van Rensburg et al. 1992; van Rensburg 1999). The new political order changed it all. The ANC (African National Congress)-led government embarked on fundamental reform, encompassing both the broader societal order and the narrower health sector. Since 1994, the reform frameworks have been detailed and mandated by a series of official policy papers and legislation at both national and provincial levels (Department of Health 1997a, 1997c). More fundamentally, the new *Constitution* lay the basis for the reform of the health sector.

Prior to the current reforms, health care services were a privilege rather than a right and the main beneficiaries were whites. The *Constitution of the Republic of South Africa* of 1996, which replaced the interim *Constitution* of 1993, gives conspicuous expression to the idea of a fundamental right to health care for all. It translates to the health care sector the values of social justice, equality under the law, and respect for human rights that were not priorities under colonial and apartheid dispensations. By doing so the Constitution clearly lays the foundation for both a liberal and egalitarian health care system and thereby signals a break with the legacy of gross inequality and guarantees everyone the right of access to basic health care services. At the same time, it enjoins the state to take reasonable measures within its available resources to achieve the progressive realization of such a right of access to health care (De Waal et al. 1999).

Outside the Constitution, there are a number of other measures which have been taken with a view to achieving equitable access to health care. Noteworthy are the provision of free health care to mothers and children under six, the *Choice on Termination of Pregnancy Act*, which gives women easy access to legal abortion, the *Medical Schemes Act*, which extends medical-aid coverage to the elderly and chronically sick, and the *Medicines and Related Substances Act*, which permits parallel importation of medicines and promotes the use of generic medicines which are more affordable. Plans are also underway to introduce a social health insurance scheme so as to require those in employment to purchase for themselves more stable and reliable medical cover. In short, the new reforms, if efficiently implemented and sustained, should provide the substance for rectifying not only racial, but also equally significant, income and geographical impediments to access to health care services.

Reforms in the Structure and Content of the Health System

UNIFYING FRAGMENTED HEALTH STRUCTURES

Note again, that in the previous dispensation health care was geographically, structurally, racially, as well as authority-wise, fragmented to the extreme, consisting of 14 health authority structures – 1 national ("white" South Africa), 10 homeland (per ethnic group), and 3 own affairs (based on race) ministries. Prime among the achievements of the new government is the dismantling of this fragmentation by unifying the segregated and divided structures. Health is now consolidated under a single national ministry supposed to oversee, support, and coordinate the entire health system of the country. The nine newly established provincial governments (PHAs) embody a "federal-like" decentralized system, with more powers entrusted unto the provinces than before. In turn, these PHAs are now developing, coordinating, and supporting the emerging district health authorities (DHAs). In this respect, the *White Paper on Local Government* (1998) introduced an entirely new phase in the restructuring of health, intending to shift the responsibility for PHC increasingly onto local authorities and communities. In turn, this implies that the current, still fragmented, provincial and municipal authority and service structures are to be integrated into consolidated district structures underscored by cooperative government structures.

DISMANTLING APARTHEID IN HEALTH

The new government decisively succeeded in dismantling apartheid structures and racially discriminatory laws and measures in the public health sector in a relatively short period of time. As part of such a de-racializing process, stern affirmative action measures which pertinently encompass a striking Africanization of the public health system and a pronounced sensitivity for gender to ensure representivity, have been introduced. The once almost "all-white" and "all-male" top management structures (prior to 1994, whites accounted for 90.2 percent of management staff at national head office, while 87.8 percent of all managers were male) has been systematically revised to reflect the race and gender composition of the population more accurately. Hence Africans, Indians, and Coloureds and women now figure prominently in the executive and management positions in the public health sector.

RECTIFYING DISTRIBUTIVE DISPARITIES IN HEALTH PROVISION

There are no quick fixes to the pronounced discrepancies and inequalities in the apportionment and distribution of health resources that have been entrenched over centuries. Current reforms aim to redress these gross inequities in a two-pronged approach implying, firstly, large-scale resource reallocation and redeployment of personnel and facilities to smooth out gross disparities, and secondly, controlling the referral and flow of patients to the various public providers and facilities to ensure a more even and appropriate spread. Among the specific redistributive measures contemplated to encourage staff to deploy and redeploy in underserviced areas are; retraining of personnel; providing incentives for staff to work in rural areas; introducing contractual obligations for those receiving subsidized training; importing Cuban doctors to serve in underresourced facilities and communities; and strengthening the public sector in order to attract staff from the private sector. Regarding the flow of public patients to providers and facilities, various measures are being devised to effect more appropriate and cost-effective referral flows. Foremost are: making PHC the first point of entry for patients utilizing the public health sector; introducing penalizing payments to restrict the bypassing of PHC facilities, and thus deterring the unjustified use of public hospital facilities; and regionalizing health care, i.e. deploying health facilities and workers in such a manner and in such numbers that patients would be able to receive the appropriate services in their respective health regions and districts, except for services of a tertiary nature.

Expanding Free Health Services to Deprived and Vulnerable Groups

A major step toward equity and accessibility in health care, and particularly to remove financial barriers to access for vulnerable groups, was the introduction and expansion of free health services. Such socialization of health care stands in sharp contrast to policy under the previous government where the deliberate strengthening and expansion of the private sector in health care was one of the mainstays in health policy. Since mid-1994, formidable strides have been made toward free health services by broadening the groups eligible for such care. In tandem with these measures, and in particular to limit the expansion of the private health sector, a number of regulatory measures have been proposed to reform the private health sector and to limit its expansion, and these apply to private providers, private hospitals, and the health insurance industry. Amongst others, are the authorization of the construction of new private hospitals by the minister; cutting of state subsidies to private hospitals in order to discourage their growth; barring doctors from share-holding or having other financial interests in private hospitals; regulating the importation of expensive technology in both the public and private sectors; controlling the dispensing of medicines by medical practitioners; introducing mandatory health insurance coverage for a defined hospital benefit package; ensuring cross-subsidization and risk-pooling in health insurance; and enhancing efficiency of and cost-containment in the health insurance market (Department of Health 1996b).

INVOLVING COMMUNITIES IN GOVERNANCE OF HEALTH

After a protracted history of undemocratic, authoritarian, and top-down government – excluding in particular the "non-white" population from decision-making processes – it became one of the prime dictates of the new government to create a people-driven culture and restore democratic involvement. In public health, the focus is on participatory health care, i.e. empowering communities to participate actively in planning, prioritizing, and monitoring health care in their specific areas and to take greater responsibility for their own health (Department of Health 1996b, 1997a, 1997c; Ministry of Provincial Affairs and Constitutional Development 1998). As a result, South Africa is witnessing the emergence of numerous novel governance structures at all levels of health, pertinently representing and involving civil society (Levendal et al. 1997). Decision-making in public health is intended to become a participatory affair and devolved to the lowest levels of the district and community.

Constraints and Negative Outcomes of Health Reforms

The aforementioned reforms have in many ways transformed the South African health care system in fundamental ways, and with effects for the good of equity, accessibility, and efficiency. These positive outcomes for the health system and for health care relate to steady moves away from discrimination and domination in the public health sector; greater accessibility of health care for disadvantaged groups; significant strides toward interprovincial equity and intraprovincial parity; unifying erstwhile racially and homeland fragmentation and greater integration of formerly segregated facilities and services; initiating health programs targeting in particular the most acute health problems (HIV/AIDS, TB, MCWH, nutrition), as well as protecting the most vulnerable groups in society; and refocusing the training of health personnel to become less hospital and high-tech bound and dependent, to render them more efficient and effective in delivering care in PHC settings, also in remote rural areas.

However, transformation has not been an altogether smooth process, and in many respects it is accompanied by negative outcomes and constrained by other factors militating against full and effective reform (van Rensburg 1999). Amongst the more important failures thus far is the absence of a national legislative framework – toward the end of 1999 there is still no National Health Bill published – leaving much in the field in a vacuum, unarticulated and uncertain, resulting in a disjointed restructuring process amongst provinces (Stuurman-Moleleki et al. 1997). But there are other negative outcomes and failures.

The broader transformation process inaugurated a process of never-ending change in the public health sector that has left few structures and staff members unaffected and unconfined. It has led to large-scale restructuring of departments and divisions, to myriad of novel codes and regulations, to mass redeployment and reshuffling staff. Irrespective of major gains for equity, fairness, and representivity, affirmative action measures started rapid and large-scale introduction of less experienced and inexperienced personnel and managers into key positions in state bureaucracies, and triggered voluntary severance packages, resignations, and dismissals of senior and experienced staff in significant numbers. These developments have had detrimental effects on continuity, career security, and staff morale. They have also led to concerns that standards are dropping (Ruff 1997; SAIRR 1997).

Despite the dismantling of apartheid, race and gender distortions in health care are bound to persist for decades to come, partly due to the backlogs created by the previous system, and partly as a result of the continuation of typically race-based provision in a class-segregated system, with the more wealthy catered for by the private sector, while the less wealthy have to rely on a less effective public health sector. The introduction of free health care was in many respects not adequately planned and budgeted for, and has led to patients flooding public health facilities and services, in many cases resulting in severe overcrowding, shortages of supplies and equipment, poor working conditions at clinics, low morale among public health staff, deterioration in the quality of care, and even abuse of scarce resources (McCoy and Barron 1996; McCoy and Khosa 1996; SAIRR 1997).

Budgetary mechanisms toward equalizing interprovincial inequity at central government level had been suspended in favor of provincial autonomy. The achievement of interprovincial equity in health has thus become uncertain, compromised, and is slipping down the agenda – more so in the light of ever more stringent budgets confronting the provinces (Barron et al. 1997; Buthelezi et al. 1997; Robb et al. 1997; Ruff 1997; Van den Heever and Brijlal 1997). There is widespread public perception that access to health services and quality of care is no better than it was (Naidoo 1997; Robb et al. 1997; Gaigher 1998).

Little has as yet materialized of the intention to rid the health system of its notorious two-class character, i.e. a weak public sector that caters "second-class" services to that majority of the population dependent upon the state, and a strong private health sector providing "first-class" services for the wealthy and insured minority. Current developments and trends point to the expansion and strengthening of the private sector, and along with this, the perpetuation of those notorious structural distortions and disparities, as well as persistent market- and provider-driven initiatives leading to excessive health spending and resultant cost-escalation. There are few signs of a strong and strengthening public sector. The trend is rather in the opposite direction, i.e. a weakening public sector. Deep inroads are being made into the public sector as the influx of profits, staff, and patients to a flourishing private sector is surging and valuable resources are increasingly lost as a result of the emigration of health professionals to other countries. Broadened access to the resources of the private sector appears unlikely. Instead, the shifting of private-sector patients (with concomitant cost-shifting) onto the already overstretched public sector appears likely (Van den Heever and Brijlal 1997; Wolvardt and Palmer 1997).

The new government is not succeeding in creating unity amid crippling pluralism in the health sector. There is a growing split, estrangement, and open conflict of interests between the public and private sectors; confusion among national, provincial, and local spheres of government; conflicting relationships between local government structures and civil organizations; unfulfilled expectations of traditional healers; frustrated interests of private health providers, medical professionals, and of pharmaceutical companies; and clashes between government, the health professions, labor unions, and the private sector on matters such as compulsory community service, parallel importation of medicines, importation of foreign (Cuban and other) doctors, stances on free health care and generic medicines, and many more.

The pending devolution of control in health care to District Health Authorities certainly poses questions regarding the competence of current local governments to assume responsibility for comprehensive primary health services. These questions become more daunting if one considers the present state of local governments, many of them weak in management capacity, poor in infrastructure, and virtually in states or on the brink of bankruptcy, further fuelled by shrinking intergovernmental grants and persistence of the culture of non-payment for services. In such circumstances, the wholesale transfer of current provincial responsibilities to local governments would in most cases be risky in the extreme (Naidoo 1997).

Table 21.1 Private–public divide in the health sector, mid-1999

CATEGORY	Total	Public sector 1999 Estimated dependants: 34,611,781 82%[**]	Private sector 1999 Estimated dependants: 7,597,709 18%[**]	Public–Private RATIO
General practitioners	19 729	5,398 27.4%	14,331[*] 72.6%	1 : 2.65
Medical specialists	7,826	1,938 24.8%	5,888[*] 75.2%	1 : 3.04
Dentists (including specialists)	4,269	316 7.4%	3,953[*] 92.6%	1 : 12.51
Pharmacists	4,410	1,047 23.7%	3,363[*] 76.3%	1 : 3.21
Physiotherapists	3,406	463 13.6%	2,943[*] 86.4%	1 : 6.36
Occupational therapists	1,986	388 19.5%	1,598[*] 80.5%	1 : 4.12
Speech therapists and audiologists	1,388	119 8.6%	1,269[*] 91.4%	1 : 10.66
Dental therapists	306	121 39.5%	185[*] 60.5%	1 : 1.53
Psychologists	3,808	222 5.8%	3,586[*] 94.2%	1 : 16.15

Sources: PERSAL Establishment Administration 1999; [*]Board of Healthcare Funders of South Africa 1999; [**]Chapter 13, *South African Health Review* 1998.

In spite of every effort to realize the set ideals during the past few years, the general performance record of civil society in terms of large-scale community participation and involvement in matters pertaining to health care is not always encouraging and is even disappointing (Levendal et al. 1997). Also such involvement and consultation often comes at a price in terms of protracted delays and even derailment caused by lengthy consultation in legislative and decision-making processes (Stuurman-Moleleki 1997). This is not ascribed to reluctance and apathy only, but is also due to lack of leadership, support, capacity, and material resources.

Devised to deal with the most acute problems and to look after the needs of the most vulnerable groups, several health and health-related programs (especially for HIV/AIDS, TB, immunization, nutrition, MCWH) had been introduced. One could say that many policies with clear objectives and targets have been set. However, the extent of health problems still to be addressed suggest that widespread implementation is far from adequate and that performance records leave much to be desired. The intent has been provided; what is needed, is the transformation of good intentions into practices which can make an impact (Floyd 1997; Jacobs et al. 1997; SAIRR 1997).

The health reforms also brought major reforms and restructuring to health care training and education, especially a determined shift toward emphasis on PHC. Medical training and specialized health care came under severe pressure as medical schools, which offer the best prospect of retaining the best of modern medicine within the public sector, are "dismantled" under the thrust of the PHC drive and financial stringency. It is questionable whether the narrow perspectives of political decision-making in this respect really understand the long-term implications (Benatar 1997).

In the final analysis, one could then say that the health reforms in South Africa opened vast potential and numerous new avenues for better, easier, accessible, and more equitable health care. However, reforms have not been altogether effective and beneficial. The overhasty pace and the political thrust of the transition in many respects also confused matters and introduced unintended negative results detrimental to the effectiveness and efficiency of the system, the well-being of staff, as well as the quality and user-friendliness of the services for patients.

Health and Disease Profiles – Daunting Challenges for Reform

Main Determinants of Health, Disease, and Death in South Africa

Health and disease are not primarily matters of health care. They are as much the result of prevailing environmental influences, cultural patterns, and behavioral risks. Therefore they do not necessarily respond to biomedical and health care interventions. Also health reforms play but a small part in the improvement of health. More important for health are the general living and working conditions of that population and the lifestyles of its members.

The prevailing socioeconomic conditions in South Africa do not spell encouraging prospects for the health and well-being of the majority of the population, especially not for the disadvantaged who are at the same time the most vulnerable to disease and death. Furthermore, there is not enough evidence to convincingly conclude that the general living and working conditions of the majority of South Africans have improved significantly over the past four to five years as to reflect positively in health indicators – despite the major strides in health reform. Poverty and unemployment are high, large proportions of the population remain undernourished and illiterate, disruption of family life is escalating, levels of crime, violence, and trauma are rising, backlogs in housing, pure drinking water and sanitation persist, mass labor migration and the influx of illegal migrants continues, and South Africans are smoking more (Bradshaw 1996; SAIRR 1997). Amid such broader trends in the environment, improvements in health care would have minor effects, if at all, on the health of South Africans. In addition, current health reforms cannot swiftly react to, or compensate for, historical neglect and backlogs in health and health care in the short term.

From the foregoing emerge a picture of gross inequalities. In fact, among the middle-income countries, South Africa of recent has the highest income inequalities in the world. The inner layers of this inequality leave particular groups within the South African society highly vulnerable (Mokaba and Bambo 1996): First, Africans carry most of the burden of poverty, and bear the highest negative and the lowest desirable indicators. Secondly, women bear most of the brunt of inequality and poverty, and constitute an ever-larger proportion of people in poverty. Thirdly, serious disparities exist among provinces and between rural and urban areas, with rural areas and provinces (especially the former homelands) with larger percentages of rural settlements faring worse than urban areas.

Table 21.2 Socioeconomic inequality: select social indicators

Indicator	African	Coloured	Indian	White	South African
Human Development Index	0.500	0.663	0.836	0.901	0.677
Gini coefficient	0.53	0.44	0.47	0.45	0.58
% Individuals in poverty	57.2	19.8	6.8	2.1	45.7
% Households in poverty	47.2	18.5	6.2	2.1	35.2
Annual household income (ZAR) urban	17,900	22,600	40,900	59,800	
% Unemployment	41	23	17	6	33
% Household with piped water in dwelling	32.7	72.2	96.8	96.9	51.4
% Household with sanitation facilities	90.1	96.8	100	99.9	92.3
% Electricity for lighting from grid	51	84	99	99	65

Source: Bradshaw 1998; Mokaba and Bambo 1996; Møller 1998.

Like the prevailing living conditions of the population, so is lifestyle and risk behavior among different groups and categories of the South African population highly variegated phenomena. In their turn, these phenomena have determining effects on health status and burden of disease. The prevalence of smoking, obesity, sexual practices, and preferences among different ethnic, gender, and age groups illustrate the vast divergence in risk-taking behavior and practices. Recently it was estimated that 56.5 percent of adults (15–64) need to change to a healthier lifestyle and that 16.5 percent fall into a high-risk category that need to be diagnosed and managed (Fourie and Steyn 1995). Results of the *South African Demographic and Health Survey 1998* show that there is almost universal knowledge (97%) of HIV/AIDS and the population is generally well-informed about how the disease is transmitted. However, this does not translate into safe sexual behavior as reflected in high rates of STD symptoms. Also the types of contraceptives most popular among women – injection, pills, and female sterilization – suggest that knowledge of HIV and STD transmission does not always synchronize with prevailing sexual practices.

Table 21.3 Burden of disease in different races – select indicators

Indicator	African	Coloured	Indian	White	South African
Crude mortality rate (1994)	10.2	7.2	7.3	6.7	9.4
Infant mortality rate/1,000	54.3	36.3	9.9	7.3	48.9
Maternal mortality rate (1992)	58	22	5	8	
Female life expectancy at birth	67	65	70	76	68
Male life expectancy at birth	60	59	64	69	62
Cervical cancer/100,000	34.6	30.4	15.1	12.3	30.5
AIDS total number AIDS (1996)					
females	5,219	202	6	25	5,452
males	4,606	172	13	492	5,283
Tuberculosis notifications (all forms)/100,000 (1996)	137.4	530.3	50.4	14.3	154.3
Measles notifications /100,000 (1995)	14.3	27.5	4.6	5.5	14.7
Measured hypertension (1998)					
men >15	10.3	12.4	9.9	15.2	11.0
women >15	13.0	17.1	9.3	12.0	13.2
Prevalence of symptomatic asthma (1998)					
men > 15	6.4	6.2	8.9	8.5	6.7
women > 15	8.5	8.1	12.5	8.1	8.6

Sources: South African Health Review 1998; Department of Health 1997b; *Epidemiological Comments* Dec. 1996/Jan. 1997; V. Møller 1998; *South African Demographic and Health Survey* 1998.

Mortality and Morbidity Profiles of the South African Population

South African society is preeminently a society in transition, and this fact is clearly reflected in its disease and death profiles. In general, mortality rates have declined mainly as a result of improved incomes, diet, and living conditions, and access to medical technology and health care (Bradshaw and Buthelezi 1996). Equally characteristic of South Africa's profiles of health and disease, are the gross differences and diversity which hinge in particular on the parameters of race/ethnicity, age, gender, and geographical location, but foremost on socio-economic conditions, cultural patterns, and resulting lifestyles and deprivation. Typical of the health and disease profiles of South Africans are the high and consistently rising prevalence of chronic and degenerative conditions such as ischaemic heart disease, cancer, hypertension, diabetes, etc., amid widespread incidence of so-called "social diseases" associated with poverty and poor living conditions, such as tuberculosis, pneumonia, measles, nutritional deficiencies, STDs, gastro-intestinal diseases, etc. To these are to be added the high prevalence of trauma caused by motor vehicle accidents, violence, assault, rape, and murder. Rightly Bradshaw (1998) refers to the "triple burden of disease" prevailing among South Africans, comprising chronic diseases of lifestyle, communicable diseases, and trauma.

Morbidity and mortality in South Africa are further characterized by extensive variations between the provinces, along the rural–urban divide, and among the ethnic groups, the latter closely linked to socioeconomic class disparities. A number of these variations in the morbidity and mortality patterns are depicted in table 21.3 according to racial/ethnic affiliation and provincial location.

Outcomes of the Reforms for Health and Health Status

Apart from the above-described outcomes of the health reforms for health policy and the health care system, it is also important to reflect on the outcomes of these reforms for the health of the population. Theoretically, the commendable gains of the past years, especially in terms of accessibility, affordability, and attainability of public health care, should also reflect in concomitant benefits for the health and well-being of the people. Whether this has been the case, remains difficult to determine for several reasons.

Firstly, it is difficult, and even impossible, to monitor the outcomes of health care reforms over the short time span of four years, and as explicated in terms of improved health status and quality of life, fulfilment of health needs, decreases in mortality and morbidity rates, higher life expectancy, etc. Second, improvements in health status indicators since 1994 (if any) are part of longer-term trends noticeable for the past decade or two – IMR between 1960 and 1994 almost halved, from 80/1,000 in 1960 to 43.1/1,000 in 1994. Despite this general decrease, enormous differentials in IMR remain for the various population groups – for Africans 54/1,000, for Coloureds 36, for Asians 9.9, and for whites 7.3/1,000. Trends in IMRs are inextricably linked to trends in socioeconomic improvement, but note that infant mortality has lately begun to increase with the impact of the HIV/AIDS pandemic. This situation is illustrated in the two scenarios depicted in table 21.4.

Table 21.4   Projected trends in infant mortality rate by race – two scenarios

Year	1990–95	1995–2000	2000–5	2005–10	2010–15	2015–20
African (A)	53.4	39.0	26.7	20.6	16.9	15.1
African (B)	53.4	49.5	46.7	43.9	41.7	40.8
Coloured	42.4	36.5	30.7	24.8	18.9	15.5
Indian	13.4	11.1	9.7	9.7	9.7	9.7
White	10.2	9.7	9.7	9.7	9.7	9.7

Notes:

A = improvement in quality of life because of better housing, electricity, clean water, and a drop in the unemployment. Rate – IMR for Africans would drop to 15/1,000, i.e. by 72% in the 30-year period.

B = general living conditions would not improve markedly. Rate – IMR for Africans would not drop below 40/1,000, i.e. by 24% only in the 30-year period.

Source: J. Catlitz 1996.

Third, the lack of information, and more specifically, the inconsistency and unreliability of current health status indicators (in particular for the African population), rules out any reliable deductions on short-term trends in health status at this point of time (Bradshaw 1997). Fourth, there is indeed ample evidence that in recent times trends in several important indices of mortality and morbidity are on the increase rather than declining – Tuberculosis and HIV/AIDS are examples. Fifth, recent gains regarding mortality, morbidity, and life expectancy could in coming years be eroded dramatically by the AIDS pandemic (SAIRR 1997). Sixth, health and disease are not matters of health care only; but are as much the result of prevailing socioeconomic conditions and lifestyle, and thus do not necessarily respond to health care interventions.

All things being equal, more accessible and affordable services should have soothing effects on the health of the population, especially those sectors of the clientele previously seriously disadvantaged and deprived. The Presidential-led programs of nutrition, free health services, mother and child health, clinic building and upgrading, certainly also have immediate effects, for example on the alleviation of hunger and undernutrition, accessible mother and child care, etc. However, looking at the outcomes of the health reforms on health, matters appear not all that promising. Three broad areas suffice to illustrate this gloomier side.

HIV/AIDS shows the fastest growing rate of contagion in the world (Williams 1998). The proportion of the sexually active population that is HIV+ has been increasing drastically. In 1994 it was approximately 5 percent of the sexually active population or half a million people, with a doubling of numbers every 13 months. In 1996 it was between 12 percent and 16 percent of the sexually active or up to 2 million people, and the doubling time was 5–12 months. The evidence of the 1998 HIV survey confirms that the epidemic continues to grow at an alarming rate with 3.6 million people infected (Department of Health 1999). South Africa could expect to accumulate between 5 and 7 million HIV-infections and about 1.5 million cases of AIDS by 2005. Unless the epidemic is turned around, expenditure on HIV/AIDS could hypothetically take up at least a third and possibly as much as 75 percent of the health budget within the next decade (Floyd 1997; SAIRR 1997) with major distorting effects on the general provision of and access to health services.

Table 21.5 HIV-infection rates in women attending antenatal clinics

Year	1993	1994	1995	1996	1997	1998
Percentage infected	4.01	7.57	10.44	14.17	17.04	22.8

Source: Bradshaw 1997:10; Department of Health 1998; Floyd 1997; SAIRR 1997.

South Africa is facing one of the worst TB epidemics in the world, with disease rates more than double those observed in other developing countries (Weyer 1997). In 1994 the incidence of TB in South Africa stood on 300/100,000 of the population, with 2,000 reported deaths for that year. More recent figures show that the incidence rate of TB has increased by 6 percent between 1995 and 1996 – from 340 to 362/100,000 of the population. An investigation by the WHO showed that South Africa had the worst TB epidemic out of 150 countries investigated. If trends continue, some 3.5 million people would become infected with TB by 2006, while multidrug-resistant TB is on the increase (SAIRR 1997; Weyer 1997). Worst is the situation in the mining industry where recently the incidence of TB is given as 3,000/100,000, as over a national rate of approximately 350/100,000 (SIMRAC 1999). The spread of TB within the mining context is grossly facilitated by an extensive migrant labor system within South Africa, as well as between South Africa and several neighboring countries. Note also that the magnitude of this bleak scenario is deepened by TB being so closely linked to HIV infection; in 1995, an estimated 23 percent of all TB cases were HIV+, increasing to 27 percent in 1996.

Ours is also a society of exceptional high levels of violence with few signs in recent years that a declining curve is emerging. During the decade 1987 to 1997, political violence alone has claimed 21,438 lives (SAIRR 1998). Trauma and fatalities as a result of road traffic accidents, assault, and murder also pitch at alarming heights with few signs of abating trends. Bradshaw (1997) records that in 1996 9,790 people died through road traffic collisions; a further 38,159 sustained serious injuries, and 86,291 slight injuries. During the period 1990–6, the average number of casualties per collision increased from 1.2 to 1.6. Furthermore, amid a relatively poor record of safety over the years, fatalities and injuries in South African mines adopt alarming proportions: between 1988 and 1995 fatalities in a total workforce of approximately 400,000 amounted to 5,005 and injuries to 75,001. Recent downward trends in figures are more ascribed to a decrease in the workforce than to improvements in the state of occupational safety (SIMRAC 1999).

A last point, with the strong emphasis on primary health care and the concomitant de-emphasizing of sophisticated hospital and specialized care, it is to be expected that certain disease conditions and patients categories will receive less attention from a treatment point of view – expensive treatment procedures and free option to utilize these have certainly diminished.

Regarding the outcomes of the health reforms on the health and well-being of the people, one could then conclude that the reforms over the past five years in all probability contributed constructively to improving the health of the population and alleviating the heavy burden of disease and ill health of the deprived and vulnerable. However, areas remain where the new policies and structures of health care as yet do not in practice make any significant difference. Only an improved standard of living and changed lifestyles would render such a difference.

Conclusion

Africa's heavy burden of disease, scarce health resources, and ailing health systems are unenviable. However, in South Africa's case, there are some hopeful signs. In the short period since 1994, transformation of the health system has been remarkable. The country's constitution, health policy, health structures, and contents of health care have changed fundamentally. The constitution is categorical about the commitment toward recognizing the injustices of the past and effecting redress so as to establish a society based on social justice, improve the quality of life for all citizens, and free the potential of each person. It thus frowns upon the historical lottery of race, income, and geographical location as the major determinant of access to health care. Instead, access to health care is cast in egalitarian terms as a right for everyone. It is apparent, however, that there are formidable obstacles to the realization of equitable access to health care. Though the transformation of the South African health care system is on track and in numerous ways irreversible, it is far from complete. Moreover, the implementation of the new policies has been slow and tardy, hampered by many difficulties, not least by forces with different convictions, aims, and interests.

References

Abdool Karim, S. S., T. T. Ziqubu-Page, and R. Arendse. 1994. *Bridging the Gap: Potential for a Health Care Partnership Between African Traditional Healers and Biomedical Personnel in South Africa.* Cape Town: Medical Research Council.

Africa South of the Sahara. 1998. 27th edition. London: Europa Publications.

Alubo, S. O. and F. Vivekananda. 1995. *Beyond the Illusion of Primary Health Care in an African Society: The Political Economy of Health Care and Crisis in Nigeria: With a Discourse on Kenya, Tanzania, Brazil, Cuba.* Stockholm: Bethany Books.

ANC (African National Congress). 1994a. *The Reconstruction and Development Programme – A Policy Framework.* Johannesburg: Umanyano Publications.

——. 1994b. *National Health Plan for South Africa.* Johannesburg: African National Congress.

Banda, E. N. and G. Walt. 1995. "The Private Health Sector in Malawi: Opening a Pandora's Box." *Journal of International Development* 7: 403–21.

Bannerman, R. H., J. Burton, and C. Wen-Chieh (eds.). 1983 *Traditional Medicine and Health Care Coverage: A Reader for Administrators and Practitioners*. Geneva: World Health Organization.

Barron P., K. Strachan, and C. Ijsselmuiden. 1997. "The Year in Review." *South African Health Review 1997*: xvii-xxiii.

Benatar, S. R. 1995. "History of Medical Ethics in South Africa." Pp. 1465–9 in W. Reich (ed.) *Encyclopedia of Bioethics*, 2nd edn. New York: Macmillan.

——. 1997. "Health Care Reform in the New South Africa." *New England Journal of Medicine* 77: 441–7.

Benatar, S. R. and H. C. J. van Rensburg. 1995. "Health Care Services in a New South Africa." *Hastings Centre Report* 25: 16–21.

Berman, P. (ed.). *Health Sector Reform in Developing Countries: Making Health Development Sustainable*. Cambridge, MA: Harvard University Press.

Bijlmakers, L. A., M. T. Bassett, and D. M. Sanders. 1996. *Health and Structural Adjustment in Rural and Urban Zimbabwe*. Uppsala: Nordiska Afrikainstitutet.

Bradshaw, D. 1996. "Health Status." *South African Health Review 1996*: 19–32.

——. 1997. "The Broad Picture: Health Status and Determinants." *South African Health Review 1997*: 1–15.

——. 1998. "Health for All – Monitoring Equity." *South African Health Review 1998*: 7–16.

Brown, R. 1998. "European Colonial Rule in Africa." *Africa South of the Sahara 1998*: 19–22.

Browne Commission (*Final Report of the Commission of Inquiry into Health Services – RP 67/1986*). 1986. Pretoria: Government Printer.

Burrows, E. H. 1958. *A History of Medicine in South Africa up to the End of the Nineteenth Century*. Cape Town: A. A. Balkema.

Buthelezi, G., P. Barron, N. Makhanya, and J. Edwards-Miller. 1997. *Measuring the Move Towards Equity from the Site of Service Delivery: Results from the Nine Provinces*. Durban: Health Systems Trust.

Calitz, J. 1996. *Population of South Africa: Updated Estimates, Scenarios, and Projections, 1990–2020*. Midrand: Centre for Policy and Information (DBSA).

Cockerham, W. C. 1998. *Medical Sociology, 7th edition*. Englewood Cliffs, NJ: Prentice-Hall.

Comoro, C. J. 1993. "Traditional Medical Practices and Western Allopathic Medicine in Tanzania: A Look at Bottlenecks Towards Universal Health Care by the Year 2000 or Beyond." *Internationale Afrikaforum* 29: 159–75.

Costello, A., F. Watson, and D. Woodward. 1994. *Human Face or Human Facade? Adjustment and the Health of Mothers and Children*. London: Centre for International Child Health.

David, A. R. 1997. "Disease in Egyptian Mummies: The Contribution of New Technologies." *The Lancet* 349: 1760–3.

Davidson, B. 1992. *The Black Man's Burden: Africa and the Curse of the Nation State*. London: James Currey.

De Beer, Cedric. 1984. "The South African Disease: Apartheid, Health, and Health Services." Johannesburg: South African Research Service.

Department of Health. 1996a. *Annual Report 1995*. Pretoria: Department of Health.

——. 1996b. *Restructuring the National Health System for Universal Primary Health Care*. Pretoria: Department of Health.

——. 1997a. *White Paper for the Transformation of the Health System in South Africa* (Notice 667 of 1997). Pretoria: Government Printers.

——. 1997b. *Health Trends in South Africa 1995/1996*. Pretoria: Department of Health.

——. 1998. *Eighth Annual National HIV Sero-Prevalence Survey of Women Attending Antenatal Clinics in South Africa 1997*. Pretoria: Department of Health.

——. 1999. *Ninth Annual National HIV Sero-Prevalence Survey of Women Attending Antenatal Clinics in South Africa 1998*. Pretoria: Department of Health.

De Waal, J., I. Currie, and G. Erasmus. 1999. *The Bill of Rights Handbook*. Kenwyn: Juta.

EIU (The Economist Intelligence Unit). 1997. *County Profiles 1997–1998/1998–1999*. London: EIU.

Epidemiological Comments. Dec. 1996/Jan. 1997. Seventh National HIV Survey of Women Attending Antenatal Clinics of the Public Health Services, 1996: 4–16.

Esterhuysen, P. (compiler). 1998. *Africa at a Glance: Facts and Figures: Quality of Life and Political Change 1997/1998*. Africa Institute of South Africa.

Fetter, B. 1993. "Health Care in Twentieth Century Africa: Statistics Theories and Policies." *Africa Today* 40: 8–23.

Field, M. G. 1989. *Success and Crisis in National Health Systems: A Comparative Approach*. New York: Routledge.

Floyd, L. 1997. "HIV/AIDS." *South African Health Review*. Durban: Health Systems Trust, pp. 187–96.

Fourie, J. and K. Steyn (eds.). 1995. *Chronic Diseases of Lifestyle in South Africa: Review of Research and Identification of Essential Health Priorities*. Cape Town: Medical Research Council.

Fyle, C. M. (ed.). 1993. *The State and Provision of Social Services in Sierra Leone Since Independence*. Oxford: Codesria.

Gaigher, R. 2000. "The political pathology of health care policy in South Africa." *Acta Academica* 32(1): 44–66.

Gill, P. 1986. *A Year in the Death of Africa: Politics, Bureaucracy, and the Famine*. London: Paladin.

Gilson, L. and A. Mills. 1995. "Health Sector Reforms in Sub-Saharan Africa: Lessons of the Last 10 Years." Pp. 277–316 in P. Berman (ed.), *Health Sector Reform in Developing Countries: Making Health Development Sustainable*. Cambridge, MA: Harvard University Press.

Gluckman Commission (*Report of the National Health Services Commission* – UG 30/1944). 1944. Pretoria: Government Printer.

Good, C. M. 1991. "Pioneer Medical Missions in Colonial Africa." *Social Science and Medicine* 32: 1–10.

Harrison, S. and M. Qose. 1998. "Health Legislation." *South African Health Review 1998*: 17–27. Durban: Health Systems Trust.

Health Systems Trust. 1995. *South African Health Review 1995*. Durban: Health Systems Trust and the Henry J. Kaiser Family Foundation.

——. 1996. *South African Health Review 1996*. Durban: Health Systems Trust and the Henry J. Kaiser Family Foundation.

——. 1997. *South African Health Review 1997*. Durban: Health Systems Trust and the Henry J. Kaiser Family Foundation.

——. 1998. *South African Health Review 1998*. Durban: Health Systems Trust and the Henry J. Kaiser Family Foundation.

Jacobs, M., A. Wigton, N. Makhanya, and B. Ngcobo. 1997. "Maternal, Child, and Women's Health." *South African Health Review 1997*: 139–52.

Kandela, P. 1993. "Academic Defiance in Sudan." *The Lancet* 342: 44, 45.

Kirby, J. P. 1993. "The Islamic Dialogue with African Traditional Religion: Divination and Health Care." *Social Science and Medicine* 36: 237–47.

Lachman, S. 1999. *A Knowledge Base of Heterosexual HIV/AIDS as a Global Problem in the 21st century*. Houghton: JB Israelsohn.

Laidler, P. W. and M. Gelfand. 1971. *South Africa: Its Medical History 1652–1898 – A Medical and Social Study*. Cape Town: Struik.

Last, M. and G. L. Chavunduka (eds.). 1986 *The Professionalisation of African Medicine*. International African Seminars, New Series, no. 1. Manchester: Manchester University Press.

Levendal, E., S. Lapinsky, and D. Mametja. 1997. "Community Involvement in Health." *South African Health Review 1997*: 129–35.

Logie, D. and S. R. Benatar. 1997. "Africa in the 21st Century: Can Despair be Turned to Hope?" *British Medical Journal* 315: 1444–6.

Magennis, R. 1996. "Organisation and Management: Private Sector." *South African Health Review 1996*: 61–3.

Mail and Guardian. 15–21 May 1998a. "Debt: The Plague that Kills Millions: Why the Poor are Picking up the Tab." Pp. 18, 19.

——. 8–14 May 1998b. "Former PM Admits Role in Genocide." P. 14.

McCoy, D. and P. Barron. 1996. *Free Health Care for Pregnant Women and Children Under Six in South Africa: An Impact Assessment*. Durban: Health Systems Trust.

McCoy, D. and S. Khosa. 1996 "Free Health Care Policies." *South African Health Review 1996*: 157–64.

McIntyre D., L. Baba, and B. Makan. 1998. "Equity in Public Sector Health Care Financing and Expenditure in South Africa." *South African Health Review 1998*: 29–43.

Miller, R. L. 1997. "Tetanus after Cranial Trauma in Ancient Egypt." *Journal of Neurology, Neurosurgery and Psychiatry* 63: 758.

Ministry of Provincial Affairs and Constitutional Development. 1998. *White Paper on Local Government*. Pretoria: CTP Printers.

Mokaba, B. and M. Bambo. 1996. "Socio-Economic Context of Health." *South African Health Review 1996*: 11–18.

Møller, V. 1998. "Quality of Life Trends in South Africa: An Update." Paper presented at the Annual Congress of the South African Sociological Association, Johannesburg, 30 June–3 July 1998.

MRC (Medical Research Council). 1991. *Changing the Health in South Africa: Towards New Perspectives in Research*. Menlo Park, California: Henry J. Kaiser Family Foundation.

Mwabu, G. 1995. "Health Care Reform in Kenya: A Review of the Process." Pp. 317–31 in P. Berman (ed.), *Health Sector Reform in Developing Countries: Making Health Development Sustainable*. Cambridge: MA: Harvard University Press.

Naidoo, S. 1997 "Local Government in the Move to a District Health System." *South African Health Review 1997*: 53–8.

Naylor, C. D. 1988. "Private Medicine and the Privatisation of Health Care South Africa." *Social Science and Medicine* 27: 1153–70.

Owen, C. P. (ed.). 1988. *Towards a National Health Service*. Cape Town: NAMDA Publishers.

Pickett, A. C. 1992. "The Oath of Imhotep: In Recognition of African Contributions to Western Medicine." *Journal of the National Medical Association* 84: 636–7.

Pretorius, E. 1995. "Coming in from the Cold: Traditional Medicine in the New South Africa." Paper read at the 14th International Human Sciences Research Council. Midrand, South Africa, August 1995.

——. 1999. "In the Home Stretch: The Legislation of African Traditional Health Care in South Africa." *Acta Academica* 31: 1–17.

Price, M. 1988. "The Consequences of Health Service Privatisation for Equality and Equity in Health Care in South Africa." *Social Science and Medicine* 27: 703–16.

Reich, W. (ed.). 1995. *Encyclopaedia of Bioethics*. 2nd edition. New York: Macmillan.

Robb, D., M. Annadale de Villiers, and K. Vallabjee. 1997. "Provincial Restructuring." *South African Health Review 1997*: 45–51.

Ruff, B. 1997. "Hospital Restructuring." *South African Health Review 1997*: 59–80.

SAIRR (South African Institute of Race Relations). 1997. *South Africa Survey 1996/1997*. Johannesburg: South African Institute of Race Relations.

——. 1998. *South Africa Survey 1997/1998*. Johannesburg: South African Institute of Race Relations.

Savage, M. and S. R. Benatar. 1990. "Analysis of Health and Health Services." In R. A. Schrire (ed.) 1990: 147–67.

Schrire, R. A. (ed.). 1990. *Critical Choices for South Africa. An Agenda for the 1990s*. Cape Town: Oxford University Press.

Sharp, B., C. Martin, J. Nawn, B. Curtis, A. Boulle, and D. Le Sueur. 1998. *A Collation of the Current Health Boundary and Facility Data for South Africa*. Cape Town: Medical Research Council.

SIMRAC (Safety in Mines Research Advisory Committee). 1999. "Communication During Presentation." Bloemfontein.

Sparks, D. L. 1998. "Economic Trends in Africa South of the Sahara, 1997." *Africa South of the Sahara 1998*: 11–18.

Stephan, J. 1983. "Legal Aspects." In R. H. Bannerman et al. 1983: 290–313.

Stuurman-Moleleki, J., L. Sait, and P. Long. 1997. "Health Legislation." *South African Health Review 1997*: 29–35.

UNDP (United Nations Development Programme). 1997. *Human Development Report 1997*. New York: Oxford University Press.

Van den Heever, A. M. and V. Brijlal. 1997. "Health Care Financing." *South African Health Review 1997*: 81–9.

Van Heyningen, E. 1990. "Epidemics and Disease: Historical Writing on Health in South Africa." *South African Historical Journal* 23: 122–33.

Van Niekerk, R. and D. M. Sanders. 1997. "Human Resource Development for Health." *South African Health Review 1997*: 91–8.

van Rensburg, H. C. J. 1991. "South African Health Care in Change." *South African Journal of Sociology* 22: 1–10.

——. 1999. "Health and Health Care in South Africa in Transition: A Macro Perspective." *Acta Academica* 31: 1–26.

van Rensburg, H. C. J. and S. R. Benatar. 1993. "The Legacy of Apartheid in Health and Health Care." *South African Journal of Sociology* 24: 99–111.

van Rensburg, H. C. J. and A. Fourie. 1988. "Privatisation of South Africa Health Care: In Whose Interest?" *Curationis* 11: 1–6.

van Rensburg, H. C. J., A. Fourie, and E. Pretorius. 1992. *Health Care in South Africa: Structure and Dynamics*. Pretoria: Academica.

van Rensburg, H. C. J. and D. Harrison. 1995. "History of Health Policy." *South African Health Review 1995*: 53–71.

Vogel, R. J. 1993. *Financing Health Care in Sub-Saharan Africa*. London: Greenwood Press.

Waite, G. 1987. "Public Health in Pre-Colonial East-Central Africa." *Social Science and Medicine* 24: 197–208.

Weiss, G. L. and L. E. Lonnquist. 1994. *The Sociology of Health, Healing and Illness*. Englewood Cliffs, NJ: Prentice-Hall.

Weyer, K. 1997. "Tuberculosis." *South African Health Review 1997*: 197–206.

WHO Report. 1996. *Fighting Disease, Fostering Development*. Geneva: WHO.

——. 1997. *Conquering Suffering, Enriching Humanity*. Geneva: WHO.

Williams, G. 1998. "Africa in Retrospect and Prospect." *Africa South of the Sahara*: 3–10.

Wolvardt, G. and N. Palmer. 1997. "Private Sector." *South African Health Review 1997*: 37–44.

World Bank. 1996. *Social Indicators of Development 1996*. Baltimore: Johns Hopkins University Press.

——. 1997. *World Development Report 1997: The State in a Changing World*. New York: Oxford University Press.

Zoneraich, S., P. Bhat, J. G. Bhat, and J. L. Mollura. 1996. "Bedside Patient Examination Originated 6000 Years Ago in Ancient Egypt." *Circulation* 94: 1792–3.

The Middle East

22

Health, Health Care, and Medical Education in the Arab World

Eugene Gallagher

To clarify the scope of this chapter and also to sharpen the reader's "sense of the comparative" in medical sociology it should be noted that this chapter has a special feature. This chapter, on the Arab world, embraces a cultural-geographic region rather than a single nation, or an entire continent.

For this reason it is important to delineate "the Arab world." Here the author makes use of the Arabic language as the defining criterion of what makes a person an Arab and, by extension, the provenance of the Arab world. In making this choice, I follow in the path of many specialists in Arab studies. A leading example is the Hungarian scholar Raphael Patai. In explicating "the Arab mind," he wrote that an Arab is "one whose mother tongue is Arabic" (Patai 1976: 43). Patai shows that linguistic identity is the major basis for social solidarity and he traces out related historical, ethnic, cultural, and geographic features of the Arab world. Mansfield (1985) and Burton (1932) stress the linguistic criterion still more by arguing that Arabic as a spoken language has a special formative energy that blankets and infuses consciousness more strongly than other languages; Burton even likens the Arabic language, as a vehicle of expression, to the faithful wife who follows her husband's mind and gives birth to his conceptions or thoughts.

One can draw up a list of countries in which Arabic is the predominant language. These countries fall into two geographic clusters: countries in southwest Asia, and countries in North Africa. The countries in the first group are: Bahrain, Iraq, Jordan, Kuwait, Lebanon, Oman, Qatar, Saudi Arabia, Syria, United Arab Emirates, and Yemen. The countries in the second group are: Algeria, Egypt, Libya, Mauritania, Morocco, The Sudan, and Tunisia.

The Arab world is centered in the Middle East, which is well known for being the cradle of the monotheistic religions of Judaism, Christianity, and Islam.

Measured by the number of adherents in the contemporary Middle East, Islam far exceeds Judaism and Christianity. However, it is a mistake to regard the Arab world as equivalent to the domain of Islam. This view, though widely held, is wrong on two counts. First, the majority of Muslims in the world are not Arab (i.e. Arabic-speaking). Turkey, Iran, Pakistan, and Indonesia all have populations that are predominantly to overwhelmingly Muslim but not Arab. Indeed, Arabs constitute much the smaller proportion – not more than one-quarter – of the world's Muslims. Second, some Arabs are not Muslims. Egypt, Lebanon, Iraq, and Jordan all have Christian minorities that have played an important part in earlier and recent history in the educational and professional development of the nation including its health services. Just as Europe is predominantly but not exclusively Christian, so the Arab world is predominantly but not exclusively Muslim. Even in the Saudi Arabia – the heartland of Islam – there are tribal groups that were historically Christian.

THE SOCIAL, DEMOGRAPHIC, AND HEALTH STATUS OF ARAB COUNTRIES

Aggregate and mean statistics that depict the health status of the Arab world as a whole would necessarily conceal sizable variations between nations and also within single nations. Despite their heterogeneity, it can nevertheless be stated that the nations of the Arab world are developing societies, not industrial societies. Even the Gulf Arab nations, stretching from Kuwait to Oman, although they enjoy what might be called an "industrial level" of wealth, are not industrial societies. They lack widespread industry and commerce; their wealth depends almost entirely on petroleum.

Tables 22.1 and 22.2 convey basic information on social, demographic, and health features of Algeria, Egypt, Lebanon, and Saudi Arabia. These nations occupy distinctive niches within the Arab world. With 66 million people, Egypt is the most populous Arab nation; Cairo, its capital, is one of the world's largest cities and presents all the problems of density and sprawl that beset metropolitan areas throughout the Third World. Algeria and Lebanon have, since the post-colonial epoch at the end of World War II, both liberated themselves from European-French domination; both have been rent by sectarian/religious violence jeopardizing the health and well-being of the population as well as economic and social progress. In addition to its wealth, Saudi Arabia sees itself as the titular leader of the Islamic world because the Muslim holy cities of Mecca and Medina are located in it.

Table 22.1 sets forth important social features of the four nations. Table 22.2 deals with demographic and health features. Over and above what the sheer numbers reveal, three general comments are in order.

First, these are nations with relatively high fertility rates and high population growth rates. Their growth is almost entirely due to natural increase (the excess of births over deaths) rather than migration. Their present populations are youthful, with many children and adolescents, and relatively few elderly persons. However, as the figures on life expectancy presage, the elderly component will

Table 22.1 Social characteristics of four leading nations in the Arab world: Algeria, Egypt, Lebanon, Saudi Arabia

| | Total population in millions (1998) | Annual growth rate (1978–1998) | Gross National Product per capita (1995) | Average years of education* (1990) | | Adult literacy rate (1995) | Dependency ratio** (1998) |
				Females	Males		
Algeria	30.1	2.7%	$1,600	1.9	3.8	62%	70
Egypt	66.0	2.3%	$790	2.3	5.0	51%	68
Lebanon	3.2	0.8%	$2,660	–	–	79%	64
Saudi Arabia	20.2	4.4%	$7,040	–	–	63%	78
The World	5,885	1.6%	–	4.5	6.6	–	59

Notes: *refers to adult population (aged 25+); **ratio of population ages 0–14 and 65+ to population 15–64.
Source: adapted from *The World Health Report* for 1998 and 1999, Geneva, Switzerland: WHO.

Table 22.2 Demographic/health characteristics for four leading nations in the Arab World: Algeria, Egypt, Lebanon, Saudi Arabia

	Infant mortality rate (1998)*	Maternal mortal-ity rate (1990)**	Total fertility rate (1998)***	Life expectancy (1998) (years) Females	Males	Total health expenditures as a percentage of GDP (1995)	Public sector health expen-ditures as a percentage of total (1995)
Algeria	44	160	5.4	70	68	4.6	73
Egypt	51	170	3.4	68	65	3.7	43
Lebanon	29	300	2.7	72	68	5.3	39
Saudi Arabia	23	130	5.8	73	70	3.1	–
The World	57	430	2.7	69	65	5.2	48

Notes: * per 1,000 live births; ** per 100,000 live births; *** average number of children born to a woman of reproduction age.
Source: adapted from *The World Health Report* for 1998 and 1999, Geneva, Switzerland: WHO.

increase rapidly in decades to come. As in other developing nations (Gallagher et al. 2000) the fertility rate, though still high by western standards, has dropped considerably within the past 20 years. Longevity is increasing substantially for the middle-aged and elderly. These four nations, along with the Arab world in general have moved a considerable distance along the path of the "epidemiologic transition." As first enunciated by Omran, this transition is the massive demographic change that nations typically undergo in the process of industrialization; they move from the earlier combination of high birth and death rates to the "mature" phase of low birth and death rates (Omran 1971). In the earlier phase, life expectancy is low (in the thirties to forties); in the latter phase, it is high, reaching into the seventies and eighties.

Second, these four Arab nations stand low in education by comparison with the world population. Further, the "female shortfall" – the deficiency of education among women compared with men – is large. The nations with greater financial resources, such as Saudi Arabia, have made rapid strides in education in recent years. The opportunities for females are not far behind those available to males in primary and secondary education, but lag behind at the postsecondary level (more will be said below about the status of women in Arab society). In the poorer Arab countries such as Yemen and Egypt, educational opportunity is limited at all levels, especially for females. Lack of schooling of course shows up later on in the form of low adult literacy.

Third, some notion of health care outlays in the four countries can be obtained from table 22.2. A rough guide to the average expenditure per person can be obtained by multiplying the per capita income (table 22.1 – Gross National Product per capita) by the percentage of national income (approximated by the gross domestic product) devoted to health expenditures (table 22.2 – Total health expenditures as a percentage of GDP). This simple arithmetic reveals that the average annual health expenditure for an Algerian is $74; for an Egyptian, $29; for a Lebanese, $141; and for a Saudi, $218. All four nations have a skewed distribution of income in which there are small proportions of well-to-do persons and many poor persons. However, Saudi Arabia is unique in that its ruling family (the house of Al Saud) is both large, with some 8,000 adult members, and immensely rich; however, the lower end of the Saudi spectrum is comparatively better off than the low end in Algeria, Egypt, and Lebanon, with corresponding favorable implications for health services and health status in the Saudi case.

ARAB VALUES AND THE SICK ROLE

Sociologists and anthropologists have frequently observed that, in developing societies, social relationships are suffused by a yearning for emotional warmth and interpersonal affiliation. Many sociological frameworks that contrast modern civilization and traditional society recognize this feature. In Talcott Parsons' (1951) well-known scheme of pattern variables, social relationships in traditional societies are particularistic, ascriptive, affective, and diffuse. These qualities enhance the sense of trust, mutual concern, and reliability within a relationship.

Nowhere in the developing world is the striving for personal bonds, for affiliation, and the glow of intimacy stronger than in Arab society. A well-known Arab rhyming aphorism goes: "Jarr qabla darr w rafeeq qabla tareeq." It translates into "[Choose] your neighbor before your house and [choose] your companion before your journey." While it cannot be taken literally, it probes into the personalistic, personalizing nature of the Arab culture that spawned it. This quality of social relationships has implications for medical care, as will be seen below.

A second characteristic of Arab society with great relevance for medical care is the high value it places upon helper roles and helping activities. Of course, all societies would cease to exist if parents did not nurture their children – nurture as a radical form of helping is vital. Yet more than in most other societies, Arab society weaves helping activities into the social fabric, so that the giving of help becomes a constitutive or basic cultural value and not merely a source of benefit to the person who is helped.

These two characteristics of Arab culture coalesce to form another strong cultural formation: a high tolerance for dependency in the sick role. Medical sociologists will recall Parsons' formulation whereby the sick person is relieved of their usual social responsibilities in proportion to the discomforts and disabilities imposed by the illness and also the requirements of treatment.

It is not within the scope of this chapter to engage in a full exploration of the sick role. However a basic question for medical sociology can be raised: should the sick role be understood as a universal, impervious to cultural modification – or is it significantly shaped into variant forms by cultural values (Gallagher and Subedi 1992)? This question has obvious import for the theory of the sick role, for medical sociology more generally, and for the delivery of culturally sensitive medical care. The view of the author is that the sick role is indeed universal within broad limits; but it is nevertheless important here to discern the nuances that impinge upon it in Arab culture.

Arab culture is notably indulgent toward sick-role dependency. Here are three case-examples that would be difficult to duplicate in American society.

1   An example of "feeding dependency" comes from the observations of an American physician who spent several years as a personal physician to the royal family, Al Saud, in Saudi Arabia. He reports the following episode (Gray 1983: 45). The patient was a 60-year-old cousin of King Khalid. He was hospitalized for ulcer distress:

> Since an ulcer diet was an important part of the treatment, the next step was to devise a diet that the prince would be willing to follow. I consulted with the dietician and recommended rice, yogurt, and camel's or goat's milk to start with. These were among the prince's favorite foods. He seemed content, provided his servant prepared the food and fed him spoonful by spoonful. I watched this nursery scene for a few moments and then left.

2   A 50-year-old female bedouin patient received hemodialysis at a tertiary care hospital in the Negev desert of southern Israel. She was married and, like most of the seminomadic Arab bedu, of low socioeconomic status. Because of vascular damage from diabetes (which was also the cause of her renal failure), her right leg was amputated. Following that, she was provided with a prosthesis, crutches, and a wheelchair. Hospital staff noted, however, that she rarely used her prosthesis or crutches; instead, her sons and grandsons regularly carried her or pushed her in the wheelchair. The patient's dependence upon kinsmen for mobility is consistent with the more general observation made by the staff (Lewando-Hunt et al. 1980: 10):

> There is a specific cultural attitude amongst the Bedouin toward the chronically sick and the handicapped which both gives them support but also encourages them to be dependent on their family. One's family is expected to adjust to one's limited functioning. They have no expectations of rehabilitation. The blind are assumed to be unable to undertake any physical activity without guidance. The deaf are not expected to know how to lip-read. Their relatives and friends learn how to communicate by gesture. In the case of the dialysis patients, there is a readiness to care for them, even unnecessarily.

3   The third example is a female adolescent patient in Kuwait who was born with severe congenital anomaly known as spina bifida. With prompt, and continuing, medical and surgical treatment she survived (Gallagher 1998). As she grew, her physical development was arrested and she resorted to a wheelchair for mobility. Also she was incontinent of urine. She and her family, who were wealthy, were instructed that she should urinate through a device known as a Foley catheter, inserted in her vagina and re-inserted every day or two. This was uncomfortable for her (as it is for many similar patients). Despite medical admonitions, her family gave in to her complaints and allowed her to urinate freely into diapers. She began to suffer an intermittent urinary/kidney infection. This led over time to chronic renal failure and necessitated her being started on hemodialysis three times weekly.

Although the cause of her kidney failure cannot be attributed solely to the family's indulgence of her discomfort with the catheter, this factor did contribute to her renal failure. In the first two case-examples, the patient's condition was not worsened by the latitude of their support system. In the case of the adolescent girl, whose medical plight was worse from the outset, it contributed to a severe yet necessary outcome, namely, hemodialysis.

ENVIRONMENTAL AND CULTURAL FACTORS CONTRIBUTING TO ILL HEALTH

The Arab world lies substantially in tropical latitudes. It has environmental and climatic conditions favorable to the spread of parasitic diseases such as malaria, schistosomiasis (spread by snails exposed to human feces), and leishmaniasis (spread by sandflies). These occur especially in regions that lack safe drinking water and sanitation. Other common parasitic diseases are onchocer-iasis (leading often to "river blindness") and helminthiasis (i.e. tapeworm infes-tation).

Cultural-sanctioned practices may also pose a health risk. Consanguineous marriage – marriage between close relatives such as first or second cousins, or uncle/niece – increases the probability of genetic disease or disability. Consan-guineous marriage – "inbreeding" – is widespread in developing societies (Bittles et al. 1991) and in tradition-oriented segments of industrial societies such as the Amish sect in the United States (McKusick et al. 1964). It raises the likelihood of genetically-determined diseases and conditions that would be rarer if marital or mating partners were drawn from a wider, more "public" pool of breeding candidates.

A Saudi study of 9,061 households conducted in 1987–8 showed that 34 percent of marriages of females in urban areas were with first cousins, 24 percent were with other relatives, and 42 percent were with non-relatives (Al-Mazrou et al. 1995). This is a high rate compared with western industrialized countries; it reflects basic features of Arab society. An individual's family status and family connections are more completely determinative of his/her life-chances than in the West. In particular, opportunities for individualized careers, occupational differ-entiation, and cultural participation are limited, and much more limited for females than for males. The stronger role of family influence and the more restricted role of non-familial influences have many implications for choice of one's marital partner.

The notion of marriage based upon love is certainly known and to some extent idealized in Arab society. However, there are few social opportunities for men and women to meet apart from situations arising from family circumstances. Although Arab life is intensely "social," virtually all the sociability and social interaction are family-based or based upon same-sex relationships. Although the experience of the large extended family living under one roof is less widespread than formerly, the smaller nuclear families retain geographic contiguity and emotional closeness with each other. One's individual life is densely filled with a round of religious feast-days and family events such as births, circumcisions, marital engagements, weddings, and funerals. Even in Arab metropolises such as Baghdad, Cairo, and Beirut, there is much less detached or alienated individu-alism than in New York or Paris.

Given this social pattern, it is not surprising that most Arab marriages are arranged by the parents or other older relatives of the marital partners. Though adverse genetic consequences of such arranged "close-in" pairings may occur, there are arguably at the same time several social advantages. Wealth and social status can be retained within the extended family. The bride and groom have the security of knowing a good deal about each other's family of origination. Guidance and support can flow more easily from a shared cohort of older relatives.

If the negative genetic consequences of consanguinity could be weighed in a scale against the foregoing positive social consequences, in the light of full, objective information, many people would opt against the prevailing marriage pattern and hope for some other ways of providing guidance to young married couples. Not surprisingly, laypersons do not figure in this manner. A study conducted in Saudi Arabia in 1988 found that, among a group of 36 families with children with metabolic and neurological disorders, many parents did not understand or accept probabilistic genetic explanations. They argued that if consanguinity were the culprit, then why were not all of their children afflicted (Panter-Brick 1991)? Many of them adhered to beliefs, such as the evil eye, that could allow for a particularized explanation why the afflicted child was different from his siblings.

THE ALLOCATION OF HEALTH RESOURCES

The Arab world faces critical dilemmas concerning the distribution of health resources for the present and projected future needs of the population. In confronting such issues, it is not distinctively different from other developing regions of the world. Indeed the industrialized nations face similar issues. One basic question is: what is the role of the physician in the overall delivery of health care, *vis-à-vis* the role of other health professionals? A related question concerns the balance between generalists and specialists within the medical profession. A further question concerns the place of the hospital in the health care delivery system.

Many health planners and public health authorities believe that there has been, worldwide, an overemphasis upon the production of physicians and the building of hospitals. This view has been clearly articulated by the World Health Organization (WHO) and expressed in its program, "Health for All by the Year 2000," frequently abbreviated to HFA/2000 (World Health Organization 1981). This program was first enunciated in 1978 in a WHO conference at Alma-Ata in the former Soviet Union.

The central official health authority in virtually every Arab nation has endorsed HFA/2000. By itself, this endorsement does not necessarily mean that there will be a major reorientation of health care priorities. While in no way degrading the strategic position of the medical profession in the delivery of health care overall, the WHO initiative aims to promote primary health care, much of which can be delivered by non-physician health professionals. It also endorses ambulatory and community care conducted outside of hospitals; additionally, WHO urges the establishment of national referral systems through which, when hospitalization is necessary, patients can be directed to the most appropriate level of care/treatment. This embraces the creation of local or district hospitals, provincial or secondary-level hospitals, and central or highly specialized tertiary-level hospitals (Barnum and Kutzin 1993). Decisions for the establishment of the foregoing, "rational," or planned scheme of health care would be made in the political or governmental domain.

In every country there is a division between health services that are politically or governmentally financed and administered, and those that are in the private sector, where market or economic forces prevail. Many countries that are currently characterized as poor and developing have a relatively small private sector; though often woefully underfinanced, the public sector is larger.

Table 22.2 gives a rough estimate of the public/private balance in Arab countries. It shows that, as a percentage of total health expenditures, the amount spent by the government (the public sector) is 73 percent in Algeria, 43 percent in Egypt, and 39 percent in Lebanon. The case of Egypt is of particular interest because of its status as the most populous Arab nation. If the balance between public/private is 43/57, this roughly implies that governmental decisions cannot reach beyond 43 percent of total health outlays and correspondingly that the bulk of spending and provision lies in the private sector. This sector includes the services of private physicians, the large majority of whom in Egypt are specialists. It includes also the services of dentists and pharmacists, the latter being exceedingly important within the overall mix of health services in Arab countries. It includes as well private hospitals. In Egypt many private hospitals are relatively small, 10–20 bed hospitals owned by private physicians who also provide most or all of the medical services to their patients.

Another critical phenomenon in the Egyptian private sector is that Islamic organizations, also organized as political parties, have an extensive network of lay and professionally-trained persons who provide free health and medical services throughout the country, in both urban and rural areas. They are of particular importance in impoverished, underserved sections of cities. A newspaper account states: "Militants provide funds to the destitute, run clinics, mediate disputes and patrol against common crime" (Hedges 1992). Because the Islamic groups are private, voluntary organizations there are no reliable official statistics about the volume of services they deliver, in comparison with public and with private-market provision. It seems clear however that their contribution is substantial.

The Islamic-based organizations are not politically neutral providers of professional and technical services. On the contrary, they make partisan claims and wield political influence. Beyond the value of the clinical services they put forth, they seek to gain political–religious allegiance and to stir enthusiasm within the Egyptian populace. They argue that, in failing to offer effective health services, the national government is impotent, inefficient, and corrupt; they hold forth their own offerings as a demonstration of what can be accomplished through religious and cultural dedication (it is not clear, however, that they are themselves free of the faults which they see in the government). In Egypt they present an unusual model of "health service in the name of politics"; on a lesser scale, similar organizations and political–religious dynamics can be found in other Arab countries and in the West Bank (Greenberg 1992).

Medical Schools in the Arab World

The eighteen countries comprising the "Arab world" (listed above) have among them, in 1999, 63 medical schools (also referred to as "medical faculties"). This figure is approximate and may be low by two or three schools. It comes from a WHO report published in 1988 (WHO 1988), supplemented by fragmentary information available to the author on schools more recently established. The report was based on a WHO questionnaire survey of all UN Member States.

Some countries (member states) gave incomplete responses. Each of the 18 nations has at least one medical school except for Qatar and Mauritania, which have none. Kuwait, Oman, and United Arab Emirates have one medical school each. At the other extreme, Iraq has six; Algeria, nine; and Egypt, nineteen. Among the oldest medical schools are: University of Baghdad (Iraq, founded in 1927); American University in Beirut (Lebanon, 1867); University of Khartoum (The Sudan, 1924); University of Damascus (Syria, 1919); and, in Egypt, University of Cairo (1827) and University of Alexandria (1942). Western colonial influence was strong in the Middle East and North Africa prior to World War II. The few medical schools started during this earlier period owe their establishment to western initiative. Later, under the recently decolonialized national governments, many schools were begun in the fifties, sixties, and seventies. The most recently established is that in United Arab Emirates, which admitted its first class in 1986.

To study the dynamics of medical education in any developing country of the globe is to seize upon a particularly symbolic fulcrum for social change in that country. This is particularly true in the Arab world. Many countries in South America, Africa, and South Asia are undergoing struggles in the effort to modernize in the fast-paced era of economic and cultural globalization. Aside from industrial and commercial development, two pivotal features of modernization are the drive toward the implementation of scientific knowledge for human betterment and toward greater respect for the rights and the potential of the individual human being. Medicine and health care tie together these two objectives. Though increasingly assisted by other health professions, the physician remains the key actor. As proto-physicians, medical students are an especially strategic group for embodying national expectations and visions.

CULTURAL TENSIONS IN MEDICAL EDUCATION

Tension is felt in all developing societies between still powerful cultural traditions and the pull toward the future. Nowhere is the tension greater than in the Arab world. Medicine is seemingly a universally acclaimed and non-controversial ingredient in the formula for progress. Medical education of course goes along with medicine. What could be more solidly aligned with the future yet culturally impartial than the preparation of the next generation of doctors?

Yet there are within the structure of medical education in the Arab world several veins of controversy – features that call into question its Arab-Islamic legitimacy. These are: (1) the struggle to reappropriate the historic medieval Arab medical heritage as a contemporary guide in the medical school curriculum; (2) the use of western languages (especially English) with medical students as the "language of instruction"; and (3) the emancipatory pressure of medical learning and activity upon the traditional proprieties of gender.

These features of controversy will be dealt with serially below.

1   In the history of western culture it is an accepted truth that in the long interval between the end of Roman imperial culture and the western Renaissance, Arab scholars studied, translated into Arabic, and promulgated classical

Greek and Roman thought. Along with astronomy and mathematics, medical taxonomy, discovery, and application were particularly important (Khairallah 1946). Especially illustrious were Ibn Sina (or Avicenna: 980–1037), Al Zahrawi (936–1035), and Ibn Rushd (or Averroes: 1126–1198) (Ahmad 1991). Many Arab–Muslim physicians and medical educators, both in the Arab world and in the West, desire that these "forgotten" names and their accomplishments be celebrated so that current medical students will identify with a heritage that rapidly lost its vigor about five centuries ago. However, the general temper of medical education nowadays, whether in North America, Europe, the Middle East, or Asia, leaves little room for concern with the history of medicine (except as a specialized scholarly discipline). The desire of medical educators for revival seems at best nostalgic; it has not worked its way into medical curricula in the Arab world.

In contrast, the prospects for fresh interest in what might be called "traditional health care, Middle Eastern style" and its incorporation into medical education seem brighter (Pillsbury 1978). Belief in the evil eye, the practice of cautery (touching afflicted portions of the body with hot irons), and potions to reverse female infertility would not find favor in medical schools. However much of the knowledge and technique possessed by community herbalists and midwives is of interest to medical educators. Just as so-called alternative medicine is being selectively adopted into western medical schools, so the equivalent process has favorable potential in the Arab world.

2   The issue concerning the use of Arabic as the language of instruction in medical education has a cultural dynamic similar to that concerning the history of Arab medicine. In both instances, it appears that an integral feature of Arabic–Muslim tradition has yielded to western cultural hegemony. In the WHO survey of medical schools, most schools list English as the language of instruction while those in former French-dominated regions – Tunisia, Morocco, Algeria, Syria, and Lebanon – list French. Some schools permit some lecturing in Arabic but virtually all written materials – textbooks, lab manuals, syllabi, teaching outlines, lecture handouts – are presented in English (or French).

Most of the faculty in Arab medical schools are Arabs. Many find it difficult to use English (or French) even though they obtained their higher degrees in European or North American universities. If non-Arabic languages are a stumbling block for faculty, it is even more so for the students. Questions arise about students who fail academically: are they simply weak students who lack intellectual capacity to master medicine – or are they bright students who are trapped by an inadequate command of the non-Arabic language of instruction (Gallagher 1989)?

On the surface, the issue seems straightforward but nevertheless difficult to resolve: should students learn medicine in their native language or another, more metropolitan language? Beneath the surface but close to it are a host of other issues which make it so difficult to settle – the nature of medicine, the place of science in medical education, the role of the physician in society, and the tensions between Arab and western culture.

One obvious fact is that almost all students in Arab medical schools are born and raised in Arab culture, and they look forward to a career of practice with

Arab patients. Given this, English often appears to be an artificial imposition. They do, however, have increasing amounts of exposure to English through the mass media and through primary and secondary education. Whether this exposure is sufficient to establish a base for learning medicine in English is hotly debated among the faculties.

Another question is this: is the physician primarily a technician who has learned a series of algorithms and techniques for treating patients – or is the physician a scientist who knows and understands the deeper, and always evolving, scientific principles that underlie techniques? Although this question vexes faculty in medical schools everywhere, it has special resonance in the Arab medical schools as suggested by this additional question: can the Arabic language and Arab–Muslim culture become a vehicle for scientific knowledge and discovery?

3   Given the strength of religio–cultural tradition in the Arab–Muslim world, it is not surprising that basic expectations about gender find expression in medical education. Medical education is gender-segregated by administrative policy throughout most of the Arab world though its stringency varies. Thus, Saudi Arabia, the most stiffly orthodox Arab nation, has separate campuses for male and female medical students; less conservative, the United Arab Emirates has separate classes, separate labs, and separate library facilities, but all using the same faculty. In Kuwait, there is no segregation policy – the prevailing patterns of interaction between male and female students approximate those in the West.

Given the sequestered and restricted movement of females in Arab public space, there is a gigantic built-in need for female physicians. As in western countries many female patients prefer female doctors; additionally, the male guardians of females – husbands, brothers, fathers, sons – do not wish their clients to be dealt with by male physicians. Thus, in most Arab countries, females constitute 40–60 percent of the total of medical students; once trained and registered, this sizable contingent of female physicians then meet the health needs of children as well as females in their society. Another factor that draws female students to medicine is that it is one of the very few professions open to females, particularly in the more conservative Arab countries. Indeed, the narrowness of vocational opportunity probably means that some female students are more concerned to prove themselves intellectually and academically in a general sense than they are specifically interested in medicine (Gallagher 1993).

A concomitant development in Arab medical education and medical care is that there is currently a shortage of academically qualified males who aspire to medical training and practice. This is an important trend that is not well understood sociologically; it has to do with the occupational aspirations of males. Many expect to find employment in private businesses of their fathers or other older male relatives, or in the national civil service (a major employer throughout the Arab world); while they may seek a university education, many of them lean away from the intensive type of professional training that medicine requires.

The relatively small number of qualified male applicants has given rise to sensitive and contentious discussions among medical educators. It has led one of the Arab Gulf countries to adopt a type of "affirmative action" policy that openly favors male applicants over female; males can matriculate with lower secondary school grades and lower entrance test scores than females. The rationale for this differential standard is not that males have been discriminated against in the past; it is, rather, that without the differential some 70–80 percent of practicing physicians would, in ten years' time, be female. There would not be enough male physicians to meet the needs of male patients. Female medical students and physicians are concerned about the "double standard" but appear to accept it as a policy necessity for the present.

One recalls that, in the United States, studies of medical student recruitment and socialization were, among other events, an important springboard for the emergence of medical sociology. The same would certainly be true for medical sociology in the Arab world. A good starting point would be precisely the aforementioned troublesome dearth of male applicants for medical school. By itself it is a highly specific and narrow problem-phenomenon in search of a sociological explanation. Its solution however would require a systematic study of student socialization and progress across the full six-year university curriculum, covering its premedical, preclinical, and clinical phases. It would also verge upon questions and concepts that lie as much in general sociology as in medical sociology, such as the life-course expectations and aspirations currently held by young Arabs in their diverse family and social milieux.

ARAB MEDICAL SOCIOLOGY

This chapter will conclude with a brief examination of the topic alluded to above, namely, what is the current status of medical sociology in the Arab world? Relatedly, what is the status of general sociology there?

Sociology made its first appearance in the Arab world in Egyptian universities in the 1920s (Zayed 1997). Since then, it established itself in many other Arab universities. However, although it has achieved some breadth, its depth and cultural impact, along with that of the other social sciences, has not been substantial. Its influence has not been strong either in the universities or in general public discourse. In his account of Arab sociology, Bagader (1997) sees several reasons for this condition. One is the language barrier. Most sociology has been written in English, French, or German and has yet to be translated into Arabic. However, once translated or adapted, sociological material then appears to be "obscure and alien" – a second reason for the low impact of sociology. The few sociology textbooks written in Arabic are "based on American textbooks . . . which enforced the notion that sociology is totally a Western discipline that does not have anything to offer to Arab society and culture" (Bagader 1997: 68–9).

Probably the status of sociology will rise as the Arab world makes further progress toward democratic political institutions and toward a culture of open public discourse. It is possible meanwhile to draw a more encouraging picture of medical sociology. As in the United States and many European countries, medical sociology has grown and prospered by the adoption of sociological concepts and perspectives into the curricula of medical and other health professional schools (Cockerham 2000). Medical schools in Oman, Kuwait, United Arab

Emirates, and Saudi Arabia have in various ways drawn upon sociology as an important source of content, and upon sociologists to teach it. Typically the sociological content is conveyed within an interdisciplinary framework – in courses dealing for example with the biopsychosocial model of disease, or with medical interviewing. As in the West, the departmental sponsorship of "interdisciplinary medical sociology" varies widely and sometimes multiplies within the same medical faculty – departments of psychiatry, family medicine, behavioral sciences, community medicine, and preventive medicine are the major sponsors but occasionally sociological content and personnel are found also in clinical departments such as pediatrics and obstetrics.

A 1986 survey of research in Arab sociology by Sabagh and Ghazella (1986) reveals virtually no work that falls clearly within the domain of medical sociology. Since that time, three foci of research activity have emerged that deserve mention here, as follows:

1 Problems that nurses in Jordan confront have been investigated by Professor Muhanna Haddad in Jordan (Haddad 1988). He finds that many nurses felt disrespected and unappreciated in their work; they had difficult working conditions, and hospital administration ignored their complaints. Moreover those who were widows were "easily suspected of immorality and sexual deviance in a traditional society" (Haddad 1988: 3).

2 The Dubai Community Psychiatric Survey, conducted by Professor Rafia Ghubash (Ghubash et al. 1994), examined the effects of rapid and massive social change on the mental health of female nationals in the metropolis of Dubai, United Arab Emirates. On the basis of data gathered in her household survey, Ghubash found: "The overall rate of psychiatric disorder in Dubai...is high in international terms and this is consonant with the hypothesis that the rapidly changing culture of Dubai is stressful to its citizens... retaining some traditional values in the face of social change does not necessarily imply an increased risk of affective and neurotic forms of psychiatric morbidity... on the contrary, insofar as it represents a choice, it may be a prudent course of action" (Ghubash et al. 1994: 131).

3 In Saudi Arabia, Professor Zohair Sebai, in the Department of Family Medicine at the King Faisal Medical Faculty at Dammam, has studied the beliefs of rural Saudi bedouin groups concerning disease causation, family planning, and medical care (1985). Sebai found, with regard to birth control, that many bedouin women had a passive, accepting attitude toward future pregnancies, while approximately one-quarter said they wanted no more pregnancies. Bedouin men, in contrast, "don't accept contraception... They always want more children, since children are a symbol of wealth, strength and vitality. They reason that it does not cost much, if anything to have one more child, as he or she will be raised with other children in the household" (Sebai 1985: 460).

The foregoing examples of research demonstrate the range of investigations being carried out by Arab investigators. For sociologists trained in the West, the Arab world offers a prodigious and intense arena of topics for research, most of them connected with processes of social change. It is not surprising, however, that there are difficult problems of access that hamper investigators coming into Arab societies as strangers. For this reason, we as medical sociologists must turn to our Arab colleagues. We hope that research training and facilitation will increase among Arab sociologists (and other social scientists) and that future accounts will report steady progress toward increasing our understanding of health and health care in the Arab world.

References

Ahmad, M. Basheer. 1991. "Contribution of Muslim Physicians and Scholars of Spain during the Period between the Ninth and Thirteenth Centuries." *Journal of the Islamic Medical Association* 23: 82–6.

Al-Mazrou, Yagob, Samir M. Farid, and Moslem Uddin Khan. 1995. "Changing Marriage Age and Consanguineous Marriage in Saudi Females." *Annals of Saudi Medicine* 15: 481–5.

Bagader, Abubaker A. 1997. "The State of Arab Sociology as Seen by an Arab Sociologist." Pp. 61–72 in Abdelkader Zghal and Ahmed Iadh Ouederni (eds.), *Questions from Arab Societies*. Proceedings of the Arab Regional Conference, International Sociological Association, Madrid, Spain.

Barnum, Howard and Joseph Kutzin. 1993. *Public Hospitals in Developing Countries – Resource Use, Cost, Financing*. Baltimore: Johns Hopkins University Press.

Bittles, A. H., W. M. Mason, J. Green, and N. A. Rao. 1991. "Reproductive Behavior and Health in Consanguineous Marriages." *Science* 252: 794–8.

Burton, Richard. 1932. Essay Accompanying Burton Translation of *One Thousand and One Nights*. New York: Blue Ribbon Books.

Cockerham, William C. 2000. "Medical Sociology at the Millennium." Pp. 417–39 in S. Quah and A. Sales (eds.), *International Handbook of Sociology*. London: Sage.

Gallagher, Eugene B. 1989. "Institutional Response to Student Difficulties with the 'Language of Instruction' in an Arab Medical College." *Journal of Higher Education* 60: 565–82.

——. 1993. "Curricular Goals and Student Aspirations in a New Arab Medical College." Pp. 135–53 in P. Conrad and E. Gallagher (eds.), *Health and Health Care in Developing Countries*. Philadelphia: Temple University Press.

——. 1998. "Psychosocial Aspects of Hemodialysis in Arab Gulf Societies." Unpublished study in progress.

Gallagher, Eugene B., Thomas F. Stewart, and Terry D. Stratton. 2000. "The Sociology of Health in Developing Countries." Pp. 387–97 in C. Bird, P. Conrad, and A. Fremont (eds.), *Handbook of Medical Sociology*, 5th edition. Saddle River, NJ: Prentice-Hall.

Gallagher, Eugene B. and Janardan Subedi. 1992. "Studying Health in Developing Societies: A Conceptually-Informed Research Agenda." *Central Issues in Anthropology* 10: 127–33.

Ghubash, Rafia, Emad Hamdi, and Paul Bebbington. 1994. "The Dubai Community Psychiatric Survey: Acculturation and the Prevalence of Psychiatric Disorder." *Psychological Medicine* 24: 121–31.

Gray, Seymour. 1983. *Beyond the Veil*. New York: Harper and Row.

Greenberg, Joel. 1992. "Winds of Islam Sweep Israel, Changing Landscape." *New York Times* (September 16): 4.

Haddad, Muhanna Yousef. 1988. "Problems of Nursing and Marital Status in Jordan." Yarmouk University, Irbid, Jordan: Department of Humanities and Social Sciences.

Hedges, Chris. 1992. "As Islamic Militants Thunder, Egypt Grows More Nervous." *New York Times* (November 13): 1.

Khairallah, Amin. 1946. *Outline of Arabic Contributions to Medicine*. Beirut: American Press.

Lewando-Hunt, Gillian, Stanley Rabinowitz, Naomi Shohat, and Gabriel M. Danvitch. 1980. "The Influence of Socio-Cultural Factors on Adaptation to Dialysis Treatment." Beersheba: Ben-Gurion University of the Negev. Unpublished report.

Mansfield, Peter. 1985. *The Arabs*, 2nd edition. London: Penguin Books.

McKusick, Victor A., John A. Hostetler, and Janice A. Egeland. 1964. "Genetic Studies of the Amish." *Bulletin of the Johns Hopkins Hospital* 115: 203–22.

Omran, Abdel R. 1971. "The Epidemiologic Transition." *Milbank Memorial Quarterly* 4: 509–38.

Panter-Brick, Catherine. 1991. "Parental Responses to Consanguinity and Genetic Disease in Saudi Arabia." *Social Science and Medicine* 33: 1295–302.

Parsons, Talcott. 1951. *The Social System*. New York: Free Press.

Patai, Raphael. 1976. *The Arab Mind*. New York: Charles Scribner's Sons.

Pillsbury, Barbara. 1978. *Traditional Health Care in the Near East – Indigenous Health Practices and Practitioners*. Washington, DC: Near East Bureau, Health and Nutrition Division, Agency for International Development.

Sabagh, George and Iman Ghazella. 1986. "Arab Sociology Today: A Survey from Within," *Annual Review of Sociology* 12: 389–97.

Sebai, Zohair M. 1985. *Health in Saudi Arabia*. Riyadh: Tihama.

World Health Organization. 1981. *Global Strategy for Health for All by the Year 2000*. Geneva: World Health Organization.

——. 1988. *World Directory of Medical Schools*, 6th edition. Geneva: World Health Organization.

Zayed, Ahmed A. 1997. "Knowledge in the Arab Countries: The Case of Egypt." Pp. 48–60 in A. Zghal and A. Ouederni (eds.), *Questions from Arab Societies*. Proceeding of the Arab Regional Conference, International Sociological Association, Madrid, Spain.

23

Health and Health Care in Israel

OFRA ANSON

In many ways, Israeli society is no different from other western societies. Yet, beyond the social characteristics, structures, processes, and organizations shared with other developed countries, there are some unique features, which affect the well-being of Israelis and the organization of their health services. These unique features of Israel are the focus of this chapter.

THE SOCIAL ORIGINS OF ILLNESS AND HEALTH

Stress

Many of the stressors, which characterize daily life in the industrial and post-industrial arena, are present in Israel: poverty, unemployment, job insecurity, inequality, disability, and family violence. There are, however, stressors that are more salient in Israel than in other developed countries. Two such chronic stressors are the collective memory of the Holocaust and the implications of the geopolitical situation of Israel.

The memory of the Holocaust, the attempt to systematically eradicate the Jewish people during World War II, is continuously maintained by several institutionalized means. Just four years after independence (1953), the Israeli Parliament established a memorial institution in Jerusalem *Yad Vashem* to collect, preserve, and present all available names, knowledge, and materials related to the Holocaust and it victims. All foreign official guests to Israel are taken to this institution at least on their first visit to the country, and the ceremony held there is prominently reported in the media. The Holocaust is part of the regular curriculum of high schools, and in an increasing number of schools, eleventh-grade students make a journey to Warsaw and Auschwitz.

On the annual memorial day, one week before the Day of Independence, all entertainment facilities are closed by law, and memorial ceremonies take place in schools, local municipalities, and other public institutions, attended by survivors, political and religious leaders. The national ceremony, in which the President, the Prime Minister, and the two Chief Rabbis participate, is broadcast by all the media. On this day, written and electronic mass media are almost solely devoted to stories of the Holocaust. The main theme of all these different, institutionalized activities is "never forget" and "never again."

With this background, it is clear how the geopolitical situation of Israel has cultivated a sense of being a garrison state, constantly fighting for its survival. During the 50 years since the War of Independence, Israel has experienced five wars, countless military operations beyond its international boarders, and over 20 years of guerilla war in south Lebanon, the result of the Israeli Defense Force's effort to maintain a security belt (buffer zone) for northern Israel, a part of the country which has suffered frequent guerilla and artillery attacks in the past. Frequent casualties, public debate regarding the necessity of this security belt, and the inability or unwillingness of the political leadership to negotiate alternative arrangements further induce stress related to the insecurity of Israeli society as a collective.

Another source of stress is the threat of terror activities. Terrorism has become a global problem, but few developed countries experience terror attacks on the civilian population as frequently as does Israel. The very nature of terrorist activity is that both its timing and location are unpredictable. The sense of permanent danger is intensified in several ways: checking of personal belongings upon entering public places such as shopping malls and hospitals; guards in schools; advertisements encouraging the public to pay attention and report any suspected parcels; and a public announcement regarding an official blockade on the occupied territories on every holiday. All these maintain and increase a sense of insecurity.

The ups and the downs of the peace process in the Middle East are another source of stress. Since the late 1980s, the results of the general elections as well as public-opinion polls clearly show that Israeli society is split regarding a peace treaty based on territorial withdrawal and the establishment of an independent Palestinian state. The scenarios presented by each side are based on unprovable assumptions, in which the Jewish history, prejudices, national security and economy, and the collective memory of the Holocaust are intertwined. Thus, while half of the populations feels under threat with any advancement in the peace process, holding the process back is stressful for the other half.

Immigration

Immigration as a stressful life event has already been discussed in this volume. While the patterns of migration into and out of Israel resembles those of many postindustrial societies, it has some unique features (Shuval and Leshem 1998). First of these is the magnitude of immigration: in 1997, 38 percent of the Israeli Jews were immigrants, and 36 percent of those born in Israel were children of immigrants. Immigration doubled the Israeli population during the first four years after independence (1948–53); immigration from former communist countries increased the population by 15 percent during the period 1989–95. Second is the open door policy, aimed at encouraging all Jews of the diaspora to immigrate to Israel (Anson et al. 1996; Bernstein 1997). This policy is grounded in the ideology that only Israel is the right and safe place for all Jewry, and that Israeli society is obliged to adapt itself to the immigrants' needs and to ease their absorption. Accordingly, major social resources are invested in both outreach efforts in the diaspora and in absorption programs.

Beyond the health risks associated with migration as a stressful life event for the individual migrant, an open door policy also entails public health risks. Israeli society must therefore handle a necessary tension between the values of free immigration on one hand, and the value of protecting and promoting its members' health, particularly at periods of mass immigration, on the other. The open door policy thus affects patterns of health, the burden on the health services, and on the quality of health care provided.

Migrants import patterns of illness, which reflect the health patterns and the available health services of their country of origin, presenting the health services with different challenges. The mass immigration during 1948–54 included refugees from post-World War II Europe, North Africa, and Asia. Many of these immigrants were in poor health, the result of malnutrition and high prevalence of infectious diseases, psychiatric conditions, chronic illnesses, and disability (Shuval 1992). Some of these conditions, such as trachoma, body lice, and trichophytosis seriously threatened public health. The physical and sanitary conditions in the temporary camps and settlements presented further health risks (Hacohen 1994). Frequent epidemics of dysentery and a polio epidemic increased infant mortality from 29 per 1,000 live births in 1947 to 52 per 1,000 in 1949.

In recent years, two distinct immigration waves, one from Ethiopia, and the other from the former communist countries, posed new challenges. The Ethiopian immigrants arrived in Israel after a long period of social disorganization, the result of a transition from their home villages to Sudan or Addis-Ababa, where they stayed for up to two years in temporary camps. Those who survived the hardships of the exodus were, of course, younger and healthier. However, intestinal parasites were highly prevalent in this group, up to 80 percent according to some reports, and, compared to the Israeli population, so were infectious diseases, in particular tuberculosis and AIDS. Immigrants from Ethiopia comprised 36 percent of the new TB cases in 1993 and 40 percent of the known HIV positive cases in 1995, though they comprise only 1.3 percent of the Jewish population (Health Israel 1998). These figures should be cautiously interpreted, however, as only Ethiopian immigrants are routinely screened for theses conditions.

The patterns of disease brought in by immigrants from the former communist countries are completely different, reflecting the difference in age structure, sanitary conditions, and the health services in these countries. The age structure of these immigrants was older than that of the Israeli population as a whole, mainly as a result of lower fertility: 19 percent were children aged 0–15 and 15

Table 23.1 Health status of immigrants from the former Soviet Union and Israeli military veterans (in percentages)

	Total no.	Age under 44	45–64	65–74	74+
Subjective health evaluation:					
Good health					
Immigrants	39	58%	25%	14%	27%
Veterans	73	85%	70%	43%	38%
Poor health					
Immigrants	22	7%	22%	44%	53%
Veterans	6	3%	4%	14%	23%
Prevalence of disease, limitation, or disability:					
Immigrants	47	21%	55%	89%	77%
Veterans	30	21%	32%	61%	60%

Source: Nirel et al. 1996.

percent were aged 65+ years, compared with 24 percent and 12 percent in the veteran population in 1996 (Central Bureau of Statistics 1998). As shown in table 23.1, high prevalence of disability, functional limitation, and chronic conditions among the immigrants increased the prevalence of these conditions in Israel.

Another aspect of the open door policy is the emphasis on rapid integration of the immigrants into the Israeli labor force, and in an occupation as similar as possible to the one held in the country of origin. Health professionals were no exclusion. Under the assumption that health professions share a universal body of knowledge and code of ethics, all immigrant health professionals could obtain a license to practice their profession upon providing their graduation certificate, physicians were required to work for one year under the supervision of a veteran colleague (Shuval 1983, 1998). Indeed, 40 percent of the professionally active physicians in 1987 graduated from foreign medical schools, between 1989 and 1997 71 percent of all new licenses to practice medicine were issued to immigrants, mainly from the former communist countries (Ministry of Health, personal communication). Similar patterns were observed for dentists and to a somewhat lesser degree for pharmacists and nurses. Reevaluation and reconsideration of this approach started during the 1970s, when most incoming health professionals had been trained in eastern Europe.

Both the structure and the content of medical education in the former communist countries are very different from those prevailing in western countries. For nurses, prerequisites and length of training were similar to programs training practical, rather than registered, nurses. Health professionals were unfamiliar with modern diagnostic and treatment technologies, and restricted communication with the West curtailed access to recent scientific knowledge. These led to questioning the quality of training and the competence of immigrants' health professionals.

The concerns regarding the quality of health care provided by immigrants coincided with an increase in the share of health expenditure in the GNP and in unemployment among physicians. In 1988, a new licensing policy was launched, first for physicians, and later applied to other health professions (Bernstein 1997). Yet, in congruence with the centrality of immigration in the Israeli value system, fully subsidized preparation courses, Hebrew and medical terminology classes were developed to assist the immigrants to qualify for the license to practice their profession in their new homeland. Table 23.2 shows that over 80 percent of the physicians, and even a higher proportion of dentists and pharmacists (who are required one year of supervised work, but no qualification examination) obtained a license three to five years after migration, dramatically increasing the supply of health care personnel. Moreover, 77 percent of the physicians, the profession most intensively studied, were employed in their profession within five years after migration (Bernstein and Shuval 1998), most of them in tenured or tenure-track, full-time, monthly salaried positions (Nirel and Nave 1996). It seems, then, that Israeli society consistently gives priority to pro-immigration values over the value of health and high quality health care.

Table 23.2   Immigration of health professionals, Israel 1989 and 1996

	Immigrated during (Absolute number)			Rate per 1,000 population	
	1989–95	1988	1996	1988/9	1996
Physicians	14,590	16,777	25,898	3.8	4.7
Dentists	1,574	4,607	7,256	1.1	1.3
Pharmacists	1,606	3,226	4,366	0.7	0.8
Nurses					
registered		15,900	23,853	3.6	3.8
practical		11,000	19,536	2.2	2.8
Total	14,341	26,900	43,389		

Sources: Ministry of Immigration 1996; Ministry of Health 1996, 1998.

Informal Coping Resources

Health is highly valued in the Israeli society. Traditionally, the maintenance of health and taking care of the ill are viewed as religious duties; saving life is a religious obligation, and treating and caring for an ill person is allowed even if it requires work on Sabbath. Physicians are highly esteemed, medicine is fully trusted, doctors enjoy high prestige and are perceived as omnipotent.

In some respects, it may be argued that Israeli society is a relatively traditional one. Only about one-fifth of the Israeli population defines itself as completely secular, another fifth as orthodox, and the rest as religious or traditional (Peres and Yuchtman-Yaar 1998). This could be one explanation for the high value of health in the Israeli value system. Symbolically, phrases such as "let us only be healthy" or "health is most important" are common in every day language, especially when troublesome incidents, daily hassles, or economic hardships are discussed.

One other aspect of the relative traditionalism of the Israeli society is the centrality of the family. Although the social processes which brought about decline in fertility and increase in divorce and out of wedlock birth rates in many postindustrial societies are notable in Israel as well, these transitions were much slower, and the Israeli family has maintained its stability to a large extent (Peres and Katz 1990). Fertility rates are higher than in other industrial societies, marriage rates exceed those of most OECD countries, and divorce rates are lower than in most European and American countries, higher only when compared to Catholic societies (table 23.3).

The stability of the Israeli family may, at least partially, be attributed to the role of religion in Israeli society. Saturday and Jewish holy days take on a civil, as well as a religious, connotation, and are national days of rest by law. From early

Table 23.3   Marriage, divorce, and fertility rates in selected countries

	Fertility per 1,000 women age 15–49 1990–1993	Marriages per 1,000 population 1993	Divorces per 1,000 population 1991–1992
Europe			
Austria	48.3	5.6	2.1
Italy	38.7	4.8	0.5
England	53.6	5.9	3.0
Hungary	45.4	5.3	2.1
Greece	40.3	6.0	0.6
France	53.9	4.7	1.9
The Americas			
USA	62.0	9.0	4.8
Canada	56.6	5.5	2.7
Uruguay	75.8	6.2	3.1
Argentina	82.0	5.7	not available
Brazil	62.6	5.0	0.6
Africa			
Tunisia	105.3	6.4	1.5
Egypt	128.5	8.5	1.4
Asia			
Iran	147.8	7.9	0.6
Turkey	149.0	7.4	0.5
Jordan	219.7	8.0	1.2
Japan	38.1	6.7	1.4
Israel	85.4	6.5	1.3

Source: UN Demographic Yearbook 1988, 1996.

afternoon on Friday and on holiday eves, businesses, services, and public trans-portation close down, with very few exceptions. Emergency services and the defense forces operate with reduced staff, and even entertainment (e.g. restau-rants, movie theaters) is available on a smaller scale. On these days, the nuclear and the extended family largely become the core of social life. In addition, life events such as marriages, births, rites of passage, and funerals are normatively celebrated with members of the extended family, enabling it to fulfill its inte-grative and regulative functions (for the role of the family in controlling health related behavior see Anson 1989; Umberson 1992).

As in other industrial societies, the Israeli family takes responsibility for the care needs of its sick members, the disabled, and the elderly (Avgar 1997). However, comparative data on long-term hospitalization and home care rates of the elderly suggest that the Israeli family is more inclined to care for its elderly than many postindustrial societies. In 1994, for example, 4.5 percent of the Israelis aged 65+ were institutionalized, compared with an average of 5.5 percent in 20 OECD countries in 1990–2; 10 percent of the elderly were provided with formal long-term home care in 1996, lower than that of most European countries (OECD 1996). Similar patterns can be found regarding institutional care for the mentally and physically disabled (Kop 1997). The Israeli family, then, is a major health resource.

Formal Support Systems

Like many other postmodern societies, Israeli society has undergone economic and social processes that have lead to the weakening of the welfare state (Quandagno 1999). At the same time, the underlying assumption that society is responsible for the education, health, and welfare of its members has persisted. The most recent manifestation of this perception is the National Health Insur-ance Law, which came into effect in 1995, by which every resident is entitled to a basic basket of services, regardless of his or her contribution (health tax). The law explicitly declares the social obligation to provide health care, based on the principles of justice, equity, and mutual help. Public education of nine years is mandatory, six-months unemployment benefits, old age and survivors' pensions, maternity, and children's allowances are universal, independent of other income. Disability pension and disabled child allowances are dependent on functional limitations only. Other welfare programs, such as single parent allowance, income supplement, and income support for the elderly serve as a safety net for lower income individuals and families. Only long-term home care is depend-ent on both income and functional ability. These programs, however, did not prevent individuals and families from falling into poverty: 16.5 percent of the population in 1996, 20.6 percent of the elderly and 21.4 percent of all children (Ministry of Health 1998).

Health, education, and welfare services are well distributed within the country, and most places are no further than 30–45 minutes drive from a hospital. At the same time, these services vary in quality and quantity, raising concern regarding the equity of the allocation of the available resources in different locations and social groups (Azaiza 1995; Swirsky et al. 1998; Shuval and Anson forthcoming).

HEALTH STATUS, HEALTH, AND ILLNESS BEHAVIOR

The Population

By the end of 1997, Israel had 5,900,000 residents, 79.7 percent Jewish (of whom over one-third were born outside of Israel), 14.7 percent Moslem Arabs, 2.1 percent Christian, and 1.6 percent Druze (Statistical Abstract of Israel 1998). Due to high fertility, children age 0–14 comprise 29.0 percent of the population, and the elderly only 9.9 percent. The median years of schooling were 12.1 in 1997, with 61.6 percent of men and 45.8 percent of women over the age 15 participating in the civilian labor force.

Health Indicators

In order to present the health status in Israel, we choose to compare the 1980 and the 1994 health indicators of Israel with the average of the European Union (hence EU), whose members enjoy a similar level or better level of economic development and comparable health and welfare systems. As there is no consistent and continuous national data collection of the incidence and prevalence of most chronic and acute conditions, the discussion will focus on mortality-based health indicators as shown in figure 23.1a and 23.1b. These data demonstrate two long-term tendencies: first, on most indicators, Israeli men appear to be healthier than EU men while the health of Israeli women is poorer than that of their EU counter-

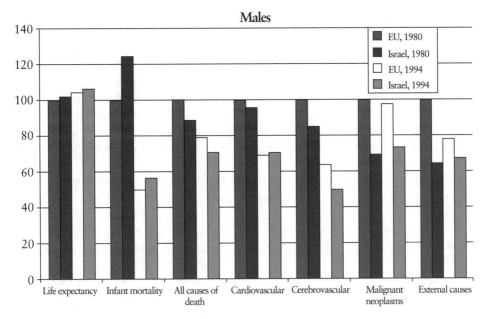

Figure 23.1a (males)   Mortality-based health indicators: relative risk, Israel and the European Union, 1980–1994 (EU 1980 = 100)

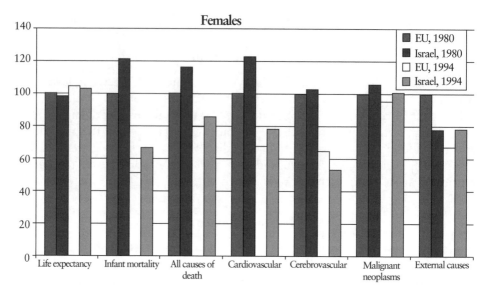

Figure 23.1b (females)

Note: Life expectancy is from birth infant mortality rate per 1,000 births, and death rates are per 100,000 in the population.

Source: Health for All European Region 1997.

parts; second, with few exceptions, age-adjusted mortality for the leading causes of death of Israeli men and women converges over time with the EU average.

Infant mortality rates in Israel are higher than the EU average throughout the 15 years examined, but Israeli male infant mortality declined faster than the rates for EU males and Israeli females. Death rates from external causes in Israel increased for both men and women compared with a decline in the EU average, but only the mortality of Israeli women from external causes exceeded that of EU women in 1994. Between 1980 and 1994, the average life expectancy at birth of EU and Israeli men increased by 3.3 years, Israeli men consistently live 1.5 years longer than EU men. The life expectancy at birth of Israeli women, however, is shorter than in the EU, and the gap declined by only six months during the 15 years studied.

These trends cannot be easily explained, especially the consistent smaller gender gap in life expectancy in Israel compared to the EU. One line of explanation is based on the hypothesis that the social origins of illness and health discussed above affect men and women differently. It is thus possible that the stress imposed by Israel's geopolitical situation varies by gender, as women, on the average, have fewer coping resources than men (Anson et al. 1993).

Further, it is also possible that the Israeli traditionalism and familism, reflected in the gendered division of labor (Azmon and Izraeli 1993) and women's greater involvement in nurturing roles (Lieblich 1993), hamper their health. Over a quarter of a century ago, Gove (1973) showed that marriage "protects" men from mortality more than it protects women. The relatively high marriage and fertility rates and the lower rates of long-term institutionalization and long-term home care services were discussed earlier in this chapter. Furthermore, compared to the EU average, Israel has fewer general hospital beds (4.1 and 2.4 per 1,000 population in 1993, respectively), compensated by shorter average lengths of stay (9.4 and 4.5 days in 1993, respectively). Much of the needs unmet by the formal health and welfare services are thus met by unpaid women family members, an overload with possibly negative affects on Israeli women's health (Avgar 1997).

Health Behavior

Another factor, which may explain men's longevity, is health behavior. Suicide rates are extremely low, alcoholism is relatively rare – Israelis consume less alcohol than Europeans (3.4 liters of wine and 9 liters of beer per person in Israel compared with 34.4 and 82.0 EU average in 1994 (Ministry of Health 1997)). Drug abuse is also relatively infrequent compared to EU members (Anderson 1995; Rahav et al. 1995), and Israeli children and youth are less likely to smoke cigarettes than their EU counterparts (WHO 1996). The proportion of adult smokers is similar to the EU average, but is gradually declining: from 37 percent in 1989 to 28 percent in 1996 (Ministry of Health 1996b). Only physical activity is relatively rare among Israelis (Heler 1994; WHO 1996).

How Israeli society has managed to prevent the dispersal of social diseases below the prevalence level of other industrial societies is not completely clear. It has been suggested that the perception of Israel as a society in continuous struggle for survival, the ongoing concern with national tasks such as security, immigration absorption, and economic strain inhibited the development of consumerism and indulgence (Shuval 1992). Others have focused on social control agencies, especially religion and the family (Shuval and Anson forthcoming). For instance, drug and alcohol consumption is less common among the married, children living with both parents, and religious youth (Rahav et al. 1995).

Illness Behavior

Israel has one of the highest average numbers of doctor visits in the western world, 9.4 visits per person per year in 1996. Of these, 4.9 visits to primary care physician, 1.8 visits to a specialist, and 2.6 dental visits (Health in Israel 1998). In 1992, the last comparative data available to us, only Germany and Switzerland reported a higher number of doctor visits than Israel (Bib-Nun and Ben-Ori 1996). As in other developed countries, utilization rates are higher among women, children under five years old, and the elderly. Judging by mortality-based health indicators, the high utilization rates cannot be explained by poor health status of the population. Shuval (1992) argued that this pattern can be explained by three factors.

1   First, the availability of readily accessible health services, with few barriers. There are 3.8 operating physicians per 1,000 population, primary care clinics are located in almost all rural settlements and urban neighborhoods, doctor visits are free of charge in three of the four sick funds (i.e. for 80% of the population), and medications are subsidized.

2 Second, a perceived need for medical care can develop against the background of chronic and acute stress, sense of failure, and the need for catharsis. The emphasis on the bio-psychosocial model and doctor–patient communication in the training program of family practitioners advances consumers' expectations for catharsis and approval.

3 Finally, medical authorization is required for various public benefits. Ground floor apartments, tax exemptions, long-term care, etc. are dependent on referrals from primary care physicals.

As in other western societies, the utilization of non-conventional medicine seems to be increasing. Many different healing systems are available; most healers are trained outside the country and practice in the private sector. As with the patterns of utilization in other developed countries, non-conventional medicine is complementary rather than alternative to conventional health care, used more often by persons whose needs were not satisfied by biomedical embedded care (table 23.4) (Bernstein and Shuval 1997).

THE HEALTH CARE SYSTEM

The Israeli health care system has some unique features, which have developed as a result of social and historical processes. Of particular note are the strong ties

Table 23.4 Satisfaction with family doctor: A comparison between users and non-users of alternative medicine practitioners (means[1] and standard deviations)

Satisfaction with	Users	Non-users
The relationships[2]	5.61 (1.65)	6.00 (1.33)
Amount of time he/she spends with you[3]	5.39 (5.87)	1.85 (1.46)
Convenience (consultation hours, distance, wait for appointment)[3]	5.02 (1.93)	5.57 (1.66)
Amount of information he/she provides[3]	5.54 (1.82)	6.00 (1.38)
Quality of care[2]	5.64 (1.71)	6.02 (1.31)
Overall[3]	5.59 (6.02)	1.69 (1.28)

Source: Bernstein and Shuval 1997.

Notes
1 On a seven-point scale from 1 = very dissatisfied to 7 = very satisfied.
2 $p < .05$.
3 $p < .01$.

between the health care and the political systems; the dual role Israeli Medical Association; the co-optation of non-conventional medicine; and the Patient's Rights Law. These will be shortly discussed.

Health Care and Politics

Long before independence, health services in Israel were established and developed not only in response to the health needs of the population, but also as a political asset in the struggle for power, while economic considerations and efficiency were largely disregarded. The first sick funds were established by regional workers' organizations in 1911. Seven years later, they merged to become one of the many services that the General Federation of Labor (*Histadruth*) provided for its members. Congruent with the Zionist and socialist ideology of the *Histadruth*, special attention was paid to rural communities. For over 60 years the medical insurance, to which all members of the *Histadruth* were entitled, was one of the main mechanisms for recruiting members, ensuring their commitment and conformity to the *Histadruth*, and through it to the Labor Movement and Parties. This triangular link proved beneficial to all parties involved and enabled the General Sick Fund to rely on the government to bail it out of frequent financial crises until the elections of 1977, when the Labor Party lost to the right-wing Likud Party (Chinitz 1996).

Similarly, *Hadassa*, the American Zionist Womens organization, established a sick fund for the self-employed farmers in 1931. The latter were not entitled to join the *Histadruth* because of their capitalist attitudes, but the rivalry between the medical delegation sent by *Hadassa* organization after WWI and the Labor Movement was no less important than the farmers' health needs. The revisionist movement, the political opposition of the socialist parties, established its own, albeit much smaller, National Labor Federation including a sick fund in 1933. Since the mid-1930s, several small sick funds were founded by physicians, refugees from Nazi Germany, to meet their employment needs and their preference to be self-employed.

The National Health Insurance Law implemented in January 1995, was also the result of political change in Israel, in the *Histadruth*, and in the Labor Party itself (Gross and Anson forthcoming). Over seven national committees recommended such legislation since Israel's independence in 1948, but the Labor Party, the *Histadruth* and its sick fund succeeded in preventing such an act which, they felt, was against their interests.[1] It was only after the Labor party lost its political hegemony both in the parliament and the *Histadruth*, the General Sick Fund's market share declined, and its deficit reached $1.5 billion, that the NHI Law was passed and implemented.

According to the Law, a legally defined service package is provided by four sick funds, financed through a progressive health-tax on incomes. Preventive care is mainly provided by Ministry of Health MCH clinics, and the Ministry also provides 55 percent of the psychiatric beds, 36 percent of acute hospitalization beds, and 12 percent of the long-term beds. Its involvement with direct care provision thus results in a conflict of interests and interferes with traditional ministerial roles (Gross and Anson forthcoming).

The Israeli Medical Association

The great majority of health professionals (except for dentists and pharmacists) are employees, organized in professional organizations. The most interesting of these is the Israeli Medical Association (IMA), which carries the dual role of professional association and trade union (Harrison 1993). As a professional association, the IMA strives to improve the quality of health care, either by advising the MOH on a variety of issues, or by organizing educational activities for its members. The IMA thus sets the qualifying exams for immigrant physicians and specialists, and is responsible for the content of specialization programs, continuing education activities, etc.

At the same time, the IMA is a trade union, which strives to improve the working conditions of its members. As such, it does not hesitate to employ proletarian strategies, that is, strikes, slowdowns, and working-to-rule every two or three years. In fact, physicians were the first to strike after independence, in the midst of the first immigration wave described above.

The tension between the physician's demand for recognition as a professional elite (Shuval 1992) and their proletarian behavior is reconciled in two main ways. First, health services are never shut down completely during industrial actions. Services are provided on a lower-scale, similar to those provided on Saturdays and holidays, along with treatments for conditions considered by the public as life threatening (e.g. cancer). Sometimes, industrial action is taken on a rotating basis, with physicians working in different hospitals, outpatient clinics, sick funds, or different parts of the country, striking on different days.

Second, legitimization for industrial struggles is sought by presenting the actions taken in terms of public interest. Overload, it is argued, whether caused by insufficient personnel or by too low wages, which force doctors to take on a second job, hinders the quality of patient care. Higher wages and additional positions in primary care and hospitals, on the other hand, will enable doctors to devote more time both to patients and to advancing their medical knowledge.

The advisory status of the IMA on licensing issues further enables it to protect the interests of its members. The patterns of absorbing immigrant physicians from the former Soviet Union demonstrate the exercise of such power. In line with the Israeli value system, the IMA supported local initiatives preparing immigrant physicians for local accreditation. However, while the structure of medical education in the former Soviet Union is highly specialized, the examination in Israel qualifies immigrants only for a general practitioner license. Physicians trained in a non English-speaking country are required to take the specialization examination together with graduates of the IMA specialization programs, regardless of their work experience and credentials from their country of origin. These procedures enhanced the elitist claims of Israeli and Anglophone trained physicians in two ways. First, many immigrant physicians were forced to enter primary care, which is perceived by both health professionals and consumers as less prestigious than hospital-based practice. Second, the intra-professional stratification criterion is based on formally recognized specialities.

Limiting immigrants access to specialist status thus promotes the interests of veteran, more established, physicians.

The Co-optation of Non-conventional Medicine

The reaction of conventional medicine to the growing utilization of non-conventional medicine described above was paradoxical. While physicians, as individuals, used some of these methods for specific conditions for themselves, members of their family, and even referred a few of their patients to practitioners they knew of (Borkan et al. 1994), the official stance of the IMA was one of total non-recognition.

A State Commission of Inquiry to examine the issue of non-conventional medicine in Israel was appointed by the Minister of Health in 1988. Its report, in 1991, included six recommendations, and sought to bridge the right of individual free choice with the State's obligation to protect its citizen's health. Only one recommendation, concerning the licensing of imported homeopathic medications, was partially implemented. In 1996 the State Comptroller heavily criticized the MOH for neglecting the commissions report. The IMA responded to that criticism with an official position paper (1997), declaring that "there is no alternative medicine...but one medicine,...and only certified physicians (M.D.) can practice it." According to the IMA, non-conventional medicine provides false hopes to patients *who think* that their needs were not met by the biomedical system and personal attention which biomedical physicians in the public sector are *unable* to provide due to *overload*.

At the same time, increasing utilization of non-conventional methods, public willingness to pay out-of-pocket for these services, and individual physician's confidence in the benefit of some complementary methods brought about a unique pattern of collaboration between non-conventional medicine and the biomedical establishment. During the period 1991–7, ten general hospitals and all four sick funds commenced outpatient clinics providing non-conventional services (Shuval 1999). The patterns that emerged, however, indicate that it is not collaboration among equals, but, rather, one that symbolically emphasizes the primacy of conventional medicine.

First, hiring policies overtly prefer biomedically-trained physicians who also practice complementary medicine. Second, a biomedically-trained physician is first to examine the patient, decides on the appropriate non-conventional method, and periodically assesses the outcome. Needless to say, no similar routine periodic supervision/assessment is practiced within biomedicine. Furthermore, in all formal publications, non-conventional practitioners are referred to as "healers" (*merapim*) rather than physicians (*rofim*), even when holding an MD. Finally, non-conventional facilities are geographically segregated from conventional medicine.

These patterns of collaboration/co-optation serve the interests of both systems. Non-conventional practitioners gain a legitimate practice setting under the prestigious biomedical umbrella, which, in the long run, may develop to full recognition. The biomedical system gains symbolic primacy and some actual control over the non-conventional medicine (Shuval 1999).

The Patient's Rights Law

As in many western countries, increased bureaucratization of health care organizations has brought about a growing alienation between consumers and providers. At the same time, processes of globalization and the spread of knowledge through written and electronic media have increased demand for the most recent technological developments, and for greater equality in decision-making between patients and physicians. It also increased awareness of the uncertainty aspect of the biomedical body of knowledge and the unavoidable limitations of the individual health practitioner. These same processes advanced the diffusion of ideas, and familiarity with the consumerist trends in the field of health around the postindustrial world. These processes were exacerbated by the elitist attitudes of medical professionals, mentioned above, and the development of black medicine, out-of-pocket payment to elite members of the profession for services ostensibly covered by one's insurance and provided in public facilities. All these processes were associated with a growing sense of dissatisfaction with the health care system, and the portrayal of physicians as arrogant and greedy. One result of these processes was the legislation of the Patient's Rights Law in 1996.

The stated purpose of the law is to guarantee patients' privacy and respect. Nevertheless, some paragraphs of the law can be interpreted in terms of deprofessionalization (Haug 1973, 1988). The law largely limits professional control over knowledge and self-regulation, two of the core sources of professional power (Anson forthcoming). Health professionals are obliged to share their knowledge with their patients, and to explain in great detail the arguments for and against all possible treatment alternatives in order to obtain informed consent.

The profession of medicine obtained social legitimization for self-regulation under the claim that professionals alone can evaluate their colleagues competence and performance, and the fundamental need to learn from mistakes and unpredicted intervention outcomes for maintaining and improving the quality of care. The Israeli Patient's Rights Law created two separate mechanisms to fulfill the dual function of self-regulation: one for promoting the quality of care, the other for social control over professional performance. The function of improving the quality of care by exploring undesired episodes, such as infections, mistakes, a patient's disappearance, or falling off the bed was assigned to an obligatory quality-control committee. The results of this committee's investigations and all the information gathered is confidential to the public and may not be presented as evidence in court. The function of social control over the performance of members of the medical team has been placed in the hands of an "inquiry committee," which is established at the request of a patient or anybody he/she authorizes. Its report goes to the person(s) who initiated the inquiry; the provider who is the subject of the complaint; the Ministry of Health; and the general administrator of the health care institution, which treated the patient. All the information collected by the inquiry committee, including the chronology taken during the discussions held, may be presented as evidence in court.

SUMMARY

Some of the unique features of health and health care in Israel were presented in this chapter. We made an effort to present the social origins of illness and health, namely the unique stressors threatening the health of Israelis and the informal and formal social support available to them. The unique patterns of health and illness behavior were shortly described. Some outstanding characteristics of the Israeli health services and policy, particularly the strong link between politics and health provision, the dual role of the Israeli Medical Association, patterns of collaboration between conventional and non-conventional medicine, and the social processes that lead to the nonpareil Patient's Rights Law, were portrayed. Other important characteristics, such as patterns of health inequalities and inequity in the allocation of the available health services, by age, gender, ethnicity, and geographical periphery have been left untouched, despite their importance.

Note

1   It should be noted that over 95 percent of the population had medical insurance before the NHI Law.

References

Anderson, Katherine. 1995. *Young People and Alcohol, Drugs and Tobacco*. WHO.

Anson, Ofra. 1989. "Marital Status and Women's Health Revisited: The Importance of a Proximate Adult." *Journal of Marriage and the Family* 51: 185–94.

——. Forthcoming. "Professionalism and the Israeli Patient's Rights Law." *Medical Law International*.

Anson, Ofra, Esther Paran, Lily Neumann, and Dov Chernichovsky. 1993. "Gender Differences in Health Perceptions and their Predictors." *Social Science and Medicine* 36: 419–27.

Anson, Ofra, Dina Pilpel, and Valentina Rolnik. 1996. "Physical and Psychological Well-Being among Immigrants Referrals to Colonoscopy." *Social Science and Medicine* 43: 1309–16.

Avgar, Amy. 1997. "Womens Health in Israel: A Feminist Perspective." *Social Work in Health Care* 25: 45–62.

Azaiza, Fu'ad. 1995. "Welfare Services in the Israeli-Arab Sector." Pp. 207–23 in *The Israeli Arabs toward the Twenty-first Century*. Jerusalem: Magnes Hebrew University Press (Hebrew).

Azmon, Yael and Dafna Izraeli. 1993. "Introduction: Women in Israel – A Sociological Overview." Pp. 1–21 in Y. Azmon and D. N. Izraeli (eds.), *Women in Israel*. London: Transaction.

Bernstein, Judith H. 1997. "Israel's Open Door Policy: Implications for Immigrant Physicians." Pp. 67–86 in J. T. Shuval and J. H. Bernstein (eds.), *Immigrant Physicians: Former Soviet Doctors in Israel, Canada and The United States*. Westport, CT: Praeger–Greenwood.

Bernstein, Judith H. and Judith T. Shuval. 1997. "Non-conventional Medicine in Israel: Consultation Patterns of the Israeli Population and Attitudes of Primary Care Physicians. *Social Science and Medicine* 44: 1341–8.

——. 1998. "The Occupational Integration of Former Soviet Physicians in Israel: Findings From A Five-Year Follow-Up Study." *Social Science and Medicine* 47: 809–19.

Bib-Nun, Gavriel and Dan Ben-Ori. 1996. *International Comparisons – OECD and Israel*. Jerusalem: Ministry of Health (Hebrew).

Borkan Jeffrey, Jon O. Neher, Ofra Anson, and Bret Smoker. 1994. "Referrals to Alternative Therapies: A Three-Site Study." *The Journal of Family Practice* 39: 545–50.

Chinitz, David. 1996. "Israel's Health Policy Breakthrough: The Politics of Reform and the Reform of Politics." *Journal of Politics, Policy and Law* 20: 909–32.

Gove, Walter R. 1973. "Sex, Marital Status, and Mortality." *American Journal of Sociology* 79: 45–67.

Gross, Revital and Ofra Anson. Forthcoming. "The Reforms in the Israeli Health Care System." In A. Twaddle (ed.), *Comparative Medical Care Reform*.

Hacohen, Debora. 1994. *Immigrants in Storm* (Olim Beseara). Jerusalem: Izhak Ben-Zvi Memorial. (Hebrew).

Harrison, Michael. 1993. "Medical Dominance or Proletarianization: Evidence from Israel." *Research in the Sociology of Health Care* 10: 73–81.

Haug, M. 1973. "Deprofessionalization: An Alternative Hypothesis for the Future." *Sociological Review Monograph* 2: 195–211.

——. 1988. "A Re-examination of the Hypothesis of Physician Deprofessionalization." *Milbank Memorial Fund Quarterly* 66: 48–56.

Heler, Arie. 1994. *Attitudes and Behavior Regarding Physical Excercise*. Tel Aviv: Modi'in Ezrahi (Hebrew).

Kop, Jacob. 1997. *Resources Allocation to Social Services, 1997*. Jerusalem: Social Policy Research Center (Hebrew).

Lieblich, Amia. 1993. "Preliminary Comparison of Israeli and American Successful Women." Pp. 195–208 in Y. Azmon and D. Izraeli (eds.), *Women in Israel*. London: Transaction.

Ministry of Health. 1996a. *Knowledge, Attitudes and Health Behavior*. Jerusalem: State of Israel (Hebrew).

——. 1996b. *Health in Israel, 1996*. Jerusalem: State of Israel (Hebrew).

——. 1997. *Health in Israel, 1996*. Jerusalem: State of Israel (Hebrew).

——. 1998. *Health in Israel, 1998*. Jerusalem: State of Israel (Hebrew).

Ministry of Immigration. 1996. *Immigration and Absorption: Data, Challenge, and Goals*. Jerusalem: State of Israel (Hebrew).

Nirel, Nurit, Bruce Rosen, Revital Gross, Aieleth Berg, and D. Yuval. 1996. *Immigrants from the Former Soviet Union in the Health System: Selected Findings from National Surveys*. Jerusalem: JDC–Brookdale Institute.

Nirel, Nurit and Giora Nave. 1996. *The Employment of Immigrant Physicians in Israel: Is it Stable?* Jerusalem: JDC-Brookdale Institute.

OECD. 1996. *Caring for Frail Elderly People: Policies in Evolution*. Paris.

Peres, Yochanan and Ruth Katz. 1990. "The Family in Israel: Change and Continuity." Pp. 9–32 in L. Shamgar and R. Bar-Yosef (eds.), *Families in Israel*. Jerusalem: Akademon (Hebrew).

Peres, Yochanan and Ephraim Yuchtman-Yaar. 1998. *Between Consent and Dissent: Democracy and Peace in the Israeli Mind*. Tel Aviv: The Israel Democracy Institute (Hebrew).

Quandagno, Jill. 1999. "Creating Capital Investment Welfare State." *American Sociological Review* 64: 1–11.

Rahav, Giora, Meir Teichman, Refael Gil et al. 1995. *The Use of Psychoactive Materials in Israel 1995: Epidemiological Survey III*. Jerusalem: Pory Institute (Hebrew).

Statistical Abstract of Israel 1998. Jerusalem: Central Bureau of Statistics.

Shuval, Judith T. 1983. *Newcomers and Colleagues: Soviet Immigrant Physicians in Israel*. Houston: Cap and Gown Press.

——. 1992. *Social Dimensions of Health: The Case of Israel*. Westpoint, CN: Praeger.

——. 1998. "Credentialling Immigrant Physicians to Israel." *Health and Place* (in press).

——. 1999. "The Bear's Hug: Patterns of Pragmatic Collaboration and Coexistence of Complementary Medicine and Biomedicine in Israel." In S. Saks and C. Benoit (eds.), *Professional Identities in Transition*. Monograph no. 71. Stockholm: Gotenberg University, Almqvist & Weksell International.

Shuval, Judith T. and Ofra Anson. Forthcoming. *Health Is the Essence – Social Structure and Health in Israel*. Jerusalem: Magnes, Hebrew University Press (Hebrew).

Shuval, Judith T. and Eli Leshem. 1998. "The Sociology of Migration in Israel: A Critical View." Pp. 3–50 in E. Leshem and J. T. Shuval (eds.), *Immigration to Israel: Sociological Perspectives*. New Brunswick: Transaction.

Swirsky, Barbara, Hatim Kanaaneh, and Amy Avgar. 1998. *Health Care in Israel*. Tel Aviv: Adva.

Umberson, Debra. 1992. "Gender, Marital Status and Social Control of Health Behavior." *Social Science and Medicine* 34: 907–17.

UN Demographic Yearbook. 1996. New York: United Nations.

Asia and the Pacific Region

24

Medicine and Health Care in Australia

Deborah Lupton

Australia is a wealthy, First World country of approximately 19 million people which was founded as a penal colony by the English in 1788. The states and territories of Australia were federated in 1901, and government operates at both the federal and the state/territory level. The British antecedents of the modern Australian state has had much influence upon contemporary Australian culture. Australia is still a member of the British Commonwealth and has the Queen of England as her head of state, although there are currently influential moves towards republicanism.

Well into the mid-twentieth century, Australian governments upheld the principles of the racist White Australia Policy, which sought to prevent non-white people from emigrating to and settling in Australia. As a result, the Australian population was dominated by people of Anglo-Celtic ethnicity with a very small minority of Aboriginal people and others of non-Anglo-Celtic ancestry. Over the past half century, however, this monocultural perspective has been challenged by a massive immigration program. Since the years following World War II, when large numbers of people emigrated to Australia from central and southern Europe, immigration programs have vastly expanded, with the most recent increase in people arriving from east and southeast Asia. By 1998, almost a quarter of the current Australian population were born overseas, of which only 7 percent were born in Britain, while 13 percent were born in Europe and 5 percent were born in east and southeast Asia. Approximately 15 percent of Australians over the age of five years speak a language other than English at home, with Italian, Greek, Cantonese, Arabic, and Vietnamese the most common languages (Australian Bureau of Statistics 1999).

Since 1996 Australia has been governed by a conservative Coalition Party, led by Prime Minister John Howard. Before Howard's party gained power, the other major party, the Australian Labor Party, had ruled for some 13 years. While the

Coalition Party can be characterized as right-wing, and the Labor Party as left-wing, in recent years both parties have developed attributes of neo-liberalism, albeit to varying degrees and with different emphases. Neo-liberalism is an approach to government which has been taken up in many western societies at the end of the twentieth century. It incorporates a focus on a relationship between citizens and the state that emphasizes the responsibility of the former to care for themselves, drawing attention away from the state acting to promote the welfare of citizens (Dean 1997).

According to the neo-liberal perspective, health care becomes seen as more of a privileged commodity than a universal right. As is discussed in greater detail below, although Australia currently has a public health insurance system, the Howard government has taken steps to protect the private health insurance industry with tax incentives rather than deciding to direct significant additional revenue to the public system. As such, it demonstrates a neo-liberal rather than welfare state approach to health care provision. Recently even some members of Labor governments, known in the past for their social welfare approach to health care provision and other public institutions, have proposed directing more resources to the private health insurance and private health provision sectors. No political party, however, has attempted to dismantle the current universal health care system, which is strongly supported by the electorate.

The health status of Australians in general rates well in comparison to other First World nations. For infants born in 1995, it has been calculated that female life expectancy is 81 years and male life expectancy 75 years. This compares favorably with the United Kingdom (79 years and 74 years respectively) and the United States (79 years and 72 years respectively). The Australian infant mortality rate also compares favorably with other western Anglophone nations. In 1994 the rate was 5.7 per 1,000 live births, compared with 6.1 for the United Kingdom and 7.5 for the United States. Like many other western nations, the Australian population is aging due to the sustained decline in fertility which followed the post-World War II baby boom (Australian Bureau of Statistics 1999).

MEDICAL SOCIOLOGY IN AUSTRALIA

Medical sociology is strong in Australian universities in terms of both teaching and research and scholarship, comprising the largest of the interest sections in the Australian Sociological Association. There are currently two dominant theoretical positions taken in Australian medical sociology: the political economy perspective and the poststructuralist perspective. The former perspective has been dominant since the 1970s, responding to a wider turn towards Marxist theory in sociology at that time. Writers in this area have focused their attentions on the ways in which health status and health care are structured via social class and other major social categories such as age, gender, and ethnicity (for book-length works, see, for example, Willis 1983; Davis and George 1988; Palmer and Short 1989; Reid and Trompf 1990, 1991; Broom 1991).

The poststructuralist perspective, which has a social constructionist orientation, is more recent, emerging in Australian sociology in the mid- to late 1980s. This perspective has now become predominant over the political economy critique in Australian research and scholarship on health and medicine. Poststructuralism in Australian medical sociology is influenced by the writings of Michel Foucault on medical power and the regulated body. Exponents focus their attention on the diffuse ways in which power operates via medicine and health care and on the importance of language in constructing notions of health and illness (for example books by Lawler 1991; Lupton 1994a, 1994b, 1995a; Petersen and Lupton 1996; Pringle 1998). Some recent textbooks on health and medicine in Australia have sought to combine both perspectives (Petersen and Waddell 1998; Germov 1999).

THE AUSTRALIAN HEALTH CARE SYSTEM

Health care in contemporary Australia is funded by a mixture of private and publicly funded insurance schemes regulated by the federal government in negotiation with state governments, who run the public hospitals. Funding for public care comes from general taxation revenue: the federal government provides funds to state governments to partially support hospital care and reimburses individuals in full or part for fees they pay to individual health care providers outside the public hospital system. State governments provide some additional funding for public hospitals and community health services through state taxation revenue. The Australian health care system can therefore be located somewhere between the universal health insurance system in Britain and the largely private health care system in the United States. This status is, to some extent, reflected in the expenditure on health services, which in Australia in 1997 was 8.3 percent of GDP compared with 6.7 percent in the United Kingdom and 14 percent in the United States (Australian Bureau of Statistics 1999).

The current Australian health care system has its antecedents in the early years of British settlement, in which public medical care was made available by the British government to convicts, the military, and free settlers. Following the cessation of the transportation of convicts in the mid-nineteenth century, the principles of laissez-faire government began to hold sway in the Australian colonies. Medical practitioners embraced these principles, dissociating themselves from government and seeking to set themselves up as entrepreneurial private practitioners. Then followed over half a century of medical entrepreneurialism largely unencumbered by state regulation.

It was not until the early twentieth century that state patronage of doctors, and with it, increased state intervention into the regulation and provision of medical care, began to emerge in Australia. As in other western countries, medical practitioners began successfully to differentiate themselves from other health care providers such as homoeopaths and to position themselves as the preeminent source of "scientific" health care. A series of licensing laws were enacted which enabled the medical profession to set itself apart legally from other practitioners and to control entry into the profession (Davis and George 1988; Lloyd 1994). From World War II onwards, this position allowed doctors to begin to have a significant influence on government health care policy and to resist government attempts to regulate their work (Willis 1983). From the 1920s, medical specializations began to develop and the various specialist associations were established (Lloyd 1994). In Australia today, general practitioners offer routine, non- surgical health care, referring patients to specialists for more specific care or surgical procedures.

Due in part to the vociferous opposition of the medical profession, it was not until 1975 that the first universal health insurance scheme, Medibank, was introduced by the reformist Whitlam Labor government. This government, however, was voted out of power only a matter of months after Medibank had been set in place. Medibank was gradually dismantled by the incumbent con-servative Fraser government, and was finally completely abandoned by 1981. Another change of government back to the Labor Party in 1983 saw the reintroduction of universal health insurance, this time under the name "Medi-care." This is the system which remains in place today, albeit with some changes introduced by the Howard government.

The proportion of people privately insured has steadily dropped since the reintroduction of the national health insurance scheme. In 1997 less than a third of the population had private health insurance compared with almost half the population in 1987 (Australian Bureau of Statistics 1999). Since gaining office, the Howard government has attempted to encourage people to seek out private health care (particularly in hospitals), therefore reducing the financial burden on the public system, and to fund this through private insurance schemes.

While medical practitioners work within a system of national insurance for health care, they retain a high level of autonomy. The majority of medical care is provided as a fee-for-service, whether offered in public or private institutions or clinics. Doctors have the right to treat private patients in public hospitals and very few of them are employed exclusively by the state as salaried employees. The government reimburses patients a set amount for each procedure they pay for. Practitioners in private practice are free to set the fees they charge for their services while those treating public patients in public hospitals may only charge the Medicare scheduled fee. It is therefore more lucrative for doctors to treat private patients. The private patient must bear the cost of any extra over the scheduled fee that their doctor charges. There are no restrictions on which doctors people may choose to attend, although a referral from a GP is required for specialist care. Those who have private medical insurance may seek such coverage for procedures or commodities that are not covered by Medicare, such as spectacles or contact lenses and dental procedures, to have some degree of choice concerning the specialist who attends them in hospital (public patients in public hospitals do not have this choice) and to gain entry to a private rather than a public hospital should they require hospitalization.

The national association of medical practitioners, the Australian Medical Association (AMA), has a powerful voice in lobbying government on behalf of its members. As noted above, historically, Australian medical practi-tioners have sought to avoid becoming salaried employees of the state, preferring instead to practice medicine as private entrepreneurs. The AMA, to which a majority of doctors belong, has traditionally opposed universal health insurance. This organization sees universal health insurance as a means of allowing government to have greater control over doctors' activities and incomes (Sax 1984).

The Australian health care system is controversial largely because of funding issues. Media coverage constantly warns of the results of underfunding of the public health care system, and the stresses placed on the system by an ageing population and increasing use of high-technology medicine, particularly in relation to hospital care. Long waiting lists and poor conditions in public hospitals are often emphasized in the mass media. For example, a study I conducted of health and medical news stories reported on the front page of a major Australian newspaper in the early 1990s (Lupton 1995b) found that issues concerning health service delivery was the most frequently reported topic. The news stories were highly political, describing disputes and controversies over policy decisions and the distribution of resources, particularly between leaders of the AMA and other medical spokespeople and government ministers and officials.

THE POSITION OF THE MEDICAL PROFESSION

As noted above, organizations of Australian medical practitioners such as the AMA have wielded a great deal of power as a lobby group in the political arena, particularly in relation to issues around health care funding and provision. Some sociologists have argued that the medical profession in western countries such as Australia has been faced with threats to its power and dominance in matters medical over the past three decades, and thus has become "deprofessionalized." They claim that doctors' autonomy to practice medicine has been challenged by the state and that patients have become more cynical, ambivalent, and consumeristic in their attitudes towards members of the medical profession (Haug 1988; McKinlay and Stoeckle 1988).

It is certainly the case in Australia that the power of the medical profession has, to some extent, been challenged by the emergence of patient consumer groups and such state-funded organizations as health complaints commissions. Patients have been encouraged by such organizations as, on the one hand, the Consumers' Health Forum and the Australian Consumers' Association, and on the other hand, right-wing policy "think tanks" (Logan et al. 1989) to view themselves as consumers: that is, to challenge medical authority if they feel it to be negligent or inaccurate and to demand second opinions and "value for money." Despite this, research suggests that many Australians do not want to adopt the consumerist approach to health care, preferring to invest their faith and trust in their doctors. Even though they may have a more jaundiced and cynical view concerning doctors now than in the past, Australians still respect members of the medical profession, particularly their "own" doctors.

One study of Sydney patients, conducted by myself and colleagues, found that although they had chosen their general practitioner in a casual manner, only a small minority of the respondents reported ever changing to another GP or even considering such a move. While they may have occasionally sought help from other doctors or alternative practitioners, the majority of respondents adhered to a satellite rather than a pluralist model of health care, preferring to return to their regular GP for care whenever possible (Lupton et al. 1991). In another, more recent study, again of patients living in Sydney, I found that the participants expressed their belief in the power of biomedicine to cure illnesses and save lives, and were particularly impressed by the advances made in high-technology surgical procedures and drug therapies. The authority and expertise that attend biomedicine and those who are medically trained still carried much weight among these patients (Lupton 1996, 1997).

These findings would suggest that the Australian medical profession retains a significant degree of social and cultural status. While Medicare does incorporate some degree of structural control over doctors' professional activities, as most general practitioners and specialists are not salaried workers in public hospitals but rather are self-employed, they are under far less government control than are practitioners in such fully public systems as the British National Health Service. Further, medical practitioners in Australia, particularly AMA officials, still have a high profile in terms of acting as influential spokespeople on medical matters in the public domain. They are frequently reported as authoritative experts in the news media in reports on medical and health issues compared with other health care providers or consumer bodies (Lupton 1995b; Lupton and McLean 1998) and hold important roles in decision-making bodies in hospitals and government agencies (Willis 1993). Although news stories in the Australian press report cases of medical negligence or misconduct, they also frequently represent doctors as skilled, heroic, and fighting to maintain high standards of patient care in the face of funding pressures for health care delivery (Lupton and McLean 1998).

In recent years, challenges to the dominance of orthodox practitioners in Australia have come from practitioners of alternative therapies, who have sought to have their therapies legitimized. Universities now offer courses in such therapies as chiropractic, homoeopathy, and acupuncture, and chiropractors and osteopaths have achieved statutory registration as legitimate health care providers in Australia. Only acupuncture is officially recognized through attracting a Medicare rebate, however, and this is only the case if it is performed by a medical practitioner. The AMA has also played an important role in opposing the entry of alternative practitioners into orthodox health care system, arguing that alternative therapies are "unscientific" (Easthope 1993). The medical profession thus far has successfully prevented alternative therapists from practising in hospitals.

One study conducted in the state of South Australia in 1993 found that one in five of the respondents had ever sought treatment from alternative practitioners (MacLennan et al. 1996). But while alternative therapies continue to gain popularity among Australians, orthodox medicine remains far and away the first source of health care. Although more Australians are seeking care from alternative therapists, they have not rejected biomedicine, but rather tend to turn to alternative therapy when they find that orthodox medicine cannot provide a cure for a particular ailment (Lloyd et al. 1993; Lupton 1998). The 1989–90 National Health Survey found that fully 20 percent of respondents had consulted an orthodox medical practitioner during the two weeks prior to the survey, while only 1.3 percent had consulted a chiropractor, 0.2 percent an acupuncturist, and 0.3 percent a naturopath during that period (Australian Bureau of Statistics 1992).

In terms of reasons for seeking alternative therapies, it would appear that the nature of the doctor–patient encounter and disillusionment with what orthodox medicine can offer for a specific ailment are important factors. One study found that the patients greatly valued the time the practitioners spent with them, the personalized and individualized attention they received, the "natural" and "holistic" qualities of the therapy and the opportunity to seek help for conditions, particularly musculoskeletal, digestive, and emotional or nervous problems, that orthodox medicine had been unable to treat (Lloyd et al. 1993). Dissatisfaction with the medical encounter and doctor – patient relationship was found to be a major reason for seeking alternative therapies by Siahpush (1998) in his study of people living in a rural region of Australia. One response to the adoption of alternative medicine by patients is the decision by doctors to incorporate such therapies as acupuncture and chiropractic into their own practices. A recent study found that 15 percent of Australian GPs were offering acupuncture as part of their services to patients (Easthope et al. 1998).

Nurses in Australia have also attempted to gain greater professional power in relation to medical practitioners. Through the legitimization of nursing training via university courses and the introduction of the "nurse practitioner," a nurse who is qualified to independently perform procedures that were previously the preserve of medical practitioners only, nurses have sought greater autonomy and a higher professional status than they held in the past (Wicks 1999). Despite these moves, nurses still remain very much subordinate to medical practitioners in terms of status, power, and influence in health care provision decision-making.

SOCIAL CAUSES OF HEALTH AND ILLNESS

Social class is a factor in patterns of health and ill health in Australia as it is in other western societies. While it is often claimed that Australia is a "classless" society compared to Britain, there are distinct social groupings related to such aspects as income, education level, area of residence, and occupation that influence health outcomes. As in other western nations, people from lower socioeconomic classes have a higher mortality rate and a lower life expectancy than do the more advantaged, and suffer from some illnesses in greater numbers. For example, it has been reported by the Australian Bureau of Statistics (1999) that those people living in areas of greater socioeconomic disadvantage tend to rate their own health status more negatively and visit their doctors more often than do those living in advantaged areas. Death rates from ischaemic heart disease, lung conditions such as bronchitis, emphysema, and lung cancer, diabetes, cerebrovascular disease (mostly strokes), suicide, and traffic accidents are higher for those living in the most disadvantaged areas. More men and women in disadvantaged areas are likely to smoke cigarettes and drink alcohol at a medium- or high-risk level, and more women from these areas are overweight or obese. People in these areas are less likely to engage in preventive health actions such as having their children immunized against infectious disease or taking part in cancer screening. There is also a social class difference in patients' perspectives on doctors. Patients who are more highly educated and who hold middle-class occupations are more likely to exhibit consumeristic attitudes toward their doctors, tending to challenge their authority to a greater extent (Lupton et al. 1991; Lupton 1997).

Ethnicity and race have an impact on health states for both better and worse among Australians. People from southern Europe who have emigrated to Australia have better health outcomes in relation to such diseases as heart disease than do Australians of British ethnicity. It has been speculated that their diet, which has less animal fat and more vegetables and grains than the standard British-style cuisine, is the reason for this. Their health risks may increase with length of residence in Australia, however, as immigrants may move towards a diet that is closer to the British style (Manderson and Reid 1994). Recent immigrants have better health than do the Australian born, most probably because they undergo stringent health checks before being granted immigrant status and are younger, on average, than the general Australian population. There is evidence to suggest that the health status of some immigrants worsens after their arrival in Australia. Immigrants may be prey to illness as a result of cultural dislocation, loneliness, and depression (Julian 1999). Men of Greek and Italian ethnicity, for example, are more at risk of coronary heart disease the longer they reside in Australia (Davis and George 1988). Refugees are more likely to suffer from psychiatric disorders than other Australians, often as a result of their enforced migration and traumatic experiences in their country of birth.

People from non-English-speaking backgrounds often find that health services available to them in Australia are culturally inappropriate or may have difficulties communicating with health workers because of poor English and a lack of available interpreters (Julian 1999). New immigrants are more likely to be employed in low-skilled, dangerous occupations and therefore to suffer from work-related injuries. Migrant women from non-English-speaking backgrounds, in particular, have a higher incidence of work-related injuries and illness and a greater incidence of mental health problems than do Australian women of English-speaking backgrounds. Their health often declines after their arrival in Australia due to problems of dislocation and social and cultural isolation, as well as poor working conditions (Alcorso and Schofield 1992).

Aboriginal people suffer the greatest socioeconomic disadvantage, and subsequently the worst health, of any other ethnic/racial group in Australia. The descendants of those Aboriginal people who survived the early decades of colonization were subjected in the twentieth century to acts of rank racial discrimination. These included the forcible removal of infants and young children from their parents, a practice which continued until the 1960s in the attempt to "assimilate" Aboriginal people into white Australian cultural mores. Members of this "stolen generation" have suffered health and psychological problems as a result of their removal from their families and being brought up in missions, orphanages, or foster homes where some were subject to physical or sexual abuse (Human Rights and Equal Opportunity Commission 1997).

Aboriginal people currently have greater rates of unemployment than do non-Aboriginal Australians, have lower education levels, suffer from problems such as alcohol abuse, petrol sniffing, and violence in greater proportions, and are far more likely to be jailed than other Australians. They are more likely to smoke cigarettes, commit suicide, or inflict self-harm. Their socioeconomic and social disadvantage is mirrored in their health states. Aboriginal men and women have significantly lower life expectancies than do non-Aboriginals and the mortality rate of Aboriginal infants is far higher than for non-Aboriginals (Gray and Saggers 1994, 1999). Although successive Australian governments have recognized the plight of Aboriginal people, few attempts thus far have proved successful in ameliorating their poor health status. As with other "Fourth World" or indigenous populations in First World countries, such as the Native Americans and Maoris, Aboriginal people argue that their lack of access to traditional culture, customs, and rituals, their enforced dependence on the colonizing culture, and their lack of opportunity to engage in self-determination due to their dispossession from the land are major sources of cultural dislocation and ill health (Reid and Lupton 1991).

CONCLUSION

The nature of the health care system and the status of the medical profession in Australia demonstrate a number of features of the history, politics, and social structure of that country. In particular, white Australia's beginnings as a British penal colony, a subsequent change to laissez-faire government and then to increased government regulation of the medical profession followed by a move toward neo-liberalism have been important in the development of the current system. So too, the power of medical associations to disrupt government initiatives to introduce universal health care has been an important influence in Australian health care policy, particularly in the twentieth century. As in other western countries, the social power of the orthodox medical profession in Australia has been subject to some challenge in recent decades on the part of consumer bodies, practitioners of alternative therapies, and other health care professionals. Although its standing may have been somewhat eroded, particularly by negative media coverage, the Australian medical profession retains a significant degree of political, social, and cultural status. Its leaders continue to influence public policy, acting as influential spokespeople on health matters in decision-making bodies and media reports. For the most part, the medical profession and the institution of scientific medicine are still held in high regard by patients in Australia.

References

Alcorso, C. and C. Schofield. 1992. *The National Non-English-Speaking Background Women's Health Strategy*. Canberra: Australian Government Publishing Service.

Australian Bureau of Statistics. 1992. *1989–90 National Health Survey: Consultations with Health Professionals, Australia*. Canberra: Australian Government Publishing Service.

——. 1999. *Australian Social Trends 1999* (Catalogue No. 4102.0). Canberra: Australian Government Publishing Service.

Broom, D. 1991. *Damned If We Do: Contradictions in Women's Health Care*. Sydney: Allen and Unwin.

Crichton, A. 1990. *Slowly Taking Control? Australian Governments and Health Care Provision 1788–1988*. Sydney: Allen and Unwin.

Davis, A. and J. George. 1988. *States of Health: Health and Illness in Australia*. Sydney: Harper and Row.

Dean, M. 1997. "Sociology After Society." Pp. 205–28 in D. Owen (ed.), *Sociology After Postmodernism*. London: Sage.

Easthope, G. 1993. "The Response of Orthodox Medicine to the Challenge of Alternative Medicine in Australia." *Australian and New Zealand Journal of Sociology* 29: 289–301.

Easthope, G., G. Gill, J. Beilby, and B. Tranter. 1998. "Acupuncture in General Practice: Practitioner Characteristics." *Medical Journal of Australia* 169: 197–200.

Germov, J. (ed.). 1999. *Second Opinion: An Introduction to Health Sociology*, revised edition. Melbourne: Oxford University Press.

Gillespie, J. 1991. *The Price of Health: Australian Governments and Medical Politics 1910–1960*. Melbourne: Cambridge University Press.

Gray, D. and S. Saggers. 1994. "Aboriginal Ill Health: The Harvest of Injustice." Pp. 119–33 in C. Waddell and A. Petersen (eds.), *Just Health: Inequality in Illness, Care and Prevention*. Melbourne: Churchill Livingstone.

——. 1999. "Indigenous Health: The Perpetuation of Inequality." Pp. 57–74 in J. Germov (ed.), *Second Opinion: An Introduction to Health Sociology*, revised edition. Melbourne: Oxford University Press.

Haug, M. 1988. "A Re-examination of the Hypothesis of Physician Deprofessionalization." *Milbank Quarterly* 66: 48–56.

Human Rights and Equal Opportunity Commission. 1997. *Bringing Them Home: Report of the National Inquiry into the Separation of Aboriginal and Torres Strait Islander Children from their Families*. Canberra: Australian Government Printing Service.

Julian, R. 1999. "Ethnicity, Health, and Multiculturalism." Pp. 77–95 in J. Germov (ed.), *Second Opinion: An Introduction to Health Sociology*, revised edition. Melbourne: Oxford University Press.

Lawler, J. 1991. *Behind the Screens: Nursing, Somology and the Problem of the Body*. Melbourne: Churchill Livingstone.

Lloyd, P. 1994. "A History of Medical Professionalisation in NSW: 1788–1950." *Australian Health Review* 17: 14–28.

Lloyd, P., D. Lupton, D. Wiesner, and S. Hasleton. 1993. "Socio-Demographic Characteristics and Reasons for Choosing Natural Therapy: An Exploratory Study of Patients Resident in Sydney." *Australian Journal of Public Health* 17: 135–44.

Logan, J., D. Green, and A. Woodfield. 1989. *Healthy Competition*. Sydney: Centre for Independent Studies.

Lupton, D. 1994a. *Medicine as Culture: Illness, Disease and the Body in Western Societies*. London: Sage.

——. 1994b. *Moral Threats and Dangerous Desires: AIDS in the News Media*. London: Taylor and Francis.

——. 1995a. *The Imperative of Health: Public Health and the Regulated Body*. London: Sage.

——. 1995b. "Medical and Health Stories on the Sydney Morning Herald's Front Page." *Australian Journal of Public Health* 19: 501–8.

——. 1996. "'Your Life in Their Hands': Trust in the Medical Encounter." Pp. 158–72 in V. James and J. Gabe (eds.), *Health and the Sociology of Emotion* (Sociology of Health and Illness Monograph Series). Oxford: Blackwell Publishers.

——. 1997. "Consumerism, Reflexivity, and the Medical Encounter." *Social Science and Medicine* 45: 373–81.

Lupton, D., C. Donaldson, and P. Lloyd. 1991. "Caveat Emptor or Blissful Ignorance? Patients and the Consumerist Ethos." *Social Science and Medicine* 33: 559–68.

Lupton, D. and J. McLean. 1998. "Representing Doctors: Discourses and Images in the Australian Press." *Social Science and Medicine* 46: 947–58.

McKinlay, J. and J. Stoeckle. 1988. "Corporatization and the Social Transformation of Doctoring." *International Journal of Health Services* 18: 191–205.

MacLennan, A., D. Wilson, and A. Taylor. 1996. "Prevalence and Cost of Alternative Medicine in Australia." *Lancet* 347: 569–73.

Manderson, L. and J. Reid. 1994. "What's Culture Got to Do with It?" Pp. 7–26 in C. Waddell and A. Petersen (eds.), *Just Health: Inequality in Illness, Care and Prevention*. Melbourne: Churchill Livingstone.

Palmer, G. and S. Short. 1989. *Health Care and Public Policy: An Australian Analysis*. Melbourne: Macmillan.

Petersen, A. and D. Lupton. 1996. *The New Public Health: Health and Self in the Age of Risk*. London: Sage.

Petersen, A. and C. Waddell. (eds.). 1998. *Health Matters: A Sociology of Illness, Prevention and Care*. Sydney: Allen and Unwin.

Pringle, R. 1998. *Sex and Medicine: Gender, Power and Authority in the Medical Profession*. Cambridge: Cambridge University Press.

Reid, J. and D. Lupton. 1991. "Introduction." Pp. xi–xxii in J. Reid and P. Trompf (eds.), *The Health of Aboriginal Australia*. Sydney: Harcourt Brace Jovanovich.

Reid, J. and P. Trompf. (eds.). 1990. *The Health of Immigrant Australia*. Sydney: Harcourt Brace Jovanovich.

——. 1991. *The Health of Aboriginal Australia*. Sydney: Harcourt Brace Jovanovich.

Sax, S. 1984. *A Strife of Interests: Politics and Policies in Australian Health Services*. Sydney: Allen and Unwin.

Siahpush, M. 1998. "Postmodern Values, Dissatisfaction with Conventional Medicine and Popularity of Alternative Therapies." *Journal of Sociology* 34: 58–70.

Wicks, D. 1999. "Nursing and Sociology: An Uneasy Relationship." Pp. 249–66 in J. Germov (ed.), *Second Opinion: An Introduction to Health Sociology*, revised edition. Melbourne: Oxford University Press.

Willis, E. 1983. *Medical Dominance: The Division of Labour In Australian Health Care*. Sydney: George Allen and Unwin.

——. "Doctoring in Australia: A View at the Bicentenary." *The Milbank Quarterly* 66: 167–81.

25

Health, Illness, and Health Policy in Japan

Masahira Anesaki and Tsunetsugu Munakata

Health Care and Socio-Behavioral Factors in Health and Illness in Japan

In this chapter, we will deal with the sociocultural factors of health and illness in contemporary Japan and the historical view of health care policies in financing and delivery of services in Japan.

The Ten Components of a Nation's Health Care

First of all, we would like to present our model describing a nation's health and health care delivery system (Anesaki 1977). Our model is comprised of ten components. Health care starts with a physician's response to a person's needs for care or treatment. The consumers or recipients of health care are not only sick, injured, or disabled, but also include healthy people who ask for preventive care and health promotion. Sometimes people who are in need of care refuse the necessary care because of mental illness or other reasons. In modern society, health care is provided by a team of health personnel who have the necessary educational qualifications to use modern technology in well- equipped health care institutions like clinics or hospitals. This type of health care produces health-related and other industries, while governments, insurers, and individuals pay for the costs. The health economy has become a large sector of any national economy. Laws and ethics regulate health care because it directly intervenes with people's lives and is a basic human right. As the protection of the population's health is a major governmental responsibility, health care is an important aspect

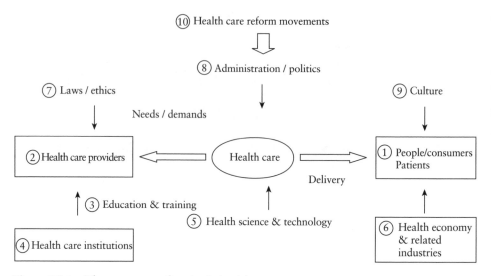

Figure 25.1 The structure of nation's health care

of civic administration and politics. People's health and health care has universal as well as cultural features. Any nation is faced often with health care reform movements, whether radical or minor.

The ten components of a nation's health care are shown in figure 25.1: (1) people/consumers, (2) health care providers, (3) health care education and training, (4) health care institutions, (5) health science and technology, (6) the health economy, (7) health-related laws and ethics, (8) health administration and politics, (9) health-related culture, and (10) reform movements. These components and the whole of health care are determined by a nation's history, economy, technology, culture, and traditions.

HEALTH AND ILLNESS IN JAPAN

In 1996, the average life expectancy in Japan was 77.01 years for men and 83.59 for women. The death rate adjusted for age was 7.4 per 1,000 for men and 4.0 per 1,000 for women. The infant mortality rate was 3.8 per 1,000 births. In each case, the Japanese figures are the best in the world. These figures reflect the high standard of living and favorable sanitation conditions in Japan. In addition, the speed at which Japan's population structure is aging is among the fastest in the world, so is the speed at which the birth rate is decreasing. These trends will force Japan to face enormous challenges in the future, as the country copes with a rapidly increasing aged population and a low birth rate.

To identify today's health problems, let us first look at the principal diseases that make up the total patient population of Japan. Hypertension, diabetes, stroke, cancer, and other diseases related to daily living habits are the principal afflictions

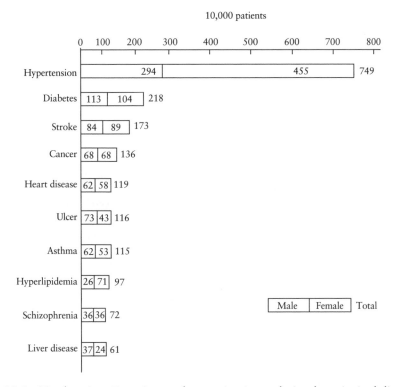

Figure 25.2 Total patient (inpatient and outpatient) population by principal disease diagnoses

Source: Ministry of Health and Welfare, 1998.

of the Japanese (Japan Ministry of Health and Welfare 1999). On one hand, Japan has created a highly managed society with excellent sanitation that enable the Japanese to live on average longer than in any other country in the world. On the other hand, it is today beset with an aging population, with more and more Japanese suffering from diseases caused by living in a highly managed, stressful society.

SOCIO-ENVIRONMENTAL FACTORS CAUSING LIFESTYLE DISEASES AND JAPANESE BEHAVIORAL CHARACTERISTICS

Diseases related to daily living habits are by nature preventable, treatable, or controllable, provided healthy habits and behaviors are followed. Thus, it is important that we know what habits are health-inducing and learn how to change any daily habits that are detrimental to health. But in reality it is difficult to develop healthy habits and behaviors even if we have sound knowledge of what is good and what is bad for us.

Why? One reason is that the environment we live in is such that it is hard to develop healthy daily behaviors. For example, in a 1991 survey, we found that, while people in most cities of the world can get to work in 30 minutes

(Munakata 1990), more than 30 percent of commuters in the greater Tokyo area have to travel over an hour to get to work (Munakata et al. 1991). A study of the neurotic tendencies of Japanese people using the General Health Questionnaire Scale (GHQ, the Japanese edition) of 60 items reveals that among those commuting 60 minutes or less, 26–28 percent had a neurotic tendency, as opposed to 33 percent for those commuting more than 60 minutes. In the case of white-collar workers in the greater Tokyo area, we found that the longer their commuting time, the more likely they are to experience daily hassles, have irregular eating habits, eat unbalanced meals, suffer from lack of sleep, drink more per week, and habitually smoke more.

Another reason has to do with the fact that the difficulty of developing healthy habits and the unhealthy daily environment people live in are correlated. That is, Japanese workers react to the source of stress at work or home that they cannot control by engaging in escapist or compensatory behaviors such as overeating, overdrinking, and watching television excessively. Consequently, to change our unhealthy daily habits we need to reconstruct the environment we live in to make it more conducive to healthy living. Also, individually the Japanese should develop effective stress-management skills. However, the Japanese personality until now has been characterized by a strong tendency to adopt self-repressive behavior traits in which they repress their feelings hoping to be well-regarded by those around them. This kind of personality is reflected in such statements as "I try hard to meet the expectations of other people," "I have a hard time expressing what's on my mind," and "I'm the type that endures hardships."

These behavior patterns make it easier for stress to accumulate, are apt to lead to neurotic tendencies, and cause people to develop unhealthy living habits to compensate for their stress. In our survey we found that, while it is true that the Japanese people's self-repressive behavior is correlated to Japanese Type-A behavior, it is precisely these behavioral patterns that have enabled the Japanese to build an industrialized society at a speed unprecedented in the world. In the United States, people with Type-A personality make all-out efforts to succeed in society by asserting themselves freely as individuals and competing openly with others and aggressively airing their views. By contrast, in Japan, Type-A people "work hard" while trying to maintain "amicable relationships" with those around them. This is reflected in such statements as "I feel like I'm betraying my colleagues if I take too many days off" or "I feel like I'm cheating the company if I don't work late." People with such attitudes become workaholics, keep irregular hours, and develop various stress-related diseases caused by daily habits including ischemic cardiac disorders.

HEALING NEGATIVE FEEDBACK OF DISEASES AND BEING ONESELF

By the beginning of the 1980s, there was so much material wealth and such positive sanitary conditions that life expectancy in Japan was, as noted, the longest in the world. But also around that time, people began to place more importance on quality than quantity, that is, on life-satisfaction. In response to this change in consumer preference, businesses came to value workers good at empathizing with the feelings of others, for such workers would be able to creatively determine what sort of goods or services would satisfy their customers. Instead of refraining from self-assertion for the sake of group harmony and devoting themselves to work, as has been the norm up to now, workers are currently expected to openly express their feelings and ideas, assert their own individuality, and demonstrate a creativity high in added value.

However, the vast majority of people in urban areas, formerly the base from which industrialization was achieved, are citizens who still strongly tend to be self-repressive. These citizens, as noted earlier, tend to live in stressful environments and continue showing stress-generating behavioral characteristics (Munakata 1991). Consequently, their neurotic condition gets worse, which compels them to take compensatory, habitual behavior against stress. If change is not forthcoming, it will be impossible to prevent the spread of diseases caused by stress-induced daily habits.

Illness is deeply related to how people live, but it is also filled with potential for changing our environment. Illness is also the subconscious expression of the demands of those who have repressed their desire for self-satisfaction in their daily lives governed by a strong social order. For example, as we found in our survey, with the exception of those who worked less than four hours a day, the more hours people worked, the shorter their sleeping hours, and fewer the number of days off per month, the more likely they were to show neurotic tendencies. People who work long hours without taking a rest tend to isolate themselves from their surroundings. To compensate, they try to meet the expectations of those around them by repressing their feelings, thus aggravating their neurotic symptoms. These symptoms in turn push them into unhealthy habits, paving the way for the onslaught of diseases related to daily living habits.

What then are the demands those who are afflicted with such diseases repress? The answer: these people live constantly worried about how they are viewed by others and repress their wish to live their own lives based on their own self-evaluation. The medical establishment continues to treat only the symptoms of such diseases. Stress that causes diseases related to daily living habit has become a real problem, for it increases workplace bullying, karoshi (death from overwork), depression, suicide, and the like.

The more serious the problem becomes, the greater the demand for a labor environment where workers would have more time for recreation and healing, including reduction in working hours, flexible working hours, working at home, working at satellite offices, and workplace amenities. It is also true that a shift in orientation has begun to take place through mental examinations, stress-management training, self-awareness seminars, and counseling services, just to name a few. The change is from a "nice guy" orientation which force people to be cooperative and self-repressive to "being oneself" orientation where people express themselves more openly without worrying about what others may think.

HISTORICAL VIEW OF HEALTH POLICIES IN JAPAN

Primitive Medicine Earlier than the Sixth Century

One of the major historical features of health care and medicine in Japan, particularly after the middle of the sixth century, is that Japan has modeled itself after a certain country during each major time period (Powell and Anesaki 1990). In ancient times the Japanese developed their own primitive medical beliefs and practices including anatomical dissections, autopsies, and an awareness of how cleanliness can prevent the spread of disease. This awareness about cleanliness, in turn, led to the development of purification rituals.

Adoption of Chinese Medicine

From earliest times, knowledge about Chinese medicine came to Japan largely through Koreans. However, direct communication between China and Japan grew from the middle of the sixth century, and Buddhism and other components of Chinese culture came into Japan. Especially during the periods of the Sui (AD 589–617) and Tang (AD 618–959) dynasties when China enjoyed remarkable prosperity and prestige, Japan's political and intellectual leaders were so eager to adopt and copy all things Chinese that priests, scholars, and artisans were sent from Japan to study in China. Buddhist medico-priests were among the many visitors from the mainland. Chinese medicine at that time was closely connected with Buddhism; charity institutions were established in the precincts of Buddhist temples and medico-priests and nurse-priests were produced in great numbers. Chinese medicine became the national medicine in Japan, and remained so until the end of the feudalistic era in 1868.

During the long dominance of Chinese medicine in Japan, there was some modification and development. Some schools, for example, emphasized the importance of observation and experiment, thereby establishing the positivist foundation of medical practice in Japan. Toward the end of the seventeenth century, scientists carried out the dissection of animals when human dissection was prohibited, and began using an anaesthetic preparation during surgical procedures at the beginning of the nineteenth century – one century earlier than the United States pioneered the use of anesthesia in the West.

Jesuit Missionary Medicine and Dutch Medicine

Before modern times, Japan had direct contact with western medicine three times: (1) Christian missionary medicine in the middle of the sixteenth century, (2) Dutch medicine through Dutch medical officers stationed at the Dutch trading house in Dejima, Nagasaki, and (3) Japanese interpreters from 1641 to 1858 under Japan's isolation policy. Even after Christian missionary activities were strictly prohibited and foreign missionaries were expelled, missionary medicine survived as "southern barbarian surgery," thanks to the usefulness of the surgical techniques. This "southern barbarian surgery" was combined with Dutch medicine that was up-to-date European medicine. This combination of western medicine and the positivistic and experimental Chinese (or Japanized Chinese) medicine paved the way for the adoption of modern western medical practice in Japan (Powell and Anesaki 1990).

German Medicine as a Model for Modern Japan until World War II

As soon as the isolation policy under the feudalistic Tokugawa Shogunate ended in 1868, Japan decided to adopt German medicine as the model for modernization, along with the German model for the constitution and military system. This decision was based upon Germany's method of modernization in which the country strengthened industry and the military. The Japanese government invited two instructors from a German army medical school to be a part of the institution that was the forerunner of the University of Tokyo Medical School. The two instructors were empowered with full authority to establish a new medical education system at Tokyo University that would disseminate western medicine all over Japan.

The Golden Age for Private Medical Practitioners

Beginning in 1876, a license to practice medicine was granted only to those trained in western medical science. This excluded practitioners of Chinese medicine who were still the majority. Their fight for inclusion in the new system was in vain against a background of officially endorsed modernism. Successful candidates for a medical practitioner's license were educated at national, municipal, and private medical schools, with the University of Tokyo School of Medicine at the top of a pyramidal structure.

The popular demand for western medical care services grew so rapidly that the demand for services exceeded the supply of medical practitioners. Those practitioners who possessed the knowledge and skills of western medicine and were protected by license enjoyed economic advantages under the free market principle.

From Public to Private Dominance of Hospitals

At the Meiji Restoration in 1868, when Japan's modernization began, there were no hospitals in Japan. The only exception was a hospital built toward the end of the feudalistic era on the advice of a Dutch doctor named Pompe van Meerdervont who had been invited by the Shogunate to help with the preparation for modernization. After the Meiji Restoration the central and local governments built public hospitals, including military hospitals for soldiers injured in the civil wars, which were mostly attached to medical schools. However, after 1887 an ordinance banned support for medical schools from prefectural taxes, and many prefectural hospitals were closed. Private hospitals then began to outnumber public hospitals. Private practitioners in particular began to convert their clinics into hospitals. This type of private practitioner-owned hospital became the majority of hospitals in Japan. By 1898, there were 136 government hospitals in Japan and 518 private ones. Except for military hospitals and leading national university hospitals (or imperial university hospitals), Japan's private sector-dominated pattern of medical care delivery was established toward the end of the nineteenth century.

Charity, Discount Clinics, and Health Insurance

Japan experienced industrial revolutions in light and then heavy industry during the Sino–Japanese War of 1894–5, the Russo–Japanese War of 1904–5, the World War of 1914–18. Under the development of a free market economy, medical fees were not regulated and doctors could charge their patients any amount they wished. The economic benefits of industrialization did not trickle down to the majority of the population while living conditions in the rapidly expanding urban centers were poor and rural remote areas were isolated from the benefits of modern medicine. High medical fees became a concern for the country.

Economic and social conditions were favorable to the growth of the labor and socialist movements. In 1910, a group of socialists was arrested on suspicion of regicide and the "conspirators" were executed. In 1911 the Emperor issued an imperial proclamation on charity medical care that looked like compensation for this dubious "high treason" case. He donated initial money to the state, and with further donations collected by public subscription, the government set up an Imperial charitable foundation to own and operate charity clinics and welfare institutions. By 1936 the foundation ran fifteen hospitals, three sanatoria, one maternity hospital, one nursery, ten visiting medical units, 12 mobile nurses units, and 61 clinics in various parts of the country.

Also in 1911, a dedicated physician, ex-businessman, and parliamentarian set up a chain of discount and low profit clinics. The clinics had such strong support, especially among the working class, that this phenomenon became a national movement in the provision of medical care. The local medical associations were afraid and thus opposed to the further development of such clinics, but the clinics had been highly successful and paved the way for the organization of medical co-ops. They also established the foundation for the introduction of health insurance. Mutual aid associations began to be organized toward the end of the nineteenth century as the predecessors of health insurance societies. The associations were set up at mines, textile companies, and government agencies such as railways, printing offices, mints, postal and telecommunications offices, and army and navy bases.

Japan's first health insurance law was passed by the Diet in 1922 and came into force in 1927; about 40 years later than the world's first health insurance law passed by the German Reichstag. It is said that the Health Insurance Bill sneaked through the Diet, overshadowed by the contentious debates that attended the passing of the Anti-Socialist Bill of 1925. This was similar to the Anti-Socialist Law of 1878 in connection with the Health Insurance Law of 1882 in Germany. Japan's first health insurance law was a provision of medical treatment for disease, injuries, and death, with some cash allowances for only 2 million employees out of an estimated 4.7 million employed workers to a maximum 180-day period.

The Road to War and its Impact on Health Care: 1930–45

Japan benefited from World War I economically. Soon, however, it suffered from the postwar trade depression, a banking crisis in 1927, and the World Depression in 1929. These economic crises affected certain sectors of society: mainly workers and small business owners in urban centers and poor tenant farmers in rural areas. Under these conditions, the health status of the people was deteriorating. The incidence of tuberculosis was high and growing, and the infant mortality-rate was also high. Many areas were without doctors, clinics, or hospitals. Even if a doctor was available, the number of insured people was so limited that most of the population could not afford to have medical care.

The early 1930s saw two notable attempts to remedy these situations. One was the movement for the development of cooperative medical care facilities led by Christian intellectuals. The other was the socialist or communist movement for medical facilities for poor workers. The first group, the cooperative movement, in association with other groups such as the agricultural cooperative association, was taken over during the war by the Japan Medical Corporation, the official body in charge of wartime medical services. However, the Corporation was dissolved after the war by the Occupation Forces. The second group, sponsored by the Communists, was found unacceptable by the authorities and their facilities were closed under pressure of the Japanese police force.

In the 1930s fanatic ultra-nationalistic ideas about how to rebuild Japan prevailed and especially inspired the younger army officers, some of whom assassinated political and business leaders whom they blamed for lack of policy and leadership. Extremists in the military took advantage of this political tension and upheaval to take Japan the way of militarism. They exerted control over the nation and invaded China and neighboring countries. Japan started the "Fifteen-years war" with China and proceeded toward involvement in the World War II.

With war underway, Japan's military forces demanded radical changes in health policy. The military force was worried about the worsening health examination records of its soldiers upon conscription, and demanded the establishment of an independent Ministry of Health and Welfare that would be responsible for the nation's health and social welfare, to make "healthy and strong soldiers." It was established in 1938. At the same time, community public health centers were starting to offer preventive health services, health education, and guidance. Also in 1938, the National Health Insurance Act, which covered self-employed people such as farmers and fishermen and their families, was enacted.

With the beginning of the Pacific War on December 8, 1941 (December 7 in the US and Europe) the country came under total wartime conditions. The National Medical Service Act of 1942 regulated all matters relating to the medical and health professions, and it set up the Japan Medical Corporation to organize and control a nationwide network of all medical facilities. The Japan Medical Corporation Plan called for two central hospitals with 500 beds each, one for the northeastern half of the country and another for the southwestern half; 47 prefectural hospitals (one for each prefecture) with 250 beds each; 588 district hospitals with 50 beds each; new clinics for communities without doctors so far; and 100,000 new beds in tuberculosis sanatoria. Since the Japan Medical Corporation was dissolved after the war ended, this effort to establish a nation-wide pyramidal medical care delivery system was never fully realized.

The war years saw some expansion of the health insurance system. By the end of the war in 1945 approximately one-third of the population was covered by some insurance. Ironically, however, the war had severely limited the availability of medical care because bombing had destroyed many facilities, production of drugs and supplies was interrupted, and male physicians had been drafted by the military. As many medical students were trained in shorter courses to meet the wartime need for medical personnel, problems of over-supply and the quality of doctors became serious after the war when doctors returned from military service.

From the War-Devastated Ruins to Universal Health Insurance: 1945–61

Japan accepted the unconditional surrender demanded in the Potsdam Proclamation by the Allies, and the war ended on August 15, 1945. General Douglas MacArthur and his American staff led the Occupation by the Allied Powers after the war ended. Their main purpose was to democratize Japan after demilitarization, so the General Headquarters (GHQ) of the Occupation Forces drafted a new constitution for Japan. It passed the Japanese Diet, was promulgated on November 3, 1946, and enforced on May 3, 1947. This new Constitution has been called the Constitution of Pacifism and Democracy. Article 25 of the Constitution is as famous as Article 1 about the emperor as the national symbol and Article 9 about the renouncement of the armed forces. Article 25 states: "All people shall have the right to maintain the minimum standards of wholesome and cultural living. In all spheres of life the state shall use its endeavors for the promotion and extension of social welfare and security and of public health." It was a revolution in Japan that the new Constitution guaranteed the people's right to life and established state responsibility to promote and improve welfare, social security, and public health (in contrast to the old Constitution). This article of the Constitution became a foundation of social and health policy as well as the legal ground for future social and health judgments (Powell and Anesaki 1990).

During the war, 40 percent of the built-up area of more than 60 cities and towns was destroyed, including atomic-bombed Hiroshima and Nagasaki. Many medical facilities were also destroyed. When the war ended the total number of hospital beds was reduced to 31,756 or 15 percent of the number available in 1941 when the war started. The clinics decreased from 45,808 in 1940 to 6,607 in 1945, a mere 15 percent of their previous number. The number of physicians went from 67,600 in 1941 to 12,800 in 1945. Health care delivery was almost paralyzed. The extremely short supply of medical care in addition to postwar hyperinflation also paralyzed health insurance that had at one time covered approximately one-third of the population.

Some Japanese intellectuals were idealistic seekers of Beveridge's plan in Britain for a welfare state in Japan. During the early period of the occupation, government committees on social security, or social insurance, were set up one after another on the recommendation from American advisors and the staff of the GHQ. Those committees and councils presented an idealistic blueprint for the future social security system based upon social insurance.

During the cold war, the Chinese Revolution, the Korean War, and Japan's Peace Treaty with free bloc countries among the Allies accompanied by the Security Treaty with the USA, the Japanese government's policies, including social policies, leaned toward the political right. Britain and other European welfare states were experiencing at the same time the controversial choice between "Butter or Cannons" (social security or armament). Japan also struggled with this issue. However, when the Korean war broke out across the Japan Sea the pacifist Constitution prohibited Japan from participating in the war directly, and Japan reaped the economic benefit of the Korean War. Japan's economy not only recovered but began booming. Universal health insurance was achieved finally in 1961, but unfortunately it still left some problems unsolved. This universal health insurance was comprised of too many kinds of employer-based health insurance societies along with many municipality-based health insurance societies. Copayment varied between the insured and their dependents as well as among the diverse societies. The same fee-schedule was applied to both privately invested medical facilities and publicly subsidized public medical facilities.

On the side of health care delivery the number of medical facilities climbed so steadily that the number of hospitals in 1947 exceeded that of 1941. At first, the government adopted a policy of focusing their restoration efforts on public hospitals because private sources could not afford to invest in building hospitals. As military forces began dwindling, army/navy hospitals and facilities for invalids were transferred to the Ministry of Health and Welfare. The Japan Medical Corporation, set up by the wartime government, was dissolved. The 688 medical facilities under the Corporation were transferred to the Ministry of Health and Welfare or returned to the local governments.

The Japanese government next nullified the major wartime medical provision, entitled "The National Medical Service Act." Instead, the government legislated a group of more specific laws such as the Medical Service Act, the Medical Practitioners Act, the Dental Practitioners Act, and the Nurses Act in 1948 to secure and improve the quality of medical facilities, physicians, dentists, and nurses. Legislation for other allied medical professions soon followed: the Dental Hygienists Act of 1948, the Clinical X-ray Technologists Act of 1951, the Dental Engineers Act of 1955, and the Clinical Laboratory Technicians Act of 1958. Considering the aging population, the Japanese government also instated legislation to regulate rehabilitation personnel, as in the Physical and Occupational Therapists Act of 1965, the Orthopedists Act of 1971, the Artificial Limb Fitters Act of 1987, and the Clinical Engineers Act of 1987.

Private Sector Dominance in the Development of Health Care Delivery

In order to address the overflow of physicians after the war, the government restricted the training of new physicians for some time after the war ended. However, because experts predicted a sharp increase in the demand for medical care after the introduction of universal health insurance, the government planned to increase the intake of medical students and even allowed the establishment of new medical schools from 1970. The "one medical school at one prefecture" policy was instituted in 1973. The government's target was to reach 150 physicians per 10,000 population by 1985, but instead it achieved this goal two years earlier than expected, in 1983.

Private sector dominance in the field of medical facilities was soon restored under Japan's high growth economy and strengthened under heavy political pressure from the Japanese Medical Association, which represented the interest of private practitioners and physician-owned private hospitals. Moreover, since 1950 private hospitals have been given the privilege of tax exemption with only a few requirements. In 1960 the new Medical Finance Corporation began to provide private hospitals with long-term and low interest loans, and in 1962 the government introduced laws to limit the increase in public hospital beds. Because of this series of policies and circumstances, private hospitals came into a favorable position in Japan.

An Epoch-Making Progress in Health Insurance Benefits followed by the 1973 "Oil Crisis"

Because the postwar development in hospitals often involved the reduction of hospital workers, strikes broke out in hospitals throughout Japan from 1960 to 1961. Sometimes physicians, led by the Japanese Medical Association (JMA), and hospital workers, led by hospital labor unions, fought with the government over their working conditions. After universal health insurance was achieved, it became a source of political contention between the Japanese Medical Association and the Japanese government. The JMA fought for conditions favorable to physicians, while the government wanted to protect health insurance finances. Eventually, high economic growth in the health care field seemed to make it possible for the government to accept the demands of the JMA.

The year 1973 was a turning point for Japan's social security. The government instituted free medical care for the aged, decreased the percentage of copayment required of dependents to 30 percent, and introduced a ceiling on the total amount of copayment. Japan also enjoyed a new universal pension scheme, one of the fruits of its high economic growth. Tragically, all of these benefits originating in Japan's high economic growth came to a halt in October of the same year, when the Fourth Arab–Israeli War began. The Organization of Arabic Oil Exporting Countries (OPEC) took advantage of oil supplies as a diplomatic weapon and restricted the oil export to the countries supporting Israel. Most western countries as well as Japan were affected, and oil prices increased by 30 to 70 percent. Japan's high economic growth, which relied upon almost all imported oil as its energy source, slowed down beginning in 1973. Eventually, the government had to take cost-containment actions in all areas, including health service fields.

The Beginning of Cost-Containment Policies

In 1980 the conservative-led government set up the Administrative Reform Council. The Council consisted of a number of specialized subcommittees and study groups. In the long-term, its objective was to privatize the public sector as much as possible to make a small government sector. This was similar to the policy of restraint that was being instituted by the Reagan administration in the United States and the Thatcher administration in the United Kingdom. The Administrative Reform Council issued specific recommendations about health and social welfare to guide the Ministry of Health and Welfare in policy formation. The Administrative Reform Council's first report on July 10, 1981, included recommendations to restrict government expenditure and to slash government subsidies by 10 percent. On the issue of medical care the report stated: "Medical care costs should be borne by the beneficiary where possible. Raise the maximum amount to be paid by beneficiaries of expensive medical treatment. Require elderly beneficiaries to bear part their medical expenses." Similarly, the third report on July 30, 1982 included a specific recommendation related to health care that Japan "rationalize medical costs to curb total medical expenditures." Finally, the fifth report of March 14, 1983 notes that the country should "transfer one-tenth of government controlled activities to local authorities over the next two years."

The government's concerns and subsequent policies tended to concentrate on health and medical expenditures and on health care financing mechanisms while ignoring problems concerning health and medical care delivery. Problems remained with the shortage and misdistribution of medical care resources (i.e. medical care personnel and facilities). Official concern grew concerning both the dramatic rise in the cost of medical care for elderly people and the ratio of medical care costs for the elderly to total national medical costs. The Health and Medical Services for the Elderly Act of 1982 (enacted in 1983) introduced a flat rate co-payment by elderly people for medical care that would restrict excessive medical care for elderly people. In addition to illness-specific medical care for the elderly this Act provided prevention health services for them like health checkups and health education. The provision of preventative health care was based upon the principle that "prevention is cheaper than cure."

Cost Containment through Health Insurance to Health Care Delivery

Socialization, or systematization, of health care financing and of health care delivery should go together in a good balance. In Japan, however, health care financing was socialized under a universal health insurance scheme, while health care delivery remained dominated by the private sector in a "laissez- faire" way. Misdistribution of health care resources rendered areas in which there were no medical care services available even when the residents paid premiums. Any patient could have free access to any medical facility with the same health insurance book, and there was no official distinction between medical facilities. Ambulatory care patients could go either to individual doctors' clinics or directly to the outpatient department (OPD) of large hospitals without any referral by family physicians. In urban areas, therefore, people often preferred large hospital outpatient departments to small clinics, which meant that the OPDs were so crowded that patients had to wait "three hours for three minutes' consultation."

Among inpatients acute and chronic patients were mixed, and the average length of stay was more than 30 days.

The increase of enrollment in medical schools continued until 1979 when the 80th and last medical school opened in Okinawa. Concern over the future potential for an excessive supply of physicians had already started. A series of amendments to the Medical Service Act began in 1985. The amendments were meant to effect cost-containment and to solve accumulated problems caused by the mainly "laissez-faire" system of health care delivery. The First Amendment to Medical Service Act asked each prefecture to demarcate secondary medical care or hospital care service zones along with the estimation of the needed number of hospital beds for each zone. In zones where the number of hospital beds exceeded the estimated number, new increases in hospital beds were not allowed. The Second Amendment in 1992 classified hospitals' function according to two opposite purposes. It designated two national medical centers and 80 university hospitals as highly advanced hospitals and specified on the other hand long-term nursing care units in hospitals. The Third Amendment in 1997 instituted informed consent to treatments in order to protect patients' rights. The Fourth Amendment is still forthcoming. Topics that will possibly be included are: clearer distinction between beds for acute patients and for chronic patients, broader disclosure of medical information, deregulation of restriction of advertisements concerning medical facilities, two-year compulsory postgraduate medical training.

Along with this series of policies regulating medical care delivery, a 1986 government committee on future supply and demand of physicians disclosed its recommendation that the intake of medical students should decrease by 10 percent before 1995. The Japanese counterpart to the Joint Commission on Accreditation of Health Care Organizations (JCAHO) in the USA, the Japan Council for Quality Health Care (JCQHC), was set up in 1995 to assess the quality of hospitals. As of May 1999, 220 hospitals were accredited. Also, care by private nurses or relatives for inpatients, which is a Japanese traditional custom, was abolished in September 1998 after a few years' preparation.

Policies on Care Delivery and Financing for the Aging Population

In 1989 the "Ten-Year Strategy to Promote Health and Welfare for the Elderly in the Twenty-first Century" (the Gold Plan) was adopted. This plan included numerical targets to be completed by the end of the twentieth century for health and welfare personnel and for domiciliary and institutional care facilities for the elderly. In 1995 those targets were revised (the New Gold Plan). To finance the care for the elderly in the twenty-first century, as prepared by the Gold Plan, the Japanese government prepared the Long-Term Nursing Care Insurance Plan of 1997. This social insurance will be enacted on April 1, 2000 when the fiscal as well as the academic year starts in Japan at the first year of the new millennium.

CONCLUSION

The national health policy and its outcome are a combined product of the ten components (noted at the beginning of this chapter) and the country's natural and sociocultural histories. The main principle of Japan's health policy after World War II has been equal access to health care for everyone, mainly through health insurance (Campbell and Ikegami 1998; Maruyama, Shimizu, and Tsurumaki 1998). This fundamental egalitarian principle has been successful, but it has sacrificed or ignored efficiency and amenity in health care delivery. Japan's health care service is at a turning point. Rationalization and competition are being introduced. In this situation, it is becoming important how equity and patients' rights should be protected.

References

Anesaki, Masahira. 1977. "Problems of Health and Medical Sociology." Pp. 401–2 in Japanese Society of Health and Medical Sociology. *Achievements and Problems of Health and Medical Sociology*. Tokyo: Kakiuchi Shuppan. (In Japanese).

Campbell, John C. and Naoki Ikegami. 1998. *The Art of Balance in Health Policy*. Cambridge: Cambridge University Press.

Japan Ministry of Health and Welfare. 1999. *A Guide Book for Understanding Disease Related to Daily Habits*. Tokyo.

Maruyama, Meridith E., Louise P. Shimizu, and Nancy S. Tsurumaki. 1995 (1st edition) and 1998 (revised edition). *Japan Health Handbook*. Tokyo, New York, London: Kodansha International.

Munakata, T. 1990. "Research Report on the Mental Health of Overseas Japanese Business People and Family." Tokyo: Japan Overseas Medical Fund.

——. 1991. *Theory of Stress Management*. Tokyo: Shogakukan.

Munakata, T., Department of Health Narashino City, and Chiba Medical Association. 1991. "A Longitudinal Study of Stress and Mental Health in a Community Population." Tokyo: Japan Ministry of Health and Welfare.

National Index of Health & Welfare: National Tendency of Health [Kokumin Eisei No Doukou]. 1998. Tokyo: Japan Health and Welfare Statistics Association.

Powell, Margaret and Masahira Anesaki. 1990. *Health Care in Japan*. London and New York: Routledge.

26

The Great Reversal: Transformation of Health Care in the People's Republic of China

Meei-shia Chen

On October 1, 1949, Mao Zedong proclaimed the founding of the People's Republic of China (PRC) from the Gate of Heavenly Peace (*Tienanmen*) of its capital, Beijing. During the three decades after 1949, the PRC, under Mao's leadership, developed a central planning socialist system that emphasized public ownership and welfare, mass-based collectivism and egalitarianism, and de-emphasized the role of the market in the delivery of various services and products. But in 1978 Deng Xiaoping took over the leadership of China and set China onto a new course: the PRC has been undergoing dramatic market reform, privatizing formerly public systems, enterprises, and institutions, de-collectivizing rural communes, emphasizing individual responsibilities, and allowing an increase in social inequality (Hinton 1990; Leung 1994; Wong 1994; Weil 1996; MacFarquhar 1997; Meisner 1999). This political, economic, and social transformation was described as "the great reversal" by Hinton (Hinton 1990), the author of the classic, *Fanshen: A Documentary of Revolution in a Chinese Village* (Hinton 1966).

During Mao's era, the PRC impressed the world by developing an innovative and successful health care system, with a great emphasis on preventive public health. This system included the development of the cooperative medical system; the use of barefoot doctors; the implementation of health programs through mass movements; the integration of traditional Chinese medicine and western medicine; and increased emphasis on the health of the rural population. However, during the past two decades of market reform, the PRC transformed its health care system into a very different one. Increasing emphasis has been placed in curative medicine and the cooperative medical system has been mostly dismantled. Barefoot doctors no longer exist – most have been professionalized by becoming village doctors and many moved to more profitable jobs. Mass mobilization is no longer an official imperative and there is a new focus on medical technology. The policy towards the integration of traditional Chinese medicine and western medicine has been shifting toward a greater reliance on western medicine; and increasingly, resources have been shifted from rural to urban areas. Indeed, the drastic transformation of health care in the PRC since the market reform was launched in 1978 represents "the great reversal" of the former health care system developed during Mao's era. In this chapter, we will (1) discuss the major components of the health care system before reform and its impact on health status; (2) describe the changes in the health care system which occurred after the reform and the consequences of these changes on health and health care; and (3) the implications of the great reversal of health care for China and the world.

HEALTH CARE BEFORE MARKET REFORM

In the century before the PRC was founded, China suffered from many devastating civil as well as anti-imperialist wars. The PRC inherited a land of depressed economic and social conditions and of people with rampant infectious, parasitic, and nutritional diseases (Sidel and Sidel 1973). Life expectancy in the immediate postwar period is estimated to have been less than 35 years and the infant mortality rate, about 250 per 1000 life births (Jamison et al. 1984). The health and medical workforces then were woefully inadequate in the face of the enormous health problems facing the Chinese people. The majority of the medical providers were traditional Chinese medical practitioners and herbalists, many of whom lacked adequate training for preventing or treating epidemic diseases (Sidel and Sidel 1973; Sidel and Sidel 1982). Nationwide preventive programs did not exist (Sidel and Sidel 1973).

Confronted with these conditions, the PRC had to develop a health care system which could effectively deal with its people's immediate health problems. The most common model adopted by developing countries facing similar health conditions at that time was a western model or modified western model. The major characteristics of this model are (1) its heavy dependence on expensively trained and highly skilled and specialized medical personnel; (2) its emphasis on high medical technology; (3) its curative orientation; and (4) its focus on individual health care rather than public health projects (Li and Wang 1995; Wilenski 1976). This model may be suitable for the industrialized countries where mortality rates have fallen along with the increase in the standard of living, level of nutrition, and sanitation. However, for the developing countries, this model proved inappropriate. Limited national resources prevented these countries from training sufficient numbers of highly-skilled western medical providers fast enough to meet urgent health care needs. Moreover, once graduated, the majority of these medical providers clustered in the urban areas, leaving rural residents with inadequate care; costly medical technology is mostly available for urban residents; curative-oriented medical services and personal health care provided by small numbers of highly-skilled medical personnel cannot effectively resolve the uncontrolled infectious and nutritional diseases of the poverty-stricken population in particularly poor rural areas (Wilenski 1976).

The PRC was one of the few countries which moved away from the conventional western model and developed an innovative system which depended heavily on less skilled health workers, whose training can be completed in a much shorter time; developed labor-intensive approaches rather than capital-intensive medical technology; emphasized prevention and primary care; and concentrated more on public health programs than on individualized care (Rifkin 1972; Rifkin 1973; Wilenski 1976; Maru 1977; Wilenski 1977; Blendon 1979; Sidel and Sidel 1982).

Soon after the revolution, the PRC developed four guidelines for its health and medical work (Wilenski 1976; Sidel and Sidel 1983). These guidelines set the framework for the development of PRC health care system for the following three decades. They are as follows:

1   The health care system should serve the workers, peasants, and soldiers;
2   Prevention should be put first;
3   Traditional Chinese medicine should be integrated with western medicine; and
4   Health work should be carried out through "mass movements."

Serving the Workers, Peasants, and Soldiers and Prevention First

Before the PRC was founded, peasants and workers were, socioeconomically, the most disadvantaged population and infectious, nutritional, and parasitic diseases were most prevalent among them. The PRC, in building a socialist country, held peasants, workers, and soldiers[1] to be the most important groups served by the state, and this was reflected in the orientation of its health care system (Sidel 1975; Wu 1975). Prevention, rather than the treatment of diseases, was also emphasized. During the three decades after 1949, the PRC, compared to virtually all countries in the world, placed much greater emphasis on preventive rather than curative health services (Jamison et al. 1984).

Major public health campaigns were launched to improve environmental sanitation; to eliminate "four pests" – rats, flies, mosquitoes, and bedbugs;[2] to eliminate venereal diseases; to control the vectors of major endemic disorders such as malaria and schistosomiasis; and to immunize the population against many infectious diseases such as smallpox, diphtheria, and tuberculosis (Heller 1973; Sidel and Sidel 1973; Wilenski 1976; Jamison et al. 1984; The Editorial Committee for New China's Historical Experience of Preventive Medicine 1991). To ensure the successful implementation of these campaigns, the PRC developed a basic preventive health infrastructure throughout the country. Many public health workers were trained and sanitation and epidemic prevention centers or stations were developed in rural communes[3] and urban districts (Heller 1973; Rifkin 1973; Sidel 1975). These centers/stations carried out and managed these public health campaigns by coordinating with health workers from production brigade health stations, commune health centers, and other health and medical institutions (Rifkin 1972; Heller 1973). The most unique feature of these campaigns was that they were carried out through mass mobilization. This mass mobilization was essential for the successful implementation of the public health campaigns and will be discussed in the later section.

Cooperative Medical System

Cooperative Medical System (CMS) (*Ho-zuo Yi-Liau*) is a financing and delivery system in rural China which provided peasants in communes with preventive services, primary care and curative services. In 1949, about 85 percent of the 800 million Chinese lived in rural areas (Sidel 1975; Hu 1976). Before the CMS was fully developed, peasants had to pay for their medical care on a fee-for-service basis (Feng et al. 1995). However, with the rural area undergoing agricultural collectivization, this fee-for-service system was becoming an anomaly within the collectivized system (Zhang 1960). Subsequently, experiments with cooperative health care organization and financing began in the mid-1950s, when the trend of agricultural collectivization was on the rise (Zhang 1992; Feng et al. 1995). Because CMS was effective in implementing preventive programs, ensuring the early diagnosis and treatment of peasants' illnesses, and consolidating the commune health organization, the Communist Party and the government encouraged and facilitated its development in rural areas (Zhang 1959). CMS was developed further and expanded rapidly in many rural communes during the Cultural Revolution in the 1960s and 1970s. Up to 1976, about 93 percent of communes had established CMS (Zhang 1985; Feng et al. 1995; Carrin et al. 1999).

Commune welfare funds and membership fees were the two major funding sources for CMS. The contribution from collective funds varied among communes, from 30 to 90 percent, with an average of 50 percent. The annual membership fees ranged from 0.5 percent to 2 percent of peasant income (Carrin et al. 1999). The membership fee was calculated from the commune's previous year's CMS expenditure and thus could change over a period of time.[4] In most communes, peasants had to pay a nominal registration fee and part of the hospital fees if they were referred to the county hospitals for the treatment of more serious diseases for which the CMS clinic did not have the appropriate skills or facilities. CMS provided health education, family planning, immunization, communicable disease reporting, and other preventive services, and basic medical care (Zhu 1989). A management committee composed of brigade leaders, barefoot doctors, and peasants managed the CMS (Zhang 1966; Zhu 1989). The barefoot doctor – to be discussed later – was the key health worker for the CMS.

Because the commune financed CMS itself (primarily with collective funds and membership fees), it was highly motivated to contain the cost of CMS (Wen and Hays 1976). The cost-containment strategies were carried out at four levels. First, the central state and local governments encouraged communes to ensure a successful implementation of the "prevention first" policy and public health campaigns so that fewer diseases would occur in the commune and consequently would reduce the medical expenses of CMS. Secondly, the CMS endeavored to provide patients with preventive or primary care before peasants' disease became worse as they were aware that it is more costly to treat diseases once they have become more serious. Thirdly, in order to reduce the cost of drugs, CMS avoided the over-use or abuse of drugs and the communes grew, collected, manufactured, and utilized extensively local herb medicine rather than more expensive western medicine. Fourthly, CMS limited the referrals to county hospitals where the cost of care was higher than that provided by the CMS clinics. The barefoot doctor served as the gatekeeper for these referrals (Zhang 1965a; Zhang 1965b; Kwangchow Provincial Institute of Maternal and Child Health Care 1978; Hu 1981; Zhu et al. 1989).

CMS provided peasants with access to basic care regardless of their economic situation. It also saved the peasants' time which they previously had to spend in traveling long distances to seek medical care; CMS made the primary care services accessible and available from the barefoot doctors or other health workers at the level of production team and production brigade, geographically close to the peasants. In addition, it strengthened the status of the commune health center and the training of its personnel as funding was ensured (Zhang 1965a; Feng et al. 1995).

In urban areas, the two major types of health financing and delivery systems were the Public Expense Medical Service (*Qong-fei yi-liao*) and Labor Insurance Medical Service (*Laobao yi-liao*). The former, introduced in 1951 and financed by the government, covered the state cadres and students, accounting for approximately 2 percent of the population in China. The latter, also introduced in 1951 and financed by the factories and firms, covered fully the medical expenses of their workers and staff members and 50 percent of those of their family members (Hu 1976).

Barefoot Doctors

The term, "barefoot doctor (Chi Jiao Yi Sheng)"[5] was the nickname the peasants in Shanghai rural area affectionately gave to their fellow peasants who spent part of their time farming and part of their time doing medical work (*ban nong ban yi*) in the late 1950s (Report of An Investigation from Shanghai 1968). In 1958 – at the beginning of the Great Leap Forward[6] and at the peak of agricultural collectivization and socialist idealism (Zhu et al. 1989; Meisner 1999) – a large number of physicians in Shanghai organized themselves to go to the rural areas and train, in short term classes, a great number of peasants as health-workers. The idea was that the peasant health-workers, while providing their fellow peasants with health and medical services, would not be divorced from production (Report of An Investigation from Shanghai 1968; Peking Review 1974; Peking Review 1975). During the Cultural Revolution, at the same time as the CMS was expanding rapidly in rural communes, the number of barefoot doctors was also increasing dramatically (Zhu et al. 1989). By 1978, there were 1.8 million barefoot doctors in rural China (Chen et al. 1993). On average, there were about 3 barefoot doctors in each production brigade (Wang 1975).

Each production team chose its barefoot doctor. The most important criteria was his/her willingness to "serve the people" in an unselfish way. Other criteria such as education, age, and personal interests were secondary (Sidel 1972a; Ronaghy and Solter 1974; Huang 1988). The pattern of training of the barefoot doctors differed among communes. However, all emphasized prevention and the treatment of common illnesses and the training period was about three to six months (Wang 1975). The training program was carried out most often in the county hospitals and sometimes in commune health centers or in the production brigade by a mobile medical team coming from the urban areas (Lyle 1980). Great emphasis was placed on the on-the-job supervised experience and continuing education,[7] of which the expenses were paid by CMS (Wang 1975; Lyle 1980).

The work of the barefoot doctors varied among communes or among production brigades within the commune (Sidel 1972a). However, they had in common certain duties including preventive work such as health education, immunization, environmental sanitation, first aid, and public health campaigns and the provision of primary care for common or less serious illnesses (Sidel 1972b; Hu 1976). Note that these duties are also the major work of the CMS, as barefoot doctors were responsible for carrying out the work of the CMS. The barefoot doctor received his/her income similarly to his fellow peasants. The commune worker's income depended on the total income of his/her commune and the number of "work points" that he/she collected. The barefoot doctor's health and medical work was also considered part of agricultural work and calculated by "work points" (Sidel and Sidel 1983; White 1998).

The system of barefoot doctors in rural China, in comparison with the western model of health personnel training, has several unique features. First, a large number of barefoot doctors can be trained in a short period of time to meet the urgent health and medical personnel needs of rural areas. Second, because the barefoot doctors work together with their fellow peasants, they know who is ill and what diseases to watch for at various seasons better than western-trained medical providers coming from urban or other areas. Third, the barefoot doctor, having the same role (i.e. being a peasant) as the patients treated by him/her, can serve better as the advocate of his/her patients than a highly-skilled medical provider coming from a different area. Further, engaging both in farming and health work helps reduce the gap between manual and intellectual work and consequently avoids the problem of the elite medical provider having a much higher status than that of patients, as is often the case in a society based on the western medical model (Report of An Investigation from Shanghai 1968; Wei 1975; Miao 1976; Sidel and Sidel 1983). Fourth, the use of barefoot doctors popularized not only health care but also health knowledge, and consequently health care was no longer a privilege for certain groups and medical providers were not the only ones who had access to medical knowledge (Chinese Medical Association 1974; Chu and Tien 1974; Wang 1975).

Lastly, the use of barefoot doctors de-professionalized medical providers and revolutionized the conventional western medical education.[8] The western medical professions are usually resistant to the training of less-skilled health workers who can perform simple health work and treat common diseases on the ground that these health workers would lower the professional standard (Kao 1974; Wilenski 1976). The use of barefoot doctors broke this professional resistance and created a new role for health workers. In sum, the PRC, using its imagination, trained a great supply of barefoot doctors within a relatively short period of time by maximizing its use of its most abundant resource – labor, and minimizing its dependence on expensive high technology or highly-skilled medical personnel. As a result of this policy, the PRC was able to successfully meet the great challenge of the serious lack of medical personnel in rural areas (Wang 1975; Wilenski 1976).

Mass Mobilization in Health Work

To the CCP, the revolutionary war could only be waged and won by mobilizing and depending on the masses (Mao 1934; Xu 1960; Wilenski 1976). This tradition was based on the conviction that ordinary people, given the right kind of knowledge, appropriate motivation, and power, can resolve complex problems (Horn 1972; Chin 1973). The "mass line" approach was applied to health work because Chinese leaders recognized that rapid and dramatic improvement in the health status of the masses could not be achieved without the full participation of the masses (Yang 1958; Sidel and Sidel 1983). By getting the Chinese people involved in the health campaign, they became more knowledgeable and more conscious about their own health problems and thus were more likely to change their behavior in order to protect their health. Another dominant theme for the PRC's nation-building under Mao's leadership was the national pursuit of "self-reliance (*zi li geng sheng*)." The mass line approach in health is also based on China's "self-reliance" policy, in which ordinary Chinese people were mobilized to solve their own health problems (Sidel 1975; Wilenski 1976).

Mass mobilization was realized mainly through "patriotic health movements." These health campaigns were usually nationwide. Although the campaigns were conducted about four to five times throughout the year, the most intensive mobilization was usually carried out during the slack season of the agricultural and industrial work. The patriotic health movement committee at each of the national, provincial, county, commune, and brigade levels was responsible for the implementation of the movement (Guizhou South East Miao and Dong Minority Autonomy Region Local History Editorial Committee 1993; Guangzhou Local History Editorial Committee 1995). The committee at the brigade level was often chaired by the brigade barefoot doctor (Jamison et al. 1984). During the campaign, all means of communication (e.g. newspapers, radio, pamphlets, wall posters, cartoons, lectures, group discussions, drama, street propaganda, exhibits, etc.) were used to encourage the people to engage in simple public health activities from street cleaning to burying snails (Wilenski 1976; Sandbach 1977; Schwartz 1977; Sidel and Sidel 1982). The campaign stressed preventive work including immunization, environmental sanitation, and the elimination of disease-causing pests.

Integration of Traditional Chinese Medicine with Western Medicine

Traditional Chinese Medicine (TCM) is the oldest form of medical knowledge and practice in world history. Over four thousand years of Chinese civilization, TCM has been essential to the maintenance of the health and thus the survival of the Chinese people. With the introduction of western medicine into China in the late nineteenth century, however, the efficacy of TCM and its practitioners have been under critical challenge. Strongly influenced by western scientific ideology and impressed with the remarkable advancement of western technology, many Chinese people favored western scientific medicine over their own traditional medicine. Western medical practitioners and others in Chinese society have criticized TCM as "unscientific," "superstitious," and "unreliable" (Croizier 1968; Lee 1981). Traditional medicine has been similarly undermined in many other developing countries. Very few countries, in developing their national health care system, were able to maintain the status of the practitioners of their national traditional medicine. Nor were they able to incorporate these practitioners into their formal health care system successfully (Wilenski 1976). Indeed, the health care system the PRC inherited was based on the western model which greatly suppressed TCM practitioners (Chen 1947; Wilenski 1976).

When the PRC was founded, China had very few western- trained medical providers and the majority of them practiced in urban areas. Nevertheless, more than ten times the number of traditional practitioners were available in both rural and urban areas (Sidel and Sidel 1973; Wilenski 1976). It was necessary to rely on them in order to serve the people more effectively. As a result, the PRC declared in the early 1950s the integration of traditional and western medicines as one of the four basic guidelines for the organization of the PRC's health care system (Wilenski 1976; Sidel and Sidel 1982; Guangzhou Local History Editorial Committee 1995). From 1954 to 1960 Mao intensified the PRC's policy of promoting traditional medicine. State policy stipulated that western medicine must learn from TCM in their practices as a part of their continuing education. Further, schools of western medicine were required to include TCM in their curricula. Many national TCM colleges were built and TCM practitioners trained (Croizier 1968; Hillier and Jewell 1983; Huang and Lin 1986). Intensive research into the efficacy of TCM, including acupuncture and various herbal remedies, was conducted and the new discovery of TCM remedies were made (Wilenski 1976; Anching Local History Editorial Committee 1996).

Rural Emphasis in Health and Medical Work

Many of the PRC's public health programs such as patriotic health campaigns started right after the founding of the state in both urban and rural areas. However, the PRC's policy toward the provision of rural medical services was not firmly established until 1965 (Hu 1976; Wilenski 1977). A greater proportion of the public health workers trained during the 1950s were concentrated in urban areas and many more medical and sanitation facilities were built in urban areas (Heller 1973), while most of the resources of the Ministry of Public Health were spent in urban areas as well (Lyle 1980). This situation was becoming dissatisfactory for some state leaders who were concerned about the rural population's needs. By 1955, Mao had started criticizing the Ministry of Public Health for being more responsive to urban than to rural medical needs (Lampton 1977). Indeed, until the mid-1960s, only 20–40 percent of the physicians were located in rural areas where about 85 percent of the population resided (Hu 1976). The famous June 26 directive issued by Mao in 1965 initiated severe criticism of the urban bias of the Ministry of Public Health and set the new directions for rural emphasis in medical and health work:

> Tell the Ministry of Public Health that it only works for 15 percent of the entire population. Furthermore, this 15 percent is made up mostly of the "overlords." The broad ranks of the peasants cannot obtain medical treatment and also do not receive medicine. The Ministry of Public Health is not a people's ministry. It should be called the Urban Public Health Ministry or, the Ministry of Public Health for Urban Overlords....In medicine and health, put the stress on the rural areas! (Wilenski 1976; Mao 1974)

Mao's directive also inspired a huge flow of urban physicians and health workers into the countryside in the "rotation" *(Xia Xiang)* (Qien 1965; The Chinese Communist Party Committee of the Peking Tuberculosis Research Institute 1975; Yuan 1975). It was estimated that in some urban hospitals, up to one-third of the staff was practicing in rural areas. These medical providers spent about six months to one year – usually in mobile medical teams – in rural areas. During their rotations, they provided medical care and preventive services, trained barefoot doctors, organized and educated the community in health protection and promotion, and obtained their own "re-education" by learning about the peasants' health problems (Sidel 1972b). Many of these urban medical and health providers – approximately 100,000 – settled in rural areas (Maddin 1974; Wu 1975). After Mao's directive was issued, the state placed much greater emphasis on the health and medical work of the rural areas. For example, the central government allocated about 60 percent of the national health expenditures to the rural areas after the Cultural Revolution. This compared to 20–30 percent before 1965 (Hu 1980).

The Impact of the Health Care System

The above-described health care system developed in PRC before market reforms, although impressive in many aspects, also had its problems. For example, even a decade after Mao's criticism of the Ministry of Public Health for its urban bias, medical care remained more accessible and of higher technical quality in urban areas (Sidel and Sidel 1983). The financial self-reliance of the CMS gave the commune the total control of its own people's medical care and health protection but also led to disparity of care among communes, with the rich ones having an adequate system but the poor ones receiving inadequate care (Huang 1988). The quality of barefoot doctors was uneven because of their highly decentralized training (Hsu 1974). Some barefoot doctors were criticized for occasionally attempting to perform tasks too complex for their level of skill and training (Hsu 1974; Sidel and Sidel 1983). In addition, in the poor communes, barefoot doctors' turnover rates were high because of their low income and heavy workload (Hsu 1974). Further, despite the national policy of encouraging the integration of TCM and western medicine, traditional medical practitioners continued to have less status than western medical doctors (Sidel and Sidel 1983).

Nevertheless, as pointed out by Sidel and Sidel (1983), the above problems are small compared to the internationally-recognized achievement the PRC made in developing a successful health care system, breaking with the conventional western model, and developing innovative programs suitable for the unique conditions which China faced during the first three decades after the founding of the state. Indeed, impressed with this achievement, the World Health Organization made the PRC's health care system the model for its worldwide Primary Health Care initiative formulated at the 1978 Alma Ata conference (Jamison et al. 1984; Yang et al. 1991; Chen et al. 1993; White 1998). Furthermore, the PRC's unique health care innovations have profoundly influenced how the health care professionals in other developing countries think about designing health care programs suitable for their own countries rather than copying blindly the western model (Jamison et al. 1984).

The improvement in the Chinese people's health status after 1949 is also internationally recognized: many epidemic diseases such as smallpox, cholera, and venereal diseases have been eliminated and parasitic diseases such as schistosomiasis and malaria have been greatly reduced; life expectancy rose from less than 35 years in the immediate post-1949 period to almost 70 years in the early 1980s; infant mortality rate declined from an estimated 250 per 1000 life births in 1950 to a rate lower than 50 in 1981. In 1980, the PRC's life expectancy was longer than many countries with substantially higher income levels. The increase in life expectancy in the PRC between 1960 and 1980 exceeded other countries in the world to a very significant extent.[9] The World Bank report on China's health sector hailed this success in health to be the "first Chinese health care revolution (Jamison et al. 1984)." It should be noted, however, that the PRC's success in health care was not the only factor contributing to this great improvement in health status. Increasing levels of education, availability of food, more equal distribution of food, and the improvements in water supply and sanitation all contributed to this impressive advancement in Chinese people's health status (Jamison et al. 1984). Indeed, the PRC's health and medical work was only one part – albeit an integral part – of the restructuring of the whole Chinese society.

The characteristics of any country's health care system are determined by the country's political and economic system (Hsu 1977; Albrecht and Tang 1990). The unique public health programs and health care system the PRC developed during the three decades after 1949, as pointed out by many researchers (e.g. Liang et al. 1973; Vogel 1973; Hsu 1977; Blendon 1979; Parmelee et al. 1982; Sidel and Sidel 1982), were possible because of the particular configuration of political, economic, social, and ideological conditions during that period of time. However, the market reform orchestrated under Deng's leadership completely undermined these foundations and the health care system based on these foundations would soon crumble. The reformed health care system would in turn reflect the political, economic, social, and ideological characteristics of the new societal structure developed by Deng and other market reformers.

HEALTH CARE SYSTEM UNDER MARKET REFORM

The health condition faced by the PRC in the late 1970s, when Deng and his government launched the market reform, was substantially better than that confronting the PRC in 1949. Nevertheless, the Chinese people in this period continued to be afflicted by many old and new health problems. Parasitic and infectious diseases were still prevalent in some part of China, particularly in rural areas. Furthermore, China was undergoing a health transition, with chronic diseases such as cancer, heart disease, and stroke replacing infectious and endemic diseases as leading causes of deaths (Jamison et al. 1984; Bumgarner 1990; Zhang and Chen 1996; Ministry of Health 1997).

This change in health condition, although serious, should have been a manageable challenge for the PRC's market reformers, considering that the reformers had inherited from Mao's era (1) a well-organized health care system which had been proved to be effective in improving Chinese people's health; and (2) a much larger health care workforce than in earlier decades after 1949.[10] Therefore, it seemed logical that the PRC would use the already-established health care system to continue the nation's previous endeavor to eradicate the infectious and endemic diseases still prevalent particularly in rural areas. For the prevention, control, and treatment of the newly-emerging chronic diseases, it might also have seemed natural for the health sector to continue adopting the existing programs (such as the "prevention first" emphasis and the mass mobilization program) while further upgrading and refining the health workers' skills and developing new programs for the prevention and control of chronic diseases. However, the PRC's reformers did not follow this path.

As a result of the market reforms that were underway, the system of rural communes had by the early 1980s been largely dismantled, agricultural production was de-collectivized, and a new "household responsibility system"[11] was introduced. The market reform and the responsibility system also swept through urban areas. The PRC devolved economic decision-making to individual enterprises and institutions that would operate on a profit-making basis (Meisner 1999). The market reform in both the rural and urban areas undermined the political, financial, economic, and ideological foundation of the health care system and consequently the former system has been collapsing. Furthermore, the reformers, many of whom were victims of the Cultural Revolution (the most prominent being Deng Xiaoping himself who was ousted from power twice during 1966 to 1976 (Weil 1996)), dismissed all policies – including health care innovations – developed, expanded, or popularized during the Cultural Revolution (Zhu et al. 1989; Chen et al. 1993). The health policies and programs described earlier were consequently abandoned rapidly after the reform. Instead, the reformers moved the PRC's health care system toward a western model – curative-oriented, personal care-oriented, high-technology-oriented, hospital-based, capital-intensive, commodified, and urban-biased – the exact model that the PRC had rejected during the early years of the founding of the state (Yang et al. 1991; Smith 1993; Henderson et al. 1994).

The Neglect of Public Health Programs and the Move toward Curative Services

Along with the market reform, the government stipulated that health care financing be based on the principle of financial self-sufficiency (*Zi Fu Ying Kui*) (World Bank 1992). As a result, the economic environment created by the reform all over China has become inhospitable to public health goals. The epidemic prevention center no longer has adequate funds from the government[12] for widespread surveillance, sanitation, control, or immunization programs. In an effort to become self-sufficient financially, the center has been providing services that have few health benefits but which can help the center recover costs,[13] rather than providing essential preventive services or implementing public health programs that are not profitable[14] (World Bank 1992). Further, the center has been charging fees for preventive health services such as immunization and treatment services for infectious diseases such as tuberculosis. As a result, the access to such services, particularly for the poor, has been reduced (Hsiao 1984; World Bank 1992, 1997; Tang and Gu 1996). Organizationally, because each health institution is financially independent, the center no longer has the power to solicit the collaboration from other health institutions[15] (World Bank 1992).

Many other health institutions have been oriented toward treatment and curative services with a relative neglect of preventative public health programs because the former are more profitable (Wegman 1982; World Bank 1992; Cheung 1995; Bloom 1998; Cai et al. 1998; Henderson and Stroup 1998). The health sector has increased the percentage of health expenditure for hospitals and treatment costs but decreased that for prevention programs. Increasing amounts of health-care funds are being used to purchase advanced medical technology while the funding for disease prevention has stagnated (Henderson et al. 1988). In short, prevention now has very low priority in health budget planning (Hu 1987; World Bank 1992).

The Dismantling of the Cooperative Medical System

The CMS was integrally linked to the collectivization system (White 1998). "Without the agricultural collectivization movement, there would not have existed a rural cooperative medical system," Qien Xinzhong, PRC's former Public Health Minister, candidly pointed out (Qien 1993). With the disappearance of communes and the completion of the de-collectivization in rural areas, the political and ideological backing and financial support for the CMS from the state was eroded (Young 1986; Zhu et al. 1989; Chen et al. 1993; Liu et al. 1995). Regardless of the strong support for the CMS among peasants, the CMS were entirely dismantled. In fact, some villages wanted to maintain their CMS but were discouraged from doing so (Chen et al. 1993). As a result, the percentage of villages having CMS decreased from more than 90 percent in 1976 to 4.8 percent in 1986 (Feng et al. 1995). In the 1990s, even with the backing of local government and the encouragement of the central state, this percentage was only increased to 7 percent in 1997 (Tang 1997).

With the collapse of CMS, most villages could not afford to pay their health workers a salary and thus these workers had to move on to other jobs. Many village health clinics (formerly brigade health stations) were sold to individual medical practitioners or contracted out to them. Before the market reform, all health clinics were collectively owned but by 1990 this proportion had been reduced to only 47 percent (Feng et al. 1995). Primary health care in rural areas has largely fallen under private control (Aldis 1989; Hillier and Zheng 1990). By the late 1990s, about 90 percent of peasants were paying for their health care out of their own pockets on the fee-for-service basis (Aldis 1989; World Bank 1997). This lack of insurance protection and limited access to care is particularly serious in poor rural areas (Henderson and Cohen 1982; Gu et al. 1993). The profit-orientation of the private practitioners leads to the neglect of preventive services and the move toward the provision of curative services because the former are not as profitable as the latter. Peasants even have to pay for preventive services such as immunization and maternal and child health services (Aldis 1989; Zhu et al. 1989; Chen et al. 1993; Feng et al. 1995).

Alarmed by the serious problem of financial access to health care in rural – particularly poor – areas, the PRC government has been promoting rural health prepayment schemes – similar to the Health Maintenance Organization in the US (Cretin et al. 1990; Ho 1995; Tang 1997; Bloom and Tang 1999). Nevertheless, participation in such schemes is voluntary, and studies have reported that few peasants are persuaded of the value of insurance schemes and consequently many are reluctant to engage in the risk-sharing these schemes are based upon. In fact, some such plans have collapsed (Tang 1997; Bloom and Tang 1999; Carrin et al. 1999). This insurance plan may be possible in villages with sucessful enterprises which generate high profit rates (Khan et al. 1996) but is difficult in poorer areas (Gu et al. 1993; Tang 1997).

The market reform has also had significant impact on health care in urban areas. Two major insurance systems – the Public Expense Medical Service and Labor Insurance Medical Service – have been undergoing profound changes. The cost of these two insurance systems has been escalating since the reform due to, among other reasons, general inflation, aging of the population, rapid adoption of high-tech medicine, and the abusive use of expensive drugs (Liu and Hsiao 1995). For example, the annual rate of increase for the periods 1952–78, 1978–85, and 1985–9 was 3.1, 8.2, and 24.4 percent respectively (Liu and Hsiao 1995). This cost escalation and the eroding ability of the state to transfer sufficient funds to the insurance system has led the state to rationalize the systems by instituting a nationwide copayment policy and decentralizing the financial responsibility to cities and enterprises (Bo and Dong 1993; Gu and Liang 1993; Ding 1994; Cai 1995; Grogan 1995; Zhou 1995).

Consequently, public employees and state enterprise workers are no longer guaranteed free health services. Further, this rationalization also led to a great inequality in financial access among cities and among enterprises; the public employees in the poorer cities and workers in the enterprises with low or no profit rates have to pay a higher percentage of copayments and are covered by fewer services. In addition, as an increasing number of people migrate to the cities and the number of joint ventures and collective and private enterprises grows (which the government does not require to provide health insurance coverage for), an increasing number of people in urban areas are left uncovered by any form of health insurance (Grogan 1995).

From "Barefoot Doctors" to "Village Doctors"

Before the reform, the commune's work point system and the collective funding of the CMS supported the work being done by barefoot doctors (Cheung 1995). Unsurprisingly, with the dismantling of the communes and the CMS, the number of barefoot doctors decreased from 1.8 million in 1975 to 1.4 million in 1982 and then to 1.2 million in 1984[16] (Sidel and Sidel 1983; Zhu et al. 1989; Smith 1993). The household responsibility system and the increase in the price of agricultural products after 1978 made agricultural work more lucrative. Therefore, many barefoot doctors spent less time in health work than on farming. Further, many found jobs in township or village enterprises, engaged in trades, or migrated to cities to find higher-income jobs (Zhu et al. 1989).

One of the most important themes of Deng's reform is its emphasis on "expert" (professional skills) over "red" (political attitudes) (Meisner 1999). With the reform underway, barefoot doctors are required to take examinations and once passed, they are certified as "village doctors." The training period has become longer – six months or more (Zhu et al. 1989). Upgrading the barefoot doctors' skills is imperative as the demand for better quality health services grows stronger and the treatment of the more prevalent chronic diseases is more complex. However, the training now focuses more on theoretical rather than practical issues and more on clinical and curative treatments than on prevention (Sidel and Sidel 1982; Koplan et al. 1985). Many barefoot doctors want to become certified because certification advances one's reputation and brings higher income, possible government employment, promotion, or subsidies (Chen et al. 1993; Smith 1993; White 1998). Most village doctors are in private practice and thus are profit-driven. There have been many reports of over-prescribed drugs, unnecessary injections, and other artificially induced demands and as a result, practitioners neglect less profitable activities like providing preventive services (Young 1989). In sum, the professionalization of barefoot doctors, in which they were transformed into village doctors, and the subsequent privatization of health-care has led to the loss of the innovative essence of the barefoot doctor system – the fact that it was designed to be a de- professionalized grass-roots health care system, intended to meet the needs of peasants. Health care is back under the control of medical professionals.

Mass Mobilization Dropped out of Health Work

The integration of health work with mass movements has been ostensibly dropped out of the national guidelines for health work (see, e.g., World Bank 1992; Xu 1995). In Mao's era, the commune would subsidize peasants, based on the work point system, for participating in the patriotic health campaigns (Cheung 1995). Now that this system no longer exists, the number of peasants involved and their time spent in the health programs decreased dramatically

(Sleigh et al. 1998). The patriotic health movement committees at various levels
lack the authority to call for the participation of the health workers and peasants. This is partly due to the shortage of funding and the decreased integration
between levels – village, township, and county – of health authorities (Cheung
1995). The mass-based organizations that helped mobilize people for health
campaigns before the reform, including the Women's Federation and Communist
Youth League, do not have the government's support for their involvement in the
campaigns (Cheung 1995). Most organizations have been streamlined under the
market reform and as a result their ability to get involved in additional activities
such as health mass-movement is greatly reduced.[17] The inspiring atmosphere of
cooperation for the community's health promotion and the ideology of "serving
the people," which were an integral part of the success of the mass-mobilization
for health in Mao's era, have been replaced by competitive value of the market and
an ideology which holds that "getting rich is glorious" (Sidel 1993; Cheung 1995).

From the Integration of Traditional Chinese Medicine with Western Medicine to a Greater Reliance on Western Medicine

The support for TCM remains an important aspect of the PRC's national health
policy (World Bank 1992; Xu 1995). But there are clear indications that, in
comparison with the before-reform era, TCM is not as prominent and in contrast,
there is increasing reliance on western medicine (Zhang 1981; New 1982; Sidel
and Sidel 1982; New and Cheung 1984; Zhu et al. 1989). As a result of the
reforms herbal gardens are nowadays not as common as they were before the
reforms (New 1982). Many herbal medicine stores have been closed. The research
on TCM or herbal medicine is now a lower priority in the local government's
health agenda (Zhang 1981). With the dismantling of the communes, there is no
more collective support or funding for organizing the mass-scale expeditions to
collect, grow, and produce traditional Chinese or herbal medicine. A study of the
villages of southwest of Yunnan Province, for example, revealed that before the
reform 40–80 percent of the medicines used in these villages were based on TCM.
But by the 1990s about 80 percent of their medicines relied on western pharmaceuticals (White 1998). Foreign pharmaceutical companies, in collusion with
hospital interests, have been importing a great quantity of western pharmaceuticals into the Chinese medical care market. The manufacturers of TCM, not as
competitive, are losing their market share (China Times 1998).

The Shift of Emphasis from Rural to Urban Areas

The inequality between rural and urban areas in health resources and health
status declined during Mao's era, particularly after Mao's June 26 directive was
declared in 1965. However, this trend has been reversed under Deng's market
reform (Henderson 1990). After the reform, the state health budget for the urban
areas increased significantly at the expense of the rural areas (Smith 1993; Liu et
al. 1995; Hillier and Shen 1996; Bloom 1998). The state has been providing and
allocating greater resources to train highly-skilled medical personnel, construct
capital-intensive medical facilities and hospitals, and purchase capital-intensive

equipment, all of which tend to be concentrated in urban areas (Young 1989; Hsiao 1995; Bloom 1998; Liu et al. 1999). As a result, the local and national governments have been withdrawing their resources from rural areas. The ratio of health expenditure per capita between urban and rural areas increased from three times in 1981 to five times in 1990s (Hillier and Shen 1996). Rural health centers have also experienced serious shortage of skilled personnel. Moreover, their personnel receive little supervision and in-service training (Young 1989; Shi 1993; Liu et al. 1995).

Although "serving peasants, workers, and soldiers" is still part of the national rhetoric, peasants and workers are no longer the major national health care concern. Peasants must for the most part provide for their own in their health maintenance and promotion. The "iron rice bowl" (*Tie Fan Wan*) policy, in which workers are guaranteed of free health care and other welfare benefits, has been completely dismantled (Leung 1994; Wong 1994). Most workers have to pay a significant portion of their medical costs and many do not have insurance coverage. Furthermore, the protection of workers' health and safety in the workplace, an issue taken seriously by the state during the rule of Mao, has been deteriorating as the central state and particularly the local governments are now driven by an overriding economic imperative to generate high rates of profit (Chen and Chan 1999). Given this significant decline in health and welfare benefits, it is not surprising that many peasants and workers have been reportedly feeling betrayed or abandoned by the state (Weil 1996; Hinton 1990).

The Impact of the Market Reform on Health Care Access and Health Status

The market reform after 1978 has led to impressive economic growth in China. The gross national product has increased 9 percent annually since the reform was launched (Liu et al. 1999) and the per capita disposable income (income after tax) has increased 6.1 percent annually (after adjusting for inflation), more than three times the rate in the US (Hsiao and Liu 1996). Nevertheless, this economic growth has not brought equally improved access to health care or better health status to the Chinese people. Although the PRC's total health expenditure has been increasing rapidly – 10.9 percent per year between 1978 to 1993 (Bloom 1998) – access to health care has not improved for majority of the population. The percentage of the population uninsured has increased considerably, from 29 percent in 1981 to 79 percent in 1993 (World Bank 1997). The majority of the uninsured population live in rural areas. Furthermore the central state and local governments have exacerbated this problem by shifting health care resources to urban areas.

Consequently, the gap in access to health care and health status between rural and urban areas has been widening drastically (Shi 1993; Liu et al. 1995; Bloom 1998). Further, while the two urban health insurance systems, Public Expense Medical Service and Labor Insurance Medical Service, cover only 15 percent of China's total population, they absorb two-thirds of the state's budget on health (World Bank 1997). This inequity of health care access between urban and rural areas is growing worse. In a recent study of poor rural counties it was found that

30 percent of the county villages had no village doctors; 28 percent of peasants did not seek medical care because they could not afford the costs; and 25 percent had to borrow money and 6 percent had to sell their assets to pay for their medical care (Hsiao and Liu 1996). Another survey conducted in 1994 indicated that about 59 percent of rural patients refused professional recommendations for hospitalization because of their inability to pay, compared to 40 percent of urban patients (Liu et al. 1999). In addition, about 30–50 percent of the rural poor become poor because of the financial losses incurred from their illness (Hsiao 1995; Liu et al. 1999). The gap in access to health care between various socio-economic groups within both rural and urban areas has also been increasing as the income disparity between socioeconomic groups widens (World Bank 1992; Grogan 1995; Hsiao 1995; Bloom 1998; Liu et al. 1999).

The change in Chinese people's health status after the reform is mixed. The overall health status of the Chinese people has generally improved after the reform but at a much slower pace than during Mao's era. The incidence of infectious diseases has decreased while that of chronic diseases has increased (Liu et al. 1999). A recent study indicated that the height of children aged two to five increased from 1975 to 1992 but the increase has not been equal for rural and urban areas (Shen et al. 1996). Changes in other health status indicators are in fact alarming. Despite the rapid economic growth, the infant mortality rate has stopped declining since the early 1980s (World Bank 1997; Liu et al. 1999). The under-five mortality rate, a robust and reliable national health indicator, has stagnated since mid-1980s. This causes concern, as the rate for many countries undergoing similar economic growth did not plateau as PRC's did. There have been reports of unexpected outbreaks of communicable diseases in some areas (Zhang 1985; Zhu et al. 1989; Liu et al. 1995; Hillier and Shen 1996; World Bank 1997). The average life expectancy has changed little, from 68 in 1982 to 69 in 1993 (Hsiao and Liu 1996).

In almost every health status indicator, urban population does better than the rural population and this gap is clearly increasing (Bloom 1998; Liu et al. 1999). For example, while the infant mortality rate in urban areas has been steadily declining since the early 1980s, the rate in rural areas increased in the 1990s. In fact, a study of 30 poverty-stricken counties in China found a distressing trend: the infant mortality rate in these poor regions increased from 50 per 1000 live births in the late 1970s to 72 in the late 1980s (Liu et al. 1999). With income inequality increasing in both rural and urban areas (Hinton 1990; Weil 1996; Meisner 1999), health inequality between different income groups in both areas is also likely to grow worse.

Implications of PRC's Health Care Transformation

The great reversal of the health care system in China before and after the market reform represents a dramatic example of how a health care system can be affected by drastic changes in the political, economic, and social systems. Most studies on the PRC's health care system and its transformation have praised the design and implementation of effective public health and medical care programs and the improvement of Chinese people's health status up to the reform and lamented the dismantling of such programs after the reform was launched. Some researchers warned the PRC of the potential problems of adopting the western medical model – i.e. the development of curative and tertiary care at the expense of public health programs and primary and secondary care; the emphasis on urban medical care at the expense of rural health care; increasing health inequality between urban and rural areas and between income groups; escalating health care costs; and other problems confronting the industrialized countries whose health care system is run primarily by market forces and on the western medical model. The authors of the three major World Bank reports on the PRC's health care (Jamison et al. 1984; World Bank 1992; World Bank 1997) present the most significant example of researchers[18] who both praise the PRC's previous health care achievement and warn of the dangers of health care reform. These authors warned the PRC not to follow the western medical model which relies greatly on curative and high-tech medicine[19] and not to let market forces dictate health care provision.[20] Indeed, for reasons yet to be studied – probably in response to the suggestions of the World Bank and other foreign researchers or because of a fear that the health care may deteriorate to the extent that it might endanger the state's legitimacy – the PRC has reinitiated and encouraged the rural cooperative medical systems since 1994 (Bloom and Tang 1999; Carrin et al. 1999).

Is it possible for the PRC to reestablish the successful health care programs developed and carried out before market reform? Several factors make it rather unlikely. First, the reversal of the PRC's former political, economic, and social system under the market reform, as mentioned previously, has undermined the foundation of the former health care system. Secondly, another important factor leading to the PRC's unique health care system was the strong national confidence derived from Mao's policy of self-reliance. This instilled in popular consciousness the conviction that the Chinese people could mold a unique future by their own efforts. In a great contrast, after the reform, there has been a rebirth of blind admiration of the West and subsequently, a loss of national confidence (Meisner 1999). In health care, the PRC ended its policy of strict technological self-reliance and started importing medical technology from the West shortly after the reform. Furthermore, there is widespread admiration for the western medical model among health professionals and within the state (Blendon 1981; Sidel and Sidel 1983). Moreover, the fact that the PRC will soon be joining the World Trade Organization, thus becoming more integrated with the world system, makes China even more vulnerable to western influence. Thirdly, while "serving the people" and working for the collective good was the ideological norm in Mao's era, the competitive values of the market dominate the reformed society. Fourthly, the reformed health care system has already generated great disparity between regions and socioeconomic groups and created vested – both domestic and foreign – interests which have benefited and are still reaping profits from the new system (see, e.g., Bell 1998; China Times 1998). In the light of the above factors, this chapter has to end on a pessimistic note: short of another social revolution, it may not be possible to reintroduce the former health care system developed during Mao's era. Consequently, the current reformed western model-oriented system may well continue to determine the course of development of China's health care system.

Acknowledgment

I thank the Center for East Asian Studies of the University of Chicago for making the university library facilities accessible to me as Associate Member of the Center; William Hinton for his helpful comments; Stephen Daniel Rosenberg for his editing assistance; and Cheng Ping-ping for her clerical assistance.

Notes

1 Majority of soldiers were from peasants in rural areas.

2 Originally sparrows were designated as one of the four pests. However, when it was found that elimination of sparrows led to ecological problems, bedbugs replaced sparrows as one of the four pests (Horn 1969).

3 Communes, with about 10,000 to 60,000 population, were the basic economic, political, and social units in rural China. They developed during the late 1950s when land reform was implemented and collectivization was carried out. The smallest subdivision of the commune is the production team, with several hundred members who live close to each other. Several teams combine to form production brigade, which usually have wider responsibility in health and other collective responsibilities. A commune is typically composed of about ten to thirty production brigades. The commune is the lowest level of formal state power in the rural areas and is responsible for its people's education, welfare, health, and other collective matters. Above the commune are the county and provincial authorities (Sidel and Sidel 1982).

4 For example, in 1972, a commune in Chekiang Province had fewer serious illnesses than before and grew and used herbal medicine more extensively and, as a result, the annual membership fee in 1973 was reduced from 1 yuan (equivalent to US $0.45 then) to 0.35 yuan (Hu 1976).

5 The term "barefoot" reflects the fact that the role of these medical workers is mainly peasants. But they did wear shoes most of the time particularly when they perform health and medical work (Sidel and Sidel 1982).

6 Great Leap Forward was an ideological and economic movement PRC carried out in China from 1958 to 1960. The ideological basis of this movement is that the economic development should rely on the "revolutionary enthusiasm" of the masses. The economic aspect of the movement aimed at the industrialization of the rural areas in order to resolve the potential problems of unemployment in the cities and the underemployment in rural areas (Meisner 1999).

7 For example, in a production brigade in Fujien, a barefoot doctor's continuing education regarding gynecology, internal medicine, surgery, immunization, and Chinese medicine accumulated to more than four years within her 16 years of practice as a barefoot doctor (Huang 1988).

8 Under the western medical model, medical providers are professionalized: only those who have a long professional education and are licensed or certified to practice are legally allowed to provide medical services.

9 According to World Bank's estimates, PRC's life expectancy increased by 27 years between 1960 to 1980, in comparison with 15 years for low-income countries, 9 years for middle-income countries, and 4 years for industrial capitalist countries (Jamison et al. 1984).

10 For example, in the 1980s, with the exception of dentists, the medical personnel (including western medical doctors, medical assistants, traditional medical practitioners, and nurses) to population ratios were better than the average in developing

countries (Jamison et al. 1984) and these ratios were a result of an increase of many folds since 1949 (Sidel and Sidel 1982).

11 In the household responsibility system, a peasant family is held responsible for the production of a given lot and can sell the production over the quota paid to the local government to the free market and keep the profit (Weil 1996).

12 For example, the funding for the Epidemic Prevention Service, the national level institution for prevention programs, as the percentage of GDP reduced from 0.11 percent in 1978 to 0.04 percent in 1993 (World Bank 1997).

13 For example, the epidemic prevention center had been testing water quality for factories, certifying foods and cosmetics for hygiene for the enterprises' commercial use, and conducting physical examinations of industrial workers for which a fee could be charged (World Bank 1992). Further, a 1994 survey revealed that the county epidemic prevention stations, by charging for preventive service and other specialized services such as lab tests or physical examinations of enterprises' employees, raised 56 percent of their budgets themselves and the county maternal and child health centers raised 67 percent (Bloom 1998).

14 For example, the environmental sanitation programs have been neglected (World Bank 1992). Using the control of schistosomiasis as an example, it was reported that, due to the neglect of the public health programs, snail habitat was increasing and the spread of heavy infestation was wide and persistent since the early 1980s (World Bank 1992).

15 During Mao's era, the barefoot doctors and other health workers from the production brigade health station and commune health center were the major workforce for public health campaigns. These health workers, under the market reform era, are independent providers and thus the epidemic prevention center no longer has the power to engage them in the public health programs.

16 The number of barefoot doctors reported in various studies differed slightly. For example, Young's study (Young 1986) indicated 1.6 million in 1975 and 1.28 million in 1986, different from those of other studies. Nevertheless, all studies reported the general trend of decrease.

17 Chronic diseases are partly related to unhealthy lifestyles, such as smoking, heavy salt intake, and increased dietary animal fat consumption. Because these behaviors are prevalent among the Chinese population, the individualized approach to promote healthy behavior will not be efficient. The more effective approach is the mass mobilization, the old strategy used before the market reform. The workplace and environmental pollution also contributes to chronic diseases such as cancer and respiratory diseases. Mass mobilization is also an effective method to raise the awareness of the mass of the problem and resolve the problem through mass participation.

18 World Bank's authors represent an outstanding example particularly because its three reports on PRC's health care warned PRC of the problems of privatization and market forces in health care. This position is curious because it contrasts, in fact contradicts, with World Bank's long-time position of promoting privatization of the health care and welfare system in Latin American and other countries (for World Bank's promotion of privatization, see, for example, Danaher (1994) and Paul and Paul (1995)).

19 World Bank reports pointed out the ineffectiveness of the western medical model which relies greatly on curative and high-tech medicine in dealing with chronic diseases.

20 World Bank report (World Bank 1992) warned that if PRC continued with the current fee-for-service system and let the market forces run the system, a disastrous

situation – an uncontrollable skyrocketing health care expenditure and serious health inequality – would occur.

References

Albrecht, Gary L. and Xiaoyin Tang. 1990. "Rehabilitation in the People's Republic of China: A Reflection of Social Structure and Culture." *Advances in Medical Sociology* 1: 235–67.

Aldis, William L. 1989. "Privatisation of Care in China." *The Lancet* 2: 1456–7.

Anching Local History Editorial Committee. 1996. "Medical and Health Organizations (in Chinese)." Pp. 1091–112 in *The History of Anqing*. Anhui: Huangshan Books.

Bell, Allison. 1998. "Opportunities in Chinese Health Reforms." *National Underwriter* 102: 37–9.

Blendon, Robert J. 1979. "Can China's Health Care be Transplanted without China's Economic Policies?" *The New England Journal of Medicine* 300: 1453–8.

——. 1981. "Public Health Versus Personal Medical Care. The Dilemma of Post-Mao China." *The New England Journal of Medicine* 304: 981–3.

Bloom, Gerald. 1998. "Primary Health Care. Meets the Market in China and Vietnam." *Health Policy* 44: 233–52.

Bloom, Gerald and Tang Shenglan. 1999. "Rural Health Prepayment Schemes in China: Towards A More Active Role for Government." *Social Science and Medicine* 48: 951–60.

Bo, Xianfeng and Jianzhen Dong. 1993. "Analysis and Forecast of Medical System Reform (in Chinese)." Pp. 191–211 in Jiang Liu, Lu Xueyi, and Dan Tienlun (eds.), *China in 1992–1993: The Analysis and Forecast of Societal Situations*. Beijing: Chinese Social Sciences Press.

Bumgarner, J. Richard. 1990. "Public Policies for the Health Transition in China: Preventing Exposure to Behavioral and Environmental Risk." *Environmental Impact Assessment Review* 10: 405–16.

Cai, Renhua. 1995. "The Interest Group Relations in the Public Expense Medical Service Reform (in Chinese)." Pp. 16–29 in Ministry of Health Policy and Management Expert Committee (ed.), *The Health Insurance System for Public Employees and Workers: Reform Papers*. Beijing: Ministry of Health, People's Republic of China.

Cai, Wen-Wei, James S. Marks, H. C. Charles, You-Xien Zhuang, and Jeffrey R. Harris. 1998. "Increased Cesarean Section Rates and Emerging Patterns of Health Insurance in Shanghai, China." *American Journal of Public Health* 88: 777–80.

Carrin, Guy, Ron Aviva, Hui Yang, Hong Wang, Tuohong Zhang, Licheng Zhang, Shuo Zhang, Yide Ye, Jiaying Chen, Qicheng Jiang, Zhaoyang Zhang, Jun Yu, and Xuesheng Li. 1999. "The Reform of the Rural Cooperative Medical System in the People's Republic of China: Interim Experience in 14 Pilot Counties." *Social Science and Medicine* 48: 961–72.

Chen, Meei-shia and Anita Chan. 1999. "China's 'Market Economics in Command': Footwear Workers' Health in Jeopardy." *International Journal of Health Services* 29: 793–811.

Chen, Xiao-Ming, Teh-Wei Hu, and Zihua Lin. 1993. "The Rise and Decline of the Cooperative Medical System in Rural China." *International Journal of Health Services* 23: 731–42.

Chen, Yunliang. 1947. *An Outline of History of Medicine in China* (Chinese). Guangzhou: Kwongwah Printing Co.

Cheung, Yin-Bun. 1995. "Community Mobilization and Health Care in Rural China." *Community Development Journal* 30: 317–26.

Chin, Robert. 1973. "The Changing Health Conduct of the 'New Man.'" Pp. 113–23 in Myron E. Wegman, Tsung-Yi Lin, and Elizabeth F. Purcell (eds.), *Public Health in the People's Republic of China*. New York: Josiah Macy, JR. Foundation.

China Times. 1998. "Imported Western Medicine Occupied the Market; China's Local Medicine Lost Its Market (in Chinese)." Section 14, November 23, 1998.

Chinese Medical Association. 1974. "Child Health Care in New China." *American Journal of Chinese Medicine* 2: 149–58.

Chu, Li and Chieh-Yun Tien. 1974. "Medical and Health Service." Pp. 194–208 in Chu Li and Chieh-Yun Tien (eds.), *Inside A People's Commune*. Peking: Foreign Languages Press.

Cretin, Shan, Naihua Duan, Albert P. Williams, Xingyuan Gu, and Yuanqiu Shi. 1990. "Modeling the Effect of Insurance on Health Expenditures in the People's Republic of China." *Health Services Research* 25: 667–85.

Croizier, Ralph C. 1968. *Traditional Medicine in Modern China: Science, Nationalism, and the Tensions of Cultural Change*. Cambridge, MA: Harvard University Press.

Danaher, Kevin. 1994. *50 Years is Enough*. Boston. MA: South End Press.

Ding, Yendi. 1994. "The Thoughts on the Reform of the Public Expense Medical Service (in Chinese)." *Sociological Research* 3: 121–4.

Feng, Xueshan, Shenglan Tang, Gerald Bloom, Malcolm Segall, and Xingyuan Gu. 1995. "Cooperative Medical Schemes in Contemporary Rural China." *Social Science and Medicine* 41: 1111–18.

Grogan, Colleen M. 1995. "Urban Economic Reform and Access to Health Care Coverage in the People's Republic of China." *Social Science and Medicine* 41: 1073–84.

Gu, Shengzu and Zhexi Liang. 1993. "The Medical Services Utilization by the Elderly and the Reform of the Medical Care System in China (in Chinese)." *Sociological Research* 6: 56–65.

Gu, Xingyuan, Gerald Bloom, Shenglan Tang, Yingya Zhu, Shouqi Zhou, and Xingbao Chen. 1993. "Financing Health Care in Rural China: Preliminary Report of A Nationwide Study." *Social Science and Medicine* 36: 385–91.

Guangzhou Local History Editorial Committee. 1995. "The History of Physical Education and Health Work (in Chinese)." In *The History of Guangzhou*. Guangzhou, Guangdong: Guangzhou Press.

Guizhou South East Miao and Dong Minority Autonomy Region Local History Editorial Committee. 1993. *History of Health Work* (Chinese). Guiyang, Guizhou: Guizhou People's Press.

Heller, Peter S. 1973. "The Strategy of Health-Sector Planning." Pp. 62–107 in Myron E. Wegman, Tsung-Yi Lin, and Elizabeth F. Purcell (eds.), *Public Health in the People's Republic of China*. New York: Josiah Macy, JR. Foundation.

Henderson, Gail. 1990. "Increased Inequality in Health Care." Pp. 263–82 in Deborah Davis and Ezra F. Vogel (eds.), *Chinese Society on the Eve of Tiananmen: The Impact of Reform*. Massachusetts: The Council on East Asian Studies.

Henderson, Gail, John Akin, Li Zhiming, Jin Shuigao, Ma Haijiang, and Ge Keyou. 1994. "Equity and the Utilization of Health Services: Report of an Eight-Province survey in China." *Social Science and Medicine* 39: 687–99.

Henderson, Gail E. and Myron S. Cohen. 1982. "Health Care in the People's Republic of China: A View from Inside the System." *American Journal of Public Health* 72: 1238–45.

Henderson, Gail E., Elizabeth A. Murphy, Samuel T. Sockwell, Jiongliang Zhou, Qingrui Shen, and Zhiming Li. 1988. "High-Technology Medicine in China: The Case of

Chronic Renal Failure and Hemodialysis." *The New England Journal of Medicine* 318: 1000–4.

Henderson, Gail and Scott T. Stroup. 1998. "Preventive Health Care: Privatization and the Public Good." Pp. 184–269 in Andrew G. Walder (ed.), *Zouping in Transition: The Process of Reform in Rural North China*. Massachusetts: Harvard University.

Hillier, S. M. and J. A. Jewell. 1983. *Health Care and Traditional Medicine in China, 1800–1982*. London: Routledge and Kegan Paul.

Hillier, Sheila and Xiang Zheng. 1990. "Privatisation of Care in China." *The Lancet* 335: 414.

Hillier, Sheila and Jie Shen. 1996. "Health Care Systems in Transition: People's Republic of China Part I: An Overview of China's Health Care System." *Journal of Public Health Medicine* 18: 258–65.

Hinton, William. 1966. *Fanshen: A Documentary of Revolution in A Chinese Village*. New York: Random House, Vintage Books.

——. 1990. *The Great Reversal: The Privatization of China, 1978–1989*. New York: Monthly Review Press.

Ho, Lok Sang. 1995. "Marker Reforms and China's Health Care System." *Social Science and Medicine* 41: 1065–72.

Horn, Joshua S. 1969. *Away With All Pests: An English Surgeon in People's China, 1954–1969*. New York: Monthly Review Press.

——. 1972. "Building A Rural Health Service in the People's Republic of China." *International Journal of Health Services* 2: 377–83.

Hsiao, William C. 1984. "Transformation of Health Care in China." *The New England Journal of Medicine* 310: 932–6.

——. 1995. "The Chinese Health Care System: Lessons for Other Nations." *Social Science and Medicine* 41: 1047–55.

Hsiao, William C. L. and Yuanli Liu. 1996. "Economic Reform and Health-Lessons from China." *The New England Journal of Medicine* 335: 430–2.

Hsu, Robert C. 1977. "The Political Economy of Rural Health Care in China." *Review of Radical Political Economy*. 9: 134–40.

——. 1974. "The Barefoot Doctors of the People's Republic of China – Some Problems." *The New England Journal of Medicine* 291: 124–27.

Hu, Teh-Wei. 1976. "The Financing and the Economic Efficiency of Rural Health Services in the People's Republic of China." *International Journal of Health Services* 6: 239–49.

——. 1980. "Health Care Services in China's Economic Development." Pp. 229–57 in Robert F. Dernberger (ed.), *China's Development Experience in Comparative Perspective*. Cambridge: Harvard University Press.

——. 1981. "Issues of Health Care Financing in the People's Republic of China." *Social Science and Medicine* 15: 233–7.

——. 1987. "Western Technology for China's Hospitals." *The China Business Review* 14: 29–31.

Huang, Xizhe and Xishiao Lin. 1986. *The Health Career of Contemporary China, Vol. 1* (in Chinese). Shanghai: China Social Science Publishing Co.

Huang, Shu-Min. 1988. "Transforming China's Collective Health Care System: A Village Study." *Social Science and Medicine* 27: 879–88.

Jamison, Dean T., John R. Evans, Timothy King, Ian Porter, Nicholas Prescott, and Andre Prost. 1984. *China: The Health Sector*. Washington DC: The World Bank.

Kao, John J. 1974. "Psychiatry in the People's Republic of China: A Prospectus." *American Journal of Chinese Medicine* 2: 441–4.

Khan, M. Mahmud, Naisu Zhu, and Jack C. Ling. 1996. "Community-Based Health Insurance in China: Bending to the Wind of Change." *World Health Forum* 17: 58–62.

Koplan, Jeffrey P., Alan R. Hinman, Robert L. Parker, You-Long Gong, and Ming-Ding Yang. 1985. "The Barefoot Doctor: Shanghai County Revisited." *American Journal of Public Health* 75: 768–70.

Kwangchow, Provincial Institute of Maternal and Child Health Care. 1978. "Rural Child Health Care in Kwangtung Province." *Chinese Medical Journal* 4: 85–8.

Lampton, David M. 1977. *The Politics of Medicine in China*. Boulder, CO: Westview Press.

Lee, Rance P. L. 1981. "Chinese and Western Medical Care in China's Rural Commune: A Case Study." *Social Science and Medicine* 15A: 137–48.

Leung, Joe C. B. 1994. "Dismantling the 'Iron Rice Bowl': Welfare Reforms in the People's Republic of China." *International Journal of Social Policy* 23: 341–61.

Li, Weiping and Mei Wang. 1994. "A Comparative Study of the Health Status and Its Influencing Factors between China and U.S.A. (in Chinese)" *Technology and Development, Special Issue on the Development in China* 4: 36–9.

Liang, Matthew H., Philip S. Eichling, Lawrence J. Fine, and George J. Annas. 1973. "Chinese Health Care: Determinants of the System." *American Journal of Public Health* 63: 102–10.

Liu, Xingzhu and William C. L. Hsiao. 1995. "The Cost Escalation of Social Health Insurance Plans in China: Its Implication for Public Policy." *Social Science and Medicine* 41: 1095–101.

Liu, Yuanli, William C. L. Hsiao, Qing Li, Xingzhu Liu, and Minghui Ren. 1995. "Transformation of China's Rural Health Care Financing." *Social Science and Medicine* 41: 1085–93.

Liu, Yuanli, William C. Hsiao, and Karen Eggleston. 1999. "Equity in Health and Health Care: The Chinese Experience." *Social Science and Medicine* 49: 1349–56.

Lyle, Katherine Ch'iu. 1980. "China's Health System: Determinants." *American Journal of Chinese Medicine* 8: 199–220.

MacFarquhar, Roderick. 1997. *The Politics of China*, 2nd edition. New York: Cambridge University Press.

Maddin, W. Stuart. 1974. "Integration of Tradition and Modern Medicine." Pp. 3–11 in Joseph R. Quinn (ed.), *China Medicine As We Saw It*. US Public Health Service: DHEW Publications.

Mao, Zedong. 1934. "Be Concerned about the Mass's Life and Pay Attention to the Work Method (in Chinese)." Pp. 122–7 in The Publication Committee of the Selections of Mao Zedong in the Central Committee of the Chinese Communist Party (ed.), *Selections of Mao Zedong*. Beijing: People's Press.

——. 1974. "Directive on Public Health Work (in Chinese)." Pp. 232–3 in Stuart Schram (ed.), *Chairman Mao Talks to the People*. New York: Pantheon.

Maru, Rushikesh M. 1977. "Health Manpower Strategies for Rural Health Services in India and China: 1949–1975." *Social Science and Medicine* 11: 535–47.

Meisner, Maurice. 1999. *Mao's China and After*. New York: The Free Press.

Miao, Yu. 1976. "Stabilize and Expand the Achievement of Rural Health Revolution (in Chinese)." *Red Flag* 9: 57–60.

Ministry of Health. 1997. "The Work on Health Statistics (in Chinese)." Pp. 419–33 in *The Annual Review of Public Health in China*. Beijing: Ministry of Health, People's Republic of China.

New, Peter Kong-Ming. 1982. "Changing Health Policies in the PRC: Another Perspective." *Medical Anthropology Newsletter* 13: 1–2.

New, Peter Kong-Ming and Yuet-Wah Cheung. 1984. "The Evolution of Health Care in China: A Backward Look to the Future." *Medicine Anthropology* 8: 169–79.

Parmelee, Donna E., Gail Henderson, and Myron S. Cohen. 1982. "Medicine Under Socialism: Some Observations on Yugoslavia and China." *Social Science and Medicine* 16: 1389–96.

Paul, Susanne S. and James A. Paul. 1995. "The World Bank, Pensions, and Income (In)Security in the Global South." *International Journal of Health Services* 25: 697–726.

Peking Review. 1974. "Growth of 'Barefoot Doctors' in the Country." *Peking Review* 17: 6.

——. 1975. "Co-operative Medical Service and Barefoot Doctors in China's Rural Areas." *Peking Review* 18: 20–1.

Qien, Xinzhong. 1965. "Several Problems Concerning the Work of Rural Mobile Medical Teams." *Red Flag* 13: 1–9.

——. 1993. "Preface (in Chinese)." In Zhang Zikuan (ed.), *On Cooperative Medical System*. Taiyuan, Shanxi: Shanxi People's Press.

Report of an Investigation from Shanghai. 1968. *An Assessment of the Orientation of the Revolution in Medical Education as seen in the Growth of Barefoot Doctors* (Chinese). Beijing: People's Press.

Rifkin, Susan B. 1972. "Health Care for Rural Areas." Pp. 137–49 in Joseph R. Quinn (ed.), *Medicine and Public Health in the People's Republic of China*. USA: DHEW Publication.

——. 1973. "Public Health in China – Is the Experience Relevant to Other Less Developed Nations?" *Social Science and Medicine* 7: 249–57.

Ronaghy, Hossain A. and Steven Solter. 1974. "Is the Chinese 'Barefoot Doctor' Exportable to Rural Iran?" *The Lancet* 1: 1331–3.

Sandbach, F. R. 1977. "Farewell to the God of Plague – The Control of Schistosomiasis in China." *Social Science and Medicine* 11: 27–33.

Schwartz, Dan. 1977. "A Comparison between the Chinese Approach and 'Western' Health Education Principles." *International Journal of Health Education* 10: 1–15.

Shen, Tiefu, Jean-Pierre Habicht, and Ying Chang. 1996. "Effect of Economic Reforms on Child Growth in Urban and Rural Areas of China." *The New England Journal of Medicine* 335: 400–6.

Shi, Leiyu. 1993. "Health Care in China: A Rural–Urban Comparison after the Socioeconomic Reforms." *Bulletin of the World Health Organization* 71: 723–36.

Sidel, Victor W. 1972a. "The Barefoot Doctors of the People's Republic of China." *The New England Journal of Medicine* 286: 1292–300.

——. 1972b. "Some Observations on the Health Services in the People's Republic of China." *International Journal of Health Services* 2: 385–95.

——. 1975. "Medical Care in the People's Republic of China." *Archives of Internal Medicine* 135: 916–26.

——. 1993. "New Lessons from China: Equity and Economics in Rural Health Care." *American Journal of Public Health* 83: 1665–6.

Sidel, Victor W. and Ruth Sidel. 1973. *Serve the People: Observations on Medicine in the People's Republic of China*. New York: Beacon Press.

Sidel, Ruth and Victor W. Sidel. 1982. *The Health of China*. Boston: Beacon Press.

Sidel, Victor W. and Ruth Sidel. 1983. "The People's Republic of China-Mass Mobilization." Pp. 209–39 in Victor W. Sidel and Ruth Sidel (eds.), *A Healthy State: An International Perspective on the Crisis in United States Medical Care*. New York: Pantheon Books.

Sleigh, A., Xueming Li, S. Jackson, and Kengling Huang. 1998. "Eradication of Schistosomiasis in Guangxi, China. Part 1: Setting, Strategies, Operations, and Outcomes, 1953–92." *Bulletin of the World Health Organization* 76: 361–72.

Smith, Christopher J. 1993. "(Over)Eating Success: The Health Consequences of the Restoration of Capitalism in Rural China." *Social Science and Medicine* 37: 761–70.

Tang, Sheng-Lan. 1997. "Community-Based Health Insurance." *World Health Forum* 18: 63–4.

Tang, Sheng-Lan and Xing-Yuan Gu. 1996. "Bringing Basic Health Care to the Rural Poor." *World Health Forum* 17: 404–8.

The Chinese Communist Party Committee of the Peking Tuberculosis Research Institute. 1975. "Implementing Chairman Mao's Directive 'In Medical and Health Work, Put the Stress on the Rural Areas'." *Chinese Medical Journal* 1: 237–40.

The Editorial Committee for New China's Historical Experience of Preventive Medicine. 1991. *The Historical Experience of New China's Preventive Medicine, Vol. 1*. Beijing: People's Health Press.

Vogel, Ezra F. 1973. "Organization of Health Services." Pp. 51–61 in Myron E. Wegman, Tsung-Yi Lin, and Elizabeth F. Purcell (eds.), *Public Health in the People's Republic of China*. New York: Josiah Macy, JR. Foundation.

Wang, Virginia Li. 1975. "Training of the Barefoot Doctor in the People's Republic of China: From Prevention to Curative Service." *International Journal of Health Services* 5: 475–88.

Wegman, Myron E. 1982. "Public Health in China." *American Journal of Public Health* 72: 978–9.

Wei, Ge. 1975. "Further Improve Rural Health Work (in Chinese)." *Red Flag* 9: 36–8.

Weil, Robert. 1996. *Red Cat, White Cat*. New York: Monthly Review Press.

Wen, Chi-Pang and Charles W. Hays. 1976. "Health Care Financing in China." *Medical Care* 14: 241–54.

White, Sydney D. 1998. "From 'Barefoot Doctor' to 'Village Doctor' in Tiger Spring Village: A Case Study of Rural Health Care Transformations in Socialist China." *Human Organization* 57: 480–90.

Wilenski, Peter. 1976. *The Delivery of Health Services in the People's Republic of China*. Canada, Ottawa: International Development Research Center.

——. 1977. "Health Organization in Developing Countries: Innovations in the People's Republic of China." *The Medical Journal of Australia* 1: 29–31.

Wong, Linda. 1994. "Privatization of Social Welfare in Post-Mao China." *Asian Survey* 34: 307–25.

World Bank. 1992. *China: Long-Term Issues and Options in the Health Transition*. Washington, DC: The World Bank.

——. 1997. *Financing Health Care: Issues and Options for China*. Washington, DC: The World Bank.

Wu, Chieh-Ping. 1975. "Medicine and Health (I) For Workers, Peasants and Soldiers." *Peking Review* 8: 9–22.

Xu, Wenbo. 1995. "Flourishing Health Work in China." *Social Science and Medicine* 41: 1043–5

Xu, Yunbei. 1960. "Develop the Great People's Health Work (in Chinese)." *Red Flag* 6: 9–22.

Yang, Jie. 1958. "The Victory of the Control of Four Pests is the Victory of Mass Line (in Chinese)." *Red Flag* 4: 31–4.

Yang, Pei-Lin, Vivian Lin, and James Lawson. 1991. "Health Policy Reform in the People's Republic of China." *International Journal of Health Services* 21: 481–91.

Young, Mary. 1986. "Changes in Rural Health Care in China." *Hospital Practice* 21: 107–9.

———. 1989. "Impact of the Rural Reform on Financing Rural Health Services in China." *Health Policy* 11: 27–42.

Yuan, Yung-ts'ai. 1975. "Brilliant 'June 26' Directive Shows Me the Way Forward." *Chinese Medical Journal* 1: 241–6.

Zhang, Kong-Lai and Wei Chen. 1996. "Health Care System in Transition: People's Republic of China. Part II: The Chinese Health Care System's Response to HIV-AIDS." *Journal of Public Health Medicine* 18: 226–68.

Zhang, Zikuan. 1959. "Concerning the Medical Care System for the People's Commune (in Chinese)." P. 1 in *On Cooperative Medical System*, edited by Zikuan Zhang in 1993. Taiyuan, Shanxi: Shanxi People's Press.

———. 1960. "Aggressively Promoting Collective Health Care System (in Chinese)." Pp. 3–5 in *On Cooperative Medical System*, edited by Zikuan Zhang in 1993. Taiyuan, Shanxi: Shanxi People's Press.

———. 1965a. "Strengthening the Management of the Cooperative Medical System (in Chinese)." P. 8 in *On Cooperative Medical System*, edited by Zikuan Zhang in 1993. Taiyuan, Shanxi: Shanxi People's Press.

———. 1965b. "Many Benefits for Cooperative Medical System (in Chinese)." P. 13 in *On Cooperative Medical System*, edited by Zikuan Zhang in 1993. Taiyuan, Shanxi: Shanxi People's Press.

———. 1966. "The Tentative Management Rules for the Cooperative Medical System in Ma Cheng County (in Chinese)." Pp. 38–47 in *On Cooperative Medical System*, edited by Zikuan Zhang in 1993. Taiyuan, Shanxi: Shanxi People's Press.

———. 1985. "Strengthening the Research on the Rural Health Care System (in Chinese)." Pp. 67–75 in *On Cooperative Medical System*, edited by Zikuan Zhang in 1993. Taiyuan, Shanxi: Shanxi People's Press.

———. 1992. "The Review of the Early Historical Situation of Cooperative Medical System (in Chinese)." Pp. 102–9 in *On Cooperative Medical System*, edited by Zikuan Zhang in 1993. Taiyuan, Shanxi: Shanxi People's Press.

———. 1981. "Please Save the Herbal Medicine and Pharmaceuticals: The Investigation of the Herbal Medicine and Herbal Pharmaceuticals in Fujian Provice (in Chinese)." Pp. 58–64 in *On Rural Health and Primary Health Care*, edited by Zikuan Zhang in 1993. Taiyuan, Shanxi: Shanxi People's Press.

Zhou, Caiming. 1995. "In the Reform of the Medical Insurance System (in Chinese)." Pp. 3–15 in Ministry of Health Policy and Management Expert Committee (ed.), *The Health Insurance System for Public Employees and Workers: Reform Sections*. Beijing: Ministry of Health, People's Republic of Health.

Zhu, Jianhua, Yang Zhu, and Yungjun Guo. 1989. *The History of the People's Republic of China* (Chinese). Harbin, China: Heilongjiang People's Press.

Index